Second Edition

Literacy
for the 21st Century

A Balanced Approach

GAIL E. TOMPKINS

California State University, Fresno

Merrill
Prentice Hall

Upper Saddle River, New Jersey
Columbus, Ohio

Library of Congress Cataloging-in-Publication Data
Tompkins, Gail E.
    Literacy for the 21st century : a balanced approach / Gail E. Tompkins.—2nd ed.
        p.   cm.
    Rev. ed. of : Literacy for the twenty-first century. c1997.
    Includes bibliographical references and index.
    ISBN 0-13-017297-9
        1. Language arts (Elementary) 2. Literature—Study and teaching (Elementary) 3.
    Reading (Elementary) 4. Literacy. I. Title: Literacy for the twenty-first century. II.
    Tompkins, Gail E. Literacy for the twenty-first century. III. Title

    LB1576.T657   2001   00–028375
    372.6—dc21

Vice President and Publisher: Jeffery W. Johnston
Editor: Linda Ashe Montgomery
Development Editor: Linda Scharp McElhiney
Editorial Assistant: Jennifer Day
Production Editor: Mary M. Irvin
Design Coordinator: Karrie Converse-Jones
Text Design: Jill Little
Cover Design: Diane C. Lorenzo
Cover Art: Mary O'Keefe Young
Production Manager: Pamela D. Bennett
Director of Marketing: Kevin Flanagan
Marketing Manager: Amy June
Marketing Services Manager: Krista Groshong

This book was set in Galliard by The Clarinda Company and was printed and bound by Courier Kendallville, Inc. The cover was printed by Phoenix Color Corp.

Photo Credits: All photos supplied by Gail E. Tompkins

Merrill
Prentice Hall

10 9 8 7 6 5 4 3 2 1
ISBN: 0–13–017297–9

About the Author

Gail E. Tompkins is a Professor at California State University, Fresno, in the Department of Literacy and Early Education, where she teaches courses in reading, language arts, and writing for pre-service teachers and students in the reading/language arts master's degree program. She directs the San Joaquin Valley Writing Project and works regularly with teachers, both by teaching model lessons in classrooms and by leading staff development programs. Recently Dr. Tompkins was inducted into the California Reading Association's Reading Hall of Fame in recognition of her publications and other accomplishments in the field of reading. She has also been awarded the prestigious Provost's Award for Excellence in Teaching at California State University, Fresno.

Previously, Dr. Tompkins taught at Miami University in Ohio and at the University of Oklahoma in Norman where she received the prestigious Regents' Award for Superior Teaching. She was also an elementary teacher in Virginia for eight years.

Dr. Tompkins is the author of three books published by Merrill/Prentice Hall: *Teaching Writing: Balancing Process and Product*, 3rd ed. (2000), *50 Literacy Strategies* (1998), and *Language Arts: Content and Teaching Strategies*, 4th ed. (1998). She has written numerous articles related to reading and language arts that have appeared in *The Reading Teacher, Language Arts,* and other professional journals.

Preface

Facing the Challenge: How Do Today's Teachers Chart a Course to Create Competent, Literate Citizens for Tomorrow?

Helping children become literate is one of the greatest challenges facing teachers today. As some teachers and researchers tout and defend one approach after another, parents are frightened that the new instructional methods aren't getting the job done. The media fuels the controversy with reports lamenting failing test scores and criticism that many schools are failing to produce literate citizens who can function competently.

I have written this textbook to blaze a pathway toward implementing a thoughtful, balanced approach to teaching reading and writing, a pathway that incorporates the most effective teaching approaches and strategies.

The second edition of *Literacy for the Twenty-First Century: A Balanced Approach* builds on the research-based approaches to literacy instruction outlined in the first edition, the most popular new reading methods textbook in a decade.

Why Is This Reader-Friendly Textbook a Best-Seller? Here's What Professors and Their Students Tell Us:

- This comprehensive text presents several sound approaches to literacy instruction and guides teachers toward best practice in teaching skills as well as and strategies.
- It functions equally well as a core text for traditional introduction to reading methods courses and for the newer literacy "block" courses.
- The ten principles of effective reading instruction outlined in Chapter 1 provide a strong, easily understood foundation for the entire book.
- The text is written with preservice teachers in mind; however, those teachers pressed into service in accelerated credential programs will find the book invaluable as a resource to get up and running quickly.
- The easily accessible Compendium of Instructional Procedures at the back of the book offers 38 clearly articulated instructional methods, an invaluable resource and quick reference.
- The text includes many lively descriptions of how real teachers teach reading and writing effectively, through vignettes opening each chapter and colorful part opening sections that present visual reinforcement of each major approach to teaching literacy.
- The Review section at the end of each chapter includes a chart that contrasts effective and ineffective instructional practices related to the chapter topic.

What Is New in the Second Edition?

1. Increased coverage of comprehension: an entire chapter is devoted to the most recent research on facilitating students' comprehension. This chapter details

how to help students understand and make meaning from text, once they have learned to decode it.

2. Still more on comprehension: check out the video free to adopters of this text in which the author herself presents her analysis of field-tested ideas to improve students' comprehension.

3. More ways to use technology effectively as a resource. Not only are there more Technology Links features, but there are many website addresses provided throughout the text. These addresses are accompanied by brief annotations so readers can assess their usefulness.

4. More ways to use technology effectively as a teaching tool. The Companion Website for the second edition (www.prenhall.com/tompkins) offers opportunities for self-assessment; analysis, synthesis, and application of concepts; updated web addresses; and special information for teachers required to pass state tests in teaching reading in order to obtain credentials.

5. Much more on assessment tools, including ideas for alternative assessment.

6. Suggestions for the creative use of traditional basal readers, including the "guided reading" approach.

7. A new full-color opener for Part III, featuring a middle school content-area unit on medieval life.

What Is the Purpose of This Textbook?

My goal in this text is to show beginning teachers how to teach reading and writing effectively, how to create a classroom climate where literacy flourishes, and how to empower the diverse array of students in today's classrooms to function competently as literate adults in the twenty-first century. To that end, I have based the text on four contemporary theories of literacy learning: constructivist, interactive, socio-linguistic, and reader response theories.

Readers will learn how to implement a reading program with skills and strategies taught in context using a whole-part-whole organizational approach. The approach I take can, I believe, best be described as "balanced." Literature provides the major focus for reading instruction and for integrating the language arts. You will learn how to teach vital skills and useful strategies within the context of authentic reading and writing experiences. I have carefully selected the principles, skills, strategies, and examples of literature that will empower the beginning teacher to get up to speed quickly. In creating this textbook, I used knowledge I gleaned from a host of teachers who have been students in my beginning reading course over the years, and I also sifted through the array of practices and procedures proven effective in today's classrooms and with today's diverse student populations. Although there are many other useful ideas and strategies that can accomplish the goal of producing literate students, I have deliberately and painstakingly chosen research-based, classroom-tested ideas—the best of the best—as the focus of this textbook.

It is widely recognized that today's teachers need as many approaches and strategies in their repertoire as possible. However, I have carefully culled out a critical path for beginning teachers to follow. Why? Because it is important for beginning teachers of reading and writing to learn a few things well at the outset so that they are prepared to hit the ground running as they confidently implement effective methods. If you know how to be effective from the first day, you will have the confidence necessary to add to your bag of tricks as your experience guides you.

So, could it be argued that there are many more principles for effective teaching of reading and writing than the ten I outline in Chapter 1? Sure. But I am certain that the ten principles I present there will be memorable, useful, helpful, and effective. Does this textbook cover every permutation of every practice option? No. But I am sure that the 38 procedures outlined in detail in the Compendium at the back of the text constitute a memorable, useful, helpful, and effective critical mass of practice options on which you can build.

This textbook is neither an encyclopedia of reading methods nor a comprehensive history of reading. Rather, it is intended as a practical application of knowledge obtained from these encyclopedias and histories and, more important, from the experiences of hundreds of teachers across the country. Not only is the focus on practical application—the reason professors will adopt this book—but that focus is also the reason beginning teachers will keep this book.

How Is This Textbook Organized?

This book is organized into four sections. The three chapters in the first section address the question "What is a balanced approach to literacy instruction?" Chapter 1 sets out ten basic instructional principles on which to build balanced literacy instruction. These ten principles describe how effective teachers teach reading and writing. Chapter 2 explains the reading and writing processes that teachers use to teach reading and writing, no matter whether teachers are teaching literature focus units, literature circles, reading and writing workshop, or content area units. Chapter 3 describes both traditional and authentic assessment procedures.

Part II examines the question "How do children learn to read and write?" Chapter 4 is devoted to the special needs of emergent readers and writers (kindergartners and first graders). The basics of the alphabetic principle—phonemic awareness, phonics, and spelling—are explained in Chapter 5. Chapter 6 explains word recognition and word identification and how students become fluent readers.

Answering the question "How do readers and writers construct meaning?" is the focus of Chapters 7 and through 9. Chapter 7 is devoted to vocabulary and how students refine their understanding of the meanings of words. Chapter 8 focuses on comprehension—the five comprehension processes, the metacognitive strategies that capable readers use, and comprehension activities during each stage of the reading process. Chapter 9 presents information about the structure of stories, informational books, and poetry. Students use their knowledge of the structure of texts in comprehending what they read.

The five chapters in Part IV answer the question "How do teachers organize literacy instruction?" Chapters on literature focus units, literature circles, reading and writing workshop, basal reading textbooks, and content area units show teachers how to set up their instructional programs based on the reading and writing processes described in Chapter 2.

What Are the Special Features?

I have included nine special features to increase the effectiveness of the text and to address the most current resources in the field of literacy.

Principles of Effective Reading Instruction. I set out a list of ten principles of effective reading instruction in Chapter 1, and these principles provide the foundation for the entire textbook. Near the end of each chapter (except Chapter 1), the Review section includes a feature in which I contrast effective and ineffective instructional practices related to the chapter topic. Instructors and students alike will find these features very interesting.

Vignettes. Starting with Chapter 2, I begin each chapter with a vignette in which you will see how a real teacher teaches the topic addressed in the chapter. These vignettes are rich and detailed, with chapter-opener photos, dialogue, student writing samples, and illustrations. Readers will be drawn into the story of literacy instruction in a real classroom as they build background and activate prior knowledge about the chapter's topic. Throughout the chapter, I refer readers to the vignette so that they can apply the concepts they are reading about and make connections to the world of practice.

Website Addresses. Annotated Internet website addresses are listed as margin notes in each chapter. These websites are suggested as resources that readers might use to extend their learning and read the most up-to-date information about guided reading, interactive writing, fluency, comprehension, literature circles, and other literacy topics. Instructors and students are also encouraged to visit Merrill/Prentice Hall's Companion Website at www.prenhall.com/tompkins.

Technology Links. Readers will learn about innovative uses of technology in teaching reading and writing through the Technology Links. Among the topics I present in these special features are screen reading using captioned text on television to develop reading fluency, electronic dialoguing to write back and forth to a reading buddy to respond to literature, videotape portfolios to document student learning, and interactive electronic books on CD-ROM to teach high-frequency words and phonics skills.

Chapter on the Reading and Writing Processes. In Chapter 2 I describe the reading and writing processes. These two processes provide the foundation for the chapters on how to organize the instructional programs, literature focus units (Chapter 10), literature circles (Chapter 11), reading and writing workshop (Chapter 12), basal reading textbooks (Chapter 13), and thematic units (Chapter 14).

Chapter on Breaking the Code. Chapter 5 focuses on the phonological system: phonemic awareness, phonics, and spelling. Phonics is a controversial topic in reading, and the position I take in this chapter is that phonics and related topics are part of a balanced literacy program and are best taught in the context of real literature using a whole-part-whole approach.

Chapter on Fluency. In Chapter 6 I explain that students in the primary grades need to develop strong word recognition skills so that they can automatically read hundreds and hundreds of words in order to become fluent readers. That is, they can read quickly and with expression by the time they are third graders. Students also need to develop word identification tools, including phonemic and morphological analysis, so that they can decode unfamiliar words as they are reading.

Chapter on Comprehension. Chapter 8 delves into five comprehension processes and how teachers teach and assess each process. I set out 12 strategies that readers and writers use and explain the difference between strategies and skills. To emphasize the importance of helping children become strategic readers, I compare more-capable readers will less-capable readers and writers and conclude that more-capable students have both more skills and more strategies, but what really separates the two groups is that more-capable readers are more strategic.

Compendium of Instructional Procedures. For your ready reference, the Compendium at the back of the book provides a comprehensive review of 38 instructional procedures used in literature-based reading classrooms, with step-by-step directions and student samples. The procedures are highlighted when they are mentioned in the text to cue readers to consult the Compendium for more detailed information.

ACKNOWLEDGMENTS

Many people helped and encouraged me during the development of this text. My heartfelt thanks go to each of them. First, I want to thank my students at California State University, Fresno, who taught me while I taught them, and the teacher-consultants in the San Joaquin Valley Writing Project, who shared their expertise with me. Their insightful questions challenged and broadened my thinking.

Thanks, too, go to the teachers who welcomed me into their classrooms, showed me how they used literature in innovative ways, and allowed me to learn from them and their students. In particular, I want to express my appreciation to the teachers and students who appear in the vignettes: Eileen Boland, Tenaya Middle School, Fresno, CA; Jessica Bradshaw, Rocky Hill Elementary School, Exeter, CA: Roberta Dillon, Armona Elementary School, Armona, CA: Whitney Donnelly, Williams Ranch School, Penn Valley, CA; Laurie Goodman, Parkview Middle School, Armona, CA; Judy Hoddy, Hennessey School, Grass Valley, CA; Sally Mast, Thomas Elementary School, Fresno, CA; Kristi Ohashi, Terry Elementary School, Selma, CA; Jill Peterson, Mickey Cox Elementary School, Clovis, CA; Judy Roberts, Lincoln Elementary School, Madera, CA; Camilla Simmons, Charles Wright School, Merced, CA, and Darcy Williams, Aynesworth Elementary School, Fresno, CA. Thanks, too, to Sonja Wiens, Leavenworth Elementary School, Fresno, CA; Kimberly Clark, Aynesworth Elementary School, Fresno, CA; Lisa Coronado and Wendy Magill, Lincoln Elementary School, Madera, CA; Bob Dickinson, Williams Ranch School, Penn Valley, CA; Judith Salzberg and Mr. Lee, Charles Wright School, Merced, CA; Kim Ransdell, Armona Elementary School, Armona, CA, and their students also appeared in photos in the book. I also want to acknowledge Jenny Reno and the teachers and students at Western Hills Elementary School, Lawton, OK, and Carol Ochs, Jackson Elementary School, Norman, OK, who have been a part of each of the books I have written. I want also to thank the reviewers of my manuscript for their comments and insights: Judy A. Abbott, West Virginia University; Joanne E. Bernstein, Brooklyn College; Jean M. Casey, California State University, Long Beach; Carolyn L. Piazza, Florida State University; Thomas C. Potter, California State University, Northridge; Cheryl Rosaen, Michigan State University; and Sharyn Walker, Bowling Green State University.

Finally, I am indebted to Jeff Johnston and his team at Merrill/Prentice Hall in Columbus, Ohio, who produce so many high-quality publications. I am honored to be a Merrill author. Linda Scharp McElhiney continues to be the guiding force behind my work. I want to express my appreciation to Mary Irvin, who supervised the production of this book, and to Jonathan Lawrence, who has again dealt so expertly with production details and copyediting.

Discover the Companion Website Accompanying This Book

The Prentice Hall Companion Website: A Virtual Learning Environment

Technology is a constantly growing and changing aspect of our field that is creating a need for content and resources. To address this emerging need, Prentice Hall has developed an online learning environment for students and professors alike— Companion Websites—to support our textbooks.

In creating a Companion Website, our goal is to build on and enhance what the textbook already offers. For this reason, the content for each user-friendly website is organized by chapter and provides the professor and student with a variety of meaningful resources. Common features of a Companion Website include:

For the Professor

Every Companion Website integrates **Syllabus Manager™**, an online syllabus creation and management utility.

- **Syllabus Manager™** provides you, the instructor, with an easy, step-by-step process to create and revise syllabi, with direct links into Companion Website and other online content without having to learn HTML.

- Students may log on to your syllabus during any study session. All they need to know is the web address for the Companion Website and the password you've assigned to your syllabus.

- After you have created a syllabus using **Syllabus Manager™**, students may enter the syllabus for their course section from any point in the Companion Website.

- Clicking on a date, the student is shown the list of activities for the assignment. The activities for each assignment are linked directly to actual content, saving time for students.

- Adding assignments consists of clicking on the desired due date, then filling in the details of the assignment—name of the assignment, instructions, and whether or not it is a one-time or repeating assignment.

- In addition, links to other activities can be created easily. If the activity is online, a URL can be entered in the space provided, and it will be linked automatically in the final syllabus.

❦ Your completed syllabus is hosted on our servers, allowing convenient updates from any computer on the Internet. Changes you make to your syllabus are immediately available to your students at their next logon.

For the Student

❦ **Chapter Objectives**—outline key concepts from the text.

❦ **Interactive Self-quizzes**—complete with hints and automatic grading that provide immediate feedback for students

After students submit their answers for the interactive self-quizzes, the Companion Website **Results Reporter** computes a percentage grade, provides a graphic representation of how many questions were answered correctly and incorrectly, and gives a question by question analysis of the quiz. Students are given the option to send their quiz to up to four email addresses (professor, teaching assistant, study partner, etc.)

❦ **Message Board**—serves as a virtual bulletin board to post–or respond to–questions or comments to/from a national audience

❦ **Chat**—real-time chat with anyone who is using the text anywhere in the country—ideal for discussion and study groups, class projects, etc.

❦ **Web Destinations**—links to www sites that relate to chapter conent

❦ **Additional Resources**—access to chapter-specific or general content that enhances material found in the text

To take advantage of these and other resources, please visit the LITERACY IN THE 21ST CENTURY Companion Website at

www.prenhall.com/tompkins

Brief Contents

Contents

PART II
How Do Children Learn to Read and Write?   116

4   Working With Emergent Readers and Writers   120

5   Breaking the Alphabetic Code   160

PART V
Compendium of Instructional Procedures   491

Special Features

How Effective Teachers . . .

Technology Link

Assessment Tools

Part I
What Is a Balanced Approach to Literacy Instruction?

Mrs. Peterson shares objects from a book box—white vegetables, a bunny, and a children's version of *Dracula*—as she introduces *Bunnicula: A Rabbit-Tale of Mystery.*

Text Set

Featured Selection
Howe, D., & Howe, J. (1979). *Bunnicula: A rabbit-tale of mystery.* New York: Atheneum.

Related Books
Howe, J. (1982). *Howliday Inn.* New York: Atheneum.
Howe, J. (1984). *The celery stalks at midnight.* New York: Atheneum.
Howe, J. (1987). *Nighty-nightmare.* New York: Atheneum.
Howe, J. (1989). *Harold and Chester in Scared silly: A Halloween treat.* New York: Morrow.
Howe, J. (1990). *Hot fudge.* New York: Morrow.
Howe, J. (1992). *Return to Howliday Inn.* New York: Atheneum.

About the Author
Howe, J. (1994). *Playing with words.* Katonah, NY: Richard C. Owen.

Mrs. Peterson joins a small group of sixth graders to talk about the fifth chapter in a grand conversation. Students also refer to their reading logs to read favorite sentences, highlight difficult vocabulary words, and make predictions about what will happen next.

Bunnicula
A Rabbit-Tale of
Mystery

Students write responses in reading logs after they read each chapter. They focus on connecting the story to their own lives and write about what they might do in a similar situation. They also note difficult vocabulary words and write a favorite sentence.

As an exploring step activity, Mrs. Peterson shares information about author James Howe and reads aloud his autobiography *Playing With Words*. Some students decide to write letters to the author to ask him about how he thought of the clever story idea.

Bunnicula is a word that the author invented by combining the words *bunny* and *Dracula*. Mrs. Peterson teaches a minilesson on portmanteau words, including *brunch*, *flurry*, and *motel*. Then students practice matching the portmanteau word with the two words that were combined to form it at the Word Work Center.

Students extend their learning as they develop projects. This student shares vampire jokes and riddles with classmates during a sharing session.

These girls share their "Count Dracula's Vampire Facts" poster with the class. One student reads each fact aloud and classmates decide whether the fact is true or false. Then the student lifts the red tab to check the answer.

Chapter 1

Becoming an Effective Teacher of Reading

— Chapter Questions —

What does an effective teacher of reading do?

Which instructional practices are most effective for teaching reading and writing?

What is a balanced approach to literacy?

The children of the twenty-first century will face many challenges that will require them to use reading and writing in different forms. As we begin the new millennium, teachers are learning research-based approaches to teach reading and writing that will prepare their students for the future. Teachers make a significant difference in children's lives, and this book is designed to help you become an effective reading teacher. Researchers have examined many teaching practices and have drawn some important conclusions about the most effective ones. We must teach students the processes of reading and writing, as well as how to use reading and writing as learning tools. Bill Teale (1995) challenges us to teach students to think with and through reading and writing, to use reading and writing to get a wide variety of things done in their lives, and to use reading and writing for pleasure and insight.

Let's start with some definitions. "Literacy" used to mean knowing how to read, but the term has been broadened to encompass both reading and writing. Now literacy means the competence "to carry out the complex tasks using reading and writing related to the world of work and to life outside the school" (*Cases in Literacy,* 1989, p. 36). Educators are also identifying other literacies that they believe will be needed in the twenty-first century (Harris & Hodges, 1995). Our reliance on radio and television for conveying ideas has awakened us to the importance of "oracy," the ability to express and understand spoken language. Visual literacy, the ability to create meaning from illustrations, is also receiving a great deal of attention.

The term "literacy" is being used in other ways as well. Teachers are introducing even very young children to computers and developing their "computer literacy." Similarly, math and science educators speak of mathematical and scientific literacies. Hirsch (1987) called for another type of literacy, "cultural literacy," as a way to introduce children "to the major ideas and ideals from past cultures that have defined and shaped today's society" (p. 10). Literacy, however, is not a prescription of certain books to read or concepts to define. Rather, according to Rafferty (1999), it is a tool, a way to learn about the world and a means to participate more fully in the technological society of the twenty-first century.

Both reading and writing are processes of constructing meaning. Sometimes children describe reading as "saying all the words right," or writing as "making all your letters neatly," but when they do they are focusing only on the surface features of reading and writing. In actuality, readers create meaning for the words in the book based on their own knowledge and experiences. Similarly, writers take ideas and organize them using their knowledge of spelling and grammar to transcribe their thoughts onto paper or computer screens. Phonics, decoding, and reading aloud are all part of reading, but the essence of reading is the creation of meaning. By the same token, spelling, handwriting, and using capital letters correctly are parts of writing, but without ideas to communicate, neat handwriting isn't very important.

In this chapter, I introduce the ten principles of an effective reading program. Each principle is stated in terms of what an effective reading teacher does. Ernest Boyer, in his book *The Basic School* (1995), explains that we really do know what works in elementary schools. From the research that has been conducted in the last 25 years and the effective practices used in good schools today, we can identify the characteristics of a quality literacy program and incorporate them in our own teaching.

www.ciera.org

Ten Research-Based Principles.
Strategies for improving the reading achievement of America's children.

1. EFFECTIVE TEACHERS OF READING CREATE A COMMUNITY OF LEARNERS

Reading classrooms are social settings in which students read, discuss, and write about literature. Together, students and their teachers create the classroom community, and the type of community they create strongly influences students' learning. Effective teachers establish a community of learners in which students are motivated to learn and are actively involved in reading and writing activities. Teachers and students work collaboratively and purposefully. Perhaps the most striking quality of classroom communities is the partnership that the teacher and students create. Students are a "family" in which all the members respect one another and support each other's learning. Students value culturally and linguistically diverse classmates and recognize that all students make important contributions to the classroom (Wells & Chang-Wells, 1992).

Students and teachers work together for the common good of the community. Consider the differences between renting and owning a home. In a classroom community, students and the teacher are joint "owners" of the classroom. Students assume responsibility for their own learning and behavior, work collaboratively with classmates, complete assignments, and care for the classroom. In traditional classrooms, in contrast, the classroom is the teacher's and students are simply "renters" for the school year. This doesn't mean that, in a classroom community, teachers abdicate their responsibility to the students. Teachers retain all of their roles as guide, instructor, monitor, coach, mentor, and grader. Sometimes these roles are shared with students, but the ultimate responsibility remains with the teacher.

Ten Characteristics of Classroom Communities

Classroom communities have specific characteristics that are conducive to learning and which support students' interactions with literature. Ten of the characteristics are:

1. *Responsibility.* Students are responsible for their learning, their behavior, and the contributions they make in the classroom. They see themselves as valued and contributing members of the classroom community.
2. *Opportunities.* Children have opportunities to read and write for genuine and meaningful purposes. They read real books and write for real audiences—their classmates, their parents, members of their community. They rarely use workbooks or drill-and-practice sheets.
3. *Engagement.* Students are motivated to learn and actively involved in reading and writing activities. Students sometimes choose which books to read, how they will respond to a book, and which reading and writing projects they will pursue.
4. *Demonstration.* Teachers provide demonstrations of literacy skills and strategies, and children observe in order to learn what more capable readers and writers do.
5. *Risk-taking.* Students are encouraged to explore topics, make guesses, and take risks.
6. *Instruction.* Teachers are expert readers and writers, and they provide instruction through **minilessons** (see the Compendium for more information about this and all other highlighted terms in this chapter) on procedures, skills, and strategies related to reading and writing.
7. *Response.* Children share personal connections to stories, make predictions, ask questions, and deepen their comprehension as they write in reading logs and participate in **grand conversations.** When they write, children share their rough

drafts in writing groups to get feedback on how well they are communicating, and they celebrate their published books by sharing them with classmates.

8. *Choice.* Students often make choices about the books they read and the writing they do within the parameters set by the teacher. When given opportunities to make choices, students are often more highly motivated to read and write, and they value their learning experience more because it is more meaningful to them.

9. *Time.* Children need large chunks of time to pursue reading and writing activities. It doesn't work well for teachers to break the classroom schedule into many small time blocks. Two to three hours of uninterrupted time each day for reading and writing instruction is recommended. It is important to minimize disruptions during the time set aside for literacy instruction, and administrators should schedule computer, music, art, and other pull-out programs so that they do not interfere. This is especially important in the primary grades.

10. *Assessment.* Teachers and children work together to establish guidelines for assessment so that children can monitor their own work and participate in the evaluation.

These ten characteristics are reviewed in Figure 1–1.

How to Create a Classroom Community

Teachers are more successful when they take the first two weeks of the school year to establish the classroom environment (Sumara & Walker, 1991). Teachers can't assume that children will be familiar with the procedures and routines or that they will instinctively be cooperative, responsible, and respectful of classmates. Teachers explicitly explain classroom routines, such as how to get supplies out and put them away and how to work with classmates in a cooperative group, and set the expectation that students will adhere to the routines. Next, they demonstrate literacy procedures, including how to choose a book from the classroom library to read, how to provide feedback about a classmate's writing, and how to participate in a grand conversation about a book. Third, teachers model ways of interacting with students, responding to literature, respecting classmates, and assisting classmates with reading and writing projects.

Teachers are the classroom managers. They set expectations and clearly explain to children what is expected of them and what is valued in the classroom. The classroom rules are specific and consistent, and teachers also set limits. For example, children might be allowed to talk quietly with classmates when they are working, but they are not allowed to shout across the classroom or talk when the teacher is talking or when students are making a presentation to the class. Teachers also model classroom rules themselves as they interact with students. According to Sumara and Walker (1991), the process of socialization at the beginning of the school year is planned, deliberate, and crucial to the success of the literacy program.

Not everything can be accomplished during the first two weeks, however. Teachers continue to reinforce classroom routines and literacy procedures. One way is to have student leaders model the desired routines and behaviors. When this is done, other students are likely to follow the lead. Teachers also continue to teach additional literacy procedures as students are involved in new types of activities. The classroom community evolves during the school year, but the foundation is laid during the first two weeks.

Teachers develop a predictable classroom environment with familiar routines and literacy procedures. Children feel comfortable, safe, and more willing to take risks and experiment in a predictable classroom environment. This is especially true for students from varied cultures, students learning English as a second language, and less capable readers and writers.

Figure 1–1   Ten characteristics of a community of learners

Characteristic	Students' Role	Teacher's Role
Responsibility	Students are responsible for fully participating in the classroom, including completing assignments, participating in groups, and cooperating with classmates.	Teachers set guidelines and have the expectation that students will be responsible. Teachers also model responsible behavior.
Opportunities	Students take advantage of learning opportunities provided in class. They read independently during reading workshop, and they share their writing during sharing time.	Teachers provide opportunities for students to read and write in genuine and meaningful activities, not contrived practice activities.
Engagement	Students are actively involved in reading and writing activities. They are motivated and industrious because they are reading real literature and are involved in activities they find meaningful.	Teachers make it possible for students to be engaged by the literature and activities they provide for students. Also, by planning units with students and allowing them to make choices, they motivate students to complete assignments.
Demonstration	Students observe the teacher's demonstrations of skills and strategies that readers and writers use.	Teachers demonstrate what readers and writers do and use think-alouds to explain their thinking during the demonstrations.
Risk-taking	Students explore what they are learning, take risks as they ask questions, and make guesses. They expect not to be laughed at or made fun of. They view learning as a process of exploration.	Teachers encourage students to take risks, make guesses, and explore their thinking. They deemphasize students' need to get things "right."
Instruction	Students look to the teacher to provide instruction on procedures, concepts, strategies, and skills related to reading and writing. Students participate in minilessons and then apply what they have learned in their own reading and writing.	Teachers provide instruction through minilessons. During minilessons, teachers provide information and make connections to the reading and writing in which students are involved.
Response	Students respond to books they are reading in reading logs and grand conversations. They share their writing in writing groups and get feedback from classmates.	Teachers provide opportunities for students to share and respond to reading and activities. Students are a supportive audience for classmates.
Choice	Students make choices about some books they read, some writing activities, and some projects they develop within parameters set by the teacher.	Teachers encourage students to choose some of the books they read and some of the writing activities and projects they develop.
Time	Students have large chunks of time for reading and writing activities. They work on projects over days and weeks and understand when assignments are due.	Teachers organize the class schedule with large chunks of time for reading and writing activities. They plan units with students and together set deadlines.
Assessment	Students understand how they will be assessed and graded, and they participate in their assessment. They collect their work in progress in folders and choose which work they will place in portfolios.	Teachers set grading plans with students before beginning each unit, meet with students in assessment conferences, and assist students in collecting work for portfolios.

The classroom community also extends beyond the walls of the classroom to include the entire school and the wider community. Within the school, students become "buddies" with students in other classes and get together to read and write in pairs (Morrice & Simmons, 1991). When parents and other community members come into the school, they demonstrate the value they place on education by working as tutors and aides, sharing their cultures, and demonstrating other types of expertise (Graves, 1995).

Professional Resources for Reading Teachers

As you begin teaching, you will want to continue to learn about reading and writing instruction and ways to become a more effective teacher. Through professional organizations, you can stay abreast of the newest research and ways to implement the research in your classroom. Two organizations dedicated to improving literacy instruction are the International Reading Association (IRA) and the National Council of Teachers of English (NCTE). Both organizations publish journals for classroom teachers, and both also organize yearly conferences that are held in major cities around the United States. In addition, these organizations have state and local affiliate groups you can join. Through these local groups, you can meet other teachers with similar interests and concerns and form support networks.

www.mcrel.org

Literacy Resources Online.
Links to a wide variety of resources and reports about reading and writing.

In addition, teachers learn more about teaching writing by participating in workshops sponsored by the National Writing Project (NWP). Since it began more than 25 years ago at the University of California, Berkeley, the NWP has spread to more than 150 sites located in almost every state. For example, the Gateway Writing Project serves the St. Louis area, and the Capital Writing Project serves the Washington, DC, area. You may be able to attend in-service workshops that are scheduled in school districts near each affiliate group. After you have a few years' teaching experience, you might be interested in applying to participate in a special summer institute. Figure 1–2 provides information about ways to continue learning about teaching reading and writing.

2. EFFECTIVE TEACHERS OF READING UNDERSTAND HOW CHILDREN LEARN

Understanding how children learn, and particularly how they learn to read, influences the instructional approaches that effective teachers use. A generation ago, behaviorists influenced how teachers taught reading. According to behavioral theory, students learn to read by learning a series of discrete, sequenced skills (Skinner, 1968), and teachers applied this theory by drilling students on skills and having them complete skills worksheets.

Reading instruction has changed considerably in the past 25 years, thanks to four intertwining theories of learning, language, and literacy. These theories are the constructivist, interactive, sociolinguistic, and reader response theories. They are overviewed in Figure 1–3. In the figure, the theories are drawn as though they were parts of a jigsaw puzzle in order to show that they are linked.

Constructivist Learning Theories

Jean Piaget's (1969) theoretical framework differed substantially from behaviorist theories. Piaget described learning as the modification of students' cognitive structures, or schemata, as they interact with and adapt to their environment. Schemata

Figure 1–2 Ways to learn more about teaching reading and writing

☞ Join these literacy organizations:

International Reading
  Association (IRA)
800 Barksdale Road
P.O. Box 8139
Newark, DE 19711
www.reading.org

National Council of
  Teachers of English (NCTE)
1111 Kenyon Road
Urbana, IL 61801
www.ncte.org

☞ Attend conferences sponsored by local professional organizations, IRA and NCTE affiliate groups, and national organizations.

☞ Subscribe to one or more of these journals and magazines about reading, children's literature, and writing:

Book Links
P.O. Box 1347
Elmhurst, IL 60126

CBC Features
Children's Book Council, Inc.
350 Scotland Rd.
Orange, NJ 07050

The Horn Book
Park Square Building
31 Saint James Avenue
Boston, MA 02116

Language Arts
National Council of Teachers
  of English
1111 Kenyon Road
Urbana, IL 61801

The New Advocate
480 Washington Street
Norwood, MA 02062

Primary Voices K–6
National Council of Teachers
  of English
1111 Kenyon Road
Urbana, IL 61801

The Reading Teacher
International Reading
  Association
800 Barksdale Road
P.O. Box 8139
Newark, DE 19711

Teaching K–8
P.O. Box 54808
Boulder, CO 80322

Voices From the Middle
National Council of Teachers
  of English
1111 Kenyon Road
Urbana, IL 61801

Writing Teacher
P.O. Box 791437
San Antonio, TX 78279

☞ Check the International Reading Association's online journal, *Reading Online* (www.readingonline.org)

☞ Subscribe to a literacy-related listserv, such as RTEACHER at Listserv@listserv.syr.edu.

☞ Visit local children's bookstores and libraries to preview newly published children's books and meet children's authors when they visit.

☞ Attend writing workshops sponsored by the local affiliate of the National Writing Project (NWP) or apply to participate in a summer invitational institute. To locate the NWP affiliate group nearest you, contact the National Writing Project, School of Education, University of California, Berkeley, CA 94720.

| Figure 1–3 | The four learning theories |

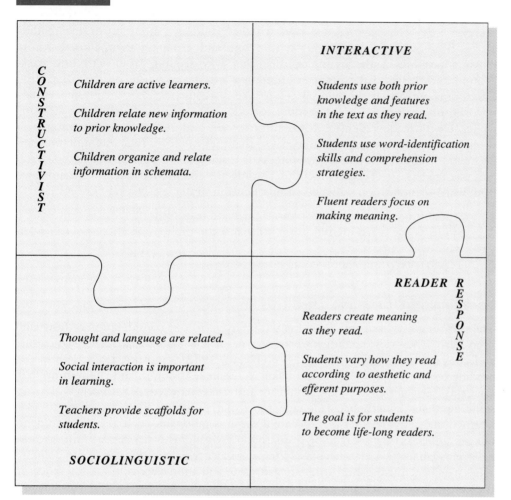

are like mental filing cabinets, and new information is organized with prior knowledge in the filing system. Piaget also posited that children are active and motivated thinkers and learners. This definition of learning and children's role in learning requires a reexamination of the teacher's role. Instead of being dispensers of knowledge, teachers engage students with experiences so that they modify their schemata and construct their own knowledge. The key concepts are:

1. Children are active learners.
2. Children relate new information to prior knowledge.
3. Children organize and integrate information in schemata.

Interactive Learning Theories

The interactive theories describe what readers do as they read. They emphasize that readers focus on comprehension, or making meaning, as they read (Rumelhart, 1977; Stanovich, 1980). Readers construct meaning using a combination of

www.sedl.org

Applying Technology to Restructuring and Learning.
Models of constructivist learning environments supported by technology.

text-based information (information from the text) and reader-based information (information from readers' backgrounds of knowledge, or schemata). These theories echo the importance of schemata described in the constructivist theories. In the past, educators have argued over whether children's attention during reading moves from noticing the letters on the page and grouping them into words to making meaning in the brain, or the other way around, from activating background knowledge in the brain to examining letters and words on the page. Educators now agree that the two processes take place interactively, at the same time.

The interactive model of reading includes an executive function, or decision maker. Fluent readers identify words automatically and use word-identification skills when they come across unfamiliar words so that they can focus their attention on comprehension. The decision maker monitors the reading process and the skills and strategies that readers use. Teachers focus on reading as a comprehension process and teach both word-identification skills and comprehension strategies. The key concepts are:

1. Students use both their prior knowledge and features in the text as they read.
2. Students use word-identification skills and comprehension strategies to understand what they read.
3. Teachers help students become fluent readers.

Sociolinguistic Learning Theories

The sociolinguists contribute a cultural dimension to our consideration of how children learn. They view reading and writing as social activities that reflect the culture and community in which students live (Heath, 1983; Vygotsky, 1978, 1986). According to Lev Vygotsky, language helps to organize thought, and children use language to learn as well as to communicate and share experiences with others. Understanding that children use language for social purposes allows teachers to plan instructional activities that incorporate a social component, such as having students talk about books they are reading or share their writing with classmates. And, because children's language and concepts of literacy reflect their cultures and home communities, teachers must respect students' language and appreciate cultural differences in their attitudes toward learning and becoming literate.

Social interaction enhances learning in two other ways: scaffolding and the zone of proximal development (Dixon-Krauss, 1996). Scaffolding is a support mechanism that teachers and parents use to assist students. Vygotsky suggests that children can accomplish more difficult things in collaboration with adults than they can on their own. For example, when teachers assist students to read a book they could not read independently or help students revise a piece of writing, they are scaffolding. Vygotsky also suggests that children learn very little when they perform tasks that they can already do independently. He recommends the zone of proximal development, the range of tasks between students' actual developmental level and their potential development. More challenging tasks done with the teacher's scaffolding are more conducive to learning. As students learn, teachers gradually withdraw their support so that eventually students perform the task independently. Then the cycle begins again. The key concepts are:

1. Thought and language are interrelated.
2. Social interaction is important in learning.
3. Teachers provide scaffolds for students.
4. Teachers plan instruction based on students' zone of proximal development.

www.csunix1.lvc.edu

Vygotsky's Theory of Cognitive Development. *Learn about Lev Vygotsky and the educational contributions of his theory.*

Reader Response Learning Theories

Louise Rosenblatt (1978, 1983) and other reader response theorists consider how students create meaning as they read. These theories extend the constructivist theories about schemata and making meaning in the brain, not the eyes. According to reader response theorists, students do not try to figure out the author's meaning as they read. Instead, they negotiate or create a meaning that makes sense based on the words they are reading and their own background knowledge. Reader response theorists agree with Piaget that readers are active and responsible for their learning.

Rosenblatt (1991) explains that there are two stances or purposes for reading. When readers read for enjoyment or pleasure, they assume an aesthetic stance, and when they read to locate and remember information, they read efferently. Rosenblatt suggests that these two stances represent the ends of a continuum and that readers often use a combination of the two stances when they read, whether they are reading stories or informational books. For example, when students read *Nature's Green Umbrella* (Gibbons, 1994), an informational book about tropical rain forests, they may read efferently to locate information about the animals that live in rain forests. Or they may read aesthetically, carried off—in their minds, at least—on an expedition to the Amazon River. When students read a novel such as *Sarah, Plain and Tall* (MacLachlan, 1985), a story about a mail-order bride, they usually read aesthetically as they relive life on the prairie a century ago. Students are encouraged to step into the story and become a character and to "live" the story. This conflicts with more traditional approaches in which teachers ask students to recall specific information from the story, thus forcing students to read efferently, to take away information. Reader response theory suggests that when students read efferently rather than aesthetically, they do not learn to love reading and may not become lifelong readers. The key concepts are:

1. Readers create meaning as they read.
2. Students vary how they read depending on whether they are reading for aesthetic or efferent purposes.
3. The goal of literacy instruction is for students to become lifelong readers.

3. EFFECTIVE TEACHERS OF READING SUPPORT CHILDREN'S USE OF THE FOUR CUEING SYSTEMS

Language is a complex system for creating meaning through socially shared conventions (Halliday, 1978). English, like other languages, involves four cueing systems:

❧ the phonological or sound system
❧ the syntactic or structural system
❧ the semantic or meaning system
❧ the pragmatic or social and cultural use system

Together these four systems make communication possible, and children and adults use all four systems simultaneously as they read, write, listen, and talk. Information about the four cueing systems is summarized in Figure 1–4.

| | Figure 1–4 | Relationships among the four cueing systems |

Type	Terms	Uses in the Elementary Grades
Phonological System The sound system of English with approximately 44 sounds and more than 500 ways to spell the 44 sounds	❧ Phoneme (the smallest unit of sound) ❧ Grapheme (the written representation of a phoneme using one or more letters) ❧ Phonics (teaching sound-symbol correspondences and spelling rules)	❧ Pronouncing words ❧ Detecting regional and other dialects ❧ Decoding words when reading ❧ Using invented spelling ❧ Reading and writing alliterations and onomatopoeia ❧ Noticing rhyming words ❧ Dividing words into syllables
Syntactic System The structural system of English that governs how words are combined into sentences	❧ Syntax (the structure or grammar of a sentence) ❧ Morpheme (the smallest meaningful unit of language) ❧ Free morpheme (a morpheme that can stand alone as a word) ❧ Bound morpheme (a morpheme that must be attached to a free morpheme)	❧ Adding inflectional endings to words ❧ Combining words to form compound words ❧ Adding prefixes and suffixes to root words ❧ Using capitalization and punctuation to indicate beginnings and ends of sentences ❧ Writing simple, compound, and complex sentences ❧ Combining sentences
Semantic System The meaning system of English that focuses on vocabulary	❧ Semantics (meaning)	❧ Learning the meanings of words ❧ Discovering that some words have multiple meanings ❧ Studying synonyms, antonyms, and homonyms ❧ Using a dictionary and thesaurus ❧ Reading and writing comparisons (metaphors and similes)
Pragmatic System The system of English that varies language according to social and cultural uses	❧ Function (the purpose for which a person uses language) ❧ Standard English (the form of English used in textbooks and by television newscasters) ❧ Nonstandard English (other forms of English)	❧ Varying language to fit specific purposes ❧ Reading and writing dialogue in dialects ❧ Comparing standard and nonstandard forms of English

The Phonological System

There are approximately 44 speech sounds in English. Students learn to pronounce these sounds as they learn to talk, and they learn to associate the sounds with letters as they learn to read and write. Sounds are called phonemes, and they are represented in print with diagonal lines to differentiate them from graphemes (letter or letter combinations). Thus, the first grapheme in *mother* is *m*, while the phoneme is /m/. The phoneme in *soap* that is represented by the grapheme *oa* is called "long o" and written /ō/.

The phonological system is important for both oral and written language. Regional and cultural differences exist in the way people pronounce phonemes. For example, people from Massachusetts pronounce sounds differently from people from Georgia. Similarly, the English spoken in Australia is different from American English. Children who are learning English as a second language must learn to pronounce English sounds, and sounds that are different from those in their native language are particularly difficult to learn. For example, Spanish does not have /th/, and children who have immigrated to the United States from Mexico and other Spanish-speaking countries have difficulty pronouncing this sound. They often substitute /d/ for /th/ because both sounds are articulated in similar ways (Nathenson-Mejia, 1989). Younger children usually learn to pronounce the difficult sounds more easily than older children and adults.

Children use their knowledge of the phonological system as they learn to read and write. In a purely phonetic language, there would be a one-to-one correspondence between letters and sounds, and teaching students to sound out words would be a simple process. But English is not a purely phonetic language because there are 26 letters and 44 sounds and many ways to combine the letters to spell some of the sounds, especially vowels. Consider these ways to spell long *e: sea, green, Pete, me,* and *people.* And sometimes the patterns used to spell long *e* don't work, as in *head* and *great.* Phonics, which describes the phoneme-grapheme correspondences and related spelling rules, is an important part of reading instruction. Students use phonics information to decode words, but phonics instruction is not a complete reading program because only about half of our words can be decoded easily and because good readers do much more than just decode words when they read. This is an important point because the advertisements for some commercial phonics programs claim that they are complete programs.

Children in the primary grades also use their understanding of the phonological system to create invented or temporary spellings. First graders might, for example, spell *home* as *hm* or *hom,* and second graders might spell *school* as *skule,* based on their knowledge of phoneme-grapheme relationships and the English spelling patterns. As children learn more phonics and gain more experience reading and writing, their spellings become more conventional. For students who are learning English as a second language, their spellings often reflect their pronunciations of words (Nathenson-Mejia, 1989).

The Syntactic System

The syntactic system is the structural organization of English. This system is the grammar that regulates how words are combined into sentences. The word *grammar* here means the rules governing how words are combined in sentences, not parts of speech. Children use the syntactic system as they combine words to form sentences. Word order is important in English, and English speakers must arrange words into a sequence that makes sense. Young Spanish-speaking children who are learning English as a second language, for example, learn to say "This is my red sweater," not "This is my sweater red," which is the literal translation from Spanish.

Children use their knowledge of the syntactic system as they read. They anticipate that the words they are reading have been strung together into sentences. When they come to an unfamiliar word, they recognize its role in the sentence even if they don't know the terms for parts of speech. In the sentence "The horses galloped through the gate and out into the field," students may not be able to decode the word *through*, but they can easily substitute a reasonable word or phrase, such as *out of* or *past*.

Many of the capitalization and punctuation rules that elementary students learn reflect the syntactic system of language. Similarly, when children learn about simple, compound, and complex sentences they are learning about the syntactic system.

Another component of syntax is word forms. Words such as *dog* and *play* are morphemes, the smallest meaningful units in language. Word parts that change the meaning of a word are also morphemes. When the plural marker *-s* is added to *dog* to make *dogs*, for instance, or the past-tense marker *-ed* is added to *play* to make *played*, these words now have two morphemes because the inflectional endings change the meaning of the words. The words *dog* and *play* are free morphemes because they convey meaning while standing alone. The endings *-s* and *-ed* are bound morphemes because they must be attached to free morphemes to convey meaning. Compound words are two or more morphemes combined to create a new word. *Birthday*, for example, is a compound word made up of two free morphemes.

During the elementary grades, children learn to add affixes to words. Affixes that are added at the beginning of a word are prefixes, and affixes added at the end are suffixes. Both kinds of affixes are bound morphemes. The prefix *un-* in *unhappy* is a bound morpheme, and *happy* is a free morpheme because it can stand alone as a word.

The Semantic System

The third language system is the semantic or meaning system. Vocabulary is the key component of this system. As children learn to talk, they acquire a vocabulary that is continually increasing. Researchers estimate that children have a vocabulary of 5,000 words by the time they enter school, and they continue to acquire 3,000 to 4,000 words each year during the elementary grades (Lindfors, 1987; Nagy, 1988). Considering how many words children learn each year, it is unreasonable to assume that they learn words only through formal instruction. They learn many, many words informally through reading and through social studies and science lessons.

Children learn approximately 8 to 10 words a day. A remarkable achievement! As children learn a word, they move from a general understanding of the meaning of the word to a better-developed understanding, and they learn these words through real reading, not by copying definitions from a dictionary. Researchers have estimated that students need to read a word 4 to 14 times to make it their own, and this is only possible when students read and reread books and write about what they are reading.

The Pragmatic System

The fourth language system is pragmatics, which deals with the social aspects of language use. People use language for many purposes, and how they talk or write varies according to their purpose and audience. Language use also varies among social classes, ethnic groups, and geographic regions. These varieties are known as dialects. School is one cultural community, and the language of school is Standard English. This dialect is formal—the one used in textbooks, newspapers, and magazines and by television newscasters. Other forms, including those spoken in urban ghettos, in Appalachia, and by Mexican Americans in the Southwest, are generally classified as nonstandard English. These nonstandard forms of English are alternatives in which the phonology, syntax, and semantics differ from those of Standard English. These forms are neither inferior nor substandard. They reflect the communities of speakers, and the speakers communicate as effectively as those who use Standard English. The goal is for children to add Standard English to their repertoire of language registers, not to replace their home dialect with Standard English.

As children who speak nonstandard English read texts written in Standard English, they often translate what they read into their dialect. Sometimes this occurs when children are reading aloud. For example, a sentence written "They are going to school" might be read aloud as "They be goin' to school." Emergent or beginning readers are not usually corrected when they translate words into nonstandard dialects as long as they don't change the meaning, but older, more fluent readers should be directed to read the words as they are printed in the book.

Effective teachers understand that children use all four cueing systems as they read and write. For example, when students read the sentence "Jimmy is playing ball with his father" correctly, they are probably using information from all four systems. When a child substitutes *dad* for *father* and reads "Jimmy is playing ball with his dad," he might be focusing on the semantic or pragmatic system rather than the phonological system. When a child substitutes *basketball* for *ball* and reads "Jimmy is playing basketball with his father," he might be relying on an illustration or his own experience playing basketball. Because both *basketball* and *ball* begin with *b*, he might have used the beginning sound as an aid in decoding, but he apparently did not consider how long the word *basketball* is compared with the word *ball*. When the child changes the syntax, as in "Jimmy, he play ball with his father," he may speak a nonstandard dialect. Sometimes a child reads the sentence as "Jump is play boat with his father," so that it doesn't make sense. The child chooses words with the correct beginning sound and uses appropriate parts of speech for at least some of the words, but there is no comprehension. This is a serious problem because the child doesn't seem to understand that what he reads must make sense.

You will learn ways to apply this information on the cueing systems in upcoming chapters. The information on the phonological system will be applied to phonics in Chapter 5, "Breaking the Alphabetic Code," and the information on the syntactic system will be applied to words and sentences in Chapter 6, "Developing Fluent Readers and Writers," and Chapter 7, "Learning About the Meanings of Words." The information on the semantic and pragmatic systems will be applied to vocabulary and comprehension in Chapter 7 and in Chapter 8, "Facilitating Students' Comprehension."

4. EFFECTIVE TEACHERS TEACH THE READING AND WRITING PROCESSES

Reading and writing are similar meaning-making processes, and students are involved in many similar activities as they read and write (Butler & Turbill, 1984). For example, both reading and writing begin with students activating prior knowledge and making plans, and students revise and refine their understanding as they move through the reading and writing processes.

The Reading Process

Effective teachers understand the steps in the reading and writing processes and teach students how to use the processes as they read and write. The reading process involves five steps:

1. *Prereading.* Students activate prior knowledge or build new understanding about the topic, the genre, the author, or something else related to the book.
2. *Reading.* Students read the book using one of several approaches, such as independent reading, guided reading, shared reading, guided reading, or listening to the teacher read aloud.
3. *Responding.* Students react to the book, ask questions, and express their feelings through **reading logs** and **grand conversations.**
4. *Exploring.* Students participate in word-study activities, examine the structure of the text, learn reading skills and strategies, or focus on other technical aspects of reading.
5. *Applying.* Students apply what they have learned to create projects in reading, writing, oral language, or the arts.

During an author unit on Beverly Cleary, students create puppets and present puppet shows for their classmates.

The Writing Process

In recent years, the emphasis in writing instruction has shifted from the finished product that students have written to the process they use as they gather and organize ideas, draft their ideas, and refine and polish their compositions. The teacher's role has changed from merely assigning and grading the finished product to working with students through the writing process. The writing process also includes five steps:

1. *Prewriting.* This is the "getting ready to write" step. Students gather and organize ideas for writing.
2. *Drafting.* Students write a rough draft. The focus in this step is for children pour out their ideas rather than to make the writing perfect. They will have opportunities to revise and edit their writing in the next two steps.
3. *Revising.* Students share their rough drafts, get feedback from classmates about how well they are creating meaning, and then make revisions based on the feedback they receive.
4. *Editing.* Students proofread to identify mechanical errors and then correct errors in spelling, capitalization, punctuation, and grammar.
5. *Publishing.* Students put their papers into final form and share their final copies with real audiences.

Even though these processes are described step by step, they are not necessarily sequential processes. Students do not always proceed through them in the same order; instead, they work in recurring cycles. The labeling of the steps is an aid to introducing and discussing the activities in the reading and writing processes. In the classroom, the steps merge and repeat. It is important that teachers plan literacy activities so that students can connect reading and writing. Figure 1–5 overviews the steps in the reading and writing processes.

The Reading-Writing Connection

Research shows that students learn to read and write better when the two processes are connected. Shanahan (1988) identified seven instructional principles for relating reading and writing:

1. Teachers provide daily opportunities for students to read literature and write in response to their reading.
2. Teachers introduce reading and writing in kindergarten and provide opportunities for young children to read and write for genuine purposes.
3. Teachers understand that students' reading and writing reflect the developmental nature of the reading-writing relationship.
4. Teachers make the reading-writing connection explicit to students by providing opportunities for them to share their writing with classmates, publish their own books, and learn about authors.
5. Teachers emphasize that the quality of students' reading and writing experiences depends on the processes they have used. For example, as students reread and talk about literature they deepen their comprehension, and as they revise their writing they communicate more effectively.
6. Teachers emphasize the communicative functions of reading and writing and involve students in reading and writing for genuine communication purposes.
7. Teachers teach reading and writing in meaningful contexts with literature.

Figure 1–5   Steps in the reading and writing processes

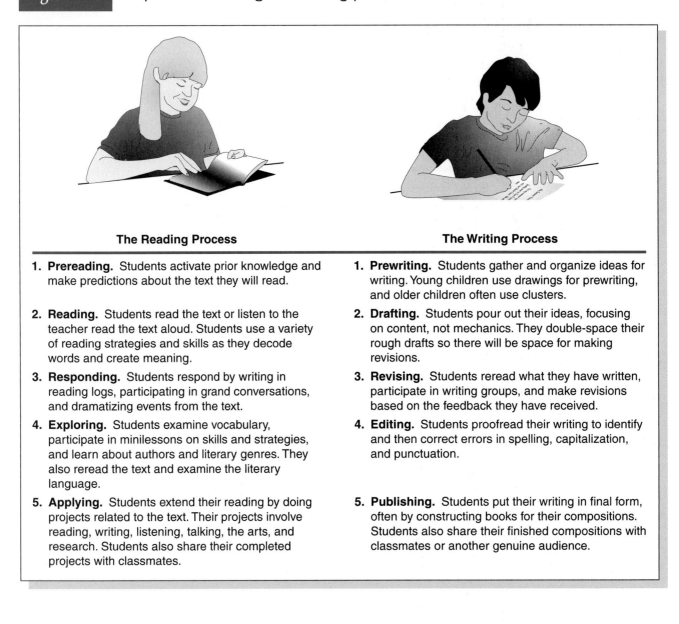

The Reading Process

1. **Prereading.** Students activate prior knowledge and make predictions about the text they will read.

2. **Reading.** Students read the text or listen to the teacher read the text aloud. Students use a variety of reading strategies and skills as they decode words and create meaning.

3. **Responding.** Students respond by writing in reading logs, participating in grand conversations, and dramatizing events from the text.

4. **Exploring.** Students examine vocabulary, participate in minilessons on skills and strategies, and learn about authors and literary genres. They also reread the text and examine the literary language.

5. **Applying.** Students extend their reading by doing projects related to the text. Their projects involve reading, writing, listening, talking, the arts, and research. Students also share their completed projects with classmates.

The Writing Process

1. **Prewriting.** Students gather and organize ideas for writing. Young children use drawings for prewriting, and older children often use clusters.

2. **Drafting.** Students pour out their ideas, focusing on content, not mechanics. They double-space their rough drafts so there will be space for making revisions.

3. **Revising.** Students reread what they have written, participate in writing groups, and make revisions based on the feedback they have received.

4. **Editing.** Students proofread their writing to identify and then correct errors in spelling, capitalization, and punctuation.

5. **Publishing.** Students put their writing in final form, often by constructing books for their compositions. Students also share their finished compositions with classmates or another genuine audience.

Effective teachers integrate the reading and writing processes in their balanced reading programs and encourage students to use both reading and writing as tools for learning.

You will learn more about the reading and writing processes and the connection between them in Chapter 2, "Teaching the Reading and Writing Processes."

5. EFFECTIVE TEACHERS SCAFFOLD CHILDREN'S READING AND WRITING EXPERIENCES

Teachers scaffold or support children's reading and writing as they demonstrate, guide, and teach, and they vary the amount of support they provide according to their instructional purpose and the children's needs. Sometimes teachers model how experienced readers read, or they record children's dictation when the writing is too difficult for children to do on their own. At other times, they carefully guide children as they read a leveled book or proofread their writing. Teachers also provide plenty of time for children to read and write independently and to practice skills they have learned. Teachers use five levels of support, moving from the greatest amount to the least as children assume more and more of the responsibility for themselves (Fountas & Pinnell, 1996). Figure 1–6 summarizes these five levels—modeled, shared, interactive, guided, and independent—of reading and writing.

Teachers working with kindergartners through eighth graders use all five levels. For instance, when teachers introduce a new writing form or teach a reading strategy or skill, they use demonstrations or modeling. Or, when teachers want children to practice a strategy or skill they have already taught, they might use a guided or independent literacy activity. The purpose of the activity, not the activity itself, determines which level of support is used. Teachers are less actively involved in directing independent reading and writing, but the quality of instruction that children have received is clearest when children work independently because they are applying what they have learned.

www.learningfirst.org

Every Child Reading. An action paper adopted by twelve educational organizations to ensure that all children learn to read well.

Modeled Reading and Writing

Teachers provide the greatest amount of support when they demonstrate or model how expert readers read and expert writers write while children observe. When teachers read aloud to children, they are modeling. They read fluently and with expression, and they talk about the strategies they use while they are reading. When they are modeling writing, teachers write a composition on chart paper or using an overhead projector so that all children can see what the teacher does and what is being written. Teachers use this level to demonstrate how to make small books and how to do new writing forms and formats, such as poems and letters. Often teachers talk about or reflect on their reading and writing processes as they read and write to show students the types of decisions they make and the strategies they use.

Four purposes of modeling are:

1. To demonstrate fluent reading and writing.
2. To demonstrate how to use reading and writing strategies, such as predicting, monitoring, and revising.
3. To demonstrate the procedure for a new reading or writing activity.
4. To demonstrate how reading and writing conventions and other skills work.

Shared Reading and Writing

At this level, children and the teacher "share" the reading and writing tasks. Teachers use shared reading to read big books with primary-grade children. The teacher does most of the reading, but children join in the reading of familiar and

Figure 1–6 A continuum of literacy instruction

Activity	Modeled Reading and Writing	Shared Reading and Writing
Reading	Teacher reads aloud, modeling how good readers read fluently and with expression. Books too difficult for students to read themselves are used. Examples: reading aloud and listening centers.	Teacher and students read big books together, with the students following as the teacher reads and then repeating familiar refrains. Books students can't read by themselves are used. Example: buddy reading.
Writing	Teacher writes in front of students, creating the text, doing the writing, and thinking aloud about writing strategies and skills. Example: demonstrations.	Teacher and students create the text together; then the teacher does the actual writing. Students may assist by spelling words. Example: language experience approach.

repeated words and phrases. Upper-grade teachers also use shared reading. When children are reading a book that is too difficult for them to read independently, the teacher may read aloud while the children follow along, reading aloud softly or silently.

Teachers at different grade levels use shared writing in a variety of ways. Primary-grade teachers often use the **language experience approach** to write children's dictation on paintings and brainstorm lists of words on the chalkboard, for example, while upper-grade teachers may take children's dictation when they make **K-W-L charts,** draw **story maps** and **clusters,** and write class collaboration poems.

The most important way that sharing differs from modeling is that children actually participate in the activity rather than simply observe the teacher. In the shared reading activity, children follow along as the teacher reads, and in shared writing, they suggest the words and sentences that the teacher writes. Three purposes for shared reading and writing are:

1. To involve children in reading and writing activities that they could not do independently.
2. To provide opportunities for children to experience success in reading and writing.
3. To provide practice before children read and write independently.

Interactive Reading and Writing

Children assume an increasingly important role in interactive reading and writing activities. At this level, children no longer observe the teacher read or write, repeat familiar words, or suggest what the teacher will write. Instead, children are more actively involved in reading and writing. They support their classmates by sharing the reading and writing responsibilities, and their teacher provides assistance when needed. **Choral reading** and **readers theatre** are two examples of interactive reading. In choral reading, children take turns reading lines of a poem, and in readers theatre, they assume the roles of characters and read lines in a script. In both of these interac-

Interactive Reading and Writing	Guided Reading and Writing	Independent Reading and Writing
Teacher and students read together and take turns reading. The teacher helps students read fluently and with expression. Instructional-level books are used. Examples: choral reading and readers theatre.	Teacher plans and teaches small homogeneous group reading lessons using instructional-level books. Focus is on supporting and observing students' use of strategies. Example: guided reading groups.	Students choose and read self-selected books independently. Teachers conference with students to monitor their progress. Examples: reading workshop and reading center.
Teacher and students create the text and share the pen to do the writing. Teacher and students talk about writing conventions. Examples: interactive writing and daily news.	Teacher plans and teaches lesson on a writing procedure, strategy, or skill, and students participate in supervised practice activities. Examples: class collaborations and sentence frames.	Students use the writing process to write stories, informational books, and other compositions. Teacher monitors students' progress. Examples: writing workshop and writing center.

tive reading activities, the children support each other by actively participating and sharing the work. Teachers provide support by helping students with unfamiliar words or reading a sentence with more expression.

Interactive writing is a recently developed writing activity in which children and the teacher create a text and "share the pen" to write the text on chart paper (Button, Johnson, & Furgerson, 1996; Collom, 1998). The text is composed by the group, and the teacher assists children as they write the text word by word on chart paper. Children take turns writing known letters and familiar words, adding punctuation marks, and marking spaces between words. The teacher helps children to spell all words correctly and use written language conventions so that the text can be easily read. All children participate in creating and writing the text on chart paper, and they also write the text on small white boards. After writing, children read and reread the text using shared and independent reading.

Four purposes of interactive reading and writing are:

1.   To practice reading and writing high-frequency words.
2.   To teach and practice phonics and spelling skills.
3.   To successfully read and write texts that children could not do independently.
4.   To have children share their reading and writing expertise with classmates.

Guided Reading and Writing

Teachers continue to support children's reading and writing during guided literacy activities, but the children do the actual reading and writing themselves. In guided reading, small homogeneous groups of children meet with the teacher to read a book at their instructional level. The teacher introduces the book and guides children as they begin reading. Then children continue reading on their own while the teacher monitors their reading. After reading, children and the teacher discuss the book, and children often reread the book.

Teachers plan structured writing activities in guided writing and then supervise as children do the writing. For example, when children make pages for a class **alphabet book** or write formula poems, they are doing guided writing because the teacher has set up the writing activity. Teachers also guide children's writing when they conference with children as they write, participate in **writing groups** to help children revise their writing, and proofread with children.

Teachers use guided reading and writing to provide instruction and assistance as children are actually reading and writing. Four purposes of guided reading and writing activities are:

1. To support children's reading in instructional-level materials.
2. To teach literacy procedures, concepts, skills, and strategies during minilessons.
3. To introduce different types of writing activities.
4. To teach children to use the writing process—in particular, how to revise and edit.

Independent Reading and Writing

Children do the reading and writing themselves during independent reading and writing activities. They apply and practice the procedures, concepts, strategies, and skills they have learned. Students may be involved in reading workshop or literature circles. During independent reading, they usually choose the books they read and work at their own pace. Similarly, during independent writing, children may be involved in writing workshop or work at a writing center. They usually choose their own topics for writing and move through the steps of the writing process at their own pace as they develop and refine their writing.

Through independent reading experiences, children learn the joy of reading and, teachers hope, become lifelong readers. And, through independent writing experiences, children come to view themselves as authors. Three purposes of independent reading and writing activities are:

1. To create opportunities for children to practice reading and writing procedures, concepts, strategies, and skills that have been taught.
2. To provide authentic literacy experiences in which students choose their own topics, purposes, and materials.
3. To develop lifelong readers and writers.

6. EFFECTIVE TEACHERS USE LITERATURE AND OTHER MATERIALS TO TEACH READING

One of the biggest questions facing reading teachers today is whether to use literature published as trade books or commercial reading programs (often called basals) for reading instruction. Twenty years ago almost all teachers used basal readers and relied on them for their entire reading program (Anderson, Hiebert, Scott, & Wilkinson, 1985; Shannon, 1989). Often students were divided into small groups by ability, and they met in small groups with the teacher to read selections and practice reading skills with the teacher. They also completed workbook pages and did little writing except filling in the blanks on worksheets.

Basal reading programs have been a staple of American reading instruction for generations, and they have several advantages. They have been judged as successful, especially as measured by students' achievement on standardized tests, and teachers—especially beginning teachers—feel secure using the step-by-step guidance provided by teacher's manuals.

Basals are leveled by grade. A third-grade textbook, for example, is written at the third-grade reading level and is typically used for reading instruction in third-grade classrooms. Across the grades, basals present reading materials that are increasingly difficult, and teachers can use basals to provide instruction and practice for students who are reading at these levels. Unfortunately, not all students can read grade-level textbooks. The books are too easy for some students and too difficult for others. Especially at the first-grade level, basals are too difficult for many children, and matching individual children to selections at their own level is difficult when using a textbook (Fountas & Pinnell, 1996).

Traditionally, the stories and informational selections used in basals were developed around a hierarchy of skills and contained a tightly controlled vocabulary. The short, contrived selections designed for skills practice and the abundance of accompanying skills-based workbook activities were probably the greatest drawbacks of these programs. Today, many published reading programs have replaced most of the contrived selections with "real" literature or excerpts from trade books.

During the same 20-year period, there has been a proliferation of literature for children published as hardcover and paperback trade books, and teachers have begun using trade books in place of textbooks, often with remarkable results (Dekker, 1991; Egawa, 1990; O'Brien, 1991; Swift, 1993). Teachers who use literature as the core of their reading programs have become convinced that exposing children to literature and helping them make choices about their literacy experiences creates both proficient and lifelong readers (Cullinan, 1992; Danielson & LaBonty, 1994; Goodman, Shannon, Freeman, & Murphy, 1988; Zarrillo, 1991).

Effective teachers choose a wide variety of stories, informational books, and books of poetry at varying reading levels for their classroom libraries, and they have these books available for children to read independently during reading workshop. They identify featured books for small groups of students to read during literature circles and other featured books that the whole class reads together in literature focus units. These books should represent the finest in children's literature. Often they have won prestigious awards, such as the Caldecott Medal, which is given each year for the best illustrated picture book for children, and the Newbery Medal, which is given each year for the book deemed the best written for children. The American Library Association presents these awards. Well-known winners of the Caldecott Medal include *Snowflake Bentley* (Martin, 1998), *Officer Buckle and Gloria* (Rathmann, 1995), *Smoky Night* (Bunting, 1994), *Hey, Al* (Yorinks, 1986), and *Jumanji* (Van Allsburg, 1981). Newbery Award books include *Holes* (Sachar, 1998), *The Giver* (Lowry, 1993), *Shiloh* (Naylor, 1991), *Sarah, Plain and Tall* (MacLachlan, 1985), and *Julie of the Wolves* (George, 1972).

To locate highly recommended trade books to use with elementary students, teachers consult reference books such as *Valerie and Walter's Best Books for Children: A Lively, Opinionated Guide for Listeners and Readers From Birth to Age 14* (Lewis & Mayes, 1998); journals that review newly published trade books, such as *Horn Book,* a publication of the American Library Association, for recommendations about the best trade books for children; and websites devoted to children's literature. Figure 1–7 presents a list of resources that teachers can consult for guidance in choosing trade books for their classroom libraries and featured books for literature circles and literature focus units.

www.nea.org

🕸 *Read Across America. Invitation to participate in this annual event to promote literacy development.*

Resources about choosing trade books

Reference Books

Adventuring with books. A booklist for Pre-K–grade 6. (1997). Urbana, IL: National Council of Teachers of English.

Donavin, D. (Ed.). (1992) *Best of the best for children* (2nd ed.). Chicago, IL: American Library Association.

Gunning, T. G. (1998). *Best books for beginning readers.* Boston: Allyn & Bacon.

Lewis, V. V., & Mayes, W. M. (1998). *Valerie and Walter's best books for children: A lively, opinionated guide for listeners and readers from birth to age 14.* New York: Avon Books.

Odean, K. (1997). *Great books for boys.* New York: Ballantine Books.

Odean, K. (1998). *Great books for girls.* New York: Ballantine Books.

Journals

Book Links
Horn Book
The New Advocate
School Library Journal

Websites

www.ala.org/alsc/
Association for Library Service to Children (ALSC)

www.carolhurst.com
Carol Hurst's Children's Literature Site

www.cbcbooks.org
The Children's Book Council

www.beyondbasals.com
Children's Literature: Beyond Basals

www.acs.ucalgary.ca/dkbrown
Children's Literature Web Guide

www.scils.rutgers.edu/special.kay/
Kay Vandergrift's Special Interest Page

www.ala.org/yalsa/
Young Adult Library Services Association (YALSA)

Listservs

listserv@rutvml.rutgers.edu
Children's Literature Criticism and Theory
To subscribe, send this e-mail message: Subscribe CHILDLIT

listserv@bingvmb.cc.binghamton.edu
Children and Youth Literature
To subscribe, send this e-mail message: Subscribe KIDLIT-L

It is also important that teachers incorporate multicultural literature in their reading programs. Multicultural literature helps students appreciate diversity and become more tolerant of members of minority groups and more aware of other cultures (Edwards, Beasley, & Thompson, 1991; May, 1993). Reading multicultural literature presents students with the opportunity to "walk a mile" in an African American's shoes in books like *The Watsons Go to Birmingham—1963* (Curtis, 1995) or travel to America with a family of recent immigrants in *How Many Days to America? A Thanksgiving Story* (Bunting, 1988).

The position taken in this book is that effective teachers of reading use literature, whether published as trade books or contained in commercial reading programs, to teach reading. Literature is the core of a balanced literacy program because of its universal appeal. As they read, students meet characters they can relate to and heroes who grapple with all of life's tragedies, joys, and triumphs. Students learn about the world around them and are vicariously transported to other lands or back or forward in time to experience lives very different from their own. Literature also helps children understand how the institutions of society and the forces of nature affect them. Through reading, students learn about the power of language to narrate a story or to persuade. Literature is our cultural heritage and should be central to our curriculum.

You will learn ways to use basal textbooks and trade books in Chapters 10 through 14. In these chapters, you will learn how to develop and teach literature focus units, literature circles, reading and writing workshop, and content-area units, and how to teach using basal reading textbooks.

7. EFFECTIVE TEACHERS OF READING ORGANIZE LITERACY INSTRUCTION IN FOUR WAYS

Effective teachers put literature at the center of their instructional programs, and they combine opportunities for students to read and write with lessons on literacy skills and strategies. Teachers choose among four instructional approaches for their reading programs:

1. ***Literature focus units.*** All students in the class read and respond to the same book, and the teacher supports students' learning through a variety of related activities. Books chosen for literature focus units should be of high quality; teachers often choose books for literature focus units from a district- or state-approved list of books that all children are expected to read at that grade level.

2. ***Literature circles.*** Teachers select five or six books for a text set. These books range in difficulty level to meet the needs of all children in the classroom, and they are often related in theme or written by the same author. Teachers collect five or six copies of each book and give a book talk to introduce the books. Then students choose a book to read from a text set and form a group to read and respond to the book they have chosen.

3. ***Reading and writing workshop.*** Students individually select books to read and then read independently and conference with the teacher about their reading. Similarly, in writing workshop, students write books on topics that they choose and the teacher conferences with them about their writing. Usually teachers set aside a time for reading and writing workshop, and all children read and write while the teacher conferences with small groups of children. Sometimes, however, when the teacher is working with guided reading groups, the remainder of the class works in reading and writing workshop.

4. ***Basal reading programs.*** Commercially developed reading programs are known as basal readers. These programs include a textbook or anthology of stories and other reading selections and accompanying skill sheets, books, and related instructional materials at each grade level. Instructional manuals and testing materials are also included. Teachers usually divide students into small homogeneous groups, and then teachers meet with groups to read selections and teach skills. They use guided reading to scaffold students' reading and monitor their progress. The companies tout these books as complete reading programs, but effective teachers integrate basal reading programs with other instructional approaches.

These four approaches are used at all grade levels, from kindergarten through eighth grade, and effective teachers usually use a combination of these approaches. Students need a variety of reading opportunities, and some books that students read are more difficult and require more support from the teacher. Some teachers alternate literature focus units or literature circles with reading and writing workshop and basal readers, while others use some components from each approach throughout the school year. Figure 1–8 presents a comparison of the four approaches.

As you continue reading, you will often see the terms *literature focus units, literature circles, reading and writing workshop,* and *basal reading programs* used because they are the instructional approaches advocated in this text. In addition, entire chapters are devoted to each of these instructional approaches in Part 4, "How Do Teachers Organize Literacy Instruction?"

Figure 1–8 Four instructional approaches

Features	Literature Focus Units	Literature Circles
Description	Teacher and students read and respond to one text together as a class or in small groups. Teachers choose texts that are high-quality literature, either trade books or from a basal reader textbook. After reading, students explore the text and apply their learning by creating projects.	Teachers choose five or six books and collect multiple copies of each book. Students each choose the book they want to read and form groups or "book clubs" to read and respond to the book. They develop a reading and discussion schedule, and the teacher often participates in the discussions.
Strengths	❧ Teachers develop units using the reading process. ❧ Teachers select picture books, chapter books, or use selections from basal reader textbooks for units. ❧ Teachers scaffold reading instruction as they read with the whole class or small groups. ❧ Teachers teach minilessons on reading skills and strategies. ❧ Students explore vocabulary and literary language. ❧ Students develop projects to extend their reading.	❧ Books are available at a variety of reading levels. ❧ Students are more strongly motivated because they choose the books they read. ❧ Students have opportunities to work with their classmates. ❧ Students participate in authentic literacy experiences. ❧ Activities are student-directed, and students work at their own pace. ❧ Teachers may participate in discussions to help students clarify misunderstandings and think more deeply about the book.
Drawbacks	❧ Students all read the same book whether they like it or not or whether it is at their reading level or not. ❧ Many of the activities are teacher-directed.	❧ Teachers often feel a loss of control since students are reading different books. ❧ Students must learn to be task-oriented and use time wisely in order to be successful. ❧ Sometimes students choose books that are too difficult or too easy for them.

8. EFFECTIVE TEACHERS USE READING AND WRITING AS TOOLS FOR LEARNING IN THE CONTENT AREAS

Language is a powerful learning tool, and reading and writing are valuable ways to learn in all content areas. Effective teachers encourage students to use reading and writing in meaningful ways in thematic units so that they learn information better and refine their literacy competencies. Thaiss (1986) identified three benefits students gain from using reading and writing as learning tools:

1. Students understand and remember better when they use reading and writing to explore what they are learning.

Reading and Writing Workshop	Basal Reading Programs
Students choose books and read and respond to them independently during reading workshop and write books on self-selected topics during writing workshop. Teachers monitor students' work through conferences. Students share the books they read and the books they write with classmates during a sharing period.	Teachers group students into small homogeneous groups for reading instruction and use commercially developed basal readers that are graded according to difficulty so that students can read selections at their instructional level. Teachers use guided reading to scaffold students so they can be successful. Students read independently and teachers provide assistance as needed. Teachers also use running records to monitor students' reading.
❧ Students read books appropriate for their reading levels. ❧ Students are more strongly motivated because they choose the books they read. ❧ Students work through the steps of the writing process during writing workshop. ❧ Teachers teach minilessons on reading skills and strategies. ❧ Activities are student-directed and students work at their own pace. ❧ Teachers have opportunities to work individually with students during conferences.	❧ Students read selections at their instructional level. ❧ Teachers teach word-identification skills and vocabulary words. ❧ Teachers teach strategies and skills and provide structured practice opportunities. ❧ Teachers monitor students' reading. ❧ Teachers are available to reteach strategies as needed. ❧ The instructor's guide provides detailed instructions for teachers.
❧ Teachers often feel a loss of control since students are reading different books and working at different steps of the writing process. ❧ Students must learn to be task-oriented and use time wisely in order to be successful.	❧ Students do not select the books they read and may not be interested in the books. ❧ The reading lesson is very structured. ❧ Programs include many skill workbooks and worksheets.

Students use reading and writing during a content-area unit on immigration.

2. Students' literacy learning is reinforced when they read and write about what they are learning.
3. Students learn best through active involvement, collaborative projects, and interaction with classmates, the teacher, and the world.

Social studies and science topics are often integrated into thematic units. For example, students might study life in the oceans, Native Americans, or World War II. Teachers often use content-area textbooks as a major resource for teaching a unit, but these materials are often difficult for students to read. Teachers can use a variety of activities to support students as they read content-area textbooks. They have students generate a list of questions about the topic of the chapter and then read to locate answers. Or, they might create a graphic organizer about the content presented in the chapter and help students complete the diagram during a discussion prior to reading the chapter. Or, they may have students read an informational book or story on the same topic first. When teachers introduce the vocabulary and revisit concepts prior to reading, students' background knowledge is activated and they are better able to comprehend the information presented in the chapter.

In addition to the content-area textbook, teachers collect informational books, stories, and poems for a text set related to the unit. Books of children's literature are very useful in teaching social studies and science concepts (Farris & Fuhler, 1994; Freeman & Person, 1992; Tunnell & Ammon, 1993). For example, students learn about ecosystems when they read *Cactus Hotel* (Guiberson, 1991), the human body through *The Magic School Bus Inside the Human Body* (Cole, 1989), and oviparous (egg-laying) animals in *Chickens Aren't the Only Ones* (Heller, 1981). After they read, students often take notes or write in learning logs, and then they use the information in creating reports, murals, and other displays and projects. As students read informational books, they also learn about expository text—how it is organized, how to read charts and diagrams, and how to use an index.

In Chapter 14, "Reading and Writing in the Content Areas," you will learn more about how to develop thematic units and how to use reading and writing as learning tools. You will read about ways to adapt content-area textbooks to make them more useful and how to use text sets of books together with content-area textbooks.

9. EFFECTIVE TEACHERS OF READING USE A VARIETY OF ASSESSMENT PROCEDURES TO DOCUMENT STUDENT LEARNING

Teachers understand that students learn to read and write by doing lots of reading and writing and applying skills and strategies in real reading and writing, not by doing exercises on isolated literacy skills. This understanding affects the way they assess students. No longer does it seem enough to grade students' vocabulary exercises or ask them to answer multiple-choice comprehension questions on reading passages that have no point beyond the exercise. Similarly, it no longer seems appropriate to measure success in writing by means of spelling and grammar tests. Instead, teachers need assessment information that tells about the complex achievements that students are making in reading and writing.

Teachers use assessment procedures that they develop and others that are commercially available to:

❦ monitor students' learning

❦ identify students' reading levels

❦ diagnose students' reading problems

❦ identify strengths and weaknesses in students' writing

❦ analyze students' spelling development

❦ document students' learning

❦ showcase students' best work

❦ assign grades

And, teachers use the results of standardized achievement tests as indicators of students' literacy levels and their strengths and weaknesses, as well as to assess the effect of their instruction.

Assessment is more than testing; it is an integral and ongoing part of teaching and learning (Glazer, 1998). Figure 1–9 shows the teach-assess cycle. Effective teachers identify their goals and plan their instruction at the same time as they develop their assessment plan. The assessment plan involves three components: preassessing, monitoring, and assessing.

Preassessing

Teachers assess students' background knowledge before reading in order to determine whether students are familiar with the topic they will read about. They also check to see that students are familiar with the genre, vocabulary, skills, and strategies. Then, based on the results of the assessment, teachers either help students

Figure 1–9 The teach-assess cycle

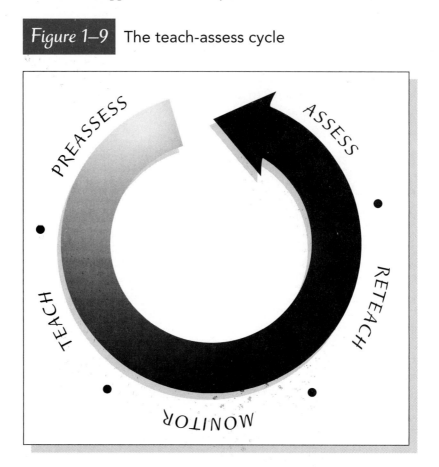

develop more background knowledge or move on to the next step of their instructional plan. Some preassessment tools are:

- ❧ creating a **K-W-L chart**
- ❧ **quickwriting** or quickdrawing about a topic
- ❧ discussing a topic with students
- ❧ completing an **anticipation guide**
- ❧ brainstorming a list of characteristics about a topic

Monitoring

Teachers often monitor students' progress in reading and writing as they observe students participating in literacy activities. Students might participate in conferences with the teacher, for example, and talk about what they are reading and writing, the strategies and skills they are learning to use, and problem areas. They reflect on what they do well as readers and writers and on what they need to learn next. Here are some monitoring tools:

- ❧ listening to students read aloud
- ❧ making **running records** of students' oral reading "miscues" or errors
- ❧ conferencing with students during reading and writing workshop

❦ listening to comments students make during **grand conversations** and other book discussions

❦ reading students' **reading log** entries and rough drafts of other compositions

❦ examining students' work in progress

Assessing

Teachers assess and grade students' learning at the end of a unit. Besides grading students' written assignments, teachers collect other assessment information through the following activities:

❦ observing students' presentation of oral language projects, such as puppet shows, oral reports, and story retellings

❦ examining students' art and other visual projects

❦ analyzing students' comprehension through charts, dioramas, murals, Venn diagrams, and other **story maps** they have made

❦ examining all drafts of students' writing to document their use of the writing process

❦ checking students' use of newly taught vocabulary in their compositions and other projects

❦ analyzing students' spelling using their compositions

Teachers also have students keep track of their progress using checklists that list assignments and other requirements. Then at the end of the unit, teachers collect and grade students' assignments. Figure 1–10 shows a checklist from a third-grade literature focus unit on fables, featuring Arnold Lobel's award-winning book *Fables* (1980), a collection of 20 brief stories with a moral at the end, written in Aesop's style. Students read Lobel's book and other fables in their basal reading textbooks and other trade books in the classroom during the unit. They also participate in a variety of literacy activities, some of which are included on the checklist. Students check off items on the checklist during the unit, and at the end they assess their own work before submitting it to the teacher.

You will learn more about how to monitor, document, and grade student learning in Chapter 3, "Assessing Students' Literacy Development."

10. EFFECTIVE TEACHERS OF READING ADOPT A BALANCED APPROACH TO LITERACY INSTRUCTION

Recent years have witnessed a great deal of controversy about the best way to teach reading. On one side are the proponents of a skills-based or phonics approach; on the other side are advocates of a holistic, literature-based approach. Teachers favoring each side cite research to support their views, and state legislatures are joining the debate by mandating systematic, intensive phonics instruction in the primary grades. Today many teachers agree with Richard Allington that there is "no quick fix" and no one program to meet the needs of all children (Allington & Walmsley, 1995). Many teachers recognize value in both points of view and recommend a "balance" or combination of holistic and skills approaches (Baumann, Hoffman, Moon, & Duffy-Hester, 1998).

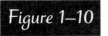 An assessment checklist for a literature focus unit on fables

---

Fables

Name _____ Date _____

Student's
Check

Teacher's
Check

☐ 1. Read these fables:
     ____ *Fables*
     ____ "The Ant and the Grasshopper"
     ____ "The Lion and the Mouse"
     ____ "The Tortoise and the Hare"   ☐

☐ 2. Write about the fables in your reading log.   ☐

☐ 3. Write information about fables in your log.   ☐

☐ 4. Draw and write about the opposites in a fable.   ☐

☐ 5. Make a chart to show the moral of one fable.   ☐

☐ 6. Do a group oral or written retelling of a fable.   ☐

That is the perspective taken in this text. The first nine principles of effective teaching have outlined many of the components of a balanced literacy approach.

A balanced approach to literacy, according to Spiegel (1998), is a decision-making approach through which teachers make thoughtful and purposeful decisions about how to help students become better readers and writers. A balanced approach "is built on research, views the teacher as an informed decision maker who develops a flexible program, and is constructed around a comprehensive view of literacy" (Spiegel, 1998, p. 117).

Fitzgerald (1999) identified three principles of a balanced literacy approach. First, teachers develop students' skills knowledge, including decoding skills, their strategy knowledge for comprehension and responding to literature, and their affective knowledge, including nurturing students' love of reading. Second, instructional approaches that are sometimes viewed as opposites are used to meet students' learning needs. Phonics instruction and reading workshop, for instance, are two very different instructional programs that are used in a balanced literacy approach. Third, students read a variety of reading materials, ranging from trade books to leveled books with controlled vocabulary and basal reading textbooks.

Even though balanced programs vary, they usually embody these characteristics:

1. Literacy is viewed comprehensively, as involving both reading and writing.
2. Literature is at the heart of the program.
3. Skills and strategies are taught both directly and indirectly.
4. Reading instruction involves learning word recognition and identification, vocabulary, and comprehension.
5. Writing instruction involves learning to express meaningful ideas and use conventional spelling, grammar, and punctuation to express those ideas.
6. Students use reading and writing as tools for learning in the content areas.
7. The goal of a balanced literacy program is to develop lifelong readers and writers. (Baumann & Ivey, 1997; McIntyre & Pressley, 1996; Spiegel, 1998; Strickland, 1994/1995; Weaver, 1998)

www.ciera.org

Every Child a Reader. Information on eight topics related to the balanced approach to literacy instruction.

No longer do teachers need to choose a side—either whole language or phonics—because a balanced approach recognizes the contributions of many different approaches and perspectives. Reutzel (1998/1999) urges teachers to pay attention to "our reading past" and to incorporate the contributions of the many approaches that have been proven effective.

Review

This chapter set out 10 principles of effective teaching of reading:

1. Effective teachers of reading create a community of learners in their classrooms.
2. Effective teachers of reading understand how children learn.
3. Effective teachers of reading support children's use of the four cueing systems.
4. Effective teachers teach the reading and writing processes.
5. Effective teachers scaffold children's reading and writing experiences.
6. Effective teachers use literature and other instructional materials to teach reading.
7. Effective teachers organize literacy instruction in literature focus units, literature circles, reading and writing workshop, and basal reading programs.
8. Effective teachers use reading and writing as tools for learning in the content areas.
9. Effective teachers of reading use a variety of assessment procedures to document student learning.
10. Effective teachers adopt a balanced approach to literacy instruction.

These principles were drawn from research over the past 30 years about how children learn to read and the "best teaching practices" used in successful elementary schools. These principles suggest a balanced reading program. In the chapters that follow, you will learn how to develop and implement a balanced reading program for kindergarten through eighth grade.

References

Allington, R., & Walmsley, S. (Eds.). (1995). *No quick fix: Rethinking literacy programs in America's elementary schools.*New York: Teachers College Press.

Anderson, R. C., Hiebert, E. H., Scott, J. A., & Wilkinson, I. A. G. (1985). *Becoming a nation of readers.* Washington, DC: National Institute of Education.

Baumann, J. F., Hoffman, J. V., Moon, J., & Duffy-Hester, A. M. (1998). Where are teachers' voices in the phonics/whole language debate? Results from a survey of U.S. elementary teachers. *The Reading Teacher, 51,* 636–650.

Baumann, J. F., & Ivey, G. (1997). Delicate balances: Striving for curricular and instructional equilibrium in a second-grade, literature/strategy-based classroom. *Reading Research Quarterly, 23,* 244–275.

Boyer, E. (1995). *The basic school: A community for learning.* Princeton, NJ: Carnegie Foundation for the Advancement of Teaching.

Butler, A., & Turbill, J. (1984). *Towards a reading-writing classroom.* Portsmouth, NH: Heinemann.

Button, K., Johnson, M. J., & Furgerson, P. (1996). Interactive writing in a primary classroom. *The Reading Teacher, 49,* 446–454.

Cases in literacy: An agenda for discussion. (1989). Newark, DE: International Reading Association and the National Council of Teachers of English.

Collom, S. (1998). *Sharing the pen: Interactive writing with young children.* Fresno: California State University, Fresno, and San Joaquin Valley Writing Project.

Cullinan, B. E. (Ed.). (1992). *Invitation to read: More children's literature in the reading program.* Newark, DE: International Reading Association.

Danielson, K. E., & LaBonty, J. (1994). *Integrating reading and writing through children's literature.* Boston: Allyn & Bacon.

Dekker, M. M. (1991). Books, reading, and response: A teacher-researcher tells a story. *The New Advocate, 4,* 37–45.

Dixon-Krauss, L. (1996). *Vygotsky in the classroom.* White Plains, NY: Longman.

Edwards, P. A., Beasley, K., & Thompson, J. (1991). Teachers in transition: Accommodating reading curriculum to cultural diversity. *The Reading Teacher, 44,* 436–437.

Egawa, K. (1990). Harnessing the power of language: First graders' literature engagement with *Owl moon. Language Arts, 67,* 582–588.

Farris, P. J., & Fuhler, C. J. (1994). Developing social studies concepts through picture books. *The Reading Teacher, 47,* 380–391.

Fitzgerald, J. (1999). What is this thing called "balance"? *The Reading Teacher, 53,* 100–107.

Fountas, I. C., & Pinnell, G. S. (1996). *Guided reading: Good first teaching for all children.* Portsmouth, NH: Heinemann.

Freeman, E. B., & Person, D. G. (Eds.). (1992). *Using nonfiction trade books in the elementary classroom: From ants to zeppelins.* Urbana, IL: National Council of Teachers of English.

Glazer, S. M. (1998). *Assessment is instruction: Reading, writing, spelling, and phonics for all learners.* Norwood, MA: Christopher-Gordon.

Goodman, K. S., Shannon, P., Freeman, Y. S., & Murphy, S. (1988). *Report card on basal readers.* Katonah, NY: Richard C. Owen.

Graves, D. H. (1995). A tour of Segovia School in the year 2005. *Language Arts, 72,* 12–18.

Halliday, M. A. K. (1978). *Language as social semiotic: The social interpretation of language and meaning.* Baltimore: University Park Press.

Harris, T. L., & Hodges, R. E. (Eds.). (1995). *The literacy dictionary: The vocabulary of reading and writing.* Newark, DE: International Reading Association.

Heath, S. B. (1983). Research currents: A lot of talk about nothing. *Language Arts, 60,* 999–1007.

Hirsch, E. D., Jr. (1987). *Cultural literacy: What every American needs to know.* Boston: Houghton Mifflin.

Lewis, V. V., & Mayes, W. M. (1998). *Valerie and Walter's best books for children: A lively, opinionated guide for listeners and readers from birth to age 14.* New York: Avon Books.

Lindfors, J. W. (1987). *Children's language and learning* (2nd ed.). Englewood Cliffs, NJ: Prentice Hall.

May, S. A. (1993). Redeeming multicultural education. *Language Arts, 70,* 364–372.

McIntyre, E. & Pressley, M. (Eds.). (1996). *Balanced instruction: Strategies and skills in whole language.* Norwood, MA: Christopher-Gordon.

Morrice, C., & Simmons, M. (1991). Beyond reading buddies: A whole language cross-age program. *The Reading Teacher, 44,* 572–578.

Nagy, W. E. (1988). *Teaching vocabulary to improve reading comprehension.* Urbana, IL: ERIC Clearinghouse on Reading and Communication Skills and the National Council of Teachers of English and the International Reading Association.

Nathenson-Mejia, S. (1989). Writing in a second language: Negotiating meaning through invented spelling. *Language Arts, 66,* 516–526.

O'Brien, K. L. (1991). A look at one successful literature program. *The New Advocate, 4,* 113–123.

Piaget, J. (1969). *The psychology of intelligence.* Paterson, NJ: Littlefield, Adams.

Rafferty, C. D. (1999). Literacy in the information age. *Educational Leadership, 57,* 22–25.

Reutzel, D. R. (1998/1999). On balanced reading. *The Reading Teacher, 52,* 322–324.

Rosenblatt, L. (1978). *The reader, the text, the poem: The transactional theory of the literary work.* Carbondale, IL: Southern Illinois University Press.

Rosenblatt, L. (1983). *Literature as exploration* (4th ed.). New York: Modern Language Association.

Rosenblatt, L. (1991). Literature—S.O.S.! *Language Arts, 68,* 444–448.

Rumelhart, D. E. (1977). Toward an interactive model of reading. In S. Dornic (Ed.), *Attention and performance* (Vol. 6). Hillsdale, NJ: Erlbaum.

Shanahan, T. (1988). The reading-writing relationship: Seven instructional principles. *The Reading Teacher, 41,* 636–647.

Shannon, P. (1989). *Broken promises: Reading instruction in twentieth-century America.* New York: Bergin & Garvey.

Skinner, B. F. (1968). *The technology of teaching.* New York: Appleton-Century-Crofts.

Spiegel, D. L. (1998). Silver bullets, babies, and bath water: Literature response groups in a balanced literacy program. *The Reading Teacher, 52,* 114–124.

Stanovich, K. (1980). Toward an interactive-compensatory model of individual differences in the development of reading fluency. *Reading Research Quarterly, 16,* 32–71.

Strickland, D. S. (1994/1995). Reinventing our literacy programs: Books, basics, and balance. *The Reading Teacher, 48,* 294–306.

Sumara, D., & Walker, L. (1991). The teacher's role in whole language. *Language Arts, 68,* 276–285.

Swift, K. (1993). Try reading workshop in your classroom. *The Reading Teacher, 46,* 366–371.

Teale, B. (1995). Dear readers. *Language Arts, 72,* 8–9.

Thaiss, C. (1986). *Language across the curriculum in the elementary grades.* Urbana, IL: ERIC Clearinghouse on Reading and Communication Skills and the National Council of Teachers of English.

Tunnell, M. O., & Ammon, R. (Eds.). (1993). *The story of ourselves: Teaching history through children's literature.* Portsmouth, NH: Heinemann.

Vygotsky, L. S. (1978). *Mind in society.* Cambridge, MA: Harvard University Press.

Vygotsky, L. S. (1986). *Thought and language.* Cambridge, MA: MIT Press.

Weaver, C. (Ed.). (1998). *Reconsidering a balanced approach to reading.* Urbana, IL: National Council of Teachers of English.

Wells, G., & Chang-Wells, G. L. (1992). *Constructing knowledge together: Classrooms as centers of inquiry and literacy.* Portsmouth, NH: Heinemann.

Zarrillo, J. (1991). Theory becomes practice: Aesthetic teaching with literature. *The New Advocate, 4,* 221–233.

Children's Book References

Bunting, E. (1994). *Smoky night.* San Diego, CA: Harcourt Brace.

Bunting, E. (1988). *How many days to America? A Thanksgiving story.* New York: Clarion.

Cole, J. (1989). *The magic school bus inside the human body.* New York: Scholastic.

Curtis, C. P. (1995). *The Watsons go to Birmingham—1963.* New York: Delacorte.

George, J. C. (1972). *Julie of the wolves.* New York: Harper & Row.

Gibbons, G. (1994). *Nature's green umbrella: Tropical rain forests.* New York: Morrow.

Guiberson, B. Z. (1991). *Cactus hotel.* New York: Henry Holt.

Heller, R. (1981). *Chickens aren't the only ones.* New York: Grosset & Dunlap.

Lobel, A. (1980). *Fables.* New York: HarperCollins.

Lowry, L. (1993). *The giver.* Boston: Houghton Mifflin.

MacLachlan, P. (1985). *Sarah, plain and tall.* New York: Harper and Row.

Martin, J. B. (1998). *Snowflake Bentley.* Boston: Houghton Mifflin.

Naylor, P. R. (1991). *Shiloh.* New York: Atheneum.

Rathmann, P. (1995). *Officer Buckle and Gloria.* New York: Putnam.

Sachar, L. (1998). *Holes.* New York: Farrar, Straus & Giroux.

Van Allsburg, C. (1981). *Jumanji.* Boston: Houghton Mifflin.

Yorinks, A. (1986). *Hey, Al.* New York: Farrar, Straus & Giroux.

Chapter 2

Teaching the Reading and Writing Processes

— Chapter Questions —

What are the steps in the reading process?

What are the steps in the writing process?

How are the two processes alike?

How do teachers use these two processes in teaching reading and writing?

Mrs. Lentz's Seventh Graders Use the Reading Process

The seventh graders in Mrs. Lentz's class are reading the Newbery Award–winning book *The Giver* (Lowry, 1993). In this futuristic story, 12-year-old Jonas is selected to become the next Keeper of the Memories, and he discovers the terrible truth of his community. Mrs. Lentz has a class set of paperbacks of the book, and her students use the reading process as they read and explore the book.

To introduce the book to her students, she asks them to get into small groups and brainstorm lists of all the things they would change about life if they could. They write the lists on butcher paper. Their lists include getting $200 for allowance every week, no more homework, no AIDS, no crime, no gangs, no parents, no taking out the garbage, and being allowed to drive a car at age 10. The groups hang their lists on the chalkboard and share their lists. Then Mrs. Lentz puts check marks by many of the items, seeming to agree with the points. Next she explains that the class is going to read a story about life in the future. She explains that *The Giver* takes place in a planned utopian, or "perfect," society with the qualities that she checked on students' brainstormed lists.

She passes out copies of the book and uses shared reading as she reads the first chapter aloud and students follow along in their books. Then the class talks about the first chapter, and they ask a lot of questions: Why were there so many rules? Doesn't anyone drive a car? What does "released" mean? Why are children called a "Seven" or a "Four"? What does it mean that people are "given" spouses—don't they fall in love and get married? Why does Jonas have to tell his feelings? Why can't he keep them to himself? Classmates share their ideas and are eager to continue reading. Mrs. Lentz's reading aloud of the first chapter and the questions that the students raise cause everyone in the class to become interested in the story, even several students who often try to remain uninvolved in class activities. The power of this story grabs them all.

The class sets up a schedule for reading and discussion. Every three days they will come together to talk about the chapters they have read, and over two weeks the class will read and talk about the story. They will also write in **reading logs** (see the Compendium for more information about this and all other highlighted terms in this chapter) after reading the first chapter and then five more times as they are reading. In their reading logs, students write reactions to the story. Maria wrote this journal entry after she finished reading the book:

> *Jonas had to do it. He had to save Gabriel's life because the next day Jonas's father was going to release (kill) him. He had it all planned out. That was important. He was very brave to leave his parents and his home. But I guess they weren't his parents really and his home wasn't all that good. I don't know if I could have done it but he did the right thing. He had to get out. He saved himself and he saved little Gabe. I'm glad he took Gabriel. That community was supposed to be safe but it really was dangerous. It was weird to not have colors. I guess that things that at first seem to be good are really bad.*

Ron explored some of the themes of the story:

> *Starving. He has memories of food. He's still hungry. But he's free. Food is safe. Freedom is surprises. Never saw a bird before. Same-same-same. Before he was starved for colors, memories and choice. Choice. To do what you want. To be who you can be. He won't starve.*

Alicia thought about a lesson her mother taught her as she wrote:

> *As Jonas fled from the community he lost his memories so that they would go back to the people there. Would they learn from them? Would they remember them? Or would life go on just the same? I think you have to do it yourself if you are going to learn. That's what my mom says. Somebody else can't do it for you. But Jonas did it. He got out with Gabe.*

Tomas wrote about the Christmas connection at the end of the story:

> *Jonas and Gabe came to the town at Christmas. Why did Lois Lowry do that? Gabe is like the baby Jesus, I think. It is like a rebirth—being born again. Jonas and his old community didn't go to church. Maybe they didn't believe in God. Now Jonas will be a Christian and the people in the church will welcome them. Gabe won't be re-leased. I think Gabe is like Jesus because people tried to release Jesus.*

During their discussions, which Mrs. Lentz calls **grand conversations,** students talk about many of the same points they raise in their journal entries. The story fascinates her students—at first they think about how simple and safe life would be, but then they think about all the things they take for granted that they would have to give up to live in Jonas's ordered society. They talk about bravery and making choices, and applaud Jonas's decision to flee with Gabriel. They also speculate about Jonas's and Gabe's new lives in Elsewhere. Will they be happy? Will they ever go back to check on their old community? Will other people escape to Elsewhere?

The students collect "important" words from the story for their **word wall**. After reading Chapters 4, 5, and 6, students add these words to the word wall:

leisurely pace	bikeports	regulated
invariably	gravitating	rehabilitation
serene	chastised	rule infraction
the wanting	stirrings	reprieve
relinquish	chastisement	assignment

Sometimes students choose unfamiliar or long words, but they also choose words like *assignment* that are important to the story. Students refer to the list for words and their spellings for the various activities they are involved in. Later during the unit, Mrs. Lentz teaches a minilesson about root words using some of these words.

Mrs. Lentz teaches a series of **minilessons** about reading strategies and skills as students read the story. The day after students read about colors in the story, she teaches a minilesson on the visualization strategy. She begins by rereading excerpts from Chapters 7 and 8 about Jonas being selected to be the next Receiver and asks students to try to draw a picture of the scene in their minds. Mrs. Lentz asks students to focus on the sights, sounds, smells, and feelings, and she talks about the importance of bringing a story to life in their minds as they read. Then students draw pictures of their visualizations and share them in small groups.

To review spelling patterns and phonics rules, Mrs. Lentz does a **making words** activity. She divides the class into six groups and gives each group a different set of letter cards that can be sorted to spell a word from the word wall: *stirrings, release, memories, receiver, fascinated,* or *ceremony.* She asks the students in each group to arrange the letter cards to spell as many different words as they can. Letters from *ceremony,* for example, can be used to spell *me, my, on, no, eye, men, more, core, corn, mercy,* and *money.* Then they arrange all of the letters to spell the word wall word.

Another minilesson is about literary opposites. Mrs. Lentz explains that authors often introduce conflict and develop themes using contrasts or opposites. She asks students to think of opposites in *The Giver.* One example that she suggests is *safe* and *free.* Other opposites that the students suggest include:

alive—released	color—black and white
choice—no choice	conform—do your own thing
rules—anarchy	stirrings—the pill
families—family units	memories—no memories

Mrs. Lentz asks students to think about how the opposites relate to the development of the story and how Lois Lowry made the opposites explicit in *The Giver.* Students talk about how the community seemed safe at the beginning of the story, but chapter by chapter Lowry uncovered the shortcomings of the community. They also talk about themes of the story reflected in these opposites. Mrs. Lentz ends the minilesson by asking students to look for opposites in other stories they read.

After they finish reading the book, students have a **read-around** in which they select and read aloud favorite passages to the class. Then students make a **quilt** about the story. Each student prepares a quilt piece made of construction paper and writes a favorite quote on the square. One quilt square is shown in Figure 2–1. The students decide to use white, gray, and black for most of the quilt square to represent the sameness of Jonas's community, and they add color in the center to represent Elsewhere.

Students also choose projects that they will work on individually or in small groups to apply their reading of *The Giver.* One student makes a **book box** with objects related to the story, and two other students read *Hailstones and Halibut Bones* (O'Neill, 1989) and then write their own collection of color poetry. One student

www.ipl.org

Ask the Author: Lois Lowry Biographical information about the author and answers to frequently asked questions.

Figure 2–1 One square for a quilt on *The Giver*

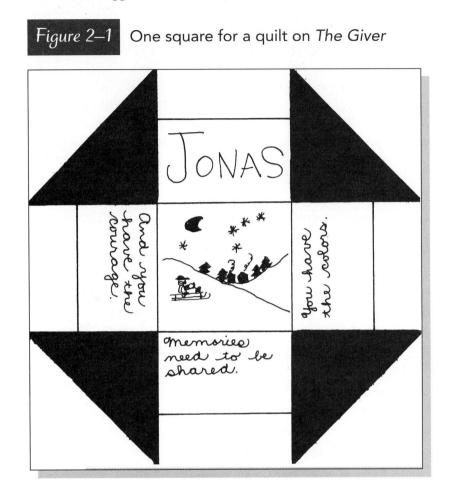

makes an **open-mind portrait** of Jonas to show his thoughts the night he decided to escape with Gabe. Some students read other books with similar themes or other books by Lois Lowry, and they share their books with the class during a **book talk**. Other students write about memories of their own lives. They use the writing process to draft, refine, and publish their writing. They share their published pieces at a class meeting at the end of the unit.

The reading process that Mrs. Lentz uses represents a significant shift in thinking about what people do as they read. Mrs. Lentz understands that readers construct meaning as they negotiate the texts they are reading, and that they use their life and literature experiences and knowledge of written language as they read. She knows that it is quite common for two people to read the same story and come away with different interpretations, and that their understanding of the story will depend on things that have happened in their own lives. Meaning does not exist on the pages of the book readers are reading; instead, comprehension is created through the interaction between readers and the texts they are reading.

The reading process involves a series of steps during which readers construct interpretations as they read and respond to the text. The term *text* includes all reading materials—stories, maps, newspapers, cereal boxes, textbooks, and so on; it is not limited to basal reader textbooks. The writing process is a similar recursive process involving a variety of activities as students gather and organize ideas, draft their compositions, revise and edit the drafts, and, finally, publish their writings.

Reading and writing have been thought of as the flip sides of a coin—as opposites; readers decoded or deciphered written language, and writers encoded or produced written language. Then researchers began to note similarities between reading and writing and talked of both of them as processes. Now reading and writing are viewed as parallel processes of meaning construction, and readers and writers use similar strategies for making meaning with text.

THE READING PROCESS

Reading is a process in which readers comprehend and construct meaning. During reading, the meaning does not go from the page to readers. Instead, reading is a complex negotiation among the text, readers, and their purpose for reading that is shaped by many factors:

- Readers' knowledge about the topic
- Readers' knowledge about reading and written language
- The language community to which readers belong
- The match between readers' language and the language used in the text
- Readers' culturally based expectations about reading
- Readers' expectations about reading based on their previous experiences (Weaver, 1988)

The reading process involves five steps: prereading, reading, responding, exploring, and applying. These steps are overviewed in Figure 2–2.

Step 1: Prereading

The reading process does not begin as readers open a book and read the first sentence. The first step is preparing to read. In the vignette, Mrs. Lentz developed her students' background knowledge and stimulated their interest in *The Giver* as they brainstormed lists and talked about how wonderful life would be in a "perfect" world. As readers prepare to read, they make connections, set purposes, and plan for reading.

Making Connections. Readers activate their background knowledge or schemata about the book or other text they plan to read. They make connections to personal experiences, to literary experiences, or to thematic units in the classroom. The topic of the book, the title, the author, the genre, an illustration, a comment someone makes about the text, or something else may trigger this activation, but for readers to make meaning with the text, schemata must be activated. For instance, readers who love horses and are very knowledgeable about them often choose horse books like *Misty of Chincoteague* (Henry, 1963) to read. Those who like books written by Beverly Cleary or Dr. Seuss choose books by their favorite authors.

Sometimes teachers collect objects related to the book and create a **book box** to use in introducing the book to the class. As you saw on pages 2–5, Mrs. Peterson

Figure 2–2	Key features of the reading process

Step 1: Prereading

- 🦚 Students set purposes.
- 🦚 Students connect to prior personal experiences.
- 🦚 Students connect to prior literary experiences.
- 🦚 Students connect to thematic units or special interests.
- 🦚 Students make predictions.
- 🦚 Students preview the text.
- 🦚 Students consult the index to locate information.

Step 2: Reading

- 🦚 Students make predictions.
- 🦚 Students apply skills and strategies.
- 🦚 Students read independently; with a partner; using shared reading or guided reading; or listen to the text read aloud.
- 🦚 Students read the illustrations, charts, and diagrams.
- 🦚 Students read the entire text from beginning to end.
- 🦚 Students read one or more sections of text to learn specific information.
- 🦚 Students take notes.

Step 3: Responding

- 🦚 Students write in a reading log.
- 🦚 Students participate in a grand conversation or instructional conversation.

Step 4: Exploring

- 🦚 Students reread and think more deeply about the text.
- 🦚 Students make connections with personal experiences.
- 🦚 Students make connections with other literary experiences.
- 🦚 Students examine the author's craft.
- 🦚 Students identify memorable quotes.
- 🦚 Students learn new vocabulary words.
- 🦚 Students participate in minilessons on reading procedures, concepts, strategies, and skills.

Step 5: Applying

- 🦚 Students construct projects.
- 🦚 Students use information in thematic units.
- 🦚 Students connect with related books.
- 🦚 Students reflect on their interpretation.
- 🦚 Students value the reading experience.

collected objects related to *Bunnicula: A Rabbit-Tale of Mystery* (Howe & Howe, 1979). She painted fabric vegetables white and added two little "fang" holes in each one and placed them in the box. She also added a small black-and-white stuffed bunny and a book about vampires. As she introduced the book, she showed students the objects, talked about each one, and asked students to speculate on how they might be related to the story.

Setting Purposes. The two overarching purposes for reading are pleasure and information. When students read for pleasure or enjoyment, they read aesthetically, to be carried into the world of the text; when they read to locate information or for directions about how to do something, they read efferently (Rosenblatt, 1978). Often readers use elements of both purposes as they read, but usually one purpose is more primary to the reading experience than the other. For example, when students pick up *The Sweetest Fig* (1993), one of Chris Van Allsburg's picture book fantasies, their primary purpose is enjoyment. They want to experience the story, but at the same time, they search for the white dog, a trademark that Van Allsburg includes in all of his books, and they compare this book with others of his they have read. As they search for the white dog or make comparisons, they add efferent purposes to their primarily aesthetic reading experience.

Purpose-setting is usually directed by the teacher during literature focus units, but in reading workshop students set their own purposes because everyone is reading different self-selected books. For teacher-directed purpose-setting, teachers explain how students are expected to read and what they will do after reading. The goal of teacher-directed purpose-setting is to help students learn how to set personally relevant purposes when they are reading independently (Blanton, Wood, & Moorman, 1990). Students should always have a purpose for reading, whether they are reading aesthetically or efferently, whether reading a text for the first time or the tenth. Readers are more successful when they have a single purpose for reading the entire selection. A single purpose is more effective than multiple purposes, and sustaining a single purpose is more effective than presenting students with a series of purposes as they read.

When readers have purposes for reading, their comprehension of the selection is enhanced in three ways, whether teachers provide the purpose or students set their own purpose (Blanton et al., 1990). First of all, the purpose guides the reading process that students use. Having a purpose provides motivation and direction for reading, as well as a mechanism that students use for monitoring their reading. As they monitor their reading, students ask themselves whether or not they are fulfilling their purpose.

Second, setting a purpose activates a plan for readers to use while reading. Purpose-setting causes students to draw on background knowledge, consider strategies they might use as they read, and think about the structure of the text they are reading. Third, students are better able to sort out important from unimportant information as they read when they have a purpose for reading. Teachers direct students' attention to relevant concepts as they set purposes for reading and show them how to connect the concepts they are reading about to their prior knowledge about a topic.

Third, students read differently depending on the purpose for reading, and the instructional procedures that teachers use also vary according to the purpose for reading. When students are reading stories, teachers might use the **Directed Reading-Thinking Activity** (DRTA) to help students predict and then read to confirm or reject their predictions, or have students create **story maps** to focus their attention on plot, characters, or another element of story structure. When students are reading informational books and content-area textbooks, teachers might use an **anticipation guide** to activate prior knowledge, or use **cubing** to explore a concept from different viewpoints.

In contrast to teacher-directed purpose-setting, students set their own purposes for reading during literature circles, reading workshop, and at other times when they choose their own books to read. Often they choose materials that are intrinsically interesting or which describe something they want to learn more about. As students gain experience in reading, identify favorite authors and illustrators, and learn about genre, they have other criteria to use in choosing books and setting purposes for reading. When teachers conference with students, they often ask them about their purposes for reading and why they choose particular books to read.

Planning for Reading. Students often preview the reading selection during the prereading step. They look through the selection and check its length, the reading difficulty of the selection, and the illustrations in order to judge the general suitability of the selection for them as readers. Previewing serves an important function as students connect their prior knowledge, identify their purpose for reading, and take their first look at the selection. Teachers set the guidelines for the reading experience, explain how the book will be read—independently, in small groups, or as a class—and set the schedule for reading. Setting the schedule is especially important when students are reading a chapter book. Often teachers and students work together to create a two-, three-, or four-week schedule for reading and responding and then write the schedule on a calendar to which students can refer.

Students make other types of plans depending on the type of selection they will read. Those who are preparing to read stories make predictions about the characters and events in the story. Students often use the title of the selection and the illustration on the cover of the book or on the first page as a basis for their predictions. If they have read other books by the same author or other selections in the same genre, students also use this information in making their predictions. Sometimes students share their predictions orally as they talk about the selection, while at other times they write and draw their predictions as the first entry in their **reading logs**.

When students are preparing to read informational books, they preview the selection by flipping through the pages and noting section headings, illustrations, diagrams, and other charts. Sometimes they examine the table of contents to see how the book is organized, or consult the index to locate specific information they want to read. They may also notice unfamiliar terminology and other words they can check in the glossary, ask a classmate or the teacher about, or look up in a dictionary. Teachers also use **anticipation guides, prereading plans** (PRePs), and the survey step of the **SQ3R study strategy** as they introduce informational books and content-area textbooks.

Students often make notes in learning logs as they explore informational books and content-area textbooks. They do **quickwrites** and quickdraws to activate prior knowledge and explore the concepts to be presented in the selection, write down important terminology, and draw **clusters, data charts,** and other diagrams they will complete as they read. As they move through the remaining steps in the reading process, students add other information to their learning logs.

Step 2: Reading

In this step, students read the book or other selection. They use their knowledge of decoding and word identification, sight words, strategies, skills, and vocabulary while they read. Fluent readers are better able to understand what they are reading because they identify most words automatically and use decoding skills when necessary. They also apply their knowledge of the structure of text as they create meaning. They continue reading as long as what they are reading fits the meaning they are constructing. When something doesn't make sense, readers slow down, back up, and reread until they are making meaning again.

Students may read the entire text or only read sections. When students are reading aesthetically, they usually read the entire text, but when they are reading efferently, they may be searching for specific information and read only until they locate that information. Also, students may decide to put a book down if it does not capture their interest, if it is too difficult to read, or if it doesn't have the information they are searching for. It is unrealistic to assume that students will always read entire texts or finish reading every book they begin.

Outside of school, readers usually read silently and independently. Sometimes, however, people listen as someone else reads. Young children often sit in a parent's lap and look at the illustrations as the parent reads a picture book aloud. Adults also listen to books read aloud on cassette tapes. In the classroom, teachers and students use five types of reading: shared reading, guided reading, independent reading, buddy reading, and reading aloud to students. Teachers choose the type of reading experience according to the purpose for reading, students' reading levels, and the number of copies available.

Shared Reading. Teachers use shared reading to read aloud books and other texts that children can't read independently (Holdaway, 1979). Often primary-grade teachers use big books or texts written on charts so that both small groups and whole-class groups can see the text and read along with the teacher. Teachers model what fluent readers do as they involve students in enjoyable reading activities (Fountas & Pinnell, 1996). After the text is read several times, teachers use the text to teach phonics concepts and high-frequency words. Students can also read small versions of the book independently or with partners, and the pattern or structure used in the text can be used for writing activities (Slaughter, 1993).

Shared reading is part of a balanced literacy program for beginning readers in the primary grades. Teachers read aloud books that are appropriate for children's interest level but too difficult for them to read for themselves. The books chosen for shared reading are available in both big-book and small-book formats and are close to children's reading level, but still beyond their ability to read independently. As an instructional strategy, shared reading differs from reading aloud to students because students see the text as the teacher reads. Also, students often join in the reading of predictable refrains and rhyming words, and after listening to the teacher read the text several times, students often remember enough of the text to read along with the teacher. The steps in a shared reading lesson are listed in Figure 2–3.

Shared reading is also used to read chapter books with older students when the books are too difficult for students to read independently. Teachers distribute copies of the chapter book to all students, and students follow along in the book as the teacher reads aloud. Sometimes students take turns reading sections aloud, but the goal is not for everyone to have a turn reading, as in round-robin reading. Students who want to read and are fluent enough to keep the reading meaningful volunteer to read. Often teachers begin reading, and when a student wants to take over the reading, he or she begins reading aloud with the teacher. Then the teacher drops off and the student continues reading. After a paragraph or a page, another student joins in and the first student drops off. Many teachers call this "popcorn reading."

Guided Reading. Teachers use guided reading to work with small groups of four or five students who are reading at the same level (Clay, 1991). They select a book that students can read at their instructional level, with approximately 90–94% accuracy. Teachers support students' reading and their use of reading strategies during guided reading (Depree & Iversen, 1996; Fountas & Pinnell, 1996). Students do the actual reading themselves, although the teacher may read aloud with children to get them started on the first page or two. Emergent readers often mumble the words softly as they read, and this helps the teacher keep track of students' reading and the strategies

Figure 2–3 Steps in a shared reading lesson

1. Prereading

Teachers select books that are available in big book format with text that is large enough for students to see. It is also important that the books are interesting so that students will want to listen to them read aloud several times and read them themselves. Teachers talk about the book or other text by activating or building background knowledge on topics related to the book and by reading the title and the author's name aloud. Often teachers also have students make predictions before beginning to read.

2. Reading

Teachers read aloud the book or other text using a pointer (a dowel rod with a pencil eraser on the end) to track as they read. They read with good expression and highlight key vocabulary words and repetitive patterns. They invite children to join in reading the repetitive refrains, rhymes, and other familiar words. During the first reading teachers make very few stops, but they do stop once or twice for students to make more predictions. Depending on students' interest, teachers may stop after the first reading to talk about the book, or they reread the book once or twice and encourage students to join in the reading.

3. Responding

Students and the teacher talk about the book in a grand conversation, and students share their responses to the book. Teachers clarify misconceptions, expand on children's comments, and ask higher-level questions, such as "What would happen if . . . ?" and "What did this book make you think of?" After the grand conversation, students draw or write in reading logs or share the pen to write a sentence or two interactively about the book.

4. Exploring

Teachers and students reread the big book over a period of several days. Children take turns turning the pages and using the pointer to track the reading. Teachers invite children to join in reading familiar and predictable words, and children increasingly read more and more of the words. Teachers also take advantage of opportunities to teach capitalization and punctuation marks, use graphophonic cues, and model reading. As students gain experience reading the text, they often reread the book using small books, too.

Also during the exploring step, students add important words to the word wall, and teachers present minilessons on phonics concepts, skills and strategies, and high-frequency words. Teachers also present more information about the author and illustrator and introduce a text set with other books by the same author and illustrator.

5. Applying

Students often create "innovations," or their own versions of the book using the pattern used in the book. Sometimes students collaborate to write a class book, and at other times they write individual books. Also, students read small books if they haven't already read them. Another possible applying activity is to have students create art projects related to the book.

In guided reading, small groups of students read and discuss the story with the teacher.

they are using. Older students who are more fluent readers usually read silently during guided reading. Guided reading is not round-robin reading, in which students take turns reading pages aloud to the group.

Guided reading lessons usually last 25 to 30 minutes. When the students first arrive for the small-group lesson, they often reread, either individually or with a buddy, familiar books used in previous guided reading lessons. For the new guided reading lesson, students read books that they have not read before. Beginning readers usually read small picture books at one sitting, but older students who are reading longer chapter books take several days to several weeks to read their books. The steps in a guided reading lesson are listed in Figure 2–4.

Teachers observe students as they read during guided reading lessons. They spend a few minutes observing each student, either sitting in front of the student or beside the student. Teachers observe the student's behaviors for evidence of strategy use and confirm the student's attempts to identify words and solve reading problems. Some of the strategies and problem-solving behaviors that teachers look for include:

🦎 self-monitoring

🦎 checking predictions

🦎 sounding out unfamiliar words

🦎 determining if the word makes sense

🦎 checking that a word is appropriate in the syntax of the sentence

🦎 using all sources of information

Figure 2–4 Steps in a guided reading lesson

1. Prereading

Teachers introduce the new book and prepare students to read. Teachers often begin by activating or building background knowledge on a topic related to the book. Then they show the cover of the book, say the title, and talk about the book and have students make predictions. Often teachers continue with a book walk to overview the book, but do not read the book. Then teachers introduce crucial new vocabulary. Sometimes teachers ask students to look through the book to locate known words and unknown words essential to the meaning of the book. One other activity that is often included in this first step is teaching or reviewing a skill or strategy that students can use as they read the book.

2. Reading

Teachers guide students through several readings of the book. During the first reading, students and the teacher often read the first page or two together. Then students read the book individually, reading aloud, softly, to themselves, or silently, depending on their reading level. Teachers prompt for strategies and word identification as needed, and then they move from student to student to listen in as the student reads. Teachers do a running record as one or two of the students read aloud. After students finish reading the book, teachers often invite students to reread the book twice, once with the teacher, with a partner, or individually.

3. Responding

After reading, students think about the book and make personal and literary connections. Activities include:

- Discuss the book with the group using a grand conversation.
- Ask inferential and critical level questions, such as:

    What would happen if . . . ?
    Why did . . . ?
    If . . . , what might have happened next?
    If you were . . . , what would you . . . ?
    What did this book make you think of?
    What did you like best about this book?

- Share the pen to write a sentence interactively about the book.
- Have students draw and write in reading logs.

4. Exploring

Teachers teach minilessons and students practice making words and sentences. Three types of exploring activities are:

- *Minilessons.* Teachers discuss a skill or strategy that was evident in the text or teach a skill or strategy and have students practice it as they reread. Teachers also teach phonics during these minilessons.
- *Word work.* Teachers have students review known high-frequency words and then introduce a new word and have students write the word using magnetic letters, writing on a white board, or forming letters using waxy pipe cleaners.
- *Sentence work.* Teachers write sentences from the book on sentence strips and cut the strips apart. Then students put the words together to re-create the sentence.

5. Applying

Students practice and apply skills and strategies they are learning at literacy centers.

❧ attempting to read an unfamiliar word

❧ self-correcting

❧ chunking phrases to read more fluently

Teachers take notes about their observations and use the information in deciding what minilessons to teach and what books to choose for children to read.

Teachers also take **running records** of one or two children during each guided reading lesson and use this information as part of their assessment. Teachers check to see that the books children are reading are at their instructional level and that they are making expected progress and continuing to progress to increasingly more difficult levels of books.

Independent Reading. When students read independently, they read silently by themselves, for their own purposes, and at their own pace (Hornsby, Sukarna, & Parry, 1986). In order for students to read independently, the reading selections must be at their reading level. Primary-grade students often read the featured selection independently during literature focus units, but this is often after they have already read the selection once or twice with assistance from the teacher. In the upper grades, many students read chapter books independently, but less capable readers may not be able to read the featured book independently. Students also read related books at varied reading levels from the text set independently as part of these units.

During reading workshop, students almost always read independently. They choose the books they want to read, and they need to learn how to choose books that are written at an appropriate level of difficulty. Even children in kindergarten can do a variation of independent reading when they look at books, creating their own text to accompany the illustrations.

Independent reading is an important part of a balanced reading program because it is the most authentic type of reading. This type of reading is what most people do when they read, and this is the way students develop a love of reading and come to think of themselves as readers. The reading selection, however, must be at an appropriate level of difficulty so that students can read it independently. Otherwise, teachers use one of the other four types of reading to support students and make it possible for them to participate in the reading experience.

Buddy Reading. In buddy reading, students read or reread a selection with a classmate. Sometimes students read with buddies because it is an enjoyable social activity, and sometimes they read together to help each other. Often students can read selections together that neither student could read individually. Buddy reading is a good alternative to independent reading because students can choose books they want to read and then read at their own pace. By working together they are often able to figure out unfamiliar words and talk out comprehension problems.

As teachers introduce buddy reading, they show students how to read with buddies and how to support each other as they read. Unless the teacher has explained the approach and taught students how to work collaboratively, buddy reading often deteriorates into the stronger of the two buddies reading aloud to the other student, and that is not the intention of this type of reading. Students take turns reading aloud to each other or read in unison. They often stop and help each other identify an unfamiliar word or take a minute or two at the end of each page to talk about what they have read. Buddy reading is a valuable way of providing the practice that beginning readers need to become fluent readers; it is also an effective way to work with students with special learning needs and students who are learning English.

Reading Aloud to Students. In kindergarten through eighth grade, teachers read aloud to students for a variety of purposes each day. During literature focus units, teachers read aloud featured selections that are appropriate for students' interest level but too difficult for students to read themselves. Sometimes it is also appropriate to read the featured selection aloud before distributing copies of the selection for students to read with buddies or independently. When they read aloud, teachers model what good readers do and how good readers use reading strategies. Reading aloud also provides an opportunity for teachers to think aloud about their use of reading strategies.

Reading aloud to students is not the same as "round-robin" reading, a practice that is no longer recommended in which students take turns reading paragraphs aloud as the rest of the class listens. Round-robin reading has been used for reading chapter books aloud, but it is more commonly used for reading chapters in content-area textbooks, even though there are more effective ways to teach content-area information and read textbooks. For more information on using content-area textbooks, see Chapter 14, "Reading and Writing in the Content Areas."

Round-robin reading is no longer recommended, for several reasons (Opitz & Rasinski, 1998). First, if students are going to read aloud, they should read fluently. When less capable readers read, their reading is often difficult to listen to and embarrassing to them personally. Less capable readers need reading practice, but performing in front of the entire class is not the most productive way for them to practice. They can read with buddies and in small groups during guided reading. Second, if the selection is appropriate for students to read aloud, they should be reading independently. Whenever the reading level of the text is appropriate for students, they should be reading independently. During round-robin reading, students often only follow along just before it is their turn to read. Third, round-robin reading is often tedious and boring, and students lose interest in reading.

The advantages and drawbacks for each type of reading are outlined in Figure 2–5. In the vignette at the beginning of this chapter, Mrs. Lentz used a combination of these approaches. She used shared reading as she read the first chapter aloud, with students following in their own copies of *The Giver*. Later, students read together in small groups, with a buddy, or independently. As teachers plan their instructional programs, they include reading aloud to students, teacher-led student reading, and independent reading each day.

Step 3: Responding

During the third step, readers respond to their reading and continue to negotiate the meaning. Two ways that students make tentative and exploratory comments immediately after reading are by writing in reading logs and participating in grand conversations.

Writing in Reading Logs. Students write and draw their thoughts and feelings about what they have read in **reading logs**. Rosenblatt (1978) explains that as students write about what they have read, they unravel their thinking and, at the same time, elaborate on and clarify their responses. When students read informational books, they sometimes write in reading logs, as they do after reading stories and poems, but at other times they make notes of important information or draw charts and diagrams to use in thematic units.

Figure 2–5 Advantages and disadvantages of the five types of reading

Type	Advantages	Drawbacks
Shared Reading Teacher reads aloud while students follow along using individual copies of book, a class chart, or a big book.	❧ Access to books students could not read themselves. ❧ Teacher models fluent reading. ❧ Opportunities to model reading strategies. ❧ Students practice fluent reading. ❧ Develops a community of readers.	❧ Multiple copies, a class chart, or a big book needed. ❧ Text may not be appropriate for all students. ❧ Students may not be interested in the text.
Guided Reading Teachers support students as they apply reading strategies and skills to read a text.	❧ Teach skills and strategies. ❧ Teacher provides direction and scaffolding. ❧ Opportunities to model reading strategies. ❧ Use with unfamiliar texts.	❧ Multiple copies of text needed. ❧ Teacher controls the reading experience. ❧ Some students may not be interested in the text.
Independent Reading Students read a text independently and often choose the text themselves.	❧ Develops responsibility and ownership. ❧ Self-selection of texts. ❧ Experience is more authentic.	❧ Students may need assistance to read the text. ❧ Little teacher involvement and control.
Buddy Reading Two students read or reread a text together.	❧ Collaboration between students. ❧ Students assist each other. ❧ Use to reread familiar texts. ❧ Develops reading fluency. ❧ Students talk and share interpretations.	❧ Limited teacher involvement. ❧ Less teacher control.
Reading Aloud to Students Teacher or other fluent reader reads aloud to students.	❧ Access to books students could not read themselves. ❧ Teacher models fluent reading. ❧ Opportunities to model reading strategies. ❧ Develops a community of readers. ❧ Use when only one copy of text is available.	❧ No opportunity for students themselves to read. ❧ Text may not be appropriate for all students. ❧ Students may not be interested in the text.

Students usually make reading logs by stapling together 10 to 12 sheets of paper at the beginning of a literature focus unit or reading workshop. At the beginning of a thematic unit, students make **learning logs** to write in during the unit. They decorate the covers, keeping with the theme of the unit, write entries related to their reading, and make notes related to what they are learning in **minilessons**. Teachers monitor students' entries during the unit, often reading and responding to students' entries. Because these journals are learning tools, teachers rarely correct students' spellings. They focus their responses on the students' ideas, but they expect students to spell the title of the book and the names of characters accurately. At the end of the unit, teachers review students' work and often grade the journals based on whether students completed all the entries and on the quality of the ideas in their entries.

Participating in Grand Conversations. Students also talk about the text with classmates in **grand conversations, instructional conversations,** or other literature discussions. Peterson and Eeds (1990) explain that in this type of discussion students share their personal responses and tell what they liked about the text. After sharing personal reactions, they shift the focus to "puzzle over what the author has written and . . . share what it is they find revealed" (p. 61). Often students make connections between the text and their own lives or between the text and other literature they have read. If they are reading a chapter book, they also make predictions about what they think will happen in the next chapter.

Teachers often participate in grand conversations, but they act as interested participants, not leaders. The talk is primarily among the students, but teachers ask questions regarding things they are genuinely interested in learning more about and share information in response to questions that students ask. In the past, many discussions have been "gentle inquisitions" during which students recited answers to factual questions teachers asked about books that students were reading (Eeds & Wells, 1989). Teachers asked these questions in order to determine whether or not students read and understood an assignment. While teachers can still judge whether or not students have read the assignment, the focus in grand conversations is on clarifying and deepening students' understanding of the story they have read. Teachers and students have similar instructional conversations after reading content-area textbooks and informational books.

These grand conversations can be held with the whole class or in small groups. Young children usually meet together as a class, while older students often prefer to talk with classmates in small groups. When students meet together as a class there is a shared feeling of community, and the teacher can be part of the group. When students meet in small groups they have more opportunities to participate in the discussion and share their interpretations, but fewer viewpoints are expressed in each group and teachers must move around, spending only a few minutes with each group. Some teachers compromise and have students begin their discussions in small groups and then come together as a class and have each group share what their group discussed.

Step 4: Exploring

During this step, students go back into the text to explore it more analytically. They reread the selection, examine the author's craft, and focus on words from the selection. Teachers also present minilessons on procedures, concepts, strategies, and skills.

Rereading the Selection. As students reread the selection, they think again about what they have read. Each time they reread a selection, students benefit in specific

Primary-grade students often reread stories during the exploring step of the reading process.

ways (Yaden, 1988). They deepen their comprehension and make further connections between the selection and their own lives or between the selection and other literature they have read. Students often reread a basal reader story, a picture book, or excerpts from a chapter book several times. If the teacher used shared reading to read the selection with students in the reading step, students might reread it with a buddy once or twice, read it with their parents, and, after these experiences, read it independently.

Examining the Author's Craft. Teachers plan exploring activities to focus students' attention on the structure of text and the literary language that authors use. Students notice opposites in the story, use **story boards** to sequence the events in the story, and make **story maps** to highlight the plot, characters, and other elements of story structure. Another way students learn about the structure of stories is by writing books based on the selection they have read. In sequels, students tell what happens to the characters after the story ends. Stories such as *Jumanji* (Van Allsburg, 1981), a fantasy about a board game that comes to life, suggest another episode at the end of the story and invite students to create a sequel. Students also write innovations, or new versions, for the selection, in which they follow the same sentence pattern but use their own ideas. First graders often write innovations for Bill Martin, Jr.'s, *Brown Bear, Brown Bear, What Did You See?* (1983) and *Polar Bear, Polar Bear, What Did You Hear?* (1992), and older students write innovations for *Alexander and the Terrible, Horrible, No Good, Very Bad Day* (Viorst, 1977).

Teachers share information about the author of the featured selection and introduce other books by the same author. Sometimes teachers help students make comparisons among several books written by a particular author. They also provide information about the illustrator and the illustration techniques used in the book. To focus on literary language, students often reread favorite excerpts in **read-arounds** and write memorable quotes on **quilts** that they create.

Focusing on Words and Sentences. Teachers and students add "important" words to **word walls** after reading and post these word walls in the classroom. Students refer to the word walls when they write, using these words for a variety of activities during the exploring step. Students make word **clusters** and posters to highlight particular words. They also make word chains, do **word sorts,** create semantic feature analysis charts to analyze related words, and play word games.

Teachers choose words from word walls to use in minilessons, too. Words can be used to teach phonics skills, such as beginning sounds, rhyming words, vowel patterns, *r*-controlled vowels, and syllabication. Other concepts, such as root words and affixes, compound words, contractions, and metaphors, can also be taught using examples from word walls. Sometimes teachers decide to teach a minilesson on a particular concept, such as words with the *-ly* suffix, because five or six words representing the concept are listed on the word wall.

Students also locate "important" sentences in books they read. These sentences might be important because of figurative language, because they express the theme or illustrate a character trait, or simply because students like them. Students often copy the sentences on sentence strips to display in the classroom and use in other exploring activities. Also, students can copy the sentences in their reading logs.

Teaching Minilessons. Teachers present minilessons on reading procedures, concepts, strategies, and skills during the exploring step. (To review the steps in a minilesson, check the section on minilessons in the Compendium.) In a minilesson, teachers introduce the topic and make connections between the topic and examples in the featured selection students have read. In this way, students are better able to connect the information teachers are presenting with their own reading process. In the vignette, Mrs. Lentz presented minilessons on the visualization strategy and on root words and affixes using examples from *The Giver*.

Step 5: Applying

During the applying step, readers extend their comprehension, reflect on their understanding, and value the reading experience. Building on the initial and exploratory responses they made immediately after reading, students create projects. These projects can involve reading, writing, talk and drama, art, or research and may take many forms, including murals, **readers theatre** scripts, and **individual books and reports,** as well as reading other books by the same author. Usually students choose which projects they will do rather than having the entire class do the same project. Sometimes, however, the class decides to work together on a project. In Mrs. Lentz's class, for example, some students wrote color poems, while others read books and wrote about memories. A list of projects is presented in Figure 2–6. The purpose of these activities is for students to expand the ideas they read about, create a personal interpretation, and value the reading experience.

THE WRITING PROCESS

The focus in the writing process is on what students think and do as they write. The five steps are prewriting, drafting, revising, editing, and publishing. The labeling and numbering of the steps does not mean that the writing process is a linear series of neatly packaged categories. Research has shown that the process involves recurring cycles, and labeling is only an aid to identifying and discussing writing activities. In

Figure 2–6 Projects students develop during the extending stage

Art Projects

1. Experiment with the illustration techniques (e.g., collage, watercolor, line drawing) used in a favorite book. Examine other books illustrated with the same technique.
2. Make a diagram or model using information from a book.
3. Create a collage to represent the theme of a book.
4. Design a book jacket for a book, laminate it, and place it on the book.
5. Decorate a coffee can or a potato chip can using scenes from a book. Fill the can with quotes from characters in the story. Other students can guess the identity of the characters. Or fill the can with quotes from a poem with words missing. Other students guess the missing words.
6. Construct a shoebox or other miniature scene of an episode for a favorite book (or use a larger box to construct a diorama).
7. Make illustrations for each important event in a book.
8. Make a map or relief map of a book's setting or something related to the book.
9. Construct the setting of the book in the block center, or use other construction toys such as Lego's or Lincoln Logs.
10. Construct a mobile illustrating a book.
11. Make a roll-movie of a book by drawing a series of pictures on a long strip of paper. Attach ends to rollers and place in a cardboard box cut like a television set.
12. Make a comic strip to illustrate the sequence of events in a book.
13. Make a clay or soap model of a character.
14. Prepare bookmarks for a book and distribute them to classmates.
15. Prepare flannel board pictures to use in retelling the story.
16. Use or prepare illustrations of characters for pocket props to use in retelling the story.
17. Use or prepare illustrations of the events in the story for clothesline props to use in retelling the story.
18. Experiment with art techniques related to the mood of a poem.
19. Make a mural of the book.
20. Make a book box and decorate it with scenes from a book. Collect objects, poems, and illustrations that represent characters, events, or images from the book to add to the box.
21. Make an open-mind portrait to probe the thoughts of one character.

Writing Projects

22. Write a review of a favorite book for a class review file.
23. Write a letter about a book to a classmate, friend, or pen pal.
24. Dictate or write another episode or sequel for a book.
25. Create a newspaper with news stories and advertisements based on characters and episodes from a book.
26. Make a five-senses cluster about the book.
27. Write a letter to a favorite character (or participate in a class collaboration letter).
28. Write a simulated letter from one book character to another.
29. Copy five "quotable quotes" from a book and list them on a poster.
30. Make a scrapbook about the book. Label all items in the scrapbook and write a short description of the most interesting ones.
31. Write a poem related to the book. Some types of poems to choose from are acrostic, concrete poem, color poem, "I wish" poem, "If I were" poem, haiku, or limerick.

Figure 2–6 continued

32. Write a lifeline related to the book, the era, the character, or the author.
33. Write a business letter to a company or organization requesting information on a topic related to the book.
34. Keep a simulated journal from the perspective of one character from the book.
35. Write a dictionary defining specialized vocabulary in a book.
36. Write the story from another point of view (e.g., write the story of *The Little Red Hen* from the perspective of the lazy characters).
37. Make a class collaboration book. Each child dictates or writes one page.
38. Write a letter to a famous person from a character in a book.
39. Make a ladder to accomplishment listing the steps taken to achieve some goal.

Reading Projects

40. Read another book by the same author.
41. Read another book by the same illustrator.
42. Read another book on the same theme.
43. Read another book in the same genre.
44. Read another book about the same character.
45. Read and compare another version of the same story.
46. Listen to and compare a tape, filmstrip, film, or video version of the same story.
47. Tape-record a book or an excerpt from it to place in the listening center.
48. Read a poem that complements the book aloud to the class. Place a copy of the poem in the book.
49. Tape-record a book using background music and sound effects.

Drama and Talk Projects

50. Give a readers theatre presentation of a book.
51. Improvise the events in a book.
52. Write a script and present a play about a book.
53. Make puppets and use them in retelling a book.
54. Dress as a character from the book and answer questions from classmates about the character.
55. Have a grand conversation with a small group or the whole class about a book.
56. Write and present a rap about the book.
57. Videotape a commercial for a book.
58. Interview someone in the community who is knowledgeable about a topic related to the book.

Literary Analysis Projects

59. Make a chart to compare the story with another version or with the film version of the story.
60. Make a character cluster.
61. Make a character sociogram.
62. Make a plot diagram of the book.
63. Make a plot profile of the book.

Research Projects

64. Research the author of the book and compile information in a chart or summary. Place the chart or summary in the book.
65. Research a topic related to the book. Present the information in a report.

 Key features of the writing process

---

Step 1: Prewriting

🌱 Students write on topics based on their own experiences.
🌱 Students engage in rehearsal activities before writing.
🌱 Students identify the audience to whom they will write.
🌱 Students identify the function of the writing activity.
🌱 Students choose an appropriate form for their compositions based on audience and function.

Step 2: Drafting

🌱 Students write a rough draft.
🌱 Students emphasize content rather than mechanics.

Step 3: Revising

🌱 Students reread their own writing.
🌱 Students share their writing in writing groups.
🌱 Students participate constructively in discussions about classmates' writing.
🌱 Students make changes in their compositions to reflect the reactions and comments of both teacher and classmates.
🌱 Between the first and final drafts, students make substantive rather than only minor changes.

Step 4: Editing

🌱 Students proofread their own compositions.
🌱 Students help proofread classmates' compositions.
🌱 Students increasingly identify and correct their own mechanical errors.
🌱 Students meet with the teacher for a final editing.

Step 5: Publishing

🌱 Students publish their writing in an appropriate form.
🌱 Students share their finished writing with an appropriate audience.

---

the classroom, the steps merge and recur as students write. The key features of each step in the writing process are shown in Figure 2–7.

Step 1: Prewriting

Prewriting is the "getting ready to write" step. The traditional notion that writers have a topic completely thought out and ready to flow onto the page is ridiculous. If writers wait for ideas to fully develop, they may wait forever. Instead, writers begin tentatively—talking, reading, writing—to see what they know and what direction they want to go in. Prewriting has probably been the most neglected step in the writing process; however, it is as crucial to writers as a warm-up is to athletes. Murray (1982) believes that at least 70% of writing time should be spent in prewriting. During the prewriting step, students choose a topic, consider purpose, audience, and form, and gather and organize ideas for writing.

Choosing a Topic. Choosing a topic for writing can be a stumbling block for students who have become dependent on teachers to supply topics. For years, teachers have supplied topics by suggesting gimmicky story starters and relieving students of the "burden" of topic selection. These "creative" topics often stymied students, who were forced to write on topics they knew little about or were not interested in. Graves (1976) calls this "writing welfare." Instead, students need to choose their own writing topics.

Some students complain that they don't know what to write about, but teachers can help them brainstorm a list of three, four, or five topics and then identify the one topic they are most interested in and know the most about. Students who feel they cannot generate any writing topics are often surprised that they have so many options available. Then, through prewriting activities, students talk, draw, read, and even write to develop information about their topics.

Asking students to choose their own topics for writing does not mean that teachers never give writing assignments; teachers do provide general guidelines. They may specify the writing form, and at other times they may establish the function, but students should choose their own content.

Considering Purpose. As students prepare to write, they need to think about the purpose of their writing. Are they writing to entertain? To inform? To persuade? Setting the purpose for writing is just as important as setting the purpose for reading, because purpose influences decisions students make about audience and form.

Considering Audience. Students may write primarily for themselves—to express and clarify their own ideas and feelings—or they may write for others. Possible audiences include classmates, younger children, parents, foster grandparents, children's authors, and pen pals. Other audiences are more distant and less well known. For example, students write letters to businesses to request information, articles for the local newspaper, or stories and poems for publication in literary magazines.

Children's writing is influenced by their sense of audience. Britton and his colleagues (1975) define audience awareness as "the manner in which the writer expresses a relationship with the reader in respect to the writer's understanding" (pp. 65–66). Students adapt their writing to fit their audience just as they vary their speech to meet the needs of the people who are listening to them.

Considering Form. One of the most important considerations is the form the writing will take: A story? A letter? A poem? A journal entry? A writing activity could be handled in any one of these ways. As part of a science thematic unit on hermit crabs, for instance, students could write a story about a hermit crab, draw a picture and label body parts, explain how hermit crabs obtain shells to live in, or keep a log of observations about the pet hermit crabs in the classroom. There is an almost endless variety of forms that children's writing may take. A list of these forms is presented in Figure 2–8. Students need to experiment with a wide variety of writing forms and explore the potential of these functions and formats.

Through reading and writing, students develop a strong sense of these forms and how they are structured. Langer (1985) found that by third grade, students responded in distinctly different ways to story- and report-writing assignments; they organized the writing differently and included varied kinds of information and elaboration. Similarly, Hidi and Hildyard (1983) found that elementary students could differentiate between stories and persuasive essays. Because children are clarifying the distinctions between various writing forms during the elementary grades, it is important that teachers use the correct terminology and not label all children's writing "stories."

Decisions about function, audience, and form influence each other. For example, if the function is to entertain, an appropriate form might be a story, script, or poem—

Figure 2–8 Writing forms

acrostic poems	diamante poems	paragraphs
advertisements	dictionaries	pattern books
"All About the Author"	directions	personal narratives
alphabet books	double-entry journals	persuasive letters
announcements	editorials	poems for two voices
apologies	e-mails	postcards
applications	essays	posters
autobiographies	explanations	preposition poems
awards	fables	questions
bibliographies	five-senses poems	quickwrites
biographies	folktales	reading logs
book jackets	found poems	readers theatre scripts
book reports	greeting cards	research reports
books	haiku poems	retellings
brochures	hink-pinks	reviews
bumper stickers	"I am" poems	riddles
captions	idioms	schedules
cartoons	"If I were . . ." poems	scripts
charts	instructions	sentences
cinquain poems	interviews	sequels
clusters	invitations	signs
color poems	"I wish . . ." poems	simulated journals
comics	jokes	stories
comparisons	K-W-L charts	story boards
computer programs	labels	story maps
crossword puzzles	learning logs	study guides
cubing	letters	thank-you notes
daily news charts	letters to the editor	tongue twisters
data charts	lists	Venn diagrams
definitions	lyrics	word-finds
descriptions	maps	wordless picture books
dialogue	newspapers	words
diagrams	notes	word walls

and these three forms look very different on a piece of paper. Whereas a story is written in the traditional block format, scripts and poems have unique page arrangements. Scripts are written with the character's name and a colon, and the dialogue is set off. Action and dialogue, rather than description, carry the story line in a script. In contrast, poems have unique formatting considerations, and words are used judiciously. Each word and phrase is chosen to convey a maximum amount of information.

Gathering and Organizing Ideas. Students engage in activities to gather and organize ideas for writing. Graves (1983) calls what writers do to prepare for writing "rehearsal" activities. Rehearsal activities take many forms, including:

1. *Drawing.* Drawing is the way young children gather and organize ideas for writing. Primary-grade teachers often notice that students draw before they write and, thinking that they are eating dessert before the meat and vegetables, insist that

they write first. But many young children cannot write first because they don't know what to write until they see what they draw (Dyson, 1982, 1986).

2. *Clustering.* Students make **clusters** (weblike diagrams) in which they write the topic in a center circle and then draw rays from the circle for each main idea. Then they add details and other information on rays drawn from each main idea. Through clustering, students organize their ideas for writing. Clustering is a better prewriting strategy than outlining because it is nonlinear.

3. *Talking.* Students talk with their classmates to share ideas about possible writing topics, try out ways to express an idea, and ask questions.

4. *Reading.* Students gather ideas for writing and investigate the structure of various written forms through reading. They may retell a favorite story in writing,

Technology Link   Computer Programs for Writers

A variety of word-processing programs, desktop publishing programs, and graphics packages support students who use the process approach to writing (Cochran-Smith, 1991; DeGroff, 1990). Students revise and edit their rough drafts more easily when they use word processors, and they print out neat and "clean" final copies without the drudgery of recopying their compositions (Strickland, 1997). They use digital cameras, graphics packages, and drawing and painting programs to create illustrations. And, with desktop publishing programs, students create professional-looking newspapers, brochures, and books. Here's a list of writing-related computer programs:

Type of Program	*Title*
Integrated packages	Claris Works
	Microsoft Works
	The Writing Center
Word-processing programs	Amazing Writing Machine
	Kid Works II
	Kidwriter Gold
	Mac Write Pro
	Microsoft Word
	Magic Slate
	Talking Text Writer
	Writer's Helper
Desktop publishing programs	Big Book Maker
	The Children's Writing and Publishing Center
	Make-a-Book
	Newspaper Maker
	Newsroom
	Pagemaker
	Print Shop
	Publish It!

write new adventures for favorite story characters, or experiment with repetition, onomatopoeia, or another poetic device used in a poem they have read. Informational books also provide raw material for writing. For example, if students are studying polar bears, they read to gather information about the animal—its habitat and predators, for example—that they may use in writing a report.

5. *Role-playing.* Children discover and shape ideas they will use in their writing through role-playing. During thematic units and after reading stories, students can reenact events to bring an experience to life. Teachers should choose a particular critical moment for students to reenact. For example, after reading *Sarah, Plain and Tall* (MacLachlan, 1985), children might reenact the day Sarah took the wagon to town. This is a critical moment: Does Sarah like them and their prairie home well enough to stay?

Type of Program	Title
	Ready, Set, Go!
	Super Print
	Toucan Press
Graphics packages	Bannermania
	PrintShop Deluxe
	SuperPrint
Drawing and painting programs	DazzleDraw
	Freehand
	Kid Pix Studio Deluxe
	Kid Works Deluxe
Presentation software	Kid Pix Slide Show
Digital cameras	QuickTake
	XapShot
Hypermedia programs	HyperCard
	HyperStudio
	Multimedia Workshop
Keyboarding programs	Kid Keys
	Kids on Keys
	Microtype: The Wonderful World of Paws
	Type to Learn

It's a good idea to make the first writing project a class collaboration so students can review word-processing procedures. The next several writing projects should be short so that students can concentrate on working through the word-processing procedures. Often one or two students will assume an important new status as "computer expert" because of special interest or expertise. These experts help other students with word-processing tasks and using the printer.

Step 2: Drafting

Students write and refine their compositions through a series of drafts. During the drafting step, they focus on getting their ideas down on paper. Because writers don't begin writing with their compositions already composed in their minds, students begin with tentative ideas developed through prewriting activities. The drafting step is the time to pour out ideas, with little concern about spelling, punctuation, and other mechanical errors.

Students skip every other line when they write their rough drafts to leave space for revisions. They use arrows to move sections of text, cross-outs to delete sections, and scissors and tape to cut apart and rearrange text, just as adult writers do. They write only on one side of a sheet of paper so it can be cut apart or rearranged. As computers become more available in elementary classrooms, revising, with all its moving, adding, and deleting of text, will be much easier. However, for students who hand-write their compositions, the wide spacing is crucial. Teachers might make small x's on every other line of students' papers as a reminder to skip lines as they draft their compositions.

Students label their drafts by writing *Rough Draft* in ink at the top or by using a ROUGH DRAFT stamp. This label indicates to the writer, other students, parents, and administrators that the composition is a draft in which the emphasis is on content, not mechanics. It also explains why the teacher has not graded the paper or marked mechanical errors.

Instead of writing drafts by hand, students can use computers to compose rough drafts, polish their writing, and print out final copies. There are many benefits of using computers for word processing. Students are often more motivated to write, and they tend to write longer pieces. Their writing looks neater, and they can use spellcheck programs to identify and correct misspelled words. Even young children can word-process their compositions using Magic Slate and other programs designed for beginning writers. To learn more about word-processing and other writing-related computer programs for elementary students, check the Technology Link on pages 64 and 65.

During drafting, students may need to modify their earlier decisions about purpose, audience, and, especially, the form their writing will take. For example, a composition that began as a story may be transformed into a report, letter, or poem. The new format allows the student to communicate more effectively. The process of modifying earlier decisions continues into the revising step.

As students write rough drafts, it is important for teachers not to emphasize correct spelling and neatness. In fact, pointing out mechanical errors during the drafting step sends students a false message that mechanical correctness is more important than content (Sommers, 1982). Later, during editing, students clean up mechanical errors and put their composition into a neat, final form.

Step 3: Revising

During the revising step, writers refine ideas in their compositions. Students often break the writing process cycle as soon as they complete a rough draft, believing that once they have jotted down their ideas, the writing task is complete. Experienced writers, however, know they must turn to others for reactions and revise on the basis of these comments. Revision is not just polishing; it is meeting the needs of readers by adding, substituting, deleting, and rearranging material. *Revision* means "seeing again," and in this step writers see their compositions again with the help of classmates and the teacher. The revising step includes three activities: rereading the rough draft, sharing the rough draft in a writing group, and revising on the basis of feedback.

Rereading the Rough Draft. After finishing the rough draft, writers need to distance themselves from the draft for a day or two, then reread it from a fresh perspective, as a reader might. As they reread, students make changes—adding, substituting, deleting, and moving—and place question marks by sections that need work. It is these trouble spots that students ask for help with in their writing groups.

Sharing in Writing Groups. Students meet in writing groups to share their compositions with classmates. They respond to the writer's rough draft and suggest possible revisions. Writing groups provide a scaffold in which teachers and classmates talk about plans and strategies for writing and revising (Applebee & Langer, 1983; Calkins, 1983).

Writing groups can form spontaneously when several students have completed drafts and are ready to share their compositions, or they can be formal groupings with identified leaders. In some classrooms writing groups form when four or five students finish writing their rough drafts. Students gather around a conference table or in a corner of the classroom and take turns reading their rough drafts aloud. Classmates in the group listen and respond, offering compliments and suggestions for revision. Sometimes the teacher joins the writing group, but if the teacher is involved in something else, students work independently.

In other classrooms, the writing groups are assigned. Students get together when all students in the group have completed their rough drafts and are ready to share their writing. Sometimes the teacher participates in these groups, providing feedback along with the students. Or, the writing groups can function independently. For these assigned

Students share their rough drafts and get feedback from classmates and the teacher during writing groups.

groups, each cluster is made up of four or five students, and a list of groups and their members is posted in the classroom. The teacher puts a star by one student's name, and that student serves as a group leader. The leader changes every quarter.

Making Revisions. Students make four types of changes to their rough drafts: additions, substitutions, deletions, and moves (Faigley & Witte, 1981). As they revise, students might add words, substitute sentences, delete paragraphs, and move phrases. Students often use a blue or red pen to cross out, draw arrows, and write in the space left between the double-spaced lines of their rough drafts so that revisions will show clearly. That way teachers can examine the types of revisions students make by examining their revised rough drafts. Revisions are another gauge of students' growth as writers.

Step 4: Editing

Editing is putting the piece of writing into its final form. Until this step, the focus has been primarily on the content of students' writing. Once the focus changes to mechanics, students polish their writing by correcting spelling mistakes and other mechanical errors. The goal here is to make the writing "optimally readable" (Smith, 1982). Writers who write for readers understand that if their compositions are not readable, they have written in vain because their ideas will never be read.

Mechanics are the commonly accepted conventions of written Standard English. They include capitalization, punctuation, spelling, sentence structure, usage, and formatting considerations specific to poems, scripts, letters, and other writing forms. The use of these commonly accepted conventions is a courtesy to those who will read the composition.

Students learn mechanical skills best through hands-on editing of their own compositions, not through workbook exercises. When they edit a composition that will be shared with a genuine audience, students are more interested in using mechanical skills correctly so they can communicate effectively. Calkins (1980) compared how teachers in two third-grade classrooms taught punctuation skills. She found that the students in the class who learned punctuation marks as a part of editing could define or explain more marks than the students in the other class, who were taught punctuation skills in a traditional manner, with instruction and practice exercises on each punctuation mark. The results of this research, as well as other studies (Bissex, 1980; Elley, Barham, Lamb, & Wyllie, 1976; Graves, 1983), suggest that it is more effective to teach mechanical skills as part of the writing process than through practice exercises.

Students move through three activities in the editing step: getting distance from the composition, proofreading to locate errors, and correcting errors.

Getting Distance. Students are more efficient editors if they set the composition aside for a few days before beginning to edit. After working so closely with a piece of writing during drafting and revising, they are too familiar with it to notice many mechanical errors. With the distance gained by waiting a few days, children are better able to approach editing with a fresh perspective and gather the enthusiasm necessary to finish the writing process by making the paper optimally readable.

Proofreading. Students proofread their compositions to locate and mark possible errors. Proofreading is a unique type of reading in which students read slowly, word by word, hunting for errors rather than reading quickly for meaning (King, 1985). Concentrating on mechanics is difficult because of our natural inclination to read for meaning. Even experienced proofreaders often find themselves reading for meaning and thus overlooking errors that do not inhibit meaning. It is important, therefore, to

Figure 2–9   Proofreaders' marks

Delete	ℯ	Most whales are ~~big and~~ huge creatures.
Insert	∧	**called** A baby whale is ∧ a calf.
Indent paragraph	¶	¶Whales look a lot like fish, but the two are quite different.
Capitalize	≡	In the United s̲tates it is illegal to hunt whales.
Change to lower case	/	Why do beached W̸hales die?
Add period	⊙	Baleen whales do not have any teeth⊙
Add comma	⌄	Some baleen whales are blue whales ⌄gray whales and humpback whales.
Add apostrophe	⌄	People are the whale⌄s only enemy.

take time to explain proofreading to students and to demonstrate how it differs from regular reading.

To demonstrate proofreading, teachers take a piece of student writing and copy it on the chalkboard or display it on an overhead projector. The teacher reads it several times, each time hunting for a particular type of error. During each reading, the teacher reads the composition slowly, softly pronouncing each word and touching the word with a pencil or pen to focus attention on it. The teacher marks possible errors as they are located.

Errors are marked or corrected with special proofreaders' marks. Students enjoy using these marks, the same ones that adult authors and editors use. Proofreaders' marks that elementary students can learn to use in editing their writing are presented in Figure 2–9.

Editing checklists help students focus on particular types of errors. Teachers can develop checklists with two to six items appropriate for the grade level. A first-grade checklist, for example, might include only two items—perhaps one about capital letters at the beginning of sentences and a second about periods at the end of sentences. In contrast, a middle-grade checklist might include items such as using commas in a series, indenting paragraphs, capitalizing proper nouns and adjectives, and spelling homonyms correctly. Teachers revise the checklist during the school year to focus attention on skills that have recently been taught.

A sample third-grade editing checklist is presented in Figure 2–10. The writer and a classmate work together as partners to edit their compositions. First, students proofread their own compositions, searching for errors in each category on the

Figure 2–10 A third-grade editing checklist

EDITING CHECKLIST

Author   Editor

1. I have circled the words that might be misspelled.

2. I have checked that all sentences begin with capital letters.

3. I have checked that all sentences end with punctuation marks.

4. I have checked that all proper nouns begin with a capital letter.

Signatures:

Author: _____ Editor: _____

checklist, and, after proofreading, check off each item. After completing the checklist, students sign their names and trade checklists and compositions. Now they become editors and complete each other's checklist. Having writer and editor sign the checklist helps them to take the activity seriously.

Correcting Errors. After students proofread their compositions and locate as many errors as they can, they use red pens to correct the errors individually or with an editor's assistance. Some errors are easy to correct, some require use of a dictionary, and others involve instruction from the teacher. It is unrealistic to expect students to locate and correct every mechanical error in their compositions. Not even published books are always error-free! Once in a while, students may change a correct spelling or punctuation mark and make it incorrect, but they correct far more errors than they create.

Editing can end after students and their editors correct as many mechanical errors as possible, or after students meet with the teacher in a conference for a final editing. When mechanical correctness is crucial, this conference is important. Teachers proofread the composition with the student, and they identify and make the remaining corrections together, or the teacher makes check marks in the margin to note errors for the student to correct independently.

Step 5: Publishing

In this step, students bring their compositions to life by writing final copies and by sharing them orally with an appropriate audience. When they share their writing with real audiences of classmates, other students, parents, and the community, students come to think of themselves as authors.

Making Books. One of the most popular ways for children to publish their writing is by making books. Simple booklets can be made by folding a sheet of paper into quarters, like a greeting card. Students write the title on the front and use the three remaining sides for their composition. They can also construct booklets by stapling sheets of writing paper together and adding covers made out of construction paper. Sheets of wallpaper cut from old sample books also make sturdy covers. These stapled booklets can be cut into various shapes, too. Students can make more sophisticated books by covering cardboard covers with contact paper, wallpaper samples, or cloth. Pages are sewn or stapled together, and the first and last pages (endpapers) are glued to the cardboard covers to hold the book together. Directions for making one type of hardcover book are shown in Figure 2–11.

Sharing Writing. Students read their writing to classmates or share it with larger audiences through hardcover books placed in the class or school library, plays performed for classmates, or letters sent to authors, businesses, and other correspondents. Here are some other ways to share children's writing:

❦ Submit the piece to writing contests

❦ Display the writing as a mobile

❦ Contribute to a class anthology

❦ Contribute to the local newspaper

❦ Make a shape book

❦ Record the writing on a cassette tape

❦ Submit it to a literary magazine

❦ Read it at a school assembly

❦ Share it at a read-aloud party

❦ Share it with parents and siblings

❦ Display poetry on a "poet-tree"

❦ Send it to a pen pal

❦ Display it on a bulletin board

❦ Make a big book

❦ Design a poster about the writing

❦ Read it to foster grandparents

❦ Share it as a puppet show

❦ Display it at a public event

❦ Read it to children in other classes

Through this sharing, students communicate with genuine audiences who respond to their writing in meaningful ways. Sharing writing is a social activity that helps children develop sensitivity to audiences and confidence in themselves as authors. Dyson (1985) advises that teachers consider the social interpretations of sharing—the students' behavior, the teacher's behavior, and the interaction between students and teacher—within the classroom context. Individual students interpret sharing differently. Beyond just providing the opportunity for students to share writing, teachers need to teach students how to respond to their classmates. Teachers themselves serve as a model for responding to students' writing without dominating the sharing.

www.sdcoe.k12.ca.us

Publishing Student Work.
Links to sites on the Internet that publish students' writing.

www.cyberkids.com

Cyberkids.
An online magazine written by children for children ages seven to eleven.

Figure 2–11 Directions for making hardcover books

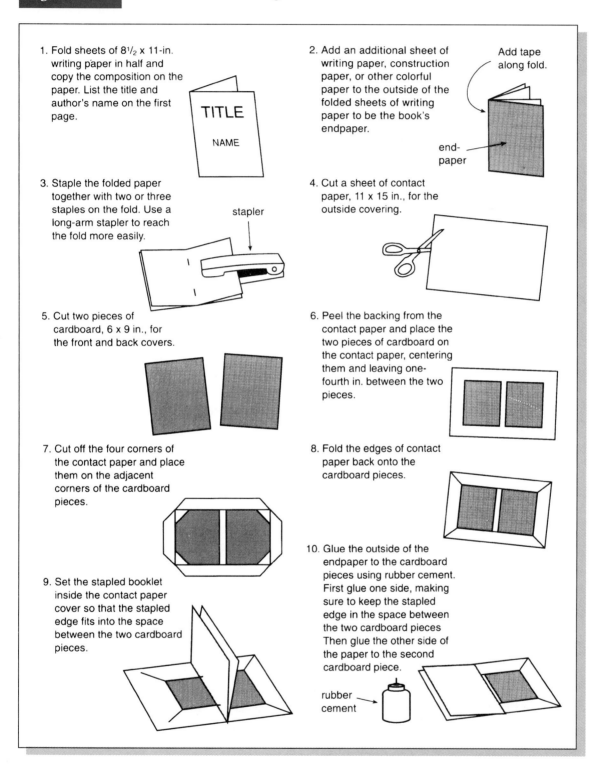

1. Fold sheets of 8½ x 11-in. writing paper in half and copy the composition on the paper. List the title and author's name on the first page.

TITLE

NAME

2. Add an additional sheet of writing paper, construction paper, or other colorful paper to the outside of the folded sheets of writing paper to be the book's endpaper.

Add tape along fold.

end-paper

3. Staple the folded paper together with two or three staples on the fold. Use a long-arm stapler to reach the fold more easily.

stapler

4. Cut a sheet of contact paper, 11 x 15 in., for the outside covering.

5. Cut two pieces of cardboard, 6 x 9 in., for the front and back covers.

6. Peel the backing from the contact paper and place the two pieces of cardboard on the contact paper, centering them and leaving one-fourth in. between the two pieces.

7. Cut off the four corners of the contact paper and place them on the adjacent corners of the cardboard pieces.

8. Fold the edges of contact paper back onto the cardboard pieces.

10. Glue the outside of the endpaper to the cardboard pieces using rubber cement. First glue one side, making sure to keep the stapled edge in the space between the two cardboard pieces Then glue the other side of the paper to the second cardboard piece.

rubber cement

9. Set the stapled booklet inside the contact paper cover so that the stapled edge fits into the space between the two cardboard pieces.

WHY ARE READING AND WRITING SIMILAR PROCESSES?

In both reading and writing the goal is to construct meaning, and the reading and writing processes have comparable activities at each step (Butler & Turbill, 1984). Figure 2–12 shows the similarities between reading and writing activities at each step. Notice the activities listed for the third step, responding and revising, for example. Fitzgerald (1989) analyzed these two activities and concluded that they draw on similar processes of author-reader-text interaction. Similar analyses can be made for reading and writing activities in all of the other steps, as well.

Tierney (1983) explains that reading and writing are multidimensional and involve concurrent, complex transactions between writers, between writers as readers, between readers, and between readers as writers. Writers participate in several types of reading activities. They read other authors' works for ideas and to learn about the structure of stories, but they also read and reread their own work—to problem-solve, discover, monitor, and clarify. The quality of these reading experiences seems closely tied to success in writing. "Readers as writers" is a newer idea, but readers are involved in many of the same activities that writers use. They generate ideas, organize, monitor, problem-solve, and revise. Smith (1983) believes that reading influences writing skills because readers unconsciously "read like writers":

> To read like a writer we engage with the author in what the author is writing. We can anticipate what the author will say, so that the author is in effect writing on our behalf, not showing how something is done but doing it with us. . . . Bit by bit, one thing at a time, but enormous numbers of things over the passage of time, the learner learns through reading like a writer to write like a writer. (pp. 563–564)

Also, both reading and writing are recursive, cycling back through various parts of the process, and, just as writers compose text, readers compose their meaning.

Teachers can help students appreciate the similarities between reading and writing in many ways. Tierney (1983) explains: "What we need are reading teachers who act as if their students were developing writers and writing teachers who act as if their students were readers" (p. 151). These are some ways to point out the relationships between reading and writing:

❦ Help writers assume alternative points of view as potential readers.

❦ Help readers consider the writer's purpose and viewpoint.

❦ Point out that reading is much like composing, so that students will view reading as a process, much like the writing process.

❦ Talk with students about the reading and writing processes.

❦ Talk with students about reading and writing strategies.

Readers and writers use a number of strategies for constructing meaning as they interact with print. As readers, we use a variety of problem-solving strategies to make decisions about an author's meaning and to construct meaning for ourselves. As writers we also use problem-solving strategies to decide what our readers need as we construct meaning for them and for ourselves. Comparing reading to writing, Tierney and Pearson (1983) described reading as a composing process because readers compose and refine meaning through reading, much like writers compose and refine meaning through writing.

Figure 2–12 **A comparison of the reading and writing processes**
Adapted from Butler and Turbill, 1984.

		What Readers Do	**What Writers Do**
Step	1	*Prereading*	*Prewriting*

Step 1

Prereading

Readers use knowledge about
- the topic
- reading
- literature
- language systems

Readers' expectations are cued by
- previous reading/writing experiences
- format of the text
- purpose for reading
- audience for reading

Readers make predictions.

Prewriting

Writers use knowledge about
- the topic
- writing
- literature
- language systems

Writers' expectations are cued by
- previous reading/writing experiences
- format of the text
- purpose for writing
- audience for writing

Writers gather and organize ideas.

Step 2

Reading

Readers
- use word-identification strategies
- use comprehension strategies
- monitor reading
- create meaning

Drafting

Writers
- use transcription strategies
- use meaning-making strategies
- monitor writing
- create meaning

Step 3

Responding

Readers
- respond to the text
- interpret meaning
- clarify misunderstandings
- expand ideas

Revising

Writers
- respond to the text
- interpret meaning
- clarify misunderstandings
- expand ideas

Step 4

Exploring

Readers
- examine the impact of words and literary language
- explore structural elements
- compare the text to others

Editing

Writers
- identify and correct mechanical errors
- review paragraph and sentence structure

Step 5

Applying

Readers
- go beyond the text to extend their interpretations
- share projects with classmates
- reflect on the reading process
- make connections to life and literature
- value the piece of literature
- feel success
- want to read again

Publishing

Writers
- produce the finished copy of their compositions
- share their compositions with genuine audiences
- reflect on the writing process
- value the composition
- feel success
- want to write again

Langer (1985) followed this line of thinking in identifying four strategies that both readers and writers use to interact with text. The first strategy is generating ideas: both readers and writers generate ideas as they get started, as they become aware of important ideas and experiences, and as they begin to plan and organize the information. Formulating meaning is the second strategy—the essence of both reading and writing. Readers and writers formulate meaning by developing the message, considering the audience, drawing on personal experience, choosing language, linking concepts, summarizing, and paraphrasing. Assessing is the third strategy. In both reading and writing, students review, react, and monitor their understanding of the message and the text itself. The fourth strategy is revising, in which both readers and writers reconsider and restructure the message, recognize when meaning has broken down, and take appropriate action to change the text to improve understanding.

There are practical benefits of connecting reading and writing. Reading contributes to students' writing development, and writing contributes to students' reading development. Shanahan (1988) has outlined seven instructional principles for relating reading and writing so that students develop a clear conception of literacy:

1. Involve students in reading and writing experiences every day.
2. Introduce the reading and writing processes in kindergarten.
3. Expect students' reading and writing to reflect their stage of literacy development.
4. Make the reading-writing connection explicit to students.
5. Emphasize both the processes and the products of reading and writing.
6. Emphasize the functions for which students use reading and writing.
7. Teach reading and writing through authentic literacy experiences.

These principles are incorporated into a balanced literacy program in which students read and write books and learn to view themselves as readers and writers.

Review

Teachers incorporate the five steps of the reading process—prereading, reading, responding, exploring, and applying—in planning for instruction. Teachers include shared reading, guided reading, independent reading, buddy reading, and reading aloud to students in their instructional programs. Teachers also use the five steps of the writing process—prewriting, drafting, revising, editing, and publishing—in teaching students how to write and refine their compositions. The goal of both reading and writing is to construct meaning, and the two processes involve similar activities at each step. Researchers recommend that teachers connect reading and writing because they are mutually supportive processes. The feature on page 76 presents guidelines for effectively teaching the reading and writing processes to students.

How Effective Teachers . . .

Teach the Reading and Writing Processes

⭐ Effective Practices

1. Teachers use the five-step reading process to plan an integrated, balanced instructional program.
2. Teachers and students set purposes for reading.
3. Teachers incorporate different types of reading: shared reading, guided reading, independent reading, buddy reading, and reading aloud to students.
4. Students respond to their reading as they participate in grand conversations and write in reading logs.
5. Students reread the selection, examine the author's craft, and focus on words during the exploring step.
6. Teachers teach skills and strategies during the exploring step.
7. Teachers provide opportunities for students to complete self-selected projects.
8. Teachers view reading and writing as processes of creating meaning.
9. Teachers teach students how to use each of the five steps in the writing process.
10. Teachers involve students in genuine and meaningful reading and writing activities.

⭐ Ineffective Practices

1. Teachers segment instruction, with separate reading and skills programs.
2. Teachers and students don't set purposes for reading, or set inappropriate purposes.
3. Teachers use only one type of reading.

4. Teachers ask questions to assess children's understanding of the reading selection.

5. Teachers assign students worksheets to practice vocabulary words and check comprehension skills.
6. Teachers don't coordinate skills instruction with literature.
7. Teachers assign more practice activities and worksheets.
8. Teachers see reading and writing as instructional activities.
9. Teachers assign single-draft writing activities.
10. Teachers assign worksheets and other practice activities.

References

Applebee, A. N., & Langer, J. A. (1983). Instructional scaffolding: Reading and writing and natural language activities. *Language Arts, 60,* 168–175.

Bissex, G. L. (1980). *Gyns at wrk: A child learns to write and read.* Cambridge: Harvard University Press.

Blanton, W. E., Wood, K. D., & Moorman, G. B. (1990). The role of purpose in reading instruction. *The Reading Teacher, 43,* 486–493.

Britton, J., Burgess, T., Martin, N., McLeod, A., & Rosen, H. (1975). *The development of writing abilities (11–18).* London: Schools Council Publications.

Butler, A., & Turbill, J. (1984). *Towards a reading-writing classroom.* Portsmouth, NH: Heinemann.

Calkins, L. M. (1980). When children want to punctuate: Basic skills belong in context. *Language Arts, 57,* 567–573.

Calkins, L. M. (1983). *Lessons from a child: On the teaching and learning of writing.* Portsmouth, NH: Heinemann.

Clay, M. M. (1991). *Becoming literate: The construction of inner control.* Portsmouth, NH: Heinemann.

Cochran-Smith, M. (1991). Word processing and writing in elementary classrooms: A critical review of related literature. *Review of Educational Research, 61,* 107–155.

DeGroff, L. (1990). Is there a place for computers in whole language classrooms? *The Reading Teacher, 43,* 568–572.

Depree, H., & Iversen, S. (1996). *Early literacy in the classroom: A new standard for young readers.* Bothell, WA: Wright Group.

Dyson, A. H. (1982). The emergence of visible language: Interrelationships between drawing and early writing. *Visible Language, 6,* 360–381.

Dyson, A. H. (1985). Second graders sharing writing: The multiple social realities of a literacy event. *Written Communication, 2,* 189–215.

Dyson, A. H. (1986). The imaginary worlds of childhood: A multimedia presentation. *Language Arts, 63,* 799–808.

Eeds, M., & Wells, D. (1989). Grand conversations: An exploration of meaning construction in literature study groups. *Research in the Teaching of English, 23,* 4–29.

Elley, W. B., Barham, I. H., Lamb, H., & Wyllie, M. (1976). The role of grammar in a secondary school English curriculum. *Research in the Teaching of English, 10,* 5–21.

Faigley, L., & Witte, S. (1981). Analyzing revision. *College Composition and Communication, 32,* 400–410.

Fitzgerald, J. (1989). Enhancing two related thought processes: Revision in writing and critical thinking. *The Reading Teacher, 43,* 42–48.

Fountas, I. C., & Pinnell, G. S. (1996). *Guided reading: Good first teaching for all children.* Portsmouth, NH: Heinemann.

Graves, D. H. (1976). Let's get rid of the welfare mess in the teaching of writing. *Language Arts, 53,* 645–651.

Graves, D. H. (1983). *Writing: Teachers and children at work.* Exeter, NH: Heinemann.

Hidi, S., & Hildyard, A. (1983). The comparison of oral and written productions in two discourse modes. *Discourse Processes, 6,* 91–105.

Holdaway, D. (1979). *The foundations of literacy.* Portsmouth, NH: Heinemann.

Hornsby, D., Sukarna, D., & Parry, J. (1986). *Read on: A conference approach to reading.* Portsmouth, NH: Heinemann.

King, M. (1985). Proofreading is not reading. *Teaching English in the Two-Year College, 12,* 108–112.

Langer, J. A. (1985). Children's sense of genre. *Written Communication, 2,* 157–187.

Murray, D. H. (1982). *Learning by teaching.* Montclair, NJ: Boynton/Cook.

Opitz, M. F., & Rasinski, T. V. (1998). *Good-bye round robin: 25 effective oral reading strategies.* Portsmouth, NH: Heinemann.

Peterson, R., & Eeds, M. (1990). *Grand conversations: Literature groups in action.* New York: Scholastic.

Rosenblatt, L. (1978). *The reader, the text, the poem: The transactional theory of the literary work.* Carbondale: Southern Illinois University Press.

Shanahan, T. (1988). The reading-writing relationship: Seven instructional principles. *The Reading Teacher, 41,* 636–647.

Slaughter, J. P. (1993). *Beyond storybooks: Young children and the shared book experience.* Newark, DE: International Reading Association.

Smith, F. (1982). *Writing and the writer.* New York: Holt, Rinehart and Winston.

Smith, F. (1983). *Essays into literacy.* Portsmouth, NH: Heinemann.

Sommers, N. (1982). Responding to student writing. *College Composition and Communication, 33,* 148–156.

Strickland, J. (1997). *From disk to hard copy: Teaching writing with computers.* Portsmouth, NH: Boynton-Cook/Heinemann.

Tierney, R. J. (1983). Writer-reader transactions: Defining the dimensions of negotiation. In P. L. Stock (Ed.), *Forum: Essays on theory and practice in the teaching of writing* (pp. 147–151). Upper Montclair, NJ: Boynton/Cook.

Tierney, R. J., & Pearson, P. D. (1983). Toward a composing model of reading. *Language Arts, 60,* 568–580.

Weaver, C. (1988). *Reading process and practice: From socio-psycholinguistics to whole language.* Portsmouth, NH: Heinemann.

Yaden, D. B., Jr. (1988). Understanding stories through repeated read-alouds: How many does it take? *The Reading Teacher, 41,* 556–560.

Children's Book References

Henry, M. (1963). *Misty of Chincoteague.* Chicago: Rand McNally.

Howe, D., & Howe, J. (1979). *Bunnicula: A rabbit-tale of mystery.* New York: Atheneum.

Lowry, L. (1993). *The giver.* Boston: Houghton Mifflin.

MacLachlan, P. (1985). *Sarah, plain and tall.* New York: Harper & Row.

Martin, B., Jr. (1983). *Brown bear, brown bear, what do you see?* New York: Holt, Rinehart & Winston.

Martin, B., Jr. (1992). *Polar bear, polar bear, what do you hear?* New York: Holt, Rinehart & Winston.

O'Neill, M. (1989). *Hailstones and halibut bones.* New York: Doubleday.

Van Allsburg, C. (1981). *Jumanji.* Boston: Houghton Mifflin.

Van Allsburg, C. (1993). *The sweetest fig.* Boston: Houghton Mifflin.

Viorst, J. (1977). *Alexander and the terrible, horrible, no good, very bad day.* New York: Atheneum.

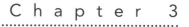

Chapter 3

Assessing Students' Literacy Development

— Chapter Questions —

Which assessment tools do teachers use to monitor students' learning in reading and writing?

How do students use portfolios?

How do teachers assign grades?

Mrs. Peterson Conducts End-of-Quarter Conferences

During the last week of the third quarter, Mrs. Peterson conferences with each of her sixth graders to review and reflect upon their work during the quarter. Students bring their three language arts folders to their conferences. One folder contains students' work from a literature focus unit on *Tuck Everlasting* (Babbitt, 1975), the story about a family who drinks from a magic spring and never grows older or dies. During this three-week unit, students:

- read and responded to the book
- focused on reading skills and strategies through a series of **minilessons** (see the Compendium for more information about this and all other highlighted terms in this chapter)
- put words on the class **word wall**
- participated in other exploring activities
- created projects to apply their learning

Students kept track of assignments using an assignment sheet and placed all of their work in their unit folders. At the end of the unit, Mrs. Peterson collected the students' folders, reviewed the work in them, and assigned grades using the point system listed on the assignment sheets.

The second folder contains students' work from literature circles when students divided into small groups and read and responded to one of six books. The groups read one of these books:

- *The Lion, the Witch and the Wardrobe* (Lewis, 1950)
- *Bunnicula: A Rabbit-Tale of Mystery* (Howe & Howe, 1979)
- *Shiloh* (Naylor, 1991)
- *The Midnight Fox* (Byars, 1968)
- *Julie of the Wolves* (George, 1972)
- *Hatchet* (Paulsen, 1987)

During this two-week unit, students chose the book they wanted to read after Mrs. Peterson gave brief **book talks** about each book. Then students divided into literature circle groups. Each group determined its own schedule for the two weeks. They read the book, conducted **grand conversations,** and wrote in **reading logs.** During the first week, Mrs. Peterson taught daily minilessons to the whole class to review the structural elements of stories—plot, character, setting, point of view, and theme—and then asked students to think about how the author of the book they were reading used these elements and what the relative importance of each element was in the book. Mrs. Peterson moved from group to group as students read, responded, and discussed the story elements. At the end of the unit, each literature circle reported to the class on its book and about how the author wove the story elements together. Each group prepared a chart to highlight one of the story elements, and students presented the charts to the class during the sharing time.

Students kept track of their work during this unit on assignment sheets, too. After the unit ended, Mrs. Peterson collected students' folders, reviewed them, and assigned grades using the point system listed on the assignment sheets.

During the last four weeks of the quarter, students are doing reading and writing workshop. They are choosing and reading books that interest them. Several are reading other books by Gary Paulsen or other books in C. S. Lewis's Chronicles of Narnia series. Mrs. Peterson encourages students to choose books that are a "good fit" for them—neither too hard nor too easy. During the four-week unit, students are expected to read at least two books. Students document their reading by writing reactions in reading logs, and they conference once a week with Mrs. Peterson.

During writing workshop, students use the writing process to compose stories, poems, essays, how-to manuals, and other types of writing. Most students use a computer to print out their final copies, and then they bind them into books. Students are expected to complete two books during the four-week unit. The weekly assignment sheet that Mrs. Peterson's students use during reading and writing workshop is shown in Figure 3–1.

Mrs. Peterson collects other types of assessment information about her students on a regular basis during this quarter. She does the following activities:

🐾 listens to students read aloud excerpts of books they are reading and takes **running records** to check their fluency

🐾 reviews students' reading logs to check for comprehension

🐾 listens to comments students make during grand conversations to monitor comprehension

🐾 checks their understanding of story elements as they develop charts during literature circles

🐾 analyzes spelling errors in students' reading logs and on students' rough drafts during editing conferences in writing workshop

🐾 uses rubrics to assess students' compositions

🐾 observes students and makes anecdotal notes each week to monitor their work habits and learning

Mrs. Peterson keeps a literacy folder for each student in which she places the assessment information she collects as well as notes from each conference. She brings these folders to the conferences at the end of the third quarter and will add the notes she makes during this conference to the folders.

During the last week of the quarter, Mrs. Peterson conferences with each student. She spends approximately 15 minutes talking with each student about his or her work and making plans for the next quarter. She uses a conference sheet to take notes about these conferences, and both she and the student sign this sheet. A copy of the conference sheet is shown in Figure 3–2. At the conference, Mrs. Peterson accomplishes these things:

🐾 reviews the student's work during the three units and the grades the student received

Figure 3–1 Record sheet used by Mrs. Peterson's sixth graders

Weekly Assignment Sheet

Name _____ Week _____

READING WORKSHOP

1. What books did you read?

2. Did you write in your reading log?

3. Did you conference with Mrs. Peterson?

4. What did you do during Reading Workshop?

M	T	W	Th	F

WRITING WORKSHOP

1. What did you write?

2. Did you use the writing process?

   ❧ prewriting   ❧ drafting   ❧ revising   ❧ editing   ❧ publishing

3. Did you conference with Mrs. Peterson?

4. What did you do during Writing Workshop?

M	T	W	Th	F

Figure 3–2 Mrs. Peterson's assessment form

End-of-Quarter Conference Sheet

Name _____   Date _____

Unit 1

Unit 2

Unit 3

_____

Items Chosen for Portfolio

_____

Accomplishments

_____

Concerns and Issues

_____

Goals for the Next Quarter

_____

Grades | □ | Reading | | □ | Writing | | □ | Work Habits |

_____   _____
Student   Teacher

❦ examines the items the student has chosen to add to his or her portfolio and asks the student to explain why these items were chosen

❦ presents some of the assessment information she has collected about the student

❦ determines the student's reading and writing grades for the report card

❦ sets goals with the student for the next quarter

❦ completes the conference sheet

After the conference, students finish writing reflections to attach to the new portfolio items and then add them to their portfolios. Students will take the rest of the unit folders home with their report cards. They will also take a copy of the conference sheet with their goals for the next quarter.

Today Mrs. Peterson conferences with Ted. They go over his three unit folders and set goals for the next quarter. Ted explains that he really didn't like *Tuck Everlasting* and didn't work as hard as he usually does. He says that the unit grade he received—B—reflects the grade he would give the book. Ted asks if he can choose five items from the other two units because he really doesn't have anything in this unit folder that he wants to put into his portfolio, and Mrs. Peterson agrees.

Ted participated in the literature circle reading *Bunnicula: A Rabbit-Tale of Mystery* (Howe & Howe, 1979), and he says that this is one of his favorite books. Through his reading log and participation in grand conversations, Ted demonstrated his comprehension of the story and his knowledge of story structure. Mrs. Peterson recalls that Ted asked her about humor and whether or not it was an element of story structure. He says that he now thinks humor is the glue that holds the story together because it is a combination of characters, plot, setting, and point of view. He tells Mrs. Peterson that he has concluded that he likes stories like *Bunnicula* that are told in the first person best.

Ted shows Mrs. Peterson his reading log, written from Harold the dog's viewpoint, and a chart he has made about the humor in the book that he wants to place in his portfolio. Mrs. Peterson agrees. Ted's grade for this literature circle unit is an A on his assignment sheet, and Ted agrees that he deserved it.

During reading workshop, Ted has continued reading Bunnicula sequels, including *Howliday Inn* (Howe, 1981), *The Celery Stalks at Midnight* (Howe, 1983), *Nighty-Nightmare* (Howe, 1987), and *Return to Howliday Inn* (Howe, 1992). He made an audiotape of his reading of excerpts from each of the books, and this is one of the items he wants to put in his portfolio. He is especially proud of the voices he uses for each character. Mrs. Peterson praises Ted for his enthusiasm and the number of books he has read in reading workshop. His grade for reading workshop will be an A. She also asks if the Bunnicula books are challenging him, or if they are easy for him. He admits that they are "sort of easy" and agrees to choose some more challenging books during the next quarter.

During writing workshop, Ted has written and mailed a letter to author James Howe. He wants to put a copy of the letter in his portfolio, along with the response he is eagerly awaiting. He became interested in vampires through the Bunnicula books and has researched them. Now he is finishing a book he's calling "What's True and What's Not About Vampires," and he wants to place it in his portfolio, too. He is preparing his final copy on the computer so that it will be neat. Mrs. Peterson talks with Ted about his writing process. He talks about how he draws a series of small boxes representing each page on a sheet of paper during prewriting to plan his book. He tries to plan out the entire book in his head, and then he writes the book straight through, paying little attention to revising. He met with Mrs. Peterson several days earlier to edit his book, and although there were several places where he might have made some revisions, he didn't want to. Mrs. Peterson expresses her concern that he isn't giving adequate attention to revising and that this is affecting the quality of his writing. His grade for writing workshop will be a B.

During the last several minutes of the conference, Ted sets goals for the next quarter. For reading, he wants to read ten books and agrees to choose more challenging books. For writing, he reluctantly agrees to take time to revise his work, and, because Ted enjoys word processing, Mrs. Peterson suggests that he do both his rough drafts and final copies on the computer. Ted also volunteers that he would like to try his hand at writing a play during writing workshop in the next quarter. He had attended a play with his family and learned about scripts. Now he wants to write one. He thinks perhaps that he will feature Bunnicula, Harold, and Chester in the play.

The conference ends, Ted returns to his desk, and Mrs. Peterson calls another student to the conference table.

···

Assessing students' literacy development is a difficult task. Although it may seem fairly easy to develop and administer a criterion-referenced test, tests often cannot measure the complex ways students use reading and writing. Tests in which students match characters and events or write the meanings of words do not measure comprehension very well, and a test on punctuation marks, for example, does not indicate students' ability to use punctuation marks correctly in their own writing. Instead, tests typically evaluate students' ability to add punctuation marks to a set of sentences created by someone else, or to proofread and spot punctuation errors in someone else's writing.

Traditional assessment reflects outdated views of how students learn to read and write, and it provides an incomplete assessment of students' literacy abilities. Tests and other traditional assessment procedures focus on only a few aspects of what readers do as they read, and of what writers do as they write. Traditional reading assessment fails to use authentic reading tasks or to help teachers find ways to help students succeed.

Assessment is an integral part of teaching and learning. The purpose of classroom assessment is to inform and influence instruction. Through assessment, teachers learn about their students, about themselves as teachers, and about the impact of the instructional program. Similarly, when students reflect on their learning and use self-assessment, they learn about themselves as learners and also about their learning. Figure 3–3 presents guidelines for classroom assessment and describes how teachers can use assessment tools in their classrooms.

www.cse.ucla.edu

National Center for Research on Evaluation, Standards, and Student Testing. Presents results of research about educational testing in the United States.

Figure 3–3 Guidelines for classroom assessment

1. Select Appropriate Assessment Tools

Teachers identify their purpose for assessment and choose an appropriate assessment tool. To gauge students' reading fluency, for example, teachers can do a running record, and to judge whether or not students are comprehending, they can examine students' reading logs and listen to their comments during a grand conversation.

2. Use a Variety of Assessment Tools

Teachers learn how to use and then regularly use a variety of assessment tools that reflect current theories about how children learn and become literate, including running records, anecdotal notes, and reading logs.

3. Integrate Instruction and Assessment

Teachers use the results of assessment to inform their teaching. They observe and conference with students as they teach and supervise students during reading and writing activities. When students do not understand what teachers are trying to teach, teachers need to try other instructional procedures.

4. Focus on the Positive

Teachers focus on what students can do, not what they can't do. Too often teachers want to diagnose students' problems and then remediate or "fix" these problems, but teachers should focus on how to facilitate students' development as readers and writers.

5. Examine Both Processes and Products

Teachers examine both the processes and the products of reading and writing. Teachers notice the strategies that students use as well as assess the products they produce through reading and writing.

6. Use Multiple Contexts

Teachers assess students' literacy development in a variety of contexts, including literature focus units, literature circles, reading and writing workshop, basal reader programs, and thematic units. Multiple contexts are important because students often do better in one type of activity than another.

7. Work With Individual Students

In addition to making whole-class assessments, teachers make time to observe, conference with, and do other assessment procedures with individual students in order to develop clear understandings of the student's development as a reader or writer.

8. Encourage Self-Assessment

Students' reflection on and self-assessment of their progress in reading and writing should be an integral part of assessment.

LITERACY ASSESSMENT TOOLS

Teachers use a variety of literacy assessment tools and procedures to monitor and document students' reading and writing development. These tools examine students' ability to identify words, read fluently, comprehend what they are reading, use the writing process, and spell words. Many of these tools are informal and created by teachers, but others have been developed, standardized, and published by researchers. Teachers also use assessment tools to diagnose struggling students' reading and writing problems. Many of these assessments are used with individual students, and even though it takes time to administer individual assessments, the information the teacher gains is useful and valuable. Giving a paper-and-pencil test to the entire class rarely provides much useful information. Teachers learn much more about their students as they listen to individual students read, watch individual students write, and talk with individual students about their reading and writing.

Assessing Students' Concepts About Print

www.sedl.org

Reading Assessment Database. Database of reading assessment tools for kindergarten through third grade.

Young children learn concepts about print as they observe written language in their environment, listen to parents and teachers read books aloud, and experiment with reading and writing themselves. They learn basic concepts about letters, words, writing, and reading, and they demonstrate this knowledge when they turn the pages in a book, participate in **interactive writing** activities, and identify letters, words, and sentences on classroom charts.

Marie Clay (1985) developed the Concepts About Print Test (CAP Test) to more formally assess young children's understanding of written language concepts. The test has 24 items, and it is administered individually in 10 minutes. As the teacher reads the story aloud, the child looks at a test booklet with a story that has a picture on one facing page and text on the other. The child is asked to open the book, turn pages, and point out particular features of the text, including letters, words, sentences, and punctuation marks, as the story is read.

─────────── *Assessment Tools: Concepts About Print* ───────────

Marie Clay developed the Concepts About Print Test (CAP Test) to assess young children's understanding of concepts about print. These three types of concepts are assessed:

1. Book-orientation concepts
2. Directionality concepts
3. Letter and word concepts

There are two forms of the CAP Test booklet, *Sand* (Clay, 1972) and *Stones* (Clay, 1979). In both forms, the same 24 items are assessed. Teachers can use the CAP Test booklets or any big book or small book. They administer the test by reading a book to the child and asking the child to point to the first page of the story, show the direction of print, and point to letters, words, and punctuation marks. It is important that teachers carefully observe children as they respond and mark their responses on a scoring sheet. For more information, see *An Observational Survey of Early Literacy Assessment* (Clay, 1993).

Teachers can also create their own versions of the CAP Test and use the test with any story they are reading with a child. As with the CAP Test, teachers' adaptations examine children's understanding that print carries the meaning, directionality of print, tracking of print, and letter, word, and sentence representation.

As they read any big book or small book with a child, teachers ask the child to show book-orientation concepts, directionality concepts, and letter and word concepts. Teachers can use the CAP Test scoring sheet shown in Figure 3–4 or develop one of their own to monitor children's growing understanding of these concepts.

Figure 3–4 Concepts About Print Test scoring sheet

CAP Test Scoring Sheet

Name _____ Date _____

Title of Book _____

Check the items that the child demonstrates.

1. Book-Orientation Concepts
   ☐ Shows the front of a book.
   ☐ Turns to the first page of the story.
   ☐ Shows where to start reading on a page.

2. Directionality Concepts
   ☐ Shows the direction of print across a line of text.
   ☐ Shows the direction of print on a page with more than one line of print.
   ☐ Points to track words as the teacher reads.

3. Letter and Word Concepts
   ☐ Points to any letter on a page.
   ☐ Points to a particular letter on a page.
   ☐ Puts fingers around any word on a page.
   ☐ Puts fingers around a particular word on a page.
   ☐ Puts fingers around any sentence on a page.
   ☐ Points to the first and last letters of a word.
   ☐ Points to a period or other punctuation mark.
   ☐ Points to a capital letter.

Summary Comments:

Assessing Students' Phonemic Awareness and Phonics

Students learn about the alphabetic principle (that letters represent sounds) in the primary grades. Through phonemic awareness instruction, students learn strategies for segmenting, blending, and substituting sounds in words, and through phonics instruction they learn about consonant and vowel sounds and phonics generalizations. Teachers often monitor students' learning as they participate in phonemic awareness and phonics activities in the classroom. When they sort picture cards according to beginning sounds or identify rhyming words in a familiar song, students are demonstrating their knowledge of phonemic awareness. Similarly, when students use magnetic letters to spell words ending in -*at,* such as *bat, cat, hat, mat, rat,* and *sat,* they are demonstrating their phonics knowledge.

Phonics instruction is usually completed in the primary grades, but some older students who are struggling readers have not acquired all of the phonics skills. Cunningham (1990) developed The Names Test to measure older students' ability to decode unfamiliar words. She created a list of 50 first and last names, including both one-syllable and multisyllabic names representing many common phonics elements. Duffelmeyer, Kruse, Merkley, and Fyfe (1994) expanded the test to 70 names in order to increase its validity. Teachers administer this test individually. They ask students to read the list of names, and mark which names students read correctly and which they pronounce incorrectly. Then teachers analyze students' errors to determine which phonics elements students have not acquired in order to plan for future instruction.

--------- *Assessment Tools: Phonemic Awareness and Phonics* ---------

Teachers in kindergarten and first grade teach and monitor students' growing phonemic awareness using a variety of classroom activities and these test instruments:

> Phonemic Awareness in Young Children (Adams, Foorman, Lundberg & Beeler, 1997)
> Test of Phonological Awareness (Torgesen & Bryant, 1994)
> Yopp-Singer Test of Phonemic Segmentation (Yopp, 1995)

Teachers use these assessments from Clay's *Observational Survey* to assess young children's knowledge of letters of the alphabet, phonics, and words:

> Letter Identification (Clay, 1993)
> Word Test (Clay, 1993)
> Dictation Task (Clay, 1993)

Teachers in grades 3 through 8 use The Names Test (Cunningham, 1990; Duffelmeyer et al., 1994) to assess older students' knowledge of phonics.

Assessing Students' Word Identification and Fluency

The goal of word identification is for students to read words accurately, rapidly, and automatically. Teachers listen to students read aloud to determine whether they can read words automatically and have strategies for unlocking unfamiliar words. Chil-

Teachers take running records as they listen to students read books aloud.

dren in the primary grades learn to read high-frequency sight words, such as *said* and *what,* and apply phonics skills to "sound out" other unfamiliar words. Older students extend this knowledge by learning how to break multisyllabic words into syllables to facilitate pronunciation.

Students who read fluently are better able to comprehend what they read because they have the mental energy to focus on what they are reading. Teachers monitor students' fluency as they listen to students read aloud. They check to see that students read with appropriate speed, intonation, and pausing.

Teachers often take **running records** of students' oral reading to assess their word identification and reading fluency (Clay, 1985). With a running record, teachers calculate the percentage of words the student reads correctly and then analyze the miscues or errors. Teachers make a series of check marks on a sheet of paper as the child reads each word correctly. Teachers use other marks to indicate words that the student substitutes, repeats, pronounces incorrectly, or doesn't know. While teachers can make the running record on a blank sheet of paper, it is much easier to duplicate a copy of the page or pages the student will read and take the running record next to or on top of the actual text. Making a copy of the text is especially important for middle- and upper-grade students who read more complex texts and read them more quickly than younger students do.

After identifying the words that the student read incorrectly, teachers calculate the percentage of words the student read correctly. Teachers use the percentage of words read correctly to determine whether the book or other reading material is too easy, too difficult, or appropriate for the student at this time. If the student reads 95% or more of the words correctly, the book is easy or at the independent reading level for that child. If the student reads 90–94% of the words correctly, the book is at the student's instructional level. If the student reads fewer than 90% of the words correctly, the book is too difficult for the student to read: it is at the student's frustration level.

Running records are easy for teachers to take, although teachers need some practice before they are comfortable with the procedure. Figure 3–5 presents a running record done with a sixth grader in Mrs. Peterson's classroom. This student was reading the beginning of Chapter 1 of *Bunnicula: A Rabbit-Tale of Mystery* (Howe & Howe, 1979) when the running record was taken.

Teachers categorize and analyze the student's errors to identify patterns of error, as shown at the bottom of Figure 3–5. Then teachers use this information as they plan minilessons and other word-study activities. Another way to analyze students' errors is called miscue analysis (K. S. Goodman, 1976). "Miscue" is another word for "error," and it suggests that students used the wrong cueing system to figure out the word. For example, if a student reads "Dad" for "Father," the error is meaning-related because the student over-relied on the semantic system. If a student reads "Feather" for "Father," the error is more likely graphophonic (or phonological), because the student over-relied on the beginning sound in the word and didn't evaluate whether or not the word made sense semantically. The Dad/Father and Feather/Father miscues are both syntactically correct because a noun was substituted for a noun. Sometimes, however, students substitute words that don't make sense syntactically. For example, if a student reads "tomorrow" for "through" in the sentence "Father walked through the door," the error doesn't make sense either semantically or syntactically, even though both words begin with *t*.

Teachers can categorize students' miscues or errors according to the semantic, graphophonic, and syntactic cueing systems in order to examine what word-identification strategies students are using. As they categorize the miscues, teachers should ask themselves these questions:

🌿 Does the reader self-correct the miscue?

🌿 Does the miscue change the meaning of the sentence?

🌿 Is the miscue phonologically similar to the word in the text?

🌿 Is the miscue acceptable within the syntax (or structure) of the sentence?

Assessment Tools: Word Identification and Fluency

Being able to rapidly identify words without having to use word analysis skills is an important part of becoming a fluent reader. Teachers often have students read lists of high-frequency words or word cards with the high-frequency words written on them. Students individually read the lists of words and teachers mark which words students can read correctly. By third grade, students should be able to read the 100 most frequently used words (see page 187). Teachers can also use Fry's New Instant Word Lists (1980) or another graded word list of high-frequency words to assess students' word-identification skills.

Teachers take running records (Clay, 1993) to monitor students' oral reading, and assess their fluency. They categorize students' miscues or errors according to the semantic, graphophonic, and syntactic cueing systems in order to examine what word-identification strategies students are using.

Figure 3–5 Running record and analysis

Reprinted with the permission of Atheneum Books for Young Readers, an imprint of Simon and Schuster Children's Publishing Division. From Bunnicula: *A Rabbit-Tale of Mystery* by Deborah Howe and James Howe. Text copyright © 1979 James Howe.

Text	Running Record
I shall never forget the first time I laid these	✓ $\frac{will}{shall}$ ✓ ✓ ✓ ✓ ✓ ✓
now tired old eyes on our visitor. I had been	$\frac{—}{now}$ $\frac{tie\text{-}red}{tired}$ ✓ ✓ ✓ ✓ ✓ ✓
left home by the family with the admonition	✓ ✓ ✓ ✓ ✓ ✓ $\frac{T}{admonition}$
to take care of the house until they returned.	✓ ✓ ✓ ✓ ✓ ✓ ✓ ✓
That's something they always say to me when	✓ ✓ ✓ ✓ ✓ ✓ ✓ ✓
they go out: "Take care of the house, Harold.	✓ ✓ ✓ ✓ ✓ ✓ ✓ ✓
You're the watchdog." I think it's their	✓ ✓ $\frac{wa\text{-}wash\text{-}watchdog}{watchdog}$ ✓ ✓ ✓
way of making up for not taking me with	✓ ✓ ✓ ✓ ✓ ✓ ✓ ✓
them. As if I wanted to go anyway. You can't	✓ ✓ ✓ ✓ ✓ ✓ ✓ ✓ ✓
lie down at the movies and still see the screen.	$\frac{lay}{lie}$ ✓ ✓ ✓ ✓ ✓ ✓ ✓ ✓
And people think you're being impolite if you	$\frac{—}{And}$ ✓ ✓ ✓ ✓ $\frac{impo\text{-}impo\text{-}T}{impolite}$ ✓ ✓
fall asleep and start to snore, or scratch	✓ ✓ ✓ ✓ ✓ ✓ $\frac{scrap}{scratch}$
yourself in public. No thank you, I'd rather	✓ ✓ ✓ ✓ ✓ ✓ ✓
be stretched out on my favorite rug	✓ $\frac{streaked}{stretched}$ ✓ ✓ ✓ ✓
in front of a nice, whistling radiator.	✓ ✓ ✓ ✓ ✓ $\frac{radio}{radiator}$

Analysis

Total words   128
Errors   11
Accuracy rate   92%   (instructional level)

This student read the text with interest, enthusiasm, and good expression. After reading, the student was able to talk about what he had read and to make predictions about Harold's role in the story. The errors are:

Substitution	will/shall	streaked/stretched
	lay/lie	radio/radiator
	scrap/scratch	
Omission	now	and
Mispronounced	tie-red/tired	
Teacher told	admonition	impolite
Prolonged decoding	watchdog	

Most of the errors were multisyllabic words, which the student was unable to break apart. A series of minilessons on breaking apart multisyllabic words to decode them is recommended for this student. The first two substitution errors did not affect meaning, and the two omission errors did not affect meaning either.

Figure 3–6 Miscue analysis of the student's errors from running record

Student _____ Date _____

Text _____

WORDS			SEMANTICS	PHONOLOGY	SYNTAX
Text	Student	Self-corrected?	Similar meaning?	Graphophonic similarity?	Syntactically acceptable?
shall	will		✓		✓
tired	tie-red			✓	
lie	lay		✓	✓	✓
scratch	scrap			✓	
stretched	streaked			✓	✓
radiator	radio			✓	✓

Analysis:

This student seems to rely on graphophonic similarities—particularly beginning sounds—more than semantic similarities. The student did not self-correct any words.

The errors that interfere with meaning and the errors that are syntactically unacceptable are the most serious because the student doesn't realize that reading should make sense. Errors can be classified and charted, as shown in Figure 3–6. These errors were taken from the sixth grader's running record presented in Figure 3–5. Only words that students mispronounce or substitute can be analyzed. Repetitions and omissions are not calculated.

Assessing Students' Comprehension

Comprehension is the goal of reading, and students demonstrate their comprehension in many ways. The comments they write in reading logs and make during **grand**

conversations and **instructional conversations** provide evidence. Children's interest in a book is sometimes an indicator, too. When children dismiss a book as "boring," they may really mean that it is confusing.

Story retelling and **cloze procedure** are two informal assessment activities. In a story retelling, teachers ask students to retell the story in their own words, and this approach is especially useful with emergent readers (Gambrell, Pfeiffer, & Wilson, 1985; Morrow, 1985). In the cloze procedure, teachers take an excerpt of 100 to 300 words from a selection students have read, delete every fifth word from the passage, and replace the deleted words with blanks. Then students read the passage and write the missing words in the blanks. Students use their knowledge of the topic, narrative or expository structure, English word order, and the meaning of the words in the sentences to successfully guess the missing words.

Teachers use commercial tests called informal reading inventories (IRIs) to determine students' reading levels. The reading levels are expressed as grade-level scores—second-grade level or sixth-grade level, for example. The IRI is an individually administered reading test and is typically composed of graded word lists, graded passages from stories and informational books, and comprehension questions. This inventory can also be used to assess students' reading strengths and weaknesses.

The graded word lists consist of 10 to 20 words at each grade level, from first grade through eighth. Students read the lists of words until they reach a point when the words become too difficult for them. This indicates an approximate level for students to begin reading the graded reading passages. In addition, teachers can note the decoding skills that students use to identify words presented in isolation.

The graded reading passages are series of narrative and expository passages, ranging in difficulty. Students read these passages orally or silently and then answer a series of comprehension questions. The questions are designed to focus on main ideas, inferences, and vocabulary. Teachers use scoring sheets to record students' performance, and they analyze the results to see how readers use strategies in context, how they identify unknown words, and how they comprehend what they read.

Students' scores on the IRI can be used to calculate their independent, instructional, and frustration reading levels. At the independent level, students can read the text comfortably and without assistance. Students read books at this level for pleasure and during reading workshop. At the instructional level, students can read textbooks and trade books successfully with teacher guidance. Books selected for literature focus units and literature circles book clubs should be at students' instructional levels. At the frustration level, the reading materials are too difficult for students to read, so students often don't understand what they are reading. As the name implies, students become very frustrated when they attempt to read trade books and textbooks at this level. When books featured in literature focus units are too difficult for some students to read, teachers need to make provisions for these students. Teachers can use shared reading, buddy reading, or reading aloud to students.

IRIs are also used to identify students' listening capacity levels. Teachers read aloud passages written at or above students' frustration levels and ask students the comprehension questions. If students can answer the questions, they understand the passage. Teachers then know that students can comprehend books and texts at that level when they are read aloud and that students have the potential to improve their reading comprehension to this level.

www.eduplace.com

Literacy Development and Assessment. Examines the match between assessment and instruction, and provides a comprehensive list of professional references.

——————————————— *Assessment Tools: Comprehension* ———————————————

The traditional way to check on students' comprehension is to ask questions after reading, but there are better ways to assess comprehension. Teachers can examine students' entries in reading logs, note students' comments during grand conversations, and consider how students apply what they have learned in the projects they develop after reading. Two informal assessments are story retellings and cloze procedure.

Teachers use informal reading inventories (IRIs) to diagnose students' reading levels. A variety of commercially published IRIs are available, including the following:

> Analytical Reading Inventory (Woods & Moe, 1999)
> Classroom Reading Inventory (Silvaroli, 1997)
> The Flynt/Cooter Reading Inventory for the Classroom (Flynt & Cooter, 1998)

Other IRIs accompany basal reading series, and teachers can construct their own using textbooks or trade books written at each reading level.

Assessing Students' Vocabulary

www.ericae.net

Authentic Reading Assessment.
A clearinghouse for articles and books about assessment and assessment tools.

Students need to understand the meaning of words they read; otherwise, they have problems decoding words and understanding what they are reading. Elementary students learn the meanings of 3,000 or more words each year, or 8–10 new words every day, and they learn most of these words informally or without direct instruction (Stahl, 1999).

Teachers monitor students' use of new vocabulary as they talk and write about books they are reading for content-area units. In addition to determining whether students know the meaning of specific words, teachers consider whether students can differentiate among related words, such as *grumpy, surly, crabby, stern, rude, discourteous, snarling, grouchy,* and *waspish.* Another way to examine vocabulary knowledge is to ask students to name synonyms or antonyms of words. Teachers also monitor students' knowledge about root words and affixes. For example, if students know that *legible* means "readable," can they figure out what *illegible* means?

There are very few vocabulary tests available, so teachers often depend on informal measures of students' vocabulary knowledge. Some of the comprehension questions on informal reading inventories focus on the meanings of words, and students' answers to these items provide one indication of students' vocabulary knowledge.

Assessing Students' Writing

Teachers assess both the process students use as they write and the quality of students' compositions. They observe as students use the writing process to develop their compositions, and they conference with students as they revise and edit their writing. Teachers notice, for example, whether students use writing strategies to gather and organize ideas for writing, whether they use feedback from classmates in revising their writing, and whether they think about their audience when they write. They also have students keep all drafts of their compositions in writing folders so that they can document their writing processes.

As students' writing develops, it becomes more complex in a variety of ways. One of the most obvious changes is that it gets longer. Longer doesn't mean better, but as students write longer pieces their writing often shows other signs of growth, too. Four ways that elementary students' writing develops are:

1. *Ideas.* Students' writing is creative, and they develop the main ideas and provide supporting details. Their writing is tailored to both purpose and audience.
2. *Organization.* Writers present ideas in a logical sequence and provide transitions between ideas. The composition is divided into paragraphs. For stories, students organize their writing into beginning, middle, and end, and for informational pieces, topic sentences clarify the organization.
3. *Language.* Students use words effectively, including figurative language. They choose language that is appropriate for purpose and audience. Students use Standard English word forms and sentence constructions. They also vary the types of sentences they write.
4. *Mechanics.* Students use correct spelling, punctuation, and capitalization. The composition is formatted appropriately for the writing form (e.g., letters, poems, plays, or stories), and the final copy is neat (Tompkins, 2000).

Teachers develop rubrics, or scoring guides, to assess students' growth as writers (Farr & Tone, 1994). Rubrics make the analysis of writing simpler and the assessment process more reliable and consistent. Rubrics may have four, five, or six levels, with descriptors related to ideas, organization, language, and mechanics at each level. Some rubrics are general and appropriate for almost any writing assignment, while others are designed for a specific writing assignment. Figure 3–7 presents two rubrics. One is a general five-level rubric for middle-grade students, and the other is a four-level rubric for assessing sixth graders' reports on ancient Egypt. In contrast to the general rubric, the report rubric includes specific components that students were to include in their reports.

Both teachers and students can use rubrics to assess writing. They read the composition and highlight words in the rubric that best describe the composition. The score is determined by examining the highlighted words and determining which level has the most highlighted words.

www.nwrel.org

6 + 1 Traits of Writing.
The Northwest Regional Educational Laboratory's model for assessing and teaching writing, involving seven writing traits.

———————— *Assessment Tools: Writing* ————————

Teachers monitor students' use of the writing process as they write and often take anecdotal notes as they observe students and meet with them in conferences. They also ask students to keep all drafts of their writing in writing folders in order to document students' movement through the writing process.

Teachers use rubrics to assess the quality of students' compositions. Some rubrics are general and can be used for almost any writing assignment, while others are designed for a specific writing assignment. Sometimes teachers use rubrics developed by school districts; at other times they develop their own rubrics to assess the specific components and qualities they have stressed in their classrooms. Rubrics should have four to six achievement levels and address ideas, organization, language, and mechanics.

In addition, kindergarten and first-grade teachers can administer Clay's Writing Vocabulary Test, part of the *Observational Survey* (1993), to examine how many words young children can write in 10 minutes.

Figure 3–7   Two rubrics for assessing students' writing

Middle-Grade Writing Rubric
5   EXCEPTIONAL ACHIEVEMENT
☞ Creative and original ☞ Clear organization ☞ Precise word choice and figurative language ☞ Sophisticated sentences ☞ Essentially free of mechanical errors
4   EXCELLENT ACHIEVEMENT
☞ Some creativity, but more predictable than an exceptional paper ☞ Definite organization ☞ Good word choice but not figurative language ☞ Varied sentences ☞ Only a few mechanical errors
3   ADEQUATE ACHIEVEMENT
☞ Predictable paper ☞ Some organization ☞ Adequate word choice ☞ Little variety of sentences and some run-on sentences ☞ Some mechanical errors
2   LIMITED ACHIEVEMENT
☞ Brief and superficial ☞ Lacks organization ☞ Imprecise language ☞ Incomplete and run-on sentences ☞ Many mechanical errors
1   MINIMAL ACHIEVEMENT
☞ No ideas communicated ☞ No organization ☞ Inadequate word choice ☞ Sentence fragments ☞ Overwhelming mechanical errors

Assessing Students' Spelling

The choices students make as they spell words are important indicators of their knowledge of both phonics and spelling. For example, a student who spells phonetically might spell *money* as *mune*, and other students who are experimenting with long

Figure 3–7 *continued*

Rubric for Assessing Reports on Ancient Egypt
4 EXCELLENT REPORT
____ Three or more chapters with titles
____ Main idea clearly developed in each chapter
____ Three or more illustrations
____ Effective use of Egypt-related words in text and illustrations
____ Very interesting to read
____ Very few mechanical errors
____ Table of contents
3 GOOD REPORT
____ Three chapters with titles
____ Main idea somewhat developed in each chapter
____ Three illustrations
____ Some Egypt-related words used
____ Interesting to read
____ A few mechanical errors
____ Table of contents
2 AVERAGE REPORT
____ Three chapters
____ Main idea identified in each chapter
____ One or two illustrations
____ A few Egypt-related words used
____ Sort of interesting to read
____ Some mechanical errors
____ Table of contents
1 POOR REPORT
____ One or two chapters
____ Information in each chapter rambles
____ No illustrations
____ Very few Egypt-related words used
____ Hard to read and understand
____ Many mechanical errors
____ No table of contents

vowels might spell the word as *monye* or *monie*. No matter how they spell the word, students are demonstrating what they know about phonics and spelling. Teachers classify and analyze the words students misspell in their writing to gauge students' level of spelling development and to plan for instruction. The steps in classifying and analyzing students' spelling are explained in Figure 3–8.

Teachers can analyze the errors in students' compositions, or they can analyze students' errors on weekly spelling tests or diagnostic tests such as Bear's Elementary

Figure 3–8 How to analyze students' spelling

Teachers analyze children's spelling by examining their writing and classifying the words not spelled conventionally according to the five stages of spelling development (discussed in Chapter 5, "Breaking the Alpabetic Code"). The steps are:

1. Make a spelling analysis chart.

Teachers draw a chart with columns for each of the stages of spelling development at the bottom of the child's writing sample or on another sheet of paper.

2. Categorize the student's misspelled words.

Teachers identify the misspelled words in the child's writing sample and classify them according to stage of development. They list each spelling error in one of the stages, ignoring proper nouns, capitalization errors, and poorly formed or reversed letters. They write both the student's spelling and the correct spelling in parentheses to make analysis easier.

3. Determine the stage of spelling development.

Teachers count the number of errors in each category and mark the stage with the most errors as the student's level. They also examine the misspelled words to identify the spelling concepts the student is using but confusing for further instruction.

A first grader named Marc wrote this composition about a bomb scare at his school:

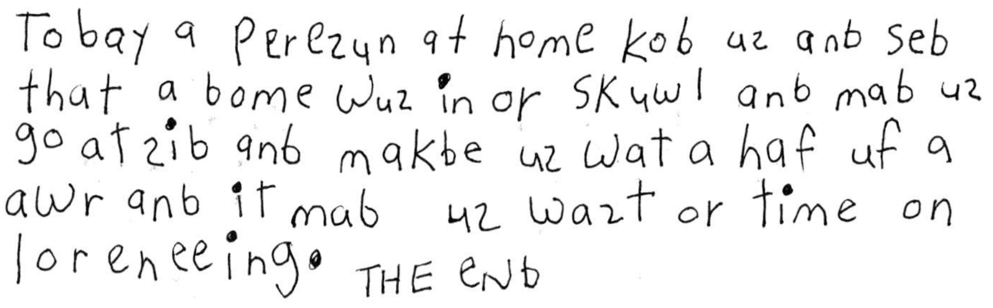

Marc reverses *b* and *s*, and these two reversals make his writing more difficult to decipher. Here is a translation of Marc's composition:

Today a person at home called us and said that a bomb was in our school and made us go outside and made us wait a half of an hour and it made us waste our time on learning. The end.

Emergent	Letter Name	Within-Word Patterns	Syllables and Affixes	Derivational Relations
	kod (called)	bome (bomb)	peresun (person)	
	sed (said)	or (our)	loreneeing (learning)	
	wus (was)	skuwl (school)		
	mad (made)	makde (made)		
	at (out)	uf (of)		
	sid (side)	awr (hour)		
	wat (wait)	or (our)		
	haf (half)			
	mad (made)			
	wazt (waste)			

Marc spelled 56% of the words correctly, and most of his spelling errors were in the Letter Name and Within-Word Patterns stages, which is typical of first graders' spelling.

Qualitative Spelling Inventory for grades K–6 and his Upper Level Qualitative Spelling Inventory for grades 6–8 (Bear, Invernizzi, Templeton, & Johnston, 2000). These tests include 20–25 spelling words listed according to difficulty and can easily be administered to small groups or whole classes. Other spelling tests are available to provide grade-level scores.

Assessment Tools: Spelling

Teachers monitor students' spelling development by examining misspelled words in the compositions that students write. They can classify students' spelling according to the five stages of spelling development and plan instruction on the basis of this analysis. Teachers also examine students' misspellings in weekly spelling tests and diagnostic tests, including the following:

> Elementary Qualitative Spelling Inventory (Grades K–6) (Bear et al., 2000)
> Upper Level Qualitative Spelling Inventory (Grades 6–8) (Bear et al., 2000)
> Qualitative Inventory of Spelling Development (Henderson, 1990)
> Test of Written Spelling—3 (Larsen & Hammill, 1994)

After teachers mark spellings as correct or incorrect on the tests, they should analyze students' errors in order to determine which skills they can use correctly, which skills they are using but confusing, and which skills they are not yet using.

Assessing Students' Attitudes and Motivation

Students' attitude and motivation affect their success in learning to read and write (Walberg & Tsai, 1985). Students who view themselves as successful readers and writers are more likely to be successful, and students and their families who value literacy are more likely to be motivated to read and write.

Teachers conference with students and parents to understand students' reading and writing habits at home, their interests and hobbies, and their view of themselves as readers and writers. Teachers can help students select more interesting books when they know more about them and their interests, and they can get parents more involved in reading activities at home.

Researchers have developed several survey instruments that teachers can use to assess students' attitudes about reading and writing. Two surveys designed for third through sixth graders are the Reader Self-Perception Scale (Henk & Melnick, 1995) and the Writer Self-Perception Scale (Bottomley, Henk, & Melnick, 1997/1998). On these surveys, students respond to statements such as "I think I am a good reader" and "I write better than my classmates do" using a five-level Likert scale (responses range from "strongly agree" to "strongly disagree"). Then teachers score students' responses and interpret the results to determine both overall and specific attitude levels.

McKenna and Kear (1990) developed the Elementary Reading Attitude Survey to assess first- through sixth-grade students' attitudes toward reading in school and reading for fun. The test includes 20 questions about reading that begin with the stem "How do you feel . . . ?" Students respond by marking one of four pictures of Garfield, the cartoon cat. Each picture of Garfield depicts a different emotional state, ranging from positive to negative. This survey enables teachers to quickly estimate students' attitudes toward reading.

─────────── *Assessment Tools: Attitudes and Motivation* ───────────

Students' attitudes, values, and motivation play a significant role in their literacy learning, and teachers monitor students' attitudes informally as they talk with students about books they are reading and compositions they are writing.

Researchers have developed three instruments that measure upper-grade students' perceptions of themselves as readers and writers. They probe students' past literacy successes, students' comparison of themselves with their peers, input the student has received from teachers and classmates, and feelings students experience during reading and writing. These three surveys are:

Elementary Reading Attitude Survey (McKenna & Kear, 1990)
Reader Self-Perception Scale (Henk & Melnick, 1995)
Writer Self-Perception Scale (Bottomley et al., 1997/1998)

All three instruments are readily available because they have been published in *The Reading Teacher.*

Monitoring Students' Progress

Teachers monitor students' learning day by day, and they use the results of their monitoring to inform their teaching (Baskwill & Whitman, 1988; K. S. Goodman, Goodman, & Hood, 1989). As they monitor students' learning, teachers learn about their students, about themselves as teachers, and about the impact of the instructional program. Five ways to monitor students' progress are:

1. *Observe students as they read and write.* Effective teachers are "kid watchers," a term Yetta Goodman (1978) coined and defined as "direct and informal observation of students" (p. 37). To be an effective kid watcher, teachers must understand how children learn to read and write. Some observation times should be planned when the teacher focuses on particular students and makes anecdotal notes about the students' involvement in literacy events. The focus is on what students do as they read or write, not on whether or not they are behaving properly or working quietly. Of course, little learning can occur in disruptive situations, but during these observations the focus is on literacy, not behavior.

2. *Take anecdotal notes of literacy events.* Teachers write brief notes as they observe students, and the most useful notes describe specific events, report rather than evaluate, and relate the events to other information about the student (Rhodes & Nathenson-Mejia, 1992). Teachers make notes about students' reading and writing activities, the questions students ask, and the strategies and skills they use fluently or indicate confusion about. These records document students' growth and pinpoint problem areas for future minilessons or conferences. Mrs. Peterson's anecdotal notes about sixth-grade students in the literature circle reading *Bunnicula: A Rabbit-Tale of Mystery* (Howe & Howe, 1979) appear in Figure 3–9.

3. *Conference with students.* Teachers talk with students to monitor their progress in reading and writing activities as well as to set goals and help students solve problems. Figure 3–10 presents a list of seven types of conferences that teachers have with students. Often these conferences are brief and impromptu, held at students' desks as the teacher moves around the classroom. At other times the conferences are

Figure 3–9 Mrs. Peterson's anecdotal notes about a literature circle

March 2

Met with the *Bunnicula* literature circle as they started reading the book. They have their reading, writing, and discussion schedule set. Sari questioned how a dog could write the book. We reread the Editor's Note. She asked if Harold really wrote the book. She's the only one confused in the group. Is she always so literal? Mario pointed out that you have to know that Harold supposedly wrote the book to understand the first-person viewpoint of the book. Talked to Sari about fantasy. Told her she'll be laughing out loud as she reads this book. She doubts it.

March 3

Returned to *Bunnicula* literature circle for first grand conversation, especially to check on Sari. Annie, Mario, Ted, Rod, Laurie, and Belinda talked about their pets and imagine them taking over their homes. Sari is not getting into the book. She doesn't have any pets and can't imagine the pets doing these things. I asked if she wanted to change groups. Perhaps a realistic book would be better. She says no. Is that because Ted is in the group?

March 5

The group is reading Chapters 4 and 5 today. Laurie asks questions about white vegetables and vampires. Rod goes to get an encyclopedia to find out about vampires. Mario asks about DDT. Everyone—even Sari—involved in reading.

March 8

During a grand conversation, students compare the characters Harold and Chester. The group plans to make a Venn diagram comparing the characters for the sharing on Friday. Students decide that character is the most important element, but Ted argues that humor is the most important element in the story. Other students say humor isn't an element. I asked what humor is a reaction to—characters or plot? I checked journals and all are up to date.

March 10

The group has finished reading the book. I share sequels from the class library. Sari grabs one to read. She's glad she stayed with the book. Ted wants to write his own sequel in writing workshop. Mario plans to write a letter to James Howe.

March 12

Ted and Sari talk about *Bunnicula* and share related books. Rod and Mario share the Venn diagram of characters. Annie reads her favorite part, and Laurie shows her collection of rabbits. Belinda hangs back. I wonder if she has been involved. I need to talk to her.

Figure 3–10 Seven types of conferences

1. On-the-Spot Conferences

Teachers visit briefly with students at their desks to monitor some aspect of the students' work or to check on progress. These conferences are brief; the teacher may spend less than a minute at each student's desk.

2. Prereading or Prewriting Conferences

The teacher and student make plans for reading or writing at the conference. At a prereading conference, they may talk about information related to the book, difficult concepts or vocabulary words related to the reading, or the reading log the student will keep. At a prewriting conference, they may discuss possible writing topics or how to narrow a broad topic.

3. Revising Conferences

A small group of students and the teacher meet to get specific suggestions about revising their compositions. These conferences offer student writers an audience to provide feedback on how well they have communicated.

4. Book Discussion Conferences

Students and the teacher meet to discuss the book they have read. They may share reading log entries, discuss plot or characters, compare the story to others they have read, or make plans to extend their reading.

5. Editing Conferences

The teacher reviews students' proofread compositions and helps them correct spelling, punctuation, capitalization, and other mechanical errors.

6. Minilesson Conferences

The teacher meets with students to explain a procedure, strategy, or skill (e.g., writing a table of contents, using the visualization strategy when reading, capitalizing proper nouns).

7. Assessment Conferences

The teacher meets with students after they have completed an assignment or project to talk about their growth as readers or writers. Students reflect on their competencies and set goals.

planned and students meet with the teacher at a designated conference table, as Mrs. Peterson did with her sixth graders in the vignette at the beginning of this chapter.

   4. *Collect students' work samples.* Teachers have students collect their work in folders to document learning. Work samples might include reading logs, audiotapes of students' reading, photos of projects, videotapes of puppet shows and oral presentations, and books students have written. Students often choose some of these work samples to place in their portfolios.

Teachers monitor students' learning as they work with small groups of students.

IMPLEMENTING PORTFOLIOS IN THE CLASSROOM

Portfolios are systematic and meaningful collections of artifacts documenting students' literacy development over a period of time (Graves & Sunstein, 1992; Porter & Cleland, 1995; Tierney, Carter, & Desai, 1991). These collections are dynamic and reflect students' day-to-day reading and writing activities as well as across-the-curriculum activities. Students' work samples provide "windows" on the strategies that students use as readers and writers. Not only do students select pieces to be placed in their portfolios; they also learn to establish criteria for their selections. Because of students' involvement in selecting pieces for their portfolios and reflecting on them, portfolio assessment respects students and their abilities. Portfolios help students, teachers, and parents see patterns of growth from one literacy milestone to another in ways that are not possible with other types of assessment.

Why Are Portfolio Programs Worthwhile?

There are many reasons why portfolio programs complement balanced reading programs. The most important one is that students become more involved in the assessment of their work and more reflective about the quality of their reading and writing. Other benefits include the following:

❦ Students feel ownership of their work.

❦ Students become more responsible about their work.

🦗 Students set goals and are motivated to work toward accomplishing them.

🦗 Students reflect on their accomplishments.

🦗 Students make connections between learning and assessing.

🦗 Students' self-esteem is enhanced.

🦗 Students recognize the connection between process and product.

🦗 Portfolios eliminate the need to grade all student work.

🦗 Portfolios are used in student and parent conferences.

🦗 Portfolios complement the information provided in report cards.

www.loretto.org

🕸 *Building a Portfolio Learning Environment. Details about how to develop and use portfolios in elementary classrooms.*

Rolling Valley Elementary School in Springfield, Virginia, implemented a portfolio program schoolwide several years ago. The students overwhelmingly reported that by using portfolios they were better able to show their parents what they were learning and also better able to set goals for themselves (Clemmons, Laase, Cooper, Areglado, & Dill, 1993). The teachers also reported that by using portfolios they were able to assess their students more thoroughly and that their students were better able to see their own progress.

Collecting Work in Portfolios

Portfolios are folders, large envelopes, or boxes that hold students' work. Teachers often have students label and decorate large folders and then store them in plastic crates or large cardboard boxes. Students date and label items as they place them in their portfolios, and they often attach notes to the items to explain the context for the

Students conference with the teacher about items they select for their portfolios.

activity and why they selected this particular item. Students' portfolios should be stored in the classroom in a place where they are readily accessible to students. Students like to review their portfolios periodically and add new pieces to them.

Students usually choose the items to place in their portfolios within the guidelines provided by the teacher. Some students submit the original piece of work; others want to keep the original, so they place a copy in the portfolio instead. In addition to the reading and writing samples that can go directly into portfolios, students also record oral language and drama samples on audiotapes and videotapes to place in their portfolios. (To learn more about videotape portfolios, check the Technology Link on page 106.) Large-size art and writing projects can be photographed, and the photographs can be placed in the portfolio. The following types of student work might be placed in a portfolio:

"All About . . . " books
alphabet books
autobiographies
biographies
books
choral readings (on audiotape)
clusters
drawings, diagrams, and charts
learning log entries
letters to pen pals, businesses, and authors (copies, because the originals have been sent)
lists of books read
newspaper articles
open-mind portraits
oral reading (on audiotape or videotape)
oral reports (on videotape)
poems
projects
puppets (on photographs)
puppet shows (on videotape)
quickwrites
readers theatre presentations (on audiotape or videotape)
reading log entries
reports
simulated journal entries
stories
story boards

This variety of work samples reflects the students' literacy programs. Samples from literature focus units, literature circles, reading and writing workshop, basal reading programs, and content-area units should be included.

One piece of writing from a third grader's portfolio is shown in Figure 3–11. This sample is a simulated letter written to Peter Rabbit from Mr. McGregor as a project during a literature focus unit on *The Tale of Peter Rabbit* (Potter, 1902). The student's teacher taught a minilesson on persuasive writing, and this student applied what he had learned in his letter. He placed it in his portfolio because he thought it "looked good" and because his classmates had really liked it when he shared it with them. His prewriting, the rough draft, and a scoring rubric were attached to the final copy shown in the figure. The scoring rubric is also shown.

Technology Link   Videotape Portfolios

Teachers can document students' learning using a camcorder in ways that reading logs, lists of books students have read, and conference notes cannot (Herrell & Fowler, 1998). The saying that "a picture is worth a thousand words" really is true! Students each bring a blank VCR tape at the beginning of the school year for their video portfolios. A sheet of paper is attached to each tape case to note dates and topics of the tapings. This sheet becomes the table of contents for the videotape.

When a camcorder is first introduced, students are distracted and "mug" for the camera, but after a few days they get used to it. Using a camcorder frequently is the best way to acclimate students. The teacher and student videographers film students as they are involved in a variety of literacy activities:

❧ Record individual students reading aloud at the beginning of the year and at the end of each grading period.

❧ Film students during reading and writing workshop.

❧ Document student-teacher conferences.

❧ Film oral performances, including puppet shows, readers theatre presentations, book talks, and reports.

❧ Include group activities such as grand conversations and read-arounds.

❧ Document students' work on projects—especially projects such as dioramas, book boxes, and murals—that can't be saved in traditional portfolio folders.

Keeping a camcorder in the classroom with batteries charged allows students and the teacher to capture ongoing classroom activities.

Creating video portfolios is too heavy a burden if teachers do all of the videotaping. Students—even second and third graders—can learn how to use the camcorder. Teachers identify guidelines for videotaping and establish routines for regular taping. They also experiment to determine how to get the best sound quality for individual and group activities, how long to film episodes, and how to transition between episodes. Aides and parent volunteers can be enlisted to assist, too.

Video portfolios often have jerky starts and abrupt stops, and sometimes the audio is difficult to hear, but nevertheless they are a meaningful record of students' literacy development and reading and writing activities spanning a school year. Even though video portfolios are rarely polished productions, they are valuable documentation for students, teachers, and parents.

The student and teacher scored the letter together using the rubric and rated it a 4 out of a possible 5 points. First, the child used the friendly letter format, so a check mark was placed on that line. Second, in the letter he had applied what he learned about persuasion. He suggested a deal to Peter and made a threat about what will happen if the rabbit comes back into the garden. A check mark was also placed on the second line. Next, he used character names and other information from the story in the persuasive argument, so the third item was checked, too. Fourth, the student and teacher looked at the spelling and other conventions. The

Figure 3–11 A third grader's simulated letter and scoring guide

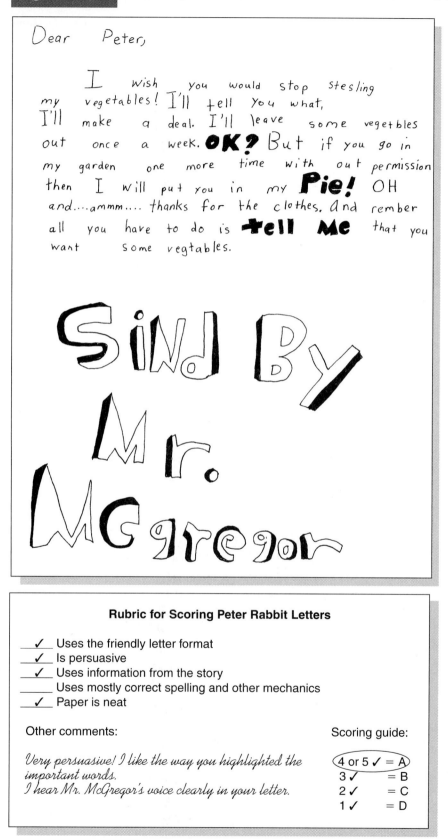

Dear   Peter,

     I   wish   you   would   stop   stesling   my   vegetables!   I'll   tell   you   what,   I'll   make   a   deal.   I'll   leave   some   vegetbles   out   once   a   week. **OK?** But   if   you   go   in   my   garden   one   more   time   with   out   permission   then   I   will   put   you   in   my   **Pie!**   OH   and....ammm.... thanks   for   the   clothes.   And   rember   all   you   have   to   do   is   **tell Me**   that   you   want   some   vegtables.

Sind By
Mr.
McGregor

Rubric for Scoring Peter Rabbit Letters

_✓_ Uses the friendly letter format
_✓_ Is persuasive
_✓_ Uses information from the story
_____ Uses mostly correct spelling and other mechanics
_✓_ Paper is neat

Other comments:

Very persuasive! I like the way you highlighted the important words.
I hear Mr. McGregor's voice clearly in your letter.

Scoring guide:

4 or 5 ✓ = A
3 ✓ = B
2 ✓ = C
1 ✓ = D

teacher pointed out five misspelled words (*stesling–stealing, vegetbles–vegetables, rember–remember, vegtables–vegetables,* and *sind–signed*) and checked to see if they had been corrected on the rough draft during editing. All but one had, but the student had failed to use the corrected spellings in his final draft. After some consideration, the student and his teacher decided not to add a check mark on this item, even though the errors were minor and did not interfere with reading the letter. The student recognized that he needed to be more careful when he made his final copy. Finally, the paper was neat, and the fifth item was checked. In addition, the teacher commended this student for his lively writing style and the way he highlighted important words in his letter.

Many teachers collect students' work in folders, and they assume portfolios are basically the same as work folders; however, the two types of collections differ in several important ways. Perhaps the most important difference is that portfolios are student-oriented, while work folders are usually teachers' collections. Students choose which samples will be placed in portfolios, while teachers often place all completed assignments in work folders (Clemmons et al., 1993). Next, portfolios focus on students' strengths, not their weaknesses. Because students choose items for portfolios, they choose samples that best represent their literacy development. Another difference is that portfolios involve reflection (D'Aoust, 1992). Through reflection, students pause and become aware of their strengths as readers and writers. They also use their work samples to identify the literacy procedures, concepts, skills, and strategies they already know and the ones they need to focus on.

Involving Students in Self-Assessment

A portfolio is not just a collection of work samples; instead, it is a vehicle for engaging students in self-evaluation and goal-setting (Clemmons et al., 1993). Students can learn to reflect on and assess their own reading and writing activities and their development as readers and writers (Stires, 1991). Teachers begin by asking students to think about their reading and writing in terms of contrasts. For reading, students identify the books they have read that they liked most and least, and ask themselves what these choices suggest about themselves as readers. They also identify what they do well in reading and what they need to improve about their reading. In writing, students make similar contrasts. They identify the compositions they thought were their best and others that were not so good, and think about what they do well when they write and what they need to improve. By making these comparisons, students begin to reflect on their literacy development.

Teachers use minilessons and conferences to talk with students about the characteristics of good readers and writers. In particular, they discuss:

- ❦ what fluent reading is
- ❦ what reading skills and strategies students use
- ❦ how students demonstrate their comprehension
- ❦ how students value books they have read
- ❦ what makes a good project to extend reading
- ❦ what makes an effective piece of writing
- ❦ what writing skills and strategies students use
- ❦ how to use writing rubrics
- ❦ how the effective use of mechanical skills is a courtesy to readers

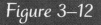 **Figure 3–12** Two students' self-assessments of items placed in their portfolios

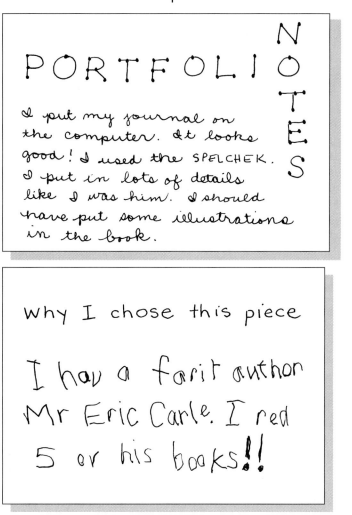

As students learn about what it means to be effective readers and writers, they acquire the tools they need to reflect on and evaluate their own reading and writing. They learn how to think about themselves as readers and writers and acquire the vocabulary to use in their reflections, such as "goal," "strategy," and "rubric."

Students write notes on items they choose to put into their portfolios. In these self-assessments, students explain their reasons for the selection and identify strengths and accomplishments in their work. In some classrooms students write their reflections and other comments on index cards, while in other classrooms they design special comment sheets that they attach to the items in their portfolios. Two students' self-assessments are shown in Figure 3–12. In the first one, "Portfolio Notes," a fifth grader assesses his simulated journal, written from the viewpoint of Benjamin Franklin. In the second, a first grader writes about having read five books written and illustrated by Eric Carle. This note is attached to her reading workshop book list for the week.

Clemmons et al. (1993) recommend collecting baseline reading and writing samples at the beginning of the school year and then conducting portfolio review conferences with students at the end of each grading period. At these conferences, the teacher and student talk about the items placed in the portfolio and the self-assessments the student has written. Together they also set goals for the next grading period. Students talk about what they want to improve or what they want to accomplish during the next grading period, and these points become their goals.

Self-assessment can also be used for an assessment at the end of the school year. Coughlan (1988) asked his seventh-grade students to "show me what you have learned about writing this year" and "explain how you have grown as a written language user, comparing what you knew in September to what you know now" (p. 375). These upper-grade students used a process approach to develop and refine their compositions, and they submitted all drafts with their final copies. Coughlan examined both the content of students' compositions and the strategies they used in thinking through the assignment and writing their responses. He found this "test" to be a very worthwhile project because it "forced the students to look within themselves . . . to realize just how much they had learned" (p. 378). Moreover, students' compositions verified that they had learned about writing and that they could articulate that learning.

Showcasing Students' Portfolios

At the end of the school year, many teachers organize "Portfolio Share Days" to celebrate students' accomplishments and to provide an opportunity for students to share their portfolios with classmates and the wider community (Porter & Cleland, 1995). Often family members, local business people, school administrators, local politicians, college students, and others are invited to attend. Students and community members form small groups, and students share their portfolios, pointing out their accomplishments and strengths. This activity is especially useful in involving community members in the school and showing them the types of literacy activities in which students are involved as well as how students are becoming effective readers and writers.

These sharing days also help students accept responsibility for their own learning—especially those students who have not been as motivated as their classmates. When less-motivated students listen to their classmates talk about their work and how they have grown as readers and writers, these students often decide to work harder the next year.

ASSIGNING GRADES

www.eduplace.com

Grading and Scoring. Information about evaluating students' learning, including letter grades and report cards.

Assigning grades is one of the most difficult responsibilities placed on teachers. "Grading is a fact of life," according to Donald Graves (1983, p. 93), but he adds that teachers should use grades to encourage students, not to hinder their achievement. The assessment procedures described in this chapter encourage students because they document what students can do as they read and write. Reviewing and translating this documentation into grades is the difficult part, but two effective techniques are unit assignment sheets and "show-me" tests.

Unit Assignment Sheets

One way for teachers to monitor students' progress and grade their achievements is to use assignment sheets. Teachers create the assignment sheet as they plan the unit, duplicate copies for each student, and then distribute them at the beginning of the unit. All assignments are listed on the sheet along with how they will be graded. These sheets can be developed for any type of unit—literature focus units, literature circles, reading and writing workshop, and content-area units. Teachers can also create assignment sheets to use with literacy centers.

An assignment sheet for a fifth-grade unit on *The Sign of the Beaver* (Speare, 1983) is shown in Figure 3–13. Students receive a copy of the assignment sheet at the beginning of the unit and keep it in their unit folders. Then, as they complete the assignments, they check them off, and it is easy for the teacher to make periodic checks to monitor students' progress. At the end of the unit, the teacher collects the unit folders and grades the work.

Assignments can be graded as "done" or "not done," or they can be graded for quality. Teachers of middle- and upper-grade students often assign points to each activity on the assignment sheet so that the total point value for the unit is 100 points. Activities that involve more time and effort earn more points. The maximum number of points possible for each assignment is listed in parentheses in Figure 3–13.

Figure 3–13 An assignment sheet for a literature focus unit

Checklist for *The Sign of the Beaver*

Name _____ Date _____

Student's Check		Teacher's Check
_____	1. Read *The Sign of the Beaver*.	_____
_____	2. Make a map of Matt's journey in 1768. (10)	_____
_____	3. Keep a simulated journal as Matt or Attean. (20)	_____
_____	4. Do a word sort by characters. (5)	_____
_____	5. Listen to Elizabeth George Speare's taped interview and do a quickwrite about her. (5)	_____
_____	6. Do an open-mind portrait about one of the characters. (10)	_____
_____	7. Make a Venn diagram to compare/contrast Matt or Attean with yourself. (10)	_____
_____	8. Contribute to a model of the Indian village or the clearing.	_____
_____	9. Write a sequel or do another project. (20) My project is _____	_____
_____	10. Read other books from the text set. (10) _____ _____ _____	_____
_____	11. Write a self-assessment about your work, behavior, and effort in this unit. (10)	_____

TOTAL POINTS _____

"Show-Me" Tests

Writing is not just a tool for learning during content-area units; students can also use writing to demonstrate what they have learned during a unit. Third-grade teacher Whitney Donnelly developed an innovative approach that she calls "show-me" tests to document and grade her students' learning. Teachers begin by reviewing the key concepts in a thematic unit with students, and then they have students choose one of the concepts to write and draw about on the test. Students divide a piece of a paper into two parts. On one part they draw pictures, diagrams, maps, or charts to describe the concept, and they label the drawings with key words and phrases. On the other part of the paper, they write about the concept. Then teachers grade the test according to the number of components related to the key concept students included in their drawings or writings.

A third grader's test on the skeletal system is presented in Figure 3–14. Students could choose to draw and write about one of three major systems in the human body: the skeletal, circulatory, or digestive system. In their tests, students were to draw at least three pieces of information and write three important things about the system. This student drew three pictures of the skeleton system, illustrating different kinds of bones, and he wrote about two functions of the skeleton—to give the body shape and to protect organs. He also points out that the bones, joints, and muscles work together to help a person move. Two other things that the class studied about the skeletal system that this child did not mention are that bone marrow helps keep blood healthy and that there are 206 bones in the body. In the middle of the written part, the child included unrelated information about the functions of the heart, lungs, and brain. Out of a possible score of 6, the child received a 5. There are a few misspelled words and missing punctuation marks in the test, but they do not affect the grade since they do not interfere with the information presented.

Figure 3–14   A third grader's "show-me" test

Review

Assessment is more than testing; it is an essential part of teaching and learning. In classroom assessment, teachers examine both the processes of reading and writing and the artifacts that students produce. Teachers use a variety of literacy assessment tools to monitor students' progress, determine students' reading levels, assess students' comprehension, document students' growth as writers, and analyze students' spelling development. Teachers help students collect their work samples in portfolios and document their literacy development. Teachers use assignment sheets to monitor students' work during literature focus units, reading and writing workshop, and thematic units, and to assign grades. Effective practices for assessing students' literacy learning are reviewed in the feature below.

How Effective Teachers . . .

Assess Students' Literacy Development

✦ Effective Practices

1. Teachers use a variety of informal and formal assessment tools to assess students' literacy development.
2. Teachers take running records to assess students' reading fluency.
3. Teachers use informal reading inventories to determine students' comprehension levels.

4. Teachers document students' growth, and students assess their own growth as writers using rubrics.
5. Teachers analyze students' spellings to determine the stage of development and plan for instruction.
6. Teachers conference with students about their attitudes and motivation for reading and writing, and they also use surveys to better understand their students.
7. Teachers monitor students' learning using observation and anecdotal notes, conferences, checklists, and collections of students' work samples.
8. Teachers have students choose work samples to document their literacy development for portfolios.
9. Teachers encourage students to self-assess their work samples and set goals for future learning.

10. Teachers use assignment sheets for literature focus units, literature circles, reading and writing workshop, and content-area units.

✦ Ineffective Practices

1. Teachers use tests to assess students' literacy development.

2. Teachers listen to students read aloud, but they don't analyze students' errors.
3. Teachers ask students to answer a series of questions orally or in writing to assess their comprehension.
4. Teachers grade students' writing according to how well ideas are developed and according to mechanical correctness.
5. Teachers mark students' spelling as correct or incorrect but do not analyze the types of mistakes students are making.
6. Teachers don't consider the role of attitude and motivation in learning to read and write.

7. Teachers collect and grade students' assignments.

8. Teachers file students' work samples in folders.

9. Teachers always do the assessing; they don't give students opportunities to self-assess their work.
10. Teachers score students' daily work and tests to determine grades.

References

Adams, M., Foorman, B., Lundberg, I., & Beeler, C. (1997). *Phonemic awareness in young children.* Baltimore: Paul H. Brookes Publishing Company.

Baskwill, J., & Whitman, P. (1988). *Evaluation: Whole language, whole child.* New York: Scholastic.

Bear, D. R., Invernizzi, M., Templeton, S., & Johnston, F. (2000). *Words their way: Word study for phonics, vocabulary, and spelling instruction* (2nd ed.). Upper Saddle River, NJ: Merrill/Prentice Hall.

Bottomley, D. M., Henk, W. A., & Melnick, S. A. (1997/1998). Assessing children's views about themselves as writers using the Writer Self-Perception Scale. *The Reading Teacher, 51,* 286–296.

Clay, M. M. (1972). *Sand—the Concepts about Print Test.* Portsmouth, NH: Heinemann.

Clay, M. M. (1979). *Stones—the Concepts about Print Test.* Portsmouth, NH: Heinemann.

Clay, M. M. (1985). *The early detection of reading difficulties: A diagnostic survey with recovery procedures.* Portsmouth, NH: Heinemann.

Clay, M. M. (1993). *An observational survey of early literacy assessment.* Portsmouth, NH: Heinemann.

Clemmons, J., Laase, L., Cooper, D., Areglado, N., & Dill, M. (1993). *Portfolios in the classroom: A teacher's sourcebook.* New York: Scholastic.

Coughlan, M. (1988). Let the students show us what they know. *Language Arts, 65,* 375–378.

Cunningham, P. (1990). The Names Test: A quick assessment of decoding ability. *The Reading Teacher, 44,* 124–129.

D'Aoust, C. (1992). Portfolios: Process for students and teachers. In K. B. Yancy (Ed.), *Portfolios in the writing classroom* (pp. 39–48). Urbana, IL: National Council of Teachers of English.

Duffelmeyer, F. A., Kruse, A. E., Merkley, D. J., & Fyfe, S. A. (1994). Further validation and enhancement of the Names Test. *The Reading Teacher, 48,* 118–128.

Farr, R., & Tone, B. (1994). *Portfolio and performance assessment.* Orlando: Harcourt Brace.

Flynt, E. S., & Cooter, R. B., Jr. (1998). *The Flynt/Cooter reading inventory for the classroom* (3rd ed.). Upper Saddle River, NJ: Merrill/Prentice Hall.

Fry, E. B. (1980). The new instant word lists. *The Reading Teacher, 34,* 284–289.

Gambrell, L. B., Pfeiffer, W., & Wilson, R. (1985). The effects of retelling upon reading comprehension and recall of text information. *Journal of Educational Research, 78,* 216–220.

Goodman, K. S. (1976). Behind the eye: What happens in reading. In H. Singer & R. B. Ruddell (Eds.), *Theoretical models and processes of reading* (2nd ed., pp. 470–496). Newark, DE: International Reading Association.

Goodman, K. S., Goodman, Y. M., & Hood, W. J. (1989). *The whole language evaluation book.* Portsmouth, NH: Heinemann.

Goodman, Y. M. (1978). Kid watching: An alternative to testing. *National Elementary Principals Journal, 57,* 41–45.

Graves, D. H. (1983). *Writing: Teachers and students at work.* Portsmouth, NH: Heinemann.

Graves, D. H., & Sunstein, B. S. (Eds.). (1992). *Portfolio portraits.* Portsmouth, NH: Heinemann.

Henderson, E. (1990). *Teaching spelling.* Boston: Houghton Mifflin.

Henk, W. A., & Melnick, S. A. (1995). The Reader Self-Perception Scale (RSPS): A new tool for measuring how children feel about themselves as readers. *The Reading Teacher, 48,* 470–482.

Herrell, A. L., & Fowler, J. P., Jr. (1998). *Camcorder in the classroom: Using the videocamera to enliven curriculum.* Upper Saddle River, NJ: Merrill/Prentice Hall.

Larsen, S. C., & Hammill, D. D. (1994). *Test of written spelling* (3rd ed.). Austin, TX: Pro-Ed.

McKenna, M. C., & Kear, D. J. (1990). Measuring attitudes toward reading: A new tool for teachers. *The Reading Teacher, 43,* 626–639.

Morrow, L. M. (1985). Retelling stories: A strategy for improving children's comprehension, concept of story structure, and oral language complexity. *Elementary School Journal, 85,* 647–661.

Porter, C., & Cleland, J. (1995). *The portfolio as a learning strategy.* Portsmouth, NH: Heinemann.

Rhodes, L. K., & Nathenson-Mejia, S. (1992). Anecdotal records: A powerful tool for ongoing literacy assessment. *The Reading Teacher, 45,* 502–511.

Silvaroli, N. J. (1997). *Classroom reading inventory* (8th ed.). Boston: McGraw-Hill.

Stahl, S. A. (1999). *Vocabulary development.* Cambridge, MA: Brookline Books.

Stires, S. (1991). Thinking through the process: Self-evaluation in writing. In B. M. Power & R. Hubbard (Eds.), *The Heinemann reader: Literacy in process* (pp. 295–310). Portsmouth, NH: Heinemann.

Tierney, R., Carter, M., & Desai, L. (1991). *Portfolio assessment in the reading-writing classroom.* Norwood, MA: Christopher-Gordon.

Tompkins, G. E. (2000). *Teaching writing: Balancing process and product* (3rd ed.). New York: Merrill/Prentice Hall.

Torgesen, J. K., & Bryant, B. R. (1994). *Test of phonological awareness.* Austin, TX: Pro-Ed.

Walberg, H. J., & Tsai, S. (1985). Correlates of reading achievement and attitude: A national assessment study. *Journal of Educational Research, 78,* 159–167.

Woods, M. L., & Moe, A. J. (1999). *Analytical reading inventory* (6th ed.). Upper Saddle River, NJ: Merrill/Prentice-Hall.

Yopp, H. K. (1995). A test for assessing phonemic awareness in young children. *The Reading Teacher, 49,* 20–28.

Children's Book References

Babbitt, N. (1975). *Tuck everlasting.* New York: Farrar, Straus & Giroux.

Byars, B. (1968). *The midnight fox.* New York: Viking.

George, J. C. (1972). *Julie of the wolves.* New York: Harper & Row.

Howe, D., & Howe, J. (1979). *Bunnicula: A rabbit-tale of mystery.* Boston: Atheneum.

Howe, J. (1981). *Howliday Inn.* Boston: Atheneum.

Howe, J. (1983). *The celery stalks at midnight.* Boston: Atheneum.

Howe, J. (1987). *Nighty-nightmare.* Boston: Atheneum.

Howe, J. (1992). *Return to Howliday Inn.* Boston: Atheneum.

Lewis, C. S. (1950). *The lion, the witch and the wardrobe.* New York: Macmillan.

Naylor, P. R. (1991). *Shiloh.* New York: Atheneum.

Paulsen, G. (1987). *Hatchet.* New York: Viking.

Potter, B. (1902). *The tale of Peter Rabbit.* New York: Warne.

Speare, E. G. (1983). *The sign of the beaver.* Boston: Houghton Mifflin.

Part II
How Do Children Learn to Read and Write?

Mrs. Hoddy collects a text set of books related to *Rosie's Walk* to use in this literature focus unit. The books include stories as well as informational books about hens and foxes, and they vary in difficulty level. Mrs. Hoddy reads some of the books aloud, and other students read to themselves.

watch out for the fox

Students take turns dramatizing the story using puppets and other props. Through drama, first graders internalize the structure of the story.

Mrs. Hoddy's first graders listen as their teacher reads aloud Pat Hutchins's *Rosie's Walk*; students follow along in their own copies as she reads. Later, they will reread the story in guided reading groups.

Students use storyboards to retell the story and sequence the events. These storyboards were made by cutting apart two copies of the book and backing the pages on sheets of poster board.

Debra and Caitlin reread the story together. As students reread with buddies, they learn high-frequency words, model reading strategies for each other, and become more fluent readers.

At the writing center, Mark is making an "All About Foxes" book. He writes one fact about foxes on each page. On this page, he is writing that foxes are mammals.

ROSIE is home saf.

After students learn about foxes, Mrs. Hoddy writes facts that students dictate on sentence strips. Students reread the sentences and examine the words in each sentence. They underline the words in the sentences using a different color marking pen for each sentence. Later they will cut the words apart, put each sentence in an envelope, and then rebuild the sentences in a center activity. Through these activities, students practice high-frequency words, develop a concept of "sentence," and learn about foxes in preparation for writing "All About Foxes" books.

Chapter 4

Working With Emergent Readers and Writers

— Chapter Questions —

How do teachers foster young children's interest in literacy?

How do teachers adapt reading instruction for emergent readers?

How do teachers adapt writing instruction for young children?

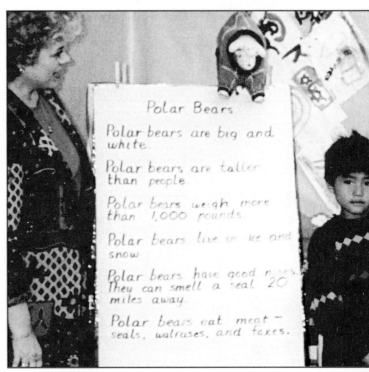

Mrs. Mast's Students Read "The Three Bears"

The kindergartners in Mrs. Mast's classroom listen as their teacher reads Paul Galdone's *The Three Bears* (1972) at the beginning of a weeklong focus unit on this familiar folktale. After Mrs. Mast reads *The Three Bears* aloud, the children talk about the story in a **grand conversation** (see the Compendium for more information about this and all other high-lighted terms in this chapter). "You shouldn't leave your front door unlocked," Angela re-minds her classmates. Kayleen adds, "Goldilocks was bad. You shouldn't go into someone else's house like that. You could get shot and killed." Other students mention the repeti-tion of threes in the story and ask questions about how dangerous bears are and whether or not the bears in the story might have killed Goldilocks in real life. Mrs. Mast assures the class that they will learn more about bears during the week.

Mrs. Mast puts pictures of Papa Bear, Mama Bear, Baby Bear, and Goldilocks in a pocket chart and sets out word cards with the bears' names. She also sets out letter cards for each name so that children can build the names of the characters. These word cards for the key words in the book constitute a **word wall** for kindergartners. During center time, children often sort the word cards, matching them to the pictures of the charac-ters, and use the letter cards to spell the characters' names, matching the letters to the word cards.

During the week, Mrs. Mast reads two other versions of the folktale, both entitled *Goldilocks and the Three Bears* (Brett, 1987; Cauley, 1981), and a related book, *Deep in the Forest* (Turkle, 1976), a wordless picture book about a small bear who has an adven-ture similar to Goldilocks's.

After Mrs. Mast has read all three versions of the folktale, the children compare them and decide that they like Cauley's version the best. They feel that her version is more satisfy-ing than Galdone's or Brett's because at the end of Cauley's, Goldilocks is home with her mother, being scolded for what she did and warned not to go into other people's houses.

Mrs. Mast sets up five literacy centers that are related to the literature focus unit. Dur-ing the week, students work at each center, either on their own or with the assistance of an adult. The five centers are:

1. *Listening center.* Children listened to a tape recording of Galdone's version of *The Three Bears*, following along in copies of the book.
2. *Literacy play center.* Children use puppets of the three bears and Goldilocks to use in retelling the story. A flannel board with pictures related to the story is also avail-able in the center.
3. *Reading center.* Children reread Galdone's version as a small group with a fifth grader or a parent volunteer. Mrs. Mast also has "bear" books in the center for stu-dents to look at.
4. *Writing center.* Children write in **reading logs** with the assistance of the aide and work on their pages for the class "Book of Threes."

5.   *Skills center.* Mrs. Mast works with small groups of students on literacy skills. Her topics this week are phonemic awareness, letter sounds, and building words. She asks students to break these spoken words from the story into sounds: *bowl, chair, bed, house, sleep, my,* and *bear.* Next, she asks students to notice the *G* in *Goldilocks* and *B* in *bear* as she writes the words on a small chalkboard. She has a collection of small objects and pictures, many beginning with *G* and *B,* in a tub. Objects include a *book, ghost, zebra, bear, green crayon, letter, button, girl, banana, gold ring,* and *gate.* Children sort the objects into three categories: *B, G,* and "other." Mrs. Mast varies the amount of time she spends on each of these activities according to which students are in the group and what skills they already know.

Later in the week, Mrs. Mast shares the wordless book *Deep in the Forest* (Turkle, 1976) with the class. First she shows each illustration in the book without saying very much. Then she goes through the book a second time, and she and her students create the story to accompany the illustrations. The children quickly notice the twist on this story. Goldilocks has become a bear cub, and he causes a ruckus in a home belonging to a human family. The students dramatize the story using props such as bowls, chairs, and towels laid on the floor for beds. They also sequence **story boards** made by cutting apart two copies of the book.

Mrs. Mast focuses on the repetition of threes in this folktale and in others with which the children are familiar, such as "The Three Little Pigs" and "The Three Billy Goats Gruff." The children in Mrs. Mast's class usually make a **collaborative book** as a project in each literature focus unit, and for this unit they decide to make a "Book of Threes." Each child chooses something related to bears or the story—three chairs, three bears, three jars of honey, three bear caves, three polar bears, three bowls of porridge, and so on. They draw pictures of the objects and add a title for their page. Figure 4–1 shows one page from the book. On this page, Mario has drawn the three bears from the story and labeled them *MB* for Mama Bear, *BB* for Baby Bear, and *PB* for Papa Bear. He has also numbered the bears 1, 2, and 3. Like many young children, Mario often reverses *B,* as he did in the title and started to do on *MB* and *PB.* Mrs. Mast usually ignores reversed letters because she understands that as children have more experience with reading and writing, they begin using the correct forms. However, as Mario was writing his page, the child sitting next to him pointed out the reversed letter and encouraged him to cross out the backward *B* and write the correct form above it. After children complete their pages, they get into a circle to share them with classmates. Then Mrs. Mast helps students compile the pages into a book. One child creates the cover page, and the book is bound together. Mrs. Mast adds the book to the classroom library, and children look at it often.

At the writing center, children make their own "Book of Threes." They take three sheets of paper and write pages as they did for the class book. Then they add a construction paper cover and compile the pages. The aide at the center helps students bind the book together using yarn, brads, or staples, depending on the child's choice.

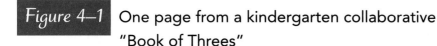

Figure 4–1   One page from a kindergarten collaborative "Book of Threes"

Because the children ask so many questions about bears—What do they eat? Are the bears in the story grizzly bears? What about polar bears?—Mrs. Mast reads *Alaska's Three Bears* (Gill, 1990), which is about brown or grizzly bears, black bears, and polar bears. Students are fascinated by the three kinds—another three—and they make three charts of information. Mrs. Mast uses the **language experience approach** to take the children's dictation as they make a shared writing chart with information about each of the three types of bears. Here is their chart about polar bears:

Polar Bears

Polar bears are big and white.
Polar bears are taller than people.
Polar bears weigh more than 1,000 pounds.
Polar bears live in ice and snow.
Polar bears have good noses. They can smell a seal 20 miles away.
Polar bears eat meat—seals, walruses, and foxes.

Mrs. Mast laminates the chart, and students read and reread it each day. Soon children have memorized most of the sentences. After they reread the chart, children pick out and circle particular letters and words such as *polar bears* with a pen for writing on laminated charts.

Mrs. Mast notices a note to Goldilocks on the classroom message board, and she takes the note and jots an answer in a childlike handwriting. Soon more children are writing notes to Goldilocks from the perspective of a bear. Most of the children realize that Mrs. Mast is pretending to be Goldilocks, and they are anxious for her to write notes back to them. One note reads:

GOOOOS	*Goldilocks,*
D U NO	*Don't you know (that it is)*
DDZTO GOTO	*dangerous to go to*
A BearH?	*a bear's house?*
BS.	*Be safe.*
FMBear	*From Mother Bear*

Mrs. Mast writes back:

Dear Mother Bear,
I have learned a good lesson.
I will never go into a bear's house again.
Love, Goldilocks

The children have been writing notes and sending pictures back and forth to classmates for several months, but this is the first time they assume the role of a character in a book they are reading.

At the end of the unit, Mrs. Mast places one copy of each of "The Three Bears" books, the story boards for Galdone's version of the book, and three small teddy bears—one brown, one black, and one white—in a small "traveling" bag. Children will take turns taking the traveling bag home to share with their parents.

Mrs. Mast's language arts block is fast-paced, taking into account young children's short attention spans, their need for active involvement, and their desire to manipulate materials. Her schedule is:

8:30–8:45   *Morning Message*
               Mrs. Mast talks briefly with students about their news and compiles important news and daily activities in a paragraph-length message that she writes using shared writing. Afterwards, Mrs. Mast reads the message aloud twice and children join in to read familiar words.

8:45–9:15   *Shared Reading*
               Mrs. Mast uses shared reading to read the focus book or related books. After reading, children participate in a grand conversation or other whole-class activity.

Figure 4-2 Mrs. Mast's unit plan for "The Three Bears"

	ACTIVITY	MONDAY	TUESDAY	WEDNESDAY	THURSDAY	FRIDAY
8:30–8:45	Morning Message	→				
8:45–9:15	Shared Reading/Reading Aloud	Read Galdone's *The Three Bears* using a big book. Grand conversation	Read Cauley's *Goldilocks and the Three Bears*. Grand conversation	Read *Alaska's Three Bears*. Grand conversation	Make charts on three kinds of bears: Grizzly bears, Black bears, Polar bears	Read *Deep in the Forest*. Retell story. Grand conversation
9:15–10:00	Guided Reading/Centers	Meet with guided reading groups while students work at literacy centers →				
10:00–10:25	Recess and Snack	→				
10:25–10:55	Other Focus Book Activities	Begin word wall. Sequence *The Three Bears* story boards. Talk about threes in story	Read Brett's *Goldilocks and the Three Bears*. Compare three versions	Talk about threes in folktales. Make a class "Book of Three." Compile the book	Fifth-grade reading buddies read "bear" books	Dramatize *Deep in the Woods*. Sequence story boards. Graph favorite story
10:55–11:00	Songs, Poems, and Fingerplays	→				

9:15–10:00   *Guided Reading and Centers*
During guided reading groups, children read leveled books and Mrs. Mast teaches phonics lessons with small groups of children while the rest of the class works at the centers related to the focus book set up in the classroom. Children rotate through the literacy centers so that each week they work at all five centers. Other centers, including blocks, a water and sand tray, and a restaurant center, are available for children to use as time permits.

10:00–10:25   *Recess and Snack*

10:25–10:55   *Other Focus Book Activities*
Students work in groups or together as a class in other reading and writing activities or related drama and art activities. One day each week, fifth graders come to Mrs. Mast's class to read books to the kindergartners using assisted reading.

10:55–11:00   *Songs, Poems, and Fingerplays*
Mrs. Mast leads the class in songs, poems, fingerplays, and other oral language activities. Whenever possible, she relates the wordplay activities to the featured book.

Mrs. Mast's lesson plan for the week-long literature focus unit on "The Three Bears" is shown in Figure 4–2.

---

www.ericeece.org

Clearinghouse on Elementary and Early Childhood Education. Special topics related to emergent literacy, listserv discussion groups, and Internet links.

Literacy is a process that begins well before the elementary grades and continues into adulthood, if not throughout life. It used to be that five-year-old children came to kindergarten to be "readied" for reading and writing instruction, which would formally begin in first grade. The implication was that there was a point in children's development when it was time to begin teaching them to read and write. For those not ready, a variety of "readiness" activities would prepare them for reading and writing. Since the 1970s this view has been discredited by the observations of both teachers and researchers (Clay, 1989). The children themselves demonstrated that they could recognize signs and other environmental print, retell stories, scribble letters, invent print-like writing, and listen to stories read aloud. Some children even taught themselves to read.

This new perspective on how children become literate—that is, how they learn to read and write—is known as emergent literacy, a term which New Zealand educator Marie Clay is credited with coining. Studies from 1966 on have shaped the current outlook (Clay, 1967; Durkin, 1966; Holdaway, 1979; Taylor, 1983; Teale, 1982; Teale & Sulzby, 1989). Now, researchers are looking at literacy learning from the child's point of view. The age range has been extended to include children as young as one or two who listen to stories being read aloud, notice labels and signs in their environment, and experiment with pencils. The concept of literacy has been broadened to include the cultural and social aspects of language learning, and children's experiences with and understandings about written language—both reading and writing—are included as part of emergent literacy.

Teale and Sulzby (1989) paint a portrait of young children as literacy learners with these characteristics:

🎋 Children begin to learn to read and write very early in life.

🎋 Young children learn the functions of literacy through observing and participating in real-life settings in which reading and writing are used.

🎋 Young children's reading and writing abilities develop concurrently and interrelatedly through experiences in reading and writing.

🎋 Through active involvement with literacy materials, young children construct their understanding of reading and writing.

In the vignette at the beginning of this chapter, Mrs. Mast's students exemplified many of these characteristics.

Teale and Sulzby describe young children as active learners who construct their own knowledge about reading and writing with the assistance of parents and other literate persons. These caregivers help by demonstrating literacy as they read and write, by supplying materials, and by structuring opportunities for children to be involved in reading and writing. The environment is positive, with children experiencing reading and writing in many facets of their everyday lives and observing others who are engaged in literacy activities.

FOSTERING YOUNG CHILDREN'S INTEREST IN LITERACY

Children's introduction to written language begins before they come to school. Parents and other caregivers read to young children, and children observe adults reading. They learn to read signs and other environmental print in their community. Children experiment with writing and have their parents write for them. They also observe adults writing. When young children come to kindergarten, their knowledge about written language expands quickly as they participate in meaningful, functional, and genuine experiences with reading and writing.

Concepts About Print

Through experiences in their homes and communities, young children learn that print carries meaning and that reading and writing are used for a variety of purposes. They read menus in restaurants to know what foods are being served, write and receive letters to communicate with friends and relatives, and read and listen to stories for enjoyment. Children also learn about language purposes as they observe parents and teachers using written language for all these purposes.

Children's understanding about the purposes of reading and writing reflects how written language is used in their community. While reading and writing are part of daily life for almost every family, families use written language for different purposes in different communities (Heath, 1983). Young children have a wide range of literacy experiences in both middle-class and working-class families, even though those experiences might be different (Taylor, 1983; Taylor & Dorsey-Gaines, 1987). In some communities, written language is used mainly as a tool for practical purposes such as paying bills, while in other communities, reading and writing are also used for leisure-time activities. In still other communities, written language serves even wider functions, such as debating social and political issues.

Young children learn concepts about print as they exchange letters at the message center.

Mrs. Mast and other primary-grade teachers demonstrate the purposes of written language and provide opportunities for students to experiment with reading and writing in many ways:

- 🌿 posting signs in the classroom
- 🌿 making a list of classroom rules
- 🌿 using reading and writing materials in literacy play centers
- 🌿 writing notes to students in the class
- 🌿 exchanging messages with classmates
- 🌿 reading and writing stories
- 🌿 making posters about favorite books
- 🌿 labeling classroom items
- 🌿 drawing and writing in journals
- 🌿 writing morning messages
- 🌿 recording questions and information on charts
- 🌿 writing notes to parents
- 🌿 reading and writing letters to pen pals
- 🌿 reading and writing charts and maps

Young children learn concepts about print as they observe print in their environment, listen to parents and teachers read books aloud, and experiment with reading and writing themselves. They learn basic concepts about letters, words, writing, and reading, concepts about combining letters to create words and combining words to compose sentences, and terms for positions in words and text such as *beginning, middle,* and *end* (Clay, 1991, 1993). Three types of concepts about print are:

1. ***Book-orientation concepts.*** Students learn how to hold books and turn pages, and they learn that the text, not the illustrations, carries the message.
2. ***Directionality concepts.*** Students learn that print is written and read from left to right and from top to bottom on a page, and they match voice to print, pointing word by word to text as it is read aloud. Students also notice punctuation marks and learn their names and purposes.
3. ***Letter and word concepts.*** Students learn to identify letter names and match upper- and lowercase letters. They also learn that words are composed of letters, that sentences are composed of words, that a capital letter highlights the first word in a sentence, and that spaces mark boundaries between words and between sentences (Clay, 1991).

Children develop these three concepts about print as they learn to read and write, and during the primary grades, they refine their concepts about print through increasingly sophisticated reading and writing experiences. It is important that children understand the terms that teachers use in literacy instruction, such as *letter, word,* and *sentence.*

Concept of a Word. Children's understanding of the concept of a "word" is an important part of becoming literate. Young children have only vague notions of language terms, such as *word, letter, sound,* and *sentence,* that teachers use in talking about reading and writing (Downing, 1970, 1971–1972). Researchers have found that young children move through several levels of awareness and understanding about this terminology during the primary grades (Downing & Oliver, 1973–1974).

Preschoolers equate words with the objects the words represent. As they are introduced to reading and writing experiences, children begin to differentiate between objects and words, and finally they come to appreciate that words have meanings of their own. Templeton (1980) explains children's development with these two examples:

> When asked if "dog" were a word, a four-year-old acquaintance of mine jumped up from the floor, began barking ferociously, and charged through the house, alternatively panting and woofing. Confronted with the same question, an eight-year-old friend responded "of course 'dog' is a word," and went on to explain how the spelling represented spoken sounds and how the word *dog* stood for a particular type of animal. (p. 454)

Several researchers have investigated children's understanding of a word as a unit of language. Papandropoulou and Sinclair (1974) identified four stages of word consciousness. At the first level, young children do not differentiate between words and things. At the next level, children describe words as labels for things. They consider words that stand for objects as words, but they do not classify articles and prepositions as words because words such as *the* and *with* cannot be represented with objects. At the third level, children understand that words carry meaning and that stories are built from words. At the fourth level, more fluent readers and writers describe words as autonomous elements having meanings of their own with definite semantic and syntactic relationships. Children might say, "You make words with letters." Also, at this level children understand that words have different appearances: they can be spoken, listened to, read, and written.

Environmental Print. Children move from recognizing environmental print to reading decontextualized words in books. Young children begin reading by recognizing logos on fast-food restaurants, department stores, grocery stores, and commonly

www.ets.uidaho.edu

The Emergent Literacy Project. Find out why emergent literacy should be part of an early childhood program.

used household items within familiar contexts (Harste, Woodward, & Burke, 1984). They recognize the golden arches of McDonald's and say "McDonald's," but when they are shown the word *McDonald's* written on a sheet of paper without the familiar sign and restaurant setting, they cannot read the word. Researchers have found that young emergent readers depend on context to read familiar words and memorized texts (Dyson, 1984; Sulzby, 1985). Slowly, children develop relationships linking form and meaning as they learn concepts about written language and gain more experience reading and writing.

When children begin writing, they use scribbles or single letters to represent complex ideas (Clay, 1975; Schickedanz, 1990). As they learn about letter names and phoneme-grapheme correspondences, they use one, two, or three letters to stand for words. At first they run their writing together, but they slowly learn to segment words and leave spaces between words. They sometimes add dots or lines as markers between words or draw circles around words. They also move from capitalizing words randomly to using capital letters at the beginning of sentences and to marking proper nouns and adjectives. Similarly, children move from using a period at the end of each line of writing to marking the ends of sentences with periods. Then they learn about other end-of-sentence markers and, finally, punctuation marks that are embedded in sentences.

Letters of the Alphabet

Most children come to school with some knowledge about the letters of the alphabet. Hiebert (1981) found that by the age of three, children could name an average of 10 letters. They usually know the names of letters in their names and letters found in environmental print, such as the *M* in *McDonald's* and the *K* in *Kmart*. In addition to learning the names of the letters, they notice the features of letters and discriminate among letters. They notice that letters are used in both reading and writing, and they make letters and letter-like forms as they scribble.

The two most important ways that children learn the letters of the alphabet are by talking about letters and using them in authentic literacy activities (McGee & Richgels, 1989). For years, kindergarten teachers have taught the letters of the alphabet by featuring one letter each week. Students listened to the teacher read stories featuring a character whose name began with the letter, practiced writing the letter, and tasted foods beginning with the featured letter. However, children do not learn letters in any particular order or in a linear sequence. Researchers do not suggest any particular order for teaching the letters; instead, teachers should take advantage of the letters in children's names and then move to other letters children are interested in learning.

Learning to recognize and form letters is an important component of emergent literacy, and researchers have found that letter knowledge is a strong predictor of children's success in learning to read in first grade (Durrell, 1958; Walsh, Price, & Gillingham, 1988). According to McGee and Richgels (1989), it is children's ability to learn about letter features and to think metacognitively about letters that is the important contribution of learning the alphabet. Clay (1975) also found that children use their knowledge of letter features when they write both mock letters and conventional letters.

Children's understanding of the role of letters is developmental, and they move through several stages as they learn the letter names and use them in reading and writing: (1) the sign stage, (2) the syllable stage, and (3) the phoneme stage. Preschool children often assume that letters are signs or symbols representing a person or object (Ferreiro & Teberosky, 1982). Dyson (1984) reported that five-year-old Dexter wrote an *N* and said, "N spell my grandmama" (p. 262). Dexter's grandmother's name was Hele*n,* but even though her name ended with an *n,* Dexter didn't think of *n* as a letter or as representing /n/; rather, it was a written sign for his grandmother. Next, students begin using a single letter to represent a syllable or part of a word. They write *DOR* for *dinosaur,* with one letter representing each syllable. Finally, children use letters to represent phonemes; this is invented spelling. As they create invented spellings, children show their understanding of the alphabetic principle.

Students learn several concepts about letters, including how to recognize the two forms of each letter (upper- and lowercase), how to form the letters, and a word or object that exemplifies each letter. Then students apply this knowledge about letters as they learn phonics.

Children need to learn how to form the letters correctly for handwriting. To teach children how to form letters, teachers can create brief directions for forming letters and sing the directions using a familiar tune. For example, to form a lowercase letter *a,* try "All around and make a tail" sung to the tune of "Row, Row, Row Your Boat." As teachers sing the directions, they model the formation of the letter in the air using large arm motions. Then students sing along and practice forming the letter in the air. Later they practice using sponge wands (sponge paintbrushes) dipped in water at the chalkboard or dry-erase pens on white boards.

Handwriting research suggests that moving models are much more effective than still models in teaching children how to handwrite. Therefore, worksheets on the letters aren't very useful because children often don't form the letters correctly. Researchers recommend that children watch teachers form letters and then practice forming them themselves after they see how the letter is formed. Also, teachers supervise students as they write so that they can correct children who form letters incorrectly. It is important that students write circles counterclockwise, starting from 1:00, and form most lines from top to bottom and left to right across the page.

Teachers play three roles in children's alphabet learning, according to McGee and Richgels (1989):

1. *Capitalize on children's interests.* Teachers provide letter activities that children enjoy and talk about letters when children are interested in talking about letters. Teachers know what features to comment on because they observe students during reading and writing activities to find out what letters and features of letters children are exploring. Children's questions also provide insights into what they are curious about.

2. *Talk about the role of letters in reading and writing.* Teachers talk about how letters represent sounds and how letters combine to spell words, and they point out capital letters and lowercase letters. Teachers often talk about the role of letters during modeled writing, in **language experience approach** activities, and through **interactive writing.**

3. *Teach routines and provide a variety of opportunities for alphabet learning.* Teachers use children's names and environmental print in literacy activities, do interactive writing, encourage children to use invented spellings, share **alphabet books,** and play letter games.

Teachers begin teaching letters of the alphabet using two sources of words—children's own names and environmental print. Teachers help children focus on individual

www.ericir.syr.edu

AskERIC Lesson Plans.
Sample lesson plans for grades K–2 on letters of the alphabet, phonics, and trade books.

letters in these words. The first letters of children's names are very useful, as are prominent letters in other words—for example, the *K* in *Kmart*.

Teachers teach children to sing the alphabet song so that children will have a strategy to use to identify a particular letter. Students learn to sing the alphabet song and point to each letter until they reach the unknown letter. This is an important strategy because it gives them a real sense of independence in identifying letters.

Teachers post children's names in the classroom and use them for a variety of activities. Children quickly learn to recognize their own names and the names of their classmates. At first teachers focus on initial letters, and then children spell their names and classmates' names. They find their friends' names on word cards in a pocket chart, and they recognize their names on sign-in sheets. Teachers can also focus on each child's name when the child is spotlighted as "Child of the Week." The teacher writes the child's name on a word card and then makes letter cards for each letter of the child's name. Then the spotlighted child spells his or her name and arranges the letters to spell the name. Later, classmates practice arranging the letters. Teachers keep the children's names and letter cards in a pocket chart and use them at the alphabet center.

Teachers provide routines, activities, and games for talking about and manipulating letters. During these familiar, predictable activities, teachers and students say letter names, share alphabet books, manipulate magnetic letters, and write letters on white boards. At first the teacher structures and guides the activity, but with experience, the students internalize the routine and can do it independently, often at a literacy center. Here are 12 routines or activities:

1. *Environmental print.* Teachers collect food labels, traffic signs, and other environmental print for children to use in identifying letters. Children can sort labels and other materials to find examples of a letter being studied.

2. *Alphabet books.* Teachers read aloud alphabet books to build vocabulary and teach students to identify words that represent each letter. Also, students consult alphabet books to think of words when making books about a letter.

3. *Magnetic letters.* Students use magnetic letters to pick out all of the examples of one letter from a collection of letters or to match upper- and lowercase forms. They can arrange the letters in alphabetical order and use the letters to spell their names and other familiar words.

4. *Stamping letters.* Students use letter stamps and ink pads to stamp letters, and use letter sponges to paint letters on paper or in little booklets. They also use letter-shaped cookie cutters to make cookies and to cut out clay letters.

5. *Key pictures and words.* Students learn a key picture or object so that they will associate words and sounds with each letter. Teachers use alphabet charts with a sample picture of a familiar object for each letter. It is crucial that children are familiar with the objects, or they won't remember the key words. Teachers can recite the alphabet with children, pointing to each letter and saying: "A—Apple, B—Bear, C—Cat," and so on. Later, as children transition from letter names to sounds, they add another component: "A—Apple /a/, B—Bear /b/, C—Cat /k/," and so on.

6. *Letter cans.* Teachers collect coffee cans or shoeboxes, one for each letter of the alphabet. They write the upper- and lowercase letters on the outside of the container and place several familiar objects in each container to represent the letter. Teachers use these cans when they introduce the letters, and students use the cans at

a center. They take the object out of the container and then match it to picture cards or other small objects.

7. *Letter frames.* Teachers make circle-shaped letter frames from tagboard, collect large plastic bracelets, or shape pipe cleaners or Wikki-Stix (pipe cleaners covered in wax) into circles for students to use to highlight particular letters on charts or in big books. Students also use transparent, removable highlighting tape to mark a particular letter on charts and in books.

8. *"Show-me" cards.* Students each fold a sheet of paper to make a triangular letter holder. Then they write letters on cards and place them in the letter holder as the teacher names the letters. Children also arrange the letters into words and place the letters in the holder.

9. *Letter books and posters.* Children make letter books with pictures of objects beginning with a particular letter on each page. They add letter stamps, stickers, or pictures cut from magazines. For posters, the teacher draws a large letter form on a chart and children add pictures, stickers, and letter stamps.

10. *Spell words aloud.* Students spell high-frequency words such as *the, is, you,* and *are* aloud as they write them to reinforce the letter names and the spelling of the word.

11. *Focus on literature.* Teachers connect the alphabet to books they are reading, using the name of a character or another important word in a story to reinforce a letter of the alphabet. For example, focus on *C* when reading Clifford stories, or teach *V* when reading *The Very Hungry Caterpillar.*

12. *High-frequency word wall.* Teachers create a **word wall** with a sheet of construction paper for each letter and add a key word picture for each letter. They begin by writing the children's names and then add high-frequency words, color words, and other words children are learning.

The Morning Message

Teachers use a combination of modeled and shared writing to write the morning message. The teacher begins by talking about the day and upcoming events, and students share their news with the class. Then the teacher or the students and teacher working together compose the morning message (Kawakami-Arakaki, Oshiro, & Farran, 1989). The teacher writes the morning message on chart paper as students watch. The message includes classroom news that is of interest to students. Here is an example of a morning message:

> Today is Wednesday, February 14. Happy Valentine's Day! Be sure to mail your valentines this morning. Our party is at 1:30. We will open valentines and have delicious snacks and drinks. Mrs. Gonzales and Mrs. Jenkins are coming to help with the party. We will have a good time!

While writing the message, the teacher demonstrates that writing is done from left to right and top to bottom. Then the teacher reads the message aloud, pointing to each word as it is read. The class talks about the meaning of the message, and the teacher uses the message to point out spelling, capitalization, or punctuation skills. Afterwards, children are encouraged to reread the message and pick out familiar

Figure 4–3 Literacy play centers

Post Office Center

mailboxes	pens	packages	address labels
envelopes	wrapping paper	scale	cash register
stamps (stickers)	tape	package seals	money

Hairdresser Center

hair rollers	empty shampoo bottle	wig and wig stand	ribbons, barrettes, clips
brush and comb	towel	hairdryer (cordless)	appointment book
mirror	posters of hair styles	curling iron (cordless)	open/closed sign

Office Center

typewriter/computer	stapler	pens and pencils	message pad
calculator	hole punch	envelopes	rubber stamps
paper	file folders	stamps	stamp pad
notepads	in/out boxes	telephone	

Restaurant Center

tablecloth	silverware	tray	vest for waiter
dishes	napkins	order pad and pencil	hat and apron for chef
glasses	menus	apron for waitress	

Travel Agency Center

travel posters	maps	wallet with money and	cash register
travel brochures	airplane, train tickets	credit cards	suitcases

Medical Center

appointment books	hypodermic syringe	bandages	prescription bottles
white shirt/jacket	(play)	prescription pad	and labels
medical bag	thermometer	folders (for patient	walkie-talkie (for
stethoscope	tweezers	records)	paramedics)

Grocery Store Center

food packages	grocery cart	money	cents-off coupons
plastic fruit and	price stickers	grocery bags	advertisements
artificial foods	cash register	marking pen	

Veterinarian Center

stuffed animals	white shirt/jacket	medicine bottles	popsicle stick splints
cages (cardboard	medical bag	prescription labels	hypodermic syringe
boxes)	stethoscope	bandages	(play)

Bank Center

teller window	play money	deposit slips	signs
checks	roll papers for coins	money bags	receipts

words. As the school year progresses, the morning message grows longer and students may assume a greater role in reading and writing the message.

Through the routine of writing morning messages, young children learn a variety of things about written language. Reading and writing are demonstrated as integrated processes, and children learn that written language can be used to convey information. They learn about the direction of print, the alphabet, spelling, and other conventions used in writing. Children also learn about appropriate topics for messages and how to organize ideas into sentences.

Literacy Play Centers

Young children learn about the purposes of reading and writing as they use written language in their play. As they construct block buildings, children write signs and tape them on the buildings. As they play doctor, children write prescriptions on slips of paper. And as they play teacher, children read stories aloud to classmates who are pretending to be students or to doll and stuffed animal "students." Young children use these activities to reenact familiar, everyday activities and to pretend to be someone or something else. Through these literacy play activities, children use reading and writing for a variety of purposes.

Housekeeping centers are probably the most common play centers in primary classrooms, but these centers can be transformed into a grocery store, a post office, or a medical center by changing the props. They become literacy play centers when materials for reading and writing are included. Food packages, price stickers, and money are props in grocery store centers; letters, stamps, and mailboxes are props in post office centers; and appointment books, prescription pads, and folders for patient records are props in medical centers. A variety of literacy play centers can be set up in classrooms, and they can often be coordinated with literature focus units and themes. Ideas for nine literacy play centers are offered in Figure 4–3. Each center includes authentic literacy materials that children can experiment with and use to learn more about the purposes of written language.

www.ciera.org

Center for the Improvement of Early Reading Achievement. Reports about innovative emergent literacy programs.

Mailboxes: Exchanging Messages With Classmates

Children discover the social purposes of reading and writing by drawing and writing messages to exchange with classmates. Either a classroom set of mailboxes made from milk cartons or a small bulletin board can be used as the message center. Students write to classmates to say hello, offer a compliment, share news, trade telephone numbers, and offer birthday wishes. They practice writing their names and their classmates' names and a few words. They also gain practice reading the messages they receive. Teachers write brief messages to classmates, too, for many of the same purposes. Examples of one kindergarten teacher's messages to her students are presented in Figure 4–4. The messages are brief, but they convey the teacher's interest in and caring for her students.

YOUNG CHILDREN EMERGE INTO READING

Young children move through a series of three stages as they learn to read (Juel, 1991). The stages are (1) emergent reading, (2) beginning reading, and (3) fluent reading. During the emergent reading stage, children gain an understanding of the communicative purpose of print. They notice environmental print, dictate stories for

Figure 4—4 A kindergarten teacher's messages

Juan,
Happy Birthday to you!
How old are you?
　　　　Love,
　　　　Ms. R.

Dear Lee,
I like the big building
you made in the Blocks
Center.
　　　　Love,
　　　　Ms. R.

Dear Aleta,
Would you like to read
with me today?
　　　　Love,
　　　　Ms. R.

Natasha,
Thank you for cleaning
Snowball's cage. You are
a good helper.
　　　　Love,
　　　　Ms. R.

the teacher to record, and reread predictable books after they have memorized the pattern. From this foundation, children move into the beginning reading stage. In this stage, children learn sound-symbol correspondences and begin to decode words. In the third stage, children can decode words quickly and automatically. They have become fluent readers and concentrate their cognitive energy on comprehension. In this chapter, we focus on the emergent stage.

Teachers who work with emergent readers use many of the same instructional approaches used with older students, such as literature focus units, guided reading, and reading workshop. Teachers adapt these approaches to provide enough scaffolding so that young children are successful. One adaptation for reading workshop, for example, is for children to read interactive electronic books available on CD-ROM. Children can choose the level of support they want. They can read these books independently, highlight unfamiliar words for the computer to identify, or follow along as the computer reads the book. Check the Technology Link on page 137 to learn more about these innovative texts.

Other instructional approaches have been developed specifically for emergent readers. Three of these approaches are shared reading, assisted reading, and the language experience approach.

Technology Link   INTERACTIVE ELECTRONIC BOOKS

Beginning readers can read interactive electronic books available on CD-ROM. The text and illustrations are displayed page by page on the computer screen. The text can be read aloud with each word or phrase highlighted as it is read, students can read the book themselves and ask the computer to identify unfamiliar words, or students can read along with the computer to develop their reading fluency. Music and sound effects accompany each program. Many programs have reading logs, writing activities, word identification, and other interactive activities. Electronic books are available for Macintosh and IBM computers with color monitors and CD-ROM drives. Four companies that sell electronic books are Scholastic, Broderbund, Tom Snyder Productions, and Computer Curriculum Corporation.

Scholastic's "WiggleWorks: Beginning Literacy System" is a set of 24 electronic books, including Norman Bridwell's *Clifford the Big Red Dog* (1963), arranged into three levels of difficulty. The program includes paperback copies of books, audiocassettes, and teaching guides. For information, contact Scholastic at 800-325-6149.

Broderbund's electronic books for grades K–3 are called "The Living Books Framework." Mercer Mayer's *Just Grandma and Me* (1992) and Jack Prelutsky's *The New Kid on the Block* (1984) are included in two sets, and some books are available in both English and Spanish. Paperback copies, teaching guides, and audiocassettes are included. For information, contact Broderbund at 800-474-8840.

"Reading Magic Library" from Tom Snyder Productions includes five animated stories that let students choose what happens next. Two of the titles are retellings of folktales, and the others are created for this program. For information, contact Tom Snyder Productions at 800-342-0236.

Computer Curriculum Corporation has a wider range of electronic books, and some are designed for students learning English as a second language. Programs include Discover English (preschool and kindergarten), First Adventures (grades 1–3), Reading Adventures (grades 2–5), and Reading Investigations (grades 3–6). For information, contact Computer Curriculum Corporation at 800-455-7910.

Guidelines for selecting electronic books for classroom use include:

1.   Choose electronic books that are high-quality children's literature and available as trade books.

2.   Check to see that the software is compatible with your computer.

3.   Preview the software before purchasing it.

4.   Determine that the electronic book is interactive.

5.   Examine the related activities, such as writing journal entries and creating new versions of the book.

6.   Check that technical support is available from the manufacturer by telephone or on-line.

Shared Reading

Teachers use shared reading to read aloud books that are appropriate for children's interest level but too difficult for them to read for themselves (Holdaway, 1979). Teachers use the five steps of the reading process in shared reading, as Mrs. Mast did in the vignette at the beginning of the chapter. The steps in shared reading are presented

www.eduplace.com

Shared Reading. Read about the theoretical basis for shared reading and the benefits of using this approach.

in Figure 4–5, showing how the activities fit into the stages. Through the reading process, teachers model what fluent readers do as they involve students in enjoyable reading activities (Fountas & Pinnell, 1996). After the text is read several times, teachers use the text to teach phonics concepts and high-frequency words. Students can also read small versions of the book with partners or independently, and the pattern or structure used in the text can be used for writing activities (Slaughter, 1993).

The books chosen for shared reading are available in both big book and small book formats and are close to children's reading level, but still beyond their ability to read independently. As an instructional strategy, shared reading differs from reading aloud to students because students see the text as the teacher reads. Also, students often join in the reading of predictable refrains and rhyming words, and after listening to the teacher read the text several times, students often remember enough of the text to read along with the teacher. Through shared reading, teachers also demonstrate how print works, provide opportunities for students to use the prediction strategy, and increase children's confidence in their ability to read.

Big Books. Big books are greatly enlarged picture books that teachers use in shared reading, most commonly with primary-grade students. In this technique, developed in New Zealand, teachers place an enlarged picture book on an easel or chart stand where all children can see it. Then they read it with small groups of children or the whole class (Holdaway, 1979). Trachtenburg and Ferruggia (1989) used big books with their class of transitional first graders and found that making and reading big books dramatically improved children's reading scores on standardized achievement tests. The teachers reported that children's self-concepts as readers were decidedly improved as well.

Many picture books can be purchased in big book format, and teachers can make big books themselves by printing the text of a picture book on large sheets of posterboard and adding illustrations. The steps in making a big book are illustrated in Figure 4–6.

Almost any type of picture book may be turned into a big book, but predictable books, nursery rhymes, songs, and poems are the most popular. Heald-Taylor (1987) lists these types of big books that teachers can make:

🌱 *Replica book.* An exact copy of a picture book.

🌱 *Newly illustrated book.* A familiar book with new illustrations.

🌱 *Adapted book.* A new version of a familiar picture book.

🌱 *Original book.* An original book composed by students or the teacher.

With the big book on a chart stand or easel, the teacher reads it aloud, pointing to every word. Before long, students join in the reading. Then the teacher rereads the book, inviting students to help with the reading. The next time the book is read, the teacher reads to the point that the text becomes predictable, such as the beginning of a refrain, and the students supply the missing text. Having students supply the missing words is important because it leads to independent reading. When students have become familiar with the text, they are invited to read the big book independently (Slaughter, 1983).

Predictable Books. The stories and other books that teachers use for shared reading with young children often have repeated words and sentences, rhyme, or other patterns. Books that use these patterns are known as predictable books. These books are a valuable tool for emergent readers because the repeated words and sentences,

| *Figure 4–5* | Steps in a shared reading lesson |

---

1. Prereading

- ❧ Activate or build background knowledge on a topic related to the book.
- ❧ Show the cover of the book and tell the title.
- ❧ Talk about the author and illustrator.
- ❧ Talk about the book and have students make predictions.

2. Reading

- ❧ Use a big book or text printed on a chart.
- ❧ Use a pointer to track during reading.
- ❧ Read expressively with very few stops during the first reading.
- ❧ Highlight vocabulary and repetitive patterns.
- ❧ Reread the book once or twice and encourage students to join in the reading.

3. Responding

- ❧ Discuss the book using a grand conversation.
- ❧ Ask inferential and critical level questions, such as "What would happen if . . . ?" and "What did this book make you think of?"
- ❧ Share the pen to write a sentence interactively about the book.
- ❧ Have students draw and write in reading logs.

4. Exploring

- ❧ Reread the book using small books.
- ❧ Add important words to the word wall.
- ❧ Teach minilessons on skills and strategies.
- ❧ Present more information about the author and illustrator.
- ❧ Provide a text set with other books by the same author and illustrator.

5. Applying

- ❧ Write an innovation using the pattern used in the book.
- ❧ Create an art project related to the book.

---

patterns, and sequences enable children to predict the next sentence or episode in the story or other book (Bridge, 1979; Heald-Taylor, 1987; Tompkins & Webeler, 1983). Four types of predictable books are:

1. *Repetitive sentences.* Phrases and sentences are repeated over and over in some books. Sometimes each episode or section of the text ends with the same words or a refrain, and in other books the same statement or question is repeated. In *The Little Red Hen* (Galdone, 1973), the animals repeat "Not I" when the Little Red Hen asks them to help her plant the seeds, harvest the wheat, and bake the bread; after their refusals to help, the hen says, "Then I will."

Figure 4–6 Steps in making a big book

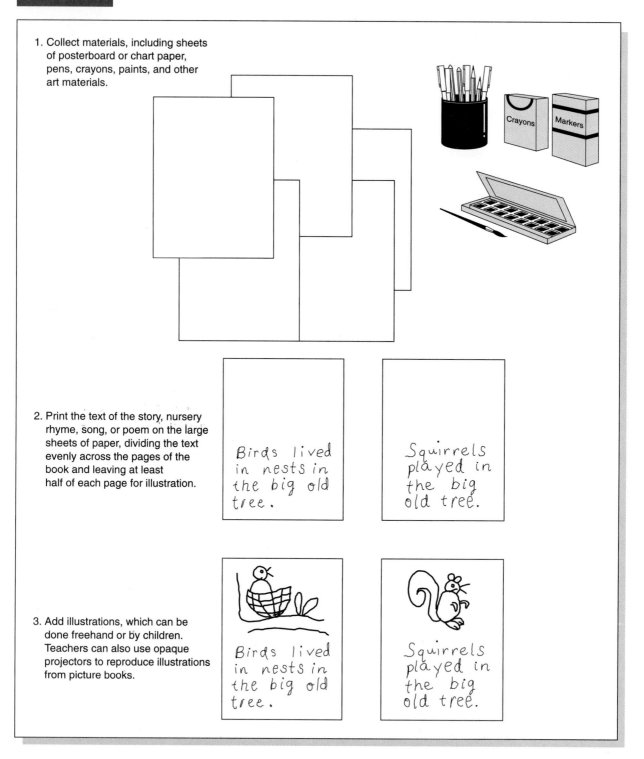

1. Collect materials, including sheets of posterboard or chart paper, pens, crayons, paints, and other art materials.

2. Print the text of the story, nursery rhyme, song, or poem on the large sheets of paper, dividing the text evenly across the pages of the book and leaving at least half of each page for illustration.

   Birds lived in nests in the big old tree.

   Squirrels played in the big old tree.

3. Add illustrations, which can be done freehand or by children. Teachers can also use opaque projectors to reproduce illustrations from picture books.

   Birds lived in nests in the big old tree.

   Squirrels played in the big old tree.

Figure 4–6 continued

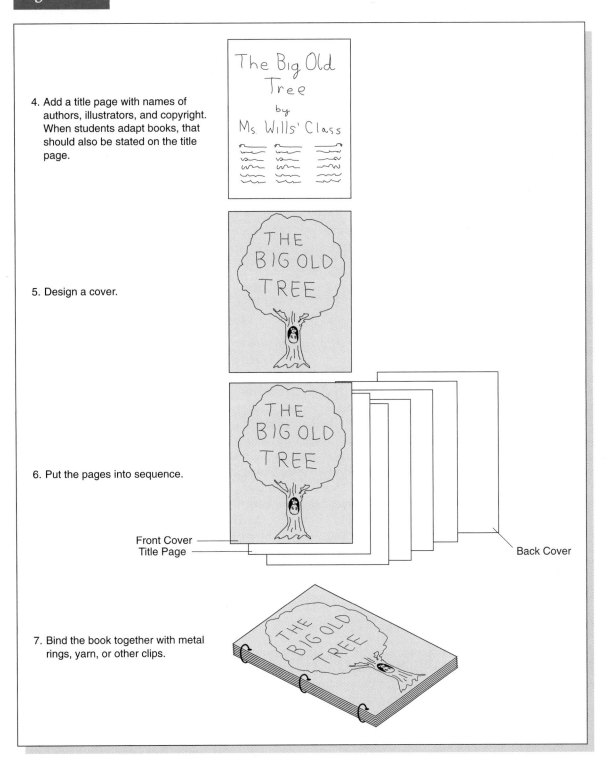

4. Add a title page with names of authors, illustrators, and copyright. When students adapt books, that should also be stated on the title page.

5. Design a cover.

6. Put the pages into sequence.

Front Cover
Title Page
Back Cover

7. Bind the book together with metal rings, yarn, or other clips.

Kindergartners read a predictable book about a dog named Spot in a guided reading group.

2. ***Repetitive sentences in a cumulative structure.*** The phrases or sentences are repeated and expanded in each episode in some books. In *The Gingerbread Boy* (Galdone, 1975), for instance, the Gingerbread Boy repeats and expands his boast as he meets each character on his run away from the Little Old Man and the Little Old Woman.

3. ***Rhyme and rhythm.*** Rhyme and rhythm are important devices in some books. The sentences have a strong beat, and rhyme is used at the end of each line or in another poetic scheme. Also, some books have an internal rhyme within lines rather than at the end of rhymes. One example is Dr. Seuss's *Hop on Pop* (1963).

4. ***Sequential patterns.*** Some books use a familiar sequence, such as months of the year, days of the week, numbers 1 to 10, or letters of the alphabet, to structure the text. For example, *The Very Hungry Caterpillar* (Carle, 1969) combines number and day-of-the-week sequences as the caterpillar eats through an amazing array of foods during the week.

A list of predictable books illustrating each of these patterns is presented in Figure 4–7.

Assisted Reading

Assisted reading extends the familiar routine of parents reading to their children (Hoskisson, 1975). A child and a teacher sit together to read a book. At first, the teacher does most of the reading, and gradually the child assumes more and more of the reading until the child is doing most of it, with the teacher supplying only a few unfamiliar words. Aides and parent volunteers can also use assisted reading one-on-one with children to introduce them to concepts about print. The main drawback is that one-on-one reading is time-consuming. Even spending ten minutes a week with each child can take more than three hours per week with a class of 20 students.

Figure 4–7 Predictable books

Repetitive Sentences

Asch, F. (1981). *Just like Daddy.* New York: Simon & Schuster.

Bennett, J. (1985). *Teeny tiny.* New York: Putnam.

Brown, R. (1981). *A dark, dark tale.* New York: Dial.

Carle, E. (1973). *Have you seen my cat?* New York: Philomel.

Carle, E. (1984). *The very busy spider.* New York: Philomel.

Carle, E. (1990). *The very quiet cricket.* New York: Philomel.

Gag, W. (1956). *Millions of cats.* New York: Coward-Mc-Cann.

Galdone, P. (1973). *The little red hen.* New York: Seabury.

Guarino, D. (1989). *Is your mama a llama?* New York: Scholastic.

Hill, E. (1980). *Where's Spot?* New York: Putnam.

Hutchins, P. (1972). *Good-night, owl!* New York: Macmillan.

Hutchins, P. (1986). *The doorbell rang.* New York: Morrow.

Martin, B., Jr. (1983). *Brown bear, brown bear, what do you see?* New York: Holt, Rinehart & Winston.

Martin, B., Jr. (1992). *Polar bear, polar bear, what do you hear?* New York: Holt, Rinehart & Winston.

Peek, M. (1981). *Roll over!* Boston: Houghton Mifflin.

Peek, M. (1985). *Mary wore her red dress.* New York: Clarion.

Rosen, M. (1989). *We're going on a bear hunt.* New York: Macmillan.

Weiss, N. (1987). *If you're happy and you know it.* New York: Greenwillow.

Weiss, N. (1989). *Where does the brown bear go?* New York: Viking.

Westcott, N. B. (1988). *The lady with the alligator purse.* Boston: Little, Brown.

Wickstrom, S. K. (1988). *Wheels on the bus.* New York: Crown.

Williams, S. (1989). *I went walking.* San Diego: Harcourt Brace Jovanovich.

Repetitive Sentences in a Cumulative Structure

Brett, J. (1989). *The mitten.* New York: Putnam.

Flack, M. (1932). *Ask Mr. Bear.* New York: Macmillan.

Fox, H. (1986). *Hattie and the fox.* New York: Bradbury.

Galdone, P. (1975). *The gingerbread boy.* New York: Seabury.

Kellogg, S. (1974). *There was an old woman.* New York: Parents.

Kraus, R. (1970). *Whose mouse are you?* New York: Macmillan.

Tolstoi, A. (1968). *The great big enormous turnip.* New York: Watts.

Westcott, N. B. (1980). *I know an old lady who swallowed a fly.* Boston: Little, Brown.

Zemach, H. (1969). *The judge.* New York: Farrar, Straus & Giroux.

Zemach, M. (1983). *The little red hen.* New York: Farrar, Straus & Giroux.

Rhyme and Rhythm

Brown, M. (1987). *Play rhymes.* New York: Dutton.

de Paola, T. (1985). *Hey diddle diddle and other Mother Goose rhymes.* New York: Putnam.

Messenger, J. (1986). *Twinkle, twinkle, little star.* New York: Macmillan.

Sendak, M. (1962). *Chicken soup with rice.* New York: Harper & Row.

Seuss, Dr. (1963). *Hop on Pop.* New York: Random House.

Seuss, Dr. (1988). *Green eggs and ham.* New York: Random House.

Sequential Patterns

Alain. (1964). *One, two, three, going to sea.* New York: Scholastic.

Carle, E. (1969). *The very hungry caterpillar.* Cleveland: Collins-World.

Carle, E. (1977). *The grouchy ladybug.* New York: Crowell.

Carle, E. (1987). *A house for a hermit crab.* Saxonville, MA: Picture Book Studio.

Domanska, J. (1985). *Busy Monday morning.* New York: Greenwillow.

Keats, E. J. (1973). *Over in the meadow.* New York: Scholastic.

Mack, S. (1974). *10 bears in my bed.* New York: Pantheon.

Numeroff, L. J. (1985). *If you give a mouse a cookie.* New York: HarperCollins.

Numeroff, L. J. (1991). *If you give a moose a muffin.* New York: HarperCollins.

Wood, A. (1984). *The napping house.* San Diego: Harcourt Brace Jovanovich.

Reading Buddies. One way to make assisted reading more feasible in classrooms is to use a class of upper-grade students in a cross-age reading buddies program with primary-grade children. Older students read books aloud to younger children, and they also read with the children using assisted reading. The effectiveness of cross-age tutoring is supported by research (Cohen, Kulik, & Kulik, 1982), and teachers report that students' reading fluency and attitudes toward school and learning improve (Labbo & Teale, 1990; Morrice & Simmons, 1991).

Teachers arranging a buddy-reading program decide when students will get together, how long each session will last, and what the schedule will be. Primary-grade teachers explain the program to their students and talk about activities the buddies will be doing together, and upper-grade teachers explain to their students how to work with young children. In particular, they should teach students how to read aloud and encourage younger children to make predictions, how to use assisted reading, how to select books to appeal to younger children, and how to help them respond to books. Then older students choose books to read aloud and practice reading them until they can read the books fluently. At the first meeting, students pair off, get acquainted, and read together. They also talk about the books they read and perhaps write in special **reading logs.** Buddies also may want to go to the library and choose the books they will read at the next session.

There are significant social benefits to cross-age tutoring programs, too. Children get acquainted with other children they might otherwise not meet, and they learn how to work with older or younger children. As they talk about books they have read, students share personal experiences and interpretations. They also talk about reading strategies, how to choose books, and their favorite authors or illustration styles. Sometimes reading buddies write notes back and forth, or the two classrooms plan holiday celebrations together. These activities strengthen the social connections between the children.

www.ed.gov

A Compact for Reading.
Read about ways to improve family involvement in education.

Traveling Bags of Books. A second way to encourage more one-on-one reading is to involve parents in the program by using traveling bags of books. Teachers collect text sets of four or five books on various topics for children to take home and read with their parents (Reutzel & Fawson, 1990). For example, teachers might collect copies of *Hattie and the Fox* (Fox, 1986), *The Gingerbread Boy* (Galdone, 1975), *Flossie and the Fox* (McKissack, 1986), and *Rosie's Walk* (Hutchins, 1968) for a traveling bag of fox stories. Then children and their parents read one or more of the books using assisted reading and draw or write a response to the books they have read in the reading log that accompanies the books in the traveling bag. Children keep the bag at home for several days, often rereading the books each day with their parents, and then return it to school so that another child can borrow it. Text sets for ten traveling bags are listed in Figure 4–8. Many of these text sets include combinations of stories, informational books, and poems. Teachers can also add small toys, stuffed animals, audiotapes of one or more of the books, or other related objects to the bags.

Teachers often introduce traveling bags at a special parents' meeting or open-house get-together at which they explain to parents how to use assisted reading to read with their children. It is important that parents understand that their children may not be familiar with the books and that children are not expected to be able to read them independently. Teachers also talk about the responses children and parents write in the reading log and show sample entries from the previous year.

Figure 4–8 Text sets for traveling bags

Books About Airplanes

Barton, R. (1982). *Airport.* New York: Harper & Row.
McPhail, D. (1987). *First flight.* Boston: Little, Brown.
Petersen, D. (1981). *Airplanes* (A new true book). Chicago: Childrens Press.
Ziegler, S. (1988). *A visit to the airport.* Chicago: Childrens Press.

Books About Dogs

Barracca, D., & Barracca, S. (1990). *The adventures of taxi dog.* New York: Dial.
Bridwell, N. (1963). *Clifford the big red dog.* New York: Greenwillow.
Cole, J. (1991). *My puppy is born.* New York: Morrow.
Reiser, L. (1992). *Any kind of dog.* New York: Greenwillow.

Books by Ezra Jack Keats

Keats, E. J. (1962). *The snowy day.* New York: Viking.
Keats, E. J. (1964). *Whistle for Willie.* New York: Viking.
Keats, E. J. (1967). *Peter's chair.* New York: Harper & Row.
Keats, E. J. (1969). *Goggles.* New York: Macmillan.
Keats, E. J. (1970). *Hi cat!* New York: Macmillan.

Books About Frogs and Toads

Lobel, A. (1970). *Frog and toad are friends.* New York: Harper & Row.
Mayer, M. (1974). *Frog goes to dinner.* New York: Dial.
Pallotta, J. (1990). *The frog alphabet book: And other awesome amphibians.* Watertown, MA: Charlesbridge.
Watts, B. (1991). *Frog.* New York: Lodestar.
Yolen, J. (1980). *Commander Toad in space.* New York: Coward-McCann.

Books About Mice

Cauley, L. B. (1984). *The town mouse and the country mouse.* New York: Putnam.
Henkes, K. (1991). *Chrysanthemum.* New York: Greenwillow.
Lionni, L. (1969). *Alexander and the wind-up mouse.* New York: Pantheon.
Lobel, A. (1977). *Mouse soup.* New York: Harper & Row.
Numeroff, L. J. (1985). *If you give a mouse a cookie.* New York: Harper & Row.

Books About Numbers

Aker, S. (1990). *What comes in 2's, 3's, & 4's?* New York: Simon & Schuster.
Bang, M. (1983). *Ten, nine, eight.* New York: Greenwillow.
Giganti, P., Jr. (1992). *Each orange had 8 slices: A counting book.* New York: Greenwillow.
Tafuri, N. (1986). *Who's counting?* New York: Greenwillow.

Books About Plants

Ehlert, L. (1991). *Red leaf, yellow leaf.* San Diego: Harcourt Brace Jovanovich.
Fowler, A. (1990). *It could still be a tree.* Chicago: Childrens Press.
Gibbons, G. (1984). *The seasons of Arnold's apple tree.* San Diego: Harcourt Brace Jovanovich.
King, E. (1990). *The pumpkin patch.* New York: Dutton.
Lobel, A. (1990). *Alison's zinnia.* New York: Greenwillow.

Books About Rain

Branley, F. M. (1985). *Flash, crash, rumble, and roll.* New York: Harper & Row.
Polacco, P. (1990). *Thunder cake.* New York: Philomel.
Shulevitz, U. (1969). *Rain rain rivers.* New York: Farrar, Straus & Giroux.
Spier, P. (1982). *Rain.* New York: Doubleday.

Books About the Three Bears

Cauley, L. B. (1981). *Goldilocks and the three bears.* New York: Putnam.
Galdone, P. (1972). *The three bears.* New York: Clarion Books.
Tolhurst, M. (1990). *Somebody and the three Blairs.* New York: Orchard Books.
Turkle, B. (1976). *Deep in the forest.* New York: Dutton.

Books About Trucks

Crews, D. (1980). *Truck.* New York: Greenwillow.
Owen, A. (1990). *Bumper to bumper.* New York: Knopf.
Rockwell, A. (1984). *Trucks.* New York: Dutton.
Rockwell, A. (1986). *Big wheels.* New York: Dutton.
Siebert, D. (1984). *Truck song.* New York: Harper & Row.

Language Experience Approach

The **language experience approach** (LEA) is based on children's language and experiences (Ashton-Warner, 1965; Stauffer, 1970). In this approach, children dictate words and sentences about their experiences, and the teacher writes down what the children say. The text they develop becomes the reading material. Because the language comes from the children themselves and the content is based on their experiences, they are usually able to read the text easily. Reading and writing are connected, as students are actively involved in reading what they have written.

Using this approach, students can create individual booklets. They draw pictures on each page or cut pictures from magazines to glue on each page, and then they dictate the text that the teacher writes beside the illustration on each page. Students can also make a class book, or they can each create one page to be added to a class book. For example, as part of the unit on "The Three Bears," Mrs. Mast's students wrote a collaborative book on bears. Students each chose a fact they knew about bears for their page. They drew an illustration and dictated the text for Mrs. Mast to record. An example of one page from the class book is shown in Figure 4–9. Mrs. Mast took the students' dictation rather than having the children write the book themselves because she wanted it to be written in conventional spelling so that students could read and reread the book.

Teachers also take children's dictation to write charts about what the class is learning about literature or in connection with social studies or science units. Students in Mrs. Mast's kindergarten class, for example, dictated the facts they learned about grizzly, black, and polar bears in the vignette at the beginning of this chapter.

It is a great temptation to change the child's language to the teacher's own, in either word choice or grammar, but editing should be kept to a minimum so that children do not get the impression that their language is inferior or inadequate.

Figure 4–9   One page from a kindergarten class book about bears

Polar bears live in ice and snow.

Jesse

As children become familiar with dictating to the teacher, they learn to pace their dictation to the teacher's writing speed. At first, children dictate as they think of ideas, but with experience they watch as the teacher writes and supply the text word by word. This change also provides evidence of children's developing concept of a word.

The language experience approach is an effective way to help children emerge into reading. Even students who have not been successful with other types of reading activities can read what they have dictated. There is a drawback, however; teachers provide a "perfect" model when they take children's dictation—they write neatly and spell words correctly. After language experience activities, some young children are not eager to do their own writing. They prefer their teacher's "perfect" writing to their own childlike writing. To avoid this problem, young children should also be doing **interactive writing** and independent writing at the same time they are participating in language experience activities. This way, they will learn that sometimes they do their own writing and at other times the teacher takes their dictation.

YOUNG CHILDREN EMERGE INTO WRITING

Many young children become writers before entering kindergarten, and the rest are introduced to writing during their first year of school (Harste et al., 1984; Temple, Nathan, Burris, & Temple, 1988). Young children's writing development follows a pattern similar to children's reading development: (1) emergent writing, (2) beginning writing, and (3) fluent writing. In the first stage, emergent writing, children make scribbles to represent writing. The scribbles may appear randomly on a page at first, but with experience children line up the letters or scribbles from left to right and from top to bottom. Children also begin to "read," or tell what their writing says. The next stage, beginning writing, marks children's growing awareness of the alphabetic principle. Children use invented spelling to represent words, and as they learn more about sound-symbol correspondences their writing approximates conventional spelling. The third stage is fluent writing, when children use conventional spelling and other conventions of written language, including capital letters and punctuation marks. By second or third grade, all students should be fluent writers.

Opportunities for writing begin on the first day of kindergarten and continue on a daily basis through the primary grades, regardless of whether children have already learned to read or write letters and spell words. Children often begin using a combination of art and scribbles or letter-like forms to express themselves, and their writing moves toward conventional forms as they apply concepts they are learning about written language.

Young children participate in many of the same types of writing activities that older students do. They use scribbles, letters, and words to label pictures they have drawn, describe experiences in journals, write letters to family members, and make books to share information. In their writing, children use a combination of adult spelling and invented spelling, or they have an idiosyncratic approach of using letters and other marks to represent words.

Introducing Young Children to Writing

Children are introduced to writing as they watch their parents and teachers write and as they experiment with drawing and writing. Teachers help children emerge into writing as they show them how to use invented spelling, teach **minilessons** about written language, and involve children in writing activities.

Teachers demonstrate to children through morning messages and language experience approach activities that people use written language to represent their thoughts. However, adult models can be very intimidating to young children who feel at a loss to produce adult writing that is neatly written and spelled conventionally. Teachers can contrast their writing—adult writing—with the "kid" writing that children can do. Young children's writing takes many different forms. It can be scribbles or a collection of random marks on paper. Sometimes children are imitating adults' cursive writing as they scribble. Children can string together letters that have no phoneme-grapheme correspondences, or they can use one or two letters to represent entire words. Children with more experience with written language can invent spellings that represent more sound features of words, and they can apply spelling rules. A child's writings of "Abbie is my good dog. I love her very much" over a year and a half are presented in Figure 4–10. The child's "kid" writing moves from using

Figure 4–10   Stages of development in a child's "kid" writing

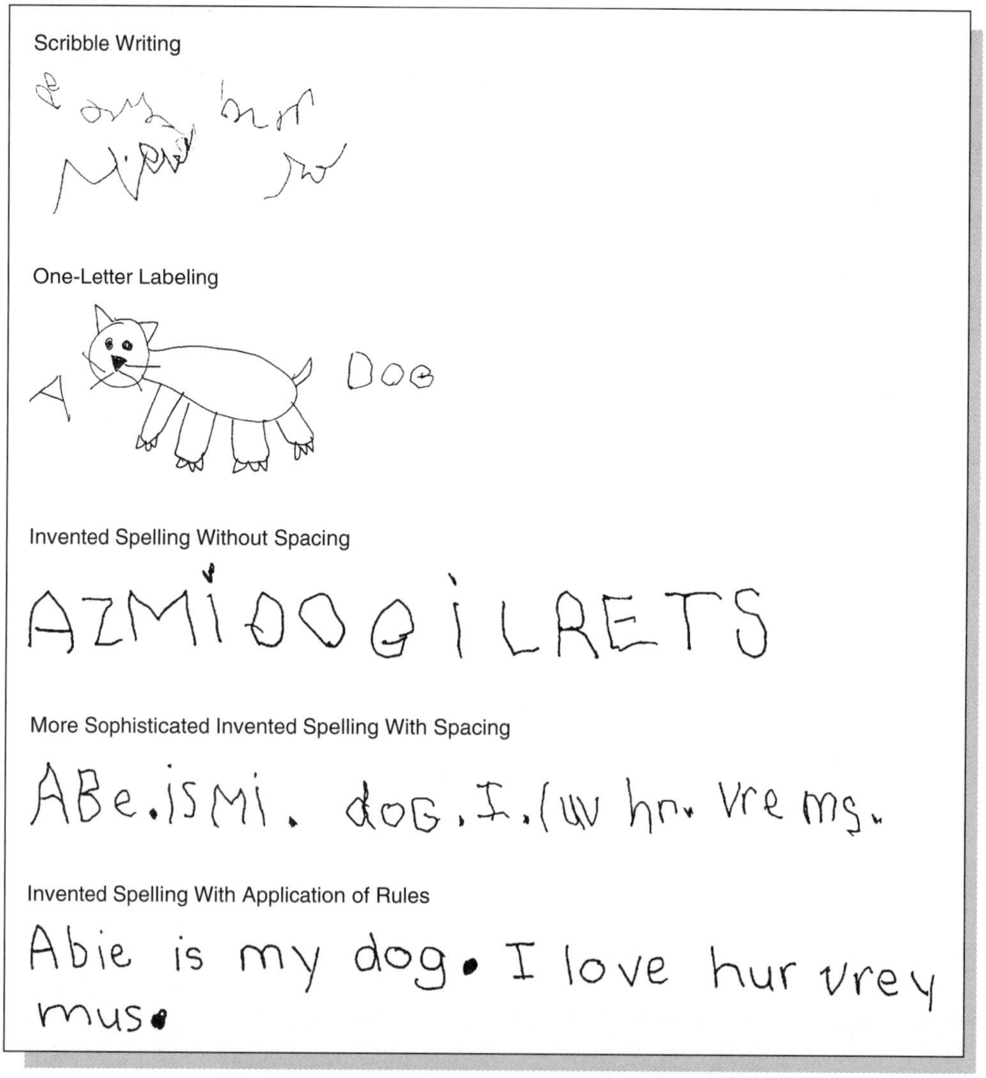

Scribble Writing

One-Letter Labeling

Invented Spelling Without Spacing

AZMI DOG i LRETS

More Sophisticated Invented Spelling With Spacing

ABe.isMi. doG.I.(uv hr. vre ms.

Invented Spelling With Application of Rules

Abie is my dog. I love hur vrey mus.

scribbles to using single letters to represent words, then to invented spelling, and finally to conventional spelling. In the fourth example, the child is experimenting with using periods to mark spaces between words.

Invented spelling is an important concept for young children because it gives them permission to experiment with written language when they write. Too often children assume they should spell like adults do, but they cannot. Without this confidence, children do not want to write, or they ask teachers to spell every word or copy text out of books or from charts. Invented spelling teaches students several strategies for writing, and it allows them to invent spellings that reflect their knowledge of written language.

Young children's writing grows out of talk and drawing. As children begin to write, their writing is literally their talk written down, and they can usually express in writing the ideas they talk about. At the same time, children's letter-like marks develop from their drawing. With experience, children differentiate between drawing and writing. Some kindergarten teachers explain to children that they should use crayons when they draw and use pencils when they write. Teachers can also differentiate where on a page children write and draw. The writing might go at the top or bottom of a page, or children can use paper with space for drawing at the top and lines for writing at the bottom.

Interactive Writing

In **interactive writing,** children and the teacher create a text together and "share the pen" as they write the text on chart paper (Button, Johnson, & Furgerson, 1996; McCarrier, Pinnell, & Fountas, 2000). The text is composed by the group, and the teacher guides children as they write the text word by word on chart paper. Children take turns writing known letters and familiar words, adding punctuation marks, and marking spaces between words. All children participate in creating and writing the text on chart paper, and they also write the text on small white boards, small chalkboards, or on paper as it is written on the chart paper. After writing, children read and reread the text using shared reading and independent reading.

Students use interactive writing to write class news, predictions before reading, retellings of stories, thank-you letters, reports, math story problems, and many other types of group writings (Collom, 1998). Two interactive writing samples are shown in Figure 4–11. The one at the top of the page was written by a kindergarten class during a health unit, and the second sample is a first-grade class's interactive writing of a math story problem. After writing this story problem, students wrote other subtraction problems individually. The boxes drawn around some of the letters and words represent correction tape that was used to correct misspellings or poorly formed letters. In the kindergarten sample, students took turns writing individual letters; in the first-grade sample, students took turns writing entire words.

Through interactive writing, students learn concepts about print, letter-sound relationships and spelling patterns, handwriting concepts, and capitalization and punctuation skills. Teachers model conventional spelling and use of conventions of print, and students practice segmenting the sounds in words and spelling familiar words. Students use the skills they learn through interactive writing when they write independently.

During interactive writing, teachers help students spell all words conventionally. They teach high-frequency words such as *the* and *of,* assist students in segmenting sounds and syllables in other words, point out unusual spelling patterns such as *pieces* and *germs,* and teach other conventions of print. Whenever students misspell a word or form a letter incorrectly, teachers use correction tape to cover the mistake and help students make the correction. For example, when a student wrote the numeral *8* to spell *ate* in the second sample in Figure 4–11, the teacher explained the *eight–ate* homophone, covered the numeral with correction tape, and helped the child "think out" the spelling of the word, including the silent *e*. Teachers emphasize the importance of using conventional spelling as a courtesy to readers, not that a student made a mistake. In contrast to the emphasis on conventional spelling in interactive writing, students are encouraged to use invented spelling and other spelling strategies when writing independently. They learn to look for familiar words posted on classroom word walls or in books they have read, think about spelling patterns and rimes, or ask a classmate for help. Teachers also talk about purpose and explain that in personal writing and rough drafts, students do use invented spelling. Increasingly, however, students want to use conventional spelling and even ask to use the correction tape to fix errors they make as they write.

Figure 4–11   Two samples of interactive writing

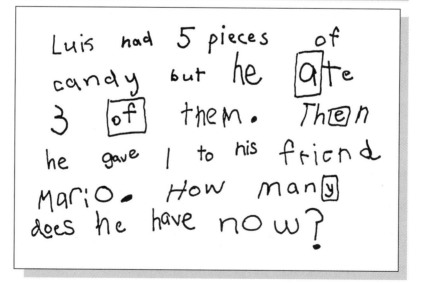

Adapting the Writing Process for Young Children

Teachers often simplify the writing process for young children by abbreviating the revising and editing steps of the writing process. At first children's revising is limited to reading the text to themselves or to the teacher to check that they have written all that they want to say. Revising becomes more formal as children learn about audience and decide they want to "add more" or "fix" their writing to make it appeal to their classmates. Some emergent writers ignore editing altogether—as soon as they have dashed off their drafts, they are ready to publish or share their writing. However, others change a spelling, fix a poorly written letter, or add a period to the end of the text as they read over their writings. When children begin writing, teachers accept children's writing as it is written and focus on the message. As children gain experience with writing, teachers encourage them to "fix" more and more of their errors. Guidelines for adapting the writing process for emergent writers are presented in Figure 4–12.

Writing Centers. Writing centers can be set up in kindergarten classrooms so that children have a special place where they can go to write. The center should be located at a table with chairs, and a box of supplies, including pencils, crayons, a date stamp, different kinds of paper, journal notebooks, a stapler, blank books, notepaper, and envelopes, should be stored nearby. The alphabet, printed in upper- and lowercase letters, should be available on the table for children to refer to as they write. In addition, there should be a crate for children to file their work in. They can also share their completed writings by sending them to classmates or sharing while sitting in a special seat called the "author's chair."

Young children draw and write in journals and make books at the writing center.

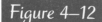

Figure 4–12 Guidelines for adapting the writing process for emergent writers

Step 1: Prewriting

Prewriting is as important to young children as it is to other writers. Children write about topics they know well and have the vocabulary to express ideas about. Topics include personal experiences, classroom activities, stories students have listened to read aloud or have read independently, and thematic unit topics. Children use drawing to gather and organize ideas before writing. Children often talk about the topic or dramatize it before beginning to write.

Step 2: Drafting

Young children usually write single-draft compositions. They add words to accompany drawings they have already made. The emphasis is on expressing ideas, not on handwriting skills or conventional spelling. Often children write in small booklets of paper, and they write equally well on lined or unlined paper.

Step 3: Revising

Teachers downplay this step until children have learned the importance of revising to meet the needs of their readers. At first children reread their writings to see that they have included everything they wanted to say, and they make very few changes. As they gain experience, they begin to make changes to make their writing clearer and add more information to make their writing more complete.

Step 4: Editing

Like revising, this step is deemphasized until children have learned conventional spellings for some words and have gained control over rules for capitalizing words and adding punctuation marks. To introduce editing, teachers help children make one or two corrections by erasing the error and writing the correction in pencil on the child's writing. Teachers do not circle errors on a child's paper with a red pen. As children become more fluent writers, teachers help them make more corrections.

Step 5: Publishing

Children read their writings to their classmates and share their drawings. Through sharing, children develop a concept of audience and learn new ways of writing from their classmates. Kindergartners and first graders usually do not recopy their writings, but sometimes the teacher or an assistant types the final copy, changing the child's writing into conventional form. When adults recopy children's writing, however, they send a strong message that the children's writing is inadequate, unless there is a good reason for converting the kid writing to adult writing.

When children come to the writing center, they draw and write in journals, compile books, and write messages to classmates. Teachers should be available to encourage and assist children at the center. They can observe children as they invent spellings and can provide information about letters, words, and sentences as needed. If the teacher cannot be at the writing center, perhaps an aide, a parent volunteer, or an upper-grade student can assist.

Figure 4–13 presents two **reading log** entries created by kindergartners and first graders at the writing center. The top sample shows a kindergartner's response to *If You Give a Mouse a Cookie* (Numeroff, 1985). The child's kid writing says, "I love

Figure 4–13 Two emergent writers' reading log entries

chocolate chip cookies." The bottom sample was written by a first grader after reading *Are You My Mother?* (Eastman, 1960). The child wrote, "The bird said, 'Are you my mother, you big ole Snort?'" After students shared their log entries during a grand conversation, this student added, "The mommy said, 'Here is a worm. I am here. I'm here.'" Notice that the part that the mother says is written as though it were coming out of the bird's mouth and going up into the air.

Young children also make books based on the books they have read at the writing center. For example, they can use the same patterns as in *Polar Bear, Polar Bear, What Do You Hear?* (Martin, 1991), *If You Give a Mouse a Cookie* (Numeroff, 1985), and *If the Dinosaurs Came Back* (Most, 1978) to create innovations, or new versions of familiar stories. A first grader's four-page book about a mouse named Jerry, written after reading *If You Give a Mouse a Cookie,* is shown in Figure 4–14. In these writing projects, children often use invented spelling, but they are encouraged to spell famil-

Figure 4–14   A first grader's innovation for *If You Give a Mouse a Cookie*

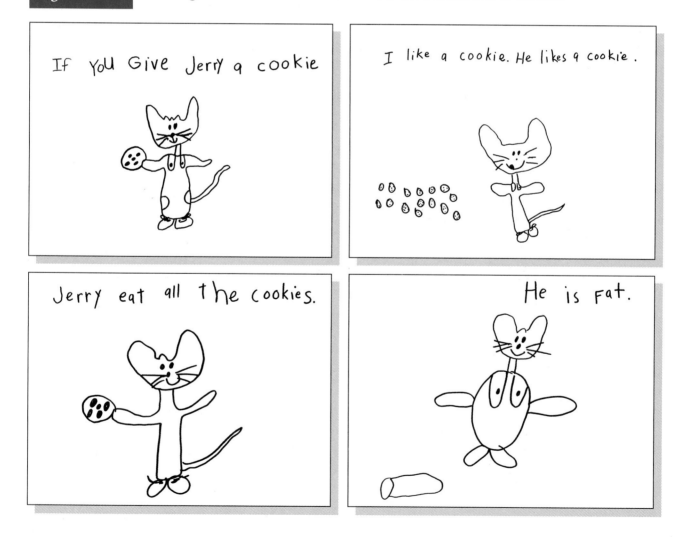

iar words correctly. They also learn to use the books they are reading to check the spelling of characters' names and other words from the story.

The Author's Chair. In primary-grade classrooms a special chair should be designated as the author's chair (Graves & Hansen, 1983). This chair might be a rocking chair, a lawn chair with a padded seat, a wooden stool, or a director's chair, and it should be labeled "Author's Chair." Children and the teacher sit in the chair to share books they have read and other books they have written, and this is the only time anyone sits in the chair.

When teachers sit in the chair to read books aloud to children, they name the author of the book and, if possible, tell a little something about the author. In this way, children gain an awareness of authors, the people who write books. Children also sit in the author's chair to share books and other compositions they have written. Sitting in the special author's chair helps children to gradually realize that they are authors. Graves and Hansen (1983) identify three stages in children's growing awareness of authors and of themselves as authors:

1. *Authors write books.* After hearing many books read to them and reading books themselves, children develop the concept that authors are the people who write books.
2. *I am an author.* Sharing the books they have written with classmates from the author's chair helps children view themselves as authors.
3. *If I wrote this published book now, I wouldn't write it this way.* Children learn that they have options when they write, and this awareness grows after experimenting with various writing functions, forms, and audiences.

When children share their writings, one child sits in the author's chair and a group of children sits on the floor or in chairs in front of the author's chair. The child sitting in the author's chair reads the book or other piece of writing aloud and shows the accompanying illustrations. Then children who want to make a comment raise their hands, and the author chooses several children to ask questions, give compliments, and make comments. Then the author chooses another child to share and takes a seat in the audience.

Review

Emergent literacy is the new way of looking at how children begin to read and write. Children's emergent literacy provides a foundation for their later literacy learning. Teachers foster young children's interest in written language through morning messages, literacy play centers, and mailboxes for exchanging messages. Literature focus units and reading workshop are used in kindergarten and the primary grades for reading instruction. Shared reading and language experience approach are ways to introduce young children to reading. As children emerge into writing they move from scribbling to using letters to represent their thoughts, and they refine their "kid" writing as they learn about phoneme-grapheme correspondences and spelling patterns. Effective teaching practices for working with emergent readers and writers are reviewed in the feature on page 156.

How Effective Teachers . . .

Work With Emergent Readers and Writers

✦ **Effective Practices**	✦ **Ineffective Practices**
1. Teachers provide developmentally appropriate reading and writing activities for children beginning on the first day of kindergarten.	1. Teachers provide readiness activities to prepare children for reading and writing instruction.
2. Teachers teach concepts about print through shared reading, language experience approach, and other instructional strategies.	2. Teachers rarely model reading and writing for children.
3. Teachers include literacy materials in play centers.	3. Teachers do not include materials for functional reading and writing activities in play centers.
4. Teachers use shared reading with big books.	4. Teachers only use small books.
5. Teachers provide opportunities for daily reading and writing experiences.	5. Teachers emphasize play and provide few opportunities for reading and writing.
6. Teachers adapt the writing process and emphasize the prewriting, drafting, and publishing steps.	6. Teachers rarely have children do writing and do not introduce the writing process.
7. Teachers introduce "kid" writing and encourage children to use invented spelling.	7. Teachers assume that children can't write because they can't write like adults.
8. Teachers set up a writing center, mailboxes, and an author's chair in their classrooms.	8. Teachers do not have a writing center in their classrooms.
9. Teachers use interactive writing to teach concepts about print, letters of the alphabet, high-frequency words, and other skills and strategies.	9. Teachers focus on teaching handwriting, not writing.
10. Teachers use predictable books and encourage children to use the pattern in order to read and write independently.	10. Teachers assume that children can't read independently, so they don't show them how to use the patterns in predictable books.

References

Ashton-Warner, S. (1965). *Teacher.* New York: Simon & Schuster.

Bridge, C. A. (1979). Predictable materials for beginning readers. *Language Arts, 56,* 503–507.

Button, K., Johnson, M. J., & Furgerson, P. (1996). Interactive writing in a primary classroom. *The Reading Teacher, 49,* 446–454.

Clay, M. M. (1967). The reading behaviour of five year old children. *New Zealand Journal of Educational Studies, 2,* 11–31.

Clay, M. M. (1975). *What did I write? Beginning writing behavior.* Portsmouth, NH: Heinemann.

Clay, M. M. (1989). Foreword. In D. S. Strickland & L. M. Morrow (Eds.)., *Emerging literacy: Young children learn to read and write.* Newark, DE: International Reading Association.

Clay, M. M. (1991). *Becoming literate: The construction of inner control.* Portsmouth, NH: Heinemann.

Clay, M. M. (1993). *An observational survey of early literacy achievement.* Portsmouth, NH: Heinemann.

Cohen, P., Kulik, J. A., & Kulik, C. (1982). Educational outcomes of tutoring: A meta-analysis of findings. *American Educational Research Journal, 19,* 237–248.

Collom, S. (Ed.). (1998). *Sharing the pen: Interactive writing with young children.* Fresno: California State University, Fresno, and the San Joaquin Valley Writing Project.

Downing, J. (1970). The development of linguistic concepts in children's thinking. *Research in the Teaching of English, 4,* 5–19.

Downing, J. (1971–1972). Children's developing concepts of spoken and written language. *Journal of Reading Behavior, 4,* 1–19.

Downing, J., & Oliver, P. (1973–1974). The child's conception of "a word." *Reading Research Quarterly, 9,* 568–582.

Durkin, D. (1966). *Children who read early.* New York: Teachers College Press.

Durrell, D. D. (1958). Success in first-grade reading. *Journal of Education, 140,* 1–48.

Dyson, A. H. (1984). "N spell my Grandmama": Fostering early thinking about print. *The Reading Teacher, 38,* 262–271.

Ferreiro, E., & Teberosky, A. (1982). *Literacy before schooling.* Portsmouth, NH: Heinemann.

Fountas, I. C., & Pinnell, G. S. (1996). *Guided reading: Good first teaching for all children.* Portsmouth, NH: Heinemann.

Graves, D. H., & Hansen, J. (1983). The author's chair. *Language Arts, 60,* 176–183.

Harste, J., Woodward, V., & Burke, C. (1984). *Language stories and literacy lessons.* Portsmouth, NH: Heinemann.

Heald-Taylor, G. (1987). How to use predictable books for K–2 language arts instruction. *The Reading Teacher, 40,* 656–661.

Heath, S. B. (1983). *Ways with words.* New York: Oxford University Press.

Hiebert, E. H. (1981). Developmental patterns and interrelationships of preschool children's print awareness. *Reading Research Quarterly, 16,* 236–260.

Holdaway, D. (1979). *The foundations of literacy.* Portsmouth, NH: Heinemann.

Hoskisson, K. (1975). The many facets of assisted reading. *Elementary English, 52,* 312–315.

Juel, C. (1991). Beginning reading. In R. Barr, M. L. Kamil, P. Mosenthal, & P. D. Pearson (Eds.), *Handbook of reading research* (Vol. 2, pp. 759–788). New York: Longman.

Kawakami-Arakaki, A., Oshiro, M., & Farran, S. (1989). Research to practice: Integrating reading and writing in a kindergarten curriculum. In J. Mason (Ed.), *Reading and writing connections* (pp. 199–218). Boston: Allyn & Bacon.

Labbo, L. D., & Teale, W. H. (1990). Cross-age reading: A strategy for helping poor readers. *The Reading Teacher, 43,* 362–369.

McCarrier, A., Pinnell, G. S., & Fountas, I. C. (2000). *Interactive writing: How language and literacy come together, K–2.* Portsmouth, NH: Heinemann.

McGee, L. M., & Richgels, D. J. (1989). "K is Kristen's": Learning the alphabet from a child's perspective. *The Reading Teacher, 43,* 216–225.

Morrice, C., & Simmons, M. (1991). Beyond reading buddies: A whole language cross-age program. *The Reading Teacher, 44,* 572–577.

Papandropoulou, I., & Sinclair, H. (1974). What is a word? Experimental study of children's ideas on grammar. *Human Development, 17,* 241–258.

Reutzel, D. R., & Fawson, P. C. (1990). Traveling tales: Connecting parents and children in writing. *The Reading Teacher, 44,* 222–227.

Schickedanz, J. A. (1990). *Adam's righting revolutions: One child's literacy development from infancy through grade one.* Portsmouth, NH: Heinemann.

Slaughter, J. P. (1983). Big books for little kids: Another fad or a new approach for teaching beginning reading? *The Reading Teacher, 36,* 758–762.

Slaughter, J. P. (1993). *Beyond storybooks: Young children and the shared book experience.* Newark, DE: International Reading Association.

Stauffer, R. G. (1970). *The language experience approach to the teaching of reading.* New York: Harper & Row.

Sulzby, E. (1985). Kindergartners as readers and writers. In M. Farr (Ed.), *Advances in writing research. Vol. 1: Children's early writing development* (pp. 127–199). Norwood, NJ: Ablex.

Taylor, D. (1983). *Family literacy: Young children learning to read and write.* Exeter, NH: Heinemann.

Taylor, D., & Dorsey-Gaines, C. (1987). *Growing up literate: Learning from inner-city families.* Portsmouth, NH: Heinemann.

Teale, W. H. (1982). Toward a theory of how children learn to read and write. *Language Arts, 59,* 555–570.

Teale, W. H., & Sulzby, E. (1989). Emerging literacy: New perspectives. In D. S. Strickland & L. M. Morrow (Eds.), *Emerging literacy: Young children learn to read and write* (pp. 1–15). Newark, DE: International Reading Association.

Temple, C., Nathan, R., Burris, N., & Temple, F. (1988). *The beginnings of writing.* Boston: Allyn & Bacon.

Templeton, S. (1980). Young children invent words: Developing concepts of "word-ness." *The Reading Teacher, 33,* 454–459.

Tompkins, G. E., & Webeler, M. (1983). What will happen next? Using predictable books with young children. *The Reading Teacher, 36,* 498–502.

Trachtenburg, R., & Ferruggia, A. (1989). Big books from little voices: Reaching high risk beginning readers. *The Reading Teacher, 42,* 284–289.

Walsh, D. J., Price, G. G., & Gillingham, M. G. (1988). The critical but transitory importance of letter naming. *Reading Research Quarterly, 23,* 108–122.

Children's Book References

Brett, J. (1987). *Goldilocks and the three bears*. New York: Sandcastle.

Bridwell, N. (1963). *Clifford the big red dog*. New York: Four Winds Press.

Carle, E. (1969). *The very hungry caterpillar*. Cleveland: Collins-World.

Cauley, L. B. (1981). *Goldilocks and the three bears*. New York: Putnam.

Eastman, P. D. (1960). *Are you my mother?* New York: Random House.

Fox, M. (1986). *Hattie and the fox*. New York: Bradbury Press.

Galdone, P. (1972). *The three bears*. Boston: Houghton Mifflin.

Galdone, P. (1973). *The little red hen*. New York: Seabury.

Galdone, P. (1975). *The gingerbread boy*. New York: Seabury.

Gill, S. (1990). *Alaska's three bears*. Homer, AK: Paws IV.

Hutchins, P. (1968). *Rosie's walk*. New York: Macmillan.

Martin, B., Jr. (1991). *Polar bear, polar bear, what do you hear?* New York: Henry Holt.

Mayer, M. (1992). *Just Grandma and me*. Novato, CA: Broderbund.

McKissack, P. C. (1986). *Flossie and the fox*. New York: Dial.

Most, B. (1978). *If the dinosaurs came back*. San Diego: Harcourt Brace.

Numeroff, L. J. (1985). *If you give a mouse a cookie*. New York: Harper & Row.

Prelutsky, J. (1984). *The new kid on the block*. New York: Greenwillow.

Seuss, Dr. (1963). *Hop on pop*. New York: Random House.

Turkle, B. (1976). *Deep in the forest*. New York: Dutton.

Chapter 5

Breaking the Alphabetic Code

— Chapter Questions —

What is phonemic awareness?

Why do children need to be phonemically aware in order to learn phonics?

Which phonics concepts are most important for children to learn?

How do teachers teach phonics?

How do children learn to spell?

Mrs. Hoddy Teaches Phonics With Literature

The first graders in Mrs. Hoddy's classroom are involved in an author study on Eric Carle. They are reading many of the books Carle has written and illustrated, including *The Very Hungry Caterpillar* (1969), *The Very Busy Spider* (1984), *The Very Quiet Cricket* (1990), and *The Very Lonely Firefly* (1995). Mrs. Hoddy has a class set of *The Very Hungry Caterpillar* and several copies of each of the other books that she places on a special shelf in the classroom library for students to read and reread. She also has audiotapes of the books that she uses in the listening center.

For each book, Mrs. Hoddy begins by reading the book aloud to the students, and then students talk about the book, sharing their impressions and reactions. They make comparisons among the Eric Carle books they've read, pointing out the repetitive patterns, the themes, and Carle's unique illustration techniques. Students have watched *Eric Carle: Picture Writer* (Carle, 1993), a videotape of the author-illustrator demonstrating his illustration techniques, and they are creating their own books with bright tissue paper collage illustrations using the same illustration techniques that Eric Carle does.

Students read and reread books in small groups, at the listening center, with buddies, and independently. They add important vocabulary words from each story to the **word wall** (see the Compendium for more information about this and all other highlighted terms in this chapter) and participate in word-identification activities. Mrs. Hoddy reviews the letter-writing form, and students write letters to Eric Carle, telling him which of his books they like the best and about the books they are making with tissue paper collage illustrations.

Mrs. Hoddy teaches **minilessons** on phonics regularly during the author unit on Eric Carle. She uses a whole-part-whole approach. She begins by sharing the book with students, giving them opportunities to read and respond to the book—the "whole." Then she focuses on skills and teaches minilessons on phonics using words from the story, and students practice the skills at the phonics center. The minilessons and practice activities are the "part." Afterwards, students apply the skills they are learning through reading and writing activities—the "whole" again. During this unit, students will continue reading Carle's books and write their own books.

After reading *The Very Hungry Caterpillar*, Carle's story about a caterpillar that eats through a large quantity of food before spinning a chrysalis, Mrs. Hoddy uses this book to teach a series of phonics minilessons. In one lesson with the whole class she reviews the days of the week and focuses on the *-ay* rime using the days of the week and the words *bay, may, say, pay, ray, way, day, lay, play,* and *stay*. She begins by pointing out the days of the week on the calendar and reviewing with students what foods the caterpillar in the story ate each day. She writes the days of the week on the chalkboard and asks students to pronounce the words and note that they all rhyme. Then she asks one child to come to the chalkboard and circle the rime *-ay*. Next, she writes *say, may, play*, and several other

-*ay* words on the chalkboard for children to decode. Then she distributes a small magic slate to each child, and students each write their favorite day of the week at the top of their slates and circle the -*ay* rime. Then students take turns suggesting rhyming words to write on their slates. Mrs. Hoddy walks around the classroom, checking to see that students are sounding out the beginning sound and adding the rime correctly. For the last two minutes of the minilesson, she reviews the -*ill* rime that she taught last week, and students write *bill, still, will, mill, kill, gill, hill,* and *pill* on their magic slates.

Mrs. Hoddy alternates teaching minilessons to the whole class with teaching minilessons to small groups of students. She introduces new concepts, skills, and generalizations to the whole class and then reinforces, reviews, and extends the lessons with small groups. These groups change often, and students are grouped together according to their need to learn a specific skill.

One group of five students, for example, is still developing phonemic awareness—the ability to orally segment spoken words. Mrs. Hoddy meets with this group to orally segment words from the story, including *egg, moon, leaf, sun, food, pie, cheese, cupcake,* and *night.* When Mrs. Hoddy meets with the group, she brings along a copy of *The Very Hungry Caterpillar* and says to the group, "Let's find some interesting words in this book to break into sounds. How about *egg?*" The children respond, "e-g." Students break the words into sounds and say the sounds together as a group, and then children take turns segmenting the words individually.

Another group of ten students reviews these six beginning sounds—/b/, /f/, /h/, /l/, /p/, and /s/—using words from the story. Mrs. Hoddy sets out six plastic baskets with a beginning sound written on the front of each basket. Then she shows students these objects and pictures—a butterfly puppet, the number 4 cut out of cardboard, a photo of a house, a lollipop, a jar of pickles, and a drawing of the sun—and students place each object in front of the appropriate basket. Then Mrs. Hoddy reads these words, which she has written on word cards:

b:	butterfly, better, beautiful, big
f:	five, four, fat, food
h:	house, hole, hungry, he
l:	light, lay, little, leaf, lollipop, look
p:	pushed, pop, pickle, piece, pears
s:	Sunday, Saturday, sun, salami, sausage

Students identify the beginning sound and place the cards in the appropriate basket. Afterwards, students add pictures on the back of each word card. Then they think of other words beginning with each sound and draw pictures representing the words on cards. They write the word on the back of the card and add these cards to the appropriate baskets. Later Mrs. Hoddy will place these materials in the phonics center.

Mrs. Hoddy passes out copies of *The Very Hungry Caterpillar* to another group of students, who look through the book to find examples of CVCe words (one-syllable words with a long vowel sound and ending with an *e*). Students locate these words and write them on cards that they place in the pocket chart:

came, ate, cake, ice, cone, slice, pie, ache, hole. They also locate several words (e.g., *one, more*) that are exceptions to the rule. Mrs. Hoddy explains that *one* is a sight word and that the *r* in *more* overpowers the *o* and changes the sound, just like the *r* in *car* (a familiar word) is stronger than the *a*. The students reread the words several times, and all but two students are able to read the cards easily. Mrs. Hoddy excuses the rest of the group and continues to work with the remaining two children for several more minutes. She gives them magic slates and asks them to draw three lines and write an *e:* ___ ___ ___ e. Then she dictates *came* for the two children to write. They carefully sound out the word and spell it correctly. Then Mrs. Hoddy repeats the process with *hole* and *cone*. She makes a note to give these students more practice later the next day with these CVCe words.

With another group of six students, Mrs. Hoddy uses a set of word cards with the words *caterpillar, little, morning, sun, ate, plum, Thursday, strawberries, chocolate, pickle, lollipop, cupcake, watermelon, stomachache, green, leaf, big, butterfly*, and *beautiful*. As she shows the cards, students read the words. Then she has them read the words a second time and break the words into syllables. Children clap as they say each syllable: *cat-er-pill-ar*. After students take turns saying each word, syllable by syllable, Mrs. Hoddy guides the students as they sort the word cards into four piles: one-syllable words, two-syllable words, three-syllable words, and four-syllable words. Then Mrs. Hoddy explains that these cards will be placed in the phonics center for children to practice sorting by the number of syllables in the word.

Several days later, Mrs. Hoddy teaches the entire class a minilesson on **making words.** She divides the class into groups of three and passes out packs of letter cards that together spell *caterpillar*. First, students arrange the letter cards to spell the words *cat, pat*, and *rat*. Then they spell *it, pit*, and *lit*. Next, *cap, lap, tap*, and *trap*. Then, *car, are, art, part*, and *cart*. Children volunteer some other words they can make: *eat, late, ape*, and *tape*. Finally, Mrs. Hoddy asks students to guess the big word that the letters spell all together. They know it is a word on the word wall. Quickly, Jonas guesses that the word is *caterpillar* and all the children arrange the letters to spell the word. The next day, Mrs. Hoddy will repeat this activity in small groups, and she will take notes about the words that students in each group can make. Then she will put the materials in the spelling center.

There are many phonics skills that Mrs. Hoddy could have chosen to teach through *The Very Hungry Caterpillar*. She could focus on one consonant sound—the /v/ in *very*, the /h/ in *hungry*, the /k/ in *caterpillar*, or the /b/ in *beautiful butterfly*, for example. Or she could have used the words *green leaf* from the story to focus on two vowel patterns used to spell long *e*. In order to show students how phonics can help them when they read, Mrs. Hoddy uses words from the book they are reading for minilessons, whenever possible.

Mrs. Hoddy knows which phonics concepts, rules, and skills her first graders need to learn, and she develops minilessons and other activities using words drawn from the books she is reading during literature focus units. Together with the other first-grade teachers at her school, Mrs. Hoddy has developed a checklist of phonics skills that she is responsible for teaching. A copy of the checklist is shown in Figure

First-grade phonics checklist

Phonemic Awareness

____ segmenting ____ blending ____ rhyming

Consonants

____ b	____ f	____ j	____ m	____ qu	____ t
____ c (k)	____ g	____ k	____ n	____ r	____ v
____ d	____ h	____ l	____ p	____ s	____ w

Blends	**Digraphs**	**Rimes**
____ bl	____ ch	____ at
____ dr	____ sh	____ ill
____ fl	____ th	____ op
____ st	____ wh	____ ate
____ tr		____ ike
		____ ay

Short Vowels	**Long Vowels**	**Rules**
____ a (fan)	____ a (came, pail)	____ CVC
____ e (web)	____ e (be, feet, eat)	____ CVCe
____ i (sit)	____ i (ice, bite)	____ *r*-controlled
____ o (not)	____ o (go, soap)	____ syllables
____ u (cup)	____ u (mule)	

5–1. The skills on this checklist include phonemic awareness, consonants, consonant blends and digraphs, rimes, short and long vowels, and vowel rules. Mrs. Hoddy chooses topics for minilessons from this checklist, and she uses one copy of the checklist to keep track of the skills she has introduced, practiced, and reviewed. She also makes copies of the checklist for each student and uses the checklists to document which skills children have learned. She uses the information on these checklists in putting together small groups for minilessons and related activities.

The alphabetic principle suggests a one-to-one correspondence between phonemes (or sounds) and graphemes (or letters), such that each letter consistently represents one sound. English, however, is not a purely phonetic language. The 26 letters represent approximately 44 phonemes, and three letters—*c, q,* and *x*—are superfluous because they do not represent unique phonemes. The letter *c,* for example, can represent either /k/ as in *cat* or /s/ as in *city,* and it can be joined with *h* for the digraph /ch/. To further complicate the situation, there are more than 500 spellings to represent the 44 phonemes. Consonants are more consistent and predictable than vowels. Long *e,* for instance, is spelled 14 different ways in common words! Consider, for example, *me, seat, feet, people, yield, baby,* and *cookie.* How a word is spelled depends on several factors, including the location of the sound in the word and whether or not the word entered English from another language (Horn, 1957).

Researchers estimate that words are spelled phonetically approximately half the time (Hanna, Hanna, Hodges, & Rudorf, 1966), and the nonphonetic spelling of many words reflects morphological information. The word *sign,* for instance, is a shortened form of *signature,* and the spelling shows this relationship. Spelling the word phonetically (i.e., *sine*) might seem simpler, but the phonetic spelling lacks semantic information (Venezky, 1999).

Other reasons for this mismatch between phonemes, graphemes, and spellings can be found by examining events in the history of the English language (Tompkins & Yaden, 1986). The introduction of the printing press in England in 1476 helped to stabilize spelling. The word *said,* for example, continues to be spelled as it was pronounced in Shakespeare's time. Our pronunciation does not reflect the word's meaning as the past tense of *say* because pronunciations have continued to evolve in the last 500 years but few spellings have been "modernized." In addition, 75% of English words have been borrowed from other languages around the world, and many words—especially those acquired more recently—have retained their native spellings. For example, *souvenir* was borrowed from French in the middle 1700s and retains its French spelling. Its literal meaning is "to remember."

The English spelling system can't be explained by the alphabetic principle alone because it is not merely a reflection of phoneme-grapheme correspondences. Our spelling system includes morphological, semantic, and syntactic elements, and it has been influenced by historical events.

PHONEMIC AWARENESS

Phonemic awareness is children's basic understanding that speech is composed of a series of individual sounds, and it provides the foundation for "breaking the code" (Yopp, 1992). When children can choose a duck as the animal whose name begins with /d/ from a collection of toy animals, identify *duck* and *luck* as rhyming words in a song, or blend the sounds /d/, /u/, and /k/ to pronounce *duck,* they are phonemically aware. (Note that the emphasis is on the sounds of spoken words, not reading letters or pronouncing letter names.) Developing phonemic awareness enables children to use sound-symbol correspondences to read and spell words. Phonemic awareness is not sounding out words for reading, nor is it using spelling patterns to write words; rather, it is the foundation for phonics.

www.sil.org

Lingualinks Library. Read about how to develop young children's phonemic awareness concepts.

Phonemes are the smallest units of speech, and they are written as graphemes, or letters of the alphabet. In this book, phonemes are marked using diagonal lines (e.g., /d/) and graphemes are italicized (e.g., *d*). Sometimes phonemes (e.g., /k/ in *duck*) are spelled with two graphemes (*ck*).

Understanding that words are composed of smaller units—phonemes—is a significant achievement for young children because phonemes are abstract language units. Phonemes carry no meaning, and children think of words according to their meanings, not their linguistic characteristics (F. Griffith & Olson, 1992). When children think about ducks, for example, they think of feathered animals that swim in ponds, fly through the air, and make noises we describe as "quacks." They don't think of "duck" as a word with three phonemes or four graphemes, as a word beginning with /d/ and rhyming with *luck*. Phonemic awareness requires that children treat speech as an object and that they shift their attention away from the meaning of words to the linguistic features of speech. This focus on phonemes is even more complicated because phonemes are not discrete units in speech. Often they are slurred or clipped in speech. Think about the blended initial sound in *tree* and the ending sound in *eating*.

Components of Phonemic Awareness

Students who have developed phonemic awareness can manipulate spoken language in these five ways:

❦ match words with sounds

❦ isolate a sound in a word

❦ blend individual sounds to form a word

❦ substitute sounds in a word

❦ segment a word into its constituent sounds (Yopp, 1992)

www.teams.lacoe.edu

Patti's Electronic Classroom.
Levels of phonemic awareness are discussed in the kindergarten and grade 1 classroom.

www.ertp.santacruz.
k12.ca.us

Phonemic Awareness Instruction.
Sample activities for teaching sound blending, sound segmentation, and other components.

Children develop these components of phonemic awareness in two ways. First, they learn through a language-rich environment as they sing songs, play with words, chant rhymes, and listen to parents and teachers read wordplay books to them (F. Griffith & Olson, 1992). Yopp (1995) recommends that teachers read books with wordplay aloud and encourage students to talk about the way the author manipulated words. Teachers make comments, such as "Did you notice how ——— and ——— rhyme?" and "This book is fun because of all the words beginning with the /m/ sound." Once students are very familiar with the book, they can create new verses or make other variations. Books such as *Cock-a-doodle-moo!* (Most, 1996) and *The Baby Uggs Are Hatching* (Prelutsky, 1982) stimulate children to experiment with sounds and create nonsense words. Teachers help children attend to the smaller units of language when they read books with alliterative or assonant patterns, such as *Faint Frogs Feeling Feverish and Other Terrifically Tantalizing Tongue Twisters* (Obligado, 1983). A list of wordplay books for young children is shown in Figure 5–2.

Second, teachers teach **minilessons** and play games such as "I Spy" to help students understand that their speech is composed of sounds (Ball & Blachman, 1991; Hohn & Ehri, 1982; Lundberg, Frost, & Peterson, 1988). The goal of phonemic awareness activities is for children to learn how to break down and manipulate spoken words.

Teachers teach minilessons focusing on each of these strategies using familiar songs with improvised lyrics, riddles and guessing games, and wordplay books. These activities should be playful and gamelike, and they should be connected to literature focus units and thematic units whenever possible. Five types of activities are sound matching, sound isolation, sound blending, sound addition and substitution, and segmentation.

Sound Matching Activities. In sound matching, children choose one of several words beginning with a particular sound or say a word that begins with a particular sound (Yopp, 1992). For these games, teachers use familiar objects (e.g., feather, toothbrush, book) and toys (e.g., small plastic animals, toy trucks, artificial fruits and vegetables), as well as pictures of familiar objects.

Teachers can play a sound-matching guessing game (Lewkowicz, 1994). For this game, teachers collect two boxes and pairs of objects to place in the boxes (e.g., forks, mittens, erasers, combs, and books). One item from each pair is placed in each box. After the teacher shows students the objects in the boxes and they name them together, two children play the game. One child selects an object, holds it, and pronounces the initial (or medial or final) sound. The second child chooses the same object from the second box and holds it up. Children check to see if the two players are holding the same object.

| *Figure 5–2* | Wordplay books to enhance children's phonemic awareness |

Ahlberg, J., & Ahlberg, A. (1978). *Each peach pear plum.* New York: Scholastic.

Cameron, P. (1961). *"I can't," said the ant.* New York: Coward McCann.

Degan, B. (1983). *Jamberry.* New York: Harper & Row.

Deming, A. G. (1994). *Who is tapping at my window?* New York: Penguin.

Ehlert, L. (1989). *Eating the alphabet: Fruits and vegetables from A to Z.* San Diego: Harcourt Brace Jovanovich.

Galdone, P. (1968). *Henny Penny.* New York: Scholastic.

Hague, K. (1984). *Alphabears.* New York: Henry Holt.

Hoberman, M. A. (1982). *A house is a house for me.* New York: Penguin.

Hutchins, P. (1976). *Don't forget the bacon!* New York: Mulberry Books.

Kuskin, K. (1990). *Roar and more.* New York: Harper & Row.

Lewiston, W. (1992). *"Buzz," said the bee.* New York: Scholastic.

Martin, B., Jr., & Archambault, J. (1987). *Chicka chicka boom boom.* New York: Simon & Schuster.

Most, B. (1991). *A dinosaur named after me.* San Diego: Harcourt Brace Jovanovich.

Most, B. (1996). *Cock-a-doodle-moo!* San Diego: Harcourt Brace.

Obligado, L. (1983). *Faint frogs feeling feverish and other terrifically tantalizing tongue twisters.* New York: Puffin.

Prelutsky, J. (1982). *The baby uggs are hatching.* New York: Mulberry.

Prelutsky, J. (1989). *Poems of A. Nonny Mouse.* New York: Knopf. (See also the second volume in the series.)

Raffi. (1987). *Down by the bay.* New York: Crown.

Sendak, M. (1990). *Alligators all around: An alphabet.* New York: Harper & Row.

Seuss, Dr. (1963). *Hop on pop.* New York: Random House. (See also other books by the author.)

Shaw, N. (1986). *Sheep in a jeep.* Boston: Houghton Mifflin. (See also other books in this series.)

Showers, P. (1991). *The listening walk.* New York: Harper & Row.

Slate, J. (1996). *Miss Bindergarten gets ready for kindergarten.* New York: Dutton.

Slepian, J., & Seidler, A. (1967). *The hungry thing.* New York: Scholastic.

Sweet, M. (1992). *Fiddle-I-fee: A farmyard song for the very young.* Boston: Little, Brown.

Tallon, R. (1979). *Zoophabets.* New York: Scholastic.

Westcott, N. B. (1988). *Down by the bay.* New York: Crown.

Winthrop, E. (1986). *Shoes.* New York: Harper & Row.

Zemach, M. (1976). *Hush, little baby.* New York: Dutton.

Children also identify rhyming words as part of sound-matching activities. Students name a word that rhymes with a given word and identify rhyming words from familiar songs and stories. As children listen to parents and teachers read Dr. Seuss books such as *Hop on Pop* (1963) and other wordplay books, students refine their understanding of rhyme.

Sound Isolation Activities. Teachers say a word and then children identify the sounds at the beginning, middle, or end of the word, or teachers and children isolate sounds as they sing familiar songs. Yopp (1992) created new verses to the tune of "Old MacDonald Had a Farm":

What's the sound that starts these words:
Chicken, chin and cheek?
(wait for response)
/ch/ is the sound that starts these words:
Chicken, chin, and cheek.
With a /ch/, /ch/ here, and a /ch/, /ch/ there,
Here a /ch/, there a /ch/, everywhere a /ch/, /ch/.
/ch/ is the sound that starts these words:
Chicken, chin, and cheek. (p. 700)

Teachers change the question at the beginning of the verse to focus on medial and final sounds. For example:

> What's the sound in the middle of these words?
> Whale, game, and rain. (p. 700)

And for final sounds:

> What's the sound at the end of these words?
> Leaf, cough, and beef. (p. 700)

Teachers also set out trays of objects and ask students to choose the one object that doesn't belong because it doesn't begin with the sound. For example, from a tray with a toy pig, a puppet, a teddy bear, and a pen, the teddy bear doesn't belong.

Sound Blending Activities. Children blend sounds together in order to combine them to form a word. For example, children blend the sounds /d/, /u/, and /k/ to form the word *duck*. Teachers play the "What am I thinking of?" guessing game with children by identifying several characteristics of the item and then saying the name of the item, articulating each of the sounds slowly and separately (Yopp, 1992). Then children blend the sounds together and identify the word, using the phonological and semantic information that the teacher provided. For example:

> I'm thinking of a small animal that lives in the pond when it is young. When it is an adult, it lives on land and it is called a /f/, /r/, /ŏ/, /g/. What is it?

The children blend the sounds together to pronounce the word *frog*. In this example, the teacher connects the game with a thematic unit, thereby making the game more meaningful for students.

Sound Addition and Substitution Activities. Students play with words and create nonsense words as they add or substitute sounds in words in songs they sing or in books that are read aloud to them. Teachers read wordplay books such as Pat Hutchins's *Don't Forget the Bacon!* (1976), in which a boy leaves for the store with a mental list of four items to buy. As he walks, he repeats his list, substituting words each time. "A cake for tea" changes to "a cape for me" and then to "a rake for leaves." Children suggest other substitutions, such as "a game for a bee."

Students substitute sounds in refrains of songs (Yopp, 1992). For example, students can change the "Ee-igh, ee-igh, oh!" refrain in "Old MacDonald Had a Farm" to "Bee-bigh, bee-bigh, boh!" to focus on the initial /b/ sound. Teachers can choose one sound, such as /sh/, and have children substitute this sound for the beginning sound in their names and in words for items in the classroom. For example, *Jimmy* becomes *Shimmy, José* becomes *Shosé,* and *clock* becomes *shock.*

Segmentation Activities. One of the more difficult phonemic awareness activities is segmentation, in which children isolate the sounds in a spoken word (Yopp, 1988). An introductory segmentation activity is to draw out the beginning sound in words. Children enjoy exaggerating the initial sound in their own names and other familiar words. For example, a pet guinea pig named Popsicle lives in Mrs. Hoddy's classroom, and the children exaggerate the beginning sound of her name so that it is pronounced as "P-P-P-Popsicle." Children can also pick up objects or pictures of objects and identify the initial sound. A child who picks up a toy tiger says, "This is a tiger and it starts with /t/."

From that beginning, children move to identifying all the sounds in a word. Using a toy tiger again, the child would say, "This is a tiger, /t/, /i/, /g/, /er/."

Yopp (1992) suggests singing a song to the tune of "Twinkle, Twinkle, Little Star" in which children segment entire words. Here is one example:

Listen, listen
To my word
Then tell me all the sounds you heard: coat
(slowly)
/k/ is one sound
/ō/ is two
/t/ is last in coat
It's true. (p. 702)

After several repetitions of the verse segmenting other words, the song ends this way:

Thanks for listening
To my words
And telling all the sounds you heard! (p. 702)

Teachers also use Elkonin boxes to teach students to segment words. This activity comes from the work of Russian psychologist D. B. Elkonin (Clay, 1985). As shown in Figure 5–3, the teacher shows an object or picture of an object and draws a series of boxes, with one box for each sound in the name of the object or picture. Then the teacher or a child moves a marker into each box as the sound is pronounced. Children can move small markers onto cards on their desks, or the teacher can draw the boxes on the chalkboard and use tape or small magnets to hold the larger markers in place. Elkonin boxes can also be used for spelling activities. When a child is trying to spell a word, such as *duck,* the teacher can draw three boxes, do the segmentation activity, and then have the child write the letters representing each sound in the boxes. Spelling boxes for *duck* and other words with two, three, or four sounds are also shown in Figure 5–3.

In these activities, students are experimenting with oral language. They do not usually read or write letters and words during phonemic awareness activities, because the focus is on speech. However, once children begin reading and writing, these activities reinforce the segmentation and blending activities they have learned. The phonemic awareness activities stimulate children's interest in language and provide valuable experiences with books and words. Effective teachers recognize the importance of building this foundation before children begin reading and writing. Guidelines for phonemic awareness activities are reviewed in Figure 5–4.

Why is Phonemic Awareness Important?

The relationship between phonemic awareness and learning to read is extremely important, and researchers have concluded that at least some level of phonemic awareness is a prerequisite for learning to read (Tunmer & Nesdale, 1985; Yopp, 1985). In fact, phonemic awareness seems to be both a prerequisite for and a consequence of learning to read (Liberman, Shankweiler, Fischer, & Carter, 1974; Perfitti, Beck, Bell, & Hughes, 1987; Stanovich, 1980). As they become phonemically aware, children recognize that speech can be segmented into smaller units, and this knowledge is very useful when children learn about sound-symbol correspondences and spelling patterns.

Researchers have concluded that children can be explicitly taught to segment and manipulate speech, and children who receive training in phonemic awareness do better in both reading and spelling (P. L. Griffith, 1991; Juel, Griffith, & Gough, 1986).

www.reading.org

Phonemic Awareness and the Teaching of Reading.
The International Reading Association's position paper on the importance of phonemic awareness.

Figure 5-3 How to use Elkonin boxes for segmentation activities

1. The teacher shows students an object or the picture of an object, such as a duck, a bed, a game, a bee, a cup, or a cat.

2. The teacher prepares a diagram with a series of boxes, corresponding to the number of sounds heard in the name of the object. For example, the teacher draws three boxes side by side to represent the three sounds heard in the word *duck*. The teacher can draw the boxes on the chalkboard or on small cards for each child to use. The teacher also prepares markers to place on the boxes.

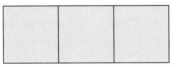

3. The teacher or students say the word slowly and move markers onto the boxes as each sound is pronounced.

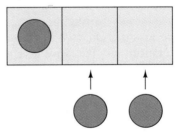

4. Elkonin boxes can also be used when spelling words. The teacher draws a series of boxes corresponding to the number of sounds heard in the word, and then the child and teacher pronounce the word, pointing to each box or sliding markers into each box. Then the child writes the letters representing each sound or spelling pattern in the boxes.

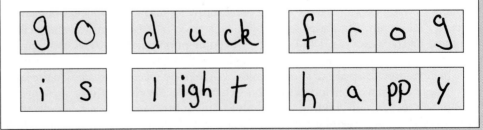

Figure 5–4 Guidelines for phonemic awareness activities
Adapted from Griffith and Olson, 1992; and Yopp, 1992.

1. Use Oral Activities

Phonemic awareness activities are oral activities. Objects and pictures are used instead of word cards, and children usually do not read or write letters and words during these activities. However, after children learn to identify the letters of the alphabet, reading and writing can be added.

2. Emphasize Experimentation

These language activities are intended to be fun, and teachers avoid drills and rote memorization activities. Children experiment with language as they sing songs, play word games, notice rhyming words, and create new words.

3. Plan Group Activities

Children do activities in a group, since language is a social activity. Teachers can read wordplay books and sing wordplay songs with the whole class, but for other activities teachers usually work with small groups.

4. Read Wordplay Books

Teachers read and reread wordplay books and encourage students to experiment with rhyming words, alliteration, and other wordplay.

5. Teach Minilessons

Teachers teach explicit minilessons on segmenting, blending, and rhyming sounds in words. These lessons are a regular part of literature focus units. Teachers also teach phonemic awareness incidentally as children play with words and recite poems.

6. Connect to Reading and Writing

Phonemic awareness activities must be incorporated into the context of authentic reading and writing activities. After children gain some understanding of phonemes, the activities can be connected to big books children are reading and to the invented spelling that children use as they write in journals and make books.

7. Allow for Individual Differences

Teachers recognize that children develop phonemic awareness at different rates and therefore allow for individual differences. Some children will catch on to the concept of phonemes right away, while others may not understand the activities for a while.

Phonemic awareness can also be nurtured in spontaneous ways by providing children with language-rich environments and emphasizing wordplay as teachers read books aloud to children and engage them in singing songs, chanting poems, and telling riddles.

Moreover, phonemic awareness has been shown to be the most powerful predictor of later reading achievement (Juel et al., 1986; Lomax & McGee, 1987; Tunmer & Nesdale, 1985). In a study comparing children's progress in learning to read in whole-language and traditional reading instruction, Klesius, Griffith, and Zielonka (1991) found that children who began first grade with strong phonemic awareness did well regardless of the kind of reading instruction they received. And neither type of instruction was better for children who were low in phonemic awareness at the beginning of first grade.

PHONICS

www.cdipage.com

*Phonics.
Learn about the
history of phonics instruction,
the debate about teaching
phonics, and research in
support of phonics
instruction.*

Phonics is the set of relationships between phonology (the sounds in speech) and orthography (the spelling patterns of written language). The emphasis is on spelling patterns, not individual letters, because there is not a one-to-one correspondence between phonemes and graphemes in English. Sounds are spelled in different ways. There are several reasons for this variety. One reason is that the sounds, especially vowels, vary according to their location in a word (e.g., *go–got*). Adjacent letters often influence how letters are pronounced (e.g., *bed–bead*), as do vowel markers such as the final *e* (e.g., *bit–bite*) (Shefelbine, 1995).

Language origin, or etymology, of words also influences their pronunciation. For example, the *ch* digraph is pronounced in several ways. The three most common are /ch/ as in *chain* (English), /sh/ as in *chauffeur* (French), and /k/ as in *chaos* (Greek). Neither the location of the digraph within the word nor adjacent letters account for these pronunciation differences. In all three words the *ch* digraph is at the beginning of the word and is followed by two vowels, the first of which is *a*. Some letters in words are not pronounced, either. In words such as *write*, the *w* is no longer pronounced, even though it probably was at one time. The same is true in *knight, know,* and *knee.* "Silent" letters in words such as *sign* and *bomb* reflect their parent words *signature* and *bombard* and have been retained for semantic, not phonological, reasons (Venezky, 1999).

Phonics Concepts, Skills, and Generalizations

Teachers teach sound-symbol correspondences, how to blend sounds together to decode words and segment sounds for spelling, and the most useful phonics generalizations or "rules." There is no simple way to explain all of the types of phonics information that students need to learn. Nor can they be listed in a clean, sequential order, since they are built on children's foundation of phonemic awareness. But the most important are letters of the alphabet, consonants, vowels, blending, rimes and rhymes, and phonics generalizations. Most of these concepts are taught in the primary grades, but students continue to refine their knowledge of the phonological system during the middle grades.

Letters of the Alphabet. Children learn many things about the alphabet as preschoolers and during the kindergarten year (McGee & Richgels, 1989). They learn to name the letters, notice letter features, and form upper- and lowercase letters in handwriting. At first they notice letters in environmental print, such as letters spelling the name of a familiar store or restaurant, and the letters in their own name. Kindergarten teachers help students focus on the letters in classmates' names, in familiar words, and in literature. For example, teachers might point out that two students in the class, Jesse and John, have names beginning with *J,* or that Miki's name starts like Max's in *Where the Wild Things Are* (Sendak, 1963).

One of the most useful ways to teach the alphabet is by singing the alphabet song. Once children know the song, they can use it as a strategy to figure out the

Kindergartners sing a song about the letters of the alphabet and stand up when the letter that begins their name is sung.

names of unfamiliar letters. They locate the unfamiliar letter on an alphabet chart and then sing the song, pointing to each letter until they reach the unfamiliar letter. Learning and using this strategy gives young children a great deal of independence in using written language. They also use their knowledge of letter names as they invent spellings. As young children attempt to write "I love you," for example, they may spell it *I lv u*, with or without spaces between words. They recognize the letter *I* and write it for the word *I*. As they pronounce *love*, they focus on the initial consonant, *l*, or the two consonants *l* and *v*, which they can figure out by matching the sounds to the letter names as they say these letters. The last word, *you*, is easy to represent because they hear the name of the letter *u* clearly.

The concept that words are composed of letters and that these letters have names is abstract, but through many meaningful experiences with written language, young children learn about the letters and that letters are used in words that they read and write. (For more information on teaching the letters of the alphabet, see Chapter 4, "Working With Emergent Readers and Writers.")

Consonants. Phonemes are classified as either consonants or vowels. The consonants are *b, c, d, f, g, h, j, k, l, m, n, p, q, r, s, t, v, w, x, y,* and *z*. Most consonants represent a single sound consistently, but there are some exceptions. *C*, for example, does not represent a sound of its own. When it is followed by *a, o,* or *u* it is pronounced /k/ (e.g., *castle, coffee, cut*), and when it is followed by *e, i,* or *y* it is pronounced /s/ (e.g., *cell, city, cycle*). *G* represents two sounds, as the word *garage* illustrates. It is usually pronounced /g/ (e.g., *glass, go, green, guppy*), but when *g* is followed by *e, i,* or *y* it is pronounced /j/, as in *giant*. *X* is also pronounced differently according to its location in a word. At the beginning of a word it is often pronounced /z/, as in *xylo-*

phone, but sometimes the letter name is used, as in *X-ray.* At the end of a word, *x* is pronounced /ks/, as in *box.*

The letters *w* and *y* are particularly interesting. At the beginning of a word or a syllable they are consonants (e.g., *wind, yard*), but when they are in the middle or at the end they are vowels (e.g., *saw, flown, day, by*).

Two kinds of combination consonants are blends and digraphs. Consonant blends occur when two or three consonants appear next to each other in words and their individual sounds are "blended" together, as in *grass, belt,* and *spring.* Consonant digraphs are letter combinations for single sounds that are not represented by either letter. The four most common are *ch* as in *chair* and *each, sh* as in *shell* and *wish, th* as in *father* and *both,* and *wh* as in *whale.* Another consonant digraph is *ph,* as in *graph* and *photo.*

Vowels. The remaining five letters—*a, e, i, o,* and *u*—represent vowels, and *w* and *y* are vowels when used in the middle and at the end of syllables and words. Vowels often represent several sounds. The two most common are short (marked with the symbol ˘, called a breve) and long sounds (marked with the symbol ¯, called a macron). The short vowel sounds are /ă/ as in *cat,* /ĕ/ as in *bed,* /ĭ/ as in *win,* /ŏ/ as in *hot,* and /ŭ/ as in *cup.* The long vowel sounds—/ā/, /ē/, /ī/, /ō/, and /ū/—are the same as the letter names, and they are illustrated in the words *make, feet, bike, coal,* and *mule.* Long vowel sounds are usually spelled with two vowels, except when the long vowel is at the end of a one-syllable word (or a syllable), as in *be* or *belong* and *try* or *tribal.*

When *y* is a vowel at the end of a word, it is pronounced as long *e* or long *i,* depending on the length of the word. In one-syllable words such as *by* and *cry,* the *y* is pronounced as long *i,* but in longer words such as *baby* and *happy,* the *y* is pronounced as long *e.*

Vowel sounds are more complicated than consonant sounds, and there are many vowel combinations representing long vowels and other vowel sounds. Consider these combinations:

> *ai* as in *nail*
>
> *au* as in *laugh* and *caught*
>
> *aw* as in *saw*
>
> *ea* as in *peach* and *bread*
>
> *ew* as in *sew* and *few*
>
> *ia* as in *dial*
>
> *ie* as in *cookie*
>
> *oa* as in *soap*
>
> *oi* as in *oil*
>
> *oo* as in *cook* and *moon*
>
> *ou* as in *house* and *through*
>
> *ow* as in *now* and *snow*
>
> *oy* as in *toy*

Most vowel combinations are vowel digraphs or diphthongs. When two vowels represent a single sound, the combination is a vowel digraph (e.g., *nail, snow*), and when the two vowels represent a glide from one sound to another, the combination is a diphthong. Two vowel combinations that are consistently diphthongs are *oi* and *oy,* but other combinations, such as *ou* as in *house* (but not in *through*) and *ow* as in *now* (but not in *snow*), are diphthongs when they represent a glided sound. In *through,* the *ou* represents the /o͞o/ sound as in *moon,* and in *snow* the *ow* represents the /ō/ sound.

When the letter *r* follows one or more vowels in a word, it influences the pronunciation of the vowel sound, as shown in the words *car, air, are, ear, bear, first, for, more, murder,* and *pure.* Students learn many of these words as sight words.

The vowels in the unaccented syllables of multisyllabic words are often softened and pronounced "uh," as in the first syllable of *about* and *machine,* and the final syllable of *pencil, tunnel, zebra,* and *selection.* This vowel sound is called schwa and is represented in dictionaries with a ə, which looks like an inverted *e.*

Blending Into Words. Readers "blend" or combine sounds in order to decode words. Even though children may identify each sound in a word, one by one, they must be able to blend them together into a word. For example, in order to read the short-vowel word *best,* children identify /b/, /ĕ/, /s/, and /t/ and then combine them to form the word. For long-vowel words, children must identify the vowel pattern as well as the surrounding letters. In *pancake,* for example, children identify /p/, /ă/, /n/, /k/, /ā/, and /k/ and recognize that the *e* at the end of the word is silent and marks the preceding vowel as long. Shefelbine (1995) emphasizes the importance of blending and suggests that students who have difficulty decoding words usually know the sound-symbol correspondences but cannot blend the sounds together into recognizable words. The ability to blend sounds together into words is part of phonemic awareness, and students who have not had practice blending speech sounds into words are likely to have trouble blending sounds into words in order to decode unfamiliar words.

Rimes and Rhymes. One-syllable words and syllables in longer words can be divided into two parts, the onset and the rime. The onset is the consonant sound, if any, that precedes the vowel, and the rime is the vowel and any consonant sounds that follow it (Treiman, 1985). For example, in *show, sh* is the onset and *ow* is the rime, and in *ball, b* is the onset and *all* is the rime. For *at* and *up* there is no onset; the entire word is the rime. Research has shown that children make more errors decoding and spelling final consonants than initial consonants and that they make more errors on vowels than on consonants (Treiman, 1985). These problem areas correspond to rimes, and educators now speculate that onsets and rimes could provide an important key to word identification.

Children can focus their attention on a rime, such as *ay,* and create rhyming words, including *bay, day, lay, may, ray, say,* and *way,* as Mrs. Hoddy did in the vignette at the beginning of this chapter. These words can be read and spelled by analogy because the vowel sounds are consistent in rimes. Wylie and Durrell (1970) identified 37 rimes that can be used to produce nearly 500 common words. These rimes and some words made from them are presented in Figure 5–5.

Phonics Generalizations. Because English does not have a one-to-one correspondence between sounds and letters, linguists have created generalizations or rules to clarify English spelling patterns. One rule is that *q* is followed by *u* and pronounced /kw/, as in *queen, quick,* and *earthquake.* There are very few, if any, exceptions to this rule. Another generalization that has few exceptions relates to *r*-controlled vowels: *r* influences the preceding vowel so that the vowel is neither long nor short. Examples are *car, market, birth,* and *four.* There are exceptions, however, and one example is *fire.*

Many generalizations aren't very useful because there are more exceptions than words that conform to the rule (Clymer, 1963). A good example is this rule for long

Figure 5–5 The 37 rimes and common words using them

rime	words	rime	words
-ack	black, pack, quack, stack	-ide	bride, hide, ride, side
-ail	mail, nail, sail, tail	-ight	bright, fight, light, might
-ain	brain, chain, plain, rain	-ill	fill, hill, kill, will
-ake	cake, shake, take, wake	-in	chin, grin, pin, win
-ale	male, sale, tale, whale	-ine	fine, line, mine, nine
-ame	came, flame, game, name	-ing	king, sing, thing, wing
-an	can, man, pan, than	-ink	pink, sink, think, wink
-ank	bank, drank, sank, thank	-ip	drip, hip, lip, ship
-ap	cap, clap, map, slap	-ir	birth, dirt, first, girl
-ash	cash, dash, flash, trash	-ock	block, clock, knock, sock
-at	bat, cat, rat, that	-oke	choke, joke, poke, woke
-ate	gate, hate, late, plate	-op	chop, drop, hop, shop
-aw	claw, draw, jaw, saw	-ore	chore, more, shore, store
-ay	day, play, say, way	-or	for, or, short, torn
-eat	beat, heat, meat, wheat	-uck	duck, luck, suck, truck
-ell	bell, sell, shell, well	-ug	bug, drug, hug, rug
-est	best, chest, nest, west	-ump	bump, dump, hump, lump
-ice	ice, mice, nice, rice	-unk	bunk, dunk, junk, sunk
-ick	brick, pick, sick, thick		

vowels: When there are two vowels side by side, the long vowel sound of the first one is pronounced and the second is silent. Teachers sometimes call this the "when two vowels go walking, the first one does the talking" rule. Examples of words conforming to this rule are *meat, soap,* and *each.* There are many more exceptions, however, including *food, said, head, chief, bread, look, soup, does, too, again,* and *believe.*

Only a few phonics generalizations have a high degree of utility for readers. The generalizations that work most of the time are the ones that students should learn because they are the most useful (Adams, 1990). Eight high-utility generalizations are listed in Figure 5–6. Even though these rules are fairly reliable, very few of them approach 100% utility. The rule about *r*-controlled vowels, mentioned above, has been calculated to be useful in 78% of words in which the letter *r* follows the vowel (Adams, 1990). Other commonly taught, useful rules have even lower percentages of utility. The CVC pattern rule—which says that when a one-syllable word has only one vowel and the vowel comes between two consonants, it is usually short, as in *bat, land,* and *cup*—is estimated to work only 62% of the time. Exceptions include *told, fall, fork,* and *birth.* The CVCe pattern rule—which says that when there are two vowels in a one-syllable word and one vowel is an *e* at the end of the word, the first vowel is long and the final *e* is silent—is estimated to work in 63% of CVCe words. Examples of conforming words are *came, hole,* and *pipe;* but two very common words, *have* and *love,* are exceptions.

Teaching Phonics

Phonics instruction is an important part of reading and writing instruction during the primary grades, but it is crucial that children are involved in real reading and writing activities as they learn phonics. Without this meaningful application of what they are learning, phonics instruction is often ineffective (Cunningham, 2000; Freppon &

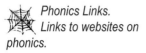

www.zaner-bloser.com

Phonics Links.
Links to websites on phonics.

Figure 5–6	The most useful phonics generalizations

Adapted from Clymer, 1963.

Pattern	Description	Examples
1. Two sounds of *c*	The letter *c* can be pronounced as /k/ or /s/. When *c* is followed by *a, o,* or *u,* it is pronounced /k/—the hard *c* sound. When *c* is followed by *e, i,* or *y,* it is pronounced /s/—the soft *c* sound.	cat cough cut cent city cycle
2. Two sounds of *g*	The sound associated with the letter *g* depends on the letter following it. When *g* is followed by *a, o,* or *u,* it is pronounced as /g/—the hard *g* sound. When *g* is followed by *e, i,* or *y,* it is usually pronounced /j/—the soft *g* sound. Exceptions include *get* and *give.*	gate go guess gentle giant gypsy
3. CVC pattern	When a one-syllable word has only one vowel and the vowel comes between two consonants, it is usually short. One exception is *told.*	bat cup land
4. Final *e* or CVCe pattern	When there are two vowels in a one-syllable word and one of them is an *e* at the end of the word, the first vowel is long and the final *e* is silent. Two exceptions are *have* and *love.*	home safe cute
5. CV pattern	When a vowel follows a consonant in a one-syllable word, the vowel is long. Exceptions include *the, to,* and *do.*	go be
6. *R*-controlled vowels	Vowels that are followed by the letter *r* are overpowered and are neither short nor long. One exception is *fire.*	car for birthday
7. *-igh*	When *gh* follows *i,* the *i* is long and the *gh* is silent. One exception is *neighbor.*	high night
8. *Kn-* and *wr-*	In words beginning with *kn-* and *wr-,* the first letter is not pronounced.	knee write

Dahl, 1991). Teachers use both direct and indirect methods for phonics instruction. They teach minilessons to introduce phonics concepts, skills, and generalizations in a systematic way, and they also take advantage of teachable moments to provide indirect instruction.

Minilessons. Teachers present **minilessons** on specific high-utility phonics concepts, skills, and generalizations as part of a systematic program. According to Shefelbine (1995), the program should be "systematic and thorough enough to enable most students to become independent and fluent readers, yet still efficient and streamlined" (p. 2). Phonics instruction is always tied to reading and writing. Teachers emphasize that they are teaching phonics so that students can decode words fluently when reading and spell words conventionally when writing.

Teachers plan for the minilesson by identifying a phonics concept, skill, or generalization and choosing words from the story to introduce the lesson. Teachers clearly and explicitly present the phonics information and provide words to use in practicing the skill, as Mrs. Hoddy did in the vignette at the beginning of this chapter. During minilessons, teachers use the following activities to provide opportunities for students to read, write, and manipulate sounds, spelling patterns, and words:

- Locate other examples of the sound or pattern in words in a book.
- Sort objects and pictures by beginning sounds.
- Cut words and pictures from newspapers and magazines for phonics posters.
- Write words on magic slates or individual dry-erase boards.
- Make a poster or book of words fitting a pattern.
- Do a **word sort** on the basis of spelling patterns.
- Arrange a group of magnetic letters or letter cards to spell words.
- Read books with many phonetically regular words, such as Dr. Seuss books and Nancy Shaw's "sheep" series (e.g., *Sheep in a Jeep*, 1986).
- Write **alphabet books** and other books featuring phonetically regular words.
- Make charts of words representing spelling patterns and other phonics generalizations, such as the two sounds of *g* and ways to spell long *o*.

The teacher presents a minilesson on /b/ as part of a literature focus unit on "The Three Bears."

Although a regular program of minilessons is important, it is essential that they do not overshadow reading and writing as meaning-making processes. Figure 5–7 reviews the guidelines for phonics instruction.

Teachers have to be knowledgeable about phonics in order to teach it well. They need to be able to draw words from students' reading materials, understand the

Figure 5–7	Guidelines for phonics instruction

Adapted from Shefelbine, 1995; Stahl, 1992; and Trachtenburg, 1990.

1. Teach High-Utility Phonics

Teachers teach the phonics concepts, skills, and generalizations that are most useful for decoding and spelling unfamiliar words. Some phonics rules, such as the CVVC long-vowel rule (e.g., *said, soap, head*), are not very useful.

2. Follow a Developmental Continuum

Teachers follow a developmental continuum for systematic phonics instruction, beginning with rhyming and ending with phonics generalizations.

3. Use a Whole-Part-Whole Instructional Sequence

Teachers plan phonics instruction that grows out of reading using a whole-part-whole sequence. Reading the literature is the whole, phonics instruction is the part, and applying the phonics in additional literacy activities is the second whole.

4. Teach Minilessons

Teachers use minilessons to clearly and directly present information about phonics skills and generalizations and provide examples from books students are reading and other common words. They also provide opportunities for students to read and write words applying the concepts they are teaching.

5. Apply Phonics Skills

Students apply what they are learning about phonics skills and generalizations through spelling, word sorts, making words, interactive writing, wordplay books such as Nancy Shaw's *Sheep in a Jeep* (1986), and other activities.

6. Use Teachable Moments

Teachers also take advantage of teachable moments when they can incorporate phonics information informally into reading and writing activities.

7. Reinforce Phonemic Awareness

Teachers reinforce students' understanding of phonemic awareness as students segment and blend written words through phonics instruction and invented spelling.

8. Review Phonics in Upper Grades

Upper-grade students review phonics generalizations and rules as part of the spelling program because some rules, such as changing the *y* at the end of a word to *i* before adding a suffix (e.g., *cherry* to *cherries*), are more useful for writing than for reading.

phonics principles operating in these words, and cite additional examples. They also need to know about exceptions so that they can explain why some words don't fit particular generalizations. Too often teachers want to purchase a packaged program, but I recommend that they plan their phonics program themselves, as Mrs. Hoddy did at the beginning of the chapter. She decided on the organization of her program using the checklist shown in Figure 5–1, and then she developed activities using words from the books her students were reading during literature focus units.

Teachable Moments. Teachers often give impromptu phonics lessons as they engage children in authentic literacy activities using children's names, titles of books, and environmental print in the classroom. During these teachable moments, teachers answer students' questions about words, model how to use phonics knowledge to decode and spell words, and have students share the strategies they use for reading and writing (Mills, O'Keefe, & Stephens, 1992). For example, as she was introducing *The Very Hungry Caterpillar,* Mrs. Hoddy pointed out that *Very* begins with *v* and that not many words start with *v.* One child mentioned that *valentine* is another *v* word, and another said that her middle name is *Victoria.* Then a child who had been quietly looking at the cover of the book said, "I think *Very* is spelled wrong. The author made a mistake," and he pronounced the word *very,* emphasizing the final long *e* sound. "*Very* should have an *e* at the end, not a *y,*" he concluded. This comment gave Mrs. Hoddy an opportunity to explain that long *e* at the end of a word is often spelled with a *y.*

Teachers also demonstrate how to apply phonics information as they read big books with the class and take children's dictation for **language experience approach** charts. As they read and spell words, teachers break words apart into sounds and apply phonics rules and generalizations. For example, as Mrs. Hoddy talked about the life cycle of butterflies, the class created the chart shown in Figure 5–8. As she wrote, she talked about plural *-s* marker on *eggs* and *caterpillars* and the interesting *tw-* blend at the beginning of *twig.* Also, each time she wrote *butterfly* and *caterpillar,* she spelled the words syllable by syllable. Then as students reread the completed chart, she prompts them on the word *pupa,* when they don't remember it, by sounding it out.

Teachers also use **interactive writing** to support children's growing awareness of phonics (Collom, 1998; McCarrier, Pinnell, & Fountas, 2000). Interactive writing is similar to the language experience approach, except that children do as much of the writing as they can themselves. Children segment words into sounds and take turns writing letters and sometimes whole words on the chart. Teachers help children to correct any errors, and they take advantage of teachable moments to review consonant and vowel sounds and spelling patterns, as well as handwriting skills and rules for capitalization and punctuation.

What Is the Role of Phonics in a Balanced Literacy Program?

Phonics is a controversial topic. Some parents and politicians, as well as even a few teachers, believe that most of our educational ills could be solved if children were taught to read using phonics. A few people still argue that phonics is a complete reading program, but that view ignores what we know about the interrelatedness of the four cueing systems. Reading is a complex process, and the phonological system works in conjunction with the semantic, syntactic, and pragmatic systems, not in isolation.

The controversy now centers on how to teach phonics. Marilyn Adams (1990), in her landmark review of the research on phonics instruction, recommends that phonics be taught within a balanced approach that integrates instruction in reading skills and

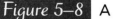 **A class chart on butterflies**

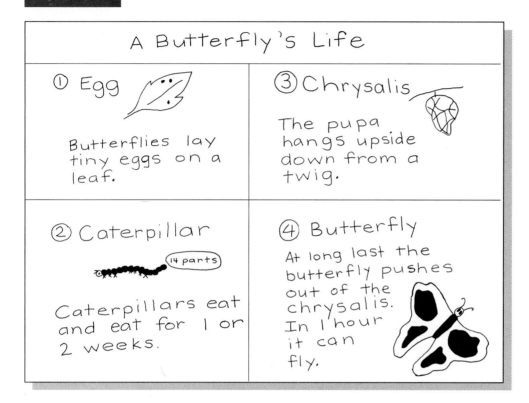

strategies with meaningful opportunities for reading and writing. She emphasizes that phonics instruction should focus on the most useful information for identifying words and that it should be systematic, intensive, and completed by the third grade.

Phonics instruction looks different today than it did a generation ago (Strickland, 1998). A generation ago, phonics instruction often involved marking letters and words on worksheets. Today, however, students learn phonics through reading and writing as well as through minilessons and game-like activities such as **making words** and **word sorts.**

SPELLING

Learning to spell is also part of "breaking the code." As children learn about sound-symbol correspondences, they apply what they are learning through both reading and writing. Children's early spellings reflect what children know about phonics and spelling patterns, and as their knowledge grows, children's spelling increasingly approximates conventional spelling.

Students need to learn to spell words conventionally so that they can communicate effectively through writing. Learning phonics during the primary grades is part of spelling instruction, but students also need to learn other strategies and information about English orthography. In the past, weekly spelling tests were the main instructional strategy. Now, they are only one part of a comprehensive spelling program.

Stages of Spelling Development

As young children begin to write, they create unique spellings, called invented spelling, based on their knowledge of sound-symbol correspondences and phonics generalizations. Charles Read (1971, 1975, 1986) found that young children use their knowledge of phonology to invent spellings. The children in Read's studies used letter names to spell words, such as U (*you*) and R (*are*), and they used consonant sounds rather consistently: GRL (*girl*), TIGR (*tiger*), and NIT (*night*). They used several unusual but phonetically based spelling patterns to represent affricates. For example, they replaced *tr* with *chr* (e.g., CHRIBLES for *troubles*) and *dr* with *jr* (e.g., JRAGIN for *dragon*). Words with long vowels were spelled using letter names: MI (*my*), LADE (*lady*), and FEL (*feel*). The children used several ingenious strategies to spell words with short vowels. The preschoolers selected letters to represent short vowels on the basis of place of articulation in the mouth. Short *i* was represented with *e*, as in FES (*fish*), short *e* with *a*, as in LAFFT (*left*), and short *o* with *i*, as in CLIK (*clock*). These spellings may seem odd to adults, but they are based on phonetic relationships.

Based on observations of children's spellings, researchers have identified five stages that children move through on their way to becoming conventional spellers. At each stage they use different types of strategies and focus on different aspects of spelling. The stages are emergent spelling, letter name spelling, within-word pattern spelling, syllables and affixes spelling, and derivational relations spelling (Bear, Invernizzi, Templeton, & Johnston, 2000). The characteristics of the five stages of spelling development are summarized in Figure 5–9.

Stage 1: Emergent Spelling. Children string scribbles, letters, and letterlike forms together, but they do not associate the marks they make with any specific phonemes. Spelling at this stage represents a natural, early expression of the alphabet and other concepts about writing. Children may write from left to right, right to left, top to bottom, or randomly across the page, but by the end of the stage they have an understanding of directionality. Some emergent spellers have a large repertoire of letter forms to use in writing, while others repeat a small number of letters over and over. They use both upper- and lowercase letters, but they show a distinct preference for uppercase letters. Toward the end of this stage, children are beginning to discover how spelling works and that letters represent sounds in words. This stage is typical of three- to five-year-olds. During the emergent stage, children learn:

❧ the distinction between drawing and writing
❧ how to make letters
❧ the direction of writing on a page
❧ some letter-sound matches

Stage 2: Letter Name Spelling. Children learn to represent phonemes in words with letters. They develop an understanding of the alphabetic principle, that a link exists between letters and sounds. At first the spellings are quite abbreviated and represent only the most prominent features in words. Children use only several letters of the alphabet to represent an entire word. Examples of early Stage 2 spelling are D (*dog*) and KE (*cookie*), and children may still be writing mainly with capital letters. Children pronounce words they want to spell slowly, listening for familiar letter names and sounds.

Stage 1: Emergent Spelling

Children string scribbles, letters, and letter-like forms together, but they do not associate the marks they make with any specific phonemes. This stage is typical of three- to five-year-olds. Children learn:

- the distinction between drawing and writing
- how to make letters
- the direction of writing on a page
- some letter-sound matches

Stage 2: Letter Name Spelling

Children learn to represent phonemes in words with letters. At first their spellings are quite abbreviated, but they learn to use consonant blends and digraphs and short-vowel patterns to spell many short-vowel words. Spellers are five- to seven-year-olds. Children learn:

- the alphabetic principle
- consonant sounds
- short-vowel sounds
- consonant blends and digraphs

Stage 3: Within-Word Pattern Spelling

Students learn long-vowel patterns and *r*-controlled vowels, but they may confuse spelling patterns and spell *meet* as *mete*, and they reverse the order of letters, such as *form* for *from* and *gril* for *girl*. Spellers are seven- to nine-year-olds, and they learn these concepts:

- long-vowel spelling patterns
- *r*-controlled vowels
- more complex consonant patterns
- diphthongs and other less common vowel patterns

Stage 4: Syllables and Affixes Spelling

Students apply what they have learned about one-syllable words to spell longer, multisyllabic words, and they learn to break words into syllables. They also learn to add inflectional endings (e.g., *-es, -ed, -ing*) and differentiate between homophones, such as *your–you're*. Spellers are often nine- to eleven-year-olds, and they learn these concepts:

- inflectional endings
- rules for adding inflectional endings
- syllabication
- homophones

Stage 5: Derivational Relations Spelling

Students explore the relationship between spelling and meaning and learn that words with related meanings are often related in spelling despite changes in sound (e.g., *wise–wisdom, sign–signal, nation–national*). They also learn about Latin and Greek root words and derivational affixes (e.g., *amphi-, pre-, -able, -tion*). Spellers are 11- to 14-year-olds. Students learn these concepts:

- consonant alternations
- vowel alternations
- Latin affixes and root words
- Greek affixes and root words
- etymologies

——————— *Assessment Tools: Spelling-by-Stage Assessment Scale* ———————

Donald Bear and his colleagues (2000, p. 36) have developed a 15-point scale to track students' spelling development in grades K–8. Teachers can use this scale to assess students' spelling development at the beginning of the school year and to monitor students' progress from year to year.

Late Derivational Relations	15
Middle Derivational Relations	14
Early Derivational Relations	13
Late Syllables and Affixes	12
Middle Syllables and Affixes	11
Early Syllables and Affixes	10
Late Within-Word Pattern	9
Middle Within-Word Pattern	8
Early Within-Word Pattern	7
Late Letter Name-Alphabetic	6
Middle Letter Name-Alphabetic	5
Early Letter Name-Alphabetic	4
Late Emergent	3
Middle Emergent	2
Early Emergent	1

In the middle of the letter name stage, students use most beginning and ending consonants and often include a vowel in most syllables. They spell *like* as *lik* and *bed* as *bad*. By the end of the stage, students use consonant blends and digraphs and short vowel patterns to spell *hat, get,* and *win,* but some students still spell *ship* as *sep.* They can also spell some CVCe words such as *name* correctly. Spellers at this stage are usually five- to seven-year-olds. During the letter name stage, students learn:

❦ the alphabetic principle

❦ consonant sounds

❦ short vowel sounds

❦ consonant blends and digraphs

Stage 3: Within-Word Pattern Spelling. Students begin the within-word pattern stage when they can spell most one-syllable short vowel words, and during this stage they learn to spell long vowel patterns and *r*-controlled vowels (Henderson, 1990). They experiment with long vowel patterns and learn that words like *come* and *bread* are exceptions that do not fit the vowel patterns. Students may confuse spelling patterns and spell *meet* as *mete,* and they reverse the order of letters, such as *form* for *from* and *gril* for *girl.* Students also learn about complex consonant sounds, including *-tch* (*match*) and *-dge* (*judge*) and less frequent vowel patterns, including *oi/oy* (*boy*), *au* (*caught*), *aw* (*saw*), *ew* (*sew, few*), *ou* (*house*), and *ow* (*cow*). Students also become aware of homophones and compare long and short vowel combinations (*hope–hop*) as they experiment with vowel patterns. Spellers at this stage are seven- to nine-years-old, and they learn these spelling concepts:

- long vowel spelling patterns
- *r*-controlled vowels
- more complex consonant patterns
- diphthongs and other less common vowel patterns

Stage 4: Syllables and Affixes Spelling. The focus is on syllables in this stage. Students apply what they have learned about one-syllable words to longer, multisyllabic words, and they learn to break words into syllables. They learn about inflectional endings (*-s, -es, -ed,* and *ing*) and rules about consonant doubling, changing the final *y* to *i,* or dropping the final *e* before adding an inflectional suffix. They also learn about homophones and compound words and are introduced to some of the more common prefixes and suffixes. Spellers in this stage are generally nine- to eleven-year-olds. Students learn these concepts during the syllables and affixes stage of spelling development:

- inflectional endings (*-s, -es, -ed, -ing*)
- rules for adding inflectional endings
- syllabication
- homophones

Stage 5: Derivational Relations Spelling. Students explore the relationship between spelling and meaning during the derivational relations stage, and they learn that words with related meanings are often related in spelling despite changes in vowel and consonant sounds (e.g., *wise–wisdom, sign–signal, nation–national*) (Templeton, 1983). The focus in this stage is on morphemes, and students learn about Greek and Latin root words and affixes. They also begin to examine etymologies and the role of history in shaping how words are spelled. They learn about eponyms (words from people's names), such as *maverick,* and *sandwich.* Spellers at this stage are 11- to 14-year-olds. Students learn these concepts at this stage of spelling development:

- consonant alternations (e.g., *soft–soften, magic–magician*)
- vowel alternations (e.g., *please–pleasant, define–definition, explain–explanation*)
- Greek and Latin affixes and root words
- etymologies

Teaching Spelling

Spelling instruction is more than weekly spelling tests. Two of the most important ways that students learn to spell are through daily reading and writing activities. As students read, they learn to visualize words so that they can recognize when a word they've written doesn't look right. Through writing, students gain valuable practice actually spelling words. In addition to reading and writing, students learn to spell through spelling activities and minilessons about phonics, spelling rules, and spelling strategies. Seven recommended activities are:

1. ***Word walls.*** Teachers use two types of **word walls** in their classrooms. One word wall features "important" words from books students are reading or social studies and science thematic units. Words may be written on a large sheet of paper hang-

www.softseek.com

Spelling Games. Download free spelling software for elementary students from this site.

First graders practice spelling skills at the computer center.

ing in the classroom or on word cards and placed in a large pocket chart. Then students refer to these word walls when they are writing. Seeing the words posted on word walls, **clusters,** and other charts in the classroom and using them in their writing helps students learn to spell the words.

The second type of word wall displays high-frequency words. Researchers have identified the most commonly used words and recommend that elementary students learn to spell 100 of these words because of their usefulness. The most frequently used words represent more than 50% of all the words children and adults write (Horn, 1926)! Figure 5–10 lists the 100 most frequently used words.

www.readingonline.org

🕸 *Making and Writing Words.*
Timothy Rasinski explains his variation of the making words activity.

2. *Making words.* Teachers choose a five- to eight-letter word (or longer words for older students) and prepare sets of letter cards for a **making words** activity (Cunningham & Cunningham, 1992; Gunning, 1995). Then students use letter cards to practice spelling words and review spelling patterns and rules. They arrange and rearrange the cards to spell one-letter words, two-letter words, three-letter words, and so forth, until they use all the letters to spell the original word. Second graders, for example, can create these words using the letters in *weather:* *a, at, we, he, the, are, art, ear, eat, hat, her, hear, here, hate, heart, wheat, there,* and *where.*

Teachers often choose words from thematic units for making words activities. For example, during a unit on the American Revolution, a fifth-grade teacher chose the word *revolutionary* and the students spelled these words:

1-letter words: I, a
2-letter words: it, in, on, an, at, to
3-letter words: lay, are, not, run, ran, oil, via, toy, tie, lie, urn, lye, rye, our, out, nut, ear, rat, lit, lot, let, vet

Figure 5–10	The 100 most frequently used words

a	for	mother	there
about	from	my	they
after	get	no	things
all	got	not	think
am	had	now	this
an	have	of	time
and	he	on	to
are	her	one	too
around	him	or	two
as	his	our	up
at	home	out	us
back	house	over	very
be	how	people	was
because	I	put	we
but	if	said	well
by	in	saw	went
came	into	school	were
can	is	see	what
could	it	she	when
day	just	so	who
did	know	some	will
didn't	like	that	with
do	little	the	would
don't	man	them	you
down	me	then	your

4-letter words: rain, tire, year, vote, only, live, love, rule, rely, your, rule, tail, near, earn, liar, turn, tear, rear, note, rate, rein, root, volt, yarn, vary, into, toil

5-letter words: learn, yearn, rerun, royal, relay, you're, early, liter, ultra, ruler, voter, lover, liver, outer, value, untie, until

6-letter words: lotion, nation, ration, turner, return, nearly, lively, tailor, revolt

9-letter words: voluntary

10-letter words: revolution

13-letter words: revolutionary

Students manipulated letter cards to spell the words, and the teacher listed the words on a chart, beginning with one-letter words and making increasingly longer words until students used all of the letters to spell *revolutionary*. As students worked, they consulted dictionaries to check the spelling of possible words and to argue (unsuccessfully) that *litter* was spelled *liter* and *volunteer* was spelled *voluntear* so that the words could be added to the chart. Students manipulated many different spelling patterns in this activity and reviewed prefixes and suffixes, homophones, and rhyming words. Some students were also introduced to new words, including *urn, ration, rye, yearn,* and *volt.*

3. *Word sorts.* Students use **word sorts** to explore, compare, and contrast word features as they sort a pack of word cards. Teachers prepare word cards for

www.carolina.cc

Wise Guys Spelling Games.
A collection of 16 spelling games for upper-grade students.

students to sort into two or more categories according to their spelling patterns or other criteria (Bear et al., 2000). Sometimes teachers tell students what categories to use and the sort is a closed sort; at other times, students determine the categories themselves and the sort is an open sort. Students can sort word cards and then return them to an envelope for future use or they can glue the cards onto a sheet of paper. Figure 5–11 shows a word sort for four vowel patterns using words with short *a* and long *a*. In this sort, students worked with partners and sorted the words into four categories (CVC, CVCe, CVVC, and CVV).

4. *Proofreading.* Proofreading is a special kind of reading that students use to locate misspelled words and other mechanical errors in rough drafts. As students learn about the writing process, they are introduced to proofreading in the editing step. More in-depth instruction about how to use proofreading to locate spelling errors and then correct these misspelled words is part of spelling instruction (Cramer, 1998). Through a series of minilessons, students can learn to proofread sample student papers and mark misspelled words. Then, working in pairs, students can correct the misspelled words.

Proofreading should be introduced in the primary grades. Young children and their teachers proofread collaborative books and dictated stories together, and students can be encouraged to read over their own compositions and make necessary corrections soon after they begin writing. This way students accept proofreading as a

Figure 5–11   A word sort of long- and short-a words

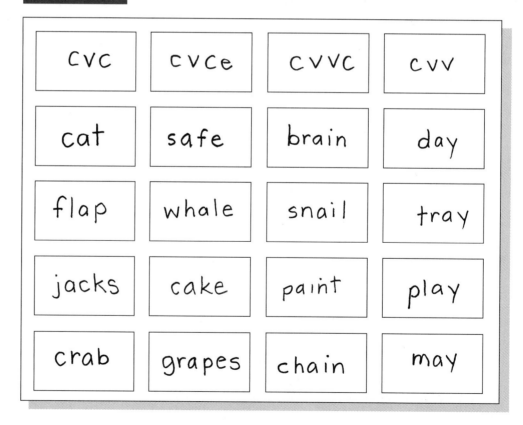

natural part of writing. Proofreading activities are more valuable for teaching spelling than are dictation activities, in which teachers dictate sentences for students to write and correctly capitalize and punctuate. Few people use dictation in their daily lives, but students use proofreading skills every time they polish a piece of writing.

5. ***Dictionary use.*** Students need to learn to locate the spelling of unfamiliar words in the dictionary. While it is relatively easy to find a "known" word in the dictionary, it is hard to locate unfamiliar words, and students need to learn what to do when they do not know how to spell a word. One approach is to predict possible spellings for unknown words, then check the most probable spellings in a dictionary.

Students should be encouraged to check the spellings of words in a dictionary as well as to use dictionaries to check multiple meanings of a word or the etymology of the word. Too often students view consulting a dictionary as punishment. Teachers must work to change this view of dictionary use. One way to do this is to appoint some students in the classroom as dictionary checkers. These students keep dictionaries on their desks, and they are consulted whenever questions about spelling, word meaning, and word usage arise.

6. ***Spelling options.*** In English, there are alternate spellings for many sounds because so many words have been borrowed from other languages and retain their native spellings. There are many more options for vowel sounds than for consonants. Even so, there are four spelling options for /f/ (*f, ff, ph, gh*). Spelling options sometimes vary according to position in the word. For example, *ff* and *gh* are only used to represent /f/ at the end of a word, as in *cuff* and *laugh*. Common spelling options for phonemes are listed in Figure 5–12.

Teachers point out spelling options as they write words on word walls and when students ask about the spelling of a word. They also can use a series of minilessons to teach upper-grade students about these options. During each lesson, students can focus on one phoneme, such as /f/ or /ar/, and as a class or small group they can develop a list of the various ways the sound is spelled in English, giving examples of each spelling. A sixth-grade chart on long *o* is presented in Figure 5–13.

7. ***Strategies for spelling unfamiliar words.*** Students need to develop a repertoire of strategies in order to spell unfamiliar words. Some of these spelling strategies are:

- inventing spellings for words based on students' phonological, semantic, and historical knowledge of words
- proofreading to locate and correct spelling errors
- locating words on word walls and other charts
- predicting the spelling of a word by generating possible spellings and choosing the best alternative
- breaking the word into syllables and spelling each syllable
- applying affixes to root words
- spelling unknown words by analogy to known words
- locating the spelling of unfamiliar words in a dictionary or other resource book
- writing a letter or two as a placeholder for a word they do not know how to spell when they are writing rough drafts and quickwrites
- asking the teacher or another person how to spell a word

www.puzzlemaker.com

Word Games and Puzzles. Create computer-generated word searches, cryptograms, and more at this site.

Figure 5–12 Common spelling options

Sound	Spellings	Examples	Sound	Spellings	Examples
long a	a-e	date	short oo	oo	book
	a	angel		u	put
	ai	aid		ou	could
	ay	day		o	woman
ch	ch	church	ou	ou	out
	t(u)	picture		ow	cow
	tch	watch	s	s	sick
	ti	question		ce	office
long e	ea	each		c	city
	ee	feel		ss	class
	e	evil		se	else
	e-e	these		x(ks)	box
	ea-e	breathe	sh	ti	attention
short e	e	end		sh	she
	ea	head		ci	ancient
f	f	feel		ssi	admission
	ff	sheriff	t	t	teacher
	ph	photograph		te	definite
j	ge	strange		ed	furnished
	g	general		tt	attend
	j	job	long u	u	union
	dge	bridge		u-e	use
k	c	call		ue	value
	k	keep		ew	few
	x	expect, luxury	short u	u	ugly
	ck	black		o	company
	qu	quite, bouquet		ou	country
l	l	last	y	u	union
	ll	allow		u-e	use
	le	automobile		y	yes
m	m	man		i	onion
	me	come		ue	value
	mm	comment		ew	few
n	n	no	z	s	present
	ne	done		se	applause
long o	o	go		ze	gauze
	o-e	note	syllabic l	le	able
	ow	own		al	animal
	oa	load		el	cancel
short o	o	office		il	civil
	a	all	syllabic n	en	written
	au	author		on	lesson
	aw	saw		an	important
oi	oi	oil		in	cousin
	oy	boy		contractions	didn't
long oo	u	cruel		ain	certain
	oo	noon	r-controlled	er	her
	u-e	rule		ur	church
	o-e	lose		ir	first
	ue	blue		or	world
	o	to		ear	heard
	ou	group		our	courage

Figure 5–13	Spelling options chart for long o

Spelling	Word	Location		
		Initial	**Medial**	**Final**
o	oh, obedient	x		
	go, no, so			x
o-e	home, pole		x	
ow	own	x		
	known		x	
	blow, elbow, yellow			x
oa	oaf, oak, oat	x		
	boat, groan		x	
ew	sew			x
ol	yolk, folk		x	
oe	toe			x
ough	though			x
eau	beau			x
ou	bouquet		x	

Instead of giving the traditional "sound it out" advice when students ask how to spell an unfamiliar word, teachers should suggest that students use a strategic "think it out" approach. This advice reminds students that spelling involves more than phonological information and suggests that students should think about spelling patterns, root words and affixes, and the shape of the word—what it looks like.

Weekly Spelling Tests

Many teachers question the usefulness of spelling tests to teach spelling, since research on invented spelling suggests that spelling is best learned through reading and writing (Gentry & Gillet, 1993; Wilde, 1992). In addition, teachers complain that lists of spelling words are unrelated to the words students are reading and writing and that the 30 minutes of valuable instructional time spent each day in completing spelling textbook activities is excessive. Even so, parents and school board members value spelling tests as evidence that spelling is being taught. Weekly spelling tests, when they are used, should be individualized so that children learn to spell the words they need for their writing.

In the individualized approach to spelling instruction, students choose the words they will study, and many of the words they choose are words they use in their writing projects. Students study 5 to 10 specific words during the week using a study strategy. This approach places more responsibility on students for their own learning. Teachers develop a weekly word list of 20 or more words of varying difficulty from which students select words to study. Words for the master list include high-frequency words, words from the word wall related to literature focus units and thematic units, and words students needed for their writing projects during the previous week. Words from spelling textbooks can also be added to the list.

www.everydayspelling.com

🕸 *Everyday Spelling.
Information about a
commercial spelling program
for elementary students.*

On Monday, the teacher administers a pretest using the master list of words, and students spell as many of the words as they can. Students correct their own pretests, and from the words they misspell they create individual spelling lists. They make two copies of their study list, using the numbers on the master list to make it easier to take the final test on Friday. Students use one copy of the list for study activities, and the teacher keeps the second copy.

Students spend approximately 5 to 10 minutes studying the words on their study lists each day during the week. Instead of "busy-work" activities such as using their spelling words in sentences or gluing yarn in the shape of the words, research shows it is more effective for students to use this study strategy:

1.   Look at the word and say it to yourself.
2.   Say each letter in the word to yourself.
3.   Close your eyes and spell the word to yourself.
4.   Write the word, and check that you spelled it correctly.
5.   Write the word again and check that you spelled it correctly.

This strategy focuses on the whole word rather than breaking the word apart into sounds or syllables. Teachers explain how to use the strategy during a minilesson at the beginning of the school year and then post a copy of the strategy in the classroom. In addition to this study strategy, sometimes students trade word lists on Wednesday or Thursday or give each other a practice test.

A final test is administered on Friday. The teacher reads the master list, and students write only those words they have practiced during the week. To make it easier to administer the test, students first list the numbers of the words they have practiced from their study lists on their test papers. Any words that students misspell should be included on their lists the following week.

This individualized approach is recommended instead of a textbook approach. Typically, textbooks are arranged in weeklong units, with lists of 10 to 20 words and practice activities that often require at least 30 minutes per day to complete. Research indicates that only 60 to 75 minutes per week should be spent on spelling instruction, as greater periods of time do not result in increased spelling ability (Johnson, Langford, & Quorn, 1981).

What Is the Controversy About Spelling Instruction?

The press and concerned parent groups periodically raise questions about invented spelling and the importance of weekly spelling tests. There is a misplaced public perception that today's children cannot spell. Researchers who are examining the types of errors students make have noted that the number of misspellings increases in grades one through four, as students write longer compositions, but that the percentage of errors decreases. The percentage continues to decline in the upper grades, although some students continue to make errors (Taylor & Kidder, 1988).

Review

The three components involved in "breaking the code" are phonemic awareness, phonics, and spelling. Phonemic awareness is the ability to segment and blend spoken words, and it provides the foundation for phonics instruction. Phonics is the set of relationships between speech sounds and spelling patterns. During the primary grades, students learn phonics in order to decode words and invent spellings. In order to become fluent readers, students need to be able to decode unfamiliar words rapidly. As young children begin writing, they use invented spelling to apply what they know about English spelling patterns. Their spelling changes to reflect phonics skills and spelling patterns they are learning. The feature below reviews the recommended practices that effective reading teachers use in assisting students to "break the code."

How Effective Teachers . . .

Assist Students in "Breaking the Code"

✱ Effective Practices

1. Teachers develop students' phonemic awareness using songs, rhymes, and wordplay books.
2. Teachers teach minilessons on segmenting and blending sounds in words using familiar words drawn from books children are reading.
3. Teachers teach phonics using a whole-part-whole approach.
4. Teachers teach the high-utility phonics concepts, skills, and generalizations.
5. Teachers teach phonics through minilessons and "teachable moments."
6. Teachers connect phonics instruction for decoding words to spelling words.
7. Teachers encourage students to apply what they know about phonics through invented spelling.
8. Teachers analyze students' spelling errors as a measure of students' understanding of phonics.
9. Teachers recognize that daily reading and writing experiences contribute to students' spelling development.
10. Teachers teach minilessons on spelling using words from students' reading and writing. They may use spelling tests, but only as part of the spelling program.

✱ Ineffective Practices

1. Teachers focus only on teaching phonics using written words.
2. Teachers don't lay a foundation for phonics instruction by teaching students about phonemic awareness.
3. Teachers teach phonics in isolation without connecting phonics to real reading and writing.
4. Teachers don't consider the usefulness of the phonics generalizations they teach.
5. Teachers depend on commercial phonics programs, including "Hooked on Phonics."
6. Teachers teach phonics using skill-and-practice activities and an abundance of worksheets and workbooks.
7. Teachers discourage students from using invented spelling.
8. Teachers consider students' spellings as right or wrong without analyzing the errors.
9. Teachers devalue the importance of reading and writing practice in students' spelling development.
10. Teachers teach spelling using spelling textbooks and weekly spelling tests.

References

Adams, M. J. (1990). *Beginning to read: Thinking and learning about print.* Cambridge, MA: MIT Press.

Ball, E., & Blachman, B. (1991). Does phoneme segmentation training in kindergarten make a difference in early word recognition and developmental spelling? *Reading Research Quarterly, 26,* 49–86.

Bear, D. R., Invernizzi, M., Templeton, S., & Johnston, F. (2000). *Words their way: Word study for phonics, vocab-ulary, and spelling instruction.* Upper Saddle River, NJ: Merrill/Prentice Hall.

Carle, E. (1993). *Eric Carle: Picture writer* (videotape). New York: Philomel.

Clay, M. M. (1985). *The early detection of reading difficul-ties* (3rd ed.). Portsmouth, NH: Heinemann.

Clymer, T. (1963). The utility of phonic generalizations in the primary grades. *The Reading Teacher, 16,* 252–258.

Collom, S. (Ed.). (1998). *Sharing the pen: Interactive writing with young children.* Fresno: California State University, Fresno, and the San Joaquin Valley Writing Project.

Cramer, R. L. (1998). *The spelling connection: Integrating reading, writing, and spelling instruction.* New York: Guilford.

Cunningham, P. M. (2000). *Phonics they use: Words for reading and writing* (3rd ed.). New York: Longman.

Cunningham, P. M., & Cunningham, J. W. (1992). Making words: Enhancing the invented spelling-decoding connection. *The Reading Teacher, 46,* 106–115.

Freppon, P. A., & Dahl, K. L. (1991). Learning about phonics in a whole language classroom. *Language Arts, 68,* 190–197.

Gentry, J. R., & Gillet, J. W. (1993). *Teaching kids to spell.* Portsmouth, NH: Heinemann.

Griffith, F., & Olson, M. (1992). Phonemic awareness helps beginning readers break the code. *The Reading Teacher, 45,* 516–523.

Griffith, P. L. (1991). Phonemic awareness helps first graders invent spellings and third graders remember correct spellings. *Journal of Reading Behavior, 23,* 215–232.

Gunning, T. G. (1995). Word building: A strategic approach to the teaching of phonics. *The Reading Teacher, 48,* 484–488.

Hanna, P. R., Hanna, J. S., Hodges, R. E., & Rudorf, E. H. (1966). *Phoneme-grapheme correspondences as cues to spelling improvement.* Washington, DC: US Government Printing Office.

Henderson, E. H. (1990). *Teaching spelling* (2nd ed.). Boston: Houghton Mifflin.

Hohn, W., & Ehri, L. (1982). Do alphabet letters help prereaders acquire phonemic segmentation skill? *Journal of Educational Psychology, 75,* 752–762.

Horn, E. (1926). *A basic writing vocabulary.* Iowa City: University of Iowa Press.

Horn, E. (1957). Phonetics and spelling. *Elementary School Journal, 57,* 233–235, 246.

Johnson, T. D., Langford, K. G., & Quorn, K. C. (1981). Characteristics of an effective spelling program. *Language Arts, 58,* 581–588.

Juel, C., Griffith, P. L., & Gough, P. B. (1986). Acquisition of literacy: A longitudinal study of children in first and second grade. *Journal of Educational Psychology, 78,* 243–255.

Klesius, J. P., Griffith, P. L., & Zielonka, P. (1991). A whole language and traditional instruction comparison: Overall effectiveness and development of the alphabetic principle. *Reading Research and Instruction, 30,* 47–61.

Lewkowicz, N. K. (1994). The bag game: An activity to heighten phonemic awareness. *The Reading Teacher, 47,* 508–509.

Liberman, I., Shankweiler, D., Fischer, F., & Carter, B. (1974). Explicit syllable and phoneme segmentation in the young child. *Journal of Experimental Child Psychology, 18,* 201–212.

Lomax, R. G., & McGee, L. M. (1987). Young children's concepts about print and meaning: Toward a model of word reading acquisition. *Reading Research Quarterly, 22,* 237–256.

Lundberg, I., Frost, J., & Peterson, O. (1988). Effects of an extensive program for stimulating phonological awareness in preschool children. *Reading Research Quarterly, 23,* 263–284.

McCarrier, A., Pinnell, G. S., & Fountas, I. C. (2000). *Interactive writing: How language and literacy come together, K–2.* Portsmouth, NH: Heinemann.

McGee, L. M., & Richgels, D. J. (1989). "K is Kristen's": Learning the alphabet from a child's perspective. *The Reading Teacher, 43,* 216–225.

Mills, H., O'Keefe, T., & Stephens, D. (1992). *Looking closely: Exploring the role of phonics in one whole language classroom.* Urbana, IL: National Council of Teachers of English.

Perfitti, C., Beck, I., Bell, L., & Hughes, C. (1987). Phonemic knowledge and learning to read are reciprocal: A longitudinal study of first grade children. *Merrill-Palmer Quarterly, 33,* 283–319.

Read, C. (1971). Pre-school children's knowledge of English phonology. *Harvard Educational Review, 41,* 1–34.

Read, C. (1975). *Children's categorization of speech sounds in English* (NCTE Research Report No. 17). Urbana, IL: National Council of Teachers of English.

Read, C. (1986). *Children's creative spelling.* London: Routledge & Kegan Paul.

Shefelbine, J. (1995). *Learning and using phonics in beginning reading* (Literacy research paper; volume 10). New York: Scholastic.

Stahl, S. A. (1992). Saying the "p" word: Nine guidelines for exemplary phonics instruction. *The Reading Teacher, 45,* 618–625.

Stanovich, K. (1980). Toward an interactive-compensatory model of individual differences in the development of reading fluency. *Reading Research Quarterly, 16,* 37–71.

Strickland, D. S. (1998). *Teaching phonics today: A primer for educators.* Newark, DE: International Reading Association.

Taylor, K. K., & Kidder, E. B. (1988). The development of spelling skills: From first grade through eighth grade. *Written Communication, 5,* 222–244.

Templeton, S. (1983). Using the spelling/meaning connection to develop word knowledge in older students. *Journal of Reading, 27,* 8–14.

Tompkins, G. E., & Yaden, D. B., Jr. (1986). *Answering students' questions about words.* Urbana, IL: ERIC

Clearinghouse on Reading and Communication Skills and National Council of Teachers of English.

Trachtenburg, P. (1990). Using children's literature to enhance phonics instruction. *The Reading Teacher, 43,* 648–654.

Treiman, R. (1985). Onsets and rimes as units of spoken syllables: Evidence from children. *Journal of Experimental Child Psychology, 39,* 161–181.

Tunmer, W., & Nesdale, A. (1985). Phonemic segmentation skill and beginning reading. *Journal of Educational Psychology, 77,* 417–427.

Venezky, R. L. (1999). *The American way of spelling: The structure and origins of American English orthography.* New York: Guilford.

Wilde, S. (1992). *You kan red this! Spelling and punctuation for whole language classrooms, K–6.* Portsmouth, NH: Heinemann.

Wylie, R. E., & Durrell, D. D. (1970). Teaching vowels through phonograms. *Elementary English, 47,* 787–791.

Yopp, H. K. (1985). Phoneme segmentation ability: A prerequisite for phonics and sight word achievement in beginning reading? In J. Niles & R. Lalik (Eds.), *Issues in literacy: A research perspective* (pp. 330–336). Rochester, NY: National Reading Conference.

Yopp, H. K. (1988). The validity and reliability of phonemic awareness tests. *Reading Research Quarterly, 23,* 159–177.

Yopp, H. K. (1992). Developing phonemic awareness in young children. *The Reading Teacher, 45,* 696–703.

Yopp, H. K. (1995). Read-aloud books for developing phonemic awareness: An annotated bibliography. *The Reading Teacher, 48,* 538–542.

Children's Book References

Barrett, J. (1978). *Cloudy with a chance of meatballs.* New York: Atheneum.

Carle, E. (1969). *The very hungry caterpillar.* New York: Philomel.

Carle, E. (1984). *The very busy spider.* New York: Philomel.

Carle, E. (1990). *The very quiet cricket.* New York: Philomel.

Carle, E. (1995). *The very lonely firefly.* New York: Philomel.

Hutchins, P. (1976). *Don't forget the bacon!* New York: Mulberry.

Most, B. (1996). *Cock-a-doodle-moo!* San Diego: Harcourt Brace.

Obligado, L. (1983). *Faint frogs feeling feverish and other terrifically tantalizing tongue twisters.* New York: Puffin.

Prelutsky, J. (1982). *The baby uggs are hatching.* New York: Mulberry.

Sendak, M. (1963). *Where the wild things are.* New York: Harper & Row.

Seuss, Dr. (1963). *Hop on pop.* New York: Random House.

Shaw, N. (1986). *Sheep in a jeep.* Boston: Houghton Mifflin.

Developing Fluent Readers and Writers

— Chapter Questions —

Why do students need to learn to read and write high-frequency words?

What strategies do students learn to use to recognize and spell unfamiliar words?

How do students become fluent readers?

Why is fluency important?

Ms. Williams's Students Learn High-Frequency Words

Ms. Williams's second graders are studying hermit crabs and their tide pool environments. A plastic habitat box sits in the center of each grouping of desks, and a hermit crab is living in each box. As students care for their crustaceans, they observe the crabs. They have examined hermit crabs up close using magnifying glasses and identified the body parts. Ms. Williams helped them draw a diagram of a hermit crab on a large chart and label the body parts. They have compared hermit crabs to true crabs and examined their exoskeletons. They have also learned how to feed hermit crabs, how to get them to come out of their shells, and how they molt. And, they've conducted experiments to determine whether hermit crabs prefer wet or dry environments.

These second graders are using reading and writing as tools for learning. Eric Carle's *A House for Hermit Crab* (1987) is the featured book for this unit. Ms. Williams has read it aloud to students several times, and students are rereading it at the listening center. *Moving Day* (Kaplan, 1996), *Pagoo* (Holling, 1990), and other story books and informational books, including *Hermit Crabs* (Pohl, 1987) and *Tide Pool* (Greenaway, 1992), are available on a special shelf in the classroom library. Ms. Williams has read some of the books aloud to students, and others they listen to at the listening center or read independently or with buddies. Students make charts about hermit crabs that they post in the classroom, and they write about hermit crabs in **learning logs** (see the Compendium for more information about this and all other highlighted terms in this chapter). One log entry is shown in Figure 6–1.

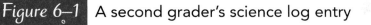 **Figure 6–1** A second grader's science log entry

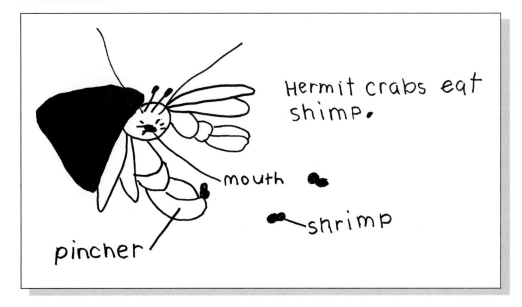

Ms. Williams and her students also write many interesting and important vocabulary words related to hermit crabs that they learn about on a **word wall** made of a sheet of butcher paper. They write these words on their word wall:

tide pool	shells	exoskeleton
starfish	sea anemone	snails
shrimp	scavenger	regeneration
enemies	lantern fish	seaweed
pebbles	coral	sea urchins
crustacean	molting	pincers
eggs	larva	larvae

Then students refer to these words as they write about hermit crabs, and Ms. Williams uses these words for various reading activities. This word wall will be displayed in the classroom only during the unit on hermit crabs.

Ms. Williams integrates many components of reading instruction, including word recognition and fluency activities, into the unit on hermit crabs. To develop her second graders' ability to recognize many high-frequency words, she uses another word wall. This word wall is different from the hermit crab word wall, which only includes words related to these ocean animals. Her high-frequency word wall is a brightly colored alphabet quilt with the most common words written on small cards, displayed permanently in the center of one wall of the classroom.

At the beginning of the school year, Ms. Williams and her students posted the 70 high-frequency words that they were familiar with from first grade on the word wall. Then each week, Ms. Williams adds three to five new words. At first the words she chose were from her list of the 100 highest-frequency words, and after finishing that list she has begun choosing words from a list of the second 100 high-frequency words. She doesn't introduce the words in the order that they are presented in the list, but she chooses words from the list that she can connect to units and words that students misspell in their writing.

This week Ms. Williams has chosen *soon, house, your,* and *you're* to add to the word wall. She chose *soon* and *house* because these words are used in *A House for Hermit Crab* and several students have recently asked her how to spell *house*. She chose the homophones *your* and *you're* because students are confusing and misspelling these two words. She has also noticed that some students are confused about contractions, and she plans to review contractions using *you're* as an example.

Ms. Williams has her students sit on the floor near the word wall to introduce the words and post them on the word wall. She uses a cookie sheet and large magnetic letters to introduce each new word. She explains that two of the new words— *house* and *soon*—are from *A House for Hermit Crab*. She scrambles the letters at the bottom of the cookie sheet and slowly builds the new word at the top of the sheet as students guess the word. She begins with *h*, adds the *ou*, and several children call out "house." Ms. Williams continues adding letters, and when they are all in place, a chorus of voices says, "house." Then Kari places the new word card in the *H* square of the word wall, and students chant and clap as they say the word and spell it. Ms. Williams begins, "House, house, h-o-u-s-e," and students echo her chant. Then she calls on Enrique to begin the chant, and students echo him. Then Ms. Williams repeats the procedure with the three remaining words.

The next day, Ms. Williams and her students use **interactive writing** to compose sentences using each of the new words. They write:

> *The hermit crab has a good shell for a <u>house</u>. He likes it but <u>soon</u> he will move. "<u>You're</u> too small for me," he says. "I have to move, but I will always be <u>your</u> friend."*

Students take turns writing these sentences on a chart, and after rereading the sentences they underline the four new words. Each week the students write sentences using the new word wall words on this chart. Ms. Williams and the students often reread the sentences they've written during previous weeks.

The next day, after students practice the word wall words, Ms. Williams takes a few minutes to review contractions so that the students understand that *you're* is a contraction of *you* and *are* and that the apostrophe indicates that a letter has been omitted. Then students volunteer other contractions. Michael identifies three: *I'm, can't,* and *don't.* The students use interactive writing to make a chart of contractions. They list the contractions and the two words that make up each contraction. Ms. Williams tells students that she'll put the chart in the word study center and that students can use the information to make books about contractions.

After this practice with high-frequency words, students participate in activities at literacy centers while Ms. Williams meets with guided reading groups. Most of the center activities relate to the unit on hermit crabs and Eric Carle's book *A House for Hermit Crab,* but students also practice reading and writing high-frequency words at two of the centers. The eight literacy centers in Ms. Williams's classroom are described in Figure 6–2.

Each morning a sixth-grade student aide comes to the classroom to monitor students' work at the centers and provide assistance as needed. Ms. Williams worked with two sixth-grade teachers to train 10 students to serve as student aides, and these students come to the classroom once every week or two on a rotating basis.

The second graders keep track of their work in centers using small booklets with eight sheets of paper that Ms. Williams calls their "center passports." Students or the student aide marks their passports with stickers or stamps at each center after they finish the assignment. They leave their written work in a basket at the center.

As a culminating activity, Ms. Williams and her students write a retelling of *A House for Hermit Crab.* The students compose the text, and Ms. Williams uses the **language experience approach** to write their rough draft on chart paper so that everyone can see it. Students learn revision strategies as they fine-tune their retelling, and then Ms. Williams types the text on five sheets of paper, duplicates copies, and compiles a booklet for each student. Students each receive a copy of the

Ms. Williams's literacy centers

---

1. Retelling Center

Students use pictures and labels with the month of the year to sequence the events in the book and retell the story.

2. Science Center

Children observe a hermit crab and make notes about its physical characteristics and eating habits in their learning logs.

3. Word Work Center

Children use magnetic letters to spell the four high-frequency words—*house, soon, your*, and *you're*—and the words from the last two weeks. They also make a book of contractions with picture and sentence examples.

4. Listening Center

Children use headphones to listen to an informational book on hermit crabs read aloud.

5. Word Wall Center

Children practice reading the word wall using the pointers at the center. Then they take a clipboard and a sheet of paper divided into 10 sections. The letters spelling h-e-r-m-i-t c-r-a-b have been written in the sections. Then children choose two words from the word wall beginning with each letter to write in each section on their papers.

6. Writing Center

Children write "I am a Hermit Crab" poems and other books about hermit crabs at the writing center.

7. Word Sort Center

Children sort vocabulary words from *A House for Hermit Crab* according to category. For example, months of the year are put in one category and ocean animals and plants in another.

8. Library Center

Children practice reading leveled books at their individual levels and other books about hermit crabs and the ocean that are placed on a special shelf in the classroom library. Ms. William includes *Hermit Crab* (Randell, 1994) (Level 8), *Hermit's Shiny Shell* (Tuchman, 1997) (Level 10), and *Moving Day* (Kaplan, 1996) (Level 7), three familiar books about hermit crabs, for students to reread.

---

booklet to read. They also add illustrations. Later they will take their booklets home to read to their families.

Ms. Williams reads their retelling aloud as students follow along, and then students join in the reading. Children do **choral reading** as they read in small groups, with classmates sitting at the same grouping of desks. The numbers on the left side indicate which group of students reads each sentence. As students read and reread the text aloud, they become increasingly fluent readers. Here is the last section of the class's retelling:

1	*Soon it was January.*
2	*Hermit Crab moved out of his house*
	and the little crab moved in.
3	*"Goodbye," said Hermit Crab.*
	"Be good to my friends."
4	*Soon Hermit Crab saw the perfect house.*
5	*It was a big, empty shell.*
1	*It looked a little plain*
	but Hermit Crab didn't care.
2	*He will decorate it*
3	*with sea urchins,*
4	*with sea anemones,*
5	*with coral,*
1	*with starfish,*
2	*with snails.*
ALL	*So many possibilities!*

The underlined words are high-frequency words that are posted on the word wall in Ms. Williams's classroom. Of the 68 words in this excerpt, 37 are high-frequency words! Also, two of the new words for this week, *soon* and *house,* are used twice.

....

*A*s students learn to read, they move from word-by-word reading with little or no expression to fluent reading. Fluency is the ability to read smoothly and with expression, and in order to read fluently, students must be able to recognize many, many words automatically. By third grade most students have moved from word-by-word reading into fluent reading, but 10–15% have difficulty learning to recognize words and their learning to read is slowed (Allington, 1998).

Students become fluent readers through a combination of instruction and lots of reading experience. Through systematic phonics instruction, students learn how to identify unfamiliar words, and as they read and reread hundreds of books during the primary grades, these words become familiar and students learn to recognize them automatically. They also learn increasingly sophisticated strategies for identifying the unfamiliar words, including syllabic and morphemic analysis in which they break words into syllables and into root words and affixes.

At the same time students are becoming fluent readers, they are also becoming fluent writers. Through phonics instruction and lots of writing practice, students learn to spell many words automatically, apply capitalization and punctuation rules, and develop writing speed. They also develop strategies for spelling longer, multisyllabic words. Developing fluency is just as important for writers because both readers and writers must be able to focus on meaning, not identifying and spelling words.

TEACHING STUDENTS TO READ AND WRITE WORDS

Teachers have two goals as they teach students to read and write words. The first is to teach students to instantly recognize a group of several hundred high-frequency words. Students need to be able to read and write these words automatically, and they usually accomplish this goal by second or third grade. The second is to equip students with strategies they can use to identify unfamiliar words—often longer, multisyllabic words they come across during reading and need to spell during writing. Students learn and refine their use of these strategies throughout the elementary grades.

The first goal is word recognition, or the quick and easy pronunciation or spelling of a familiar word, and the second is word identification, or the ability to figure out the pronunciation or spelling of an unfamiliar word using a strategy such as syllabic analysis.

Word Recognition

Students need to develop a large stock of words that they recognize instantly and automatically because it is impossible for them to analyze every word that they encounter when reading or want to spell when writing. These recognizable words are called sight words. Through repeated reading and writing experiences, students develop automaticity, the ability to quickly and accurately recognize words they read and know how to spell words they are writing (LaBerge & Samuels, 1976). The vital element in word recognition is learning each word's unique letter sequence. This knowledge about the sequence of letters is useful as students learn to spell. At the same time they are becoming fluent readers, students are also becoming fluent writers. They are learning to spell the words they write most often. Hitchcock (1989) found that by third grade most students spell 90% of the words they use correctly.

www.eduplace.com

🕸 *High-Frequency Words.*
Ideas for teaching high-frequency words.

High-Frequency Words. The most common words that readers and writers use again and again are high-frequency words. There have been numerous attempts to identify specific lists of these words and calculate their frequency in reading materials. Pinnell and Fountas (1998, p. 89) identified these 24 common words that kindergartners need to learn to recognize:

a	he	no	an
I	see	and	in
she	am	is	so
at	it	the	can
like	to	do	me
up	go	my	we

The 24 words are part of the 100 most commonly used words, and these 100 words account for more than half of the words children read and write. Children learn the rest of these 100 words in first grade. Eldredge (1995) has identified the 300 highest-frequency words used in first-grade basal readers and trade books found in first-grade classrooms. These 300 words account for 72% of the words that beginning readers read. Figure 6–3 presents Eldredge's list of 300 high-frequency words; the 100 most commonly used words are marked with an asterisk.

Some high-frequency words, such as *it* and *can*, can be sounded out using phonics, but many others, such as *are, here,* and *of,* are not phonetically regular words, and students are encouraged to learn to recognize them by sight.

High-frequency words are certainly not the only words that young children learn to read and write. For example, many kindergartners can write "I love you," and only *I* is among the 24 most common words, and only *I* and *you* are among the 100 high-frequency words. Kindergartners also read names of classmates and color words, and these words are not high-frequency words, either. Children in kindergarten and first grade learn to read and write hundreds of these "content" words in addition to the high-frequency words, but high-frequency words are important because they are so common.

It is essential that children learn to read and write high-frequency words, and many of these words are difficult to learn because they cannot be easily decoded (Cunningham, 2000). Try sounding out *to, what,* and *could* and you will see why they are called "sight" words. Because these words can't be decoded easily, it is crucial that children learn to recognize them instantly and automatically. A further complication is that many of these words are function words in sentences and don't carry much meaning. Children find it much easier to learn to recognize *whale* than *what,* because *whale* conjures up the image of the aquatic mammal, while *what* is abstract. However, *what* is used much more frequently, and children need to learn to recognize it.

Children who recognize many high-frequency words are able to read more fluently than students who do not, and fluent readers are better able to understand what they are reading. Once children can read many of these words, they gain confidence in themselves as readers and begin reading books independently. Similarly, students who can spell these words are more successful writers.

www.hunley.home. mindspring.com
Rebecca Sitton Words. Students focus on learning to spell high-frequency words in this approach to spelling instruction.

Word Walls. Teachers create word walls in their classrooms to display high-frequency words that their students are learning, as Ms. Williams did in the vignette at the beginning of the chapter (Cunningham, 2000). Some teachers use butcher paper or squares of construction paper for the word wall, and others use large pocket charts that they divide into sections for each letter of the alphabet. Word walls should be placed in a large accessible location in the classroom so that new words can be added easily and all students can see the words.

Teachers prepare word walls at the beginning of the school year and then add words to the word walls each week. Kindergarten teachers often begin the year by listing students' names on the word wall and then add the 24 highest-frequency words, one or two words per week, during the school year. First-grade teachers often add the 24 highest-frequency words to the word wall at the beginning of the year, and then add two to five words to the word wall each week during the school year. Figure 6–4 presents a first-grade word wall with just over 100 words that were added during the school year. In second grade, teachers often begin the year with the easier half of the high-frequency words already on the word wall, and they add 50 to 75 more words during the school year. Third-grade teachers often test their students' knowledge of the 100 high-frequency words at the beginning of the year, add to the word wall those words that students cannot read and write, and then continue with words from the next 200 high-frequency words.

Figure 6–3 The 300 high-frequency words

Note. From *Teaching Decoding in Holistic Classrooms* (pp. 94–95), by J. L. Eldredge, © 1995. Adapted by permission of Prentice-Hall, Inc., Upper Saddle River, NJ.

*The first 100 most frequently used words, as shown in Figure 5–10 on p. 187.

*a	children	great	looking	ran	through
*about	city	green	made	read	*time
*after	come	grow	make	red	*to
again	*could	*had	*man	ride	toad
*all	couldn't	hand	many	right	together
along	cried	happy	may	road	told
always	dad	has	maybe	room	*too
*am	dark	hat	*me	run	took
*an	*day	*have	mom	*said	top
*and	*did	*he	more	sat	tree
animals	*didn't	head	morning	*saw	truck
another	*do	hear	*mother	say	try
any	does	heard	mouse	*school	*two
*are	dog	help	Mr.	sea	under
*around	*don't	hen	Mrs.	*see	until
*as	door	*her	much	*she	*up
asked	*down	here	must	show	*us
*at	each	hill	*my	sister	*very
ate	eat	*him	name	sky	wait
away	end	*his	need	sleep	walk
baby	even	*home	never	small	walked
*back	ever	*house	new	*so	want
bad	every	*how	next	*some	wanted
ball	everyone	*I	nice	something	*was
*be	eyes	I'll	night	soon	water
bear	far	I'm	*no	started	way
*because	fast	*if	*not	stay	*we
bed	father	*in	nothing	still	*well
been	find	inside	*now	stop	*went
before	fine	*into	*of	stories	*were
began	first	*is	off	story	*what
behind	fish	*it	oh	sun	*when
best	fly	it's	old	take	where
better	*for	its	*on	tell	while
big	found	jump	once	than	*who
bird	fox	jumped	*one	*that	why
birds	friend	*just	only	that's	*will
blue	friends	keep	*or	*the	wind
book	frog	king	other	their	witch
books	*from	*know	*our	*them	*with
box	fun	last	*out	*then	wizard
boy	garden	left	*over	*there	woman
brown	gave	let	*people	these	words
*but	*get	let's	picture	*they	work
*by	girl	*like	pig	thing	*would
called	give	*little	place	*things	write
*came	go	live	play	*think	yes
*can	going	long	pulled	*this	*you
can't	good	look	*put	thought	you're
cat	*got	looked	rabbit	three	*your

Figure 6–4 A first-grade word wall

A	B	C	D
a　　　are	be	call	did
about　　as	been	called	didn't
after　　at	boy	can	do
all	but	can't	does
am	by	come	don't
and		could	down

E	F	G	H
each	find	get	had　　　him
eat	first	go	has　　　his
	for	good	have　　have
	from		he　　　how
			her
			here

I	J	K	L
I	just	know	like
if			little
in			long
into			look
is			
it			

M	N	O	P
made　　must	no	of　　　other	people
make　　my	not	on　　　our	pretty
may	now	one　　　out	
me		only　　over	
more		or	

QR	S	T	U
	said	than　　there	up
	saw	that　　these	us
	see	the　　　they	
	she	their　　this	
	so	them　　to	
	some	then　　two	
	should		

V	W	XY	Z
very	was　　where	you	
	water　　which	your	
	way　　who		
	we　　　will		
	were　　with		
	what　　words		
	when　　would		

Teachers can create word walls for older students, too. To assist struggling readers, teachers can post the 100 high-frequency words or some of the 300 high-frequency words on a word wall in the classroom, or they can make individual word walls for these students. Teachers can type up a list of words and duplicate copies to cut into bookmarks, to glue on a file folder, or to make personal dictionaries. Teachers who work with students who read and write at grade level can also make word walls to display more difficult common words. Figure 6–5 presents a list of 100 common words for fourth- through eighth-grade word walls. Some of the words, such as *himself, finally,* and *remember,* are more appropriate for fourth and fifth graders, and others, such as *independent, foreign,* and *throughout,* are more appropriate for sixth through eighth graders. These are commonly used words that students often misspell or confuse with other words.

Teachers select the words they introduce each week carefully. They choose words that students are familiar with and use in conversation. The selected words should have appeared in books students are reading or been introduced in guided reading lessons, or they should be words that students have misspelled in interactive writing activities or in other writing activities. Even though the words are listed alphabetically in Figures 6–4 and 6–5, they should not be taught in that order. In the

Figure 6–5 100 useful word wall words for students in grades 4–8

a lot	doesn't	interesting	safety
again	either	it's–its	school
all right	embarrassed	knew–new	separate
although	enough	know–no	serious
another	especially	knowledge	since
anything	etc.	language	special
around	everything	lying	something
beautiful	everywhere	maybe	success
because	excellent	necessary	their–there–they're
belief	experience	neighbor	themselves
believe	familiar	once	though
beneath	favorite	ourselves	thought
between	field	particular	threw–through
board–bored	finally	people	throughout
breathe	foreign	piece–peace	to–two–too
brought	friends	please	together
caught	frighten	possible	until
certain	hear–here	probably	usually
close–clothes	heard–herd	quiet–quite	weight
committee	height	really	were
complete	herself	receive	we're
decided	himself	recommend	where
desert–dessert	humorous	remember	whether
different	hungry	restaurant	whole–hole
discussed	immediately	right–write	your–you're

Students practice reading and spelling high-frequency words at the word work center.

vignette, Ms. Williams chose *soon* and *house* from *A House for Hermit Crab* and the homophones *your* and *you're* that students were confusing in their writing.

Teaching high-frequency words is not easy because most of the words are functional words. Many words are abstract and have little or no meaning when they are read or written in isolation. Cunningham (2000) recommends this procedure for practicing the words being placed on the word wall:

1. *Introduce the word or words in context.* The words can be presented in the context of a book students are familiar with or by using pictures or objects. For example, to introduce the words *for* and *from,* teachers might bring a box wrapped with gift paper and tied with a bow, and an attached gift tag is labeled "for" and "from." Then teachers pass out extra gift tags they have made, and students read the words *for* and *from* and briefly talk about gifts they have given and received. Teachers also clarify that *for* is not the number *four* and show students where the number *four* is written on the number chart posted in the classroom.

2. *Have students chant and clap the spelling of the words.* Teachers introduce the new word cards that will be placed on the word wall and read the words. Then they begin a chant, "For, for, f-o-r," and clap their hands. Then students repeat the chant. After several repetitions, teachers begin a second chant, "From, from, f-r-o-m," and the students repeat the chant and clap their hands as they chant. Students practice chanting and clapping the words each day that week.

3. *Have students practice reading and spelling the words in a word study center.* Students use white boards and magnetic letters to practice spelling the words. For practice reading the words, they can also sort word cards. For example, the words *for, from, four, fun, fish, fast, free, from, for, four, free,* and *fun* are written

on cards, and students sort them into three piles: one pile for *for*, a second pile for *from*, and a third pile for all other words.

4. *Have students apply the words they are learning in reading and writing activities.* Since these are high-frequency words, it is likely that students will read and write them often. Teachers can also create writing opportunities through interactive writing activities.

Through this procedure, teachers make the high-frequency words more concrete, and easily confused words are clarified and practiced. Also, students have many opportunities to practice reading and writing the words.

www.elm.maine.edu

High-Frequency Word Assessment. Read how one elementary teacher assesses her students' knowledge of the 100 high-frequency words.

Teaching and Assessing Word Recognition. Word walls are one of the most important ways that teachers teach word recognition. Reading and writing practice are two other ways. Children develop rapid word recognition by reading words. They read words in the context of stories and other books, and they read them on word lists and on word cards. Practice makes students more fluent readers and even has an impact on their comprehension. Research is inconclusive about whether it is better to have students practice reading words in context or in isolation, but most teachers prefer to have students read words in the context of stories or other books because the activity is much more authentic (I. W. Gaskins, Ehri, Cress, O'Hara, & Donnelly, 1996/1997).

Students also practice word recognition through writing because they write high-frequency words again and again. For example, when a class of first graders were studying animals, they wrote riddle books. One first grader wrote this riddle book, entitled "What Is It?":

Page 1:	*It is a bird.*
Page 2:	*It can't fly but it can swim.*
Page 3:	*It is black and white.*
Page 4:	*It eats fish.*
Page 5:	*What is it?*
Page 6:	*A penguin.*

Of the words that the child wrote, more than half are among the 24 highest-frequency words listed above! (These words are underlined.) Students can refer to the word wall when they are writing so that they can write fluently.

Because word recognition is so important in beginning reading, children's developing word recognition should be monitored and assessed on a regular basis (Snow, Burns, & Griffin, 1998). Teachers can ask students to individually read the words posted on the word wall or read high-frequency words on word cards. Kindergartners might be tested on the list of 24 words, first graders on the list of 100 words, and second and third graders on the list of 300 words. Teachers can also monitor students' use of the high-frequency words in their writing.

Word Identification

www.eduplace.com

Teaching Word-Identification Strategies. Read about the word-identification strategies, the role of phonics, how to teach the strategies, and relating word identification to writing and spelling.

Beginning readers encounter many words that they don't recognize immediately, and more fluent readers also come upon words that they don't recognize at once. Students use word-identification strategies to identify these unfamiliar words. Young children often depend on phonics to identify unfamiliar words, but older students develop a repertoire of strategies that use phonological information as well as semantic, syntactic, and pragmatic cues to identify words. Four word-identification strategies are:

🌿   Phonic analysis

🌿   By analogy

🌿   Syllabic analysis

🌿   Morphemic analysis

Writers use these same strategies to spell words as they write. As with reading, young children depend on phonics to spell many, many words, but as they learn more about words they apply more of these strategies to spelling. The word-identification strategies are summarized in Figure 6–6.

Eldredge (1995) calls these strategies "interim strategies" because students only use them until they learn to recognize words automatically. For example, fourth graders may break the word *disruption* into syllables to identify the word the first time they encounter it, but with practice they learn to recognize it automatically. And seventh graders writing a report need to spell the word *bibliography*, and they learn to spell it using their knowledge of word parts. *Biblio-* is a Greek word part meaning *books*, and *-graphy*, also a Greek word part, means *writing*. In time, students will write the word *bibliography* without breaking it into word parts or thinking about the meaning. They will write it automatically.

Figure 6–6   Word-identification strategies

Strategy	Description	Examples
Phonic Analysis	Students use their knowledge of sound-symbol correspondences and spelling patterns to decode words when reading and to spell words when writing.	*flat, peach, spring, blaze, chin*
By Analogy	Students use their knowledge of rhyming words to deduce the pronunciation or spelling of an unfamiliar word.	*creep* from *sheep*, *think* from *pink*, *include* from *dude*
Syllabic Analysis	Students break multisyllabic words into syllables and then use phonics and analogies to decode the word, syllable by syllable.	*cul-prit, tem-por-ary, vic-tor-y, neg-a-tive, sea-weed, bio-de-grad-able*
Morphemic Analysis	Students apply their knowledge of root words and affixes (prefixes at the beginning of the word and suffixes at the end) to identify an unfamiliar word. They "peel off" any prefixes or suffixes and identify the root word first. Then they add the affixes.	*trans-port, astro-naut, bi-cycle, centi-pede, pseudo-nym, tele-scope*

Phonic Analysis. Students use what they have learned about sound-symbol correspondences, phonic generalizations, and spelling patterns to decode words when they are reading and to spell words when they are writing. Even though English is not a perfectly phonetic language, phonic analysis is a very useful strategy because almost every word has some phonetically regular parts. The words *have* and *come,* for example, are considered irregular words because the vowel sounds are not predictable; however, the initial and final consonant sounds in both words are regular.

Beginning readers often try to identify words based on a partial word analysis (Gough, Juel, & Griffith, 1992). They may guess at a word using the beginning sound or look at the overall shape of the word as a clue to word identification. These are not effective techniques. Through phonics instruction, students learn to focus on the letter sequences in words so that they examine the entire word as they identify it (Adams, 1990).

Researchers report that the big difference between students who can identify words effectively and those who do not is whether or not they survey the letters in the word and analyze the interior components (Stanovich, 1992; Vellutino & Scanlon, 1987). Capable readers notice all or almost all letters in a word, while less capable readers do not completely analyze the letter sequences of words. Struggling readers with limited phonics skills often try to decode words by sounding out the beginning sound and then making a wild guess at the word without using the cueing systems to verify their guesses (I. W. Gaskins et al., 1996/1997). And, as you might guess, their guesses are usually wrong. Sometimes they don't even make sense in the context of the sentence.

Once students know some letter-sound sequences, the focus of phonics instruction should become using phonic analysis to decode and spell words. Here are the steps students follow in decoding an unfamiliar one-syllable word:

1. Determine the vowel sound in the word, and isolate that sound.
2. Blend all of the consonant sounds in front of the vowel sound with the vowel sound.
3. Isolate the consonant sound(s) after the vowel sound.
4. Blend the two parts of the word together so the word can be identified. (Eldredge, 1995, p. 108)

In order for students to use this strategy, they need to be able to identify vowels and vowel patterns in words. They also need to be able to blend sounds together to form recognizable words. In multisyllabic words, students break the word into syllables and then use the same procedure to decode each syllable. Because the location of stress in words varies, sometimes students have to try accenting different syllables to pronounce a recognizable word.

By Analogy. Students can identify some words by associating them with words they already know. This procedure is known as decoding by analogy (Cunningham, 1975–1976; R. W. Gaskins, Gaskins, & Gaskins, 1991). For example, when readers come to an unfamiliar word such as *lend,* they might think of *send* and figure the word out by analogy; for *cart,* they might notice the word *art* and use that to figure the word out. Students use analogy to figure out the spelling of unfamiliar words as well. Students might use *cat* to help them spell *that,* for example. This strategy accounts for students' common misspelling of *they* as *thay,* because *they* rhymes with *day* and *say.*

This word-identification strategy is dependent on students' phonemic awareness and phonics knowledge. Students who can break words into onsets and rimes and substitute sounds in words are more successful. Moreover, researchers have found that only students who know many sight words can use this strategy because they must be able to identify patterns in familiar words to associate with those in unfamiliar words (Ehri & Robbins, 1992). Even though some first and second graders can use this strategy, older students are more likely to use it to decode and spell words.

Teachers introduce this strategy when they have students read and write "word families" or rimes. Using the *-ill* family, for example, students can read or write *bill, chill, fill, hill, kill, mill, pill, quill, spill, still,* and *will*. Students can add inflectional endings to create even more words, including *filling, hills,* and *spilled*. Two-syllable words can also be created using these words: *killer, chilly,* and *hilltop*. Students read word cards, write the words using interactive writing, use magnetic letters to spell the words, and make rhyming word books during the primary grades to learn more about substituting beginning sounds, breaking words into parts, and spelling word parts. It is a big step, however, for students to move from these structured activities to using this strategy independently to identify unfamiliar words.

Syllabic Analysis.   During the middle grades, students learn to divide words into syllables in order to read and write multisyllabic words such as *biodegradable, admonition,* and *unforgettable*. Once a word is divided into syllables, students use phonic analysis and analogy to pronounce or spell the word. Identifying syllable boundaries is important, since these affect the pronunciation of the vowel sound. For example, compare the vowel sound in the first syllables of *cabin* and *cable*. For *cabin,* the syllable boundary is after the *b,* whereas for *cable,* the division is before the *b*. We can predict that the *a* in *cabin* will be short because the syllable follows the CVC pattern, and that the *a* in *cable* will be long because the syllable follows the CV pattern.

The most basic rule about syllabication is that there is one vowel sound in each syllable. Consider the words *bit* and *bite*. *Bit* is a one-syllable word because there is one vowel letter representing one vowel sound. *Bite* is a one-syllable word, too, because even though there are two vowels in the word, they represent one vowel sound. *Magic* and *curfew* are two-syllable words. There is one vowel letter and sound in each syllable in *magic,* but in the second syllable of *curfew,* the two vowels *ew* represent one vowel sound. Let's try a longer word. How many syllables are in *inconvenience?* There are six vowel letters representing four sounds in four syllables.

Syllabication rules are useful in teaching students how to divide words into syllables. Five of the most useful rules are listed in Figure 6–7. These 12 two-syllable words are from *A House for Hermit Crab* (Carle, 1987), the book Ms. Williams read in the vignette at the beginning of the chapter, and they illustrate all but one of the rules:

a-round	prom-ise	her-mit
pret-ty	ur-chin	nee-dles
slow-ly	o-cean	ti-dy
with-out	cor-al	com-plain

The first two rules focus on consonants, and the last three focus on vowels. The first rule, to divide between two consonants, is the most common rule, and examples from the list include *her-mit* and *pret-ty*. The second rule deals with words where three consonants appear together in a word, such as *com-plain*. The word is divided between the *m* and the *p* in order to preserve the *pl* blend. The third and fourth rules involve the VCV pattern. Usually the syllable boundary comes after the first vowel, as in *ti-dy, o-cean,* and *a-round;* however, the division comes after the consonant in

Figure 6–7   Syllabication rules

Rules	Examples
1. When two consonants come between two vowels in a word, divide syllables between the consonants.	cof-fee bor-der hec-tic plas-tic jour-ney
2. When there are more than two consonants together in a word, divide syllables keeping the blends together.	em-ploy mon-ster lob-ster en-trance bank-rupt
3. When there is one consonant between two vowels in a word, divide syllables after the first vowel.	ca-jole bo-nus fau-cet plu-ral gla-cier
4. If following the third rule does not make a recognizable word, divide syllables after the consonant that comes between the vowels.	doz-en dam-age ech-o meth-od cour-age
5. When there are two vowels together that do not represent a long-vowel sound or a diphthong, divide syllables between the vowels.	cli-ent du-et po-em cha-os li-on qui-et

cor-al because dividing the word *co-ral* does not produce a recognizable word. The syllable boundary comes after the consonant in *without,* too, but this compound word has easily recognizable word parts. According to the fifth rule, words such as *qui-et* are divided between the two vowels because the vowels do not represent a vowel digraph or diphthong. This rule is the least common, and there were no examples of it in the story.

Teachers use **minilessons** to introduce the concept of syllabication and the syllabication rules. During additional minilessons, students and teachers choose words from books students are reading and from thematic units for guided practice breaking words into syllables. After identifying syllable boundaries, students pronounce and spell the words, syllable by syllable. Teachers also mark syllable boundaries on multisyllabic words on word walls in the classroom and create center activities in which students practice dividing words into syllables and building words using word parts. For example, after the word *compromise* came up in a social studies unit, a sixth-grade

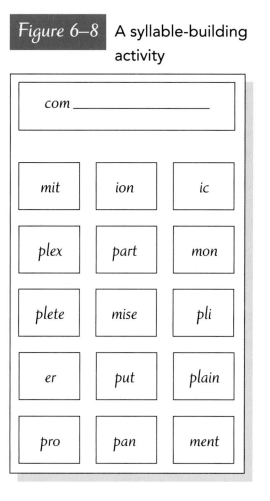

Figure 6–8 A syllable-building activity

com _____

mit	ion	ic
plex	part	mon
plete	mise	pli
er	put	plain
pro	pan	ment

teacher developed a center activity in which students created two- and three-syllable words beginning with *com-* using syllable cards. Students created these words:

comic	compliment	common
companion	complex	computer
complete	commitment	complain
compromise	comment	compartment

After building these words, students brainstormed a list of additional words beginning with *com-* including *complement, commuter, company, communicate, compass,* and *committee.* Through this activity, students become more familiar with syllables in words and the vowel patterns in syllables. The syllable cards for the center activity are presented in Figure 6–8.

Morphemic Analysis. Students examine the root word and affixes of longer unfamiliar words in order to identify the words. A root word is a morpheme, the basic part of a word to which affixes are added. Many words are developed from a single root word. For example, the Latin words *portare* (to carry), *portus* (harbor), *porta* (gate), and are the sources of at least 12 words: *deport, export, exporter, import, port, portable, porter, report, reporter, support, transport,* and *transportation.* Latin is the most common source of English root words, and Greek and English are two other sources.

Some root words are whole words, and others are parts of words. Some root words have become free morphemes and can be used as separate words, but others cannot. For instance, the word *cent* comes from the Latin root word *cent,* meaning "hundred." English treats the word as a root word that can be used independently and in combination with affixes, as in *century, bicentennial,* and *centipede.* The words *cosmopolitan, cosmic,* and *microcosm* come from the Greek root word *cosmo,* meaning "universe"; it is not an independent root word in English. A list of Latin and Greek root words appears in Figure 6–9. English words, such as *eye, tree,* and *water,* are root words, too. New words are formed through compounding—for example, *eyelash, treetop,* and *waterfall*—but other English root words, such as *read,* combine with affixes, as in *reader* and *unreadable.*

Affixes are bound morphemes that are added to words and root words. Prefixes are added to the beginning of words, as in *replay,* and suffixes are added to the end of words, as in *playing, playful,* and *player.* Like root words, some affixes are English and others come from Latin and Greek. Affixes often change a word's meaning, such as adding *un-* to *happy* to form *unhappy.* Sometimes they change the part of speech, too. For example, when *-tion* is added to *attract* to form *attraction,* the verb *attract* becomes a noun.

There are two types of suffixes: inflectional and derivational. Inflectional suffixes are endings that indicate verb tense and person, plurals, possession, and comparison, and these suffixes are English. They influence the syntax of sentences. Some examples are:

the *-ed* in *walked*

the *-ing* in *singing*

the *-s* in *asks*

the *-s* in *dogs*

the *-es* in *beaches*

the *-'s* in *girl's*

the *-er* in *faster*

the *-est* in *sunniest*

In contrast, derivational suffixes show the relationship of the word to its root word. Consider, for example, these words containing the root word *view: preview, viewer, reviewer,* and *interview.*

When a word's affix is "peeled off," the remaining word is usually a real word. For example, when the prefix *pre-* is removed from *preview,* the word *view* can stand alone, and when the suffix *-er* is removed from *viewer,* the word *view* can stand alone. Some words include letter sequences that might be affixes, but because the remaining word cannot stand alone, they are not affixes. For example, the *in-* at the beginning of *include* is not a prefix because *clude* is not a word. Similarly, the *-ic* at the end of *magic* is not a suffix because *mag* cannot stand alone as a word. Sometimes, however, Latin and Greek root words cannot stand alone. One example is *legible.* The *-ible* is a suffix, and *leg* is the root word even though it cannot stand alone. Of course, *leg*—meaning part of the body—is a word, but the root word *leg-* from *legible* is not. It is a Latin root word, meaning "to read."

A list of English, Greek, and Latin prefixes and suffixes is presented in Figure 6–10. Not surprisingly, most affixes are from Latin, as are 50–60% of words in English. White, Sowell, and Yanagihara (1989) researched affixes and identified the most common ones, and these are marked with an asterisk in Figure 6–10. White

Figure 6–9 Latin and Greek root words

Root	Language	Meaning	Sample Words
ann/enn	Latin	year	anniversary, annual, centennial, millennium, perennial, semiannual
arch	Greek	ruler	anarchy, archbishop, architecture, hierarchy, monarchy, patriarch
astro	Greek	star	aster, asterisk, astrology, astronaut, astronomy, disaster
auto	Greek	self	autobiography, automatic, automobile, autopsy, semiautomatic
bio	Greek	life	biography, biohazard, biology, biodegradable, bionic, biosphere
capit/capt	Latin	head	capital, capitalize, Capitol, captain, caption, decapitate, per capita
cent	Latin	hundred	bicentennial, cent, centennial, centigrade, centipede, century, percent
circ	Latin	around	circle, circular, circus, circumspect, circuit, circumference, circumstance
corp	Latin	body	corporal, corporation, corps, corpuscle
cosmo	Greek	universe	cosmic, cosmopolitan, microcosm
cred	Latin	believe	credit, creed, creditable, discredit, incredulity
cycl	Greek	wheel	bicycle, cycle, cyclist, cyclone, recycle, tricycle
dict	Latin	speak	contradict, dictate, dictator, prediction, verdict
graph	Greek	write	autobiography, biographer, cryptograph, epigraph, graphic, paragraph
gram	Greek	letter	cardiogram, diagram, grammar, monogram, telegram
jus/jud/jur	Latin	law	injury, injustice, judge, juror, jury, justice, justify, prejudice
lum/lus/luc	Latin	light	illuminate, lucid, luminous, luster
man	Latin	hand	manacle, maneuver, manicure, manipulate, manual, manufacture
mar/mer	Latin	sea	aquamarine, Margaret, marine, maritime, marshy, mermaid, submarine
meter	Greek	measure	centimeter, diameter, seismometer, speedometer, thermometer
mini	Latin	small	miniature, minibus, minimize, minor, minimum, minuscule, minute
mort/mors	Latin	death	immortal, mortality, mortuary, postmortem, remorseful
nym	Greek	name	anonymous, antonym, homonym, pseudonym, synonym
ped	Latin	foot	biped, pedal, pedestrian, pedicure
phono	Greek	sound	earphone, microphone, phonics, phonograph, saxophone, symphony
photo	Greek	light	photograph, photographer, photosensitive, photosynthesis
pod/pus	Greek	foot	octopus, podiatry, podium, tripod
port	Latin	carry	exporter, import, port, portable, porter, reporter, support, transportation
quer/ques/quis	Latin	seek	query, quest, question, inquisitive
scope	Latin	see	horoscope, kaleidoscope, microscope, periscope, telescope
scrib/scrip	Latin	write	describe, inscription, postscript, prescribe, scribble, scribe, script
sphere	Greek	ball	atmosphere, atmospheric, hemisphere, sphere, stratosphere
struct	Latin	build	construct, construction, destruction, indestructible, instruct, reconstruct
tele	Greek	far	telecast, telegram, telegraph, telephone, telescope, telethon, television
terr	Latin	land	subterranean, terrace, terrain, terrarium, terrier, territory
vers/vert	Latin	turn	advertise, anniversary, controversial, divert, reversible, versus
vict/vinc	Latin	conquer	convince, convict, evict, invincible, victim, victor, victory
vis/vid	Latin	see	improvise, invisible, revise, supervisor, television, video, vision, visitor
viv/vit	Latin	live	revive, survive, vital, vitamin, vivacious, vivid, viviparous
volv	Latin	roll	convolutions, evolve, evolution, involve, revolutionary, revolver, volume

Figure 6–10 Affixes

*Indicates the most commonly used affixes (White, Sowell, & Yanagihara, 1989)

Language	Prefixes	Suffixes
English	***over-** (too much): overflow **self-** (by oneself): self-employed ***un-** (not): unhappy ***un-** (reversal): untie **under-** (beneath): underground	**-ed** (past tense): played **-ful** (full of): hopeful **-ing** (participle): eating, building **-ish** (like): reddish **-less** (without): hopeless **-ling** (young): duckling ***-ly** (in the manner of): slowly ***-ness** (state or quality): kindness **-s/-es** (plural): cats, boxes **-ship** (state, or art or skill): friendship, seamanship **-ster** (one who): gangster **-ward** (direction): homeward ***-y** (full of): sleepy
Greek	**a-/an-** (not): atheist, anaerobic **amphi-** (both): amphibian **anti-** (against): antiseptic **di-** (two): dioxide **hemi-** (half): hemisphere **hyper-** (over): hyperactive **hypo-** (under): hypodermic **micro-** (small): microfilm **mono-** (one): monarch **omni-** (all): omnivorous **poly-** (many): polygon **sym-/syn-/sys-** (together): synonym	**-ism** (doctrine of): communism **-ist** (one who): artist **-logy** (the study of): zoology
Latin	**bi-** (two, twice): bifocal, biannual **contra-** (against): contradict **de-** (away): detract ***dis-** (not): disapprove ***dis-** (reversal): disinfect **ex-** (out): export ***il-/im-/in-/ir-** (not): illegible, impolite, inexpensive, irrational ***in-** (in, into): indoor **inter-** (between): intermission **milli-** (thousand): millennium ***mis-** (wrong): mistake **multi-** (many): multimillionaire **non-** (not): nonsense **post-** (after): postwar **pre-** (before): precede **quad-/quart-** (four): quadruple, quarter **re-** (again): repay ***re-/retro-** (back): replace, retroactive ***sub-** (under): submarine **super-** (above): supermarket **trans-** (across): transport **tri-** (three): triangle	**-able/-ible** (worthy of, can be): lovable, audible ***-al/-ial** (action, process): arrival, denial **-ance/-ence** (state or quality): annoyance, absence **-ant** (one who): servant **-ary/-ory** (person, place): secretary, laboratory **-cule** (very small): molecule **-ee** (one who is): trustee ***-er/-or/-ar** (one who): teacher, actor, liar **-ic** (characterized by): angelic **-ify** (to make): simplify **-ment** (state or quality): enjoyment **-ous** (full of): nervous ***-sion/-tion** (state or quality): tension, attraction **-ure** (state or quality): failure

and his colleagues recommend that the commonly used affixes be taught to middle- and upper-grade students because of their usefulness. Some of the most commonly used prefixes can be confusing because they have more than one meaning. The prefix *un-*, for example, can mean *not* (e.g., *unclear*) or it can reverse the meaning of a word (e.g., *tie–untie*).

Teaching and Assessing Word Identification. Word-level learning is an essential part of a balanced literacy program (Hiebert, 1991), and teaching minilessons about analogies and phonic, syllabic, and morphemic analysis is a useful way to help students focus on words. Minilessons grow out of meaningful literature experiences or thematic units, and teachers choose words for minilessons from books students are reading, as Ms. Williams did in the vignette. Or, at least they begin with several words from the book and then provide additional examples.

Delpit (1987) and Reyes (1991) have argued that learning words implicitly through reading and writing experiences assumes that students have existing literacy and language proficiencies and that the same sort of instruction works equally well for everyone. They point out that not all students have a rich background of literacy experiences before coming to school. Some students, especially those from nonmainstream cultural and linguistic groups, may not have been read to as preschoolers. They may not have recited nursery rhymes to develop phonemic awareness, or experimented with writing by writing letters to grandparents. Perhaps even more importantly, they may not be familiar with the routines of school—sitting quietly and listening while the teacher reads, working cooperatively on group projects, answering questions and talking about books, and imitating the teacher's literacy behaviors. Delpit and Reyes conclude that explicit instruction is crucial for nonmainstream students who do not have the same literacy background as middle-class students.

Fluent readers develop a large repertoire of sight words and use word-identification strategies to decode unfamiliar words. Less capable readers, in contrast, cannot read as many sight words and do not use as many strategies for decoding words. Researchers have concluded again and again that students who do not become fluent readers depend on explicit instruction to learn how to identify words (Calfee & Drum, 1986; R. W. Gaskins et al., 1991; Johnson & Baumann, 1984).

Many fourth-grade teachers notice that their students seem to stand still or lose ground in their reading development. It has been assumed that the increased demands for reading informational books with unfamiliar, multisyllabic words caused this phenomenon. Now researchers are suggesting that lack of instruction in word-identification strategies might be the cause of the "fourth-grade slump" (Chall, Jacobs, & Baldwin, 1990). Perhaps more minilessons on identifying multisyllabic words will help eliminate this difficulty. The guidelines for teaching word identification are summarized in Figure 6–11.

Teachers informally assess students' ability to use word-identification strategies as they observe students reading and writing and monitor their use of the strategies. They can also assess students' use of word-identification strategies by asking them to read or write a list of grade-level-appropriate words or by asking students to think aloud and explain how they decoded or spelled a particular word. It is also important that teachers check to see that students use these strategies on an "interim basis" and that through practice students learn to read and write words automatically. Fourth graders, for example, may use syllabic analysis to read or write a word such as *important,* but with practice students should learn to read and write the word automatically, without having to stop and analyze it.

Figure 6–11 Guidelines for teaching students to identify words

1. Teach as Part of a Balanced Program

Teachers present word-identification lessons as part of literature focus units and guided reading groups. A whole-part-whole approach for teaching word identification as well as other skills and strategies is recommended.

2. Teach High-Frequency Words

Teachers choose both high-frequency words and other interesting words from the reading selections for minilessons and other word-study activities. It is especially important that students learn high-frequency words in order to become fluent readers.

3. Select Words Carefully

Teachers consider the students, the text to be read, and the purpose for reading when deciding which words to focus on for word-study activities.

4. Introduce Key Words Before Reading

Introduce only a few key words before beginning to read, and teach other words during and after reading. Key words are meaningful words in the reading selection, such as characters' names, or words related to a key concept.

5. Use Shared Reading

Teachers often use shared reading to introduce trade books and selections in basal reader textbooks. As teachers read they model word-identification strategies for students.

6. Highlight High-Frequency Words

Students and teachers highlight important and interesting words from the reading selection on word walls and make word banks of high-frequency words for students to refer to when reading and spelling.

7. Teach Word-Identification Strategies

Teachers present minilessons on the four word-identification strategies and related skills: phonic analysis, analogies, syllabic analysis, and morphemic analysis.

8. Use Reading Workshop

Students need daily opportunities to read self-selected books during reading workshop, and as they read and reread books appropriate to their reading levels they apply word-identification strategies and related skills. Easy-to-read books written at the first-, second-, and third-grade levels are recommended for beginning readers.

9. Emphasize the Reading-Writing Connection

Integrated reading and writing instruction gives students many opportunities to write high-frequency words and other words related to reading selections in writing activities. Students write in reading logs, make story maps, and write innovations, or new versions of stories they are reading.

10. Focus on Fluency

The goal of word-recognition lessons is to help students become fluent readers. Fluent readers can identify most words automatically and use word-identification strategies to figure out unfamiliar words.

—————————— Assessment Tool: Word-Identification Strategies ——————————

To assess middle- and upper-grade students' ability to use word-identification strategies, prepare a set of grade-level-appropriate word cards and develop a checklist as shown below. Write the words on the checklist. Individually, ask students to read the word cards. After reading each word, ask the student to explain how he or she decoded the word and then mark the word-identification strategy. If the student already knows the word and reads it without using any word-identification strategies, check the column marked "Automatic."

Word	Phonic Analysis	By Analogy	Syllabic Analysis	Morphemic Analysis	Automatic

WHAT IS FLUENCY?

In the primary grades students learn to recognize hundreds of words automatically and learn strategies to decode unfamiliar words so that they can read fluently. Reading fluency involves two components. The first is the ability to read words accurately, rapidly, and automatically. Students need to read at least 100 words per minute in order to read fluently, and most students reach this reading speed by third grade. Students' reading speed continues to grow, and by the time they are adults they will read from 250 to 300 words per minute. The second component of reading fluency is the ability to read sentences expressively, with appropriate phrasing and intonation. Students move from word-by-word reading with little or no expression to reading in phrases, attending to punctuation, applying appropriate semantic and syntactic emphases. When they read, fluent readers' oral reading approximates talking. This component is known as prosody.

Fluent readers are better able to comprehend what they read because they can identify words easily (LaBerge & Samuels, 1976; Perfitti, 1985; Stanovich, 1986). Students who are not fluent readers often read hesitantly, in a word-by-word fashion and with great effort. These less competent readers spend too much mental energy in identifying words, leaving little energy to focus on comprehension. Readers do not have an unlimited amount of mental energy to use when they read, and they cannot focus on both word identification and comprehension at the same time. So, as students become fluent readers, they use less energy for word identification and focus more energy on comprehending what they read.

By third grade, most students have become fluent readers. They have acquired a large stock of high-frequency words that they can read automatically, and they have developed word-identification strategies, including phonic analysis and syllabic analysis, to use to figure out unfamiliar words. But some students continue to read slowly, in a halting manner and without expression. They do not read fluently, and they exemplify some of these characteristics:

- Students read slowly.
- Students cannot decode individual words.
- Students try to sound out phonetically irregular words.
- Students guess at words based on the beginning sound.
- Students do not remember a word the second or third time it is used in a passage.
- Students do not break multisyllabic words into syllables to decode them.
- Students do not break multisyllabic words into root words and affixes to decode them.
- Students point at words as they read.
- Students repeat words and phrases.
- Students read without expression.
- Students read word by word.
- Students ignore punctuation marks.
- Students do not remember or understand what they read.

Writing fluency is similar to reading fluency. Students need to be able to write quickly and easily so that their hands and arms do not hurt. Slow, laborious handwriting interferes with the expression of ideas. In addition, students must be able to spell words automatically so that they can take notes, write journal entries, and handle other writing assignments.

Promoting Reading Fluency

Nonfluent readers can learn to read fluently (Allington, 1983). These readers may need to work on their reading speed or their phrasing or on both components of fluency.

Improving Reading Speed. The best approach to improve students' reading speed is **repeated readings** (Samuels, 1979), in which students practice rereading a book or an excerpt from a book three to five times, striving to improve their reading rate and decrease the number of errors they make. Teachers often time students' reading and plot their speed on a graph so that improvements can be noted. Repeated readings also enhance students' ability to chunk words into meaningful phrases and read with more expression (Dowhower, 1987). Researchers have also found that through repeated readings, students deepen their comprehension of the books they reread (Yaden, 1988).

Teachers often incorporate repeated readings as part of guided reading when they want to assist students in rereading. Sometimes they read the passage aloud while students follow along or use echo reading in which they repeat each phrase or sentence after the teacher reads it. Then students reread the passage using **choral reading.** After several repetitions, students can reread the passage one more time, this time independently. Teachers can also set up rereading opportunities at a listening center. If students are timing their reading, then a stopwatch or other timing device can be added to the center. Teachers also use paired repeated readings in which stu-

As students reread books, they increase reading speed and develop reading fluency.

dents work together to read, reread, and evaluate their reading (P. A. Koskinen & Blum, 1986).

Teaching Phrasing. Schreider (1980) recommends teaching students how to phrase or chunk together parts of sentences in order to read. Fluent readers seem to understand how to chunk parts of sentences into meaningful units, perhaps because they have been read to or have had many reading experiences themselves, but many struggling readers do not have this ability. Consider this sentence from *Sarah, Plain and Tall* (MacLachlan, 1985): "A few raindrops came, gentle at first, then stronger and louder, so that Caleb and I covered our ears and stared at each other without speaking" (p. 47). This sentence comes from the chapter describing a terrible storm that the pioneer family endured, huddled with their animals in their sturdy barn. Three commas help students read the first part of this sentence, but then students must decide how to chunk the second part of the sentence.

Teachers can work with nonfluent readers to have them practice breaking sentences into chunks and then reading the sentences with expression. Teachers can duplicate copies of a page from a book students are reading so that students can use a pencil to mark pauses in longer sentences. Or, teachers can choose a sentence to write on the chalkboard, chunking it into phrases like this:

A few raindrops came,
gentle at first,
then stronger and louder,
so that Caleb and I
covered our ears
and stared at each other
without speaking.

After chunking, students practice reading the sentence in chunks with classmates and individually. After working with one sentence, students can choose another sentence to chunk and practice reading. Students who don't chunk words into phrases when they read aloud need many opportunities to practice chunking and rereading sentences.

Reading activities such as choral reading also help students improve their phrasing. In choral reading, students and the teacher take turns reading the text, as Ms. Williams and her students did in the vignette at the beginning of the chapter. Students provide support for each other because they are reading in small groups, and they learn to phrase sentences as they read along with classmates. Choral reading also improves students' reading speed because they read along with classmates.

One variation of choral reading is unison reading, in which the teacher and students read a text together (Reutzel & Cooter, 2000). The teacher is the leader and reads loudly enough to be heard above the group. Another variation is echo reading, in which the teacher reads a sentence with good phrasing and intonation, and then students read the same material again. If the students read confidently, the teacher moves to the next sentence. If, however, students struggle to read the sentence, the teacher repeats the first sentence. These approaches are especially useful for helping students who are learning English as a second language to develop appropriate phrasing and intonation.

Reading Practice. Students need many opportunities to practice reading and rereading books in order to develop fluency. The best books for reading practice are ones that students are interested in reading and that are written at a level just below their instructional level. Books for fluency practice should be neither too easy nor too difficult. Students should automatically recognize most words in the book, but if the book is extremely easy it provides no challenge to the reader. And, when students read books that are too difficult, they read slowly because they stop again and again to identify unfamiliar words. This constant stopping reinforces nonfluent readers' already choppy reading style.

For reading practice, students often choose "pop" literature that is fun to read but rather ordinary. These books are often more effective than some high-quality literature selections in helping children develop fluency because the vocabulary is more controlled and students can be more successful. Books like *Marvin Redpost: Kidnapped at Birth?* (Sachar, 1992), *Money Troubles* (Cosby, 1998), *Afternoon on the Amazon* (Osborne, 1995), and *Whales* (Milton, 1989) are written at the first- and second-grade level, and *Amber Brown Is Not a Crayon* (Danziger, 1994), *Chang's Paper Pony* (Coerr, 1988), and *The Cat's Meow* (Soto, 1987) are written at the third-grade level. More and more easier books that are suitable for third through sixth graders are becoming available each year, and many of these are adventure stories and informational books that appeal to boys. Many basal reading programs come with leveled practice books, and most publishers of children's books have developed series of easier books.

Teachers provide two types of daily opportunities for children to practice reading and rereading familiar stories and other books. Some activities provide assisted practice, and other activities provide students with opportunities to read independently, without assistance. In assisted practice, students have a model to follow as they read or reread. Choral reading is one example, and **readers theatre** is another. In readers theatre, students practice reading story scripts to develop fluency before reading the script to an audience of classmates. In a recent study, Martinez, Roser, and Strecker

www.sil.org

Lingualinks Library. Activities for developing fluent readers, including the neurological impress method, repeated readings, and reading along with audiotapes.

www.aaronshep.com

Stories On Stage. Scripts for readers theatre performances, how-to tips for scripting, staging, and performing, and links to related Internet sites.

Technology Link **Screen Reading: Using Captioned Television Programs to Develop Reading Fluency**

Reading captioned television programs provides students with opportunities for reading practice that is entertaining and self-correcting. On captioned television programs, sentences corresponding to the words spoken on the video are printed on the screen, much like the subtitles on foreign films. The captions can be seen on television sets that are equipped with special electronic TeleCaption decoders. These decoders can be purchased for less than $200 and can easily be attached to a television. All new televisions have the built-in circuitry to decode and display closed-captioned programming.

Captions were first developed for hearing-impaired viewers, but now they have a valuable instructional purpose: screen reading (P. S. Koskinen, Wilson, Gambrell, & Neuman, 1993). Koskinen and her colleagues found that less fluent readers and bilingual students become more motivated readers when they use captioned television and video, and they proposed that the simultaneous multisensory processing enhances learning.

Teachers can use captioned television programs when they are broadcast, or they can videotape the programs to use later. One of the best uses is to videotape a program and use it as a prereading activity to build background knowledge and introduce vocabulary. Teachers might show a video related to the text students will read, or they might show the video version of the book students will read. Many fine videos, including the Reading Rainbow programs, which feature award-winning children's literature, are available. Children with reading difficulties can also practice rereading captioned videos, and they can view the videos as independent reading activities.

Guidelines for Using Captioned Television Programs

1. Choose programs related to literature and content-area instruction as a prereading activity.
2. Introduce the program and provide key vocabulary words.
3. Plan related activities to use after viewing the program.
4. Allow students learning English as a second language and students with reading difficulties to view the program several times.
5. Create a text set of books and other reading materials to use with the program.
6. Provide opportunities for students to review the program and read related texts.
7. Create a video library.

Some captioned videos, such as Reading Rainbow programs, can be purchased from video stores and from educational publishers. Captioned programs can be videotaped from television, but copyright laws restrict the length of time they can be saved and the number of times the tapes can be used.

For more information about captioned television programs and videos, contact The National Captioning Institute, 5203 Leesburg Pike, Falls Church, VA 22041; telephone 1-800-533-WORD.

(1998/1999) found that practice reading using readers theatre scripts resulted in significant improvement in second graders' reading fluency. Other examples of assisted reading are echo reading, listening centers, shared reading, and buddy reading. Screen reading is another way to provide assisted reading practice. Check the Technology Link on page 223 for more information about how to use this underutilized technology.

In unassisted reading practice, students read independently. They do this type of reading during reading workshop and at reading centers. Another unassisted practice activity that is often used in primary-grade classrooms is reading the classroom. Students walk around the classroom reading all the words and sentences that are posted. Sometimes students dress up for this activity. They can wear glasses in which the lenses have been removed and use pointers to track what they are reading as they walk around the classroom.

Middle- and upper-grade students often participate in **read-arounds.** In this activity, students choose a favorite sentence or paragraph from a book or other reading assignment they have already read and practice reading the passage they have chosen several times. Then students take turns reading their passages aloud. They read in any order they want, and usually several students will read the same passage aloud. Teachers often plan this activity to bring closure to a book students have read or to review information presented in a content-area textbook.

Why Is Round-Robin Reading No Longer Recommended? Round-robin reading is an outmoded oral reading activity in which the teacher calls on children to read aloud, one after the other. Some teachers used round-robin reading in small groups and others used the procedure with the whole class, but neither version is advocated today. According to Opitz and Rasinski (1998), many problems are associated with round-robin reading. First of all, students may develop an inaccurate view of reading because they are expected to read aloud to the class without having opportunities to rehearse. In addition, they may develop inefficient reading habits because they slow their silent reading speed to match the various speeds of classmates when they read aloud. Students signal their inattention and boredom by misbehaving as classmates read aloud. In addition to these problems for students who are listening, round-robin reading causes problems for some students when they are called upon to read. Struggling readers are often anxious or embarrassed when they read aloud.

Most teachers now agree that round-robin reading wastes valuable classroom time that could be spent on more meaningful reading activities. Instead of round-robin reading, students should read the text independently if it is at their reading level. If it is too difficult, students can read with buddies, participate in shared reading, or listen to the teacher or another fluent reader read aloud. Also, they might listen to the teacher read the material aloud and then try reading it with a buddy or independently.

Developing Writing Fluency

To become fluent writers, students must be able to rapidly form letters and spell words automatically. Just as nonfluent readers read word by word and have to stop and decode many words, nonfluent writers write slowly, word by word, and have to stop and check the spelling of many words. In fact, some nonfluent writers write so slowly that they forget the sentence they are writing! Through varied, daily writing activities, students develop the muscular control to form letters quickly and legibly. They write high-frequency words again and again until they can spell them automatically.

Being able to write fluently usually coincides with being able to read fluently because reading and writing practice are mutually beneficial (Shanahan, 1988; Tierney, 1983).

Students become fluent writers as they practice writing, and they need opportunities for both assisted and unassisted practice. Writing on white boards during **interactive writing** lessons is one example of assisted writing practice (Tompkins, 2000). The teacher and classmates provide support for students.

Peter Elbow (1973, 1981) recommends using **quickwriting** to develop writing fluency. In quickwriting, students write rapidly and without stopping as they explore an idea. As part of the unit on hermit crabs, Ms. Williams asked the second-grade students to do a quickwrite listing what they had learned about hermit crabs. Here is Arlette's quickwrite:

> *Hermit crabs live in tide pools. They have pincers and 10 legs in all. They can pinch you very hard. Ouch! They are crabs and they molt to grow and grow. They have to buro (borrow) shells to live in becus (because) other anmels (animals) will eat them. They like to eat fish and shrimp. Sea enomes (anemones) like to live on ther (their) shells.*

Arlette listed a great deal of information that she had learned about hermit crabs. She misspelled five words, and the correct spellings are given in parentheses. Arlette was able to write such a long quickwrite and to misspell very few words because she is already a fluent writer. While she was writing, she checked the hermit crab word wall and the high-frequency word wall in the classroom in order to spell *pincers, shrimp,* and *other.* The other words she knew how to spell and wrote them automatically.

In contrast, Jeremy is not yet a fluent writer. Here is his quickwrite:

> *The hermit crab liv (lives) in a hues (house)*
>
> *he eat (eats) shimp (shrimp).*

Jeremy writes slowly and laboriously. He stops to think of an idea before writing each sentence and starts each sentence on a new line. He rarely refers to the word walls in the classroom, and he spells most words phonetically. Even though Jeremy's writing is not as fluent as Arlette's, quickwriting is a useful activity for him because he will become more fluent through practice.

Ms. Williams has her students quickwrite several times each week. They quickwrite to respond to a story she has read aloud or to write about what they are learning in science or another content area. She reads and responds to the quickwrites, and she writes the correct form of misspelled words at the bottom of the page so that students will notice the correct spelling. Once in a while she has students revise and edit their quickwrites and make a final, published copy, but her goal is to develop writing fluency, not to develop finished, polished compositions.

Why Is Copying From the Chalkboard No Longer Recommended?

Some teachers write sentences and poems on the chalkboard for students to copy in hopes that this activity will develop writing fluency. Copying isn't a very effective instructional strategy, though, because students are passively copying letters, not actively creating sentences, breaking the sentences into words, and spelling the words. In fact, sometimes students are copying sentences they cannot read, so the activity becomes little more than handwriting practice. It is much more worthwhile for students to write sentences to express their own ideas and to practice spelling words.

Assessing Students' Reading and Writing Fluency

Teachers assess reading and writing fluency by observing students as they read and write. Teachers assess students' reading fluency by listening to them read aloud and considering these points:

🦋 ***Speed.*** Do students read hesitantly, or do they read quickly enough to understand what they are reading?

🦋 ***Phrasing.*** Do students read word by word, or do they chunk words into phrases?

🦋 ***Prosody.*** Do students read in a monotone, or do they read with expression in a manner that approximates talking?

🦋 ***Automaticity.*** Do students have to decode many words, or do they read most words automatically?

By third grade, students should be fluent readers. If students have difficulty with any of the four points, teachers should provide instruction in that area in addition to reading practice to improve their fluency.

Teachers assess students' writing fluency in a similar manner. They observe students as they write and consider these points:

🦋 ***Ideas.*** Do students have trouble thinking of something to write, or do they think of ideas for writing readily?

🦋 ***Speed.*** Do students write slowly, or do they write quickly enough to complete the writing task?

🦋 ***Ease.*** Do students write laboriously or easily?

🦋 ***Automaticity.*** Do students have to sound out or locate the spelling of most words, or do they spell most words automatically?

Students should be fluent writers by third grade. If students have difficulty with any of the four points, teachers should provide instruction in that area plus lots of writing practice to improve their fluency.

Review

Students need to become fluent readers and writers by third grade. During the primary grades, students learn to recognize many high-frequency words in order to develop reading fluency. They also learn to spell these high-frequency words to become fluent writers. Teachers create word walls to call children's attention to the 100 to 300 highest-frequency words. In addi- tion, students learn to use phonic analysis, analogies, syllabic analysis, and morphemic analysis to identify unfamiliar words when reading and to spell words when writing. The feature on page 227 presents a list of recommended practices that effective teachers use to promote reading and writing fluency.

How Effective Teachers . . .

Develop Fluent Readers and Writers

✷ Effective Practices

1. Teachers teach high-frequency words because they are the most useful for students.
2. Teachers post high-frequency words on word walls in the classroom and teach students to read and spell the words using chant and clap procedures.
3. Teachers provide daily opportunities for students to practice word recognition through word study centers and reading and writing practice.
4. Teachers teach four decoding strategies and related skills—phonic analysis, by analogy, syllabic analysis, and morphemic analysis.
5. Teachers encourage students to look at every letter in a word and to decode as much of the word as possible, not to just guess at the word.
6. Teachers involve students in choral reading, repeated reading, listening centers, and other reading activities to develop their reading fluency.
7. Teachers have students choose books written at levels just below their instructional level for fluency-building activities.
8. Teachers involve students in interactive writing, quickwriting, and other writing activities to develop their writing fluency.
9. Teachers observe students as they read and write to determine whether or not they are fluent.
10. Teachers ensure that students become fluent readers and writers by third grade.

✷ Ineffective Practices

1. Teachers don't emphasize high-frequency words over less common words.
2. Teachers don't post high-frequency words in the classroom or focus students' attention on these words.
3. Teachers provide few daily opportunities for students to learn to recognize and spell many words.
4. Teachers encourage students to depend on only one or two decoding strategies—usually phonics—to figure out unfamiliar words.
5. Teachers encourage students to identify the initial sound in a word and then guess at the word.
6. Teachers use round-robin reading to help students become fluent readers.
7. Teachers don't monitor the difficulty levels of books that students use for practice reading to develop fluency.
8. Teachers have students copy from the chalkboard to develop writing fluency.
9. Teachers use silent reading to determine reading fluency and scores on spelling tests to determine writing fluency.
10. Teachers don't recognize the importance of having students become fluent readers and writers by third grade.

References

Adams, M. J. (1990). *Beginning to read: Thinking and learning about print*. Cambridge, MA: MIT Press.

Allington, R. L. (1983). Fluency: The neglected reading goal. *The Reading Teacher, 33,* 556–561.

Allington, R. L. (Ed.). (1998). *Teaching struggling readers*. Newark, DE: International Reading Association.

Calfee, R., & Drum, P. (1986). Research on teaching reading. In M. W. Wittrock (Ed.), *Handbook of research on teaching* (3rd ed.) (pp. 804–849). New York: Macmillan.

Chall, J. S., Jacobs, V. A., & Baldwin, L. E. (1990). *The reading crisis: Why poor children fall behind*. Cambridge, MA: Harvard University Press.

Cunningham, P. M. (1975–1976). Investigating a synthesized theory of mediated word identification. *Reading Research Quarterly, 11,* 127–143.

Cunningham, P. M. (2000). *Phonics they use: Words for reading and writing* (3rd ed.). New York: HarperCollins.

Delpit, L. (1987). The silenced dialogue: Power and pedagogy in educating other people's children. *Harvard Educational Review, 58,* 280–298.

Dowhower, S. L. (1987). Effects of repeated reading on second-grade transitional readers' fluency and comprehension. *Reading Research Quarterly, 22,* 389–406.

Ehri, L. C., & Robbins, C. (1992). Beginners need some decoding skill to read words by analogy. *Reading Research Quarterly, 27,* 13–26.

Elbow, P. (1973). *Writing without teachers.* Oxford: Oxford University Press.

Elbow, P. (1981). *Writing with power.* Oxford: Oxford University Press.

Eldredge, J. L. (1995). *Teaching decoding in holistic classrooms.* Englewood Cliffs, NJ: Prentice Hall.

Gaskins, I. W., Ehri, L. C., Cress, C., O'Hara, C., & Donnelly, K. (1996/1997). Procedures for word learning: Making discoveries about words. *The Reading Teacher, 50,* 312–326.

Gaskins, R. W., Gaskins, J. W., & Gaskins, I. W. (1991). A decoding program for poor readers—and the rest of the class, too! *Language Arts, 68,* 213–225.

Gough, P. B., Juel, C., & Griffith, P. L. (1992). Reading, spelling, and the orthographic cipher. In P. B. Gough, L. C. Ehri, & R. Treiman (Eds.), *Reading acquisition* (pp. 35–48). Hillsdale, NJ: Erlbaum.

Hiebert, E. H. (1991). The development of word-level strategies in authentic literacy tasks. *Language Arts, 68,* 234–240.

Hitchcock, M. E. (1989). *Elementary students' invented spellings at the correct stage of spelling development.* Unpublished doctoral dissertation, Norman, University of Oklahoma.

Johnson, D. D., & Baumann, J. F. (1984). Word identification. In P. D. Pearson (Ed.), *Handbook of reading research* (pp. 583–608). New York: Longman.

Koskinen, P. A., & Blum, I. H. (1986). Paired repeated reading: A classroom strategy for developing fluent reading. *The Reading Teacher, 40,* 70–75.

Koskinen, P. S., Wilson, R. M., Gambrell, L. B., & Neuman, S. B. (1993). Captioned video and vocabulary learning: An innovative practice in literacy instruction. *The Reading Teacher, 47,* 36–43.

LaBerge, D., & Samuels, S. J. (1976). Toward a theory of automatic information processing in reading. In H. Singer & R. Ruddell (Eds.), *Theoretical models and processes of reading* (pp. 548–579). Newark, DE: International Reading Association.

Martinez, M., Roser, N. L., & Strecker, S. (1998/1999). "I never thought I could be a star": A readers theatre ticket to fluency. *The Reading Teacher, 52,* 326–334.

Opitz, M. F., & Rasinski, T. V. (1998). *Good-bye round robin: Twenty-five effective oral reading strategies.* Portsmouth, NH: Heinemann.

Perfitti, C. A. (1985). *Reading ability.* New York: Oxford University Press.

Pinnell, G. S., & Fountas, I. C. (1998). *Word matters: Teaching phonics and spelling in the reading/writing classroom.* Portsmouth, NH: Heinemann.

Reutzel, D. R., & Cooter, R. B. (2000). *Teaching children to read: From basals to books* (3rd ed.). Upper Saddle River, NJ: Merrill/Prentice Hall.

Reyes, M. de la Luz. (1991). A process approach to literacy using dialogue journals and literature logs with second language learners. *Research in the Teaching of English, 25,* 291–313.

Samuels, S. J. (1979). The method of repeated readings. *The Reading Teacher, 32,* 403–408.

Schreider, P. A. (1980). On the acquisition of reading fluency. *Journal of Reading Behavior, 12,* 177–186.

Shanahan, T. (1988). The reading-writing relationship: Seven instructional principles. *The Reading Teacher, 41,* 636–647.

Snow, C. E., Burns, M. S., & Griffin, P. (Eds.). (1998). *Preventing reading difficulties in young children.* Washington, DC: National Academy Press.

Stanovich, K. E. (1986). Matthew effects in reading: Some consequences of individual differences in the acquisition of literacy. *Reading Research Quarterly, 21,* 360–406.

Stanovich, K. E. (1992). Speculations on the causes and consequences of individual differences in early reading acquisition. In P. B. Gough, L. C. Ehri, & R. Treiman (Eds.), *Reading acquisition* (pp. 307–342). Hillsdale, NJ: Erlbaum.

Tierney, R. J. (1983). Writer-reader transactions: Defining the dimensions of negotiation. In P. L. Stock (Ed.), *Forum: Essays on theory and practice in the teaching of writing* (pp. 147–151). Upper Montclair, NJ: Boynton/Cook.

Tompkins, G. E. (2000). *Teaching writing: Balancing process and product* (3rd ed.). Englewood Cliffs, NJ: Merrill/Prentice Hall.

Vellutino, F. R., & Scanlon, D. M. (1987). Phonological coding, phonological awareness, and reading ability: Evidence from a longitudinal and experimental study. *Merrill-Palmer Quarterly, 33,* 321–363.

White, T. G., Sowell, J., & Yanagihara, A. (1989). Teaching elementary students to use word-part clues. *The Reading Teacher, 42,* 302–308.

Yaden, D. B., Jr. (1988). Understanding stories through repeated read-alouds: How many does it take? *The Reading Teacher, 41,* 556–560.

Children's Book References

Carle, E. (1987). *A house for hermit crab*. Saxonville, MA: Picture Book Studio.

Coerr, E. (1988). *Chang's paper pony*. New York: Harper-Collins.

Cosby, B. (1998). *Money troubles*. New York: Scholastic.

Danziger, P. (1994). *Amber Brown is not a crayon*. New York: Putnam.

Greenaway, F. (1992). *Tide pool*. New York: DK Publishing.

Holling, H. C. (1990). *Pagoo*. Boston: Houghton Mifflin.

Kaplan, R. (1996). *Moving day*. New York: Greenwillow.

MacLachlan, P. (1985). *Sarah, plain and tall*. New York: Harper and Row.

Milton, J. (1989). *Whales*. New York: Random House.

Osborne, M. P. (1995). *Afternoon on the Amazon*. New York: Random House.

Pohl, K. (1987). *Hermit crabs*. Milwaukee: Raintree.

Randell, B. (1994). *Hermit crab*. Crystal Lake, IL: Rigby Books.

Sachar, L. (1992). *Marvin Redpost: Kidnapped at birth?* New York: Random House.

Soto, G. (1987). *The cat's meow*. New York: Scholastic.

Tuchman, G. (1997). *Hermit's shiny shell*. New York: Macmillan/McGraw-Hill.

Part III
How Do Readers and Writers Construct Meaning?

Ms. Boland's seventh graders are learning about medieval life in their integrated English/social studies class. They are reading and discussing Karen Cushman's *Catherine, Called Birdy* (1994), a novel written in diary form. Catherine, the author of the diary, is a young noble woman in 1290 and she provides fascinating details about life in the Middle Ages. The book's humorous tone makes it very popular.

Students meet in small groups called literature circles to discuss the book, and Ms. Boland sits in on the discussions. She helps students focus on both the events in the story and the historical information they are learning about medieval life.

Students use their social studies textbooks to learn about the Middle Ages. Students work in groups to read the three sections of the chapter. Then they report back and Ms. Boland helps to direct their focus to main ideas in each section as she lists them on the chalkboard.

Students in each group make a chart about the main ideas and details in their section of the chapter and present the information to the class.

Each group also adds important vocabulary words to "Ye Olde Word Wall," which is posted in the classroom.

To showcase their learning, Ms. Boland's students create an interactive museum about medieval life. Students, working in small groups, create displays on cathedrals; the life of a knight; food, fun, and fashion; and other topics. Students work together to research their topics using classroom resources and the Internet, and they compile the information on note cards.

As they work, students assume roles in the group, including:

➤ Facilitator, who keeps the group on task and solves problems.

➤ Research coordinator, who makes sure group members know their research topics.

➤ Internet troubleshooter, who assists group members using the Internet.

➤ Harmonizer, who helps the group work together smoothly.

➤ Supply person, who gets needed materials from Ms. Boland.

On their laptop computer, these two boys develop a PowerPoint® presentation about the life of a knight, which they will use as part of the display.

The seventh graders take the information they gathered and create accurate and creative displays to engage museum visitors. Other students at the school, parents, school board members, and other members of the community visit the museum.

Research Rubric

5 Excellent
More than four sources of information, including the Internet, were used.
Notes are written in your own words.
Time and effort clearly demonstrated in note-taking.
Bibliography is correct.

4 Very Good
Four sources of information, including the Internet, were used.
Notes are mostly written in your own words.
Above-average time and effort used in note-taking.
Bibliography has very few errors.

3 Good
Three sources of information, including the Internet, were used.
Notes are mostly written in your own words.
Average amount of time and effort used in note-taking.
Bibliography has some errors.

2 Poor

Ms. Boland and the students developed this five-point rubric to assess their research for the museum display. They developed the rubric before beginning to research so that they would understand what was expected of them.

Students' presentations take many forms, including labeled artifacts, demonstrations, and video presentations. In addition, students dress as "moving statues" on museum day and explain their displays to the visitors.

Chapter 7

Learning About the Meanings of Words

— Chapter Questions —

How do students learn vocabulary words?

What is the relationship between vocabulary knowledge and reading?

How do teachers teach vocabulary?

What are the components of word study?

Mrs. Dillon's Students Learn About Words

Before Mrs. Dillon's second graders read Kevin Henkes's *Chrysanthemum* (1991), a picture-book story about a mouse named Chrysanthemum who doesn't like her name, Mrs. Dillon brings a book box full of artificial flowers to the classroom. She talks about how she loves flowers, especially these flowers. She takes each flower out of the box as she names it: rose, gladiola, daisy, chrysanthemum, pansy, delphinium, iris, and daffodil. Children mention names of flowers they like or that grow in their gardens. Mrs. Dillon writes *Chrysanthemum* on the chalkboard, and the students are amazed by the size of the word. Dean notices the word *the* in the middle of the word. Mrs. Dillon tells the class that it is the name of one of the flowers she showed them and also the title of the book they are going to read. Mrs. Dillon's students pride themselves on being word detectives. Several of them guess the flower name right away!

Mrs. Dillon uses shared reading to introduce the book to her students. She reads the book aloud as students follow in their own copies of the book. Afterwards, students identify these interesting and important words and phrases for the **word wall** (see the Compendium for more information about this and all other highlighted terms in this chapter)—a large sheet of butcher paper hanging on the wall:

Chrysanthemum	icing on her birthday cake
happiest day	sunniest dress
absolutely perfect	Mrs. Chud
parents	wilted
bathroom mirror	absolutely dreadful
miserably	Welcome home!
Oh, pish!	precious
priceless	fascinating
winsome	Parcheesi
macaroni and cheese	ketchup
extremely pleasant	most comfortable
jealous	chocolate cake
begrudging	discontented
buttercream frosting	sprouted leaves and petals
Victoria	scrawny stem
worst nightmare	miserably
most prized possessions	good-luck charms
route to school	speechless
indescribable wonder	nice impression
class musicale	dainty Fairy Queen
Butterfly Princess	Pixie messenger

daisy	wildly funny
what's so humorous?	Mrs. Twinkle
delphinium	blushed
beamed	bloomed
longingly	marigold
carnation	lily of the valley
epilogue	huge success

There are many words in this list, such as *icing, sunniest,* and *absolutely,* that students know the meaning of but don't recognize in print. They are able to figure out how to pronounce other words, such as *wilted,* using sound-symbol correspondences, but they don't know the meaning of the words. In the story, Chrysanthemum "wilted" when someone hurt her feelings. "Does the word mean she cried?" Lizzie asks. Lizzie makes a good guess using the context clues in the story, but she isn't correct, so Mrs. Dillon dramatizes the word to clarify the meaning. They talk about how clever the author was to choose this word because flowers wilt, too. Other words, such as *scrawny, Parcheesi,* and *epilogue,* are new to them. Students don't recognize the words or know what they mean.

Mrs. Dillon won't try to teach all of these words. The ones she chooses to focus on are ones that she thinks are important to the story and also common enough that her students will read them in other books. She chooses some fun words, too. *Parcheesi* is one of the fun words. She brings in a Parcheesi game and teaches the children how to play.

Mrs. Dillon uses a variety of activities to help students learn about the words. She teaches a **minilesson** on comparatives and superlatives using *happy–happier–happiest* and *sunny–sunnier–sunniest* as examples, and students brainstorm a list of words that have comparative and superlative forms. Later, students work at the writing center to make pages for a class book on comparatives and superlatives. Children each choose a word from the brainstormed list and write the three forms of the word on a page. Then they draw pictures and write sentences using each word form to complete their page. Other word activities include:

❦ Teach a minilesson on syllables using words from the word wall. *Victoria, Chrysanthemum,* and *delphinium,* for example, all have four syllables.

❦ Introduce the concept of synonyms using words from the word wall, including *humorous, dainty, extremely, precious,* and *miserable.* Mrs. Dillon uses a children's thesaurus to locate some of the synonyms and shows the class how to use the book. Then she places the book in the word-study center and children locate words and synonyms in the thesaurus and write them on cards which they place in a pocket chart.

❦ Read other books on flowers, such as *The Rose in My Garden* (Lobel, 1984), *The Flower Alphabet Book* (Pallotta, 1988), *The Reason for a Flower* (Heller, 1983), and *Alison's Zinnia* (Lobel, 1990), and locate examples of chrysanthemums and other flowers mentioned in the story. Then students reread the books at the reading center or listen to them at the listening center.

🪰 Teach a minilesson on capitalizing names. Students learn that *chrysanthemum* is a flower, but *Chrysanthemum* is a name.

🪰 Have students make word posters illustrating a word from the word wall and using that word in a sentence at the vocabulary center.

🪰 Make a Venn diagram comparing the characters Chrysanthemum and Victoria. The Venn diagram that Mrs. Dillon's class created is shown in Figure 7–1.

At the end of the unit, one of Mrs. Dillon's students, Lizzie, talks about the words in *Chrysanthemum:*

"I thought this book was going to be hard. *Chrysanthemum* is a big word and big words are hard sometimes. But this is a good book."

Figure 7–1 A Venn diagram comparing two characters

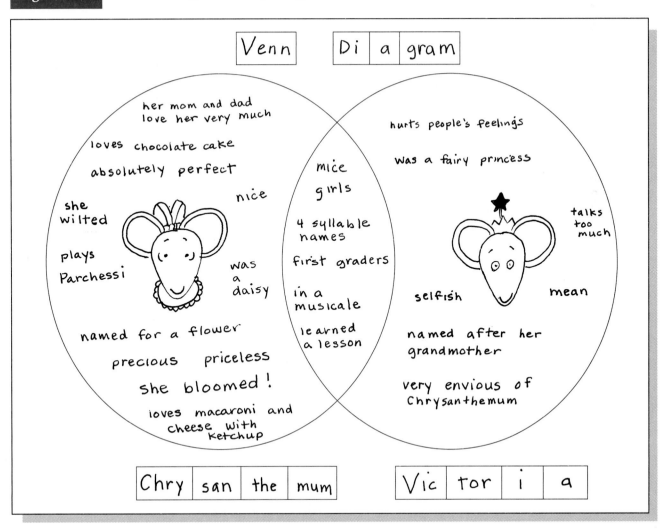

I asked whether she can read all the words in the book, and she is hesitant as she answers.

"Well, not all of them. I know *Chrysanthemum, absolutely perfect, wilted, Mrs. Chud, sunniest dress, delphinium, Mrs. Twinkle, good-luck charms, Parcheesi, . . .*" (she continues reading from the word wall).

"Can you pick out some words from the word wall that describe Chrysanthemum?"

"Yes I can. Chrysanthemum is wilted [and she dramatizes the word as Mrs. Dillon had done]. And Chrysanthemum is miserable because Victoria and Rita and the other kids hurt her feelings, and she is named after a flower, and at the end she bloomed because she likes her name now because Mrs. Twinkle named her baby Chrysanthemum. This book is love. It's good, you know."

My last question was, "How do you know these words?"

"I just do. We read and we talk about books every day. And we write lots of books. My teacher, Mrs. Dillon, says we are 'word detectives.' That means we know lots of words."

Mrs. Dillon incorporates word study throughout the reading process. She introduces a few key words before students read a book, but many other word-study activities come after reading, when students are especially interested in learning about the words in the book they have read. Mrs. Dillon creates and posts a word wall in the classroom, and her students choose the words and often write them on the word wall themselves. These words become their words. They refer to the list as they reread, write, and talk about the book, and Mrs. Dillon teaches vocabulary lessons focusing on some of the words.

··

Children learn vocabulary by being immersed in words, and Mrs. Dillon engaged her second graders with words as they read and discussed *Chrysanthemum* (Henkes, 1991). Researchers have reported again and again that reading is the best way for students to learn words. As they read, students learn many, many words incidentally, and teachers reinforce students' learning by directly teaching some difficult words that are significant to the story or important for general knowledge (Stahl, 1999).

Unfamiliar words are not equally hard or easy to learn; the degree of difficulty depends on what students already know about the word. Graves (1985) identifies four possible situations for unfamiliar words:

1. *Sight word.* Students recognize the word, know what it means when they hear someone say it, and can use it orally, but they don't recognize its written form.
2. *New word.* Students have a concept related to the word, but they are not familiar with the word, either orally or in written form.
3. *New concept.* Students have little or no background knowledge about the concept underlying the word, and they don't recognize the word itself.
4. *New meaning.* Students know the word, but they are unfamiliar with the way the word is used and its meaning in this situation.

The words in *Chrysanthemum* represented all four of these categories. Two sight words were *absolutely* and *sunniest*. As soon as Mrs. Dillon pronounced *absolutely,* the students recognized it as a familiar word that they used orally. She divided it into syllables—*ab-so-lute-ly*—so that students could decode it themselves. For *sunniest,* Mrs. Dillon explained that *sunny + est* is spelled as *sunniest,* and then the students recognized it easily. The flower words—*chrysanthemum, daisy, marigold, carnation,* and *delphinium*—were unfamiliar labels for flowers the students had seen in their neighborhood, but they knew them as "yellow flowers" or "pink flowers" or "blue flowers." Other label words that Mrs. Dillon's students learned were *wilted* and *blushed*. The students were familiar with the concepts, but they did not know the labels. They learned that *wilted* can mean that the flower "droops" or becomes limp when it needs water, and that *blushed* is when your face turns red because you are modest or embarrassed.

Mrs. Dillon taught two new concepts, and one was much easier to teach than the other. *Epilogue* was a new concept for the students, but because it is concrete, it was easy for students to learn. They understood that it was a short piece telling what happened to the characters after the story ended. *Jealousy* was a much more difficult concept because it is abstract. Mrs. Dillon talked about the concept, using as examples both Victoria's jealousy from the story and family and school experiences that children might be familiar with. Not all students understood the concept or the word, but many did.

Students learned new meanings for several words, too. They learned that *chrysanthemum* is a flower and *Chrysanthemum* is a girl's name. They knew that a *beam* can be a shaft of light as from a flashlight or a car's headlights, and they learned that the smile on a person's face can "beam," too. They learned the label *wilted* for what a flower does when it is thirsty, and they learned that a person can "wilt," too, when his or her feelings are hurt.

Of the four categories of word learning, the most difficult one for students is the one involving new concepts because they must first learn the concept and then attach a word label and learn the definition. Students benefit from receiving direct instruction on these concepts and the words to explain them.

HOW DO STUDENTS LEARN VOCABULARY WORDS?

Students' vocabularies grow at an astonishing rate—about 3,000 words a year, or roughly 7 to 10 new words every day (Nagy & Herman, 1985). By the time students graduate from high school, their vocabularies reach 25,000 to 40,000 words or more. In order to learn words at such a prolific rate, it seems obvious that students learn words both in school and outside of school, and that students learn most words incidentally, not through direct instruction. Reading has the largest impact on children's vocabulary development, but other activities are important, too. Students learn words through family activities, hobbies, and trips. Television can also have a significant impact on children's vocabularies, especially when children view educational programs and limit the amount of time they spend watching television each day. Teachers often assume that students learn words primarily through the lessons they teach, but students actually learn many more words in other ways.

Levels of Word Knowledge

Students develop knowledge about a word slowly, through repeated exposure to the word. They move from not knowing the word at all, to recognizing that they have seen a word before, and then to a level of partial knowledge where they have a general sense of the word or know one meaning. Finally, students know the word fully. They know multiple meanings of the word and can use the word in a variety of ways (Dale & O'Rourke, 1986; Nagy, 1988). The four levels or degrees of word knowledge are:

1. *Unknown word.* I don't know this word.
2. *Initial recognition.* I have seen or heard this word or I can pronounce it, but I don't know the meaning.
3. *Partial word knowledge.* I know one meaning of this word and can use it in a sentence.
4. *Full word knowledge.* I know more than one meaning or several ways to use this word. (Allen, 1999)

Once students reach the third level of word knowledge, they can usually understand the word in context and use it in their writing. Students do not reach the fourth level with all the words they learn. Stahl (1999) describes full word knowledge as "flexible." Students understand the core meaning of a word and how it changes in different contexts.

Incidental Word Learning

Students learn words incidentally, without direct instruction all the time, and because students learn so many words this way, teachers know that they do not have to teach the meaning of every unfamiliar word in a text. Students learn words from many sources, but researchers report that reading is the single largest source of vocabulary growth for students after third grade (Beck & McKeown, 1991; Nagy, 1988). In addition, the amount of time children spend reading independently is the best predictor of vocabulary growth between second and fifth grade.

Students need daily opportunities for independent reading in order to learn vocabulary words, and they need to read books that are appropriate for their reading levels. If they read books that are too easy or too hard, students will learn very few new words. Two of the best ways to provide opportunities for independent reading are reading workshop and literature circles. Through both of these activities, students have opportunities to read self-selected books that interest them and to learn words in context.

A third way teachers provide for incidental learning of vocabulary is by reading books aloud to students at every grade level, kindergarten through eighth grade. Teachers should read stories and informational books to students every day, whether during "story time" or as part of literature focus units, reading workshop, or thematic units. In fact, researchers report that students learn as many words incidentally as they listen to teachers read aloud as they do by reading themselves (Stahl, Richek, & Vandevier, 1991).

Context Clues

Students learn many words from context as they read books (Nagy, Anderson, & Herman, 1987; Nagy, Herman, & Anderson, 1985). Six types of context clues are definition, example-illustration, contrast, logic, root words and affixes, and grammar.

Students learn words as they read books and use words from the books in collaborative writing projects.

The surrounding words and sentences provide context clues. Some clues provide information about the meaning of the word, while others provide information about the part of speech and how the unfamiliar word is used in a sentence. This contextual information helps students figure out the meaning of the word. Illustrations also provide contextual information that helps readers identify words. Figure 7–2 lists six types of context clues that readers use to figure out unfamiliar words as they read sentences and paragraphs.

The six types of context clues do not operate in isolation. Two or three types of contextual information are often included in the same sentence. Also, readers' differing levels of background knowledge affect the types of word-identification strategies they can use effectively.

Consider how context clues might help students figure out the italicized words in these four sentences from *The Magic School Bus and the Electric Field Trip* (Cole, 1997):

We must have an unbroken *circuit*—circle—of wire. (p. 12)

Never use appliances with *frayed*, torn, or damaged insulation. (p. 42)

Steam is an invisible gas made of water molecules—the tiniest bits of water. (p. 20)

The *switch* pulled the contacts together, and the electric path was complete again. (p. 41)

Figure 7–2 Six types of context clues

Clue	Description	Sample Sentence
Definition	Readers use the definition in the sentence to understand the unknown word.	Some spiders spin silk with tiny organs called *spinnerets*.
Example-Illustration	Readers use an example or illustration to understand the unknown word.	Toads, frogs, and some birds are *predators* that hunt and eat spiders.
Contrast	Readers understand the unknown word because it is compared or contrasted with another word in the sentence.	Most spiders live for about one year, but *tarantulas* sometimes live for 20 years or more!
Logic	Readers think about the rest of the sentence to understand the unknown word.	An *exoskeleton* acts like a suit of armor to protect the spider.
Root Words and Affixes	Readers use their knowledge of root words and affixes to figure out the unknown word.	People who are terrified of spiders have *arachnophobia*.
Grammar	Readers use the word's function in the sentence or part of speech to figure out the unknown word.	Most spiders *molt* five to ten times.

Which sentences provided sufficient context clues to figure out the meaning of the italicized words? Which types of context clues did the author use in these sentences? In the first sentence, for example, *circle*—a synonym for *circuit*—provides useful information, but it may not provide enough information for students who do not understand concepts related to electricity.

Unfortunately, context clues rarely provide enough information in a sentence to help students learn a word. The clues may seem to be useful to someone who already knows a word, but context clues often provide only partial information, and the information can be misleading. In the third sentence, the definition of *steam* leaves out important information—that steam is dangerously hot! Researchers have concluded that context clues are relatively ineffective unless they provide definitions (Baumann & Kameenui, 1991; Nagy, 1988). Nonetheless, researchers recommend that students be taught how to use context clues because some context clues are useful and context clues do help students develop word-learning strategies to use on their own (Nagy, 1988).

Nagy, Anderson, and Herman (1987) found that students who read books at their grade level had a 1 in 20 chance of learning the meaning of any word from context. While that chance might seem insignificant, if students read 20,000 words a year, and they learn 1 of every 20 words from context, they would learn 1,000 words, or one-third of the average child's annual vocabulary growth. How much time does it take for students to read 20,000 words? Nagy (1988) has estimated that if elementary teachers provide 30 minutes of daily reading time, students will learn an additional 1,000 words a year!

The best way to teach students about context clues is by modeling. When teachers read aloud, they should stop at a difficult word and talk with students about how they can use context clues to figure out the meaning of the word. When the context provides enough information, teachers use the information and continue reading, but when the rest of the sentence or paragraph does not provide enough information, teachers model other strategies (such as looking up the word in the dictionary) to learn the meaning of the word.

It is interesting to note that both capable and less capable readers learn from context at about the same rate (Stahl, 1999). Researchers have speculated that the difference in vocabulary growth is due to differences in the amount of words that students read, not the differences in their reading achievement.

Word-learning Strategies

Capable readers use a variety of effective strategies to figure out the meaning of unknown words as they read. They might check the definition of a word in a dictionary or ask a teacher, classmate, or parent about a word. Sometimes they can use context clues to figure out the meaning of the unknown word. They also figure out a probable meaning by thinking about possible synonyms that make sense in the context of the sentence. Allen (1999) lists these 12 ways students can figure out the meaning of unknown words:

1. Look at the word in relation to the sentence.
2. Look up the word in the dictionary and see if any meanings fit the sentence.
3. Ask the teacher.
4. Sound it out.
5. Read the sentence again.
6. Look at the beginning of the sentence again.
7. Look for other key words in the sentence that might tell you the meaning.
8. Think what makes sense.
9. Ask a friend to read the sentence to you.
10. Read around the word and then go back again.
11. Look at the picture if there is one.
12. Skip it if you don't need it. (p. 23)

Less capable readers, in contrast, have fewer strategies for figuring out the meaning of unfamiliar words. They often depend on just one or two strategies, such as sounding out the word or skipping it.

Why Is Vocabulary Knowledge Important?

Vocabulary knowledge and reading achievement are closely related. Students with larger vocabularies are more capable readers, and they have a wider repertoire of strategies for figuring out the meanings of unfamiliar words than less capable readers do (McKeown, 1985). Reading widely is the best way students develop their vocabularies, and that is one reason why capable readers have larger vocabularies (Nagy, 1988; Stahl, 1999). They simply do more reading, both in school and out of school (Anderson, Wilson, & Fielding, 1986).

The idea that capable readers learn more vocabulary because they read more is an example of the Matthew effect (Stanovich, 1986). The Matthew effect suggests that "the rich get richer and the poor get poorer" in vocabulary development and other aspects of reading. Capable readers become better readers because they read more, and the books they read are more challenging and have sophisticated vocabulary words. The gulf between more capable and less capable readers grows larger because less capable readers read less and the books they read are less challenging.

TEACHING STUDENTS TO UNLOCK WORD MEANINGS

Vocabulary instruction plays an important role in balanced literacy classrooms (Rupley, Logan, & Nichols, 1998/1999). Teachers highlight important vocabulary words related to literature focus units and thematic units and teach minilessons about multiple meanings of words, etymologies, idioms, dictionary use, and other word-study skills. These lessons focus on words that students are reading and teach students how to figure out the meaning of unfamiliar words (Blachowicz & Lee, 1991). These lessons are even more important to students who are English language learners, because these students rely more heavily on direct instruction than native speakers do. Figure 7–3 lists guidelines for teaching vocabulary.

Characteristics of Effective Instruction

The goal of vocabulary instruction is for students to learn how to learn new words. According to Carr and Wixon (1986), Nagy (1988), and Allen (1999), effective vocabulary instruction exemplifies five characteristics:

1. *Connections to background knowledge.* For vocabulary instruction to be effective, students must relate new words to their background knowledge. Because learning words in isolation is rarely effective, teachers should teach words in concept clusters whenever possible.
2. *Repetition.* Students need to read, write, or say words eight to ten times or more before they recognize them automatically. Repetition helps students remember the words they are learning.
3. *Higher-level word knowledge.* The focus of instruction should be to help students develop higher-level word knowledge. Just having students memorize definitions or learn synonyms will not lead to full word knowledge.
4. *Strategy learning.* Not only are students learning the meanings of particular words through vocabulary lessons, they are developing knowledge and strategies for learning new words independently.
5. *Meaningful use.* Students need to be actively involved in word-study activities and opportunities to use the words in projects related to literature focus units and thematic units.

Teachers apply these five characteristics when they teach minilessons about vocabulary. Too often vocabulary instruction has emphasized looking up definitions of words in a dictionary, and this is not a particularly effective activity, at least not as it has been used in the past.

Minilessons. Teachers present minilessons to teach key words, vocabulary concepts, and strategies for unlocking word meanings. These lessons should focus on words that students are reading and writing and involve students in meaningful activities. Students make tentative predictions about the meaning of unfamiliar words as they read, using a combination of context clues, morphemic analysis, and their own prior knowledge (Blachowicz, 1993). Later, teachers often ask students to return to important words after reading to check their understanding of the word. For minilessons on words, vocabulary concepts, and word-learning strategies, teachers can use

Figure 7–3 Guidelines for teaching vocabulary

1. Choose Words to Study

Teachers and students choose words for vocabulary instruction from books they are reading and from thematic units. These words should not be high-frequency words, such as *what* or *because*, but content-rich words. Vocabulary instruction grows out of words that students are reading and concepts they are learning about in the classroom.

2. Highlight Words on Word Walls

Students and teachers select important and interesting words to display on word walls during literature focus units and thematic units, and they use separate word walls for each unit. Teachers highlight a few key terms before reading, and then students and teachers choose other words to add during and after reading.

3. Develop Full Word Knowledge

Students need to learn more than just single definitions of words in order to develop full word knowledge. They need to learn multiple meanings of words, how root words and affixes combine to affect meaning, synonyms, antonyms, and homonyms, word histories, and figurative meanings.

4. Teach Minilessons

Teachers teach students the meanings of individual words, vocabulary concepts, and word-learning strategies through minilessons. In a minilesson, teachers introduce the topic, present information, provide a structured practice activity, review, and provide application activities.

5. Plan Word-Study Activities

Teachers plan word-study activities so that students can explore words after reading. Activities include word posters, word maps, dramatizing words, word sorts, word chains, and semantic feature analysis.

6. Use Dictionaries and Thesauri

Students learn how to use dictionaries to learn about the meanings of words and thesauri to locate synonyms and antonyms. Teachers provide structured opportunities for students to use these books during minilessons and other word-study activities. They don't ask students to copy definitions of words or to write words in sentences or contrived stories.

7. Teach Context Clues

Words in a sentence provide clues to the meaning of other words in the sentence. They may provide definitions, comparisons, examples, or other types of information. Teachers explain the types of context clues and demonstrate how to use context clues so that students can learn words more effectively through independent reading.

8. Promote Wide Reading

Students learn only a small percentage of the 3,000 or more words they learn each year through teacher-directed lessons and activities. Wide reading is far more important in developing students' vocabularies. Teachers provide daily opportunities for students to read independently for at least 15 minutes in grades 1–3 and 30 minutes in grades 4–8. They also read aloud stories and informational books to students every day.

the following instructional procedure, which embodies the characteristics of effective vocabulary instruction:

1. *Introduce the topic.* For word study, teachers introduce the word and tie the word to students' background knowledge and the context in which the word is used. For vocabulary concepts, they identify the concept, such as synonyms, provide an explanation, and give several examples. To teach a word-learning strategy, such as context clues or using a dictionary, teachers introduce the strategy and explain how to use it to unlock a word's meaning.

2. *Provide information.* For word study, teachers define the word, identify the root word, explain the etymology of the word, and consider related words or easily confused words, if appropriate. For concepts, teachers provide additional examples; for strategies, they demonstrate the strategy.

3. *Practice.* Teachers involve students in supervised practice activities to bring together all the information presented earlier. The reading, writing, or talk activities should be meaningful so that students will understand the importance of learning the word, concept, or strategy. For a concept such as synonyms, students might choose words from a literature focus unit word wall and locate synonyms for the words, checking to make sure that they are choosing synonyms that are appropriate for the context in which the word is used in the book they are reading.

4. *Review.* Teachers and students review what they have learned, and teachers make connections to related words, concepts, or strategies. For word study, students can add the word to vocabulary notebooks, make word maps, and participate in other word-study activities. For concepts, students can make a poster to review the information they have learned. For strategies, students make a chart to review the steps in using the strategy and the contexts in which the strategy is useful.

5. *Apply.* Teachers provide opportunities for students to use what they have learned in meaningful ways.

This strategy works best for words that students have some background knowledge about and for words that are concrete. It is not suitable for words that represent unfamiliar concepts, because these require more in-depth instruction.

For example, in the first chapter of *Bunnicula: A Rabbit-Tale of Mystery* (Howe & Howe, 1979), the word *mongrel* is used in this sentence: "Now, most people might call me a *mongrel,* but I have some pretty fancy bloodlines running through these veins and Russian wolfhound happens to be one of them" (pp. 8–9). After reading the first chapter, the teacher might focus on the character of the dog named Harold and reread this sentence and ask students what the word *mongrel* means. The sentence provides some useful information about breeds that students can use to make a prediction about the meaning of the word. Students guess that a *mongrel* is a kind of dog or a breed of dog. Next the teacher shows a picture of her pet and says, "My dog is a mongrel, too. He's part collie and part German shepherd." The teacher's sentence helps to clarify the meaning of *mongrel,* and students notice the phrase "one of them" at the end of the sentence about Harold. They revise their predictions now that they understand that a mongrel is a mixed-breed dog. The teacher asks one student to check the dictionary definition, and together the class develops the word map shown in Figure 7–4. They write the category at the top, the definition on one side, the part of speech and sentence on the other side, and etymological information on the fourth side. Then the teacher displays the completed word map on

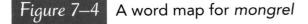

Figure 7–4   A word map for *mongrel*

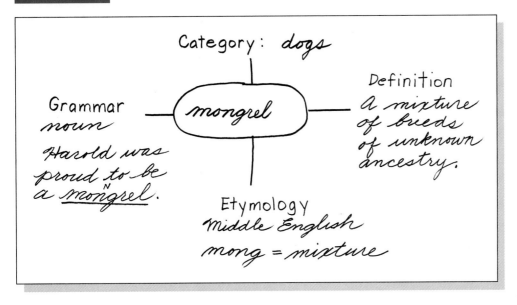

the wall, near the word wall. Students can also make copies of the word map on index cards to add to their vocabulary card files or write it in their **reading logs.**

Then several students talk about their pets and tell whether or not their dogs are mongrels. The discussion about Harold continues, and the information that he is a mixed-breed dog adds to the portrait of Harold created in the first chapter.

Using Dictionaries.   In traditional classrooms, the most common vocabulary activities involved listing new words on the chalkboard and directing students to write the words and copy the definitions from a dictionary or use the words in sentences. These activities are not effective for developing in-depth understanding and are no longer recommended (Stahl, 1999).

Looking words up in the dictionary usually isn't very effective because definitions do not provide enough useful information for students or because the words used in definition are forms of the word being defined (Allen, 1999; Stahl, 1999). Sometimes the definition that students choose—usually the first one—is the wrong one. Or, the definition they find may not make sense to them. In addition, many entries don't provide examples of how the word is used in sentences. For example, the word *pollution* is usually defined as "the act of polluting." This is not a useful definition. Students could look for an entry for *polluting,* but they won't find one. If they continue looking, they might notice an entry for *pollute,* and the first entry is "to make impure." The second definition is "to make unclean, especially with man-made waste." Even this definition provides very little useful information. Online dictionaries may be more useful to students because the entries often provide more information about words and related words.

Although parents and teachers urge students to look up unknown words in a dictionary, dictionary definitions are most useful after a person already knows the meaning of a word. Therefore, teachers play an important role in dictionary work. They contextualize the definitions that students locate by explaining the meaning of the

www.allwords.com

Online Dictionary. Children query words, hear words pronounced in one of five languages, and read definitions and related information.

www.wordcentral.com

Student Online Dictionary. Another excellent dictionary website for children; includes daily buzzwords, English experiments, and other features.

word in more detail, providing sample sentences, and comparing the word to related words and opposites.

Components of Word Study

Word knowledge involves more than learning definitions. Eight components of word study are:

- ❦ Concepts and word meanings
- ❦ Multiple meanings
- ❦ Morphemic analysis
- ❦ Synonyms
- ❦ Antonyms
- ❦ Homonyms
- ❦ Etymologies
- ❦ Figurative meanings

Students learn a variety of information about words and make connections between words and concepts. They learn one or more meanings for a word and synonyms and antonyms to compare and contrast meanings. Sometimes they confuse words they are learning with homonyms that sound or are spelled the same as the word they are learning. Students also learn that prefixes and suffixes change the meaning of a word. And, they learn about idioms and figurative sayings involving the word they are learning.

Concepts and Word Meanings.　Students use words to label concepts, and they learn words best when they are related to a concept. Consider the words *axle, groundwater, buffalo chips, wagon train, ford, fur trader, dysentery, outpost, guide, mountain men, oxen, Bowie knife, snag, cut-off, cholera, winch,* and *prairie dog.* They all relate to pioneers traveling west on the Oregon Trail. When students read a book about the Oregon Trail, for example, or during a social studies unit on the westward movement, students learn many of these words by connecting them to their Oregon Trail schema or concept. It is easier to learn a group of words relating to a concept than to learn a group of unrelated words.

Multiple Meanings of Words.　Many words have more than one meaning. For some words, multiple meanings develop for the noun and verb forms of the word, but sometimes meanings develop in other ways. The word *bank,* for example, has the following meanings:

> a piled-up mass of snow or clouds
> the slope of land beside a lake or river
> the slope of a road on a turn
> the lateral tilting of an airplane in a turn
> to cover a fire with ashes for slow burning
> a business establishment that receives and lends money
> a container in which money is saved
> a supply for use in emergencies (e.g., a blood bank)
> a place for storage (e.g., a computer's memory bank)
> to count on
> similar things arranged in a row (e.g., a bank of elevators)
> to arrange things in a row

You may be surprised that there are at least a dozen meanings for the common word *bank*. Some are nouns and others are verbs, but grammatical form alone does not account for so many meanings.

The meanings of *bank* come from three sources. The first five meanings come from a Viking word, and they are related because they all deal with something slanted or making a slanted motion. The next five meanings come from the Italian word *banca*, a money changer's table. All these meanings deal with financial banking except for the tenth meaning, "to count on," which requires a bit more thought. We use the saying "to bank on" figuratively to mean "to depend on," but it began more literally from the actual counting of money on a table. The last two meanings come from the French word *banc*, meaning "bench." Words have acquired multiple meanings as society became more complex and finer shades of meaning were necessary; for example, the meanings of *bank* as an emergency supply and a storage place are fairly new. As with many words with multiple meanings, it is just a linguistic accident that three original words from three languages with related meanings came to be spelled the same way (Tompkins & Yaden, 1986).

Students gradually acquire additional meanings for words, and they usually learn these new meanings through reading. When a familiar word is used in a new way, students often notice the new application and may be curious enough to check the meaning in a dictionary.

Morphemic Analysis. Students use their knowledge of affixes to unlock many multisyllabic words. For example, *omnivorous, carnivorous,* and *herbivorous* relate to the foods that animals eat. *Omni* means "all," *caro* means "flesh", and *herb* means "herbs or vegetation." The common word part *vorous* comes from the Latin *vorare*, meaning "to swallow up." When students know *carnivorous* or *carnivore*, they can use their knowledge of prefixes to figure out the other words.

Many English words are compound words, and the meaning is usually clear from the word parts and the context in which the word or phrase is used, as in the words *toothbrush, breakneck, earthquake,* and *anteater.* The word *fire* is used in a variety of compound words and phrases, such as *fire hydrant, firebomb, fireproof, fireplace, firearm, fire drill, under fire, set the world on fire, fire away,* and *open fire.*

Students can examine words developed from a common root, such as these words from the Latin roots *-ann* and *-enn*, which mean "year": *annual, biennial, perennial, century, centennial, bicentennial, millennium,* and *sesquicentennial.* Students figure out the meaning of the words by locating the root and identifying prefixes and affixes. Then they work together to make a cluster to highlight the words and their meanings. A sixth-grade class chart on *-ann/-enn* words is shown in Figure 7–5.

Synonyms: Words That Mean the Same. Words that have nearly the same meaning as other words are synonyms. English has so many synonyms because so many words have been borrowed from other languages. Synonyms are useful because they provide options, allowing writers to be more precise. Think of all the synonyms for the word *cold: cool, chilly, frigid, icy, frosty,* and *freezing.* Each word has a different shade of meaning: *cool* means moderately cold; *chilly* is uncomfortably cold; *frigid* is intensely cold; *icy* means very cold; *frosty* means covered with frost; and *freezing* is so cold that water changes into ice. Our language would be limited if we only had the word *cold*.

Teachers should be careful to articulate the differences among synonyms. Nagy (1988) emphasizes that teachers should focus on teaching concepts and related words, not just provide single-word definitions using synonyms. For example, to tell a child that *frigid* means *cold* only provides limited information. And, when a child

www.thesaurus.com

Online Thesaurus. Type in a word and receive a list of synonyms and antonyms.

Figure 7–5 A class chart of *-ann/-enn* words

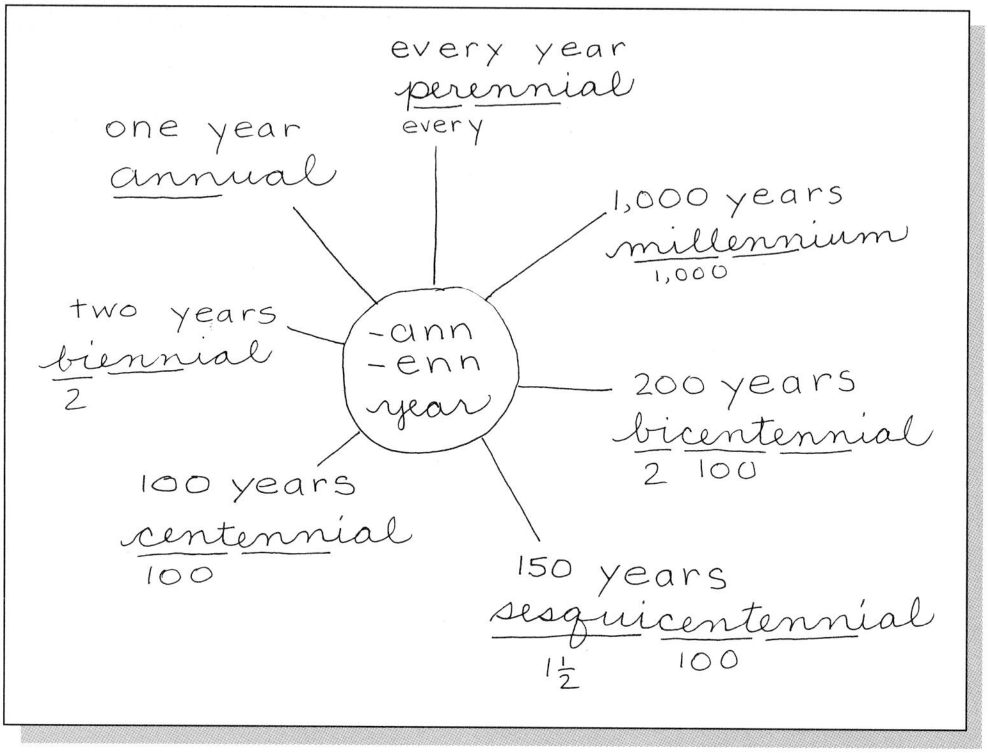

says, "I want my sweater because it's frigid in here," it shows that the child does not understand the different degrees of cold. There's a big difference between *chilly* and *frigid*.

Antonyms: Words That Mean the Opposite. Words that express the opposite meaning are antonyms. Antonyms for the word *loud*, for example, are *soft, subdued, quiet, silent, inaudible, sedate, somber, dull,* and *colorless*. These words express shades of meaning just as synonyms do, and some opposites are more appropriate for one meaning of *loud* than for another. When *loud* means *gaudy*, for instance, opposites are *somber, dull,* or *colorless*; when *loud* means *noisy*, the opposites are *quiet, silent,* or *inaudible*.

Students in the elementary grades learn to use a thesaurus to locate both synonyms and antonyms. *A First Thesaurus* (Wittels & Greisman, 1985), *Scholastic Children's Thesaurus* (Bollard, 1998), and *The American Heritage Children's Thesaurus* (Hellweg, 1997) are three excellent thesauri designed for elementary students. Students use these reference books to locate more effective words when revising their writing and for word-study activities.

Homonyms: Words That Confuse. Homonyms, also known as homophones, are words that sound alike but are spelled differently, such as *right* and *write, to, too,* and *two,* and *there, their,* and *they're*. A list of homophones is presented in Figure 7–6. Sometimes students confuse the meanings of these words, but more often they confuse the spellings of these words.

Figure 7–6 Homophones, words that sound alike but are spelled differently

air–heir	close–clothes	heroin–heroine	pain–pane	seam–seem
allowed–aloud	coarse–course	hi–high	pair–pare–pear	serf–surf
ant–aunt	colonel–kernel	hoard–horde	palette–pallet	sew–so–sow
ate–eight	complement–	hoarse–horse	passed–past	shear–sheer
ball–bawl	compliment	hoes–hose	patience–patients	shone–shown
band–banned	council–counsel	hole–whole	pause–paws	shoot–chute
bare–bear	creak–creek	hour–our	peace–piece	side–sighed
base–bass	days–daze	jam–jamb	peak–peek–pique	sighs–size
based–baste	dear–deer	knead–need	peal–peel	slay–sleigh
be–bee	dense–dents	knew–new	pedal–peddle	soar–sore
beat–beet	dew–do–due	knight–night	peer–pier	soared–sword
bell–belle	die–dye	knot–not	phase–faze	sole–soul
berry–bury	doe–dough	know–no	plain–plane	some–sum
berth–birth	dual–duel	lacks–lax	plait–plate	son–sun
billed–build	ewe–you	lead–led	pleas–please	stairs–stares
blew–blue	eye–I	leak–leek	pole–poll	stake–steak
boar–bore	fair–fare	leased–least	pore–pour	stationary–stationery
board–bored	feat–feet	lie–lye	praise–prays–preys	steal–steel
boarder–border	fined–find	links–linx	presence–presents	straight–strait
born–borne	fir–fur	load–lode	pride–pried	suite–sweet
bough–bow	flea–flee	loan–lone	prince–prints	tail–tale
brake–break	flew–flu	loot–lute	principal–principle	taught–taut
bread–bred	floe–flow	made–maid	profit–prophet	tear–tier
brews–bruise	flour–flower	mail–male	quarts–quartz	tense–tents
bridal–bridle	foaled–fold	main–mane	rain–rein–reign	their–there–they're
brows–browse	for–fore–four	maize–maze	raise–rays–raze	threw–through
buy–by–bye	forth–fourth	manner–manor	rap–wrap	throne–thrown
cache–cash	foul–fowl	marshal–martial	real–reel	tide–tied
callous–callus	gait–gate	meat–meet–mete	red–read	to–too–two
capital–capitol	genes–jeans	medal–meddle–metal	reed–read	toad–toed–towed
carat–carrot	gofer–gopher	might–mite	rest–wrest	toe–tow
cast–caste	gorilla–guerrilla	mind–mined	right–rite–write	tracked–tract
cede–seed	grate–great	miner–minor	ring–wring	troop–troupe
ceiling–sealing	grill–grille	missed–mist	road–rode–rowed	undo–undue
cell–sell	groan–grown	moan–mown	role–roll	vain–vane–vein
cellar–seller	guessed–guest	moose–mousse	roomer–rumor	wade–weighed
cent–scent–sent	hail–hale	morning–mourning	root–route	waist–waste
chews–choose	hair–hare	muscle–mussel	rose–rows	wait–weight
chic–sheik	hall–haul	naval–navel	rote–wrote	waive–wave
chili–chilly	halve–have	none–nun	rung–wrung	wares–wears
choral–coral	hangar–hanger	oar–or–ore	sac–sack	warn–worn
chord–cord–cored	hay–hey	one–won	sail–sale	way–weigh
chute–shoot	heal–heel	paced–paste	scene–seen	weak–week
cite–sight–site	hear–here	packed–pact	sea–see	wood–would
clause–claws	heard–herd	pail–pale	sealing–ceiling	yoke–yolk

Most homonyms are linguistic accidents, but *stationary* and *stationery* share an interesting history. *Stationery,* meaning paper and books, developed from *stationary.* In medieval England, merchants traveled from town to town selling their wares. The merchant who sold paper goods was the first to set up shop in one town. His shop was "stationary" because it did not move, and he came to be called the "stationer." The spelling difference between the two words signifies the semantic difference.

There are many books of homonyms for children, including Gwynne's *The King Who Rained* (1970), *A Chocolate Moose for Dinner* (1976), *The Sixteen Hand Horse* (1980), and *A Little Pigeon Toad* (1988); Maestro's *What's a Frank Frank? Tasty Homograph Riddles* (1984); *What in the World Is a Homophone?* (Presson, 1996); and *Eight Ate: A Feast of Homonym Riddles* (Terban, 1982).

Teachers in the primary grades introduce the concept of homonyms and teach the easier pairs, including *see–sea, I–eye, right–write,* and *dear–deer.* In the upper grades, teachers focus on the homophones that students continue to confuse, such as *there–their–they're* and the more sophisticated pairs, including *morning–mourning, flair–flare,* and *complement–compliment.*

Intensive study is necessary because homonyms are confusing to many students. The words sound alike and the spelling is often very similar—sometimes only one letter varies or one letter is added: *pray–prey, hole–whole.* And sometimes the words have the same letters, but they vary in sequence: *bear–bare* and *great–grate.*

Teachers teach minilessons to explain the concept of homonyms and make charts of the homophone pairs and triplets. Calling children's attention to the spelling and meaning differences helps to clarify the words. Students can also make homophone posters, as shown in Figure 7–7. On the posters, students draw pictures and write sentences to contrast the homophones. Displaying these posters in the classroom reminds students of the differences between the words.

www.wordcentral.com

Word Central: Teacher Resources. Learn about Noah Webster, how words get into the dictionary, and the history of English.

Etymologies: The History of the English Language. Glimpses into the history of the English language provide interesting information about word meanings and spellings (Tompkins & Yaden, 1986; Venezky, 1999). The English language began in 447 A.D. when the Angles, Saxons, and other Germanic tribes invaded England. This Anglo-Saxon English was first written down by Latin missionaries in approximately 750 A.D. The English of the period from 450 to 1100 is known as Old English. During this time English was a very phonetic language and followed many German syntactic patterns. Many loan words, including *ugly, window, egg, they, sky,* and *husband,* were contributed by the marauding Vikings who plundered villages along the English coast.

The English of the second period of development, Middle English (1100–1500), began with the Norman Conquest in 1066. William, Duke of Normandy, invaded England and became the English king. William, his lords, and the royals who followed him spoke French for nearly two hundred years, so French was the official language of England. Many French loan words were added to the language, and French spellings were substituted for Old English spellings. For example, in Old English *night* was spelled *niht* and *queen* was spelled *cwen.* Loan words from Dutch, Latin, and other languages were added to English during this period, too.

The invention of the printing press marks the transition from Middle English to the Modern English period (1500–present). William Caxton brought the first printing press to England in 1476, and soon books and pamphlets were being mass-produced. Spelling became standardized as Samuel Johnson and other lexicographers compiled dictionaries, even though English pronunciation of words continues to evolve. Loan words continued to flow into English from almost every language in the world. Explo-

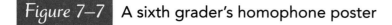

Figure 7–7 A sixth grader's homophone poster

ration and colonization in North America and around the world accounted for many of the loan words. Other words, such as *electric, democracy,* and *astronaut,* were created using Greek word parts. Figure 7–8 presents a list of loan words from languages around the world. New words are added to English every year, and the new words reflect new inventions and cultural practices. Many new words today, such as *e-mail* and *netiquette,* relate to the Internet. The word *Internet* is a new word, too. It is less than 20 years old!

Students use etymological information in dictionaries and other books about word histories to learn how particular words developed and what the words mean. Etymological information is included in brackets at the beginning or end of dictionary entries. Here is the etymological information for three words:

democracy [1576, < MF < LL < Gr demokratia, demos (people) + kratia (cracy = strength, power)]

The word *democracy* entered English in 1576 through French, and the French word came from Latin and the Latin word from Greek. In Greek, the word *demokratia* means "power to the people."

house [bef. 900, ME hous, OE hus]

House is an Old English word that entered English before 900. It was spelled *hus* in Old English and *hous* in Middle English.

moose [1603, < Algonquin, "he who strips bark"]

Figure 7–8 Loan words from around the world

African (many languages): aardvark, banjo, cola, gumbo, mumbo, jumbo, safari, trek, voodoo, zombie

American English: America, cafeteria, commuter, cowboy, frontier, hijack, jackknife, maverick, mustang, O.K., patio, pioneer, prairie, sierra, teenager, turkey, underground railroad, yankee

Arabic: alcohol, apricot, assassin, magazine, zenith, zero

Australian/New Zealand (aboriginal): boomerang, kangaroo, kiwi

Celtic: walnut

Chinese: chop suey, tea, typhoon, wok

Czech: pistol, robot

Dutch: caboose, easel, frolic, pickle, waffle, yacht

Eskimo: igloo, kayak, mukluk, parka

Finnish: sauna

French: à la carte, ballet, beef, beige, chauffeur, chic, hors d'oeuvres, restaurant, sabotage

German: dollar, kindergarten, noodle, poodle, pretzel, vampire, waltz

Greek: atom, biology, chaos, epidemic, giant, helicopter, hero, pentagon, siren, thermometer

Hawaiian: aloha, hula, lei, luau, ukelele

Hebrew: cherub, hallelujah, jubilee, kosher, rabbi

Hindi: bangle, dungaree, juggernaut, jungle, pajamas, shampoo, thug

Hungarian: goulash, paprika

Icelandic: geyser

Irish: bog, leprechaun, shamrock

Italian: carnival, extravaganza, motto, piano, pizza, solo, spaghetti, umbrella, violin

Japanese: hibachi, honcho, judo, kimono, origami

Malaysian: bamboo

Mexican Spanish: adobe, bonanza, bronco, chocolate, coyote, marijuana, ranch, tacos, tamales, tomato

Native American (many languages): barbecue, canoe, hammock, moccasin, papoose, raccoon, skunk, tepee, tomahawk

Persian: bazaar, divan, khaki, orange, peach, shawl, sherbet, turban

Polish: mazurka, polka

Polynesian: taboo, tattoo

Portuguese: albino, cobra, coconut, molasses, piranha

Russian: czar, sputnik, steppe, tundra, vodka

Scandinavian: cozy, egg, fjord, husband, knife, outlaw, rug, skate, ski, skin, sky, ugly, window

Scottish: clan, golf, slogan

South American Spanish/Portuguese: jaguar, llama

Spanish: alligator, guitar, hurricane, lasso, mosquito, potato, vanilla

Turkish: caviar, horde, khan, kiosk, yogurt

Welsh: penguin

Yiddish: bagel, chutzpah, klutz, pastrami

The word *moose* is Native American—from an Algonquin tribe in the northeastern part of the United States—and entered English in 1603. It comes from the Algonquin word for "he who strips bark."

Even though words have entered English from around the world, the three main sources of words are English, Latin, and Greek. Upper-grade students can learn to identify the languages that these words came from, and knowing the language backgrounds helps students to predict the spellings and meanings (Venezky, 1999).

English words are usually one- or two-syllable common, familiar words that may or may not be phonetically regular, such as *fox, arm, Monday, house, match, eleven, of, come, week, horse, brother,* and *dumb.* Words with *ch* (pronounced as /ch/), *sh, th,* and *wh* digraphs are usually English, as in *church, shell, bath,* and *what.* Many English words are compound words or use comparative and superlative forms, such as *starfish, toothache, fireplace, happier, fastest.*

Many words from Latin are similar to comparable words in French, Spanish, or Italian, such as *ancient, judicial, impossible,* and *officer.* Latin words have related words or derivatives, such as *courage, courageous, encourage, discourage,* and *encouragement.* Also, many Latin words have *-tion/-sion* suffixes: *imitation, corruption, attention, extension,* and *possession.*

Greek words are the most unusual. Many are long words, and their spellings seem unfamiliar. The letters *ph* are pronounced /f/, and the letters *ch* are pronounced /k/ in Greek loan words, as in *autograph, chaos,* and *architect.* Longer words with *th,* such as *thermometer* and *arithmetic,* are Greek. The suffix *-ology* is Greek, as in the words *biology, psychology,* and *geology.* The letter *y* is used in place of *i* in the middle of some words, such as *bicycle* and *myth.* Many Greek words are composed of two parts: *bibliotherapy, microscope, biosphere, hypodermic,* and *telephone.* Figure 7–9 presents lists of English, Latin, and Greek words that teachers can use for **word sorts** and other vocabulary activities.

Related words have developed from English, Latin, and Greek sources. Consider the words *tooth, dentist,* and *orthodontist. Tooth* is an English word, which explains its irregular plural form, *teeth. Dentist* is a Latin word. *Dent* means "tooth" in Latin, and the suffix *-ist* means "one who does." The word *orthodontist* is Greek. *Ortho* means "straighten" and *dont* means "tooth"; therefore, *orthodontist* means "one who straightens teeth." Other related triplets include:

book: bookstore (E), bibliography (Gr), library (L)

eye: eyelash (E), optical (Gr), binoculars (L)

foot: foot-dragging (E), tripod (Gr), pedestrian (L)

great: greatest (E), megaphone (Gr), magnificent (L)

see: foresee (E), microscope (Gr), invisible (L)

star: starry (E), astronaut (Gr), constellation (L)

time: time-tested (E), chronological (Gr), contemporary (L)

water: watermelon (E), hydrate (Gr), aquarium (L)

When students understand English, Latin, and Greek root words, they appreciate the relationships among words and their meanings.

Figurative Meanings of Words. Many words have both literal and figurative meanings. Literal meanings are the explicit, dictionary meanings, and figurative meanings

www.m-w.com

Word for the Wise. Scripts of the popular program broadcast daily on National Public Radio. Also check "Words From the Lighter Side" at the same site.

Figure 7–9 English, Latin, and Greek words

English	Latin	Greek
apple	addiction	ache
begin	administer	apology
between	advantage	arithmetic
bumblebee	beautiful	astronomy
child	capital	atmosphere
comb	confession	atomic
cry	continent	biology
cuff	couple	chaos
duckling	definition	chemical
earth	delicate	democracy
fireplace	discourage	disaster
fourteen	education	dynamic
freedom	erupt	elephant
Friday	explosion	geography
get	express	gymnastics
handsome	fraction	helicopter
have	fragile	hemisphere
horse	frequently	hieroglyphics
house	heir	kaleidoscope
kind	honest	metamorphosis
knight	honor	method
know	identify	myth
ladybug	interesting	octopus
lamb	January	phenomenal
lip	journal	photosynthesis
lock	junior	pneumonia
most	justice	pseudonym
mouth	nation	rhinoceros
nose	occupy	rhythm
out	organize	sympathy
quickly	primitive	synonym
ride	principal	telephone
silly	private	telescope
thank	procession	theater
this	salute	thermometer
twin	special	thermos
weather	uniform	trophy
whisper	vacation	type
why	valley	zodiac
wild	vegetable	zoo

are metaphorical or use figures of speech. For example, to describe *winter* as the coldest season of the year is literal, but to say that *winter has icy breath* is figurative. Two types of figurative language are idioms and comparisons.

Idioms are groups of words, such as "in hot water," that have a special meaning. Idioms can be confusing to students because they must be interpreted figuratively rather than literally. "In hot water" is an old expression meaning to be in trouble. Cox (1980) explains that hundreds of years ago there were no police officers and people had to protect themselves from robbers. When a robber tried to break into a house, the homeowner might pour boiling water from a second-floor window onto the head of the robber, who would then be "in hot water." There are hundreds of idioms in English, and we use them every day to create word pictures that make language more colorful. Some examples are "out in left field," "a skeleton in the closet," "raining cats and dogs," "stick your neck out," "a chip off the old block," and "don't cry over spilled milk."

Four excellent books of idioms for students are *Put Your Foot in Your Mouth and Other Silly Sayings* (Cox, 1980), *Scholastic Dictionary of Idioms: More than 600 Phrases, Sayings, and Expressions* (Terban, 1996), *Punching the Clock: Funny Action Idioms* (Terban, 1990), and *In a Pickle and Other Funny Idioms* (Terban, 1983). Because idioms are figurative sayings, many children—and especially those who are learning English as a second language—have difficulty learning them. It is crucial that children move beyond the literal meanings and become flexible in using language. One way for students to learn flexibility is to create idiom posters, as illustrated in Figure 7–10.

Comparisons are metaphors and similes that liken something to something else. A simile is a comparison signaled by the use of *like* or *as*. "The crowd was as rowdy as a bunch of marauding monkeys" and "My apartment was like an oven after the air-conditioning broke last summer" are two examples. In contrast, a metaphor compares two things by implying that one is something else, without using *like* or *as*.

www.eslcafe.com

*ESL Idiom Page
Lists of idioms, their meanings, and examples.*

Figure 7–10 An idiom poster

"The children were frisky puppies playing in the yard" is an example. Metaphors are stronger comparisons, as these examples show:

She's as cool as a cucumber.
She's a cool cucumber.

In the moonlight, the dead tree looked like a skeleton.
In the moonlight, the dead tree was a skeleton.

Differentiating between the terms *simile* and *metaphor* is less important than understanding the meaning of comparisons in books students read and having students use comparisons to make their writing more vivid. For example, a sixth-grade student compared anger to a thunderstorm using a simile. She wrote, "Anger is like a thunderstorm, screaming with thunder-feelings and lightning-words." Another student compared anger to a volcano. Using a metaphor, he wrote, "Anger is a volcano, erupting with poisonous words and hot-lava actions."

Students begin by learning traditional comparisons such as "happy as a clam" and "high as a kite," and then they learn to notice and invent fresh, unexpected comparisons. To introduce traditional comparisons to primary-grade students, teachers use Audrey Wood's *Quick as a Cricket* (1982). Middle- and upper-grade students can invent new comparisons for stale comparisons such as "butterflies in your stomach." In *Anastasia Krupnik,* for example, Lois Lowry (1979) substituted "ginger ale in her knees" for the trite "butterflies in her stomach" to describe how nervous Anastasia was when she had to stand up to read her poem.

Choosing Words to Study

Teachers choose the most important words from books to teach. Important words include words that are essential to understanding the text, words that may confuse students, and general utility words students will use as they read other books (Allen, 1999). Teachers should avoid words that are unrelated to the central concept of the book or unit or words that are too conceptually difficult for students. As teachers choose words to highlight and for word-study activities, they consider their students, the book being read, and the instructional context. For example, during a theme on bears, first graders listened to their teacher read these books:

The Three Bears (Galdone, 1972)
Somebody and the Three Blairs (Tolhurst, 1990)
Brown Bear, Brown Bear, What Do You See? (Martin, 1983)
Polar Bear, Polar Bear, What Do You Hear? (Martin, 1991)
Alaska's Three Bears (Cartwright, 1990)

These words were highlighted:

shaggy	fur	dangerous
meat-eating	polar bear	grizzly bear
claws	hind legs	hibernate
cubs	tame	brown bear
den	black bear	sharp teeth

These are vocabulary words—content-related words—not high-frequency words such as *who* and *this*.

Teachers use words from the word wall for minilessons and other vocabulary activities.

Students do not have to know all of the words in a book to read and comprehend it or listen to it read aloud. Researchers estimate that students can tolerate books with as many as 15% unfamiliar words (Freebody & Anderson, 1983). Of course, students vary in the percentage of unfamiliar words they can tolerate, depending on the topic of the book, the role of the unfamiliar words, and their purpose for reading. It is unrealistic for teachers to expect students to learn every word in a book or expect to have to teach every word.

Spotlighting Words on Word Walls

Teachers post **word walls,** made from large sheets of butcher paper, in the classroom, as Mrs. Dillon did in the vignette at the beginning of this chapter. Students and the teacher write interesting, confusing, and important words on the word wall. Usually students choose the words to write on the word wall and may even do the writing themselves. Teachers add other important words that students have not chosen. Words are added to the word wall as they come up in books students are reading or during a thematic unit, not in advance. Students use the word wall to locate a word they want to use during a **grand conversation** or to check the spelling of a word they are writing, and teachers use the words listed on the word wall for word-study activities.

Some teachers use pocket charts and word cards instead of butcher paper for their word walls. This way the word cards can easily be used for word-study activities, and they can be sorted and rearranged on the pocket chart. After the book or unit is completed, teachers punch holes in one end of the cards and hang them on a ring. Then the collection of word cards can be placed in the writing center for students to use in writing activities.

Word walls play an important role in vocabulary learning. The words are posted in the classroom so that they are visible to all students, and because they are so visible, students will read them more often and refer to the chart when writing. Their availability will also remind teachers to use the words for word-study activities.

Students also make individual word walls by dividing a sheet of paper into 24 boxes, labeling the boxes with the letters of the alphabet. Students put P and Q together in one box and X and Y into another box. Then students write important words and phrases in the boxes as they read and discuss the book. Figure 7–11 shows a sixth grader's word wall for *Hatchet* (1987), a wilderness survival story by Gary Paulsen.

During a unit on Martin Luther King, Jr., seventh graders highlighted these words, wrote them on index cards, and displayed them in alphabetical order on a pocket chart:

activist	Ku Klux Klan	prejudice
assassinated	Martin Luther King, Jr.	protest
discrimination	Negro	separate but equal
integration	Nobel Peace Prize	sit-in
James Earl Ray	nonviolence	slavery

Even though all of these words—and perhaps more—will be added to the word wall, not all of them will be directly taught to students. As they plan, teachers create lists of words that will probably be written on word walls during the lesson. From this list, teachers choose the key words—the ones that are critical to understanding the book or the unit—and these are the words that teachers include in minilessons.

Activities for Exploring Words

Word-study activities provide opportunities for students to explore the meaning of words listed on word walls, other words related to books they are reading, and words they are learning during social studies and science units. Through these activities, students develop concepts, learn the meanings of words, and make associations among words. None of these activities require students to simply write words and their definitions or to use the words in sentences or a contrived story.

   1. *Word posters.* Students choose a word from the word wall and write it on a small poster. Then they draw and color a picture to illustrate the word. They also use the word in a sentence on the poster. This is one way that students can visualize the meaning of a word.

   2. *Word maps.* Word maps are another way to visualize a word's meaning (Duffelmeyer & Banwart, 1992–1993; Schwartz & Raphael, 1985). Students draw a **cluster** on a small card or a sheet of paper and write a word from the word wall in the center circle. Then they draw rays from the center and write important information about the word to make connections between the word and what they are reading or studying. Three kinds of information are included in a word map: a category for the word, examples, and characteristics or associations. Figure 7–12 shows two word maps. First graders made the first cluster, on *fox,* after reading *Rosie's Walk* (Hutchins, 1968). For the examples section, they identified four stories about foxes that they had read. A fifth grader who was reading *Bunnicula: A Rabbit-Tale of Mystery* (Howe & Howe, 1979) made the second word map, on *glistened,* a word from the first chapter.

Figure 7–11 A sixth grader's word wall for *Hatchet*

A	B	C	D
alone	bush plane	Canadian wilderness	divorce
absolutely terrified	Brian Robeson	controls	desperation
arrows	bruised	cockpit	destroyed
aluminum cookset	bow & arrow	crash	disappointment
		careless	devastating
		campsite	
E	**F**	**G**	**H**
engine	fire	gut cherries	hatchet
emergency	fuselage	get food	heart attack
emptiness	fish		hunger
exhaustion	foolbirds		hope
	foodshelf		
	54 days		
I	**J**	**K**	**L**
instruments			lake
insane			
incredible wealth			
M	**N**	**O**	**PQ**
memory			pilot
mosquitoes			panic
mistakes			painful
matches			porcupine quills
mental journal			patience
moose			
R	**S**	**T**	**U**
rudder pedals	stranded		unbelievable riches
rescue	secret		
radio	survival pack		
relative comfort	search		
raspberries	sleeping bag		
roaring bonfire	shelter		
raft	starved		
V	**W**	**XY**	**Z**
visitation rights	wilderness		
viciously thirsty	windbreaker		
valuable asset	wreck		
vicious whine	woodpile		
	wolf		

Figure 7–12   Two word maps

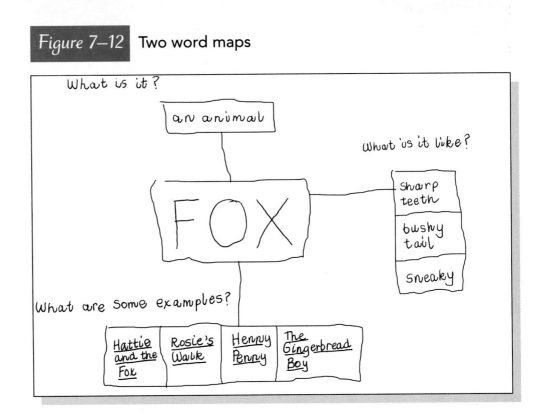

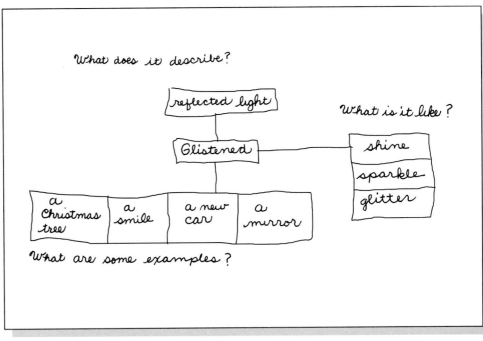

Figure 7–13 A semantic feature analysis on birds

	hatches from eggs	has feathers	has wings	can fly	can swim	migrates	is a bird of prey	is extinct
bluejay	✓	✓	✓	✓	○	○	○	○
owl	✓	✓	✓	✓	○	○	✓	○
roadrunner								
eagle								
pelican								
hummingbird								
quail								
ostrich								
dodo								
robin								
penguin								
chicken								
duck								
seagull								
peacock								
flamingo								

Code: ✓ = yes

○ = no

? = don't know

3. *Dramatizing words.* Students each choose a word from the word wall and dramatize it for classmates, who then try to guess the word. Sometimes an action is a more effective way to explain a word than a verbal definition. That's what Mrs. Dillon found when she dramatized the word *wilted* for her second graders. Dramatization is an especially effective activity for students who are learning English as a second language.

4. *Word sorts.* Students sort a collection of words taken from the word wall into two or more categories in a **word sort** (Bear, Invernizzi, Templeton, & Johnston, 2000). Usually students choose the categories they will use for the sort, but sometimes the teacher chooses them. For example, words from a story might be sorted by character, or words from a thematic unit on machines might be sorted according to type of machine. The words can be written on cards, and then students sort a pack of word cards into piles. Or, students can cut apart a list of words, sort them into categories, and then paste the grouped words together.

5. *Word chains.* Students choose a word from the word wall and then identify three or four words to sequence before or after the word to make a chain. For example, the word *tadpole* can be chained this way: *egg, tadpole, frog*; and the word *aggravate* can be chained like this: *irritate, bother, aggravate, annoy.* Students can draw and write their chains on a sheet of paper, or they can make a chain out of construction paper and write the words on each link.

6. *Semantic feature analysis.* Students select a group of related words, such as different kinds of birds, and then make a chart to classify them according to distinguishing characteristics (Heimlich & Pittelman, 1986). A semantic feature analysis on birds is presented in Figure 7–13. Students complete the semantic feature analysis by placing a check mark by the characteristics that each bird has and a circle by those the bird lacks.

Review

Students add approximately 3,000 words to their vocabularies every year. They learn some of the words through instruction that teachers provide, but they learn far more words incidentally through reading, writing, watching television, and other activities outside of school. Teachers have an important role in providing opportunities for incidental word learning through reading and teaching students how to unlock word meanings. Words should always be studied as part of meaningful reading and writing activities or content-area study. Teachers post vocabulary word walls in the classroom, teach minilessons using word wall words, and involve students in a variety of word-study activities, including word maps and word sorts. The feature on page 265 presents a list of recommended practices that effective teachers use in teaching vocabulary.

How Effective Teachers . . .

Teach Students to Learn About Words and Sentences

✴ Effective Practices

1. Teachers provide opportunities for students to read stories and informational books daily because students learn many new words through reading.
2. Teachers read aloud to students every day because students learn many new books as they listen to books read aloud.
3. Teachers support students as they develop full word knowledge and learn to use words flexibly in a variety of contexts.
4. Teachers help students to develop a repertoire of word-learning strategies in order to learn words incidentally.
5. Teachers demonstrate how to use context clues to figure out the meaning of unknown words when reading independently.
6. Teachers choose the most useful words from the word wall for vocabulary activities.
7. Teachers teach minilessons on individual words, vocabulary concepts, and word-learning strategies.
8. Teachers provide contextual support for students when they look up definitions in the dictionary.
9. Teachers teach many concepts about words, including multiple meanings, morphemic analysis, synonyms, antonyms, homonyms, etymologies, and figurative meanings.
10. Teachers involve students in meaningful word-study activities, such as word maps, dramatizing words, word sorts, and semantic feature analysis, that are related to books students are reading and units they are studying.

✴ Ineffective Practices

1. Teachers provide few opportunities for students to read books.
2. Teachers don't read aloud to students every day.
3. Teachers assume that students fully understand words when students memorize definitions or can supply synonyms.
4. Teachers advise students to use a single word-learning strategy, usually looking up unknown words in the dictionary.
5. Teachers assume students already know how to use context clues to learn new words.
6. Teachers expect that students will learn all unknown words in books they are reading.
7. Teachers only teach word meanings; they don't teach vocabulary concepts or word-learning strategies.
8. Teachers have students copy definitions from the dictionary and memorize the definitions to learn new words.
9. Teachers teach few concepts about words.
10. Teachers don't connect vocabulary instruction to books students are reading or thematic units.

References

Allen, J. (1999). *Words, words, words.* Portsmouth, NH: Heinemann.

Anderson, R. C., Wilson, P. T., & Fielding, L. G. (1986). *Growth in reading and how children spend their time*

outside of school (Technical Report No. 389). Urbana: University of Illinois, Center for the Study of Reading.

Baumann, J. F., & Kameenui, E. J. (1991). Research on vocabulary instruction: Ode to Voltaire. In J. Flood,

J. M. Jensen, D. Lapp, & J. R. Squire (Eds.), *Handbook on teaching the English language arts* (pp. 604–632). New York: Macmillan.

Bear, D. R., Invernizzi, M., Templeton, S., & Johnston, F. (2000). *Words their way: Word study for phonics, vocabulary, and spelling instruction.* Upper Saddle River, NJ: Merrill/Prentice Hall.

Beck, I., & McKeown, M. (1991). Conditions of vocabulary acquisition. In R. Barr, M. Kamil, P. Mosenthal, & P. D. Pearson (Eds.), *Handbook of reading research* (Vol. 2, pp. 789–814). White Plains, NY: Longman.

Blachowicz, C. L. Z. (1993). C(2)QU: Modeling context use in the classroom. *The Reading Teacher, 47,* 268–269.

Blachowicz, C. L. Z., & Lee, J. J. (1991). Vocabulary development in the whole literacy classroom. *The Reading Teacher, 45,* 188–195.

Carr, E., & Wixon, K. K. (1986). Guidelines for evaluating vocabulary instruction. *Journal of Reading, 29,* 588–595.

Dale, E., & O'Rourke, J. (1986). *Vocabulary building.* Columbus, OH: Zaner-Bloser.

Duffelmeyer, F. A., & Banwart, B. H. (1992–1993). Word maps for adjectives and verbs. *The Reading Teacher, 46,* 351–353.

Freebody, P., & Anderson, R. C. (1983). Effects of vocabulary difficulty, text cohesion, and schema availability on reading comprehension. *Reading Research Quarterly, 18,* 277–294.

Graves, M. (1985). *A word is a word . . . or is it?* Portsmouth, NH: Heinemann.

Heimlich, J. E., & Pittelman, S. D. (1986). *Semantic mapping: Classroom applications.* Newark, DE: International Reading Association.

McKeown, M. G. (1985). The acquisition of word meaning from context by children of high and low ability. *Reading Research Quarterly, 20,* 482–496.

Nagy, W. E. (1988). *Teaching vocabulary to improve reading comprehension.* Urbana, IL: ERIC Clearinghouse on Reading and Communication Skills and the National Council of Teachers of English and the International Reading Association.

Nagy, W. E., Anderson, R. C., & Herman, P. A. (1987). Learning word meanings from context during normal reading. *American Educational Research Journal, 24,* 237–270.

Nagy, W. E., & Herman, P. (1985). Incidental vs. instructional approaches to increasing reading vocabulary. *Educational Perspectives, 23,* 16–21.

Nagy, W. E., Herman, P. A., & Anderson, R. C. (1985). Learning words from context. *Reading Research Quarterly, 20,* 172–193.

Rupley, W. H., Logan, J. W., & Nichols, W. D. (1998/1999). Vocabulary instruction in balanced reading programs. *The Reading Teacher, 52,* 336–346.

Schwartz, R., & Raphael, T. (1985). Concept of definition: A key to improving students' vocabulary. *The Reading Teacher, 39,* 198–205.

Stahl, S. A. (1999). *Vocabulary development.* Cambridge, MA: Brookline Books.

Stahl, S. A., Richek, M. G., & Vandevier, R. (1991). Learning word meanings through listening: A sixth grade replication. In J. Zutell & S. McCormick (Eds.), *Learning factors/teacher factors: Issues in literacy research. Fortieth yearbook of the National Reading Conference* (pp. 185–192). Chicago: National Reading Conference.

Stanovich, K. E. (1986). Matthew effects in reading: Some consequences of individual differences in the acquisition of literacy. *Reading Research Quarterly, 21,* 360–406.

Tompkins, G. E., & Yaden, D. B., Jr. (1986). *Answering students' questions about words.* Urbana, IL: ERIC Clearinghouse on Reading and Communication Skills and the National Council of Teachers of English.

Venezky, R. L. (1999). *The American way of spelling: The structure and origins of American English orthography.* New York: Guilford.

Children's Book References

Bollard, J. K. (1998). *Scholastic children's thesaurus.* New York: Scholastic.

Cartwright, S. (1990). *Alaska's three bears.* Homer, AK: Paws IV Publishing Company.

Cole, J. (1997). *The magic school bus and the electric field trip.* New York: Scholastic.

Cox, J. A. (1980). *Put your foot in your mouth and other silly sayings.* New York: Random House.

Galdone, P. (1972). *The three bears.* New York: Clarion Books.

Gwynne, F. (1970). *The king who rained.* New York: Windmill Books.

Gwynne, F. (1976). *A chocolate moose for dinner.* New York: Windmill Books.

Gwynne, F. (1980). *The sixteen hand horse.* New York: Prentice Hall.

Gwynne, F. (1988). *A little pigeon toad.* New York: Simon & Schuster.

Heller, R. (1983). *The reason for a flower.* New York: Grosset & Dunlap.

Hellweg, P. (1997). *The American Heritage children's the-saurus*. Boston: Houghton Mifflin.

Henkes, K. (1991). *Chrysanthemum*. New York: Greenwillow.

Howe, D., & Howe, J. (1979). *Bunnicula: A rabbit-tale of mystery*. New York: Atheneum.

Hutchins, P. (1968). *Rosie's walk*. New York: Macmillan.

Lobel, A. (1984). *The rose in my garden*. New York: Morrow.

Lobel, A. (1990). *Alison's zinnia*. New York: Greenwillow.

Lowry, L. (1979). *Anastasia Krupnik*. Boston: Houghton Mifflin.

Maestro, G. (1984). *What's a frank Frank? Tasty homo-graph riddles*. New York: Clarion Books.

Martin, B., Jr. (1983). *Brown bear, brown bear, what do you see?* New York: Holt, Rinehart & Winston.

Martin, B., Jr. (1991). *Polar bear, polar bear, what do you hear?* New York: Henry Holt.

Pallotta, J. (1988). *The flower alphabet book*. Watertown, MA: Charlesbridge.

Paulsen, G. (1987). *Hatchet*. New York: Simon & Schuster.

Presson, L. (1996). *What in the world is a homophone?* New York: Barron's.

Terban, M. (1982). *Eight ate: A feast of homonym riddles*. New York: Clarion Books.

Terban, M. (1983). *In a pickle and other funny idioms*. New York: Clarion Books.

Terban, M. (1990). *Punching the clock: Funny action id-ioms*. New York: Clarion Books.

Terban, M. (1996). *Scholastic dictionary of idioms: More than 600 phrases, sayings, and expressions*. New York: Scholastic.

Tolhurst, M. (1990). *Somebody and the three Blairs*. New York: Orchard Books.

Wittels, H., & Greisman, J. (1985). *A first thesaurus*. New York: Golden Books.

Wood, A. (1982). *Quick as a cricket*. London: Child's Play.

Chapter 8

Facilitating Students' Comprehension

— Chapter Questions —

How do capable and less capable readers differ?

What is comprehension?

How do teachers teach and assess comprehension?

Which strategies and skills do readers and writers learn?

How do teachers teach strategies and skills?

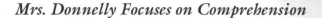

Mrs. Donnelly Focuses on Comprehension

As part of a unit on weather, Mrs. Donnelly's third-grade class reads *Cloudy With a Chance of Meatballs* (Barrett, 1978), a fantasy picture book about the town of Chewandswallow, where food and drink fall from the sky like rain three times each day. After Mrs. Donnelly introduces the book as an "absurd" fantasy, some students read it independently, others read it with a buddy, and seven students choose to read it with the teacher. Those students reading the book with Mrs. Donnelly stop reading at predetermined points and use the **say something** strategy (see the Compendium for a description of this and all other highlighted terms in this chapter) to discuss the story (Hoyt, 1999). Students ask questions, connect events to their own lives, make predictions, make comments, and express how they are feeling about the book. When students stop reading after reading the page about the salt and pepper winds and the tomato tornado, they make these comments:

> Jared: "It's real bad. I think they are going to die."
> Sara: "Yeah, at first it was fun to be in Chewandswallow but now it's not any fun at all."
> Mike: "I think they should move away."
> Vanessa: "Or turn off the weather."
> Mike: "They can't do that."
> Annie: "Well, maybe they can, like how you can turn a television on and off."
> Perry: "All I can say is that the weather is weird. It's out of control."
> Lizzy: "This story is like the *Wizard of Oz*. Dorothy and Toto were in a terrible tornado."
> Jared: "But it wasn't a tomato tornado."
> Lizzy: "No."
> Mike: "It makes me remember *The Night of the Twisters*. That's a good tornado story."

Mrs. Donnelly brings the group back to the story, and when they continue reading they learn that Mike was right: the people from Chewandswallow sail away on a raft made from a stale slice of bread. Stopping periodically as they are reading helps Mrs. Donnelly's students focus on their comprehension of the story.

After all students finish reading the book, they participate in a **grand conversation** and talk about their reactions to the book. Students talk about a variety of topics related to the story:

- how much fun it would be to have the weather bring the food
- their favorite parts of the story
- why the people moved away from Chewandswallow
- why Grandpa told the story to the children
- whether or not the story was true
- the black and white illustrations at the beginning and end of the story and the color illustrations in the middle

269

After the grand conversation, which lasted for 25 minutes, students wrote in **reading logs.** Many of them continued thinking about topics and questions raised during the grand conversation as they wrote in their reading logs. Here is Molly's entry:

> *I don't think the story was real. It seems impossible to me. I think that the reason the colors were black and white sometimes and colors sometimes was because the only real true part was with Grandpa and the kids. That was the black and white part. The color part it was make believe. It was fantasy. I love that book. I want to read it to my Mom and Dad.*

Later, in a **minilesson,** Mrs. Donnelly helps students examine how the author combined fantasy and reality in the book, and they read Judi Barrett's sequel, *Pickles to Pittsburgh* (1997), and compare it to *Cloudy with a Chance of Meatballs.* Students also create their own fantastic weather reports and write an **alphabet book** about weather. For more information about how Mrs. Donnelly's class read and responded to the book, see pages 346–349.

Josh, one of Mrs. Donnelly's students, talked to me about the book and what he does when he reads and writes. The first question I asked was, "What did you think about before you started reading this book?"

"I just looked at the cover, and I knew right away that it would be a weird book. This picture of this man getting a meatball like rain falling on his plate made me think it would be funny—like it would make me laugh. Mrs. Donnelly told us a little about this book, and I know our theme is weather, so I thought about all the stuff I know about rain, snow, clouds, and stuff. But then I read this little writing at the bottom of the page—'If food dropped like rain from the sky, wouldn't it be marvelous! Or would it?'—and I was thinking that something bad was going to happen. Maybe their rain would stop."

"What were you thinking about as you read the book?"

"Well, I wondered why the writing was in yellow boxes on some pages and in pink and orange boxes on other pages. I thought that maybe that was important, but it wasn't. And I couldn't read this word—*Chewandswallow*—at first. I didn't know it was the name of the town, but I just skipped over it and went on reading. It didn't seem important, and then I saw it way back in the book and my eyes saw that it was three words and it was easy to read."

"Mrs. Donnelly told you that *Cloudy With a Chance of Meatballs* was a fantasy, didn't she?"

"Yes, and that made me think that weird stuff would go on, and it did. I thought the weird stuff was going to start when Grandpa was making pancakes, but it didn't start until he told the story. That was sort of confusing, but I just kept reading and I figured it would make sense later on."

"After you finished reading, you wrote in your reading log, didn't you? Would you share it?"

"OK. This is my log: 'I would like to go to Chewandswallow. I want it to snow tacos and pizza and french fries and to rain Coke and hail chocolate chip cookies.

Figure 8–1   Josh's page from the class alphabet book on weather

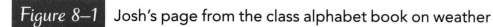

> What blows hot air and is full of rain?
>
> NOSNOOM

M is for Monsoon

A monsoon is a kind of wind that begins in the Indian Ocean. It brings lots of rain to Asia. Some places get 240 inches of rain in a year becuse of monsoons.

HOT + COLD = MONSOON

I'd like all the free food, but I wouldn't like it when the weather got bad. Some of the weather was dangerous. I thought the book would have more information about weather but it didn't. It would have been more interesting if it did.'"

"That's very interesting. How do you decide what to write in your reading log?"

"Well, I write what's on my mind and the things I want to tell Mrs. Donnelly. I think about what I liked and I write that part and then I ask myself if there's anything that was bad for me and then I write that. I ask my brain what to write and it tells me and then I write it."

"When you're reading, do you imagine that you're right there in the story?"

"I guess so. Sometimes when I'm reading, I sort of become the character that is most like me and then I think I'm there. But I didn't really do that in this book. It was too weird. I couldn't think of being there because it's something that would probably never happen."

"Was there anything that you learned when your class talked about the book after you finished reading it?"

"The colors. I was just reading the book and I didn't see that the pages, you know, were all colors during Grandpa's story and the pictures were plain at the beginning and at the end. That's what Molly said and she was right."

Also, as part of the weather unit, Mrs. Donnelly's students wrote an alphabet book on weather. Students used the writing process to draft and refine their book. Each student wrote one page on a different letter, and Josh wrote about monsoons for the *M* page. His page is shown in Figure 8–1. He talked about the page he wrote and his writing.

"How did you decide to write about monsoons?"

"Mrs. Donnelly read us this book called *Jumanji* [Van Allsburg, 1981], and it was about a monsoon. I didn't know about them but I thought it was a kind of weather. I wanted to learn about it so I did. I would like to be in a monsoon someday if I went to places like India or Asia."

"What did you do when you were revising your page?"

"Well, monsoons are not easy to understand. Everybody knows about earthquakes and tornadoes because they happen in California, but monsoons are very unusual. Mrs. Donnelly told me that I had to make sure that everyone could understand my page. I read it to Mike and Perry and they said it was good but that I needed to make a chart about how a monsoon is made. So I did and my dad helped me do it. I made it like a math problem: hot land plus cold water equals a monsoon wind. I want it to be good so everyone will like it. Everybody liked it when I read it when we sat in a circle for a read-around. Then I made a fancy *M* on my page so it would be special."

••

Josh is an effective reader and writer. He views reading and writing as meaning-making processes. He makes predictions before beginning to read, and he organizes ideas before writing. Josh can talk about connecting what he is reading and writing to his own life and to books he has read. He also regulates or monitors what he does when he reads and writes. He has a sense of his audience when he writes. Josh tolerates confusion and ambiguity when he reads and writes, and he has confidence that he'll work through these problems.

Comprehension is the goal of reading instruction. Students must comprehend what they are reading in order to learn from the experience; they must make sense of their reading in order to maintain interest; and they must derive pleasure from reading to become lifelong readers. Students who don't understand what they are reading don't find reading pleasurable and won't continue reading.

Comprehension is crucial for writers, too. As they write, students create compositions with clearly stated main ideas, relevant supporting details, effective transitions between ideas, and precise word choice. The reason why writers write is to share their ideas with readers, but compositions are unsuccessful when readers don't understand what writers have written.

COMPARING CAPABLE AND LESS CAPABLE STUDENTS

Researchers have compared students who are capable readers and writers with other students who are less successful and have found some striking differences (Baker & Brown, 1984; Faigley, Cherry, Jolliffe, & Skinner, 1985; Paris, Wasik, & Turner, 1991). The researchers have found that more capable readers

- are fluent oral and silent readers
- view reading as a process of creating meaning
- decode rapidly
- have large vocabularies
- understand the organization of stories, plays, informational books, poems, and other texts
- use a variety of strategies
- monitor their understanding as they read

Similarly, capable writers

- vary how they write depending on the purpose for writing and the audience that will read the composition
- use the writing process flexibly
- focus on developing ideas and communicating effectively
- turn to classmates for feedback on how they are communicating
- monitor how well they are communicating in the piece of writing
- use formats and structures for stories, poems, letters, and other texts
- use a variety of strategies
- postpone attention to mechanical correctness until the end of the writing process

Teachers often notice that the more capable readers and writers in their own classes exemplify many of these characteristics.

A comparison of characteristics of capable and less capable readers and writers is presented in Figure 8–2. Young students who are learning to read and write often exemplify many of the characteristics of less capable readers and writers, but older students who are less successful readers and writers also exemplify these characteristics.

Less successful readers exemplify fewer of these characteristics or behave differently when they are reading and writing. Perhaps the most remarkable difference is that more capable readers view reading as a process of comprehending or creating

Figure 8–2 Capable and less capable readers and writers

Adapted from Faigley, Cherry, Jolliffe, and Skinner, 1985; and Paris, Wasik, and Turner, 1991.

Reader Characteristics	Writer Characteristics
1. Capable readers view reading as primarily a comprehending or meaning-making process, while less capable readers view reading as a decoding, not a comprehending, process.	1. Capable writers view writing as developing ideas, while less capable writers see writing as putting words on paper.
2. Capable readers adjust their reading speed or purpose according to the reading task, while less capable readers do not.	2. Capable writers are aware of audience, purpose, and form demands and adapt writing to meet these demands, but less capable writers do not.
3. Capable readers read fluently, while less capable readers read word by word and sometimes point at words as they read. Less capable readers read slowly and move their lips as they actually say the words to themselves when reading silently.	3. Capable writers pause as they draft to think or reread what they have written, but less capable writers write without stopping to reread or think about their writing.
4. Capable readers relate what they are reading to their background knowledge, while less capable readers do not make this connection.	4. Capable writers are more concerned with ideas, while less capable writers are more concerned with mechanics and view correct spelling as the hallmark of a good writer.
5. Capable readers apply fix-up strategies effectively. Less capable readers are stumped when they come to unfamiliar words, or they skip over words and invent what they think is a reasonable text.	5. Capable writers vary the length of their writing depending on their purpose, but less capable writers assume that longer pieces of writing are better than short pieces.
6. Capable readers identify words more effectively than less capable readers do, whether the words are in context or in isolation.	6. Capable writers collaborate with classmates to write or revise their writing, but less capable writers do not collaborate as effectively.
7. Capable readers monitor their comprehension, but less capable readers don't. Neither do they realize or take action when they don't understand.	7. Capable writers assess their own writing, while less capable writers do not.
8. Capable readers have larger vocabularies than less capable readers do.	8. Capable writers make changes to communicate meaning more effectively when they revise, but less capable writers make cosmetic changes.
9. Capable readers expect to be successful, while less capable readers have low expectations for success.	9. Capable writers use many strategies and vary them according to the assignment, but less capable writers use fewer strategies and don't monitor their use.

meaning, while less capable readers focus on decoding. In writing, less capable writers make cosmetic changes when they revise, rather than changes to communicate meaning more effectively. These important differences indicate that capable students focus on comprehension and the strategies readers and writers use to understand what they read and to make sure that what they write will be comprehensible to others.

Another important difference between capable and less capable readers and writers is that those who are less successful are not strategic. They are naive. They seem reluctant to use unfamiliar strategies or those that require much effort. They do not seem to be motivated or to expect that they will be successful. Less capable readers and writers don't understand or use all steps of the reading and writing processes effectively. They do not monitor their reading and writing (Garner, 1987; Keene & Zimmermann, 1997). Or, if they do use strategies, they remain dependent on primitive strategies. For example, as they read, less successful readers seldom look ahead or back into the text to clarify misunderstandings or make plans. Or, when they come to an unfamiliar word, they often stop reading, unsure of what to do. They may try to sound out an unfamiliar word, but if that is unsuccessful they give up. In contrast, capable readers know several strategies, and if one strategy isn't successful they try another.

Less capable writers move through the writing process in a lockstep, linear approach. They use a limited number of strategies, most often a "knowledge-telling" strategy in which they list everything they know about a topic with little thought to choosing information to meet the needs of their readers or to organizing the information to put related information together (Faigley et al., 1985). In contrast, capable writers understand the recursive nature of the writing process and turn to classmates for feedback about how well they are communicating. They are more responsive to the needs of the audience that will read their writing, and they work to organize their writing in a cohesive manner.

This research on capable and less capable readers and writers has focused on comprehension differences and students' use of strategies. It is noteworthy that all research comparing readers and writers focuses on how students use reading and writing strategies, not on differences in their use of skills.

Motivation for Reading and Writing

Motivation is intrinsic and internal—a driving force within us. Often students' motivation for becoming more capable readers and writers diminishes as they reach the upper grades. Penny Oldfather (1995) conducted a four-year study to examine the factors influencing students' motivation. She found that students were more highly motivated when they had opportunities for authentic self-expression as part of literacy activities. Students she interviewed reported that they were more highly motivated when they had ownership of the learning activities. Specific activities they mentioned included opportunities to

❧ express their own ideas and opinions

❧ choose topics for writing and books for reading

❧ talk about books they are reading

❧ share their writings with classmates

❧ pursue "authentic" activities—not worksheets—using reading, writing, listening, and talking

Some students are not strongly motivated to learn to read and write, and they adopt strategies for avoiding failure rather than strategies for making meaning. These strategies are defensive tactics (Dweck, 1986; Paris et al., 1991). Unmotivated readers give up or remain passive, uninvolved in reading (Johnston & Winograd, 1985). Some students feign interest or pretend to be involved even though they are not. Others don't think reading is important, and they choose to focus on other curricular areas—math or sports, for instance. Some students complain about feeling ill or that other students are bothering them. They place the blame on anything other than themselves.

There are other students who avoid reading and writing entirely. They just don't do it. Another group of students reads books that are too easy for them or writes short pieces so that they don't have to exert much effort. Even though these strategies are self-serving, students use them because they lead to short-term success. The long-term result, however, is devastating because these students fail to learn to read and write. Because it takes quite a bit of effort to read and write strategically, it is especially important that students experience personal ownership of the literacy activities going on in their classrooms and know how to manage their own reading and writing behaviors.

THE COMPREHENSION PROCESS

Comprehension is a creative, multifaceted process in which students engage with the text (Tierney, 1990). Teachers often view comprehension as a mysterious process of making meaning or understanding what students read. It often seems mysterious because it is invisible; some students read and understand what they read, and others seem to read just as well but don't understand what they read. Sometimes comprehension problems relate to students' lack of fluency or limited vocabulary knowledge, but more often than not, students who don't comprehend seem no different from their classmates.

Three factors influence comprehension: the reader, the text, and the purpose (Irwin, 1991). The background knowledge that readers bring to the reading process influences how they understand the text as well as the strategies they know to use while reading. The text that is being read is a second factor. The author's ideas, the words the author uses to express those ideas, and how the ideas are organized and presented also affect comprehension. The purpose is the third factor. Readers vary the way they read according to their purpose. They read differently to cook a recipe, enjoy a letter from an old friend, understand the opinion expressed in an editorial, or read a novel.

Readers' comprehension varies because of these three factors. If you are a student learning how to teach reading, it seems obvious that your understanding will vary from your professor's. You and your professor have different levels of background knowledge and experience teaching reading, and you and your professor are probably reading the chapter for different purposes. Perhaps you are reading this chapter to learn the main ideas or to prepare for a test; in contrast, your professor may be reading the chapter in order to prepare to give a presentation for the next class meeting or to identify questions for a quiz. But even though comprehension varies from reader to reader, comprehension can always be supported with ideas from the text.

Judith Irwin (1991) defines comprehension as the reader's process of using prior experiences and the author's text to construct meaning that is useful to that reader for a specific purpose. For a writer, comprehension is similarly described as a process of using prior experiences to create a text that will be meaningful to that writer for a specific purpose.

www.sil.org

Lingualinks. Read more about comprehension at this website.

Readers do many things as they read in order to comprehend what they are reading, and writers do similar things to create meaningful texts. Irwin (1991) has identified five subprocesses of comprehension:

1.   Microprocesses
2.   Integrative processes
3.   Macroprocesses
4.   Elaborative processes
5.   Metacognitive processes

These subprocesses are overviewed in Figure 8–3, and instructional and assessment techniques are suggested.

Microprocesses

The microprocesses focus on sentence-level comprehension. Readers chunk ideas into phrases and select what is important from the sentence to keep in short-term memory. Students who chunk ideas into phrases read fluently, not word by word, and students who do not chunk phrases meaningfully have difficulty understanding what they are reading. For example, consider this sentence from *Cloudy With a Chance of Meatballs* (Barrett, 1978): "For lunch one day, frankfurters, already in their rolls, blew in from the northwest at about five miles an hour" (n.p.). How would you chunk the phrases? Here is one way:

For lunch one day,

frankfurters,

already in their rolls,

blew in

from the northwest

at about five miles an hour.

The commas help to chunk the text in this sentence. It is especially important that second language learners learn the ebb and flow of English phrases and sentences. Similarly, writers chunk the sentences they are writing into meaningful phrases. This chunking helps them to remember the sentence they are writing and to write fluently and with voice.

Students practice using the microprocesses whenever they read or reread sentences, paragraphs, and longer texts and chunk words into phrases as they read. Teachers listen to students read aloud to check that they are chunking words into phrases. Many less capable readers read slowly, word by word, and teachers can help students chunk words into phrases with lots of reading and rereading practice. They can also provide assisted-practice activities using **choral reading,** buddy reading, and listening centers. As students read aloud with classmates or along with an audiotape at a listening center, they listen to how more capable readers chunk words into phrases. Teachers can also write sentences from books students are reading on sentence strips and then cut the sentence apart into phrases. Then students arrange the phrase strips to complete the sentence.

Teachers can also adapt **interactive writing** activities to give students practice with chunking. Students create a long sentence, break it into phrases, and write it phrase by phrase on chart paper and on white boards.

Figure 8–3 The five comprehension subprocesses

Process	Activities	Assessment
Microprocesses. Readers chunk ideas into phrases within a sentence. Students who read word by word and do not chunk phrases meaningfully have difficulty understanding what they are reading. Similarly, writers must write fluently, chunking ideas into sentences.	Choral reading is a good activity to help children chunk text appropriately because classmates and the teacher model appropriate chunking. Interactive writing and quickwrites are effective ways to develop writing fluency.	Teachers listen to students read aloud and check for appropriate chunking. For writing, they observe students as they write.
Integrative processes. Readers infer connections and relationships between clauses and sentences by noticing pronoun substitutions, recognizing synonym substitutions, inferring cause and effect, and recognizing connectives such as *also, however*, and *unless*. In writing, students use these substitutions to clarify relationships.	Teachers use "close reading" to help students understand these connections by asking questions and directing students' attention to these relationships; for writing, they use sentence combining activities.	Teachers use "close reading" to check children's ability to use connectives and understand relationships among words in a paragraph, and they examine the paragraphs students write for these connections.
Macroprocesses. Readers organize and summarize ideas as they read; that is, they look at the big picture of the entire text as well as the smaller units in the text. For writing, they use their knowledge of story structure, expository text structures, or poetic formulas to organize their compositions.	Students learn about structural patterns of different types of text and draw graphic organizers to visually represent the main ideas. Students also do oral and written retellings and write summaries.	Teachers assess students' knowledge of macrostructures by examining students' graphic organizers, their retellings, and their compositions.
Elaborative processes. Readers elaborate on the author's message as they make connections to their own lives and other literature. Students make predictions as they read, connect their reading to prior knowledge, and identify with characters. In writing, students use classmates' feedback when they revise and provide enough details so readers can make connections.	Students learn to make connections as they talk about stories in grand conversations and write in reading logs.	Teachers observe students as they participate in grand conversations and read their reading log entries to check that they are making corrections. And teachers monitor students' compositions, checking that they provide detail so readers can make connections.
Metacognitive processes. Readers monitor their comprehension and use problem-solving strategies to read and write effectively.	Teachers model reading strategies by "thinking aloud" as they read aloud and model writing strategies during writing lessons. They provide information about literacy strategies in minilessons. Then students apply the strategies when they read and write.	Teachers observe students as they read and write and ask them to "think aloud" about the strategies they are using. Teachers also ask students to reflect on their use of strategies during a reading or writing conference.

Integrative Processes

The integrative processes deal with the semantic and syntactic connections and relationships among sentences. Here are four sentences from the beginning of *Cloudy With a Chance of Meatballs* (Barrett, 1978): "In most ways, it was very much like any other tiny town. . . . But there were no food stores in the town of Chewandswallow. They didn't need any. The sky supplied all the food they could possibly want" (n.p.). In order to comprehend the story, students need to understand that Chewandswallow is different from other towns because it didn't have any food stores and that food stores weren't needed because food and drink came down from the sky, like rain or snow.

Readers infer these connections and relationships by noticing pronoun substitutions, recognizing synonym substitutions, inferring cause and effect, and recognizing connectives such as *also, however, because,* and *unless.* Writers include these connections and relationships in paragraphs by using pronoun and synonym substitutions, providing inferential clues, and using connectives.

Teachers facilitate students' understanding of integrative processes when they are reading aloud or along with students and they stop reading to ask clarifying questions. After reading the sentences from *Cloudy With a Chance of Meatballs,* teachers might ask one or more of these questions:

What is Chewandswallow?

How is Chewandswallow different from other towns?

Why didn't this town need any food stores?

Since they had no food stores, how did the people of Chewandswallow get food?

How does the sky supply food?

This brief discussion can be done during reading, or teachers can reread the sentences after reading and then ask the questions.

Teachers can also ask these clarifying questions to assess students' ability to use integrative processes. If students have difficulty answering the questions, teachers need to ask clarifying questions like these more often and model how they make connections and relationships among sentences.

Teachers can also examine students' compositions to see if they make these connections and relationships in their writing. If students don't demonstrate knowledge of integrative processes, they can practice combining sentences. For example, combine these four sentences:

The weather came three times a day.

It came at breakfast.

It came at lunch.

It came at dinner.

These sentences might be combined this way: *The weather came three times a day, at breakfast, lunch, and dinner.* Now try combining this more complicated set of sentences:

The people lived in Chewandswallow.

The people woke up.

The people ate.

It was a shower of orange juice.

Then toast with butter and jelly blew in.

It drizzled milk.

The milk finished the meal.

Here's one combination: *The people of Chewandswallow woke up and drank a shower of orange juice. Then they ate the toast with the butter and jelly that blew in. It drizzled milk to finish the meal.* When students combine sentences, they realize the inferred connections and relationships among sentences.

Macroprocesses

Macroprocesses relate to the big picture—the entire text. The two components of the macroprocesses are recognizing the structure of text and selecting the most important information to remember (Irwin, 1991). Readers organize and summarize ideas as they read, and writers organize their ideas in order to write coherently. Both readers and writers use their knowledge of the overall structure of texts for macroprocessing. Students learn about the elements of story structure, expository text structures, and poetic formulas, and they use this knowledge about the structure of text in order to comprehend what they read. (You will learn more about the structure of text in Chapter 9.)

In order to comprehend the story *Cloudy With a Chance of Meatballs,* students have to know about the fantasy genre and recognize, as Molly did in the vignette at the beginning of the chapter, that the use of color in the illustrations represented the fantasy part of the story. Similarly, when the students in Mrs. Donnelly's classroom wrote their alphabet book about weather, they used a sequence structure to organize their book.

Students use macroprocessing when they use puppets to retell a story.

Teachers teach students about the elements of story structure, expository text structures, and poetic formulas so that students can apply this knowledge in both reading and writing. They also teach students how to use graphic organizers that emphasize the structure of a text as a comprehension aid when reading and writing. They also do **word sorts** that emphasize characters or events in a story or the main ideas in an informational book (Hoyt, 1999). Figure 8–4 shows a sentence sort contrasting reality and fantasy in *Cloudy With a Chance of Meatballs*.

Learning to differentiate between the more important and less important ideas is a part of macroprocessing, and this knowledge is crucial for both reading and writing. As students read, they choose the more important ideas to remember; when students write, they organize their compositions to focus on the more important ideas. If they are writing a story, they focus on the beginning, middle, and end; if they are writing a cause and effect essay, they explain the causes that produce an effect.

Teachers assess students' knowledge of macroprocesses through their oral and written retellings, their graphic organizers, and the summaries they write. Teachers can also examine the overall structure of the compositions students write.

Elaborative Processes

Students use the elaborative processes to go beyond literal comprehension and make inferences about what the author meant. Readers make personal connections to what they are reading and also make connections to other literature they have read. They also personalize their reading when they connect what they are reading to their prior knowledge, make predictions, identify with characters, and visualize what they are reading.

To help students reflect on their reading, Hoyt (1999) suggests the Two Words activity. In this technique, students choose two individual words to represent the book they have read. After they choose the words, they share their words, explain why they chose them, and say how they relate to the book or their own lives. For example, after reading *Cloudy With a Chance of Meatballs*, Vanessa, one of Mrs. Donnelly's students, chose *impossible* and *delicious*. She explained her choices this way: "I know this story could never happen. It is *impossible*, but I think having food fall like the rain would be *delicious*. I would like going outside and opening my mouth to get a snack."

Students are often expected to make inferences—connections that are not explicitly stated—as they read and comprehend stories. These understandings go beyond the literal information presented in the text (Keene & Zimmermann, 1997). Students have to recognize clues in the text and use them to draw conclusions. In *Miss Nelson Is Missing* (Marshall, 1977), for example, students are not explicitly told that their teacher, Miss Nelson, is pretending to be the hated substitute teacher, Miss Viola Swamp, but there are enough clues that adults and some children realize that Miss Nelson and Miss Viola Swamp are one in the same. Other children think the two are different people. They don't understand how their classmates inferred the connection and ask to have it explained to them. Many of Chris Van Allsburg's fantasies require students to use inference as well. In *The Wretched Stone* (1991), for example, some children and adults realize that the stone that captivates the crew and turns them into monkeys represents television, but others do not. Those who don't understand fail to attach importance to the clues that Van Allsburg provides: the crew watches the glowing stone for hours, they stop reading and playing music, and they neglect their duties on shipboard. Similarly, after reading Van Allsburg's *The Stranger* (1986), many students guess that the stranger is Jack Frost, but some students do not put the clues together.

Figure 8–4 A sentence sort about *Cloudy With a Chance of Meatballs*

Realism	Fantasy
The children go sledding in the snow.	People carried plates, forks and napkins with them.
People buy food in supermarkets.	There was a tomato tornado.
One flying pancake lands on Henry.	Food got larger and larger.
Grandpa told the best bedtime story.	The people abandoned the town.
Grandpa flips pancakes.	The people watch the weather report on TV to find out the menu.
	There were storms of hamburgers and showers of orange juice.
	The Sanitation Department gave up trying to clean up the extra food.

Students also make connections to books they have read previously, as two of Mrs. Donnelly's students did in the vignette. These connections are called "intertextuality" (de Beaugrande, 1980). Students also use intertextuality as they incorporate ideas and structures from the stories they have read into the stories they are writing. Here are five characteristics of intertextuality:

1. *Individual and unique.* Students' literary experiences and the connections they make among them are different.
2. *Dependent on literary experiences.* Intertextuality is dependent on the types of books students have read, their purpose for and interest in reading, and the literary communities to which students belong.
3. *Metacognitive awareness.* Most students are aware of intertextuality and consciously make connections among texts.
4. *Links to concept of story.* Students' connections among stories are linked to their knowledge about literature.
5. *Reading-writing connections.* Students make connections between stories they read and stories they write (Cairney, 1990, 1992).

Cairney's (1992) research indicates that students are aware of their past experiences with literature and use this knowledge as they read and write.

Teachers encourage students to make personal and literary connections to books during the responding step of the reading process as they participate in grand conversations and write in reading logs. Students also make connections as they assume the role of a character and make **open-mind portraits,** reenact the story, write simulated journals from the viewpoint of a character, and work on other activities in the exploring step of the reading process.

Teachers assess students' elaborative processes by checking to see that their predictions are reasonable, by listening to the comments that students make during grand conversations, and by reading their entries in reading logs. In particular, teachers should notice when students make inferences and intertextual comments during grand conversations and in their reading log entries.

Metacognitive Processes

Metacognition is students' conscious awareness of their thinking (Baker & Brown, 1984). Both readers and writers use metacognitive strategies to monitor and evaluate their comprehension. Strategies, such as predicting, visualizing, organizing, tapping prior knowledge, and self-questioning, are conscious problem-solving behaviors that students use in order to read and write effectively. The strategies are metacognitive because students think about them as they read and write, applying and regulating their use.

During the elementary grades, students' metacognitive knowledge grows as they learn about the reading and writing processes and the strategies that readers and writers use. As students gain experience, their attention in reading moves from decoding to comprehension. In writing, their focus shifts from forming letters and spelling to communicating ideas. As novice readers and writers, students apply strategies when teachers guide and direct them to, but as they become more effective readers and writers, students regulate their use of strategies independently.

Teachers introduce the strategies to students in minilessons. They model how to use the strategies and provide opportunities during guided reading and in other reading activities for students to practice using the strategies. They also teach students to

www.oise.utoronto.ca

Metacognition: Developing Your Ability to Learn. Metacognition is explained, and there are links to related sites.

reflect on their use of strategies using think-alouds, in which students talk or write about thinking about reading and writing. In the vignette at the beginning of the chapter, Josh used the think-aloud procedure to reflect on his reading and writing. Teachers can also use think-alouds to assess students' use of strategies.

—————————— *Assessment Tools: Comprehension Processes* ——————————

Teachers often use an informal reading inventory (IRI) to determine whether students comprehend reading materials at their grade level. When a student's comprehension is below grade level, teachers must examine that student's use of each comprehension subprocess to determine his or her specific problem areas. Using a familiar story, try these activities to assess a student's use of the subprocesses:

- *Microprocesses.* Ask the student to read a paragraph aloud and listen for fluency and chunking.

- *Integrative processes.* Reread a paragraph of text to the student and ask "close reading" questions about pronoun and synonym substitutions and connectives. Check to see that the student understands relationships among sentences.

- *Macroprocesses.* Have the student retell the story without looking at the illustrations. Check to see that the student structures the story events into the beginning, middle, and end and identifies the characters and setting.

- *Elaborative processes.* Ask the student to talk about a favorite character, make connections from the story to his or her own life, or make connections to other books he or she has read.

- *Metacognitive processes.* Have the student reread a paragraph and think aloud about his or her thought processes. Or, ask the student to talk about how he or she uses a strategy, such as predicting or visualizing, during reading.

www.ericir.syr.edu

ERIC Database. Search the ERIC Database for articles about comprehension.

The five comprehension subprocesses operate simultaneously during the reading and writing processes. It would be wrong to conclude that first students comprehend phrases in sentences, then sentences in paragraphs, and then the entire text. Instead, all five subprocesses work together throughout a variety of activities so that students refine their understanding. Figure 8–5 lists some comprehension activities that students use during the five steps of the reading process.

LITERACY STRATEGIES AND SKILLS

In the vignette at the beginning of the chapter, Josh applied a variety of literacy skills automatically and used problem-solving strategies in order to create meaning when he reads and writes. We all have skills we use automatically and self-regulated strategies we use thoughtfully for things we do well, such as driving defensively, playing volleyball, training a new pet, or maintaining classroom discipline. We apply skills that we have learned unconsciously and choose among skills as we think strategically. The strategies we use in these activities are problem-solving mechanisms that involve complex thinking processes.

 Ways to enhance comprehension in each step of the reading process

1. Prereading

Develop background knowledge with books, videos, and hands-on materials.
Activate background knowledge with K-W-L charts, quickwrites, and discussions.
Make predictions.
Use anticipation guides.
Prepare graphic organizers.

2. Reading

Use shared reading or read aloud to students if the text is too difficult for
    students to read.
Have students read with buddies.
Model reading strategies.
Use guided reading and monitor students' use of strategies.
Use "close reading" of short passages.
Use the "say something" activity.
Make additional predictions.

3. Responding

Discuss the text in a grand conversation.
Write in reading logs.
Use drama to reenact the story.

4. Exploring

Reread the text.
Retell the text.
Use storyboards to sequence events in the text.
Complete graphic organizers.
Examine literary opposites.
Teach lessons on reading strategies and skills.
Teach lessons on the structure of texts (e.g., plot, cause and effect).
Teach lessons about the author or genre.
Make open-mind portraits.
Examine selected sentences and paragraphs in the text.

5. Applying

Complete the K-W-L chart.
Make projects to deepen understanding.
Read other books on the same topic.
Compare related books or book and film versions.
Write reports and other books on the same topic.

When we are just learning how to drive a car, for example, we learn both skills and strategies. Some of the first skills we learn are how to start the engine, make left turns, and parallel park. With practice, these skills become automatic. Some of the first strategies we learn are how to pass another car and stay a safe distance behind other cars. At first we have only a small repertoire of strategies, and we don't always use them effectively. That's one reason why we take driving lessons from a driving instructor and have a learner's permit that requires a more experienced driver to ride along with us. These more experienced drivers teach us defensive driving strategies. We learn strategies for driving on interstate highways, on slippery roads, and at night. With practice and guidance we become more successful drivers, able to anticipate driving problems and take defensive actions.

The same is true for literacy. Strategic readers and writers control their own reading and writing and apply skills and strategies as they need them. They set purposes before reading, revise their plans as they read, and deal with the difficulties they encounter while reading and writing. Strategies allow students to monitor understanding and solve problems as they read. Students use strategies deliberately with some understanding of their usefulness or effectiveness. In order to become expert readers and writers, children must become strategic.

Reading and Writing Strategies

Capable readers and writers are actively involved in creating meaning. They select and use appropriate strategies, monitor their understanding as they read, and refine their meaning as they write (Paris & Jacobs, 1984; Schmitt, 1990). I focus on 12 strategies that elementary students use for both reading and writing. These strategies are listed in Figure 8–6.

1. *Tapping prior knowledge.* Students think about what they already know about the topic about which they will read or write. This knowledge includes information and vocabulary about topics such as dinosaurs, as well as information about authors and literary genres such as fantasies, alphabet books, and biographies. Students' knowledge is stored in schemata (or categories) and linked to other knowledge through a complex network of interrelationships. As students learn during the reading or writing task, they add the new information to their schemata.

2. *Predicting.* Students make predictions or thoughtful "guesses" about what will happen in the books they are reading. These guesses are based on what students already know about the topic and the literary genre, or on what they have read thus far. Students often make one prediction before beginning to read and several others at key points in the story or at the beginning of each chapter when reading chapter books using the **Directed Reading-Thinking Activity** (DRTA) (Stauffer, 1975). As they read, students either confirm or revise their predictions. When they are preparing to read informational books or content-area textbooks, students often preview the text in order to make predictions. They also ask questions for which they would like to find answers as they read or set purposes for reading.

When they are writing, students make plans and set purposes for the pieces they are writing. They make predictions about which ideas are important and which ones will interest their readers. They revise their plans as their writing moves in new or unexpected directions. Young children also make predictions about how long their writing will be when they count out the number of pages for their books.

3. *Organizing ideas.* Students organize ideas and sequence story events as they read, and they organize their ideas for writing using **clusters** and other graphic organizers. The way students organize ideas varies depending on whether they are reading and writing stories, informational books, or poetry. Each type of text has unique organizational patterns. When students read and write stories, they often organize the events into the beginning, middle, and end. When they read and write

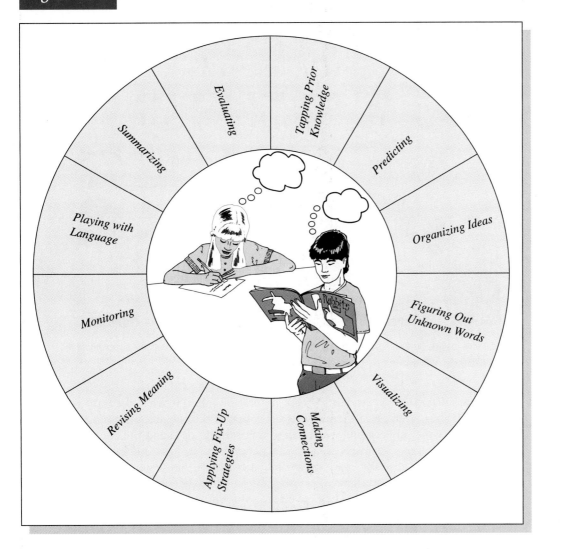

Figure 8–6 Twelve strategies that readers and writers use

informational books, they often use description, sequence, comparison, or cause-and-effect structures. When they read and write poetry, students use various poetic forms, including haiku, free verse, and acrostics.

4. *Figuring out unknown words.* Students need to decide whether to use phonic analysis, analogies, syllabic analysis, or morphemic analysis to identify an unfamiliar word or to skip over a word and continue reading. Sometimes they ask the teacher or a classmate. When students are writing, they often need to write words that they don't know how to spell. They can write several letters to serve temporarily as a placeholder, and then check the spelling later by consulting a dictionary, a classmate, or the teacher. At other times, they sound out the word or "think it out." When thinking out the spelling, they have to consider root words, affixes, spelling patterns, and whether or not the word "looks right."

Students make a quilt with memorable quotes after reading stories and informational books about the Underground Railroad.

5. *Visualizing.* Students create mental pictures of what they are reading or writing. They often place themselves in the images they create, becoming a character in the story they are reading, traveling to that setting, or facing the conflict situations that the characters themselves face. Teachers sometimes ask students to close their eyes to help visualize the story or to draw pictures of the scenes and characters they visualize. How well students use visualization often becomes clear when students view film versions of books they have read. Students who use the visualization strategy are often disappointed with the film version and the actors who perform as the characters, while students who don't visualize are often amazed by the film and prefer it to the book version.

When they are writing, students use description and sensory detail to make their writing more vivid and bring it to life for the people who will read their books. Sometimes teachers have students brainstorm lists of words related to each of the five senses and then incorporate some of the words in pieces they are writing. They also encourage students to use comparisons—metaphors and similes—to make their writing more vivid.

6. *Making connections.* Students personalize what they are reading by relating it to their own lives. They recall similar experiences or compare the characters to themselves or people they know. They connect the book they are reading to other literature they have read. Readers often make connections among several books written by one author or between two versions of the same story. Similarly, when they are writing, students make connections between what they are writing and books they have read or experiences they have had.

7. ***Applying fix-up strategies.*** When students are reading, they sometimes realize that something is not making sense or that they are not understanding what they are reading. Then they apply fix-up strategies. They may assume that things will make sense soon and continue reading, or they may reread, look at pictures, skip ahead, talk to a classmate about the book, or ask for help. Choosing an appropriate fix-up strategy is important so students can continue reading productively.

When writing, students sometimes realize that their writing isn't working the way they want it to. Then they apply fix-up strategies. They might reread what they have written to get a jump start on their writing, do more prewriting to gather and organize ideas, read a book on the topic, talk about their ideas with a classmate, or ask a classmate or the teacher to read the piece and give some feedback. Sometimes they draw a picture.

8. ***Revising meaning.*** Reading and writing are processes of making meaning, and as students read and write they are continually revising their understanding and the meaning they are creating. Students often reread for more information or because something doesn't make sense. They also study a book's illustrations, learn through the process of sharing, and get ideas from classmates during discussions. As they write in reading logs, students often gain new insights about a book.

Students meet in writing groups for classmates to read and react to their rough drafts so that writers can revise their writing and make it stronger. Writers revise on the basis of the feedback they get from classmates. As they revise, students add words and sentences, make substitutions and deletions, and move their text around to communicate more effectively. They also add titles and illustrations to clarify meaning.

9. ***Monitoring.*** Students monitor their understanding as they read, though they may only be aware of this monitoring when comprehension breaks down. Students also monitor their writing to see how well they are communicating. When they are reading and writing, students ask themselves questions to monitor their understanding, and they use fix-up strategies when they realize that understanding has broken down.

10. ***Playing with language.*** Students notice figurative and novel uses of language when they read, and they incorporate interesting language when they write. Some examples of playing with language are idioms, jokes, riddles, metaphors, similes, personification, sensory language, rhyme, alliteration, and invented words.

11. ***Summarizing.*** Readers choose important ideas to remember. Summarizing is important because big ideas are easier to remember than lots of details. As students write, they often state their big ideas at the beginning of a paragraph and then support them with facts. They want their readers to be able to pick out the important ideas. During revising, writers ask for feedback about how well their readers remember the important ideas.

12. ***Evaluating.*** Students make judgments about, reflect on, and value the books they are reading and writing. Readers think about what they have read, review the text, and evaluate their reading. They also value the books they read and what they do as readers. Writers do similar things. They ask themselves whether their own writing says what they want it to say—in other words, whether or not it is effective. They think about what they have experimented with in a particular piece of writing and reflect on the writing processes that they use. As a strategy, evaluation is not the teacher's judgment handed down to students, but rather students' own thinking about their goals and accomplishments.

Students don't use every one of these strategies every time they read or write, but effective readers and writers use most of them most of the time. Figure 8–7 shows how Mrs. Donnelly's students used these strategies in reading *Cloudy With a Chance of Meatballs* and in writing the class alphabet book about weather.

Why Is It Important That Students Become Strategic Readers and Writers? Being strategic is an important characteristic of learning. Readers and writers use strategies to generate, organize, and elaborate meaning more expertly than they can otherwise. During the elementary grades, children learn all sorts of cognitive strategies, and the acquisition of reading and writing strategies coincides with this cognitive development. As students learn to reflect on their learning, for example, they learn to reflect on themselves as readers and writers; and as they learn to monitor their learning, they learn to monitor their reading and writing. Many of the cognitive strategies that students learn have direct application to reading and writing. In this way, children's growing awarenesses about thinking, reading, and writing are mutually supportive.

Strategies are cognitive tools that students can use selectively and flexibly as they become independent readers and writers. In order for students to become independent readers and writers, they need these thinking tools. These strategies are tools for learning across the curriculum, and strategic reading and writing enhance learning in math, social studies, science, and other content areas. Children's competence in reading and writing affects all areas of the curriculum. Also, teachers can teach students how to apply reading and writing strategies (Paris et al., 1991). Just as driving instructors and more experienced drivers can teach novice drivers about defensive driving, teachers can demonstrate and explain strategic reading and writing and provide students with opportunities for guided practice.

Even though these strategies are called reading and writing strategies, they are the same strategies students use when they listen and talk and view and visually represent (Brent & Anderson, 1993; Tompkins, 1998). For example, when Mrs. Donnelly's students listen to her describe different cloud formations, they visualize the clouds in their minds and organize the information she is presenting. And when her students talk about their reflections of *Cloudy With a Chance of Meatballs,* they make connections to their own lives, revise meaning, and play with language.

Reading and Writing Skills

Skills are information-processing techniques that readers and writers use automatically and unconsciously as they construct meaning. Many skills focus at the word level, but some require readers and writers to attend to larger chunks of text. For example, at the elementary level, readers use skills such as decoding unfamiliar words, noting details, and sequencing events; and writers employ skills such as forming contractions, using punctuation marks, and capitalizing people's names. Skills and strategies are not the same thing, since strategies are problem-solving tactics selected deliberately to achieve particular goals (Paris et al., 1991). The important difference between skills and strategies is how they are used.

During the elementary grades, students learn to use five types of reading and writing skills:

1. ***Comprehension skills.*** Students use comprehension skills in conjunction with reading and writing strategies. For example, they recognize literary genres and organizational patterns. Other comprehension skills include separating facts

Figure 8–7 How third graders use reading and writing strategies

Strategy	How It Is Used When Reading *Cloudy With a Chance of Meatballs*	How It Is Used When Writing an Alphabet Book About Weather
Tapping Prior Knowledge	The teacher tells students that the book is a fantasy about weather, and students think about what they know about weather books and fantasy stories.	Students brainstorm weather words beginning with each letter of the alphabet. They choose the word for each page of the alphabet book.
Predicting	Students identify a purpose or reason for reading. They make "guesses" about what will happen next as they read, and then they read to confirm their predictions.	Students conference with the teacher, sharing their clusters before beginning to draft their page.
Organizing Ideas	Students think about the sequence of events in the story and chunk the events into three parts: beginning, middle, and end.	Students make a cluster to organize information about the word before beginning to write.
Figuring Out Unknown Words	Students skip some unfamiliar words and ask the teacher and classmates about other words. They also write unfamiliar words in their journals.	Students use invented spelling for unfamiliar words while drafting. Later, during editing, they check the spellings on the word wall, in a dictionary, or in an informational book.
Visualizing	Students visualize the events in the story or put themselves into the story and imagine the events happening to themselves.	Students think about the audience that will read their informational book. They imagine what their page in the finished book will look like.
Making Connections	Students think about how they would feel if the story happened in their community. They think about other books they have read in which impossible events occur.	Students think about what information might be interesting to readers. They think about informational books they have read that they can use as models for their books.

Figure 8–7 continued

Strategy	How It Is Used When Reading *Cloudy With a Chance of Meatballs*	How It Is Used When Writing an Alphabet Book About Weather
Applying Fix-Up Strategies	Students are confused about the realistic event at the beginning of the story, but they decide to keep reading. They notice that the pictures at the beginning and end are black and white and the ones in the fantasy are in color. They reread to figure out why.	Students decide to add a comparison of lightning and thunder to make the section on thunderstorms clearer. They read more about fog to expand that part of the book.
Revising Meaning	Students turn back a page or two when something they read doesn't make sense. Students discuss the story after reading and elaborate their understanding as they talk and listen to classmates' comments.	Students stop drafting to reread what they have read and make revisions to communicate more effectively. Students meet in writing groups to share their drafts and get feedback to use in revising.
Monitoring	As they read, students ask themselves questions to be sure they understand what they are reading. The teacher asks students to notice characteristics of fantasy in the story, and students look for characteristics as they reread it.	As they draft, students check the accuracy and completeness of the information they are writing. They put themselves in the place of their readers and ask themselves if they would find the page interesting.
Playing With Language	Students notice that the town's name—Chewandswallow—is an invented word. They make up other invented words. *Lightning* becomes *flashandboom.*	Students decide to add a riddle to introduce each letter.
Summarizing	Students identify important ideas in the story. They contrast the realism and fantasy in the story.	Students focus on the big ideas about the word and add interesting details to explain the big ideas.
Evaluating	In their journals or in conferences with the teacher, students give opinions about the story and say whether or not they liked it.	Students evaluate the effectiveness of each page and the accuracy of the information presented.

and opinions, comparing and contrasting, and recognizing literary genres and structures.

2. *Decoding and spelling skills.* Students use decoding and spelling skills as they identify words when reading and spell words when writing. They focus on spelling skills during the editing step of the writing process. Examples of decoding and spelling skills include sounding out words, breaking words into syllables, using root words and affixes to decode and spell words, and using abbreviations.

3. *Language skills.* Students use language skills to analyze words they are reading and to choose more precise words and phrases when they are writing. These skills include locating the meanings of words, noticing idioms, using figurative language, and choosing synonyms.

4. *Study skills.* Students use study skills to remember what they read during content-area units and when studying for tests. Skimming and scanning, taking notes, making clusters, and previewing a book before reading are examples of study skills.

5. *Reference skills.* Students use reference skills to read newspaper articles, locate information in dictionaries and other informational books, and use library references. These skills include alphabetizing a list of words, comparing word meanings in a dictionary, using a table of contents and an index, and reading and making graphs.

Examples of the five types of skills are presented in Figure 8–8.

Teachers often wonder when they should teach the skills listed in Figure 8–8. School districts often prepare curriculum guides or frameworks that list the skills to be taught at each grade level, and they are usually listed on scope-and-sequence charts that accompany basal reader programs. On scope-and-sequence charts, textbook makers identify the grade level at which the skill should be introduced and the grade levels at which it is practiced. These resources provide guidelines, but teachers decide which skills to teach based on their children's level of literacy development and the reading and writing activities in which their students are involved. During literature focus units and literature circles, students use many skills, and teachers often go beyond the grade-level list of skills as students use reading and writing for a variety of purposes.

Mrs. Donnelly's students used a variety of reading skills as they read *Cloudy With a Chance of Meatballs,* and they used many writing skills as they wrote their class alphabet book on weather. For example, when Mrs. Donnelly's students were checking a weather book for information about thunderstorms, they didn't start in the front of the book and hunt page by page through the book; instead, they checked the index for the location of information about thunderstorms or whatever topic they were searching for and then read that section. Using an index is a reference skill. When students wrote dialogue, they added quotation marks around the spoken words. They didn't make a conscious decision about whether or not to mark the dialogue; they automatically added the convention. Figure 8–9 provides other examples of the reading and writing skills that Mrs. Donnelly's students used.

Why Distinguish Between Skills and Strategies? Skills are more commonly associated with reading and writing instruction than strategies are, and for many years teachers and parents equated teaching skills with teaching reading. They believed that the best way to help children learn to read was to teach them a set of discrete skills, using drill-and-practice worksheets and workbooks (Smith, 1965). But research during the

Figure 8–8   Five types of skills that readers and writers use

Comprehension Skills

Chunk words into phrases
Sequence
Categorize
Classify
Separate facts and opinions
Note details
Identify cause and effect
Compare and contrast
Use context clues
Notice organizational patterns of poetry, plays,
    business and friendly letters, stories, essays, and
    reports
Recognize literary genres (traditional stories,
    fantasies, science fiction, realistic fiction,
    historical fiction, biography, autobiography,
    and poetry)

Decoding and Spelling Skills

Sound out words using phonics
Notice word families
Decode by analogy
Use classroom resources
Consult a dictionary or glossary
Apply spelling rules
Recognize high-frequency words
Divide words into syllables
Capitalize proper nouns and adjectives
Use abbreviations

Study Skills

Skim
Scan
Preview
Follow directions
Make outlines and clusters
Take notes
Paraphrase

Language Skills

Notice compound words
Use contractions
Use possessives
Notice propaganda
Use similes and metaphors
Notice idioms and slang
Choose synonyms
Recognize antonyms
Differentiate among homonyms
Use root words and affixes
Appreciate rhyme and other poetic devices
Use punctuation marks (period, question mark, excla-
    mation mark, quotation marks, comma, colon, semi-
    colon, and hyphen)
Use simple, compound, and complex sentences
Combine sentences
Recognize parts of sentences
Avoid sentence fragments
Recognize parts of speech (nouns, pronouns, verbs,
    adjectives, adverbs, conjunctions, prepositions, and
    interjections)

Reference Skills

Sort in alphabetical order
Use a glossary or dictionary
Locate etymologies in the dictionary
Use the pronunciation guide in the dictionary
Locate synonyms in a thesaurus
Locate information in an encyclopedia, atlas, or
    almanac
Use a table of contents
Use an index
Use a card catalogue
Read and make graphs, tables, and diagrams
Read and make timelines
Read newspapers and magazines
Use bibliographic forms

last 35 or more years has shown that reading is a constructive process in which readers construct meaning by interacting with texts (Pearson, Roehler, Dole, & Duffy, 1990). Writing is also a constructive process, and writers construct meaning as they compose texts. Readers and writers use strategies differently than skills: they use strategies to orchestrate higher-order thinking skills when reading and writing, whereas they use skills automatically and unconsciously when reading and writing.

While it continues to be important that students learn to use reading and writing skills automatically, of far greater importance is children's ability to use reading and

Figure 8–9 How third graders use reading and writing skills

Skills	How They Are Used When Reading *Cloudy With a Chance of Meatballs*	How They Are Used When Writing an Alphabet Book About Weather
Comprehension Skills	Students separate realism and fantasy in the story. They sequence story events. They compare real weather to the "food" weather.	Students add at least three details on each page. They reread classmates' pages to check the accuracy of information.
Decoding and Spelling Skills	Students use picture clues to read food words, including *frankfurter* and *syrup*. They sound out words like *prediction, Sanitation Department,* and *marvelous.*	During editing, students check the spelling of weather words in informational books. The teacher conferences with students about capitalization and punctuation marks.
Language Skills	Students notice weather-related words and phrases used in the story, such as "brief shower" and "gradual clearing."	Students use the " ___ is for _____ " form on each page of their books. They write in complete sentences.
Study Skills	Students scan the story looking for words for the word wall	Students skim sections of informational books as they gather information for the alphabet book. They take notes as they read. They make clusters as they prepare to write their pages.
Reference Skills	Students check the card catalogue for other books by the same author. They compare "The Chewandswallow Digest" with their local newspaper. They read weather reports and examine weather maps in their local newspaper.	Students use the index in books to locate information for the pages they are writing. They make charts and diagrams for their pages. They sort their pages into alphabetical order.

writing strategies. When skills and strategies are lumped together, teachers tend to neglect reading and writing strategies because they are more familiar with skills.

Teaching Strategies and Skills

In balanced literacy classrooms, teachers use two approaches—direct instruction and teachable moments—to teach strategies and skills (Spiegel, 1992). Teachers plan and teach minilessons on skills and strategies on a regular basis. These direct-instruction lessons are systematic and planned in conjunction with books or other selections students are reading or books that teachers are reading aloud. Students learn other strategies and skills incidentally through teachable moments as they observe and work collaboratively with teachers and classmates. In both kinds of instruction, teachers support students' learning, and students apply what they are learning in authentic literacy activities. Guidelines for skill and strategy instruction are presented in Figure 8–10.

**Figure 8–10** Guidelines for skill and strategy instruction
Adapted from Winograd and Hare, 1988; and Pressley and Harris, 1990.

1. Teach Minilessons

Teachers present minilessons to teach skills and strategies. During the lesson, teachers explain the procedure and model it. Then students practice the skill or strategy and later apply it in reading and writing activities.

2. Differentiate Between Skills and Strategies

Teachers understand that skills are automatic behaviors that readers and writers use, while strategies are problem-solving tactics, and they differentiate between skills and strategies as they teach minilessons and model how they use strategies. They are also careful to use the terms "skills" and "strategies" correctly when they talk to students.

3. Provide Step-by-Step Explanations

Teachers describe the skill or strategy step by step so that it is sensible and meaningful to students. For strategies, they can use think-aloud or talk-aloud procedures to demonstrate how the strategy is used. Teachers also explain to students why they should learn the skill or strategy, how it will make reading and writing easier, and when to use it.

4. Use Modeling

Teachers model using strategies for students in the context of authentic reading and writing activities, rather than in isolation. Students are also encouraged to model using strategies for classmates.

5. Provide Practice Opportunities

Students have opportunities to practice the skill or strategy in meaningful reading and writing activities. Teachers need to ensure that all students are successful using the skill or strategy so that they will be motivated to use it independently.

6. Apply in Content Areas

Teachers provide opportunities for students to use the skill or strategy in reading and writing activities related to social studies, science, and other content areas. The more opportunities students have to use the skill or strategy, the more likely they are to learn it.

7. Use Reflection

Teachers ask students to reflect on their use of the skill or strategy after they have had the opportunity to practice it and apply it in meaningful reading and writing activities.

8. Hang Charts of Skills and Strategies

Teachers often hang lists of skills and strategies students are learning in the classroom and encourage students to refer to them when reading and writing. Separate charts should be used for skills and strategies so that students can remember which are which.

Minilessons. **Minilessons** (Atwell, 1998) are 15- to 30-minute direct-instruction lessons designed to help students learn literacy skills and become more strategic readers and writers. In these lessons, students and the teacher are focused on a single goal; students are aware of why it is important to learn the skill or strategy, and they are explicitly taught how to use a particular skill or strategy through modeling, explanation, and practice. Then independent application takes place using authentic literacy materials. Minilessons have five steps:

1. *Introduce the skill or strategy.* The teacher names the strategy or skill and explains why it is useful. The teacher also shares examples of how and when the skill or strategy is used.
2. *Demonstrate the skill or strategy.* The teacher explains the steps of the skill or strategy and models how to use it with authentic reading and writing activities.
3. *Practice using the skill or strategy.* Students, with the teacher's guidance and support, practice the skill or strategy. The teacher provides feedback to students about how well they are doing.
4. *Review the skill or strategy.* The teacher, with the students' assistance, reviews the steps of the skill or strategy. Students reflect on what they have learned and how they would apply it in reading and writing activities. Students may also create a poster about the skill or strategy to be posted in the classroom.
5. *Apply the skill or strategy.* Students use their newly learned skill or strategy in authentic literacy activities.

Through five-step minilessons, responsibility is transferred from teacher to student (Bergman, 1992; Duffy & Roehler, 1987; Pearson & Gallagher, 1983). This minilesson procedure can be adapted to fit any skill or strategy being taught.

Figure 8–11 shows how Mrs. Donnelly used this five-step minilesson procedure to teach her third graders about literary opposites (Temple, 1992) during a literature focus unit on *Amos and Boris* (Steig, 1971), a story of unlikely friendship between a whale and a mouse. In the story, a whale named Amos rescues a shipwrecked mouse named Boris, and later Boris saves Amos when he becomes beached near Boris's home. Literary opposites are any opposites in a story—two very different settings, characters, events, and emotions in the story, for example—and most stories have more than one pair of opposites. One of the opposites in *Amos and Boris* is that the two animals, who are so different, become friends. Not only are they different in size, but one is a land animal and the other lives in the ocean.

Teachable Moments. Teachers often use informal techniques called "teachable moments" to share their knowledge as expert readers and writers. These give students opportunities to apply what they are learning in authentic reading and writing activities (Staab, 1990). Sometimes teachers take advantage of teachable moments to explain or demonstrate something with the whole class, while at other times they are used with small groups of students.

Modeling is an instructional technique that teachers use to demonstrate to students how to perform an unfamiliar reading or writing skill or strategy (Bergman, 1992). Teachers are expert readers and writers, and through modeling they show students—novice readers and writers—how to perform a strategy, skill, or other task so that students can build their own understanding of the activity. And classmates also serve as models for each other.

Teachers informally model reading and writing strategies for students whenever teachers participate in literacy activities. Young children learn concepts about books

Figure 8–11   Steps in Mrs. Donnelly's minilesson on literary opposites

1. Introduce the Strategy

Mrs. Donnelly explains that one way of organizing events and characters in stories is to think of opposites. There are many different kinds of opposites in stories: kind and mean characters, day and night settings, and happy and sad events.

2. Demonstrate the Strategy

Mrs. Donnelly reviews Jan Brett's *Town Mouse, Country Mouse* (1994) and uses the think-aloud technique to point out these opposites:

town—country	mouse—owl
plain—fancy	dark—light
mouse—cat	quiet—noisy

She writes the list on the chalkboard and stands back to reflect on it. Then she circles "plain—fancy" and thinks aloud:

> Yes, I think these are all opposites, but I like plain and fancy best. It is the most important one. It sums up the essence of this story for me. I like it. I can think about all sorts of examples of plain and fancy: Plain and fancy clothes, plain and fancy food, and plain and fancy houses. All these differences. I want to think some more. Different—alike, alike—different. That's it! I think that even though there are all these differences, the author shows me that the two mouse families were alike. How are they alike? They both wanted what they didn't have, and they both had enemies, and they both wanted to go home at the end. Oh yes, they both made it home safely and a lot smarter, too.

3. Practice the Strategy

Mrs. Donnelly asks students to reread *Amos and Boris* (Steig, 1971)—a story her students read several days before as part of a unit on whales and other animals that live in the ocean—with partners and to look for opposites. After reading, Mrs. Donnelly's third graders list these opposites:

big—little	forgetting—remembering
land animal—sea animal	hope—hopeless
helping—being helped	in the sea—out of the sea
life—death	hello—good-bye

One student makes the intertextual tie between *Amos and Boris* and "The Lion and the Mouse," pointing out that both stories have the same theme. Then Mrs. Donnelly asks students to quickwrite and draw pictures about the opposites they think are most interesting. Students share their quickwrites with classmates.

4. Review the Strategy

Mrs. Donnelly asks students to reflect on literary opposites and to think about opposites in other stories they have read. Several students also make a chart on literary opposites to hang in the classroom.

5. Apply the Strategy

Mrs. Donnelly encourages students to think about opposites in the stories they are reading during reading workshop, and she asks students about the opposites as she conferences with them. She also asks students to talk about the opposites as they share the books they have read.

Teachers model reading strategies and skills as they share big books with students.

as they watch teachers hold books, turn pages, and read from left to right and top to bottom; similarly, middle-grade students learn about revising text as they work with the teacher to revise the rough draft of a collaborative report that has been written on chart paper. As students work with teachers and observe them, they develop the understanding that readers and writers do some things automatically but at other times have to take risks, think out solutions to problems, and deal with ambiguities.

Teachers use talk-alouds to describe steps they use to apply a strategy or skill or complete a task (Baumann & Schmitt, 1986). Then teachers ask questions to guide students through the steps. In the vignette at the beginning of this chapter, Mrs. Donnelly used a talk-aloud as she introduced alphabet books to her third-grade class. She talked about how she looked at an alphabet book and what she noticed about the pattern of one letter per page with a picture and a sentence. She described the steps she used to examine an alphabet book, and then she passed out copies of various alphabet books for the students to examine. Here is an excerpt from Mrs. Donnelly's talk-aloud:

> As I looked at *The Furry Alphabet Book* by Jerry Pallotta [1991], I was thinking about all the interesting information the author and illustrator included in this book about mammals. I read the "A" page, and I noticed that there is an illustration and a paragraph of text. The text has lots of information about a rare African animal called an aye-aye. The illustration was very useful, and I thought it would help me remember the information I was reading. I thought this mammal looked a lot like a bat and thought about it eating insects, just like bats do.
>
> Then I read the "B" page, the "C" page, the "D" page, and the "E" page, and I noticed how much these pages were alike even though they were about dif-

ferent animals. They all had the upper- and lowercase letters written in a corner, a paragraph of text with lots of information, and a good illustration to show the animal and make the information easier to understand.

I always like to look to see what the author found for the hard letters, like "Q," "X," and "Z." I thought Jerry Pallotta was very smart to find animals for these letters. As I was looking for the "Q" page, I noticed that he put something special on the "P" page. He did a portrait of himself, I thought, and he added an extra fact: that people are mammals, too. For "Q," he chose quokka, a kind of small kangaroo from Australia. Then for "X," he used xukazi, the Zulu word for a female lamb, and for "Z," he described the zorilla, which is the smelliest skunk.

After the "Z" page, I found another special page about the naked mole rat, which the author said didn't deserve to be in this book because it didn't have any fur. I thought this was really cute, kind of like a secret between me and the author, so I decided to reread the book to look for more special pages, but I didn't find any more.

Then Mrs. Donnelly asked her students to look through alphabet books, to notice the format of the pages and the interesting words chosen for the "hard" letters, and to look for any special pages. Using this talk-aloud, she articulated the procedure her students were to use to investigate alphabet books in preparation for writing their own class alphabet book about weather.

In this instructional technique, teachers share with students the thought processes they go through as they use a reading or writing skill or strategy (Davey, 1983; Wade, 1990). When teaching a writing strategy such as revision, teachers can say, "I'm going to show you how I revise a rough draft." Then they read the rough draft aloud and "think aloud," presenting a running commentary on their thoughts. Teachers continue to make revisions and reread to verify the revisions, again presenting a running commentary on their thoughts. For reading strategies, teachers can do similar think-alouds on tapping prior knowledge, monitoring, and making predictions (Bergman, 1992).

Teachers also take advantage of teachable moments to share information about strategies and skills with students. They introduce, review, or extend a skill or strategy in these very brief lessons. As teachers listen to students read aloud or talk about the processes they use during reading, they often have an opportunity to teach a particular strategy or skill (Atwell, 1998). Similarly, as teachers conference with students about their writing or work with students to revise or edit their writing, teachers share information about writing skills and strategies with their students. Students also ask questions about skills and strategies or volunteer information about how they handled a reading or writing problem. Teachers who are careful observers and listen closely to their students don't miss these teachable moments.

Why Teach Skills and Strategies? Some teachers argue about whether to teach strategies and skills directly or implicitly. My position in this book is that teachers have the responsibility to teach students how to read and write, and part of that responsibility is teaching students the skills and strategies that capable readers and writers use. While it is true that students learn many things inductively through meaningful literacy experiences, direct instruction is important, too. Effective teachers do teach skills and strategies.

Researchers have compared classrooms in which teachers focused on teaching skills directly with other programs in which skills and strategies were taught inductively, and they concluded that the traditional skills programs were no more effective according to students' performance on standardized reading texts. Moreover, researchers suggest that traditional skills programs may be less effective when you take into account that students in the balanced reading programs also think of themselves as readers and writers and have more knowledge about written language.

Freppon (1991) compared the reading achievement of first graders in traditional and balanced reading classrooms and found that the balanced group was more successful. Similarly, Reutzel and Hollingsworth (1991) compared students who were taught skills with students who spent an equal amount of time reading books, and they found that neither group did better on skill tests. This research suggests that students who do not already know skills and strategies do benefit from instruction, but the instruction must stress application to authentic reading and writing activities.

Carefully planned instruction, however, may be especially important for minority students. Lisa Delpit (1987) cautions that many students who grow up outside the dominant culture are disadvantaged when certain knowledge, strategies, and skills expected by teachers are not made explicit in their classrooms. Explicitness is crucial because people from different cultures have different sets of understanding. When they teach children from other cultures, teachers often find it difficult to get their meaning across unless they are very explicit (Delpit, 1991). Delpit's writing has created a stir because she claims that African-American children and other nonmainstream children frequently are not given access to the codes of power unless literacy instruction is explicit. Too often teachers assume that children make the connection between the strategies and skills they are teaching and the future use of those strategies and skills in reading and writing, but Delpit claims that many don't.

On the other hand, several studies suggest that both mainstream and nonmainstream students learn best with balanced reading instruction. Morrow (1992) and Dahl and Freppon (1995) found that minority students in balanced reading classrooms do as well as students in skill-based classrooms, plus they develop a greater sense of the purposes of literacy and see themselves as readers and writers.

Review

Comprehension is a creative, multifaceted process that students use for reading and writing. For reading, it is the reader's process of using prior experiences and the author's text to construct meaning that is useful to that reader for a specific purpose. The five subprocesses are microprocesses, integrative processes, macroprocesses, elaborative processes, and metacognitive processes. Students use both strategies and skills for reading and writing. Strategies are problem-solving behaviors, and skills are information-processing techniques that students use automatically and unconsciously. Teachers use both direct instruction and teachable moments to teach strategies and skills in balanced reading classrooms. Ways that effective teachers facilitate students' comprehension are reviewed in the feature on page 302.

How Effective Teachers . . .

Facilitate Students' Comprehension

◼ Effective Practices

1. Teachers understand the differences between capable and less capable readers and writers.

2. Teachers use modeling and explanation to help less capable readers and writers become more like more capable readers and writers.

3. Teachers incorporate choice and authenticity into their instructional programs to influence students' motivation.

4. Teachers view comprehension as a multifaceted process involving five subprocesses.

5. Teachers incorporate comprehension activities representing all five subprocesses into the reading process.

6. Teachers monitor and assess students' ability to use all five subprocesses.

7. Teachers teach twelve strategies: tapping prior knowledge, predicting, organizing ideas, figuring out unknown words, visualizing, making connections, applying fix-up strategies, revising meaning, monitoring, playing with language, summarizing, and evaluating.

8. Teachers teach five types of skills: comprehension skills, decoding and spelling skills, language skills, study skills, and reference skills.

9. Teachers teach minilessons on skills and strategies to the whole class or to small groups, depending on students' needs.

10. Teachers take advantage of teachable moments to answer students' questions and clarify misconceptions.

◼ Ineffective Practices

1. Teachers assume that more capable readers and writers are simply more proficient than less capable readers and writers.

2. Teachers don't realize that more and less capable readers and writers think differently.

3. Teachers threaten low grades, no recess, or other forms of punishment to influence students' motivation.

4. Teachers view comprehension as a single process of making meaning; they are unfamiliar with the five subprocesses.

5. Teachers incorporate a variety of comprehension activities into their program, but they mainly focus on macroprocesses and elaborative processes.

6. Teachers rarely assess students' comprehension and do not address all five subprocesses.

7. Teachers teach very few strategies; sometimes they teach only prediction or ways to figure out unknown words.

8. Teachers teach many skills but do not always tie skills instruction to application in authentic literacy activities.

9. Teachers use direct instruction and assign many worksheets.

10. Teachers do not recognize teachable moments and rarely model strategy use or use talk-alouds and think-alouds.

References

Atwell, N. (1998). *In the middle: New understandings about writing, reading, and learning* (2nd ed.). Portsmouth, NH: Heinemann.

Baker, L., & Brown, A. L. (1984). Metacognitive skills and reading. In P. D. Pearson, M. Kamil, R. Barr, & P. Mosenthal (Eds.), *Handbook of reading research* (Vol. 1, pp. 353–394). New York: Longman.

Baumann, J. F., & Schmitt, M. C. (1986). The what, why, how, and when of comprehension instruction. *The Reading Teacher, 39,* 640–647.

Bergman, J. L. (1992). SAIL—A way to success and independence for low-achieving readers. *The Reading Teacher, 45,* 598–602.

Brent, R., & Anderson, P. (1993). Developing children's classroom listening strategies. *The Reading Teacher, 47,* 122–126.

Cairney, T. (1990). Intertextuality: Infectious echoes from the past. *The Reading Teacher, 43,* 478–484.

Cairney, T. (1992). Fostering and building students' intertextual histories. *Language Arts, 69,* 502–507.

Dahl, K. L., & Freppon, P. A. (1995). A comparison of inner-city children's interpretations of reading and writing instruction in the early grades in skills-based and whole language classrooms. *Reading Research Quarterly, 30,* 50–74.

Davey, B. (1983). Think-aloud—Modelling the cognitive processes of reading comprehension. *Journal of Reading, 27,* 44–47.

de Beaugrande, R. (1980). *Text, discourse, and process.* Norwood, NJ: Ablex.

Delpit, L. (1987). The silenced dialogue: Power and pedagogy in educating other people's children. *Harvard Educational Review, 58,* 280–298.

Delpit, L. (1991). A conversation with Lisa Delpit. *Language Arts, 68,* 541–547.

Duffy, G. G., & Roehler, L. R. (1987). Improving reading instruction through the use of responsible elaboration. *The Reading Teacher, 20,* 548–554.

Dweck, C. S. (1986). Motivational processes affecting learning. *American Psychologist, 41,* 1040–1048.

Faigley, L., Cherry, R. D., Jolliffe, D. A., & Skinner, A. M. (1985). *Assessing writers' knowledge and processes of composing.* Norwood, NJ: Ablex.

Freppon, P. A. (1991). Children's concepts of the nature and purpose of reading in different instructional settings. *Journal of Reading Behavior, 23,* 139–163.

Garner, R. (1987). *Metacognition and reading comprehension.* Norwood, NJ: Ablex.

Hoyt, L. (1999). *Revisit, reflect, retell: Strategies for improving reading comprehension.* Portsmouth, NH: Heinemann.

Irwin, J. W. (1991). *Teaching reading comprehension processes* (2nd ed). Boston: Allyn & Bacon.

Johnston, P., & Winograd, P. (1985). Passive failure in reading. *Journal of Reading Behavior, 17,* 279–301.

Keene, E. O., & Zimmermann, S. (1997). *Mosaic of thought: Teaching comprehension in a reader's workshop.* Portsmouth, NH: Heinemann.

Morrow, L. M. (1992). The impact of a literature-based program on literacy achievement, use of literature, and attitudes of children from minority backgrounds. *Reading Research Quarterly, 27,* 251–275.

Oldfather, P. (1995). Commentary: What's needed to maintain and extend motivation for literacy in the middle grades. *Journal of Reading, 38,* 420–422.

Paris, S. G., & Jacobs, J. E. (1984). The benefits of informed instruction for children's reading awareness and comprehension skills. *Child Development, 55,* 2083–2093.

Paris, S. G., Wasik, B. A., & Turner, J. C. (1991). The development of strategic readers. In R. Barr, M. L. Kamil, P. B. Mosenthal, & P. D. Pearson (Eds.), *Handbook of reading research* (Vol. 2, pp. 609–640). New York: Longman.

Pearson, P. D., & Gallagher, M. C. (1983). The instruction of reading comprehension. *Contemporary Educational Psychology, 8,* 317–344.

Pearson, P. D., Roehler, L. R., Dole, J. A., & Duffy, G. G. (1990). *Developing expertise in reading comprehension: What should be taught? How should it be taught?* (Technical Report No. 512). Champaign, IL: University of Illinois, Center for the Study of Reading.

Pressley, M., & Harris, K. R. (1990). What we really know about strategy instruction. *Educational Leadership, 48,* 31–34.

Reutzel, D. R., & Hollingsworth, P. M. (1991). Reading comprehension skills: Testing the skills distinctiveness hypothesis. *Reading Research and Instruction, 30,* 32–46.

Schmitt, M. C. (1990). A questionnaire to measure children's awareness of strategic reading processes. *The Reading Teacher, 43,* 454–461.

Smith, N. B. (1965). *American reading instruction.* Newark, DE: International Reading Association.

Spiegel, D. L. (1992). Blending whole language and systematic direct instruction. *The Reading Teacher, 46,* 38–46.

Staab, C. F. (1990). Teacher mediation in one whole literacy classroom. *The Reading Teacher, 43,* 548–552.

Stauffer, R. G. (1975). *Directing the reading-thinking process.* New York: Harper & Row.

Temple, C. (1992). Lots of plots: Patterns, meanings, and children's literature. In C. Temple & P. Collings (Eds.), *Stories and readers: New perspectives on literature in the elementary classroom* (pp. 3–13). Norwood, MA: Christopher-Gordon.

Tierney, R. J. (1990). Redefining reading comprehension. *Educational Leadership, 47,* 37–42.

Tompkins, G. E. (1998). *Language arts: Content and teaching strategies* (4th ed.). Englewood Cliffs, NJ: Merrill/Prentice Hall.

Wade, S. E. (1990). Using think alouds to assess comprehension. *The Reading Teacher, 43,* 442–453.

Winograd, P., & Hare, V. C. (1988). Direct instruction of reading comprehension strategies: The nature of teacher explanation. In C. Weinstein, E. Goetz, & P. Alexander (Eds.), *Learning and study strategies: Issues in assessment, instruction, and evaluation* (pp. 121–139). San Diego, CA: Academic Press.

Children's Book References

Barrett, J. (1978). *Cloudy with a chance of meatballs.* New York: Macmillan.

Barrett, J. (1997). *Pickles to Pittsburgh.* New York: Atheneum.

Brett, J. (1994). *Town mouse, country mouse.* New York: Putnam.

Marshall, J. (1977). *Miss Nelson is missing!* Boston: Houghton Mifflin.

Pallotta, J. (1991). *The furry alphabet book.* Watertown, MA: Charlesbridge Publishing.

Steig, W. (1971). *Amos and Boris.* New York: Farrar, Straus & Giroux.

Van Allsburg, C. (1981). *Jumanji.* Boston: Houghton Mifflin.

Van Allsburg, C. (1986). *The stranger.* Boston: Houghton Mifflin.

Van Allsburg, C. (1991). *The wretched stone.* Boston: Houghton Mifflin.

Chapter 9

Becoming Familiar With the Structure of Text

— Chapter Questions —

How are stories organized?

How are informational books organized?

How are poems structured?

How does the structure of text affect children's reading and writing?

306

Mrs. Simmons's First Graders Learn About Insects

The first graders in Mrs. Simmons's class are studying insects. They began by talking about insects and making a **K-W-L chart** (Ogle, 1986) (see the Compendium for more information about this and all other highlighted terms in this chapter), listing what they already know about insects in the "K: What We Know" column and things they want to learn in the "W: What We Want to Learn" column. At the end of the unit, students will finish the chart by listing what they have learned in the "L: What We Have Learned" column. The first graders name some of the insects they already know and ask if spiders are insects. Mrs. Simmons makes a mental note to teach a lesson comparing insects and spiders later in the unit.

The first graders read Eric Carle's insect stories: *The Very Hungry Caterpillar* (1969), a story that illustrates the life cycle of a butterfly; *The Very Quiet Cricket* (1990), a multisensory story about a cricket who is very quiet until he meets another cricket; and *The Grouchy Ladybug* (1986), a story about a ladybug who is looking for a fight and challenges every animal she meets. Mrs. Simmons encourages her students to read aesthetically and enjoy the reading experience. Later, as they reread the stories, she asks them to look for scientific information about insects, and she adds this information to the K-W-L chart.

Alberto talks about the scientific information he and his classmates found in *The Grouchy Ladybug:* "We learned that ladybugs like to eat things called aphids and we learned that ladybugs can fly. But we don't think that ladybugs are really grouchy or friendly like in the story. Something else is that they don't really try to fight with big animals like whales and rhinos."

Another day, Mrs. Simmons brings the materials to make an ant farm to the classroom. She reads *If You Were an Ant* (Calder, 1989), an informational book told through the eyes of an ant, and she asks students to try to remember the important information about ants so that they can make a chart after reading. This is their chart of 10 important facts about ants:

1. *Ants live together in colonies.*
2. *Worker ants make the nest and gather food.*
3. *The queen is the biggest ant and she lays eggs.*
4. *Ants are insects.*
5. *Ants have six legs.*
6. *Ants have combs on their front legs to comb their legs and antennae.*
7. *Ants eat caterpillars, flies, and beetles.*
8. *Ants can lift things that are 10 times heavier than they are.*
9. *Ants protect themselves by biting and stinging.*
10. *Enemies are anteaters, frogs, birds, and other ants.*

After compiling this information, Mrs. Simmons and her students follow the directions at the end of the book for making an ant farm as they make their own.

Mrs. Simmons gives students a purpose for reading or listening to each book read aloud. She asks her students to remember information for the class charts they will develop. Together they develop charts describing parts of an insect's body, comparing insects and people, sequencing the stages in the life cycle of an insect, and listing ways insects help people.

Before reading *It's a Good Thing There Are Insects* (Fowler, 1990), an easy-to-read informational book, Mrs. Simmons asks her students whether insects are helpful or hurtful. Several students comment that insects like bees can hurt people and that most people don't like insects. She tells them that after reading she will ask them to decide if insects are helpful or not. She passes out copies of the book—one for each pair of students—and invites them to look through the book and identify many of the insects in the photo illustrations with their reading buddies. Then the class reads the book using shared reading. Students read along as Mrs. Simmons reads aloud. She often purchases enough copies of a book for half of her class and has each student read with a buddy. In this way she can stretch her instructional materials budget and provide opportunities for buddy reading.

After reading, students have a **grand conversation** to talk about the book. Based on the information presented in the book, the class reaches the conclusion that insects are very helpful. From their discussion, the first graders compile this chart:

Ways Insects Help Us

1. We get silk from silkworms.
2. We get honey from bees.
3. Bees pollinate flowers.
4. Some insects are pretty to look at.
5. Ladybugs eat bad insects.

Alicia talks about this chart and how the first graders make charts: "Mrs. Simmons asked us if insects are good or bad, and we learned that they are good. We made this chart with five ways they are good. We learned about these five ways from a book that Mrs. Simmons read to us. We remembered the important stuff so we can make this chart."

Later, students use what they have learned about insects to write their own insect books. As they prepare to write, the first graders reread some of the insect books in the classroom library and the charts that the class has developed. Juan writes a book contrasting people and insects titled "I Am Not a Bug!" Two pages from his book are shown in Figure 9–1. He reflects on how he created his book: "I was just thinking about how I am not a bug and how bugs are different from people. Then I thought I could say 'I am not a bug' on every page. I looked at the chart and thought of these ways I am different. Then I just wrote my book. The best part is when I read it in the author's chair. I yelled the part 'But I am not!' and everybody laughed. That means I am a good writer."

Mrs. Simmons's students also read poems about insects from *The Random House Book of Poetry for Children* (Prelutsky, 1983) that she copied onto charts. Students

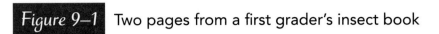

Figure 9–1 Two pages from a first grader's insect book

read the poems using **choral reading.** One of their favorites is "Wasps" (p. 74), a very short rhyming verse. Students decide to write their own poems following the rhyming pattern of "Wasps." Here are two of their pattern poems:

Ants	*Beetles*
Ants like vanilla ice cream.	*Beetles like hot dogs.*
Peanut butter sandwiches.	*Potato chips.*
Tea.	*Tea.*
Chocolate cake.	*Watermelon.*
Apple juice.	*Chocolate chip cookies.*
Me.	*Me.*

Evelyn talks about the "Ants" poem she wrote and her classmates' poems: "We wanted to make our poems like 'Wasps' so we kept tea and me because they rhyme. Then we thought about other insects and we brainstormed foods that are sweet and insects would really like. I picked my favorite foods for my poem. I think ants would like them, too."

To end the unit, Mrs. Simmons asks her students to finish the K-W-L chart. In the third column, "L: What We Have Learned," students list some of the information they have learned, including:

Insects have six legs.

The life cycle of a butterfly is: egg, caterpillar, chrysalis, and adult.

Insects usually die before their first birthday.

It is good luck to find a ladybug.

Insects hatch from eggs.

Mosquitoes and fleas are pests.

Bees give us honey.

Insects have exoskeletons.

Insects and spiders are different.

Insects' noses are on their antennae.

Insects have three body parts.

Some insects can fly, but some cannot.

There are a million different insects on Earth.

www.eric-carle.com

Eric Carle. Information about Eric Carle, his books, and his illustration techniques.

Elementary students read all three types of literature—stories, informational books, and poems—just as the students in Mrs. Simmons's classroom do. These "real" books are called trade books. Many students also use reading textbooks (often called basal readers) and social studies, science, and other content-area textbooks. Reading textbooks contain stories, informational articles, and poetry, too. In recent years there has been a great deal of controversy about whether trade books or textbooks should be used to teach reading. Lapp, Flood, and Farnan (1992) believe that textbooks and trade books are compatible and that students should read both types.

Stories, informational books, and poems have unique structures or organizational patterns. Stories are organized differently from poems and informational books. For example, *The Very Hungry Caterpillar* (Carle, 1969) is a repetitive story that chronicles the life cycle of a butterfly, while *The Icky Bug Counting Book* (Pallotta, 1992) is an informational book highlighting 26 different species of insects, one on each page. Sometimes teachers call all literature that students read and write "stories," but stories are unique. They have specific structural elements, including characters and plot. Teachers need to introduce the three types of literature and use the labels for each type correctly.

The stories students write reflect the stories they have read. De Ford (1981) and Eckhoff (1983) found that when primary-grade students read basal reading textbooks, the stories they write reflect the short, choppy linguistic style of the readers published at that time, but when students read stories published as picture books and chapter books, their writing reflects the more sophisticated language structures and literary style of these books. Dressel (1990) also found that the quality of fifth graders' writing was dependent on the quality of the stories they read and listened to read aloud, regardless of students' reading levels. Similarly, when students learn about the structure of informational books and content-area textbooks, both their reading comprehension and their nonfiction writing improve (Flood, Lapp, & Farnan, 1986; McGee & Richgels, 1985; Piccolo, 1987).

ELEMENTS OF STORY STRUCTURE

Stories give meaning to the human experience, and they are a powerful way of knowing and learning. When preschoolers listen to family members tell stories and read them aloud, they develop an understanding or concept about stories by the time they come to school. Students use and refine this knowledge as they read and write stories during the elementary grades. Many educators, including Jerome Bruner (1986), recommend using stories as a way into literacy.

Stories are available in picture-book and chapter-book formats. Picture books have brief texts, usually spread over 32 pages, in which text and illustrations combine to tell a story. The text is minimal, and the illustrations supplement the sparse text. The illustrations in many picture books are striking. Many picture books, such as *Rosie's Walk* (Hutchins, 1968), about a clever hen who outwits a fox, are for primary-grade students, but others, such as *Pink and Say* (Polacco, 1994), about a black and a white Civil War soldier, were written with middle-grade students in mind. Fairy tales have also been retold as picture books. Trina Schart Hyman's *The Sleeping Beauty* (1977) is an especially beautiful picture book. Another type of picture book is wordless picture books, such as *Tuesday* (Wiesner, 1991) and *Good Dog, Carl* (Day, 1985), in which the story is told entirely through the illustrations.

Chapter books are longer stories written in a chapter format. Most are written for older students, but Patricia Reilly Giff's series of stories about the kids at the Polk Street School, including *The Beast in Ms. Rooney's Room* (1984) and *Fish Face* (1984), is for students reading at the second-grade level. Chapter books for middle-grade students include *Charlotte's Web* (White, 1952) and *Bunnicula: A Rabbit-Tale of Mystery* (Howe & Howe, 1979). Complex stories such as *The Giver* (Lowry, 1993) are more suitable for upper-grade students. Chapter books have few illustrations, if any, and the illustrations do not play an integral role in the book.

Stories have unique structural elements that distinguish them from other forms of literature. Five story elements are plot, characters, setting, point of view, and theme. These elements work together to structure a story, and authors manipulate them to make their stories hold readers' attention.

Plot

Plot is the sequence of events involving characters in conflict situations. A story's plot is based on the goals of one or more characters and the processes they go through to attain these goals (Lukens, 1999). The main characters want to achieve a goal, and other characters are introduced to oppose the main characters or prevent them from being successful. The story events are set in motion by characters as they attempt to overcome conflict, reach their goals, and solve their problems.

The most basic aspect of plot is the division of the main events of a story into three parts: beginning, middle, and end. In *The Tale of Peter Rabbit* (Potter, 1902), for instance, the three story parts are easy to pick out. As the story begins, Mrs. Rabbit sends her children out to play after warning them not to go into Mr. McGregor's garden. In the middle, Peter goes to Mr. McGregor's garden and is almost caught. Then Peter finds his way out of the garden and gets home safely—the end of the story. Students can make a story map of the beginning-middle-end of a story using words and pictures, as the story map for *The Tale of Peter Rabbit* in Figure 9–2 shows.

Specific types of information are included in each of the three story parts. In the beginning, the author introduces the characters, describes the setting, and presents a problem. Together, the characters, setting, and events develop the plot and sustain the theme through the story. In the middle, the plot unfolds, with each event preparing readers for what will follow. Conflict heightens as the characters face roadblocks that keep them from solving their problems. How the characters tackle these problems adds suspense to keep readers interested. In the end, all is reconciled and readers learn whether or not the characters' struggles are successful.

Conflict is the tension or opposition between forces in the plot, and it is what interests readers enough to continue reading the story. Conflict usually occurs

- between a character and nature
- between a character and society
- between characters
- within a character (Lukens, 1999)

Conflict between a character and nature occurs in stories in which severe weather plays an important role, as in *Julie of the Wolves* (George, 1972), and in stories set in

---

Figure 9–2   A beginning-middle-end story map for *The Tale of Peter Rabbit*

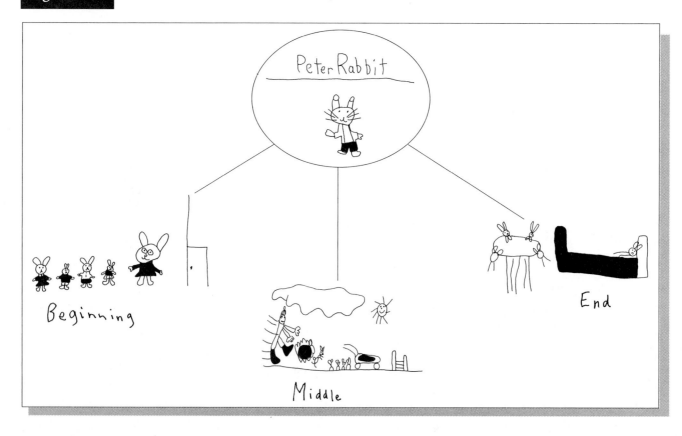

isolated geographic locations, such as *Island of the Blue Dolphins* (O'Dell, 1960), in which the Indian girl Karana struggles to survive alone on a Pacific island.

In some stories, a character's activities and beliefs differ from those of other members of the society, and the differences cause conflict between that character and the local society. One example of this type of conflict is *The Witch of Blackbird Pond* (Speare, 1958), in which Kit Tyler is accused of being a witch because she continues activities in a New England Puritan community that were acceptable in the Caribbean community where she grew up but are not acceptable in her new home. Conflict between characters is common in children's literature. In *Tales of a Fourth Grade Nothing* (Blume, 1972), for instance, the never-ending conflict between Peter and his little brother Fudge is what makes the story interesting. The fourth type of conflict is conflict within a character. In *Ira Sleeps Over* (Waber, 1972), six-year-old Ira must decide whether to take his teddy bear with him when he goes next door to spend the night with a friend. Figure 9–3 lists stories representing the four conflict situations.

The plot is developed through conflict that is introduced at the beginning of a story, expanded in the middle, and finally resolved at the end. Plot development involves four components:

1. ***A problem.*** A problem that introduces conflict is presented at the beginning of the story.
2. ***Roadblocks.*** Characters face roadblocks in attempting to solve the problem in the middle of the story.
3. ***The high point.*** The high point in the action occurs when the problem is about to be solved. This high point separates the middle and end of the story.
4. ***The solution.*** The problem is solved and the roadblocks are overcome at the end of the story.

The problem is introduced at the beginning of the story, and the characters are faced with trying to solve it. The problem determines the conflict. The problem in *Hatchet* (Paulsen, 1987) is that 13-year-old Brian is alone in the Canadian wilderness

www.garypaulsen.com

🕸 *Gary Paulsen. Visit author Gary Paulsen's website to find out about the sequels to* Hatchet.

Students learn about the structure of stories as they dramatize a familiar story.

Figure 9–3 Stores that illustrate the four types of conflict

P = primary grades (K–2): M = middle grades (3–5); U = upper grades (6–8)

Conflict Between a Character and Nature

George J. C. (1972). *Julie of the wolves.* New York: Harper & Row. (M–U)

O'Dell, S. (1960). *Island of the blue dolphins.* Boston: Houghton Mifflin. (M–U)

Paulsen, G. (1987). *Hatchet.* New York: Bradbury Press. (M–U)

Polacco, P. (1990). *Thundercake.* New York: Philomel. (P–M)

Sperry, A. (1968). *Call it courage.* New York: Macmillan. (U)

Steig, W. (1987). *Brave Irene.* New York: Farrar, Straus & Giroux. (M)

Conflict Between a Character and Society

Brett, J. (1994). *Town mouse, country mouse.* New York: Putnam. (P–M)

Bunting, E. (1994). *Smoky night.* San Diego: Harcourt Brace. (P–M)

Lowry, L. (1989). *Number the stars.* New York: Atheneum. (M–U)

Lowry, L. (1993). *The giver.* Boston: Houghton Mifflin. (U)

Nixon, J. L. (1988). *A family apart.* New York: Bantam. (M–U)

O'Brien, R. C. (1971). *Mrs. Frisby and the rats of NIMH.* New York: Atheneum. (M)

Speare, E. G. (1958). *The witch of Blackbird Pond.* Boston: Houghton Mifflin. (M–U)

Uchida, Y. (1971). *Journey to Topaz.* Berkeley, CA: Creative Arts. (U)

Conflict Between Characters

Blume, J. (1972). *Tales of a fourth grade nothing.* New York: Dutton. (M)

Bunting, E. (1994). *A day's work.* New York: Clarion. (P–M)

Cohen, B. (1983). *Molly's pilgrim.* New York: Lothrop, Lee & Shepard. (M)

Cushman, K. (1994). *Catherine called Birdy.* New York: HarperCollins. (U)

Hoban, R. (1970). *A bargain for Frances.* New York: Scholastic. (P)

Lester, H. (1988). *Tacky the penguin.* Boston: Houghton Mifflin. (P)

Say, A. (1995). *Stranger in the mirror.* Boston: Houghton Mifflin. (M–U)

Steig, W. (1982). *Doctor De Soto.* New York: Farrar, Straus & Giroux. (M)

Zelinsky, P. O. (1986). *Rumpelstiltskin.* New York: Dutton. (P–M)

Conflict Within a Character

Bauer, M. D. (1986). *On my honor.* Boston: Houghton Mifflin. (M–U)

Byars, B. (1970). *The summer of the swans.* New York: Viking. (M)

Carle, E. (1995). *The very lonely firefly.* New York: Philomel. (P)

Fritz, J. (1958). *The cabin faced west.* New York: Coward-McCann. (M)

Henkes, K. (1991). *Chrysanthemum.* New York: Greenwillow. (P)

Naylor, P. R. (1991). *Shiloh.* New York: Atheneum. (M–U)

Pinkney, A. D. (1995). *Hold fast to dreams.* New York: Morrow. (U)

Taylor, T. (1969). *The cay.* New York: Doubleday. (U)

Waber, B. (1972). *Ira sleeps over.* Boston: Houghton Mifflin. (P)

after the plane in which he is flying to visit his divorced father crashes. Conflict develops as Brian tries to survive in the wilderness. The story seems to embody conflict between a character and nature.

After introducing the problem, authors use conflict to throw roadblocks in the way of an easy solution. As characters remove one roadblock, the author devises another to further thwart the characters. Postponing the solution by introducing roadblocks is the core of plot development. Stories may contain any number of roadblocks, but many children's stories contain three, four, or five.

Brian faces many conflicts as he tries to find food to eat in the wilderness. He has to figure out how to make a fire to cook the birds, fish, and other animals he catches.

He is attacked by bees, a porcupine, and a moose. And a storm that destroys his shelter adds to the conflict.

The high point of the action occurs when the solution of the problem hangs in the balance. Tension is high, and readers continue reading to learn whether the main characters solve the problem. In *Hatchet,* readers cheer when Brian finally gets the survival pack out of the downed plane. One of the items in the pack is an emergency transmitter, and even though Brian doesn't think that it is still emitting signals, readers realize that his rescue is close at hand.

As the story ends, the problem is solved and the goal is achieved. A pilot hears the emergency signal and rescues Brian 54 days after the plane crash, long after searchers had given up hope of finding him alive. As Brian greets the pilot, readers realize that they have witnessed Brian's passage into manhood. He has survived in the wilderness, and he has survived his parents' divorce. Author Gary Paulsen has used conflict within a character, many readers conclude, to drive a riveting adventure story.

Students can chart the plot of a story using a plot profile to track the tension or excitement in a story (Johnson & Louis, 1987). Figure 9–4 presents a plot profile for *Stone Fox* (Gardiner, 1980), a story about a boy who wins a dogsled race to save his grandfather's farm. A class of fourth graders met in small groups to talk about each chapter, and after these discussions the whole class came together to decide how to mark the chart. At the end of the story, students analyzed the chart and rationalized

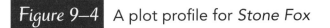

Figure 9–4 A plot profile for *Stone Fox*

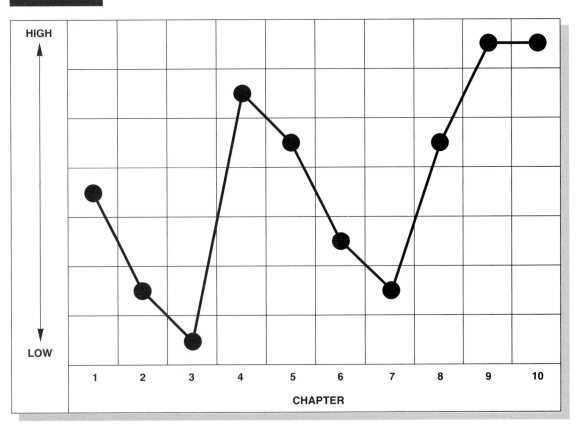

the tension dips in Chapters 3 and 7. They decided that the story would be too stressful without these dips.

Characters

Characters are the people or personified animals who are involved in the story. Characters are often the most important structural element because the story is centered around a character or group of characters. Usually, one or two fully rounded characters and several supporting characters are involved in a story. Fully developed main characters have many character traits, both good and bad; that is to say, they have all the characteristics of real people. Inferring a character's traits is an important part of reading. Through character traits we get to know a character well and the character seems to come to life. A list of stories with fully developed main characters is presented in Figure 9–5.

Characters are developed in four ways: appearance, action, dialogue, and monologue. Some description of the characters' physical appearance is usually included when they are introduced. Readers learn about characters by the description of their facial features, body shapes, habits of dress, mannerisms, and gestures. On the first page of *Tacky the Penguin* (Lester, 1988), the illustration of Tacky wearing a bright floral shirt and a purple-and-white tie suggests to readers that Tacky is an "odd bird"! Lester confirms this impression as she describes how Tacky behaves.

The second way—and often the best way—to learn about characters is through their actions. In Van Allsburg's *The Stranger* (1986), readers deduce that the stranger is Jack Frost because of what he does: he watches geese flying south for the winter, blows a cold wind, labors long hours without becoming tired, has an unusual rapport with wild animals, and is unfamiliar with modern conveniences.

Dialogue is the third way characters are developed. What characters say is important, but so is how they speak. The register of a character's language is determined by the social situation. A character might speak less formally with friends than with respected elders or characters in positions of authority. The geographic location of the story and the characters' socioeconomic status also determine how characters speak. In *Roll of Thunder, Hear My Cry* (Taylor, 1976), for example, Cassie and her family speak Black English, a dialect.

Authors also provide insight into characters by revealing their thoughts, or internal monologue. In *Sylvester and the Magic Pebble* (Steig, 1969), thoughts and wishes are central to the story. Sylvester, a donkey, foolishly wishes to become a rock, and he spends a miserable winter that way. Steig shares the donkey's thinking with us. He thinks about his parents, who are frantic with worry, and we learn how Sylvester feels in the spring when his parents picnic on the rock he has become.

Setting

In some stories the setting is barely sketched, and these are called backdrop settings. The setting in many folktales, for example, is relatively unimportant, and the convention "Once upon a time . . ." is enough to set the stage. In other stories, the setting is elaborated and essential to the story's effectiveness. These settings are called integral settings (Lukens, 1999). A list of stories with integral settings is shown in Figure 9–6. The setting in these stories is specific, and authors take care to ensure the authenticity of the historical period or geographic location in which the story is set.

Four dimensions of setting are location, weather, time period, and time. Location is an important dimension in many stories. The Boston Commons in *Make Way for*

Figure 9–5 Stories with fully developed main characters

Character	Story
Ramona	Cleary, B. (1981). *Ramona Quimby, age 8*. New York: Morrow. (M)
Leigh	Cleary, B. (1983). *Dear Mr. Henshaw*. New York: Morrow. (M)
Nick	Clements, A. (1996). *Frindle*. New York: Simon & Schuster. (M–U)
Kenny	Curtis, C. P. (1995). *The Watsons go to Birmingham—1963*. New York: Delacorte. (M–U)
Birdy	Cushman, K. (1994). *Catherine called Birdy*. New York: HarperCollins. (U)
Livingston	Edwards, P. D., & Cole, H. (1996). *Livingston Mouse*. New York: HarperCollins. (P)
Johnny	Forbes, E. (1974). *Johnny Tremain*. Boston: Houghton Mifflin. (U)
Little Willy	Gardiner, J. R. (1980). *Stone Fox*. New York: Harper & Row. (M–U)
Sam	George, J. C. (1959). *My side of the mountain*. New York: Dutton. (U)
Chrysanthemum	Henkes, K. (1991). *Chrysanthemum*. New York: Greenwillow. (P)
Tacky	Lester, H. (1988). *Tacky the penguin*. Boston: Houghton Mifflin. (P–M)
Jonas	Lowry, L. (1993). *The giver*. Boston: Houghton Mifflin. (U)
Sarah	MacLachlan, P. (1985). *Sarah, plain and tall*. New York: Harper & Row. (M)
Marty	Naylor, P. R. (1991). *Shiloh*. New York: Atheneum. (M–U)
Karana	O'Dell, S. (1960). *Island of the blue dolphins*. Boston: Houghton Mifflin. (M–U)
Gilly	Paterson, K. (1978). *The great Gilly Hopkins*. New York: Crowell. (M–U)
Charley	Ryan, P. M. (1998). *Riding Freedom*. New York: Scholastic. (M–U)
Stanley	Sachar, L. (1998). *Holes*. New York: Farrar, Straus, & Giroux. (U)
Billy	Say, A. (1990). *El Chino*. Boston: Houghton Mifflin. (M)
Matt	Speare, E. (1983). *The sign of the beaver*. Boston: Houghton Mifflin. (M–U)
Mafatu	Sperry, A. (1968). *Call it courage*. New York: Macmillan. (U)
Irene	Steig, W. (1986). *Brave Irene*. New York: Farrar, Straus & Giroux. (P–M)
Cassie	Taylor, M. (1976). *Roll of thunder, hear my cry*. New York: Dial. (U)
Moon Shadow	Yep, L. (1975). *Dragonwings*. New York: Harper & Row. (U)

Figure 9–6   Stories with integral settings

Babbitt, N. (1975). *Tuck everlasting.* New York: Farrar, Straus & Giroux. (M–U)

Bunting, E. (1994). *Smoky night.* San Diego: Harcourt Brace. (P–M)

Cauley, L. B. (1984). *The city mouse and the country mouse.* New York: Putnam. (P–M)

Choi, S. N. (1991). *Year of impossible goodbyes.* Boston: Houghton Mifflin. (U)

Curtis, C. P. (1995). *The Watsons go to Birmingham—1963.* New York: Delacorte. (M–U)

Cushman, K. (1994). *Catherine called Birdy.* New York: HarperCollins. (U)

Cushman, K. (1996). *The ballad of Lucy Whipple.* New York: Clarion. (M–U)

Fleischman, P. (1993). *Bull Run.* New York: HarperCollins. (U)

Fleischman, S. (1963). *By the great horn spoon!* Boston: Little, Brown. (M–U)

George, J. C. (1972). *Julie of the wolves.* New York: Harper & Row. (M–U)

Harvey, B. (1988). *Cassie's journey: Going west in the 1860s.* New York: Holiday House. (M)

Johnston, T. (1994). *Amber on the mountain.* New York: Dial. (P–M)

L'Engle, M. (1962). *A wrinkle in time.* New York: Farrar, Straus & Giroux. (U)

Lester, H. (1989). *Tacky the penguin.* Boston: Houghton Mifflin. (P–M)

Lowry, L. (1989). *Number the stars.* Boston: Houghton Mifflin. (M–U)

Lowry, L. (1993). *The giver.* Boston: Houghton Mifflin. (U)

McCloskey, R. (1969). *Make way for ducklings.* New York: Viking. (P)

Mead, A. (1995). *Junebug.* New York: Farrar, Straus, & Giroux. (M–U)

Myers, W. D. (1988). *Scorpions.* New York: Harper & Row. (U)

Paterson, K. (1977). *Bridge to Terabithia.* New York: Crowell. (M–U)

Paulsen, G. (1987). *Hatchet.* New York: Simon & Schuster. (U)

Polacco, P. (1988). *The keeping quilt.* New York: Simon & Schuster. (M)

Polacco, P. (1988). *Rechenka's eggs.* New York: Philomel. (P–M)

Ringgold, R. (1991). *Tar beach.* New York: Crown. (P–M)

Roop, P., & Roop, C. (1985). *Keep the lights burning, Abbie.* Minneapolis: Carolrhoda. (P–M)

Ryan, P. M. (1998). *Riding Freedom.* New York: Scholastic. (M–U)

Sachar, L. (1998). *Holes.* New York: Farrar, Straus, & Giroux. (U)

Say, A. (1990). *El Chino.* Boston: Houghton Mifflin. (M)

Speare, E. G. (1958). *The witch of Blackbird Pond.* Boston: Houghton Mifflin. (M–U)

Speare, E. G. (1983). *The sign of the beaver.* Boston: Houghton Mifflin. (M–U)

Stanley, D. (1996). *Saving Sweetness.* New York: Putnam. (P–M)

Uchida, Y. (1993). *The bracelet.* New York: Philomel. (P–M)

Wilder, L. I. (1971). *The long winter.* New York: Harper & Row. (M)

Yep, L. (1975). *Dragonwings.* New York: Harper & Row. (U)

Ducklings (McCloskey, 1969) and the Alaskan North Slope in *Julie of the Wolves* (George, 1972) are integral to those stories' effectiveness. The settings are artfully described and add something unique to the story. In contrast, many stories take place in predictable settings that do not contribute to the story's effectiveness.

Weather is a second dimension of setting and, like location, is crucial in some stories. A rainstorm is essential to the plot development in *Bridge to Terabithia* (Paterson, 1977), but in other books weather is not mentioned because it does not affect the outcome of the story. Many stories take place on warm, sunny days.

The third dimension of setting is the time period, an important element in stories set in the past or future. If *The Witch of Blackbird Pond* (Speare, 1958) and *Number the Stars* (Lowry, 1989) were set in different eras, for example, they would lose much of their impact. Today, few people would believe that Kit Tyler is a witch or that Jewish people are the focus of government persecution. In stories that take place in the future, such as *A Wrinkle in Time* (L'Engle, 1962), things are possible that are not possible today.

The fourth dimension, time, includes both time of day and the passage of time. Most stories ignore time of day, except for scary stories that take place after dark. In stories such as *The Ghost-eye Tree* (Martin & Archambault, 1985), in which two children must walk past a scary tree at night to get a pail of milk, time is a more important dimension than in stories that take place during the day, because night makes things more scary.

Many short stories span a brief period of time—often less than a day, and sometimes less than an hour. In *Jumanji* (Van Allsburg, 1981), Peter and Judy's bizarre adventure, during which their house is overtaken by exotic jungle creatures, lasts only several hours. *Hatchet* (Paulsen, 1987) takes place in less than two months. Other stories, such as *The Ugly Duckling* (Mayer, 1987), span a long enough period for the main character to grow to maturity.

Students can draw maps to show the setting of a story. These maps might show the path a character traveled or the passage of time in a story. Figure 9–7 shows a map for *Number the Stars* (Lowry, 1989). In this chapter book set in Denmark during World War II, a Christian girl and her family help a Jewish family flee to safety in Sweden. The map shows the families' homes in Copenhagen, their trip to a fishing village, and the ship they hid away on to escape to Sweden.

Point of View

Stories are written from a particular viewpoint, and this perspective determines to a great extent readers' understanding of the characters and events of the story. The four points of view are first-person viewpoint, omniscient viewpoint, limited omniscient viewpoint, and objective viewpoint (Lukens, 1999). A list of stories written from each point of view is presented in Figure 9–8.

The first-person viewpoint is used to tell a story through the eyes of one character using the first-person pronoun "I." In this point of view, the reader experiences the story as the narrator tells it. The narrator, usually the main character, speaks as an eyewitness and a participant in the events. For example, in *Alexander and the Terrible, Horrible, No Good, Very Bad Day* (Viorst, 1977), Alexander tells about a day everything seemed to go wrong for him. One limitation of this viewpoint is that the narrator must remain an eyewitness.

In the omniscient viewpoint, the author is godlike, seeing and knowing all. The author tells readers about the thought processes of each character without worrying about how the information is obtained. *Doctor De Soto* (Steig, 1982), a story about a mouse dentist who outwits a fox with a toothache, is told from the omniscient viewpoint. Steig lets readers know that the fox wants to eat the dentist as soon as his toothache is cured and that the mouse dentist is aware of the fox's thoughts and plans a clever trick.

The limited omniscient viewpoint is used so that readers know the thoughts of one character. The story is told in third person, and the author concentrates on the thoughts, feelings, and experiences of the main character or another important character. Gary Paulsen used this viewpoint for *Hatchet* (1987) in order to be able to explore Brian's thoughts as he struggled to survive in the wilderness as well as his coming to terms with his parents' divorce. And Lois Lowry used the limited omniscient viewpoint in *Number the Stars* (1989), so that Annemarie, the Christian girl, can reveal her thoughts about the lies she tells to the Nazi soldiers in this World War II story.

www.harperchildrens.com

www.randomhouse.com

www.eduplace.com

www.scholastic.com

Children's Authors. These sites include interviews with many children's authors, including Lois Lowry, Karen Cushman, Patricia MacLachlan, and Gary Paulsen.

Figure 9–7 A story map for *Number the Stars*

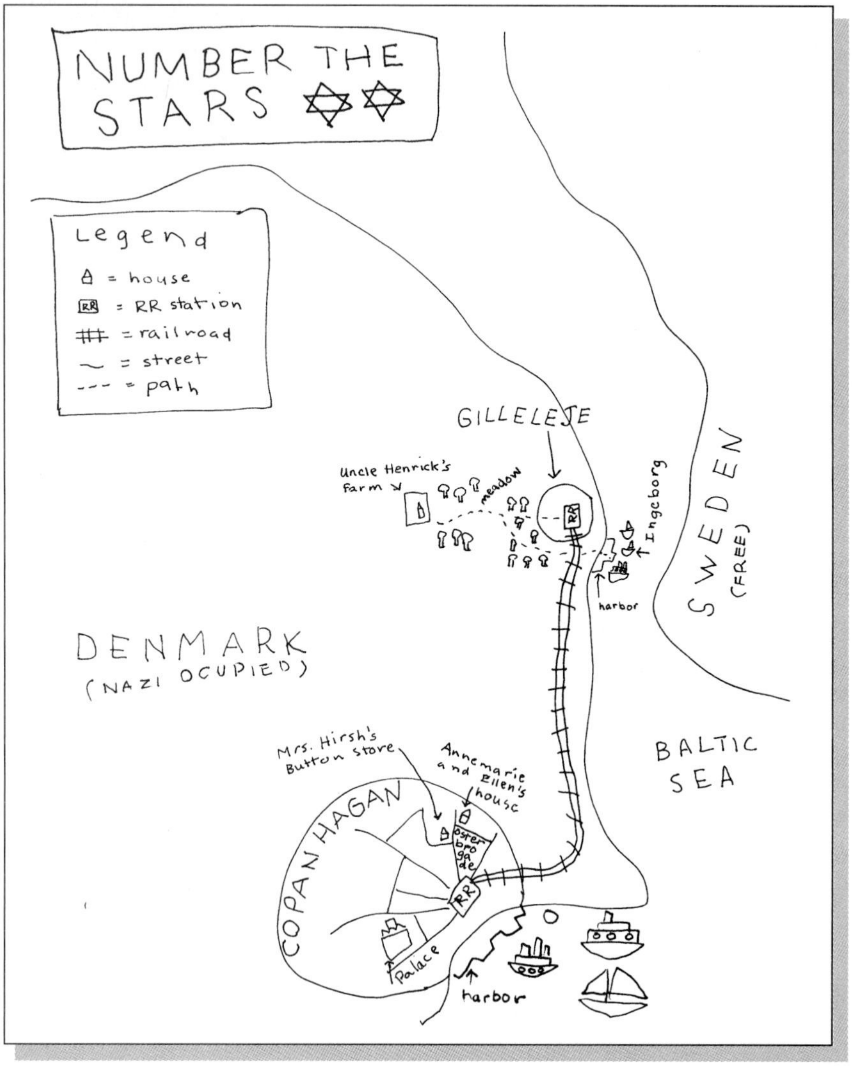

In the objective viewpoint, readers are eyewitnesses to the story and confined to the immediate scene. They learn only what is visible and audible and are not aware of what any characters think. Most fairy tales, such as *The Little Red Hen* (Zemach, 1983), are told from the objective viewpoint. The focus is on recounting events, not on developing the personalities of the characters.

Most teachers postpone introducing the four viewpoints until the upper grades, but younger children can experiment with point of view to understand how the author's viewpoint affects a story. One way to demonstrate point of view is to contrast *The Three Little Pigs* (Galdone, 1970), the traditional version of the story told from an objective viewpoint, with *The True Story of the Three Little Pigs!* (Scieszka, 1989), a self-serving narrative told by Mr. A. Wolf from a first-person viewpoint. In this satirical retelling, the wolf tries to explain away his bad image. Even first graders are struck by how different the two versions are and how the narrator filters the information.

| *Figure 9–8* | Stories that illustrate the four points of view |

First-Person Viewpoint

Bunting, E. (1994). *Smoky night.* San Diego: Harcourt Brace. (P–M)

Cushman, K. (1994). *Catherine called Birdy.* New York: HarperCollins. (U)

Howard, E. F. (1991). *Aunt Flossie's hats (and crab cakes later).* New York: Clarion. (P)

Howe, D., & Howe, J. (1979). *Bunnicula: A rabbit-tale of mystery.* New York: Atheneum. (M)

MacLachlan, P. (1985). *Sarah, plain and tall.* New York: Harper & Row. (M)

Rylant, C. (1992). *Missing May.* New York: Orchard Books. (U)

Stanley, D. (1996). *Saving Sweetness.* New York: Putnam. (P–M)

Viorst, J. (1977). *Alexander and the terrible, horrible, no good, very bad day.* New York: Atheneum. (P)

Omniscient Viewpoint

Babbitt, N. (1975). *Tuck everlasting.* New York: Farrar, Straus & Giroux. (M–U)

Grahame, K. (1961). *The wind in the willows.* New York: Scribner, (M)

Lewis, C. S. (1981). *The lion, the witch and the wardrobe.* New York: Macmillan. (M–U)

Myers, W. D. (1988). *Scorpions.* New York: Harper & Row. (U)

Steig, W. (1982). *Doctor De Soto.* New York: Farrar, Straus & Giroux. (P)

Limited Omniscient Viewpoint

Cleary, B. (1981). *Ramona Quimby, age 8.* New York: Morrow. (M)

Gardiner, J. R. (1980). *Stone Fox.* New York: Harper & Row. (M)

Lionni, L. (1969). *Alexander and the wind-up mouse.* New York: Pantheon (P)

Lowry, L. (1989). *Number the stars.* Boston: Houghton Mifflin. (M–U)

Lowry, L. (1993). *The giver.* Boston: Houghton Mifflin. (U)

Sachar, L. (1998). *Holes.* New York: Farrar, Straus, & Giroux. (U)

Objective Viewpoint

Cauley, L. B. (1988). *The pancake boy.* New York: Putnam. (P)

Lester, H. (1988). *Tacky the penguin.* Boston: Houghton Mifflin. (P–M)

Lobel, A. (1972). *Frog and Toad together.* New York: Harper & Row. (P)

Meddaugh, S. (1992). *Martha speaks.* Boston: Houghton Mifflin. (P)

Marshall, J. (1997). *Miss Nelson is missing!* Boston: Houghton Mifflin. (P–M)

Zemach, M. (1983). *The little red hen.* New York: Farrar, Straus & Giroux. (P)

Theme

Theme is the underlying meaning of a story, and it embodies general truths about human nature (Lehr, 1991; Lukens, 1999). Theme usually deals with the characters' emotions and values. Themes can be stated either explicitly or implicitly. Explicit themes are stated openly and clearly in the story, while implicit themes must be inferred from the story. Themes are developed as the characters attempt to overcome the obstacles that prevent them from reaching their goals. In a fable the theme is often stated explicitly at the end, but in most stories the theme emerges through the thoughts, speech, and actions of the characters as they seek to resolve their conflicts. In *A Chair for My Mother* (Williams, 1982), for example, a young girl demonstrates the importance of sacrificing personal wants for her family's welfare as she and her mother collect money to buy a new chair after they lose all of their belongings in a fire.

Stories usually have more one theme, and their themes usually cannot be articulated with a single word. *Charlotte's Web* (White, 1952) has several "friendship" themes, one explicitly stated and others inferred from the text. Friendship is a multidimensional theme—qualities of a good friend, unlikely friends, and sacrificing for a friend, for instance. Teachers can probe students' thinking as they work to construct a theme and move beyond one-word labels (Au, 1992).

Why Do Teachers Need to Know About Story Elements?

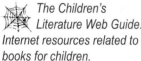

www.acs.ucalgary.ca

The Children's Literature Web Guide. Internet resources related to books for children.

Most teachers are familiar with story terms such as *character, plot,* and *setting,* but in order to plan for reading instruction, teachers need to understand how authors combine the story elements to craft stories. Teachers cannot assume that teacher's manuals or other guides will be available for every story they read with their students, or that these guides provide the necessary information about story structure. Teachers must be prepared to think about the structure of stories they will use in their classrooms.

For example, after reading *Sarah, Plain and Tall* (MacLachlan, 1985), teachers might think about how the story would be different if Sarah, not Anna, were telling the story. They might wonder if the author meant to send a message of promise of future happiness for the family by setting the story in the springtime. They also might speculate that the storm was the turning point in the story or wonder about the role of colors in the story. This kind of thoughtful reflection allows teachers to know the story better, prepare themselves to guide their students through the story, and plan activities to help students explore the story's meaning.

Teachers teach minilessons about story elements so that students can use this knowledge to enhance their comprehension. According to Irwin (1991), when students recognize the author's organization pattern, they are better able to comprehend what they are reading or listening to being read aloud. During grand conversations teachers often direct students' attention to how a particular conflict situation or viewpoint has influenced a story. Primary-grade students also use this knowledge to organize their retellings of favorite fairy tales into beginning-middle-end parts and their innovations or new versions of familiar stories like *Brown Bear, Brown Bear, What Do You See?* (Martin, 1983). And, middle-grade students use their knowledge of setting and plot as they write sequels after reading books such as *Jumanji* (Van Allsburg, 1981). Similarly, when teachers conference with students about stories they are writing, knowledge about story structure and related terminology, such as *rising action, dialogue,* and *theme,* enriches the conversation.

EXPOSITORY TEXT STRUCTURES

Stories have been the primary genre for reading and writing instruction in the elementary grades because it has been assumed that constructing stories in the mind is a fundamental way of learning (Wells, 1986). Recent research, however, suggests that children may prefer to read informational books and are able to understand them as well as they do stories (Pappas, 1993). Certainly, children are interested in learning about their world—about baleen whales, how a road is built, threats to the environment of Antarctica, or Helen Keller's courage—and informational books provide this knowledge. Even young children read informational books, as Mrs. Simmons's first graders did in the vignette.

Students often assume an efferent stance as they read informational books to locate facts, but they do not always use efferent reading (Rosenblatt, 1978). Many times students pick up an informational book to check a fact and then continue reading—aesthetically—because they are fascinated by what they are reading. They get carried away in the presentation of information, just as they do when reading stories.

At other times, students read books about topics they are interested in, and they read aesthetically, engaging in the lived-through experience of reading and connecting what they are reading to their own lives and prior reading experiences.

Russell Freedman, who won the 1988 Newbery Award for *Lincoln: A Photobiography* (1987), talks about the purpose of informational books and explains that it is not enough for an informational book to provide information: "[An informational book] must create a vivid and believable world that the reader will enter willingly and leave only with reluctance. . . . It should be just as compelling as a good story" (1992, p. 3). High-quality informational books like Freedman's encourage students to read aesthetically because they engage readers and tap their curiosity. There is a new wave of engaging and artistic informational books being published today, and these books show increased respect for children. Peter Roop (1992) explains that for years informational books were the "ugly duckling" of children's literature, but now they have grown into a beautiful swan.

Four qualities of informational books are accuracy, organization, design, and style (Vardell, 1991). First and foremost, the facts must be current and complete. They must be well researched, and, when appropriate, varying points of view should be presented. Stereotypes are to be avoided, and details in both the text and the illustrations must be authentic. Second, information should be presented clearly and logically, using organizational patterns to increase the book's readability. Third, the book's design should be eye-catching and enhance its usability. Illustrations should complement the text, and explanations should accompany each illustration. Last, the style should be lively and stimulating so as to engage readers' curiosity and wonder.

Informational books are available today on topics ranging from biological sciences, physical sciences, and social sciences to arts and biographies. *Cactus Hotel* (Guiberson, 1991) is a fine informational book about the desert ecosystem. The author discusses the life cycle of a giant saguaro cactus and describes its role as a home for desert creatures. Other books, such as *Whales* (Simon, 1989), illustrated with striking full-page color photos, and *Antarctica* (Cowcher, 1990), illustrated with dramatic double-page paintings, are socially responsible and emphasize the threats people pose to animals and the earth.

Other books present historical and geographic concepts. *A Street Through Time* (Millard, 1998), for instance, traces the evolution of one street from the Stone Age to the present day, and *Knights* (Steele, 1998) tells about the lives of knights during medieval times. These books have lavish illustrations and detailed text which provide an enriching reading experience for elementary students.

Some informational books focus on letters and numbers. While many alphabet and counting books with pictures of familiar objects are designed for young children, others provide a wealth of information on various topics. In his alphabet book *Illuminations* (1989), Jonathan Hunt presents detailed information about medieval life, and in *The Underwater Alphabet Book* (1991), Jerry Pallotta provides information about 26 types of fish and other sea creatures. Muriel and Tom Feelings present information about Africa in *Moja Means One: Swahili Counting Book* (1971), and Ann Herbert Scott presents information about cowboys in *One Good Horse: A Cowpuncher's Counting Book* (1990). In some of these books, new terms are introduced and illustrated, and in others, the term is explained in a sentence or a paragraph. Other informational books focus on mathematical concepts (Whitin & Wilde, 1992). Tana Hoban's *26 Letters and 99 Cents* (1987) presents concepts about money, *What Comes in 2's, 3's and 4's?* (Aker, 1990) introduces multiplication, and *If You Made a Million* (Schwartz, 1989) focuses on big numbers.

www.carolhurst.com

Carol Hurst's Children's Literature Site.
Reviews of informational books for social studies and science units.

Biographies are also informational books, and the biographies being written today are more realistic than in the past, presenting well-known personalities warts and all. Jean Fritz's portraits of Revolutionary War figures, such as *Will You Sign Here, John Hancock?* (1976), are among the best-known, but she has also written comprehensive biographies, including *The Great Little Madison* (1989). Fritz and other authors often include notes in the back of books to explain how the details were researched and to provide additional information. Only a few autobiographies are available to students, but more are being published each year. Autobiographies about authors and illustrators, such as Cynthia Rylant's *Best Wishes* (1992), are also popular.

Other books present information within a story context. Authors are devising innovative strategies for combining information with a story. Margy Burns Knight's *Who Belongs Here? An American Story* (1993), a two-part book, is a good example. One part is the story of Nary, a young Cambodian refugee who escapes to the United States after his parents are killed by the Khmer Rouge. This story is told in a picture-book format, with the story text accompanying each picture. The second part of the book is information about refugees, immigration laws, and cultural diversity in America. The text for this second part is printed in a different typeface and appears below the story text on each page. Additional information about America as a nation of immigrants is presented at the back of the book. The two parts work together to create a very powerful book.

Some combination informational/story books are imaginative fantasies. The Magic School Bus series is perhaps the best-known. In *The Magic School Bus Inside a Beehive* (Cole, 1996), for example, Ms. Frizzle and her class study bees and take a field trip on the magic school bus into a beehive to learn about the life cycle of honeybees, how honey is made, and bee society. The page layout is innovative, with charts and reports containing factual information presented at the outside edges of most pages.

Informational books are organized in particular ways called expository text structures. Five of the most common organizational patterns are description, sequence, comparison, cause and effect, and problem and solution (Meyer & Freedle, 1984; Niles, 1974). Figure 9–9 describes these patterns and presents sample passages and cue words that signal use of each pattern. When readers are aware of these patterns, they understand what they are reading better, and when writers use these structures to organize their writing, it is more easily understood by readers. Sometimes the pattern is signaled clearly by means of titles, topic sentences, and cue words, and sometimes it is not.

Description

In this organizational pattern, a topic is described by listing characteristics, features, and examples. Phrases such as *for example* and *characteristics are* cue this structure. Examples of books using description include *Spiders* (Gibbons, 1992) and *Mercury* (Simon, 1993), in which the authors describe many facets of their topic. When students delineate any topic, such as the Mississippi River, eagles, or Alaska, they use description.

Sequence

In this pattern, items or events are listed or explained in numerical or chronological order. Cue words for sequence include *first, second, third, next, then,* and *finally.* Caroline Arnold describes the steps in creating a museum display in *Dinosaurs All Around: An Artist's View of the Prehistoric World* (1993), and David Macaulay describes how a castle is built in *Castle* (1977). Students use the sequence pattern to write directions for completing a math problem or for the stages in an animal's life cycle. The events in a biography are often written in the sequence pattern.

www.scholastic.com

*The Magic School Bus.
Information about books in the series, videos, CD-ROMs, activities, live stage shows, and more.*

Comparison

In the comparison structure, two or more things are compared. *Different, in contrast, alike,* and *on the other hand* are cue words and phrases that signal this structure. In *Horns, Antlers, Fangs, and Tusks* (Rauzon, 1993), for example, the author compares animals with distinctive types of headgear. When students compare and contrast book and movie versions of a story, reptiles and amphibians, or life in ancient Greece with life in ancient Egypt, they use this organizational pattern.

Figure 9–9   The five expository text structures

Pattern	Description	Graphic Organizer	Sample Passage
Description	The author describes a topic by listing characteristics, features, and examples. Cue words include *for example* and *characteristics are.*		The Olympic symbol consists of five interlocking rings. The rings represent the five continents from which athletes come to compete in the games. The rings are colored black, blue, green, red, and yellow. At least one of these colors is found in the flag of every country sending athletes to compete in the Olympic games.
Sequence	The author lists items or events in numerical or chronological order. Cue words include *first, second, third, next, then,* and *finally.*	1. _____ 2. _____ 3. _____ 4. _____ 5. _____	The Olympic games began as athletic festivals to honor the Greek gods. The most important festival was held in the valley of Olympia to honor Zeus, the king of the gods. This festival became the Olympic games in 776 B.C. They were ended in A.D. 394. No Olympic games were held for more than 1,500 years. Then the modern Olympics began in 1896. Almost 300 male athletes competed in the first modern Olympics. In the 1900 games, female athletes were allowed to compete. The games have continued every four years since 1896 except during World War II.
Comparison	The author explains how two or more things are alike and/or how they are different. Cue words include *different, in contrast, alike, same as,* and *on the other hand.*	Alike / Different	The modern Olympics is very unlike the ancient Olympic games. While there were no swimming races in the ancient games, for example, there were chariot races. There were no female contestants, and all athletes competed in the nude. Of course, the ancient and modern Olympics are also alike in many ways. Some events, such as the javelin and discus throws, are the same. Some people say that cheating, professionalism, and nationalism in the modern games are a disgrace to the Olympic tradition. But according to the ancient Greek writers, there were many cases of cheating, nationalism, and professionalism in their Olympics, too.

Figure 9–9   *continued*

Pattern	Description	Graphic Organizer	Sample Passage
Cause and Effect	The author lists one or more causes and the resulting effect or effects. Cue words include *reasons why, if . . . then, as a result, therefore,* and *because.*	Cause → Effect #1 / Effect #2 / Effect #3	There are several reasons why so many people attend the Olympic games or watch them on television. One reason is tradition. The name *Olympics* and the torch and flame remind people of the ancient games. People can escape the ordinariness of daily life by attending or watching the Olympics. They like to identify with someone else's individual sacrifice and accomplishment. National pride is another reason, and an athlete's or a team's hard-earned victory becomes a nation's victory. There are national medal counts, and people keep track of how many medals their country's athletes have won.
Problem and Solution	The author states a problem and lists one or more solutions for the problem. A variation of this pattern is the question-and-answer format in which the author poses a question and then answers it. Cue words include *problem is, dilemma is, puzzle is, solved,* and *question . . . answer.*	Problem → Solution	One problem with the modern Olympics is that it has become very expensive to operate. A stadium, pools, and playing fields must be built for the athletic events, and housing is needed for the athletes who come from around the world. And these facilities are used for only 2 weeks! In 1984, Los Angeles solved these problems by charging a fee for companies who wanted to be official sponsors. Many buildings that were already built in the Los Angeles area were also used. The Coliseum where the 1932 games were held was used again, and many colleges in the area became playing and living sites.

Cause and Effect

The writer explains one or more causes and the resulting effect or effects. *Reasons why, if . . . then, as a result, therefore,* and *because* are words and phrases that cue this structure. Explanations of why dinosaurs became extinct, the effects of pollution on the environment, or the causes of the Civil War are written using this pattern. *How Do Apples Grow?* (Maestro, 1992) and *What Happens to a Hamburger?* (Showers, 1985) are two books that exemplify this structure.

Problem and Solution

In this expository structure, the writer states a problem and offers one or more solutions. In *Man and Mustang* (Ancona, 1992), for example, the author describes the problem of wild mustangs and explains how they are rescued. A variation is the question-and-answer format, in which the writer poses a question and then answers it. One question-and-answer book is . . . *If You Traveled West in a Covered Wagon* (Levine, 1986). Cue words and phrases include *the problem is, the puzzle is, solve,* and *question . . . answer.* Students use this structure when they write about why money was invented, why endangered animals should be saved, or why dams are needed to ensure a permanent water supply. They often use the problem-solution pattern in writing advertisements and other persuasive writing as well.

Students apply what they are learning about the structure of informational books as they write their own weather books.

Figure 9–10 lists other books that illustrate each of the five expository text structures.

Why Do Teachers Need to Know About Expository Text Structures?

When teachers use informational books and content-area textbooks as instructional materials, they should consider how the books are organized as they prepare for instruction. Often teachers do what Mrs. Simmons did in the vignette at the beginning of this chapter: they give students a purpose for reading and use a graphic organizer to record information after reading.

Researchers have confirmed that when students use the five expository text structures to organize their reading and writing, they are more effective readers and writers. Most of the research on expository text structures has focused on older students' use of these patterns in reading; however, elementary students also use the patterns and cue words in their writing (Langer, 1986; Raphael, Englert, & Kirschner, 1989; Tompkins, 2000).

Students also use the five expository text structures when they write informational books, essays, and other nonfiction forms. A class of second graders examined the five expository text structures and learned that authors use cue words as a secret code to signal the structures. Then the students read informational books that used

Figure 9–10 Informational books representing the expository text structures

Description

Balestrino, P. (1971). *The skeleton inside you.* New York: Crowell. (P)

Branley, F. M. (1986). *What the moon is like.* New York: Harper & Row. (M)

Fowler, A. (1990). *It could still be a bird.* Chicago: Childrens Press. (P–M)

Hansen, R., & Bell, R. A. (1985). *My first book of space.* New York: Simon & Schuster. (M)

Horvatic, A. (1989). *Simple machines.* New York: Dutton. (M)

Morris, A. (1989). *Hats, hats, hats.* New York: Mulberry Books. (P)

Patent, D. H. (1992). *Feathers.* New York: Cobblehill. (M–U)

Simon, S. (1992). *Wolves.* New York: HarperCollins. (M–U)

Sequence

Aliki. (1992). *Milk from cow to carton.* New York: HarperCollins. (P–M)

Cole, J. (1991). *My puppy is born.* New York: Morrow. (P–M)

Gibbons, G. (1993). *Pirates.* Boston: Little, Brown. (P–M)

Jaspersohn, W. (1988). *Ice cream.* New York: Macmillan. (M–U)

Lasky, K. (1983). *Sugaring time.* New York: Macmillan. (M–U)

Provensen, A. (1990). *The buck stops here.* New York: HarperCollins. (M–U)

Wheatley, N. (1992). *My place.* New York: Kane/Miller. (M–U)

Comparison

Gibbons, G. (1984). *Fire! Fire!* New York: Harper & Row. (P–M)

Lasker, J. (1976). *Merry ever after: The story of two medieval weddings.* New York: Viking. (M–U)

Markle, S. (1993). *Outside and inside trees.* New York: Bradbury Press. (M)

Munro, R. (1987). *The inside-outside book of Washington, D.C.* New York: Dutton. (M–U)

Rauzon, M. J. (1993). *Horns, antlers, fangs, and tusks.* New York: Lothrop, Lee & Shepard. (P–M)

Spier, P. (1987). *We the people.* New York: Doubleday. (M–U)

Cause and Effect

Branley, F. M. (1985). *Flash, crash, rumble, and roll.* New York: Harper & Row. (P–M)

Branley, F. M. (1985). *Volcanoes.* New York: Harper & Row. (P–M)

Branley, F. M. (1986). *What makes day and night?* New York: Harper & Row. (P–M)

Heller, R. (1983). *The reason for a flower.* New York: Grosset & Dunlap. (M)

Selsam, M. E. (1981). *Where do they go? Insects in winter.* New York: Scholastic. (P–M)

Showers, P. (1985). *What happens to a hamburger?* New York: Harper & Row. (P–M)

Problem and Solution

Cole, J. (1983). *Cars and how they go.* New York: Harper & Row. (P–M)

Heller, R. (1986). *How to hide a whippoorwill and other birds.* New York: Grosset & Dunlap. (P–M)

Lauber, P. (1990). *How we learned the earth is round.* New York: Crowell. (P–M)

Levine, E. (1988). *If you traveled on the underground railroad.* New York: Scholastic. (M–U)

Showers, P. (1980). *No measles, no mumps for me.* New York: Crowell. (P–M)

Simon, S. (1984). *The dinosaur is the biggest animal that ever lived and other wrong ideas you thought were true.* New York: Harper & Row. (M)

Combination

Aliki (1981). *Digging up dinosaurs.* New York: Harper & Row. (M)

Carrick, C. (1993). *Whaling days.* New York: Clarion (P–M)

Guiberson, B. Z. (1991). *Cactus hotel.* New York: Henry Holt. (P–M)

Hoyt-Goldsmith, D. (1992). *Hoang Anh: A Vietnamese-American boy.* New York: Holiday House. (M)

Simon, S. (1985). *Meet the computer.* New York: Harper & Row. (M–U)

Venutra, P., & Ceserani, G. P. (1985). *In search of Tutankhamun.* Morristown, NJ: Silver Burdett. (U)

each of the expository text structures, developed graphic organizers to record the information in the books, and wrote paragraphs on the same topics to exemplify each of the five organizational patterns. The graphic organizers and paragraphs are presented in Figure 9–11, and the secret code (or cue) words in each paragraph appear in boldface type. These paragraphs show that even primary-grade students can learn about expository text structures and use them to organize their writing.

POETIC FORMS

Poetry "brings sound and sense together in words and lines," according to Donald Graves, "ordering them on the page in such a way that both the writer and reader get a different view of life" (1992, p. 3). Poetry surrounds us; children chant jump-rope rhymes on the playground and dance in response to songs and their lyrics. Larrick (1991) believes that we enjoy poetry because of the physical involvement that the words evoke. Also, people play with words as they invent rhymes and ditties, create new words, and craft powerful comparisons.

Today more poets are writing for children, and more books of poems for children are being published than ever before. No longer is poetry confined to rhyming verse about daffodils, clouds, and love. Recently published poems about dinosaurs, Halloween, chocolate, baseball, and insects are very popular. Children choose to read poetry and share favorite poems with classmates. They read and respond to poems containing beautiful language and written on topics that are meaningful to them.

Three types of poetry books are published for children. A number of picture-book versions of single poems in which each line or stanza is illustrated on a page are available, such as *Paul Revere's Ride* (Longfellow, 1990). Other books are specialized collections of poems, either written by a single poet or related to a single theme, such as dinosaurs. Comprehensive anthologies are the third type of poetry books for children, and they feature 50 to 500 or more poems arranged by category. One of the best anthologies is Jack Prelutsky's *The Random House Book of Poetry for Children* (1983). A list of poetry books that includes examples of each of the three types is presented in Figure 9–12.

Poems for children assume many different forms, including rhymed verse, narrative poems, haiku, and free verse. Additional forms are useful for elementary students who write poems.

www.falcon.jmu.edu

Jack Prelutsky. Biographical information, online poems, and links to lesson plans.

www.sknox.k12.in.us

"I'd Never Eat a Beet!" A third-grade project using Jack Prelutsky's poems.

Rhymed Verse

The most common type of poetry is rhymed verse, as in *Hailstones and Halibut Bones* (O'Neill, 1989), *My Parents Think I'm Sleeping* (Prelutsky, 1985), and *Sierra* (Siebert, 1991). Poets use various rhyme schemes, and the effect of the rhyming words is a poem that is pleasurable to read and listen to when it is read aloud. Children should savor the rhyming words but not be expected to pick out the rhyme scheme.

Rhyme is the sticking point for many would-be poets. In searching for a rhyming word, children often create inane verse; for example:

> *I see a funny little goat*
> *Wearing a blue sailor's coat*
> *Sitting in an old motorboat.*

Figure 9–11 Second graders' graphic organizers and paragraphs illustrating the five expository text structures

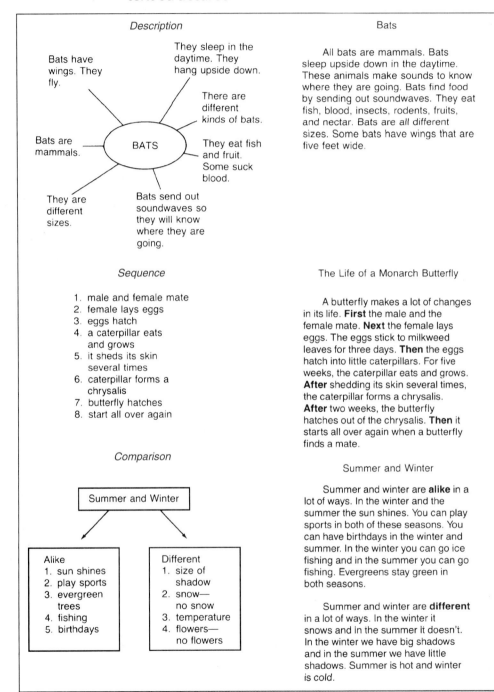

Description

Bats have wings. They fly.

They sleep in the daytime. They hang upside down.

There are different kinds of bats.

Bats are mammals.

BATS

They eat fish and fruit. Some suck blood.

They are different sizes.

Bats send out soundwaves so they will know where they are going.

Bats

All bats are mammals. Bats sleep upside down in the daytime. These animals make sounds to know where they are going. Bats find food by sending out soundwaves. They eat fish, blood, insects, rodents, fruits, and nectar. Bats are all different sizes. Some bats have wings that are five feet wide.

Sequence

1. male and female mate
2. female lays eggs
3. eggs hatch
4. a caterpillar eats and grows
5. it sheds its skin several times
6. caterpillar forms a chrysalis
7. butterfly hatches
8. start all over again

The Life of a Monarch Butterfly

A butterfly makes a lot of changes in its life. **First** the male and the female mate. **Next** the female lays eggs. The eggs stick to milkweed leaves for three days. **Then** the eggs hatch into little caterpillars. For five weeks, the caterpillar eats and grows. **After** shedding its skin several times, the caterpillar forms a chrysalis. **After** two weeks, the butterfly hatches out of the chrysalis. **Then** it starts all over again when a butterfly finds a mate.

Comparison

Summer and Winter

Alike
1. sun shines
2. play sports
3. evergreen trees
4. fishing
5. birthdays

Different
1. size of shadow
2. snow— no snow
3. temperature
4. flowers— no flowers

Summer and Winter

Summer and winter are **alike** in a lot of ways. In the winter and the summer the sun shines. You can play sports in both of these seasons. You can have birthdays in the winter and summer. In the winter you can go ice fishing and in the summer you can go fishing. Evergreens stay green in both seasons.

Summer and winter are **different** in a lot of ways. In the winter it snows and in the summer it doesn't. In the winter we have big shadows and in the summer we have little shadows. Summer is hot and winter is cold.

Figure 9–11 *continued*

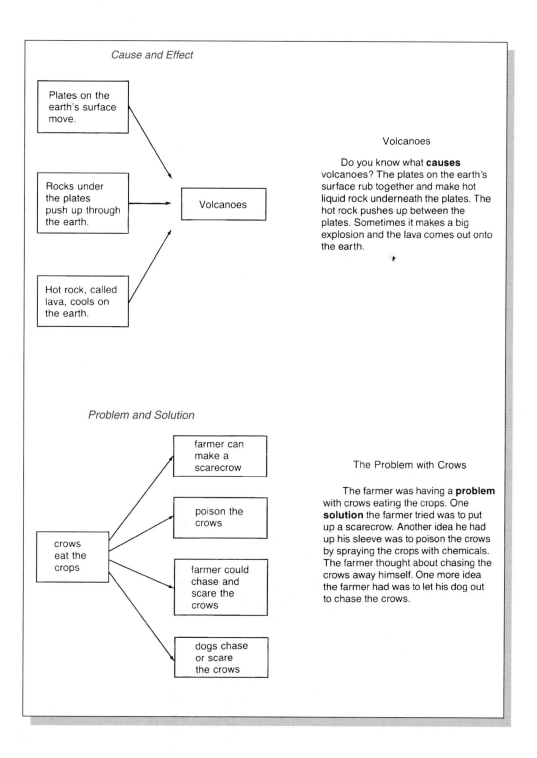

Cause and Effect

Plates on the earth's surface move.

Rocks under the plates push up through the earth. → Volcanoes

Hot rock, called lava, cools on the earth.

Volcanoes

Do you know what **causes** volcanoes? The plates on the earth's surface rub together and make hot liquid rock underneath the plates. The hot rock pushes up between the plates. Sometimes it makes a big explosion and the lava comes out onto the earth.

Problem and Solution

farmer can make a scarecrow

poison the crows

crows eat the crops

farmer could chase and scare the crows

dogs chase or scare the crows

The Problem with Crows

The farmer was having a **problem** with crows eating the crops. One **solution** the farmer tried was to put up a scarecrow. Another idea he had up his sleeve was to poison the crows by spraying the crops with chemicals. The farmer thought about chasing the crows away himself. One more idea the farmer had was to let his dog out to chase the crows.

Figure 9–12   Collections of poetry written for children

Picture Book Versions of Single Poems

Carroll, L. (1977). (Ill. by J. B. Zalben). *Lewis Carroll's Jabberwocky.* New York: Warne. (M–U)

Frost, R. (1988). (Ill. by E. Young). *Birches.* New York: Henry Holt. (U)

Lear, E. (1986). (Ill. by L. B. Cauley). *The owl and the pussycat.* New York: Putnam. (P–M)

Longfellow, H. W. (1990). (Ill. by T. Rand). *Paul Revere's ride.* New York: Dutton. (M–U)

Moore, C. (1980). *The night before Christmas.* New York: Holiday House. (P–M)

Sandurg, C. (1993). *Arithmetic.* New York: Harcourt Brace. (P–M)

Thayer, E. L. (1988). (Ill. by P. Polacco). *Casey at the bat: A ballad of the republic, sung in the year 1888.* New York: Putnam. (M–U)

Westcott, N. B. (1988). *The lady with the alligator purse.* Boston: Little, Brown. (P–M)

Specialized Collections

Fleischman, P. (1985). *I am phoenix: Poems for two voices.* New York: Harper & Row. (M–U)

Fleischman, P. (1988). *Joyful noise: Poems for two voices.* New York: Harper & Row. (M–U)

Frost, R. (1982). *A swinger of birches: Poems of Robert Frost for young people.* Owing Mills, MD: Stemmer House. (U)

George, K. O. (1998). *Old elm speaks: Tree poems.* New York: Clarion Books. (P–M)

Greenfield, E. (1988). *Under the Sunday tree.* New York: Harper & Row. (M)

Hoberman, M. A. (1998). *The llama who had no pajama: 100 favorite poems.* New York: Browndeer. (P–M)

Hopkins, L. B. (1984). *Surprises* (An I Can Read Book). New York: Harper & Row. (P)

Hopkins, L. B. (1987). *Click, rumble, roar: Poems about machines.* New York: Crowell. (M)

Janeczko, P. B. (Sel.). (1993). *Looking for your name: A collection of contemporary poems.* New York: Orchard Books. (U)

Jones, H. (Ed.). (1993). *The trees stand shining: Poetry of the North American Indians.* New York: Dial. (M–U)

Kuskin, K. (1980). *Dogs and dragons, trees and dreams.* New York: Harper & Row (P–M)

Livingston, M. C. (1985). *Celebrations.* New York: Holiday House. (M)

Lobel, A. (1983). *The book of pigericks.* New York: Harper & Row. (limericks) (P–M)

Livingston, M. C. (1986). *Earth songs.* New York: Holiday House. (See also *Sea songs* and *Space songs.*) (M–U)

McCord, D. (1974). *One at a time.* Boston: Little, Brown. (M–U)

Pomerantz, C. (1982). *If I had a paka: Poems in 11 languages.* New York: Greenwillow. (M–U)

Prelutsky, J. (1981). *It's Christmas.* New York: Scholastic. (Collections for other holidays, too.) (P–M)

Prelutsky, J. (1984). *The new kid on the block.* New York: Greenwillow. (P–M)

Prelutsky, J. (1989). *Poems of A. Nonny Mouse.* New York: Knopf. (P–M)

Prelutsky, J. (1990). *Something big has been here.* New York: Greenwillow. (P–M)

Prelutsky, J. (1993). *A Nonny Mouse writes again!* New York: Knopf. (M–U)

Prelutsky, J. (1996). *A pizza the size of the sun.* New York: Greenwillow. (P–M–U)

Siebert, D. (1984). *Truck song.* New York: Harper & Row. (P–M)

Siebert, D. (1989). *Heartland.* New York: Crowell. (M–U)

Sierra, J. (1998). *Antarctic antics: A book of penguin poems.* San Diego: Gulliver. (P–M)

Silverstein, S. (1974). *Where the sidewalk ends.* New York: Harper & Row. (P–M–U)

Stevenson, J. (1998). *Popcorn.* New York: Greenwillow. (M–U)

Wong, J. S. (1994). *Good luck gold and other poems.* New York: McElderry Books. (M–U)

Yolen, J. (1990). *Bird watch: A book of poetry.* New York: Philomel. (M–U)

Comprehensive Anthologies

de Paola, T. (Compiler). (1988). *Tomie de Paola's book of poems.* New York: Putnam. (P–M)

de Regniers, B. S., Moore, E., White, M. M., & Carr, J. (Compilers). (1988). *Sing a song of popcorn: Every child's book of poems.* New York: Scholastic. (P–M–U)

Dunning, S. Leuders, E., & Smith, H. (Compilers). (1967). *Reflections on a gift of watermelon pickle, and other modern verse.* New York: Lothrop, Lee & Shepard. (U)

Kennedy, X. J. (Complier). (1985). *The forgetful wishing well: Poems for young people.* New York: McElderry Books. (U)

Kennedy, X. J., & Kennedy, D. M. (Compilers). (1982). *Knock at a star: A child's introduction to poetry.* Boston: Little, Brown. (P–M–U)

Prelutsky, J. (Compiler). (1983). *The Random House book of poetry for children.* New York: Random House. (P–M–U)

Students read books of poetry written by Jack Prelutsky during an author study.

Certainly children should not be forbidden to write rhyming poetry, but rhyme should never be imposed as a criterion for acceptable poetry. Children may use rhyme when it fits naturally into their writing. When children write poetry, they are searching for their own voices, and they need freedom to do that. Freed from the pressure to create rhyming poetry and from other constraints, children create sensitive word pictures, vivid images, and unique comparisons.

One type of rhymed verse—limericks—can be used effectively with older students. A limerick is a short verse form popularized by Edward Lear that incorporates both rhyme and rhythm. The poem consists of five lines; the first, second, and fifth lines rhyme, while the third and fourth lines rhyme with each other and are shorter than the other three. The rhyme scheme is a-a-b-b-a. The last line often contains a funny or surprise ending, as in this limerick written by an eighth grader.

> *There once was a frog named Pete*
> *Who did nothing but sit and eat.*
> *He examined each fly*
> *With so careful an eye*
> *And then said, "You're dead meat."*

Poet X. J. Kennedy (1982) suggests introducing students to limericks by reading aloud some of Lear's verses so that students can appreciate the rhythm of the verse. One collection of Lear's limericks for elementary students is *There Was an Old Man: A Gallery of Nonsense Rhymes* (Lear, 1994). Younger children especially enjoy *AnimaLimericks* (Driver, 1994), which feature animals instead of people. Writing limericks can be a challenging assignment, but students can write limericks successfully if they write class collaboration poems. Arnold Lobel has also written a book of unique pig limericks, *Pigericks* (1983). After reading Lobel's pigericks, students will want to write "fishericks."

Narrative Poems

Poems that tell a story are narrative poems. Perhaps our best-known narrative poem is Clement Moore's classic, "The Night Before Christmas." Other narrative poems include Longfellow's *Paul Revere's Ride* (1990), illustrated by Ted Rand; Alfred Noyes's *The Highwayman* (1983), illustrated by Charles Mikolaycak; and Jeanette Winter's *Follow the Drinking Gourd* (1988), which is about the Underground Railroad.

Haiku and Related Forms

Haiku is a Japanese poetic form that contains just 17 syllables arranged in three lines of 5, 7, and 5 syllables. Haiku poems deal with nature and present a single clear image. Haiku is a concise form, much like a telegram. Because of its brevity, it has been considered an appropriate form of poetry for children to read and write. A fourth grader wrote this haiku about a spider web she saw one morning.

> *Spider web shining*
> *Tangled on the grass with dew*
> *Waiting quietly.*

Books of haiku to share with students include *Shadow Play: Night Haiku* (Harter, 1994) and *Cool Melons—Turn to Frogs! The Life and Poems of Issa* (Gollub, 1998). The artwork in these picture books may give students ideas for illustrating their haiku poems.

A poetic form similar to haiku is the cinquain, a five-line poem containing 22 syllables in a 2-4-6-8-2 syllable pattern. Cinquains often describe something, but they may also tell a story. Have students ask themselves what their subject looks like, smells like, sounds like, and tastes like, and record their ideas using a five-senses cluster. The formula is as follows.

Line 1: a one-word subject with two syllables

Line 2: four syllables describing the subject

Line 3: six syllables showing action

Line 4: eight syllables expressing a feeling or observation about the subject

Line 5: two syllables describing or renaming the subject

Students in a fourth-grade class wrote cinquains as part of a thematic unit on westward movement. One student wrote this cinquain about the transcontinental railroad:

> *Railroads*
> *One crazy guy's*
> *Transcontinental dream . . .*
> *With a golden spike it came true.*
> *Iron horse*

www.falcon.jmu.edu

Poetry for Children. E-texts of selected poems and information about haiku, limericks, and other forms of poetry.

Another student wrote about the gold rush:

> *Gold rush*
> *Forty-niners*
> *were sure to strike it rich*
> *Homesickness, pork and beans, so tired.*
> *Panning*

Another related form is the diamante (Tiedt, 1970), a seven-line contrast poem written in the shape of a diamond. This poetic form helps students apply their knowledge of opposites and parts of speech. The formula is:

Line 1: one noun as the subject

Line 2: two adjectives describing the subject

Line 3: three participles (ending in *-ing*) telling about the subject

Line 4: four nouns (the first two related to the subject and the last two related to the opposite)

Line 5: three participles telling about the opposite

Line 6: two adjectives describing the opposite

Line 7: one noun that is the opposite of the subject

A third-grade class wrote this diamante poem about the stages of life:

> *Baby*
> *wrinkled tiny*
> *crying wetting sleeping*
> *rattles diapers money house*
> *caring working loving*
> *smart helpful*
> *Adult*

Notice that the students created a contrast between *baby,* the subject represented by the noun in the first line, and *adult,* the opposite in the last line. This contrast gives students the opportunity to play with words and apply their understanding of opposites. The third word in the fourth line, *money,* begins the transition from *baby* to its opposite, *adult.*

Free Verse

Free verse is unrhymed poetry, and rhythm is less important in free verse than in other types of poetry. Word choice and visual images take on greater importance in free verse. *Nathaniel Talking* (Greenfield, 1988) and *Neighborhood Odes* (Soto, 1992) are two collections of free verse. In *Nathaniel Talking,* Eloise Greenfield writes from the viewpoint of a young African-American child who has lost his mother but not his spirit. Most of the poems are free verse, but one is a rap and several others rhyme. Greenfield uses few capital letters or punctuation marks. In *Neighborhood Odes,* Gary Soto writes about his childhood as a Mexican-American child living in Fresno, California. Soto adds a few Spanish words to his poems to sharpen the pictures the poems paint of life in his neighborhood.

In free verse, children choose words to describe something and put them together to express a thought or tell a story, without concern for rhyme or other arrangements. The number of words per line and use of punctuation vary. In the following poem, an eighth grader poignantly describes "Loneliness" using only 15 well-chosen words.

> *A lifetime*
> *Of broken dreams*
> *And promises*
> *Lost love*
> *Hurt*
> *My heart*
> *Cries*
> *In silence*

Students can use several methods for writing free verse. They can select words and phrases from brainstormed lists and **clusters** to create the poem, or they can write a paragraph and then "unwrite" it to create the poem by deleting unnecessary words. They arrange the remaining words to look like a poem.

During a literature focus unit on MacLachlan's *Sarah, Plain and Tall* (1985), a third-grade class wrote this free-form poem after discussing the two kinds of dunes in the story:

> *Dunes of sand*
> *on the beach.*
> *Sarah walks on them*
> *and watches the ocean.*
> *Dunes of hay*
> *beside the barn.*
> *Papa makes them for Sarah*
> *because she misses Maine.*

A unique type of free verse is poems for two voices. These poems are written in two columns, side by side, and the columns are read together by two readers. The two best-known books of poems for two voices are Paul Fleischman's *I Am Phoenix* (1985), which is about birds, and the Newbery Award–winning *Joyful Noise* (1988), which is about insects.

A third-grade class wrote this poem for two voices about whales as part of their across-the-curriculum unit on the ocean:

Whales	*Whales*
dive deep	*dive deep*
into the ocean	
	then surface for air
breathing	
	through blowholes
always	*always*
swimming	*looking for food*
looking for food	*swimming*

whales	whales
mammals	
	look like fish
but they aren't	but they aren't
two groups	two groups
baleen whales	
	toothed whales
the humpback whale	
	a baleen whale
fast swimmer	fast swimmer
little beluga whale	
	a toothed whale
all white	
	very unusual
the blue whale	
	a baleen whale
the biggest	
	of all
big blue	big blue
narwhal	
	a toothed whale
that looks like	
	a unicorn
killer whale	
	a toothed whale
black and white	white and black
dangerous attacker	dangerous attacker
whales	whales

Another type of free verse is found poems. Students create found poems by culling words from other sources, such as newspaper articles, stories, and informational books. Found poems give students the opportunity to manipulate words and sentence structures they don't write themselves. A small group of third graders composed the following found poem, "This Is My Day," after reading *Sarah Morton's Day: A Day in the Life of a Pilgrim Girl* (Waters, 1989):

> Good day.
> I must get up and be about my chores.
> The fire is mine to tend.
> I lay the table.
> I muck the garden.
> I pound the spices.
> I draw vinegar to polish the brass.
> I practice my lessons.
> I feed the fire again.
> I milk the goats.
> I eat dinner.
> I say the verses I am learning.
> My father is pleased with my learning.

I fetch the water for tomorrow.
I bid my parents good night.
I say my prayers.
Fare thee well.
God be with thee.

To compose the found poem, the students collected their favorite words and sentences from the book and organized them sequentially to describe the pilgrim girl's day.

Other Poetic Forms

Students use a variety of other forms when they write poems, even though few adults use these forms. These forms provide a scaffold or skeleton for students' poems. After collecting words, images, and comparisons, students craft their poems, choosing words and arranging them to create a message. Meaning is always most important, and form follows the search for meaning. Poet Kenneth Koch (1970), working with students in the elementary grades, developed some simple formulas that make it easy for nearly every child to become a successful poet. These formulas call for students to begin every line the same way or to insert a particular kind of word in every line. The formulas use repetition, a stylistic device that is more effective for young poets than rhyme. Some forms may seem more like sentences than poems, but the dividing line between poetry and prose is a blurry one, and these poetry experiences help children move toward poetic expression.

1. *"I wish . . ." poems.* Children begin each line of their poems with the words "I wish" and complete the line with a wish (Koch, 1970). In this second-grade class collaboration poem, children simply listed their wishes:

Our Wishes

I wish I had all the money in the world.
I wish I was a star fallen down from Mars.
I wish I were a butterfly.
I wish I were a teddy bear.
I wish I had a cat.
I wish I were a pink rose.
I wish it wouldn't rain today.
I wish I didn't have to wash a dish.
I wish I had a flying carpet.
I wish I could go to Disney World.
I wish school was out.
I wish I could go outside and play.

After this experience, students choose one of their wishes and expand on the idea in another poem. Brandi expanded her wish this way:

I wish I were a teddy bear
Who sat on a beautiful bed
Who got a hug every night

By a little girl or boy
Maybe tonight I'll get my wish
And wake up on a little girl's bed
And then I'll be as happy as can be.

2. *Color poems.* Students begin each line of their poems with a color. They can repeat the same color in each line or choose a different color (Koch, 1970). In this example, a class of seventh graders writes about yellow:

Yellow is shiny galoshes
splashing through mud puddles.
Yellow is a street lamp
beaming through a dark, black night.
Yellow is the egg yolk
bubbling in a frying pan.
Yellow is the lemon cake
that makes you pucker your lips.
Yellow is the sunset
and the warm summer breeze.
Yellow is the tingling in your mouth
after a lemon drop melts.

Students can also write more complex poems by expanding each idea into a stanza, as this poem about black illustrates.

Black

Black is a deep hole
sitting in the ground
waiting for animals
that live inside.
Black is a beautiful horse
standing on a high hill
with the wind
swirling its mane.
Black is a winter night sky
without stars
to keep it
company.
Black is a panther
creeping around a jungle
searching for
its prey.

Hailstones and Halibut Bones (O'Neill, 1989) is another source of color poems; however, O'Neill uses rhyme as a poetic device, and it is important to emphasize that students' poems need not rhyme.

3. *Acrostic poems.* Students write acrostic poems by taking a word and writing it vertically. They write a word or phrase beginning with each letter to complete the poem. As part of literature focus units, students can write about a book title or a character's name. This acrostic poem about *Jumanji* (Van Allsburg, 1981) was written by a fourth grader:

> *J*ungle adventure game and
> f *U*n for a while.
> *M*onkeys ransacking kitchens
> *A*nd boa constrictors slithering past.
> *N*o way out until the game is done—
> *J*ust reach the city of Jumanji.
> *I* don't want to play!

4. *Five-senses poems.* Students write about a topic using each of the five senses. Sense poems are usually five lines long, with one line for each sense, but sometimes an extra line is added, as this poem written by a sixth grader demonstrates:

> *Being Heartbroken*
>
> *Sounds like thunder and lightning*
> *Looks like a carrot going through a blender*
> *Tastes like sour milk*
> *Feels like a splinter in your finger*
> *Smells like a dead fish*
> *It must be horrible!*

It is often helpful to have students develop a five-senses cluster and collect ideas for each sense. Students select from the cluster the most vivid or strongest idea for each sense to use in a line of the poem.

5. *"If I were . . ." poems.* Children write about how they would feel and what they would do if they were something else—a dinosaur, a hamburger, sunshine (Koch, 1970). They begin each poem with "If I were" and tell what it would be like to be that thing. In this example, seven-year-old Robbie writes about what he would do if he were a dinosaur:

> *If I were a Tyrannosaurus Rex*
> *I would terrorize other dinosaurs*
> *And eat them up for supper.*

In composing "If I were . . ." poems, students use personification, explore ideas and feelings, and consider the world from a different vantage point.

6. *Preposition poems.* Students begin each line of a preposition poem with a preposition, and a delightful poetic rewording of lines often results from the attempt. Seventh grader Mike wrote this preposition poem about a movie super-hero:

> *Superman*
>
> *Within the city*
> *In a phone booth*
> *Into his clothes*
> *Like a bird*

In the sky
Through the walls
Until the crime
Among us
is defeated!

It is helpful for children to brainstorm a list of prepositions to refer to when they write preposition poems. Students may find that they need to ignore the formula for a line or two to give the content of their poems top priority, or they may mistakenly begin a line with an infinitive (e.g., "to say") rather than a preposition. These forms provide a structure or skeleton for students' writing that should be adapted as necessary.

Why Do Teachers Need to Know About Poetic Forms?

When students in the elementary grades read and recite poetry, the emphasis is on introducing them to poetry so that they have a pleasurable experience. Students need to have fun as they do choral readings of poems, pick out favorite lines, and respond to poems. Teachers need to be aware of poetic forms so that they can point out the form when it is appropriate or provide information about a poetic form when students ask. For example, sometimes when students read free verse they say it isn't poetry because it doesn't rhyme. At this time, it's appropriate to point out that poetry doesn't have to rhyme and that this poem is a poem—that this type of poetry is called free verse. Teachers might also explain that in free verse, creating an image or projecting a voice is more important than the rhyme scheme. It is not appropriate for students to analyze the rhyme scheme or search out the meaning of the poem. Instead, children should focus on what the poem means to them. Teachers introduce poetic forms when students are writing poetry. When students use poetic formulas such as color poems, acrostics, and haiku they are often more successful than when they attempt to create rhyming verse, because the formulas provide a framework for students' writing.

Review

Three broad types of literature are stories, informational books, and poetry, and they are included in basal readers and published as trade books. Each type of text has a unique structure or organization. Story elements include plot, characters, setting, point of view, and theme. Informational books are organized into expository text structures, of which the five most common patterns are description, sequence, comparison, cause and effect, and problem and solution. The most common poetic forms for children are rhymed verse, narrative poems, haiku, and free verse. Teachers need to be aware of the structure of text so that they can help students become more successful readers and writers. Guidelines for effectively teaching students about the structure of text are summarized in the feature on page 342.

How Effective Teachers . . .

Teach the Structure of Text

✳ Effective Practices

1. Teachers point out differences among stories, informational books, and poems.
2. Teachers help students set aesthetic or efferent purposes for reading.
3. Teachers include all three types of literature—stories, informational books, and poems—in text sets.
4. Teachers choose high-quality literature because they understand that students' writing reflects what they are reading.
5. Teachers teach minilessons about story elements, expository text structures, and poetic forms.
6. Teachers have students examine story elements in stories they are reading as part of literature focus units.
7. Teachers have students examine expository text structure in informational books they are reading as part of thematic units.
8. Teachers have students make charts to emphasize the structure of texts while taking notes.
9. Teachers have students examine the patterns authors use to write poems and then write poems using the same patterns.
10. Teachers have students use their knowledge of text structure when writing stories, informational books, and poems.

✳ Ineffective Practices

1. Teachers call all texts "stories" and don't differentiate among the three types of literature.
2. Teachers don't teach students to set purposes for reading.
3. Teachers don't consider whether all three types of literature are included in text sets for students to read.
4. Teachers don't consider the impact of the quality of literature on students' reading and writing development.
5. Teachers focus on other aspects of reading instruction and rarely teach about text structure.
6. Teachers don't explain that authors use plot, setting, and other elements as they develop stories.
7. Teachers don't examine the structure of the text in materials students read.
8. Teachers have students complete worksheets instead of making structural charts and diagrams.
9. Teachers don't ask students to examine the organization of poems and rarely have them write any poems.
10. Teachers focus on other aspects of writing and do not ask students to organize their writing according to text structure.

References

Au, K. H. (1992). Constructing the theme of a story. *Language Arts, 69,* 106–111.

Bruner, J. (1986). *Actual minds, possible worlds.* Cambridge, MA: Harvard University Press.

De Ford, D. (1981). Literacy: Reading, writing, and other essentials. *Language Arts, 58,* 652–658.

Dressel, J. H. (1990). The effects of listening to and discussing different qualities of children's literature on the narrative writing of fifth graders. *Research in the Teaching of English, 24,* 397–414.

Eckhoff, B. (1983). How reading affects children's writing. *Language Arts, 60,* 607–616.

Flood, J., Lapp, D., & Farnan, N. (1986). A reading-writing procedure that teaches expository paragraph structure. *The Reading Teacher, 39,* 556–562.

Freedman, R. (1992). Fact or fiction? In E. B. Freeman & D. G. Person (Eds.), *Using nonfiction tradebooks in the elementary classroom: From ants to zeppelins* (pp. 2–10). Urbana, IL: National Council of Teachers of English.

Graves, D. H. (1992). *Explore poetry.* Portsmouth, NH: Heinemann.

Irwin, J. W. (1991). *Teaching reading comprehension processes* (2nd ed.). Boston: Allyn & Bacon.

Johnson, T. D., & Louis, D. R. (1987). *Literacy through literature.* Portsmouth, NH: Heinemann.

Koch, K. (1970). *Wishes, lies, and dreams.* New York: Vintage.

Langer, J. A. (1986). *Children reading and writing: Structures and strategies.* Norwood, NJ: Ablex.

Lapp, D., Flood, J., & Farnan, N. (1992). Basal readers and literature: A tight fit or a mismatch? In K. D. Wood & A. Moss (Eds.), *Exploring literature in the classroom: Contents and methods* (pp. 35–57). Norwood, MA: Christopher Gordon.

Larrick, N. (1991). *Let's do a poem! Introducing poetry to children.* New York: Delacorte.

Lehr, S. S. (1991). *The child's developing sense of theme: Responses to literature.* New York: Teachers College Press.

Lukens, R. J. (1999). *A critical handbook of children's literature* (6th ed.). New York: Longman.

McGee, L. M., & Richgels, D. J. (1985). Teaching expository text structures to elementary students. *The Reading Teacher, 38,* 739–745.

Meyer, B. J., & Freedle, R. O. (1984). Effects of discourse type on recall. *American Educational Research Journal, 21,* 121–143.

Niles, O. S. (1974). Organization perceived. In H. L. Herber (Ed.), *Perspectives in reading: Developing study skills in secondary schools.* Newark, DE: International Reading Association.

Ogle, D. M. (1986). K-W-L: A teaching model that develops active reading of expository text. *The Reading Teacher, 39,* 564–570.

Pappas, C. (1993). Is narrative "primary"? Some insights from kindergartners' pretend readings of stories and information books. *Journal of Reading Behavior, 25,* 97–129.

Piccolo, J. A. (1987). Expository text structures: Teaching and learning strategies. *The Reading Teacher, 40,* 838–847.

Raphael, T. E., Englert, C. S., & Kirschner, B. W. (1989). Acquisition of expository writing skills. In J. M. Mason (Ed.), *Reading and writing connections* (pp. 261–290). Boston: Allyn & Bacon.

Roop, P. (1992). Nonfiction books in the primary classroom: Soaring with the swans. In E. B. Freeman & D. G. Person (Eds.), *Using nonfiction tradebooks in the elementary classroom: From ants to zeppelins* (pp. 106–112). Urbana, IL: National Council of Teachers of English.

Rosenblatt, L. (1978). *The reader, the text, the poem: The transactional theory of the literary work.* Carbondale: Southern Illinois University Press.

Tiedt, I. (1970). Exploring poetry patterns. *Elementary English, 45,* 1082–1084.

Tompkins, G. E. (2000). *Teaching writing: Balancing process and product* (3rd ed.). Upper Saddle River, NJ: Merrill/Prentice Hall.

Vardell, S. (1991). A new "picture of the world": The NCTE Orbis Pictus Award for outstanding nonfiction for children. *Language Arts, 68,* 474–479.

Wells, G. (1986). *The meaning makers: Children learning language and using language to learn.* Portsmouth, NH: Heinemann.

Whitin, D. J., & Wilde, S. (1992). *Read any good math lately? Children's books for mathematical learning, K–6.* Portsmouth, NH: Heinemann.

Children's Book References

Aker, S. (1990). *What comes in 2's, 3's, and 4's?* New York: Simon & Schuster.

Ancona, G. (1992). *Man and mustang.* New York: Macmillan.

Arnold, C. (1993). *Dinosaurs all around: An artist's view of the prehistoric world.* New York: Clarion.

Atwood, S. (1971). *Haiku: The mood of the earth.* New York: Scribner.

Blume, J. (1972). *Tales of a fourth grade nothing.* New York: Dutton.

Calder, S. J. (1989). *If you were an ant.* Englewood Cliffs, NJ: Silver Books/Silver Burdett.

Carle, E. (1969). *The very hungry caterpillar.* New York: Philomel.

Carle, E. (1986). *The grouchy ladybug.* New York: Harper & Row.

Carle, E. (1990). *The very quiet cricket.* New York: Philomel.

Cole, J. (1996). *The magic school bus inside a beehive.* New York: Scholastic.

Cowcher, H. (1990). *Antarctica.* New York: Farrar, Straus & Giroux.

Day, A. (1985). *Good dog, Carl.* New York: Green Tiger Press.

Driver, R. (1994). *AnimaLimericks.* New York: Half Moon Books.

Feelings, M., & Feelings, T. (1971). *Moja means one: Swahili counting book.* New York: Dial.

Fleischman, P. (1985). *I am phoenix: Poems for two voices.* New York: Harper & Row.

Fleischman, P. (1988). *Joyful noise: Poems for two voices.* New York: Harper & Row.

Fowler, A. (1990). *It's a good thing there are insects.* Chicago: Childrens Press.

Freedman, R. (1987). *Lincoln: A photobiography.* New York: Clarion.

Fritz, J. (1976). *Will you sign here, John Hancock?* New York: Coward-McCann.

Fritz, J. (1989). *The great little Madison.* New York: Putnam.

Galdone, P. (1970). *The three little pigs.* New York: Seabury.

Gardiner, J. R. (1980). *Stone Fox.* New York: Harper & Row.

George, J. C. (1972). *Julie of the wolves.* New York: Harper & Row.

Gibbons, G. (1992). *Spiders.* New York: Holiday House.

Giff, P. R. (1984). *The beast in Ms. Rooney's room.* New York: Bantam.

Giff, P. R. (1984). *Fish face.* New York: Bantam.

Gollub, M. (1998). *Cool melons—turn to frogs! The life and poems of Issa.* New York: Lee & Low.

Greenfield, E. (1988). *Nathaniel talking.* New York: Black Butterfly Children's Books.

Guiberson, B. Z. (1991). *Cactus hotel.* New York: Henry Holt.

Harter, P. (1994). *Shadow play: Night haiku.* New York: Simon & Schuster.

Hoban, T. (1987). *26 letters and 99 cents.* New York: Greenwillow.

Howe, D., & Howe, J. (1979). *Bunnicula: A rabbit-tale of mystery.* New York: Atheneum.

Hunt, J. (1989). *Illuminations.* New York: Bradbury.

Hutchins, P. (1968). *Rosie's walk.* New York: Macmillan.

Hyman, T. S. (1977). *The sleeping beauty.* New York: Holiday House.

Kennedy, X. J. (1982). *Knock at a star: A child's introduction to poetry.* Boston: Little, Brown.

Knight, M. B. (1993). *Who belongs here? An American story.* Gardiner, ME: Tulbury House.

Lear, E. (1994). *There was an old man: A gallery of nonsense rhymes.* New York: Morrow.

L'Engle, M. (1962). *A wrinkle in time.* New York: Farrar, Straus & Giroux.

Lester, H. (1988). *Tacky the penguin.* Boston: Houghton Mifflin.

Levine, E. (1986). *. . . If you traveled west in a covered wagon.* New York: Scholastic.

Lobel, A. (1983). *Pigericks: A book of pig limericks.* New York: Harper & Row.

Longfellow, H. W. (1990). *Paul Revere's ride.* New York: Dutton.

Lowry, L. (1989). *Number the stars.* Boston: Houghton Mifflin.

Lowry, L. (1993). *The giver.* Boston: Houghton Mifflin.

Macaulay, D. (1977). *Castle.* Boston: Houghton Mifflin.

MacLachlan, P. (1985). *Sarah, plain and tall.* New York: Harper & Row.

Maestro, B. (1992). *How do apples grow?* New York: HarperCollins.

Martin, B., Jr. (1983). *Brown bear, brown bear, what do you see?* New York: Holt, Rinehart & Winston.

Martin, B., Jr., & Archambault, J. (1985). *The ghost-eye tree.* New York: Holt, Rinehart & Winston.

Mayer, M. (1987). *The ugly duckling.* New York: Macmillan.

McCloskey, R. (1969). *Make way for ducklings.* New York: Viking.

Millard, A. (1998). *A street through time.* New York: DK Publishing.

Noyes, A. (1983). *The highwayman.* New York: Lothrop, Lee & Shepard.

O'Dell, S. (1960). *Island of the blue dolphins.* Boston: Houghton Mifflin.

O'Neill, M. (1989). *Hailstones and halibut bones.* New York: Doubleday.

Pallotta, J. (1991). *The underwater alphabet book.* Watertown, MA: Charlesbridge.

Pallotta, J. (1992). *The icky bug counting book.* Watertown, MA: Charlesbridge.

Paterson, K. (1977). *Bridge to Terabithia.* New York: Crowell.

Paulsen, G. (1987). *Hatchet.* New York: Simon & Schuster.

Polacco, P. (1994). *Pink and Say.* New York: Putnam.

Potter, B. (1902). *The tale of Peter Rabbit.* New York: Warne.

Prelutsky, J. (1983). *The Random House book of poetry for children.* New York: Random House.

Prelutsky, J. (1985). *My parents think I'm sleeping.* New York: Greenwillow.

Rauzon, M. J. (1993). *Horns, antlers, fangs, and tusks.* New York: Lothrop, Lee & Shepard.

Rylant, C. (1992). *Best wishes.* Katonwah, NY: Richard C. Owen.

Schwartz, D. (1989). *If you made a million.* New York: Lothrop, Lee & Shepard.

Scieszka, J. (1989). *The true story of the three little pigs!* New York: Viking.

Scott, A. H. (1990). *One good horse: A cowpuncher's counting book.* New York: Greenwillow.

Showers, P. (1985). *What happens to a hamburger?* New York: Harper & Row.

Siebert, D. (1991). *Sierra.* New York: HarperCollins.

Simon, S. (1989). *Whales.* New York: Crowell.

Simon, S. (1993). *Mercury.* New York: Morrow.

Soto, G. (1992). *Neighborhood odes.* San Diego: Harcourt Brace Jovanovich.

Speare, E. G. (1958). *The witch of Blackbird Pond.* Boston: Houghton Mifflin.

Steele, P. (1998). *A street through time*. New York: King-fisher.

Steig, W. (1969). *Sylvester and the magic pebble*. New York: Simon & Schuster.

Steig, W. (1982). *Doctor De Soto*. New York: Farrar, Straus & Giroux.

Taylor, M. D. (1976). *Roll of thunder, hear my cry*. New York: Dial.

Van Allsburg, C. (1981). *Jumanji*. Boston: Houghton Mifflin.

Van Allsburg, C. (1986). *The stranger*. Boston: Houghton Mifflin.

Viorst, J. (1977). *Alexander and the terrible, horrible, no good, very bad day*. New York: Atheneum.

Waber, B. (1972). *Ira sleeps over*. Boston: Houghton Mifflin.

Waters, K. (1989). *Sarah Morton's day: A day in the life of a pilgrim girl*. New York: Scholastic.

White, E. B. (1952). *Charlotte's web*. New York: Harper & Row.

Wiesner, D. (1991). *Tuesday*. New York: Clarion.

Williams, V. B. (1982). *A chair for my mother*. New York: Mulberry.

Winter, J. (1988). *Follow the drinking gourd*. New York: Knopf.

Zemach, M. (1983). *The little red hen*. New York: Farrar, Straus & Giroux.

Part IV
How Do Teachers Organize Literacy Instruction?

Mrs. Donnelly conducts a guided reading group with a small number of third graders. From their basal readers, they are reading Judi Barrett's *Cloudy with a Chance of Meatballs,* a fantasy about a town where food falls like rain, which is also available as a trade book. Students are grouped according to reading level and meet with Mrs. Donnelly to read and discuss the story.

Jason adds a word to the word wall. Important words from the story and other weather-related words are highlighted on the word wall.

Cloudy With A Chance of Meatballs

Mrs. Donnelly collects books for a text set on weather. Stories, informational books, and poems are included.

Mrs. Donnelly does a book talk to introduce students to the books displayed in the reading area.

Students use the writing process to write wacky weather reports that they will present to their classmates and parents. Mrs. Donnelly meets with Charlie to edit his weather report.

Students present their completed wacky weather reports to classmates and parents. One student videotapes the weather reports to replay later.

Mrs. Donnelly teaches a minilesson on absurdity and students brainstorm a list of other fantasies, such as *Jumanji* by Chris Van Allsburg, that include absurd elements.

Students make posters to recommend favorite books from the weather text set that they have read during reading workshop.

Mrs. Donnelly uses a combination of instructional approaches in teaching reading and writing. Students read basal reader selections using guided reading groups, read independently during reading workshop, and write weather reports during writing workshop. The approaches vary according to her goals and the books students are reading.

Chapter 10

Literature Focus Units

— Chapter Questions —

*Which books should students
read during literature focus units?*

*What components should be
included in a literature focus unit?*

*What kinds of units can
teachers develop?*

Mrs. Dillon's Students Read "The Three Little Pigs"

"Who knows the story of 'The Three Little Pigs'?" Mrs. Dillon asks her second-grade class as she holds up a double-sided doll with the faces of two of the pigs on one side and the face of the third pig and a wolf on the other side. The students talk about pigs who build houses of straw, brick, and "something else that isn't very good." They remember the nasty wolf who blows down the houses not made of bricks. Mrs. Dillon tells the students that "The Three Little Pigs" is a folktale and that most folktales have threes in them. "Sometimes there are three characters, " she says, "there might be three events, a character might have three objects, or a character does something three times." Then she asks her students to listen for threes as she reads aloud James Marshall's *The Three Little Pigs* (1989).

After she finishes reading, students move into a circle to participate in a **grand conversation** (see the Compendium for more information about this and all other highlighted terms in this chapter) about the book. Maria begins: "That wolf deserved to die. I'm glad the third pig cooked him up and ate him up." Angela says, "The first little pig and the second little pig were pretty dumb. Their houses weren't very strong." Several children agree that the third little pig was the smart one. Jim remembers that the second building material was sticks, and several children identify threes in the story: three pigs, three houses, three visits by the wolf, three tricks planned by the wolf and foiled by the third little pig.

Then Mrs. Dillon passes out paperback copies of *The Three Little Pigs* and invites the students to reread the story with partners. Afterwards, students suggest words for the class **word wall.** Their completed list includes these words:

old sow	seek their fortune	straw
house	mind your own business	wolf
lean	my chinny chin chin	annoyed
huff and puff	gobbled up	sticks
blew–blue	capital idea	bricks
sturdy	nice and solid	still hungry
loitering around	blue in the face	dazzling smile
displeasure	scrumptious turnips	splendid
shimmied	empty butter churn	frightened
mean	iron pot	

Mrs. Dillon's second graders spend two weeks reading and comparing versions of the familiar folktale "The Three Little Pigs." She has 15 paperback copies of James Marshall's *The Three Little Pigs,* as well as one or two copies of eight other versions of the folktale. She also has many other stories and informational books about pigs that students can read

Figure 10–1 Trade books used in Mrs. Dillon's literature focus unit

Versions of "The Three Little Pigs"

Bishop, G. (1989). *The three little pigs.* New York: Scholastic.

Galdone, P. (1970). *The three little pigs.* New York: Seabury.

Hooks, W. H. (1989). *The three little pigs and the fox.* New York: Macmillan.

Lowell, S. (1992). *The three little javelinas.* Flagstaff, AZ: Northland.

Marshall, J. (1989). *The three little pigs.* New York: Dial.

Scieszka, J. (1989). *The true story of the three little pigs!* New York: Viking.

Trivizas, E. (1993). *The three little wolves and the big bad pig.* New York: McElderry Books.

Zemach, M. (1988). *The three little pigs.* New York: Farrar, Straus & Giroux.

Other Stories and Informational Books About Pigs

Axelrod, A. (1994). *Pigs will be pigs.* New York: Four Winds.

Carlson, N. (1988). *I like me!* New York: Viking.

Dubanevich, A. (1983). *Pigs in hiding.* New York: Scholastic.

Galdone, P. (1981). *The amazing pig.* New York: Clarion.

Geisert, A. (1992). *Pigs from 1 to 10.* Boston: Houghton Mifflin.

Geisert, A. (1993). *Oink oink.* Boston: Houghton Mifflin.

Grossman, P. (1989). *Tommy at the grocery store.* New York: Harper & Row.

Heller, N. (1994). *Woody.* New York: Greenwillow.

Hutchins, P. (1994). *Little pink pig.* New York: Greenwillow.

Johnson, A. (1993). *Julius.* New York: Orchard.

Kasza, K. (1988). *The pigs' picnic.* New York: Scribner.

Keller, H. (1994). *Geraldine's baby brother.* New York: Greenwillow.

Kimmel, E. (1992). *The old woman and her pig.* New York: Holiday.

King-Smith, D. (1993). *All pigs are beautiful.* New York: Candlewick.

Ling, B. (1993). *Pig.* London: Dorling Kindersley.

Lobel, A. (1969). *Small pig.* New York: Harper & Row.

McPhail, D. (1993). *Pigs aplenty, pigs galore!* New York: Dutton.

Rayner, M. (1977). *Garth pig and the ice cream lady.* New York: Atheneum.

Rayner, M. (1993). *Garth pig steals the show.* New York: Dutton.

Rayner, M. (1994). *10 pink piglets: Garth pig's wall song.* New York: Dutton.

Steig, W. (1994). *Zeke Pippin.* New York: HarperCollins.

Van Leeuwen, H. (1979). *Tales of Oliver pig.* New York: Dial.

Wilhelm, H. (1988). *Oh, what a mess.* New York: Crown.

independently. These books are listed in Figure 10–1. Mrs. Dillon has arranged the books on one shelf of the classroom library, and she introduces the books to her students during a **book talk.**

During the first week of the two-week unit, Mrs. Dillon's students read the story several times—they read the story independently to themselves, the class reads the book together as a **readers theatre,** and each child reads a favorite excerpt to Mrs. Dillon. They reread the story for other purposes, too. They sequence the events using **story boards** and choose a favorite quote to use in making a **quilt** of the story. Mrs. Dillon teaches a **minilesson** on quotation marks, and then students make a booklet with dialogue among the characters in the story.

Mrs. Dillon teaches a series of minilessons on the /k/ sound at the end of short-vowel words such as *brick* or *stick* and at the end of long-vowel words such as *make* or *steak*. She chooses this minilesson because the words *brick* and *stick* are used in this story. During the minilesson, students hunt for words ending with /k/, and Mrs. Dillon writes them on the chalkboard. Then the students sort the words into two columns: words spelled with *ck* and words spelled with *k*. Together the students deduce that most short-vowel words are spelled *ck* (exceptions include *pink* and *thank*), while long-vowel words are spelled *k*. In a follow-up lesson, students practice spelling *ck* and *k* words using erasable magic slates.

Students continue to add important words to the word wall. One day they divide into four groups: first little pig, second little pig, third little pig, and big bad wolf. Each group makes a vocabulary mobile. Students draw and color a picture of the character and then add at least five words and phrases from the word wall related to that character on word cards hanging below their picture. The second little pig mobile, for example, included these words and phrases: "sticks," "build a house," "not by the hair of my chinny chin chin," "ha ha ha," and "gobbled up."

Mrs. Dillon reads a different version of "The Three Little Pigs" each day, and students compare the versions. They add information to a comparison chart they are compiling, as shown in Figure 10–2. While several of the versions are very similar, others are unique. In Hooks's Appalachian version (1989), the third little pig, Hamlet, is a girl, and she saves her brothers. In this version Hamlet builds the only house using rocks. In Lowell's southwestern version (1992), the pigs are javelinas and are pursued by a coyote, not a wolf. This story also ends happily as all three javelina brothers live together in a strong adobe house.

During the second week, students read a variety of pig books independently and work on projects that extend their interpretation of "The Three Little Pigs" stories. Some of the projects they chose are:

❧ making puppets of pigs and wolf
❧ creating a **choral reading** from the story
❧ writing several poems
❧ drawing a **story map**
❧ making a Venn diagram comparing pigs and wolves
❧ dramatizing the story
❧ writing and mailing a letter to the author
❧ making houses out of straw, sticks, and bricks
❧ writing a retelling of the story
❧ writing an "All About . . ." book about pigs

Students work on projects individually or in pairs or small groups, and then they share their projects during the last two days of the unit.

Mrs. Dillon teaches a series of minilessons this week on using *y* at the end of words. She begins the lesson by writing *by the hair of my chinny chin chin* on the chalkboard and then underlines the words *by, my,* and *chinny*. Students read the words and note that *y* in the first two words is pronounced as a long *i*, but in the third

Figure 10–2 A chart comparing versions of "The Three Little Pigs"

Book	Who Are the Three Main Characters?	Who Is the Bad Character?	What Kinds of Houses?	What Happens to the Three Characters?	What Happens to the Bad Character?
The Three Little Pigs James Marshall	3 boy pigs	wolf	1. straw 2. sticks 3. bricks	#1 eaten #2 eaten #3 lives happily ever after	He is cooked and eaten.
The Three Little Pigs Gavin Bishop	3 boy pigs	cool fox	1. straw 2. sticks 3. bricks	#1 eaten #2 eaten #3 lives happily	He is cooked and eaten.
The Three Little Pigs Paul Galdone	3 boy pigs	wolf	1. straw 2. sticks 3. bricks	#1 eaten #2 eaten #3 lives happily	He is cooked and eaten.
The Three Little Javelinas Susan Lowell	2 boy javelinas 1 girl javelina	coyote	1. tumbleweeds 2. cactus 3. adobe	#1 escapes #2 escapes #3 lives safely with her brothers	He is burned up and becomes smoke.
The Three Little Pigs and the Fox William Hooks	3 pigs: Rooter—boy Oinky—boy Hamlet—girl	fox	Only Hamlet builds a rock house.	#1 caught by fox #2 caught by fox #3 catches fox and saves her brothers	He is stuffed in a churn and floats down the river.
The Three Little Wolves and the Big Bad Pig Eugene Trivizas	3 boy wolves: #1 black #2 gray #3 white	big, bad pig	1. brick 2. concrete 3. armor-plated 4. flowers	#1 escaped #2 escaped #3 escaped to live together	He becomes a good pig and lives with the wolves.
The Three Little Pigs Margot Zemach	3 boy pigs	wolf	1. straw 2. sticks 3. bricks	#1 eaten #2 eaten #3 lives happily	He is cooked and eaten.
The True Story of the Three Little Pigs! Jon Scieszka	The wolf is the good character. He was framed.	the 3 pigs	1. straw 2. sticks 3. bricks	#1 eaten #2 eaten #3 lives happily	The "good" wolf goes to jail.

Figure 10–3 Mrs. Dillon's two-week lesson plan for "The Three Little Pigs"

	MONDAY	TUESDAY	WEDNESDAY	THURSDAY	FRIDAY
WEEK 1	Introduce "The Three Little Pigs" and 3's in fairy tales	Sequence the story boards	ML: *ck* and *k* spelling at the end of words	Do word sorts in small groups	Spell words using magic slates
	Read aloud James Marshall's *The Three Little Pigs*	ML: Comparing versions of stories	Make vocabulary mobiles in 4 groups	Reread story using readers theatre	Make quilt
	Have a grand conversation about the book; Begin word wall	Begin comparison chart	ML: Dialogue and how to use " "	Make dialogue books with quotes from each character	Also finish dialogue book
	Reread the book with partners; Introduce text set	Read Bishop's version and add information to the chart	Read Galdone's version and add to chart	Read Lowell's version and add to chart	Read Hooks's version and add to chart
WEEK 2	Independent reading of pig books				
	Work on projects			Share projects	Share projects
	ML: *y* at the end of words	ML: Focus on 1-syllable words	ML: Focus on 2-syllable words		
	Read Trivizas's version and add to chart	Read Zemach's version and add to chart	Read Scieszka's version and finish chart	Vote on favorite version and compile graph	Write letters to Mrs. Dillon. Collect materials and assignment checklists.

word it's pronounced as a long *e*. Then she asks students to think of ten other words ending in *y*. She writes students' words on a chart and then divides them into two groups according to the sound the *y* represents:

try	sunny
by	baby
sky	hairy
my	Jimmy
why	bunny

Then Mrs. Dillon spends several days teaching follow-up minilessons on using *y* at the end of words. Students also practice sorting the words (see **word sorts**) and writing and spelling the words using magic slates.

Mrs. Dillon continues to read different versions of "The Three Little Pigs" to the class this week, and they complete the chart shown in Figure 10–2. After reading all of the versions, students vote on their favorite and create a graph to show the results. Not surprisingly, Scieszka's *The True Story of the Three Little Pigs!* (1989), a story told from the wolf's viewpoint, is the class's favorite. The style of this spirited version and its surrealistic illustrations make it popular with students.

Mrs. Dillon's language arts period lasts approximately two hours each morning, and for this period she plans a variety of activities that are appropriate to the students' attention span and literacy abilities. The lesson plan shown in Figure 10–3 shows how Mrs. Dillon taught this two-week literature focus unit on "The Three Little Pigs" stories.

L iterature focus units are one of the four ways that teachers organize for literacy instruction. Teachers choose a trade book or basal reader selection and build a literature focus unit around the featured selection, as Mrs. Dillon did in the vignette. Her featured book was James Marshall's *The Three Little Pigs* (1989), and she developed a two-week unit around that book. Literature focus units include these components:

- a featured selection
- a text set of related reading materials
- multiple opportunities to read and reread the featured book as well as the text set
- ways to comprehend and respond to the featured book
- vocabulary activities
- minilessons on strategies, skills, and procedures
- projects in which students apply what they have learned

Literature focus units include activities incorporating all five steps of the reading process. Teachers involve students in prereading activities as they build background experiences and activate students' prior knowledge. Next, students read the featured book and respond to it in grand conversations and entries in **reading logs.** Students participate in exploring activities as they learn vocabulary and participate in minilessons. Last, students apply their learning as they create projects and share them with their classmates at the end of the unit. Through these activities, students become a community of readers.

CHOOSING LITERATURE FOR UNITS

Teachers choose high-quality trade books as the featured selections for literature focus units. Sometimes the books have been identified as *core* books that must be taught at their grade level, or teachers choose other high-quality books that are appropriate for students at their grade level. Teachers consider both the interest level and the reading level of the books they choose for literature focus units. The books must be interesting to children, and they must be at the appropriate reading level.

In the vignette, Mrs. Dillon was familiar with the wide range of books available for children today. Because she was knowledgeable about literature, she was able to make wise choices and connect language arts and literature. She chose one version of "The Three Little Pigs" as her main selection. Beginning with multiple copies of that book, she added other versions of the folktale and other books about pigs to create a text set.

Teachers need to consider the types of books they choose and the impact of their choices on their students. Researchers who have examined teachers' choices have found that their choices suggest an unconscious gender or racial bias because few books that are chosen feature the experiences of females or of ethnic minorities, and even fewer were written by people from these groups (Jipson & Paley, 1991; Shannon, 1986; Traxel, 1983). These researchers call this pattern the "selective tradition," and they worry about this practice because books reflect and convey sociocultural values, beliefs, and attitudes to readers. It is important that teachers be aware of the ideas conveyed by their selection patterns and become more reflective about the books they choose for classroom use.

The Best of the Best

Teachers who use literature as the basis for their reading programs must be knowledgeable about children's literature. The first step in becoming knowledgeable is to read many of the stories, informational books, and books of poetry available for children today. Many of the stories in basal readers today are also available as trade books or are excerpted from chapter books. Teachers need to locate the complete versions of basal reader selections to share with their students. Children's librarians and the salespeople in children's bookstores are very helpful and willing to suggest books for teachers.

As they read and make selections for classroom use, teachers should keep in mind guidelines for selecting literature. The most important guideline is that teachers should choose books that they like themselves. Teachers are rarely, if ever, successful in teaching books they don't like. The message that they don't like the book comes across loud and clear, even when teachers try to hide their feelings. Other guidelines for choosing stories, informational books, and poems and books of poetry are presented in Figure 10–4. The literature selections that teachers use as featured selections for literature focus units should embody these qualities.

Each year a number of books written for children are recognized for excellence and receive awards. The two best-known awards are the Caldecott Medal for excellence in illustration and the Newbery Medal for excellence in writing. Lists of the

www.chebucto.ns.ca

Electronic Resources for Youth Services: Book Reviews. Links to more than a dozen websites that review children's books.

www.ala.org

Caldecott and Newbery Medal Books. Lists of award-winning books available online.

Figure 10–4 Guidelines for selecting books

Adapted from Huck, Hepler, and Hickman, 1987; Norton, 1999;
Sutherland and Arbuthnot, 1986; and Vardell, 1991.

Stories

- Is the book a good story?
- Is the plot original and believable?
- Are the characters real and believable?
- Do the characters grow and change in the story?
- Does the author avoid stereotyping?
- Does the story move beyond the setting and have universal implications?
- Is the theme worthwhile?
- Are the style of writing and use of language appropriate?
- Does the book exemplify the characteristics of a genre?
- How does the book compare with others on the same subject or in the same genre?

Informational Books

- Does the book stimulate children's curiosity and wonder?
- Is the information accurate, complete, and up to date?
- Does the author use facts to support generalizations?
- Is the information presented without anthropomorphism (assigning human characteristics and feelings to animals, plants, or objects)?
- Are there any racial, cultural, or sexual stereotypes?
- Is the organization clear and logical?
- Is vocabulary related to the subject introduced in the text?
- Do illustrations (including photographs and charts) complement and clarify the text?
- Does the author use a lively and stimulating writing style?
- Are reference aids, such as a table of contents, a glossary, and an index, included?

Poems and Books of Poetry

- Is the poem lively, with exciting meters and rhythms?
- Does the poem emphasize the sounds of language and encourage wordplay?
- Does the poem encourage children to see or hear the world in a new way?
- Does the poem allow children to feel emotions?
- Does the poem create an image that appeals to a child's imagination?
- Is the poem good enough for children to want to hear it again and again?
- Is the cover of the book appealing to children?
- Do poems in the book meet the criteria listed above?
- Are the poems arranged on the page so as to not overwhelm children?
- Do the illustrations clarify and extend the image the poem creates, or do they merely distract the reader?

These students made cubes after reading E. B. White's Charlotte s Web, *one of the "best of the best" books.*

Caldecott and Newbery Medal and Honor Books are presented in the Appendix. Teachers should be familiar with many of these award-winning books and consider selecting one or more of them to use in their classrooms as featured selections in literature focus units.

Multicultural Literature

Multicultural literature is "literature that represents any distinct cultural group through accurate portrayal and rich detail" (Yokota, 1993, p. 157); it has generally been described as stories and books by and about people of color. Stories such as Faith Ringgold's *Tar Beach* (1991), about how an African-American child spends a hot summer evening on the roof of her New York City apartment house, and Gary Soto's *Too Many Tamales* (1993), about a Mexican-American child who loses her mother's diamond ring in a batch of tamales she is making, provide glimpses of contemporary life in two cultural groups. Other books tell the history of various cultural and ethnic groups. *So Far From the Sea* (Bunting, 1998), for instance, tells how Japanese Americans were interned in desolate camps during World War II, and *Anthony Burns: The Defeat and Triumph of a Fugitive Slave* (Hamilton, 1988) describes how slaves risked their lives to be free.

For this discussion of multicultural literature, the literature about American cultural groups has been divided into five main groups: African Americans, Asian Americans, Hispanic Americans, Native Americans, and other American groups. These umbrella labels can be deceiving, however, as there are substantial differences among the cultures within a category. For example, there are no composite Native Americans;

www.falcon.jum.edu

🕸 *Multicultural Resources for Children.*
Articles about using multicultural literature in the classroom and extensive lists of multicultural books.

www.ncrel.org

Multicultural Children's Literature. Reviews of multicultural books for children, including African-American, Asian-American, Hispanic-American, and Native American titles.

instead, Eskimos and the more than 100 Native American tribes in North America are grouped together under the Native American umbrella label. Books written for children about each of these cultures are presented in Figure 10–5. For an annotated listing of more than 300 multicultural books, see *Kaleidoscope: A Multicultural Booklist for Grades K–8* (Bishop, 1994).

1. *African Americans.* More books are available today about African Americans than about other cultural groups. Some books, such as *Follow the Drinking Gourd* (Winter, 1988), about the Underground Railroad, and *Bud, Not Buddy* (Curtis, 1999), about the harsh realities of life during the Great Depression, document events in the history of African Americans, and other books focus on contemporary events, such as *Ben's Trumpet* (Isadora, 1979), about a boy who wants to become a jazz musician.

2. *Asian Americans.* Books about Asian Americans in Figure 10–5 deal with specific Asian-American groups, not in generalities. The characters in the books go beyond common stereotypes and correct historical errors and omissions. Many of the books have been written by Asian Americans and are about their own assimilation experiences or remembrances of growing up in the United States. For example, *Angel Child, Dragon Child* (Surat, 1983) is the story of a Vietnamese-American child who adjusts to life in the United States.

3. *Hispanic Americans.* Few Hispanic-American writers are writing literature for children, and fewer books about Hispanic Americans are available than for other cultural groups, despite the fact that Hispanic Americans are one of the largest cultural groups in the United States. Two authors who are making a significant contribution are Nicholasa Mohr, who writes about life in the Puerto Rican–American community in New York, and Gary Soto, who writes about the lives of Mexican Americans in California. Both writers bring firsthand knowledge of life in a barrio (a Spanish-speaking neighborhood in the United States) to make their writing authentic (Soto, 1992; Zarnowski, 1991). Books by these two authors are included in Figure 10–5.

www.falcon.jmu.edu

Gary Soto: A Teacher Resource File. A biography, lesson plans, and links to related sites.

4. *Native Americans.* Many books are available about Native Americans, but few have been written by Native American authors. Most books about Native Americans are retellings of traditional folktales, myths, and legends, such as *The Legend of the Indian Paintbrush* (de Paola, 1988) and *Iktomi and the Boulder* (Goble, 1988). A number of biographies about Native American chiefs are also available, and other books describe Native American rituals and ceremonies, such as *Totem Pole* (Hoyt-Goldsmith, 1990), in which a contemporary Native American boy describes how his father carves a totem pole.

5. *Other American groups.* Other distinct regional and religious groups in the United States include Jewish, Amish, Cajun, and Appalachian cultures. As the majority culture, European Americans are sometimes ignored in discussions of cultural groups, but to ignore them denies the distinct cultures of many Americans (Yokota, 1993). Within the European-American umbrella category are a variety of groups, including German Americans, Italian Americans, Swedish Americans, and Russian Americans. Some books describing other American regional and religious groups are also included in Figure 10–5.

Educators recommend selecting multicultural literature that is "culturally conscious" (Sims, 1982)—that is to say, literature that accurately reflects a group's culture, language, history, and values without perpetuating stereotypes. Such literature

Figure 10–5 Multicultural books

Primary Grades

Aliki. (1976). *Corn is maize: The gift of the Indians.* New York: Crowell. (Native American)

Armstrong, J. (1993). *Cleversticks.* New York: Crown. (Asian American)

Cazet, D. (1993). *Born in the gravy.* New York: Orchard. (Hispanic)

Crews, D. (1991). *Bigmama's.* New York: Greenwillow. (African American)

de Paola, T. (1983). *The legend of the bluebonnet.* New York: Putnam. (Native American)

Dooley, N. (1991). *Everybody cooks rice.* Minneapolis: Carolrhoda. (all)

Dorros, A. (1991). *Abuela.* New York: Dutton. (Hispanic)

Garza, C. L. (1990). *Family pictures.* San Francisco: Children's Book Press. (Hispanic)

Greenfield, E. (1991). *Night on Neighborhood Street.* New York: Dial. (African American)

Hoffman, M. (1991). *Amazing Grace.* New York: Dial. (African American)

Martin, B., & Archambault, J. (1987). *Knots on a counting rope.* New York: Holt, Rinehart & Winston. (Native American)

Ringgold, F. (1991). *Tar beach.* New York: Crown. (African American)

Soto, G. (1993). *Too many tamales.* New York: Putnam. (Hispanic)

Stolz, M. (1988). *Storm in the night.* New York: HarperCollins. (African American)

Towle, W. (1993). *The real McCoy: The life of an African-American inventor.* New York: Scholastic. (African American)

Waters, K. (1990). *Lion dancer: Ernie Wan's Chinese New Year.* New York: Scholastic. (Asian American)

Middle Grades

Ancona, G. (1993). *Powwow.* Orlando: Harcourt Brace. (Native American)

Anzaldua, G. (1993). *Friends from the other side/Amigos del otro lado.* San Francisco: Children's Book Press. (Hispanic)

Bunting, E. (1998). *So far from the sea.* New York: Clarion. (Asian American)

Golenbock, P. (1990). *Teammates.* San Diego: Harcourt Brace Jovanovich. (African American)

Hamilton, V. (1985). *The people could fly: American Black folktales.* New York: Knopf. (African American)

Hewett, J. (1990). *Hector lives in the United States now: The story of a Mexican-American child.* New York: Lippincott. (Hispanic)

Jones, H. (1993). *The trees standing shining: Poetry of the North American Indians.* New York: Dial. (Native American)

Keegan, M. (1991). *Pueblo boy: Growing up in two worlds.* New York: Cobblehill. (Native American)

Lord, B. B. (1984). *In the year of the boar and Jackie Robinson.* New York: HarperCollins. (Asian American)

Mathis, S. B. (1975). *The hundred penny box.* New York: Viking. (African American)

Mead, A. (1995). *Junebug.* New York: Farrar, Straus & Giroux. (African American)

Mochizuki, K. (1993). *Baseball saved us.* New York: Lee & Low Books. (Asian American)

Mohr, N. (1979). *Felita.* New York: Dial. (Hispanic)

Soto, G. (1992). *The skirt.* New York: Delacorte. (Hispanic)

Speare, E. G. (1983). *The sign of the beaver.* Boston: Houghton Mifflin. (Native American)

Whelan, G. (1992). *Goodbye, Vietnam.* New York: Knopf. (Asian American)

Winter, J. (1988). *Follow the drinking gourd.* New York: Knopf. (African American)

Upper Grades

Armstrong, W. H. (1969). *Sounder.* New York: Harper & Row. (African American)

Cisneros, S. (1983). *The house on Mango Street.* New York: Vintage Books. (Hispanic)

Curtis, C. P. (1999). *Bud, not Buddy.* New York: Delacorte. (African American)

Denenberg, B. (1999). *The journal of Ben Uchida.* New York: Scholastic (Asian American)

George, J. C. (1972). *Julie of the wolves.* New York: Harper & Row. (Native American)

Hamilton, V. (1974). *M. C. Higgins, the great.* New York: Macmillan. (African American)

Levne, E. (1993). *Freedom's children.* New York: Putnam. (African American)

Mazer, A. (Ed.). (1993). *America street: A multicultural anthology of stories.* New York: Persea Books. (all)

Meltzer, M. (1982). *The Hispanic Americans.* New York: Crowell. (Hispanic)

Mohr, N. (1988). *In Nueva York.* Houston: Arte Publico. (Hispanic)

Myers, W. D. (1988). *Scorpions.* New York: HarperCollins. (African American)

Slote, A. (1991). *Finding Buck McHenry.* New York: HarperCollins. (African American)

Soto, G. (1992). *Neighborhood odes.* Orlando: Harcourt Brace. (Hispanic)

Uchida, Y. (1971). *Journey to Topaz.* Berkeley, CA: Creative Arts. (Asian American)

Yep, L. (1975). *Dragonwings.* New York: HarperCollins. (Asian American)

often deals with issues of prejudice, discrimination, and human dignity. According to Yokota (1993), these books should be rich in cultural details, use authentic dialogue, and present cultural issues in enough depth that readers can think and talk about them. Inclusion of cultural group members should be purposeful. They should be distinct individuals whose lives are rooted in the culture; they should never be included simply to fulfill a quota.

Multicultural literature must meet the criteria for good literature as well as for cultural consciousness. One example is *The Watsons Go to Birmingham—1963* (Curtis, 1995), an award-winning story about an African-American family living in Flint, Michigan, and the harsh realities of racial discrimination that the family encounters during a trip to Birmingham, Alabama, during the hate-filled summer of 1963. This well-written story is both historically and culturally accurate (Yokota, 1993).

www.eduplace.com

The Role of
Multicultural Literature.
Read about the importance
of cultural authenticity and
how multicultural books
promote understanding
among cultures.

Why Use Multicultural Literature? There are many reasons to use multicultural literature in elementary classrooms, whether students represent diverse cultures or not. First of all, multicultural literature is good literature. Students enjoy reading stories, informational books, and poems, and through reading they learn more about what it means to be human and that people of all cultural groups are real people with similar emotions, needs, and dreams (Bishop, 1992). Allen Say's *El Chino* (1990), for example, tells about a Chinese American who achieves his dream of becoming a great athlete, and the book provides a model for children and adults of all ethnic groups.

Second, through multicultural books, students learn about the wealth of diversity in the United States and develop sensitivity to and appreciation for people of other cultural groups (Walker-Dalhouse, 1992). *Teammates* (Golenbock, 1990), for example, tells about the friendship of baseball greats Jackie Robinson and Pee Wee Reese, and it teaches a valuable lesson in tolerance and respect. Multicultural literature also challenges racial and ethnic stereotypes by providing an inside view of a culture.

Third, students broaden their knowledge of geography and learn different views of history through multicultural literature. They read about the countries that minority groups left as they immigrated to America, and often students gain nonmainstream perspectives about historical events. For example, Yoshiko Uchida tells of her experiences in Japanese-American internment camps in the United States during World War II in *The Bracelet* (1993) and *Journey to Topaz* (1971). As they read and respond to multicultural books, students challenge traditional assumptions and gain a more balanced view of historical events and the contributions of people from various cultural groups. They learn that traditional historical accounts have emphasized the contributions of European Americans, particularly those made by men.

Fourth, multicultural literature raises issues of social injustice—prejudice, racism, discrimination, segregation, colonization, anti-Semitism, and genocide. Two books that describe the discrimination and mistreatment of Chinese Americans during the 1800s are *Chang's Paper Pony* (Coerr, 1988), a story set during the California gold rush, and *Ten Mile Day and the Building of the Transcontinental Railroad* (Fraser, 1993), a factual account of the race to complete the construction of the first railroad across North America.

Using multicultural literature has additional benefits for nonmainstream students. When students read books about their own cultural group, they develop pride in their cultural heritage and learn that their culture has made important contributions to the United States and the world (Harris, 1992a, 1992b). In addition, these students often become more interested in reading because they are able to better identify with the characters and with the events in those characters' lives.

Teachers' choices of books for instruction and for inclusion in the classroom library influence students in other ways, too. Students tend to choose familiar books and those that reflect their own cultures for reading workshop and other independent reading activities (Rudman, 1976). If teachers read aloud culturally conscious books, include them in literature focus units, and display them in the classroom library, these books become familiar and are more likely to be picked up and read independently by students.

FRAMEWORK FOR A LITERATURE FOCUS UNIT

Teachers plan literature focus units featuring popular and award-winning stories for children and adolescents. Some literature focus units feature a single book, either a picture book or a chapter book, while others feature a text set of books for a genre unit or an author study unit. Figure 10–6 presents a list of trade books, genres, and authors recommended for literature focus units for kindergarten through eighth grade. During these units, students move through the five steps of the reading process as they read and respond to stories and learn more about reading and writing.

Steps in Developing a Unit

Teachers develop a literature focus unit through a six-step series of activities, beginning with choosing the literature for the unit and setting goals, then identifying and scheduling activities, and finally deciding how to assess students' learning. Whether teachers are using trade books or basal reader selections, they develop a unit using these steps. An overview of the six steps in developing a literature focus unit is presented in Figure 10–7. Effective teachers do not simply follow directions in basal reader teacher's manuals and literature focus unit planning guides that are available for purchase in school supply stories. Teachers need to make the plans themselves because they are the ones most knowledgeable about their students, the literature books they have available, the time available for the unit, the skills and strategies they want to teach, and the activities they want to develop.

Usually literature focus units featuring a picture book are completed in one week, and units featuring a chapter book are completed in two, three, or four weeks. Genre and author units may last two, three, or four weeks. Rarely, if ever, do literature focus units continue for more than a month. When teachers drag out a unit for six weeks or longer they risk killing students' interest in that particular book or, worse yet, their love of literature or reading.

Step 1: Select the Literature. Teachers begin by selecting the reading material for the literature focus unit. The featured selection may be a story in a picture book format, a chapter book, or a story selected from a basal reading textbook. Teachers collect multiple copies of the book or books for the literature focus unit. When teachers use trade books, they have to collect class sets of the books for the unit. Many school districts have class sets of selected books available for loan to teachers; however, in other school districts, teachers have to request that administrators purchase multiple copies of books or buy them themselves through book clubs. When teachers use picture books, students can share books so only half as many books as students are needed.

www.carolhurst.com

Carol Hurst's Children's Literature Site. Book reviews, ideas for literature focus units, and professional references.

Figure 10–6   Topics for literature focus units

Books	Genres	Authors and Illustrators
Primary Grades (K–2)		
Allard, H. (1977). *Miss Nelson is missing!* Boston: Houghton Mifflin.	Number books Folk tales	Jan Brett Eric Carle
Blume, J. (1971). *Freckle juice.* New York: Bradbury Press.	Pattern stories Alphabet books	Donald Crews Tomie de Paola
Brett, J. (1989). *The mitten.* New York: Putnam.	Fairy tales	Dr. Suess
Carle, E. (1970). *The very hungry caterpillar.* New York: Viking.	Biographies	Lois Ehlert Mem Fox
Dorros, A. (1991). *Abuela.* New York: Dutton.		Tana Hoban
Galdone, P. (1972). *The three bears.* New York: Clarion.		Steven Kellogg James Marshall
Henkes, K. (1991). *Chrysanthemum.* New York: Greenwillow.		Bill Martin and John Archambault Patricia and Frederick McKissack
Hutchins, P. (1968). *Rosie's walk.* New York: Macmillan.		Bernard Most Bernard Waber
Lionni, L. (1969). *Alexander and the wind-up mouse.* New York: Knopf.		Audrey and Don Wood
Martin, B. Jr. (1983). *Brown bear, brown bear, what do you see?* New York: Holt, Rinehart & Winston.		
Most, B. (1978). *If the dinosaurs came back.* San Diego: Harcourt Brace.		
Noble, T. H. (1980). *The day Jimmy's boa ate the wash.* New York: Dial.		
Numeroff, L. (1985). *If you give a mouse a cookie.* New York: Harper & Row.		
Rylant, C. (1985). *The relatives came.* New York: Bradbury Press.		
Lester, H. (1988). *Tacky the penguin.* Boston: Houghton Mifflin.		
Middle Grades (3–5)		
Barrett, J. (1978). *Cloudy with a chance of meatballs.* New York: Macmillan.	Biography Fables	Byrd Baylor Eve Bunting
Blume, J. (1972). *Tales of a fourth grade nothing.* New York: Dutton.	Native American myths Poetry	Beverly Cleary Joanna Cole
Cleary, B. (1981). *Ramona Quimby, age 8.* New York: Morrow.	Tall tales Wordplay books	Paula Danziger Jean Fritz
Coerr, E. (1977). *Sadako and the thousand paper cranes.* New York: Putnam.		Paul Goble Eloise Greenfield
Cohen, B. (1983). *Molly's pilgrim.* New York: Morrow.		Patricia MacLachlan Ann Martin
Danziger, P. (1994). *Amber Brown is not a crayon.* New York: Putnam.		Patricia Polacco Jack Prelutsky
Gardiner, J. R. (1980). *Stone Fox.* New York: Harper & Row.		Cynthia Rylant William Steig
Lowry, L. (1989). *Number the stars.* Boston: Houghton Mifflin.		R. L. Stine Marvin Terban

Figure 10–6 continued

Books	Genres	Authors and Illustrators
Middle Grades (continued)		
MacLachlan, P. (1985). *Sarah, plain and tall.* New York: Harper & Row.		Chris Van Allsburg Jane Yolen
Mathis, S. B. (1975). *The hundred penny box.* New York: Viking.		
Naylor, P. R. (1991). *Shiloh.* New York: Macmillan.		
Paterson, K. (1977). *Bridge to Terabithia.* New York: Crowell.		
Ruckman, I. (1984). *Night of the twisters.* New York: HarperCollins.		
Speare, E. G. (1983). *The sign of the beaver.* Boston: Houghton Mifflin.		
Steig, W. (1969). *Sylvester and the magic pebble.* New York: Simon & Schuster.		
White, E. B. (1952). *Charlotte's web.* New York: Harper & Row.		
Upper Grades (6–8)		
Avi. (1991). *Nothing but the truth.* New York: Orchard.	Science fiction Myths Poetry	Lloyd Alexander Avi Karen Cushman
Babbitt, N. (1975). *Tuck everlasting.* New York: Farrar, Straus & Giroux.		Russell Freedman
Curtis, C. P. (1995). *The Watsons go to Birmingham—1963.* New York: Delacorte.		Virginia Hamilton David Macaulay
Cushman, K. (1994). *Catherine, called Birdy.* New York: HarperCollins.		Walter Dean Myers Scott O'Dell
Fox, L. (1984). *One-eyed cat.* New York: Bradbury Press.		Katherine Paterson Gary Paulsen
George, J. C. (1972). *Julie of the wolves.* New York: Harper & Row.		Richard Peck Jerry Spinelli
Hamilton, V. (1967). *Zeely.* New York: Macmillan.		Yoshiko Uchida Laurence Yep
Hinton, S. E. (1967). *The outsiders.* New York: Viking.		
Howe, D., & Howe, J. (1979). *Bunnicula: A rabbit-tale of mystery.* New York: Atheneum.		
Uchida, Y. (1971). *Journey to Topaz.* Berkeley, CA: Creative Arts.		
L'Engle, M. (1962). *A wrinkle in time.* New York: Farrar, Straus & Giroux.		
Lewis, C. S. (1950). *The lion, the witch and the wardrobe.* New York: Macmillan.		
Lowry, L. (1993). *The giver.* Boston: Houghton Mifflin.		
Paulsen, G. (1987). *Hatchet.* New York: Viking.		
Taylor, M. (1976). *Roll of thunder, hear my cry.* New York: Dial.		

Steps in developing a literature focus unit

Step 1: Select the Literature

☞ Identify the featured selection for the unit.
☞ Collect multiple copies of the featured selection for students to read individually, with partners, or in small groups.
☞ Collect related books for the text set, including stories, informational books, and poems.
☞ Identify supplemental materials, including puppets, information about the author and illustrator, and multimedia resources.

Step 2: Set Goals

☞ Identify four or five broad goals or learning outcomes for the unit.
☞ Choose skills and strategies to teach.
☞ Expect to refine these goals as the unit is developed.

Step 3: Develop a Unit Plan

☞ Read or reread the featured selection.
☞ Think about the focus for the unit and the goals or learning outcomes.
☞ Plan activities for each of the five steps of the reading process.

Step 4: Coordinate Grouping Patterns With Activities

☞ Decide how to incorporate whole-class, small-group, partner, and individual activities.
☞ Double-check that all four types of grouping are used during the unit.

Step 5: Create a Time Schedule

☞ Include activities representing all five steps of the reading process in the schedule for the literature focus unit.
☞ Incorporate minilessons to teach reading and writing procedures, concepts, skills, and strategies.
☞ Write weekly lesson plans.

Step 6: Manage Record Keeping

☞ Use unit folders in which students keep all assignments.
☞ Develop assignment checklists for students to use to keep track of their work during the unit.
☞ Monitor students' learning using observations, anecdotal notes, conferences, and work samples.

Once the book (or books) is selected, teachers collect additional related books for the text set. Books for the text set include:

☞ other versions of the same story

☞ other books written by the same author

☞ other books illustrated by the same artist

- books with the same theme
- books with similar geographic or historical settings
- books in the same genre
- informational books on a related topic
- books of poetry on a related topic

Teachers collect one or two copies of 10, 20, 30, or more books for the text set and add these to the classroom library during the focus unit. Books for the text set are placed on a special shelf or in a crate in the library center. At the beginning of the unit, teachers do a book talk to introduce the books in the text set, and then students read them during independent reading time.

Teachers also identify and collect supplemental materials related to the featured selection, including puppets, stuffed animals, and toys; charts and diagrams; **book boxes** of materials to use in introducing the book; and information about the author and illustrator. For many picture books, big book versions are also available, and these versions can be used in introducing the featured selection. Teachers also locate multi-media resources, including videotapes of the featured selection, multimedia materials to provide background knowledge on the topic, and videotapes and filmstrips about the author and illustrator.

Step 2: Set Goals. Teachers set goals for the literature focus unit. They decide what they want their students to learn during the unit, the skills and strategies they plan to teach, and the types of activities they want students to do. Teachers identify three or four broad goals for the unit and then refine these goals as they develop the unit.

Step 3: Develop a Unit Plan. Teachers read or reread the selected book or books and then think about the focus they will use for the unit. Sometimes teachers focus on

One way to make books more accessible is for students to read along as they listen to a tape of the book.

an element of story structure, the historical setting, wordplay, the author or genre, or a topic related to the book, such as weather or life in the desert. In the vignette at the beginning of this chapter, Mrs. Dillon selected Marshall's *The Three Little Pigs* and read it with her students to introduce a genre unit.

After determining the focus, teachers think about which activities they will use at each of the five steps of the reading process. For each step, teachers ask themselves these questions:

1. *Prereading*
   - ❧ What background knowledge do students need before reading?
   - ❧ What key concepts and vocabulary should I teach before reading?
   - ❧ How will I introduce the story and stimulate students' interest for reading?

2. *Reading*
   - ❧ How will students read this story?
   - ❧ What reading strategies will I model or ask students to use?
   - ❧ How can I make the story more accessible for less able readers?

3. *Responding*
   - ❧ Will students write in reading logs? How often?
   - ❧ Will students participate in grand conversations? How often?

4. *Exploring*
   - ❧ Which words will be added to the word wall?
   - ❧ Which vocabulary activities will be used?
   - ❧ Will students reread the story?
   - ❧ What skill and strategy minilessons will be taught?
   - ❧ What word-study or wordplay activities will be used?
   - ❧ How will books from the text set be used?
   - ❧ What writing, drama, and other reading activities will be used?
   - ❧ What can I share about the author, illustrator, or genre?

5. *Applying*
   - ❧ What projects might students choose to pursue?
   - ❧ How will books from the text set be used?
   - ❧ How will students share projects?

Teachers often jot notes on a chart divided into sections for each step. Then they use the ideas they have brainstormed as they plan the unit. Usually, not all of the brainstormed activities will be used in the literature focus unit, but teachers select the most important ones according to their focus and the available time. Teachers do not omit any of the reading process steps, however, in an attempt to make more time available for activities during any one step.

Step 4: Coordinate Grouping Patterns With Activities. Teachers think about how to incorporate whole-class, small-group, partner, and individual activities into their unit plans. It is important that students have opportunities to read and write independently as well as to work with small groups and to come together as a class. If the featured selection that students are reading will be read together as a class, then students need opportunities to reread it with a buddy or independently or to read related books independently. These grouping patterns should be alternated during various activities in the unit. Teachers often go back to their planning sheet and highlight activities with colored markers according to grouping patterns.

Step 5: Create a Time Schedule. Teachers create a time schedule that enables students to have sufficient time to move through the five steps of the reading process and to complete the activities planned for the literature focus unit. Literature-based reading programs require large blocks of time—at least two hours in length—in which students read, listen, talk, and write about the literature they are reading.

Teachers also plan minilessons to teach reading and writing procedures, concepts, skills, and strategies identified in their goals and those needed for students to complete the activities that teachers plan. Of course, teachers also present impromptu minilessons when students ask questions or need to know how to use a procedure, skill, or strategy, but many minilessons are planned. Sometimes teachers have a set time for minilessons in their weekly schedule, and sometimes teachers arrange their schedules so that they teach minilessons just before they introduce related activities or assignments.

Using this block of time, teachers write weekly lesson plans, as Mrs. Dillon did in Figure 10–3. Mrs. Dillon used a two-hour time block broken into four 30-minute segments. She listed the activities representing each of the five steps of the reading process during the two-week unit. The steps are not clearly separated and they do overlap, but prereading, reading, responding, exploring, and applying activities are included in the lesson plan.

Step 6: Manage Record Keeping. Teachers often distribute unit folders for students to use. They keep all work, reading logs, reading materials, and related materials in the folder. Then at the end of the unit, students turn in their completed folders for teachers to evaluate. Keeping all the materials together makes the unit easier for both students and teachers to manage.

Teachers also plan ways to document students' learning and assign grades. One type of record keeping is an assignment checklist. This sheet is developed with students and distributed at the beginning of the literature focus unit. Students keep track of their work during the unit and sometimes negotiate to change the sheet as the unit evolves. Students keep the lists in unit folders, and they mark off each item as it is completed. At the end of the unit, students turn in their completed assignment checklist and other completed work. A copy of an assignment checklist for Mrs. Dillon's literature unit on "The Three Little Pigs" is presented in Figure 10–8. While this list does not include every activity students were involved in, it does list the activities and other assignments Mrs. Dillon holds the students accountable for. Students complete the checklist on the left side of the sheet and add titles of books and other requested information.

Teachers also monitor students' learning as they observe students reading, writing, and working in small groups. Students and teachers also meet together in brief conferences during literature focus units to talk about the featured selection and other books in the text set students are reading, projects students do during the extending step of the reading process, and other assignments. Often these conferences are brief, but they give teachers insight into students' learning. Teachers make anecdotal notes of their observations and conferences, and they also examine students' work samples to monitor learning.

Figure 10–8 An assignment checklist for Mrs. Dillon's focus unit

Three Little Pigs Unit

Name _____

____1. Read *The Three Little Pigs.*

_____

_____

____2. Read to Mrs. Dillon.

____3. Make a vocabulary mobile.

____4. Make a quotes book.

____5. Make a square for the quilt.

____6. Read four pig books.

_____

_____

_____

_____

____7. Do a project.

What is your project? _____

____8. Write a letter to Mrs. Dillon.

____9. Write in your journal.

☐ draw pigs

☐ draw wolves

☐ write about the three pigs

☐ write about the wolf

Units Featuring a Picture Book

In literature focus units featuring picture books, younger children read predictable picture books or books with very little text, such as *Rosie's Walk* (Hutchins, 1968), and older students read more sophisticated picture books with more text, such as *Jumanji* (Van Allsburg, 1981). Teachers use the same six-step approach for developing units featuring a picture book for younger and older students. Second graders, for example, might spend a week reading *Tacky the Penguin* (Lester, 1988), a popular story about an oddball penguin who saves all the penguins from some hunters. During the unit, students read the story several times, share their responses to the story, participate in a variety of exploring activities, and do projects to extend their interpretations. A weeklong plan for teaching a unit on *Tacky the Penguin* is presented in Figure 10–9.

Several types of exploring activities are included in this plan. One type focuses on vocabulary. On Monday, students list words from the story on a word wall, the next day they reread the words and sort them according to the character they refer to, and

Figure 10–9 A week-long lesson plan for *Tacky the Penguin*

	MONDAY	TUESDAY	WEDNESDAY	THURSDAY	FRIDAY
8:45	Talk about penguins Begin KWL chart Begin word wall	Have students share reading log entries in small groups Reread word wall	Have students make open-mind portraits of Tacky	Reread *Tacky* in small groups while other students work on projects	Finish projects
9:15	Read *Tacky the Penguin* using guided reading Have grand conversation. Ask: Is Tacky an "odd" bird?	Reread story with reading buddies	Discuss possible projects		Sequence story boards with students who are done with their projects
9:45	BREAK				
10:00	Add words to word wall Have students write in reading logs	Sort words: 1. Tacky words 2. Other penguin words 3. Hunter words	Begin work on projects	ML: Suffix *-ly.* Show students how to peel off suffix	Share projects
10:30	Introduce text set Read aloud *Three Cheers for Tacky*	ML: Character development Make a character cluster for Tacky	Add to KWL chart Read *A Penguin Year* aloud	Read aloud two other books by Helen Lester: *Me First* *A Porcupine Named Fluffy*	
11:00	Reading Workshop/ Guided Reading Groups				Add favorite story quotes and interesting penguin facts to penguin bulletin board to make a quilt

Students learn about scarecrows during a literature focus unit on Barn Dance! *by Bill Martin, Jr., and John Archambault.*

on Thursday the teacher teaches a minilesson about peeling off the *-ly* suffix to learn the "main" word (root word). It's not typical to teach a lesson on derivational suffixes in second grade, but second graders notice that many of the words on the word wall have *-ly* at the end of them and often ask about the suffix.

Another activity examines character. The teacher gives a minilesson on characters on Tuesday. Then students make a character **cluster** about Tacky and draw open minds to show what Tacky is thinking. To make an **open-mind portrait,** students draw a portrait of the penguin, cut around the head so that it will flip open, and draw or write what Tacky is thinking on another sheet of paper that has been attached behind the paper with the portrait.

Units Featuring a Chapter Book

Teachers develop literature focus units using chapter books, such as *Bunnicula: A Rabbit-Tale of Mystery* (Howe & Howe, 1979), *Sarah, Plain and Tall* (MacLachlan, 1985), *The Sign of the Beaver* (Speare, 1983), and *Number the Stars* (Lowry, 1989). The biggest difference between picture books and chapter books is their length, and when teachers plan literature focus units featuring a chapter book, they need to decide how to schedule the reading of the book. Will students read one or two chapters each day? How often will they respond in **reading logs** or grand conversations? It is important that teachers reread the book to note the length of chapters and identify key points in the book where students will want time to explore and respond to the ideas presented in the book.

Figure 10–10 presents a four-week lesson plan for Lois Lowry's *Number the Stars*, a story of friendship and courage set in Nazi-occupied Denmark during World War II. The daily routine during the first two weeks is:

1. ***Reading.*** Students and the teacher read two chapters using shared reading.
2. ***Responding to the reading.*** Students participate in a grand conversation about the chapters they have read, write in reading logs, and add important words from the chapters to the class word wall.
3. ***Minilesson.*** The teacher teaches a minilesson on a reading strategy or presents information about World War II or about the author.
4. ***More reading.*** Students read related books from the text set independently.

The schedule for the last two weeks is different. During the third week, students choose a class project (interviewing people who were alive during World War II) and individual projects. They work in teams on activities related to the book and continue to read other books about the war. During the final week, students finish the class interview project and share their completed individual projects.

Units Focusing on a Genre

During a genre unit, students learn about a particular genre or category of literature, such as folktales or science fiction. Students read stories illustrating the genre and then participate in a variety of activities to deepen their knowledge about the genre. In these units, students participate in the following activities:

❦ reading several stories illustrating a genre

❦ learning the characteristics of the genre

❦ reading other stories illustrating the genre

❦ responding to and exploring the genre stories

❦ writing or rewriting stories exemplifying the genre

Genre studies about traditional literature, including fables, folktales, legends, and myths, are very appropriate for elementary students. A list of recommended genre units was also included in Figure 10–6.

Units Focusing on an Author or Illustrator

Students learn about authors and illustrators who write and illustrate the books they read as part of literature focus units. They need to develop concepts of author and illustrator so that students think of them as real people—real people who eat breakfast, ride bikes, and take out the garbage, just as they do. When students think of them as real people, they view reading and literature in a different, more personal way. The concepts of author and illustrator also carry over to children's writing. As they learn about authors and illustrators, students realize that they too can write and illustrate books. They can learn about the writing process from these authors, and from illustrators they can learn about using illustrations to extend the meaning of their text. Students need to be familiar with authors and illustrators so that they can have favorites and compare them.

www.sic.k12.ut.us

Authors and Illustrators. Nearly 100 links to author and illustrator sites.

Figure 10–10 A four-week lesson plan for *Number the Stars*

	MONDAY	TUESDAY	WEDNESDAY	THURSDAY	FRIDAY
WEEK 1	Build background on World War II; The Resistance movement; ML: Reading maps of Nazi-occupied Europe; Read aloud *The Lily Cupboard*	Introduce NTS; Begin word wall; Read Ch. 1 & 2; Grand conversation; Reading log; Add to word wall; Book talk on text set	Read Ch. 3 & 4; Grand conversation; Reading log; Word wall; ML: Connecting with a character; Read text set books	Read Ch. 5; Grand conversation; Reading log; Word wall; ML: Visualizing Nazis in apartment (use drama)	Read Ch. 6 & 7; Grand conversation; Reading log; Word wall; ML: Information about the author and why she wrote the book
WEEK 2	Read Ch. 8 & 9; Grand conversation; Reading log; Word wall; ML: Compare home front and war front; Read text set books	Read Ch. 10 & 11; Grand conversation; Reading log; Word wall; ML: Visualizing the wake (use drama)	Read Ch. 12 & 13; Grand conversation; Reading log; Word wall; ML: Compare characters —make Venn diagram	Read Ch. 14 & 15; Grand conversation; Reading log; Word wall; ML: Make word maps of key words	Finish book; Grand conversation; Reading log; Word wall; ML: Theme of book
WEEK 3	Plan class interview project; Choose individual projects; Independent reading/projects	Activities at Centers: 1. Story map 2. Word sort 3. Plot profile 4. Quilt			
WEEK 4	Revise interviews; Independent reading/projects		Edit interviews; Share projects	Make final copies	Compile interview book

In kindergarten or first grade, for example, many children read Eric Carle's books and experiment with his illustration techniques, while middle-grade students focus on Beverly Cleary as they read her chapter books about Ramona and her family. Many students write letters to Beverly Cleary, and she is faithful about writing back. Older students often read Chris Van Allsburg's fantasy picture books, hunt for the picture of the white dog that Van Allsburg includes in every book, and write their own fantasy stories based on *The Mysteries of Harris Burdick* (Van Allsburg, 1984). Gary Paulsen and Lois Lowry are two other contemporary authors that upper-grade students enjoy learning about. A list of recommended authors and illustrators for units was also included in Figure 10–6.

One of the best ways to interest students in learning about authors and illustrators is to teach a unit focusing on a favorite author or illustrator. In these units, students learn about the author's life and read many of his or her books. They also examine the author's or illustrator's style. Studying authors is easier than ever today, as many authors have written autobiographies, appeared in videos, and have websites on the Internet.

To plan for a unit on an author or illustrator, teachers collect books written by a particular author or illustrated by a particular illustrator, as well as related materials about the author's or illustrator's life. Six types of material are:

🌿 a collection of books written by the author or illustrated by the illustrator

🌿 audiotape or videotape versions of the books

🌿 posters about the books, author, or illustrator provided by publishers or made by students

🌿 autobiographies, biographical brochures and pamphlets, and other information about the author or illustrator

🌿 letters written by the author or illustrator to the teacher or former students

🌿 audiotapes, videotapes, and filmstrips featuring the author or illustrator

Teachers can locate a variety of materials about authors and illustrators, if they are willing to do a little extra work. They can check publishers' websites and authors' and illustrators' websites for photographs and information. One of the best websites with information about authors and illustrators is the Children's Literature Web Guide at www.acs.ucalgary.ca. Also, most publishers have pamphlets, bookmarks, and posters available for newly published books by successful authors and illustrators. The Children's Book Council (568 Broadway, New York, NY 10012) regularly publishes a newsletter with information about the promotional materials available from publishers. Teachers can subscribe, or their school library or local public library may have copies available. Librarians can be very helpful in locating information about authors and illustrators. Many librarians keep files of information about authors and illustrators that they will share with teachers.

Authors and illustrators are profiled in a variety of professional resources, such as Roginsky's (1985, 1989) two-volume resource *Behind the Covers: Interviews With Authors and Illustrators of Books for Children and Young Adults* and Cummings's *Talking With Artists* (1992). Authors and illustrators have also written autobiographical books for children, such as Patricia Polacco's *Firetalking* (1994) and James Howe's *Playing With Words* (1994). Each year more and more of these books are published, and these personal glimpses into authors' and illustrators' lives are very popular with students. Teachers can also check professional journals and magazines, including *Book Links, Language Arts, Horn Book, The New Advocate, The Reading Teacher,* and *Teaching PreK–8,* for articles about authors and illustrators.

For an author study of Chris Van Allsburg, for example, teachers collect copies of all of Van Allsburg's picture books and read them:

🐾 *The Garden of Abdul Gasazi* (1979), the story of a mean magician who turns a dog into a duck

🐾 *Jumanji* (1981), the story of two children who play a fantastic jungle adventure game

🐾 *Ben's Dream* (1982), the story of Ben's trip to famous landmarks in his dreams

🐾 *The Wreck of the Zephyr* (1983), the story of how a boy's ambition to be the greatest sailor in the world turns to ruin

🐾 *The Mysteries of Harris Burdick* (1984), a collection of black-and-white drawings with titles and captions

🐾 *The Polar Express* (1985), the story of a young child who travels to the North Pole on Christmas Eve and learns to believe in the magic of Christmas

🐾 *The Stranger* (1986), the story of Jack Frost's recuperation at the Bailey's farm after he is hit by Farmer Bailey's car

🐾 *The Z Was Zapped* (1987), an alliterative alphabet book

🐾 *Two Bad Ants* (1988), the tale of two ants venturing far from their home, told from the ants' viewpoint

🐾 *Just a Dream* (1990), the story of how Walter learns to value the environment through a series of dreams

🐾 *The Wretched Stone* (1991), a story told as a ship captain's log of how the crew turned into monkeys after staring mindlessly at a glowing stone

🐾 *The Widow's Broom* (1992), the story of a magical broom and how the villagers feared the broom because it was different

🐾 *The Sweetest Fig* (1993), the story of Monsieur Bibot, a coldhearted dentist who gets what he deserves when his long-suffering dog eats a fig with magical powers

🐾 *Bad Day at Riverbend* (1995), the story of Riverbend, a colorless, sleepy western town, and what happens when it is covered with a greasy slime of color

www.homearts.com
www.polarexpress.com
www.eduplace.com
www.wondersociety.com

🕸 *Chris Van Allsburg. Check these websites for information about this author.*

Next, teachers decide which books to focus on and read together as a class, which books students will read in small groups, and which books students will read independently. They also choose activities based on the books and plan minilesson topics. Then they develop a lesson plan according to the time and resources they have available for the unit.

A plan for a three-week author unit is presented in Figure 10–11. In this plan, the teacher spends the first two days on *Jumanji* and the next day on *The Polar Express.* Then students spend four days in book clubs. Students divide into small groups, and each day they read one of Van Allsburg's books. Students rotate through groups so that in four days they read four books. Next, students read *The Z Was Zapped* and write a class alliterative **alphabet book.** For the next two days, students read and respond to *The Wretched Stone* and *Bad Day at Riverbend* as a class, and the teacher teaches minilessons on theme using these two books as examples. During the third week, students write descriptions and stories for the illustrations in *The Mysteries of Harris Burdick* and write letters to Chris Van Allsburg. They also read and reread Van Allsburg's books in-

Figure 10–11   A three-week author unit on Chris Van Allsburg

	MONDAY	TUESDAY	WEDNESDAY	THURSDAY	FRIDAY
WEEK 1	Introduce unit Read *Jumanji* Grand conversation Word wall Reading logs Write sequels	Continue sequels Watch videotape of book Make Venn diagram to compare book and video	Continue sequels Read *The Polar Express* Grand conversation Word wall Reading logs	Introduce book clubs (small groups read a CVA book each day and write in reading logs)	Book clubs (continued)
	ML: Chris Van Allsburg	ML: Writing letters to authors	ML: Alliteration	ML: Theme	ML: Fantasy
WEEK 2	Book clubs (continued) 1. *The Sweetest Fig* 2. *The Garden of Abdul Gasazi*	Book clubs (continued) 3. *Just a Dream* 4. *The Witch's Broom* 5. *Two Bad Ants*	Read *The Z Was Zapped* Grand conversation Word wall Create class alphabet book	Read *The Wretched Stone* Grand conversation Word wall Reading log	Read *Bad Day at Riverbend* Grand conversation Word wall Reading log
					ML: Theme (continued)
WEEK 3	Share *The Mysteries of Harris Burdick*	Continue writing stories	→	Share stories	Vote on favorite CVA book
	Begin writing stories for pictures	Write letters to author	→	Mail letters	Make a cube about CVA
	Read and reread CVA books	→			Read-around

377

dependently and with buddies. To end the unit, students vote on their favorite Van Allsburg book and have a **read-around** in which they read their favorite quotes from various books aloud. They also do a **cubing** about the author and his books.

Review

Students need opportunities to read and respond to quality literature. Books that have received the Caldecott or Newbery Medal are often chosen for literature focus units. Multicultural literature should also be used as an integral part of literature focus units. Teachers develop literature focus units to highlight quality literature. Four types of literature focus units are picture book units, chapter book units, genre units, and author units. Six steps are used to develop a unit: selecting the literature, setting goals, developing the unit plan, coordinating grouping patterns with activities, creating a time schedule, and managing record keeping. Effective teaching practices for using literature focus units are reviewed in the feature below.

How Effective Teachers . . .

Develop Literature Focus Units

✴ Effective Practices

1. Teachers choose high-quality literature for literature focus units.

2. Teachers introduce students to Caldecott and Newbery Medal books.
3. Teachers select multicultural books for featured selections and for text sets.
4. Teachers determine the difficulty level of books they use for literature focus units.
5. Teachers find ways to make difficult books accessible for students.
6. Teachers provide daily opportunities for students to choose and read books at their own reading levels from text sets.
7. Teachers carefully develop literature focus units using the six-step approach described in this chapter.
8. Teachers spend approximately one week on a picture book unit and no longer than a month on other types of units.
9. Teachers use four types of literature focus units: picture book units, chapter book units, genre units, and author or illustrator units.
10. Teachers incorporate activities from all five steps of the reading process in literature focus units.

✴ Ineffective Practices

1. Teachers teach stories and other pieces without considering their literary value or interest to students.
2. Teachers don't include award-winning books in their reading program.
3. Teachers use few multicultural books.

4. Teachers do not know how to determine the difficulty level of books.
5. Teachers allow students to "sink or swim" when reading books.
6. Teachers use very few related books or don't collect books for text sets.

7. Teachers follow teacher's manuals or commercial unit plans for teaching literature focus units.

8. Teachers spend more than one week on a picture book unit and more than a month on other types of units.
9. Teachers use only one type of literature focus unit.

10. Teachers emphasize only reading and exploring activities.

References

Bishop, R. S. (1992). Multicultural literature for children: Making informed choices. In V. J. Harris (Ed.), *Teaching multicultural literature in grades K–8* (pp. 37–54). Norwood, MA: Christopher-Gordon.

Bishop, R. S. (Ed.). (1994). *Kaleidoscope: A multicultural booklist for grades K–8*. Urbana, IL: National Council of Teachers of English.

Cummings, P. (Ed.). (1992). *Talking with artists*. New York: Bradbury.

Harris, V. J. (1992a). Multiethnic children's literature. In K. D. Wood & A. Moss (Eds.), *Exploring literature in the classroom: Content and methods* (pp. 169–201). Norwood, MA: Christopher-Gordon.

Harris, V. J. (Ed.). (1992b). *Teaching multicultural literature in grades K–8*. Norwood, MA: Christopher-Gordon.

Huck, C. S., Hepler, S., & Hickman, J. (1987). *Children's literature in the elementary school* (4th ed.). New York: Holt, Rinehart & Winston.

Jipson, J., & Paley, N. (1991). The selective tradition in teachers' choice of children's literature: Does it exist in the elementary classroom? *English Education, 23,* 148–159.

Norton, D. E. (1999). *Through the eyes of a child: An introduction to children's literature* (4th ed.). Upper Saddle River, NJ: Merrill/Prentice-Hall.

Roginsky, J. (1985, 1989). *Behind the covers: Interviews with authors and illustrators of books for children and young adults* (Vols. 1–2). Englewood, CO: Libraries Unlimited.

Rudman, M. (1976). *Children's literature: An issues approach* (2nd ed.). New York: Longman.

Shannon, P. (1986). Hidden within the pages: A study of social perspective in young children's favorite books. *The Reading Teacher, 39,* 656–661.

Sims, R. B. (1982). *Shadow and substance*. Urbana, IL: National Council of Teachers of English.

Soto, G. (1992). Author for a day: Glitter and rainbows. *The Reading Teacher, 46,* 200–202.

Sutherland, Z., & Arbuthnot, M. H. (1986). *Children and books* (7th ed.). Glenview, IL: Scott Foresman.

Traxel, J. (1983). The American Revolution in children's fiction. *Research in the Teaching of English, 17,* 61–83.

Vardell, S. (1991). A new "picture of the world": The NCTE Orbis Pictus Award for outstanding nonfiction for children. *Language Arts, 68,* 474–479.

Walker-Dalhouse, D. (1992). Using African-American literature to increase ethnic understanding. *The Reading Teacher, 45,* 416–422.

Yokota, J. (1993). Issues in selecting multicultural children's literature. *Language Arts, 70,* 156–167.

Zarnoski, M. (1991). An interview with author Nicholasa Mohr. *The Reading Teacher, 45,* 100–106.

Children's Book References

Bishop, G. (1989). *The three little pigs*. New York: Scholastic.

Bunting, E. (1998). *So far from the sea*. New York: Clarion.

Coerr, E. (1988). *Chang's paper pony*. New York: Harper & Row.

Curtis, C. P. (1995). *The Watsons go to Birmingham—1963*. New York: Delacorte.

Curtis, C. P. (1999). *Bud, not Buddy*. New York: Delacorte.

de Paola, T. (1988). *The legend of the Indian paintbrush*. New York: Putnam.

Fraser, M. A. (1993). *Ten mile day and the building of the transcontinental railroad*. New York: Henry Holt.

Galdone, P. (1970). *The three little pigs*. New York: Seabury.

Goble, P. (1988). *Iktomi and the boulder*. New York: Orchard.

Golenbock, P. (1990). *Teammates*. San Diego: Harcourt Brace Jovanovich.

Hamilton, V. (1988). *Anthony Burns: The defeat and triumph of a fugitive slave*. New York: Knopf.

Hooks, W. H. (1989). *The three little pigs and the fox*. New York: Macmillan.

Howe, D., & Howe, J. (1979). *Bunnicula: A rabbit-tale of mystery*. New York: Atheneum.

Howe, J. (1994). *Playing with words*. Katonah, NY: Richard C. Owen.

Hoyt-Goldsmith, D. (1990). *Totem pole*. New York: Holiday House.

Hutchins, P. (1968). *Rosie's walk*. New York: Macmillan.

Isadora, R. (1979). *Ben's trumpet*. New York: Morrow.

Lester, H. (1988). *Tacky the penguin*. Boston: Houghton Mifflin.

Lowell, S. (1992). *The three little javelinas*. Flagstaff, AZ: Northland.

Lowry, L. (1989). *Number the stars*. Boston: Houghton Mifflin.

MacLachlan, P. (1985). *Sarah, plain and tall*. New York: Harper and Row.

Marshall, J. (1989). *The three little pigs*. New York: Dial.

Polacco, P. (1994). *Firetalking*. Katonah, NY: Richard C. Owen.

Ringgold, F. (1991). *Tar beach*. New York: Crown.

Say, A. (1990). *El Chino*. Boston: Houghton Mifflin.

Scieszka, J. (1989). *The true story of the three little pigs!* New York: Viking.

Soto, G. (1993). *Too many tamales*. New York: Putnam.

Speare, E. G. (1983). *The sign of the beaver*. Boston: Houghton Mifflin.

Surat, M. M. (1983). *Angel child, dragon child*. Milwaukee: Raintree.

Trivizas, E. (1993). *The three little wolves and the big bad pig*. New York: McElderry Books.

Uchida, Y. (1971). *Journey to Topaz*. Berkeley, CA: Creative Arts.

Uchida, Y. (1993). *The bracelet*. New York: Philomel.

Van Allsburg, C. (1979). *The garden of Abdul Gasazi*. Boston: Houghton Mifflin.

Van Allsburg, C. (1981). *Jumanji*. Boston: Houghton Mifflin.

Van Allsburg, C. (1982). *Ben's dream*. Boston: Houghton Mifflin.

Van Allsburg, C. (1983). *The wreck of the Zephyr*. Boston: Houghton Mifflin.

Van Allsburg, C. (1984). *The mysteries of Harris Burdick*. Boston: Houghton Mifflin.

Van Allsburg, C. (1985). *The polar express*. Boston: Houghton Mifflin.

Van Allsburg, C. (1986). *The stranger*. Boston: Houghton Mifflin.

Van Allsburg, C. (1987). *The Z was zapped*. Boston: Houghton Mifflin.

Van Allsburg, C. (1988). *Two bad ants*. Boston: Houghton Mifflin.

Van Allsburg, C. (1990). *Just a dream*. Boston: Houghton Mifflin.

Van Allsburg, C. (1991). *The wretched stone*. Boston: Houghton Mifflin.

Van Allsburg, C. (1992). *The widow's broom*. Boston: Houghton Mifflin.

Van Allsburg, C. (1993). *The sweetest fig*. Boston: Houghton Mifflin.

Van Allsburg, C. (1995). *Bad day at Riverbend*. Boston: Houghton Mifflin.

Winter, J. (1988). *Follow the drinking gourd*. New York: Knopf.

Zemach, M. (1988). *The three little pigs*. New York: Farrar, Straus & Giroux.

Chapter 11

Literature Circles

— Chapter Questions —

What is a literature circle?

How do teachers implement literature circles in elementary classrooms?

What are the benefits of using literature circles?

Mrs. Bradshaw's Students Read in Book Clubs

The students in Mrs. Bradshaw's multi-age classroom have divided into six small-group literature circles that they call "book clubs" to read and respond to these chapter books:

- *On My Honor* (Bauer, 1986), a story about a boy who breaks a promise to his father, with disastrous results.
- *Freckle Juice* (Blume, 1971), a humorous story about a boy who tries to rid himself of his freckles.
- *Shiloh* (Naylor, 1991), a heartwarming boy-and-dog story that has been made into a movie.
- *Bunnicula: A Rabbit-Tale of Mystery* (Howe & Howe, 1979), a fantasy about a bunny who just might be a vampire.
- *How to Eat Fried Worms* (Rockwell, 1973), a humorously revolting story about a boy who makes a bet that he can eat 15 worms in 15 days.
- *Bridge to Terabithia* (Paterson, 1977), a touching story of friendship between two lonely children.

All six of these books are good stories and popular with middle-grade students. Two have won the Newbery Medal for excellence, and one is a Newbery Honor Book (runner-up for the Newbery Medal). Mrs. Bradshaw chose these books after reflecting on the interests and needs of the students in the classroom, and based on requests and recommendations from her students. The reading levels of the books range from second to fifth grade.

Mrs. Bradshaw has a set of six of each of these books, and she introduced the books using a **book talk** (see the Compendium for more information about this and all other highlighted terms in this chapter). Students had a day to preview the books and sign up for one of the groups. After students get into groups, Mrs. Bradshaw holds a class meeting to set the guidelines for this unit. Students will have 75 minutes each day for five days to read and respond to the books. Students in each group set their own schedules for reading, discussing the book, and writing in **reading logs.** They decide how they will read the book, plan for at least three **grand conversations,** write at least three entries in their reading logs, and develop a presentation to share their book with the class at the end of the unit. Mrs. Bradshaw distributes a "Book Club Notes" sheet for students to use to keep track of their schedules and the assignments. A copy of this sheet is shown in Figure 11–1. Students keep this sheet and their reading logs in their book club folders.

The students in each book club talk about their books and make plans. Four of the groups decide to write their first reading log entry before beginning to read, and the other two groups begin reading right away. As the students read, write, and talk about their books, Mrs. Bradshaw moves from group to group and writes anecdotal notes to monitor students' progress.

Figure 11–1 Mrs. Bradshaw's schedule and assignment sheet

Book Club Notes

Name _____   Date _____

Book _____

Schedule

1	2	3	4	5

Requirements

☐ Read the book
☐ Discuss the book   1 ____   2 ____   3 ____
☐ Write in a reading log   1 ____   2 ____   3 ____
☐ Make a project

Mrs. Bradshaw joins the *Bridge to Terabithia* group as they finish reading the first chapter, and one student asks about the dedication. Mrs. Bradshaw shares that she read that Katherine Paterson wrote this book after the child of a friend of hers died, and she guesses that the Lisa mentioned in the dedication is that child. Another child asks about the setting of the story, and from the information in the first chapter, the group deduces that the story is set in a rural area outside Washington, DC. Several students comment on how vividly Paterson describes Jesse and his family. After speculating on who might be moving into the old Perkins place, they continue reading.

Next, Mrs. Bradshaw moves to the book club reading *Freckle Juice* and helps them set up their group schedule. The students in this group decide to read together. They will take turns reading aloud as the other group members follow along and help with unfamiliar words. Mrs. Bradshaw stays with this group as they read the first three pages. Then she encourages them to continue reading and moves on to another group.

The next day, the book club reading *Bunnicula: A Rabbit-Tale of Mystery* asks Mrs. Bradshaw to meet with them. They have a lot of questions and confusions about vampires and Dracula. Mrs. Bradshaw is prepared for their requests, and she brings with her the "V" and "D" volumes of an encyclopedia and several other books about vampires. She spends 20 minutes with the group, helping them find information and clarify confusions.

She also joins with the *How to Eat Fried Worms* book club as they read Chapter 3. The students ask Mrs. Bradshaw what "monshure" is, and she explains that Alan is pretending to speak French. As they continue reading Chapters 4 and 5, she points out similar instances. Once they finish reading, the group discusses the chapters they have read and talks about whether or not they would have made a similar bet. They compare themselves to Billy, the boy who eats the worms, and talk about how real the story seems and how they feel themselves tasting the worm as Billy eats it. Mrs. Bradshaw seizes the moment for an impromptu lesson on reading strategies, and she explains that good readers often seem to connect with or become a character in a story and can see, hear, smell, and even taste the same things the character does.

A few days later, Mrs. Bradshaw meets with the *Shiloh* book club as they are writing in their reading logs. Students in this group decided to write **double-entry journals.** They write interesting quotes from the book in one column and their reactions to the quotes in another column. Students are writing quotes and reactions from the last three chapters of the book. Todd chooses "I begin to see now I'm no better than Judd Travers—willing to look the other way to get something I want" (p. 124), and writes:

> *Marty IS better than Judd Travers. This book makes you realize that things are not just right and wrong and most of the time right and wrong and good and bad and fair and not fair get a little mixed up. Marty is keeping quiet about the doe for a real important reason. The deer is dead and that can't be helped but Marty can save Shiloh. He must save the dog. He's a much better person than he thinks even though he did do some wrong. Part of the reason you know he is a good person is that he knows he did the wrong things. He has a conscience. Judd don't have a conscience, none at all.*

Next, Mrs. Bradshaw meets with the *On My Honor* book club as they discuss the end of the book. Kara comments, "I don't think Joel should feel so guilty about Tony dying. It wasn't his fault." Mrs. Bradshaw asks, "Who's fault was it?" Several children say it was Tony's fault. Will explains, "He knew he couldn't swim and he went swimming anyway. That was just plain dumb." "What about Joel's dad?" Mrs. Bradshaw asks, "Was it his fault, too?" Brooke says, "His dad seems like he thinks he's guilty and he tells Joel he's sorry." Jared offers another opinion, "It was just an accident. I don't think it was anyone's fault. No one killed Tony on purpose. He just died." The group continues to talk about the effect of Tony's death on his own family and on Josh and his family.

Mrs. Bradshaw and the students in this multi-age classroom have created a community of learners. They have learned to work together in small groups. They are responsible for assignments and supportive of their classmates. They know the literacy routines and procedures to use during the book club unit. The classroom is arranged to facilitate their learning. They know where supplies are kept and how to use them. Mrs. Bradshaw assumes a number of roles during the unit. She chooses books, organizes the unit, provides information and encouragement, teaches lessons, monitors students' progress, and assesses their work.

On the fifth day, students in each book club share their projects with the class. The purpose of these projects is to celebrate the reading experience and bring closure to it. An added benefit is that students "advertise" the books during these sharing sessions, and then other students want to read them. Each group takes approximately 5 to 10 minutes to share their projects. The *How to Eat Fried Worms* group goes first. They present a book commercial. Group members tell a little about the story and dare students to eat the worms—big earthworms or night crawlers—that they have brought to school. One student, Nathan, explains that it is perfectly safe to eat the worms and extols their nutritional benefits. Even so, no one volunteers.

Next, the group reading *Freckle Juice* shares two projects. Two students share a graph they have made showing how many children in the class have freckles, and the other students present a commercial to sell a bottle of guaranteed "freckle juice."

The group reading *Bunnicula: A Rabbit-Tale of Mystery* explains that they've read a mystery about vegetables turning white, and they show some vegetables they have made out of light-colored clay as evidence. They point out two tiny marks on each vegetable. One student, Bill, pretends to be Harold, the family dog who wrote the book, and he explains that their pet rabbit—Bunnicula—who seemed to be harmless at first, may be responsible for sucking the vegetable juices out of the vegetables. Dolores displays a stuffed animal bunny dressed in a black cape to look like a vampire. The group recommends that classmates read this book if they want to find out what happens to Bunnicula. The *Shiloh* group shares information from the local ASPCA, and Angelica reads an "I Am" poem about Marty that the group has written:

> I am a boy who knows right from wrong
> but I will do anything to save that dog.
> I know how to treat a dog.
> I say, "Please don't kick him like that."
> I am afraid of Judd Travers.
> But I will do anything to save Shiloh.
> I dream of Shiloh being mine.
> I have a secret hiding place for him.
> I catch Judd Travers killing a doe out of season.

I will make mean Mr. Travers sell Shiloh to me.
I work hard for 20 hours to earn $40 to buy him.
I learn that nothing is as simple as it seems.
I am a boy who knows right from wrong
but I will do anything to save my dog.

The group reading *Bridge to Terabithia* presents a tabletop diorama they have made of the magical kingdom of Terabithia.

Last, Hector and Carlos from the group reading *On My Honor* role-play Joel and Tony, the two boys in the story. They reenact the scene where the boys decide to go swimming. They explain that Tony drowns, and then the boy playing Joel describes what it was like to search for Tony and then pretend that he didn't know what had happened to Tony. Then the other group members ask their classmates what they would have done after Tony died if they had been Joel.

After all the projects have been presented, many students trade books with classmates, and students spend the next two days independently reading any book they choose. Many students read one of the other books read during the book clubs, but some students bring other books from home to read or choose a different book from the class library.

....

Mrs. Bradshaw's students are likely to become lifelong readers because they love books and enjoy reading and discussing books. Many of them choose to read as a leisure-time activity. Books of children's literature carry readers to far-off lands and times, stretch their imaginations, expand their knowledge of people and the world, and transform them by giving life new meaning. Charlotte Huck (1998) explains: "I believe in the transforming power of literature to take you out of yourself and return you to yourself—a changed self" (p. 4). Powerful experiences with literature, like those that Mrs. Bradshaw's students experienced, heighten children's interest in reading and expand their reading abilities at the same time.

One of the best ways to nurture children's love of reading is through literature circles—small, student-led book discussion groups that meet regularly in the classroom. In the vignette, Mrs. Bradshaw called her literature circles "book clubs" (Raphael & McMahon, 1994), and some teachers call them "literature study groups" (Peterson & Eeds, 1990; Smith, 1998).

In literature circles, children meet together in small groups to read and discuss self-selected books. Harvey Daniels (1994) calls literature circles "a new kind of reading group" (p. 6). The reading materials are quality books of children's literature, including stories, poems, biographies, and informational books. What matters most is that students are reading something that interests them and is manageable. In these groups, students choose the books they want to read and form temporary groups to read. Next, they set a reading and discussion schedule. Then they read independently or with buddies and come together to talk about their reading in discussions that are like grand conversations. Sometimes the teacher meets with the group, and at other times the group meets independently. After finishing the book, students also prepare projects in order to share the book with classmates. A literature circle on one book

www.toread.com

Literature Circles.
Check this website for
more information on literature
circles.

may last from a day or two to a week or two, depending on the length of the book and the age of the students.

The characteristics of literature circles are:

1. Students choose their own reading materials from books chosen by the teacher.
2. Students form small temporary groups, based on book choice.
3. The small groups read different books.
4. Groups meet regularly according to schedules that students set up to discuss their reading.
5. Students make notes to guide their reading and discussions.
6. Students choose topics for the grand conversations and ask open-ended questions during the discussions.
7. Teachers are facilitators, not a group member or instructor.
8. Teachers evaluate literature circles by observing students during group meetings and with information learned through student self-evaluations.
9. The classroom is a community of learners, and students are actively engaged in reading and discussing the books they are reading.
10. After reading a book, students share with their classmates, and then choose new books to read (Daniels, 1994).

These characteristics exemplify the three key features of literature circles—choice, literature, and response.

KEY FEATURES OF LITERATURE CIRCLES

As teachers organize for literature circles, they make decisions about choice, literature, and response. They structure the program so that students can make choices about the literature they read, and they develop a plan for response so that students can think deeply about books they are reading and respond to them.

Choice

Students make many choices in literature circles. They choose the books they will read and the groups in which they participate. They share in setting the schedule for reading and discussing the book, and they choose the roles they assume in the discussions. They also choose how they will share the book with classmates. Teachers structure literature circles so that students have these opportunities, but even more importantly, they prepare students for making choices. Teachers prepare students by creating a community of learners in their classrooms in which students assume responsibility for their learning and can work collaboratively with classmates. In traditional classrooms children often work competitively with classmates, but in literature circles students collaborate in order to set schedules, discuss their reading, and develop responses.

Literature

The books chosen for literature circles should be interesting to students. Books that are likely to lead to good discussions have interesting plots, richly developed characters, rich language, and thought-provoking themes (Samway & Whang, 1996). The books must seem manageable to the students, especially during their first literature circles. Samway and Whang recommend choosing shorter books or picture books at first so that students don't become bogged down. It's also important that teachers have read and liked the books because they won't be able to do a convincing book talk if they haven't. In addition, they won't be able to contribute to the book discussions.

Teachers also try to connect literature circle books to literature focus units, social studies units, and other classroom activities. Sometimes it is difficult to locate related books at suitable reading levels, but often teachers can, and students benefit by making connections. For example, during a thematic unit on ancient Egypt, sixth graders might choose among these books, which range from second- to ninth-grade reading levels, for literature circles:

www.pawp.home.
pipeline.com
Bibliographies for Literature Circles. Annotated bibliographies of text sets of children's books suitable for students in grades 4–8.

- *Ancient Egypt* (Hart, 1990), a photo essay on ancient Egypt that describes many aspects of the Egyptian culture, including foods, toys and games, clothing, weapons, language and writing, and religion.
- *Cleopatra* (Stanley & Vennema, 1994), a sophisticated picture book biography of the great Egyptian queen of the period from age 18 when she became queen until her death at age 39.
- *Cleopatra VII, Daughter of the Nile* (Gregory, 1999), a fictionalized diary of 12-year-old Cleopatra set in 57 B.C. that is chock-full of intrigue and details about palace life.
- *Mummies* (Milton, 1996), an easy-to-read informational book with large print and colorful illustrations that explains the pharaohs' beliefs about life after death, the mummification process, and how pyramids were used as burial places.
- *Mummies Made in Egypt* (Aliki, 1979), a striking informational picture book that describes the techniques and reasons for the use of mummification in ancient Egypt.
- *Mummies and Their Mysteries* (Wilcox, 1993), an informational book with vivid photo illustrations that discusses mummies around the world and explains how studying them provides clues to past ways of life.
- *The Winged Cat: A Tale of Ancient Egypt* (Lattimore, 1992), a picture book story about a servant girl and a high priest who must each find the correct magic spells from the *Book of the Dead* that open the 12 gates of the netherworld to determine who is telling the truth about the death of the girl's sacred cat.
- *Tut Tut* (Scieszka, 1996), an easy time-warp story in chapter book format in which modern-day children find themselves in ancient Egypt, trying to outwit an evil high priest and escape from the mummy-making chamber.

A list of recommended books for literature circles is presented in Figure 11–2.

Response

Students meet several times during a literature circle to discuss the book and extend their comprehension of it. Through these discussions, students summarize their reading, make personal and literary connections, learn vocabulary, explore the author's use of story structure, and note literary language. Students learn that comprehension develops in layers. From an initial comprehension gained through reading, students deepen and expand their understanding through the discussions. They learn to return to the text to reread sentences and paragraphs in order to clarify a point or state an opinion. They also refine their ability to respond to books through these discussions.

Figure 11–2	Books for literature circles

Primary Grades (K–2)

Carle, E. (1987). *Have you seen my cat?* New York: Scholastic.

Carlson, N. (1988). *I like me!* New York: Viking.

Ehlert, L. (1994). *Mole's hill.* Orlando, FL: Harcourt Brace.

Galdone, P. (1968). *Henny penny.* New York: Clarion.

Guarino, D. (1989). *Is your mama a llama?* New York: Scholastic.

Hutchins, P. (1986). *The doorbell rang.* New York: Greenwillow.

Marshall, J. (1972). *George and Martha.* Boston: Houghton Mifflin.

Meddaugh, S. (1992). *Martha speaks.* Boston: Houghton Mifflin.

Numeroff, L. J. (1991). *If you give a moose a muffin.* New York: HarperCollins.

Rylant, C. (1991). *Henry and Mudge and the bedtime thumps.* New York: Simon & Schuster.

Seuss, Dr. (1960). *Green eggs and ham.* New York: Random House.

Wells, R. (1997). *McDuff moves in.* New York: Hyperion.

Middle Grades (3–5)

Bauer, M. D. (1986). *On my honor.* Boston: Houghton Mifflin.

Blume, J. (1972). *Tales of a fourth grade nothing.* New York: Dell.

Cleary, B. (1992). *Ramona the pest.* New York: Avon.

Coerr, E. (1988). *Chang's paper pony.* New York: HarperCollins.

Danziger, P. (1994). *Amber Brown is not a crayon.* New York: Putnam.

Howe, D., & Howe, J. (1980). *Bunnicula: A rabbit-tale of mystery.* New York: Atheneum.

Mathis, S. B. (1986). *The hundred-penny box.* New York: Puffin.

Naylor, P. R. (1992). *Shiloh.* New York: Atheneum.

Paterson, K. (1977). *Bridge to Terabithia.* New York: HarperCollins.

Roop, P., & Roop, C. (1985). *Keep the lights burning, Abbie.* Minneapolis, MN: Carolrhoda Books.

Smith, R. K. (1972). *Chocolate fever.* New York: Coward, McCann & Geoghegan.

Upper Grades (6–8)

Avi. (1991). *Nothing but the truth.* New York: Orchard.

Babbitt, N. (1975). *Tuck everlasting.* New York: Farrar, Straus & Giroux.

Crew, L. (1989). *Children of the river.* New York: Dell.

Cushman, K. (1994). *Catherine, called Birdy.* New York: HarperCollins.

Myers, W. D. (1988). *Scorpions.* New York: HarperCollins.

Philbrick, R. (1993). *Freak the mighty.* New York: Scholastic.

Ruckman, I. (1984). *Night of the twisters.* New York: HarperCollins.

Spinelli, J. (1990). *Maniac Magee.* New York: HarperCollins.

Taylor, M. (1976). *Roll of thunder, hear my cry.* New York: Puffin.

Uchida, Y. (1985). *Journey to Topaz.* Berkeley, CA: Creative Arts.

Yep, L. (1975). *Dragonwings.* New York: HarperCollins.

How often students meet to discuss a book varies according to the book and the students. When students are reading a picture book, they usually read the entire book before meeting to discuss it. But when they are reading chapter books, students usually meet after reading the first few chapters for an initial discussion and then several more times as they continue reading the book, as Mrs. Bradshaw's students did in the vignette at the beginning of this chapter.

Karen Smith (1998) describes the discussions her students have after they finish reading a book as "intensive study." They often involve several group meetings. At the first session, students share personal responses. They talk about the characters and events of the story, share favorite parts, and ask questions to clarify confusions. At the end of the first session, students and the teacher decide what they want to study at the

Students in a literature circle share their reading log entries.

next session. They may choose to focus on an element of story structure—character development or foreshadowing, for example. Students prepare for the second discussion by rereading excerpts from the book related to the focus they have chosen. Then, during the second session, students talk about how the author used an element of story structure in the book, and they often make charts and diagrams, such as a plot profile or an **open-mind portrait,** to organize their thoughts.

The reason why students examine the structural elements of stories is to help them develop literary insights. Teachers help by providing information, offering comments, asking insightful questions, and guiding students to make comments. Many teachers ask questions to probe students' thinking, and a list of possible questions is presented in Figure 11–3. However, Smith (1998) cautions that simply asking a list of questions is rarely productive. Teachers should adapt questions and use them judiciously to help students think more deeply about the stories. Eeds and Peterson (1991) advise teachers to listen carefully to what students say as they talk about a book and to introduce literary terminology such as *conflict, foreshadowing,* and *theme* when appropriate.

Instead of asking, for example, "What are the conflicts in the story?" teachers ask themselves that question and then comment about one conflict in the story that they found interesting. Then teachers invite students to talk about other conflicts they noticed, and finally, students reflect on the importance of the various conflict situations. Or, teachers can take advantage of a comment that a student makes about a conflict situation and then guide the discussion toward conflict situations.

Students need many opportunities to respond to literature before they will be successful in literature circles. One of the best ways to prepare students for literature circle discussions is by reading aloud to students every day and involving them in grand conversations (Smith, 1998). Teachers create a community of learners through these read-aloud experiences, and teachers can demonstrate ways to respond to literature that are reflective and thoughtful. Teachers also encourage students to respond

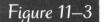

Figure 11–3   Questions to help students focus on literary elements

Adapted from Eeds and Peterson, 1991; and Peterson and Eeds, 1990.

---

1. Plot

☞ What are the conflicts in the story?
☞ How does the author develop the conflicts?
☞ What events lead to the high point in the story?
☞ What devices did the author use to develop the plot?

2. Character

☞ Which characters are fully developed and which are flat?
☞ How does the author tell us about the characters? By what they do? By how they look? By what they say? By what they think?
☞ How does the story show the development of the characters?
☞ If you were a character in the story, which character would you be? Why?

3. Setting

☞ How does the setting influence the story?
☞ Is the setting important to the story?
☞ How is time marked in the story?
☞ Does the author use flashbacks or foreshadowing?
☞ How much time passes in the story?

4. Point of View

☞ Is the story written from first person or third person?
☞ Are the characters' feelings and thoughts presented?
☞ How does the author describe the characters?

5. Theme

☞ What symbols does the author use?
☞ What universal truths does the story present?

---

to the books, and they reinforce students' comments when they share their thoughts and feelings, examine the structure of texts, and talk about their use of literacy strategies as they listened to the teacher read aloud.

Gilles (1998) examined children's talk during literature circle discussions and identified four types of talk:

1. *Talk about the book.* Children summarize their reading and talk about the book by applying what they have learned about the structure of stories and other texts as they:

☞ retell events

☞ identify main ideas

☞ summarize the plot

- discuss characters
- examine the setting
- explore themes and symbols

2. ***Talk about the reading process.*** Students think metacognitively and reflect on the process they used to read the book as they:

- reflect on how they used strategies
- explain their reading problems and how they solved them
- identify sections that they reread and why they reread them
- talk about their thinking as they were reading
- identify parts they understood or misunderstood

3. ***Talk about connections.*** Students make connections between the book and their own lives as well as to other literature they have read as they:

- explain connections to their lives
- compare this book to another book
- make connections to a film or television show they have viewed

4. ***Talk about group process and social issues.*** Children use talk to organize the literature circle and maintain the discussion. They also use talk to examine social issues and current events related to the book, such as homelessness and divorce, as they:

- decide who will be group leader
- determine the schedule, roles, and responsibilities
- draw in non-participating students
- bring the conversation back to the topic
- extend the discussion to social issues and current events

Some teachers have students assume roles and complete assignments in preparation for discussion group meetings (Daniels, 1994; Daniels & Bizar, 1998). One student is the discussion director, and this student assumes the leadership role and directs the discussion. To prepare, the discussion director chooses topics and formulates questions to guide the discussion. Other students prepare to select a passage to read aloud, identify vocabulary words for study, make personal and literary connections, summarize the reading or identify main ideas for a nonfiction text, draw a picture or make a graphic related to the book, and investigate a topic related to the book. These seven roles are detailed in Figure 11–4. Having students assume specific roles may seem artificial, but it teaches students about the types of responses they can make in literature circles.

Teachers often prepare assignment sheets for each of the roles their students assume during a literature circle and then pass out copies of the assignment sheets before students begin reading. Students complete one of the assignment sheets before each discussion. Figure 11–5 shows a "word wizard" assignment sheet that an eighth grader completed as he read *Holes* (Sachar, 1998), the story of a boy named Stanley Yelnats who is sent to a hellish correctional camp where he finds a real friend, a treasure, and a new sense of himself. As word wizard, this student chooses important words from the story to study. In the first column on the assignment sheet, the student writes the word and the page number on which it was found.

Roles students play in literature circles
Adapted from Daniels, 1994; Daniels & Bizar, 1998.

Role	Responsibilities
Discussion Director	Prepare questions to guide the group's discussion. Possible questions: 🌸 What did the reading make you think of? 🌸 What questions do you have about the reading? 🌸 What do you predict will happen next?
Passage Master (or Literary Luminary)	Choose several passages to read aloud to the group, and tell why you choose each one. These passages might be interesting, powerful, or puzzling. Also, decide how you will share the passages with the group
Word Wizard	Identify four to six words from the reading to share with the group. Be prepared to explain the meaning of the word as it is used in the text.
Connector	Find connections between the reading and your world, including happenings at school or in the community, other people, and your own life. Or, make connections with other books the same author has written or other books in the same topic.
Summarizer	Prepare a brief summary of the reading that conveys the main ideas to share with the group.
Artful Artist (or Illustrator)	Draw an illustration about the text. It might be a picture or a diagram. The illustration might relate to character, an exciting event, a prediction, or something else. Share the drawing with your group, and have them talk before you explain it.
Investigator	Locate some background information related to your reading to share with the group. Try an online computer search or check an encyclopedia to learn about the topic.

Then, in the second column, the student checks the dictionary for the word's meaning, lists several meanings when possible, and places check marks next to the meanings that are appropriate for how the word is used in the book. Students also check the etymology of the word in the dictionary, and in the third column they list the language the word came from and when it entered English.

During the discussion about the second section of *Holes*, the word *callused* became important. The student explained that *callused* means "toughened" and "hardened," and that in the story, Stanley and the other boys' hands became callused. He continued to say that the third meaning, "unsympathetic," didn't make sense. This comment provided an opportunity for the teacher to explain how *callused* could mean "unsympathetic," and students decided to make a chart to categorize characters in the story who had callused hands and those who were unsympathetic. The group

Figure 11–5 An eighth grader's literature circle role sheet

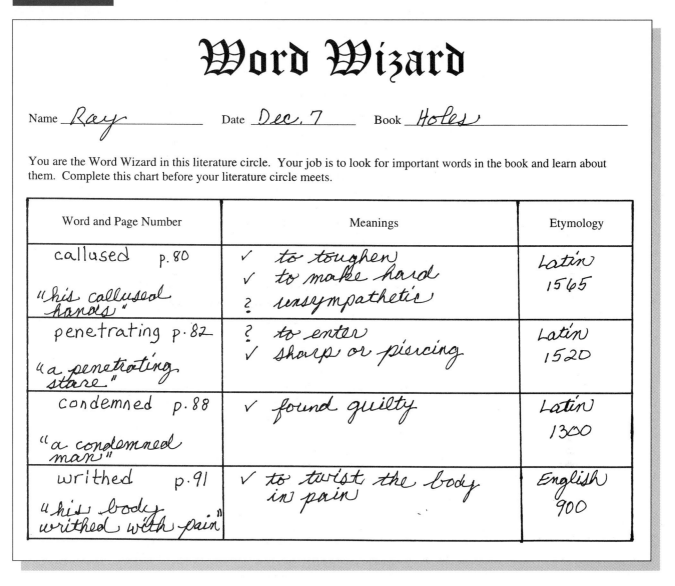

𝔚𝔬𝔯𝔡 𝔚𝔦𝔷𝔞𝔯𝔡

Name *Ray*   Date *Dec. 7*   Book *Holes*

You are the Word Wizard in this literature circle. Your job is to look for important words in the book and learn about them. Complete this chart before your literature circle meets.

Word and Page Number	Meanings	Etymology
callused p. 80 "his callused hands"	✓ to toughen ✓ to make hard ? unsympathetic	Latin 1565
penetrating p. 82 "a penetrating stare"	? to enter ✓ sharp or piercing	Latin 1520
condemned p. 88 "a condemned man"	✓ found guilty	Latin 1300
writhed p. 91 "his body writhed with pain"	✓ to twist the body in pain	English 900

concluded that the boys with callused hands were sympathetic to each other, but the adults at the correctional camp who didn't have callused hands were often unsympathetic and had callused hearts. Talking about the meaning of a single word—*callused*—led to a new and different way of looking at the characters in the story.

IMPLEMENTING LITERATURE CIRCLES

Students begin by selecting books, and then as a group they establish a schedule for reading and discussing the book. Students may meet with or without the teacher for these discussions. After reading, students create projects to share their books with the class. These literature circle activities involve all five steps of the reading process.

www.smplanet.com

Book Club. Methods and materials for setting up student-led discussion groups called book clubs.

1. *Prereading.* Teachers prepare text sets with five to seven related titles and collect six or seven copies of each book. Teachers give a brief book talk to introduce the new books, and then students sign up for the book they want to read. One way to do this is to set each book on the chalk tray and have students sign their names on the chalkboard above the book they want to read. Or, teachers can set the books on a table and place a sign-up sheet beside each book. Students need time to preview the books, and then they choose the book they want to read after considering the topic of the book and the difficulty of the text. Once in a while students don't get to read their first-choice book, but they can always read it another time, perhaps during another literature circle or during reading workshop.

The books in the text set vary in length and difficulty, but students are not placed in groups according to reading level. Students choose the books they want to read, and as they preview the books they consider how good a "fit" the book is, but that is not their only consideration. They often choose to read the book they find most interesting or the book their best friend has chosen. Students can usually manage whatever book they choose because of support and assistance from their group or through sheer determination. Once in a while, teachers counsel students to choose another book or provide an additional copy of the book so the students can practice at home or with a tutor at school.

Then students form literature circles to read each book, and usually no more than six or seven students participate in a literature circle. The group begins by setting a schedule for reading and discussing the book within the time limits that the teacher has set. Sometimes students also choose discussion roles so that they can prepare for the discussion after reading.

2. *Reading.* Students read the book independently or with a partner, depending on the difficulty level of the book. It is also possible for students to listen to a book at a listening center if they cannot read the book themselves. Students have the schedule they developed so that they know when they have to complete each reading assignment and be ready to participate in the discussion. After reading, students sometimes prepare for the discussion by noting unfamiliar words, favorite quotes, or questions to ask during the discussion in their reading logs. Or, if they have assumed discussion roles, they complete their assignments to prepare for the discussion.

3. *Responding.* After reading the first section of the book (or the entire book if it is a picture book), students meet together to talk about their reading. They participate in a grand conversation. The teacher or discussion director group begins this open-ended conversation by asking, "What did you think?" Often the teacher participates in the discussion, but sometimes students meet on their own if several groups are meeting at the same time.

Students also write in reading logs during this step. They might write reactions, use a double-entry journal format to write and respond to favorite quotes, or assume the role of a character and write a simulated journal.

4. *Exploring.* Literature discussions extend into the exploring step of the reading process. After students share their responses, teachers often teach minilessons. They may focus on an element of story structure, provide information about the author or the genre, or teach a literacy skill or strategy.

5. *Applying.* Students create a project after they finish reading. Sometimes they simply plan a way to share the book with the class, and in other classrooms they develop more extensive projects. They may examine an element of story structure in

Figure 11–6	Steps in implementing literature circles

1. Prereading

❦ Give a book talk to introduce new books.
❦ Have students sign up for the book they want to read.
❦ Form literature circles to read each book.
❦ Have the group set a schedule for reading and responding to the book.

2. Reading

❦ Have students read the book independently or with a partner.
❦ Use a listening center if the book is difficult for some students.
❦ Have students prepare for the discussion by taking notes as they read, identifying favorite quotes, or brainstorming questions to ask during the discussion.

3. Responding

❦ Have students talk about the book in a grand conversation. Begin by asking, "What did you think?"
❦ Have students share their reactions, ask questions to clarify misunderstandings, and make connections to their lives and other literature.
❦ Have students write in reading logs.

4. Exploring

❦ Teach a lesson on an element of story structure.
❦ Provide information about the author or the genre.
❦ Teach a literacy skill or strategy.

5. Applying

❦ Have students create a project.
❦ Have students meet with the teacher to evaluate the literature circle, the book, and their participation in the group.
❦ Have the group share the book and their projects with the class.

detail, research a topic related to the book, create an art or drama project, read other books by the same author, or write poems, a book, or another text related to the book. They also meet with the teacher to evaluate the literature circle, the book, and their participation in the group. Finally, the group shares the book and their projects with the rest of the class.

The steps in implementing literature circles are reviewed in Figure 11– 6.

Monitoring and Assessing Students' Learning

Teachers have a variety of options for monitoring students' work and assessing their learning during literature circles. Teachers can observe students as they participate in literature circles, monitor their work and progress using checklists and assignment

www.sasked.gov.sk.ca

Literature Circles— Assessment. Guidelines and forms to use in assessing children's learning during literature circles.

The teacher conferences with these third graders to assess their learning at the end of a literature circle.

sheets, assess students' written work, and examine their self-assessments. Specifically, teachers can participate in these four types of activities:

1. *Observing students*
   - 🌿 Observe students collaborating with classmates.
   - 🌿 Observe students reading independently.
   - 🌿 Observe students participating in discussions.
   - 🌿 Observe students' sharing of books and projects.

2. *Monitoring students' progress*
   - 🌿 Monitor students' schedules and assignment sheets.
   - 🌿 Monitor the sheets students complete for their roles in literature circles.

3. *Assessing students' work*
   - 🌿 Assess students' reading log entries.
   - 🌿 Assess students' projects.

4. *Examining students' reflections*
   - 🌿 Read students' self-assessment letters.
   - 🌿 Examine students' responses on a self-assessment checklist.
   - 🌿 Conference with students about their assessment.

Students can write self-reflections in which they discuss their participation in their group, their reactions to the book they read and discussed, and their reading process.

Figure 11–7   A second-grade evaluation form for literature circles

---

Literature Circles Report Card

Name _____   Book _____

1. How did you help your group?

2. What did you think of your book?

3. What did you say in the conversation?

4. What did you learn about your book?

5. What grade does the book get?

✳	✳✳	✳✳✳

6. What grade do you get?

✳	✳✳	✳✳✳

They can also complete assessment forms and checklists in which they self-assess their own work. A second-grade assessment checklist is shown in Figure 11– 7. Students complete this form at the end of a literature circle and then meet with the teacher to discuss their learning.

BENEFITS OF USING LITERATURE CIRCLES

Literature circles are one of the four ways to organize literacy instruction, and they are an important component of a balanced reading program. Students have opportunities to read and discuss stories and other books with their classmates in a supportive community of learners. These are some of the benefits of using literature circles:

1. Students view themselves as readers.
2. Students have opportunities to read high-quality books that they might not have chosen on their own.
3. Students read widely.

4. Students are inspired to write.
5. Students develop reading preferences.
6. Students have many opportunities to develop critical and creative thinking.
7. Students learn responsibility for completing assignments.
8. Students learn to self-assess their learning and work habits (Hill, Johnson, & Noe, 1995; Samway & Whang, 1996).

Other teacher-researchers echo these benefits and also conclude that literature circles are very effective in their classrooms (Short & Pierce, 1998).

Why Are Some Students Unmotivated to Read?

Some students, especially those in the upper grades, often say that reading is boring. They say that reading takes too long and that the words are hard to understand (Robb, 1993). Unmotivated students are rarely good readers. If students are reading simplified and uninteresting books, teachers can help them find fast-paced, action-packed stories. But the word "boring" is more likely a cover for children who are poor comprehenders. Reading isn't much fun when it doesn't make sense and it is difficult to decode. It is crucial that teachers locate books for literature circles that interest students and are written at their reading levels.

Sometimes children answer "I don't know" when teachers or classmates ask them to talk about what they are reading. An "I don't know" answer suggests that students don't understand what they are reading. Teachers need to look behind the "this is boring" and "I don't know" responses that less able readers try to hide behind and find ways to reach these students (Robb, 1993).

Ruddell (1995) researched influential reading and writing teachers—those who had a profound effect on students' lives—and found that these teachers stimulated students' internal motivation through the classroom community they created and through the literacy activities in which students were involved. Internal motivation is the innate curiosity within each of us that makes us want to figure things out. Internal motivation is social, too. We want to socialize, share ideas, and participate in group activities. Ruddell found that these influential teachers encouraged students to assume an aesthetic stance as they read and responded to books. In contrast, noninfluential teachers tried to motivate students externally, through praise, peer pressure, and grades. They encouraged students to assume an efferent stance when reading stories. Rather than exploring students' relationships with characters in discussions, they asked factual questions and judged students' responses against predetermined "correct" answers.

The types of literacy activities in which students are involved can also affect their motivation for literacy. Turner and Paris (1995) compared literacy activities like literature circles with skills-based reading programs and concluded that students' motivation was determined by the daily classroom activities. They found that open-ended activities and projects in which students were in control of the processes they used and the products they created were the most successful. Turner and Paris identified six qualities of open-ended activities: choice, challenge, control, collaboration, construction of meaning, and consequences. These qualities describe literature circles. Turner and Paris recommend that teachers consider these six qualities as they develop their instructional programs.

Review

Literature circles are small, student-led discussion groups. Students choose books to read that interest them, and they form temporary reading and discussion groups to read a particular book. The key features of literature circles are choice, literature, and response. Students meet together to talk about their reading and sometimes assume various roles for the book discussions. After students finish reading and discussing a book, they often create projects to apply their learning and share these projects with classmates. Teachers assess students' learning by monitoring their work, participating in discussions, and using checklists. Literature circles are an important component of a balanced reading program because they nurture children's love of reading. The feature below reviews how effective teachers use literature circles in their classrooms.

How Effective Teachers . . .

Conduct Literature Circles

✦ Effective Practices

1. Teachers prepare text sets with multiple copies of six or seven books.
2. Teachers give book talks to interest students in particular books.
3. Teachers have students choose the book they want to read, but provide guidance when needed.
4. Teachers allow students to set their own reading and discussion schedules.
5. Teachers have students read books independently or with a buddy, but they provide assistance when students are struggling.
6. Teachers and students participate in discussions to talk about the book and share their responses.
7. Teachers have students write in reading logs.
8. Teachers teach minilessons about story structure, authors, or other topics during book discussions.
9. Teachers have students create projects after they finish reading and share the projects with the class.
10. Teachers monitor and assess students' learning as they participate in literature circles.

✦ Ineffective Practices

1. Teacher choose high-, average-, and low-level books for students to read.
2. Teachers don't talk about the books.
3. Teachers assign students to read books based on their reading levels.
4. Teachers set reading and discussion schedules.
5. Teachers use round-robin reading to read books with students.
6. Teachers control the discussions and often ask factual questions.
7. Teachers have students complete worksheets, not write in reading logs.
8. Teachers have students complete worksheets on main ideas and other comprehension skills rather than teaching minilessons.
9. Teachers don't have students create projects or share books with classmates.
10. Teachers grade worksheets and use tests to assess students' learning.

References

Daniels, H. (1994). *Literature circles: Voice and choice in the student-centered classroom.* York, ME: Stenhouse.

Daniels, H., & Bizar, M. (1998). *Methods that matter: Six structures for best practice classrooms.* York, ME: Stenhouse.

Eeds, M., & Peterson, R. (1991). Teacher as curator: Learning to talk about literature. *The Reading Teacher, 45,* 118–126.

Gilles, C. (1998). Collaborative literacy strategies: "We don't need a circle to have a group." In K. G. Short & K. M. Pierce (Eds.), *Talking about books: Literature discussion groups in K–8 classrooms* (pp. 55–68). Portsmouth, NH: Heinemann.

Hill, B. C., Johnson, N. J., & Noe, K. L. S. (Eds.). (1995). *Literature circles and response.* Norwood, MA: Christopher-Gordon Publishers.

Huck, C. S. (1998). The power of children's literature in the classroom. In K. G. Short & K. M. Pierce (Eds.), *Talking about books: Literature discussion groups in K–8 classrooms* (pp. 3–15). Portsmouth, NH: Heinemann.

Peterson, R., & Eeds, M. (1990). *Grand conversations: Literature groups in action.* New York: Scholastic.

Raphael, T. E., & McMahon, S. I. (1994). Book club: An alternative framework for reading instruction. *The Reading Teacher, 48,* 102–117.

Robb, L. (1993). A cause for celebration: Reading and writing with at-risk students. *The New Advocate, 6,* 25–40.

Ruddell, R. B. (1995). Those influential literacy teachers: Meaning negotiators and motivation builders. *The Reading Teacher, 48,* 454–463.

Samway, K. D., & Whang, G. (1996). *Literature study circles in a multicultural classroom.* York, ME: Stenhouse.

Short, K., & Pierce, K. M. (Eds.). (1998). *Talking about books: Literature discussion groups in K–8 classrooms.* Portsmouth, NH: Heinemann.

Smith, K. (1998). Entertaining a text: A reciprocal process. In K. G. Short & K. M. Pierce (Eds.), *Talking about books: Literature discussion groups in K–8 classrooms* (pp. 17–31). Portsmouth, NH: Heinemann.

Turner, J., & Paris, S. G. (1995). How literacy tasks influence children's motivation for literacy. *The Reading Teacher, 48,* 662–673.

Children's Book References

Aliki. (1979). *Mummies made in Egypt.* New York: HarperCollins.

Bauer, M. D. (1986). *On my honor.* Boston: Houghton Mifflin.

Blume, J. (1971). *Freckle juice.* New York: Bradbury Press.

Gregory, K. (1999). *Cleopatra VII: Daughter of the Nile.* New York: Scholastic.

Hart, G. (1990). *Ancient Egypt.* New York: Knopf.

Houston, G. (1992). *My great-aunt Arizona.* New York:

Howe, D., & Howe, J. (1979). *Bunnicula: A rabbit-tale of mystery.* New York: Atheneum.

Lattimore, D. N. (1992). *The winged cat: A tale of ancient Egypt.* New York: HarperCollins.

Milton, J. (1996). *Mummies.* New York: Grosset & Dunlap.

Naylor, P. R. (1991). *Shiloh.* New York: Atheneum.

Paterson, K. (1977). *Bridge to Terabithia.* New York: Harper & Row.

Rockwell, T. (1973). *How to eat fried worms.* New York: Franklin Watts.

Sachar, L. (1998). *Holes.* New York: Farrar, Straus & Giroux.

Scieszka, J. (1996). *Tut tut.* New York: Penguin.

Stanley, D., & Vennema, P. (1994). *Cleopatra.* New York: Morrow.

Wilcox, C. (1993). *Mummies and their mysteries.* Minneapolis: Carolrhoda.

Chapter 12

Reading and Writing Workshop

— Chapter Questions —

What are the components of reading workshop?

What are the components of writing workshop?

How do teachers manage a workshop classroom?

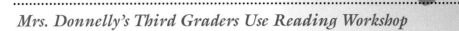

Mrs. Donnelly's Third Graders Use Reading Workshop

The 29 students in Mrs. Donnelly's third-grade classroom spend 75 minutes after lunch each day in reading and writing workshop. Mrs. Donnelly alternates reading workshop and writing workshop month by month, and this month students are involved in reading workshop. During reading workshop, they read for the first 45 minutes. As they return from lunch, they pick up the books they are reading that are stored in their desks and begin reading. Most of the students are reading Beverly Cleary chapter books, including *Ramona and Her Father* (1977), *The Mouse and the Motorcycle* (1965), and *Two Dog Biscuits* (1961), and they continue to wear the sock puppets of Cleary characters that they made as part of their just-concluded author study on Beverly Cleary. This is one of the students' favorite parts of the school day. They enter the classroom after lunch eager to read and begin reading immediately, with little or no direction from Mrs. Donnelly.

Those students who are ready for a new book browse in the classroom library and choose one. Mrs. Donnelly surveys the class as students begin reading, and stops briefly to help Noelle, who can't find her book and is beginning to clean out her desk. Then she walks to the library corner to check on four students who are browsing. Students are responsible for choosing their own books, and all but one make choices and return to their desks. She talks briefly with Marcus, who is still browsing.

Mrs. Donnelly goes to the conference table in one corner of the classroom, where she meets with students who have completed reading a book and have signed up to have a conference. She wants to conference with each child at least once a week. Sometimes she conferences individually with students; at other times, like today, she meets with small groups. She consults the sign-up list and invites four children who have finished reading Beverly Cleary books to participate in a group conference. Students bring their books (and their puppets!) and come to the table.

Mrs. Donnelly asks students to go around the table, taking turns and telling a little about their books. Jenny shares that she has finished reading *Ramona and Her Mother* (Cleary, 1984), but she liked *Ramona and Her Father* (1977) and *Ramona Forever* (1979) better. "This Ramona book is sort of dumb. She makes a toothpaste cake in the sink to get more attention and all she gets is being in trouble. She has to use that toothpaste in the sink to brush her teeth every day until it is all used up."

Mrs. Donnelly asks students if they are using the "making connections to your own life" reading strategy she taught last week in a **minilesson** (see the Compendium for more information about this and all other highlighted terms in this chapter), and students talk about how they made connections as they read. Jenny talks about some of the ways her family is like Ramona's. To end the 15-minute discussion, Mrs. Donnelly asks students what they plan to read next. Most of the students in the group have already picked out their next book. "I don't think I am going to read any more Ramona books for a while," says Jenny. "I'm sort of full of them. I think I'll read *The Magic Finger* [Dahl, 1966].

Lindy said it was good. She read it and it's real weird." Mrs. Donnelly smiles to herself, thinking about how the students have become a community of readers. Once someone in the class reads a book, it often travels around the class from student to student. Several students have begun reading Roald Dahl books, and Mrs. Donnelly decides to plan a minilesson later in the week about the British author.

As students talk, Mrs. Donnelly takes notes in her reading workshop notebook. She has a page for each student and notes the date, title, and author of the book and summarizes the conference. Mrs. Donnelly's notes about Jenny, who participated in the conference, are reproduced in Figure 12–1.

Mrs. Donnelly doesn't have her students write in **reading logs,** as many teachers do. She prefers that they spend all of the reading time doing just that—reading. They write in reading logs as part of literature focus units and literature circles. Students do, however, keep a list of all the books they have read during the year.

When the reading time ends, Mrs. Donnelly gathers the class together for 15 minutes of sharing or a minilesson. On sharing days, students who have finished reading a book and have conferenced with her take turns sharing their books with

Figure 12–1   Mrs. Donnelly's reading workshop conference notes

Jenny

2/25   *Swamp Angel* [Isaacs, 1994]. Continuing to read award books. Recognizes the Caldecott and Newbery seals on books. Asked her to pull these books from the class library and put on a special shelf and share with class. Asked what a tall tale was. Suggested that she read some of Steven Kellogg's tall tales.

3/1   *Pecos Bill* and *Paul Bunyan* [Kellogg, 1986, 1988]. Likes *Swamp Angel* better. Why? Female character and illustration techniques—paint on wood. Asks if tall tales are real. Says her parents know about Pecos Bill and Paul Bunyan but not Swamp Angel. Plans to write a tall tale at home.

3/9   *The Courage of Sarah Noble* [Dalgliesh, 1982]. Got this book from Angela. She loved it. Says she "lived this story and my heart was beating so hard." Wants to read another pioneer book that is scary. Recommended *The Cabin Faced West* [Fritz, 1958].

3/16   *Ramona Forever* [Cleary, 1979]. Excited about Beverly Cleary. Likes this one and *Ramona and Her Father* [1977] that we read together in class. Has already started *Ramona and Her Mother* [1984]. Asked about *The Cabin Faced West* and she said it was boring. Dropped it when we started reading Cleary books.

3/24   *Ramona and Her Mother.* Doesn't like this one as well as the other two Ramona books she's read. Thinks story is simplistic—"dumb." Talked about realistic fiction and compared it to historical fiction. Is applying connecting-to-your-own-life strategy. Plans to read Dahl's *The Magic Finger* [1966] next—suggested by Lindy.

the class. They give a **book talk,** in which they show the book and tell a little about it, and then they offer it to a classmate who wants to read it or put it back in the classroom library. Each student takes two or three minutes to share, and usually five or six students share each day.

On other days, Mrs. Donnelly takes these 15 minutes to teach a reading mini-lesson. She reviews how to use reading strategies such as monitoring and visualizing, and she provides opportunities for students to share how they use the strategies as they read. She also teaches reading workshop procedures, including how to select books, how to apply word-identification skills when students encounter an unfamiliar word, and how to share a book in a book talk. She also introduces new books and authors. On this day she introduces two new chapter books, *Sideways Stories From Wayside School* and *Wayside School Is Falling Down* (Sachar, 1978, 1985). She talks a little about the stories and explains how the Wayside School is organized. She reads the brief, first chapter of each book aloud and then passes out the new books to two eager students.

Mrs. Donnelly spends the last 15 minutes reading a book aloud to the class. Sometimes she reads a picture book, while at other times she reads one or two chapters from a chapter book. Today she is beginning *Strider* (1991), Beverly Cleary's sequel to *Dear Mr. Henshaw* (1983), which she finished reading yesterday. Both books are about a lonely boy named Leigh, who lives with his mother after his parents' divorce and who shows talent as a writer. From the illustration on the cover, students accurately predict that Leigh will adopt a dog, and they listen intently as Mrs. Donnelly reads aloud the first four chapters. Then students talk about the book in a **grand conversation.** They talk about their pets and agree that people who abandon dogs should be punished. They make predictions about how Leigh will change now that he has a dog, and they compare Leigh and his dog Strider to Henry and his dog Ribsy.

When Mrs. Donnelly does writing workshop, she uses a similar format. Students begin by writing for 45 minutes. They write on self-selected topics and usually prepare their writings as picture books or as chapter books with illustrations for each chapter. After students prepare the final copy of their books, they read them aloud to classmates during sharing. Then Mrs. Donnelly teaches a minilesson on writing strategies, writing workshop procedures, or other writing-related topics during the last 15 minutes.

During the school year, each of Mrs. Donnelly's students writes 20 or more books, and she keeps track of students' work in a writing workshop notebook similar to the reading workshop notebook that she keeps. During writing workshop, Mrs. Donnelly conferences with students as they revise and edit their writing, making notes about the topics students choose, the writing forms they use, their application of writing strategies, the types of revisions students make, students' questions and concerns, and possible minilesson topics.

Students are involved in authentic reading and writing projects in reading and writing workshop. They read and respond to self-selected books and write and publish books and other compositions, as the students did in Mrs. Donnelly's third-grade classroom. The workshop approach involves three key characteristics: time, choice, and response. First, in a workshop, students have large chunks of time and the opportunity to read and write. Instead of being add-ons for when students finish schoolwork, reading and writing become the core of the literacy curriculum.

Second, students have ownership of their learning through self-selection of books they read and their topics for writing. Instead of reading books selected by the teacher or reading the same book together as a group or class, students select the books they want to read, books that are suitable to their interests and reading levels. Usually students choose whatever book they want to read—a story, a book of poems, or an informational book—but sometimes teachers set parameters as Mrs. Donnelly did. During writing workshop students plan their writing projects. They choose topics related to hobbies, content-area units, and other interests, and they also select the format for their writing. Often they choose to construct books.

The third characteristic is response. In reading workshop, students respond to books they are reading in reading logs that they share with classmates and the teacher and during conversations with the teacher and classmates. Similarly, in writing workshop, students share rough drafts of books and other compositions they are writing with classmates, and they share their completed and published compositions with genuine audiences.

Reading workshop and writing workshop are different types of workshops. Reading workshop fosters real reading of self-selected stories, poems, and informational books. Students read hundreds of books during reading workshop. At the first-grade level, students might read or reread three or four books each day, totaling close to a thousand books during the school year, and older students read fewer, longer books. Even so, Cora Lee Five, a fifth-grade teacher, reported that her students read between 25 and 144 books (Five, 1988).

Similarly, writing workshop fosters real writing (and the use of the writing process) for genuine purposes and authentic audiences. Each student writes and publishes as many as 50 to 100 short books in the primary grades and 20 to 25 longer books in the middle and upper grades. As they write, students come to see themselves as authors and become interested in learning about the authors of the books they read.

Teachers often use both workshops, or if their schedule does not allow, they may alternate the two, like Mrs. Donnelly does. Schedules for reading and writing workshop at the first-, third-, sixth-, and eighth-grade levels are presented in Figure 12–2.

READING WORKSHOP

Nancie Atwell introduced reading workshop in 1987 as an alternative to traditional reading instruction. In reading workshop, students read books that they choose themselves and respond to books through writing in reading logs and conferences with teachers and classmates (Atwell, 1998). This approach represented a change in what we believe about how children learn and how literature should be used in the classroom. While traditional reading programs emphasized dependence on a teacher's guide to determine how and when particular strategies and skills should be taught, reading workshop is an individualized reading program. Atwell developed reading

Figure 12–2 Schedules for reading and writing workshop

First Grade

9:00–9:10   The teacher rereads several familiar big books with students. Then the teacher introduces a new big book and reads it with the students.

9:10–9:30   Students read matching small books independently and reread other familiar books.

9:30–9:40   Students choose one of the books they have read or reread during independent reading to draw and write a quickwrite.

9:40–9:50   Students share the favorite book and quickwrite.

9:50–10:05   The teacher teaches a reading/writing minilesson.

10:05–10:30   Students write independently on self-selected topics and conference with the teacher.

10:30–10:40   Students share their published books with classmates.

10:40–10:45   The class uses choral reading to enjoy poems and charts hanging in the classroom.

Third Grade

10:30–11:00   Students read self-selected books and respond to the books in reading logs.

11:00–11:15   Students share books they have finished reading with classmates and do informal book talks about them. Students often pass the "good" books to classmates who want to read them next.

11:15–11:30   The teacher teaches a reading/writing minilesson.

11:30–11:55   The teacher reads aloud picture books or chapter books, one or two chapters each day. After reading, students talk about the book in a grand conversation.

           — Continued after lunch —

12:45–1:15   Students write books independently.

1:15–1:30   Students share their published books with classmates.

Sixth Grade

8:20–8:45   The teacher reads aloud a chapter book to students, and students talk about their reactions in a grand conversation.

8:45–9:30   Students write independently using the writing process. They also conference with the teacher.

9:30–9:40   The teacher teaches a reading/writing minilesson.

9:40–10:25   Students read self-selected books independently.

10:25–10:40   Students share published writings and give book talks about books they have read with classmates.

Eighth Grade

During alternating months, students participate in reading workshop or writing workshop.

1:00–1:45   Students read or write independently.

1:45–2:05   The teacher presents a minilesson on a reading or writing procedure, concept, strategy, or skill.

2:05–2:15   Students share with their classmates books they have read or compositions they have published.

workshop with her middle-school students, but it has been adapted and used successfully at every grade level, first through eighth (Hornsby, Parry, & Sukarna, 1992; Hornsby, Sukarna, & Parry, 1986; McWhirter, 1990). There are several different versions of reading workshop, but they usually contain five components: reading, responding, sharing, teaching minilessons, and reading aloud to students.

Component 1: Reading

Students spend 30 to 60 minutes independently reading books and other written materials. Frank Smith (1984) claims that to learn to read, children need to read every day, and several times each day for varied purposes. Teachers need to provide plenty of time in class, and not simply assume that students will practice at home what they are learning at school. In a report entitled *Becoming a Nation of Readers,* researchers reported that, in classrooms that don't have a reading workshop component, primary-grade students typically spend only 7 to 8 minutes each day reading independently, and middle-grade students spend only about 15 minutes each day reading independently (Anderson, Hiebert, Scott, & Wilkinson, 1985). Similarly, McWhirter (1990) surveyed her eighth graders and found that 97% reported that they do not read on their own for pleasure. Moreover, research suggests that higher achievement is associated with more time allocated to academic activities (Brophy & Good, 1986).

Students choose the books that they read during reading workshop. Often they depend on recommendations from classmates. They also read books on particular topics—horses, science fiction, dinosaurs—or by favorite authors, such as Judy Blume, Chris Van Allsburg, and Dr. Seuss. Ohlhausen and Jepsen (1992) developed a

Students choose books they want to read during reading workshop from a well-stocked classroom library.

strategy for choosing books that they called the "Goldilocks Strategy." These teachers developed three categories of books—"Too Easy" books, "Too Hard" books, and "Just Right" books—using "The Three Bears" folktale as their model. The books in the "Too Easy" category were books students had read before or could read fluently. "Too Hard" books were unfamiliar and confusing, and books in the "Just Right" category were interesting and had just a few unfamiliar words. The books in each category vary according to the student's reading level. This approach works at any grade level. Figure 12–3 presents a chart about choosing books using the Goldilocks Strategy. This chart was developed by Mrs. Donnelly's students, the class that was spotlighted at the beginning of this chapter.

When students choose their own books, they take ownership of the reading. Students' reading fluency and enjoyment of reading are related to sustained encounters with interesting texts (Smith, 1984). Reading and responding to literature is the heart of reading workshop.

<u>www.teacher.</u>
<u>Scholastic.com</u>
Scholastic Book Clubs. A good source of inexpensive paperback books for reading workshop.

Figure 12–3 A third-grade chart applying the Goldilocks Strategy

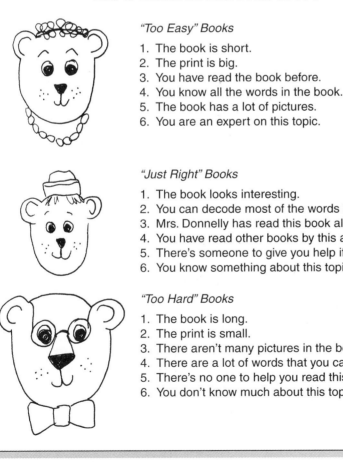

How to Choose the Best Books for YOU

"Too Easy" Books

1. The book is short.
2. The print is big.
3. You have read the book before.
4. You know all the words in the book.
5. The book has a lot of pictures.
6. You are an expert on this topic.

"Just Right" Books

1. The book looks interesting.
2. You can decode most of the words in the book.
3. Mrs. Donnelly has read this book aloud to you.
4. You have read other books by this author.
5. There's someone to give you help if you need it.
6. You know something about this topic.

"Too Hard" Books

1. The book is long.
2. The print is small.
3. There aren't many pictures in the book.
4. There are a lot of words that you can't decode.
5. There's no one to help you read this book.
6. You don't know much about this topic.

Teachers often read their own books and magazines or read a book of children's literature during reading workshop. Through their example, they are modeling and communicating the importance of reading. Teachers also conference with students about the books they are reading. As they conference, they talk briefly and quietly with students about their reading. Students may also read aloud favorite quotes or an interesting passage to the teacher.

Students read all sorts of books during reading workshop, including stories, informational books, biographies, and books of poetry. They also read magazines. Most of their reading materials are selected from the classroom library, but students also bring other books from home and borrow books from classmates, from the public library, and from the school library. Students read many award-winning books during reading workshop, but they also read series of popular books and technical books related to their hobbies and special interests. These books are not necessarily the same books that teachers use for literature focus units, but students often choose to reread books they have read earlier in the school year or the previous year in literature studies.

Teachers need to have literally hundreds of books in their class libraries, including books written at a range of reading levels, in order to have enough books so that every student can read during reading workshop. Primary teachers often worry about finding books that their emerging readers can handle independently. Wordless picture books in which the story is told entirely through pictures, alphabet books, number books, predictable books, leveled books, and books the teacher has read aloud several times are often the most accessible for kindergartners and first graders. Primary-grade children often read and reread easy-to-read books such as those in the Scholastic Bookshelf series and the Wright Group's Story Box kits. Figure 12–4 lists many trade books that might be placed in classroom libraries and used for reading workshop in kindergarten through eighth grade. Of course, many of the books listed are suitable for other grade levels, too.

Teachers need to introduce students—especially reluctant readers—to the books in the classroom library so that they can more effectively choose books to read during reading workshop. The best way to preview books is using a very brief **book talk** to interest students in the book. In a book talk, teachers tell students a little about the book, show the cover, and perhaps read the first paragraph or two (Prill, 1994–1995). Teachers also give book talks to introduce text sets of books, and students give book talks as they share books they have read with the class during the sharing part of reading workshop.

Component 2: Responding

Students usually keep **reading logs** in which they write their initial responses to the books they are reading. Sometimes students dialogue with the teacher about the book they are reading. A journal allows for ongoing written conversation between the teacher and individual students (Atwell, 1998; Staton, 1988). Responses often demonstrate students' reading strategies and offer insights into their thinking about literature. Seeing how students think about their reading helps teachers guide their learning.

Teachers play an important role in helping students expand and enrich their responses to literature (Hancock, 1993). They help students move beyond writing summaries and toward reflecting and making connections between literature and their own lives (Barone, 1990; Kelly, 1990). Excerpts from students' reading log entries about

Figure 12–4 Books for reading workshop collections

Kindergarten

Ahlberg, J., & Ahlberg, A. (1978). *Each peach, pear, plum.* New York: Scholastic.

Baker, K. (1990). *Who is the beast?* Orlando, FL: Harcourt Brace.

Barton, B. (1990). *Bones, bones, dinosaur bones.* New York: HarperCollins.

Burningham, J. (1994). *The friend.* Cambridge, MA: Candlewick.

Carlson, N. (1988). *I like me!* New York: Viking.

Crews, D. (1982). *Carousel.* New York: Greenwillow.

Cristini, E. (1984). *The pond.* New York: Picture Book Studio.

Dubanevich, A. (1983). *Pigs in hiding.* New York: Scholastic.

Ehlert, L. (1990). *Fish eyes: A book you can count on.* Orlando, FL: Harcourt Brace.

Martin, B., Jr. (1983). *Brown bear, brown bear, what do you see?* New York: Holt.

McPhail, D. (1988). *David McPhail's animals A to Z.* New York: Scholastic Hardcover.

Morris, A. (1989). *Hats, hats, hats.* New York: Mulberry Books.

Rockwell, A. (1986). *Fire engines.* New York: Dutton.

Seuss, Dr. (1963). *Hop on pop.* New York: Random House. (And other books by this author.)

Tafuri, N. (1986). *Who's counting?* New York: Mulberry Books.

Turkle, B. (1976). *Deep in the forest.* New York: Dutton.

Westcott, N. B. (1980). *The lady with the alligator purse.* New York: Lippincott.

Wood, A. (1982). *Quick as a cricket.* London: Child's Play.

First Grade

Carle, E. (1994). *Today is Monday.* New York: Philomel. (And other books by this author.)

de Paola, T. (1978). *Pancakes for breakfast.* New York: Harcourt Brace Jovanovich.

Dr. Seuss. (1988). *Green eggs and ham.* New York: Random House. (And other books by Dr. Seuss.)

Ehlert, L. (1989). *Eating the alphabet: Fruits and vegetables from A to Z.* Orlando: Harcourt Brace.

Galdone, P. (1968). *Henny penny.* New York: Clarion.

Guarino, D. (1989). *Is your mama a llama?* New York: Scholastic.

Hoberman, M. A. (1978). *A house is a house for me.* New York: Penguin.

Mayer, M. (1968). *There's a nightmare in my closet.* New York: Dial. (And other books by this author.)

Morris, A. (1989). *Bread, bread, bread.* New York: Scholastic.

Most, B. (1978). *If the dinosaurs came back.* Orlando: Harcourt Brace.

Numeroff, L. J. (1985). *If you give a mouse a cookie.* New York: Harper & Row.

Raffi. (1988). *Wheels on the bus.* New York: Crown.

Rosen, M. (1989). *We're going on a bear hunt.* New York: McElderry.

Sendak, M. (1962). *Where the wild things are.* New York: Harper & Row.

Shaw, N. (1986). *Sheep in a jeep.* Boston: Houghton Mifflin. (And other books in the series.)

Walsh, E. S. (1989). *Mouse paint.* Orlando: Harcourt Brace.

Wood, A. (1984). *The napping house.* Orlando: Harcourt Brace Jovanovich.

Ziefert, H. (1993). *Harry's bath.* New York: Bantam.

Second Grade

Blume, J. (1971). *Freckle juice.* New York: Dell.

Brett, J. (1989). *The mitten.* New York: Putnam.

Cazet, D. (1993). *Never spit on your shoes.* New York: Orchard.

Coerr, E. (1986). *The Josefina story quilt.* New York: Harper & Row.

Conrad, P. (1989). *The tub people.* New York: Harper & Row.

Fletcher, N. (1993). *Penguin.* London: Dorling Kindersley.

Fowler, A. (1990). *It could still be a tree.* Chicago: Childrens Book Press.

Gibbons, G. (1993). *Pirates: Robbers of the high seas.* Boston: Little, Brown.

Giff, P. R. (1984). *The beast in Ms. Rooney's room.* New York: Bantam. (And other books in the series.)

Heller, R. (1981). *Chickens aren't the only ones.* New York: Grosset & Dunlap. (And other books by this author.)

Kasza, K, (1987). *The wolf's chicken stew.* New York: Putnam.

Kellogg, S. (1979). *Pinkerton, behave!* New York: Dial.

Kroll, S. (1993). *Andrew wants a dog.* New York: Hyperion.

Lester, H. (1988). *Tacky the penguin.* Boston: Houghton Mifflin.

Noble, T. H. (1980). *The day Jimmy's boa ate the wash.* New York: Dial.

Numeroff, L. (1993). *Dogs don't wear sneakers.* New York: Simon & Schuster.

Sachar, L. (1992). *Monkey soup.* New York: Knopf.

Zemach, M. (1983). *The little red hen.* New York: Farrar, Straus & Giroux.

Figure 12–4 continued

Third Grade

Brenner, B. (1978). *Wagon wheels.* New York: Harper & Row.

Cherry, L. (1993). *The great Kapok tree.* Orlando: Harcourt Brace Jovanovich.

Cleary, B. (1981). *Ramona Quimby, age 8.* New York: Morrow. (And other books in the series.)

Cohen, B. (1983). *Molly's pilgrim.* New York: Bantam.

Cole, J. (1992). *The magic school bus on the ocean floor.* New York: Scholastic.

Dahl, R. (1966). *The magic finger.* New York: Puffin.

Danziger, P. (1994). *Amber Brown is not a crayon.* New York: Putnam.

Hulme, J. N. (1991). *Sea squares.* New York: Hyperion.

Maestro, B. (1993). *The story of money.* New York: Mulberry Books.

Martin, B., Jr. & Archambault, J. (1986). *White Dynamite and Curley Kidd.* New York: Henry Holt.

Prelutsky, J. (1985). *My parents think I'm sleeping.* New York: Greenwillow.

Sachar, L. (1978). *Sideways stories from Wayside School.* New York: Avon Books.

Shannon, G. (1994). *Still more stories to solve: Fourteen folktales from around the world.* New York: Greenwillow.

Spier, P. (1980). *People.* New York: Doubleday.

Viorst, J. (1972). *Alexander and the terrible, horrible, no good, very bad day.* New York: Atheneum.

Wells, R. E. (1993). *Is a blue whale the biggest thing there is?* Morton Grove, IL: Whitman.

Yolen, J. (1980). *Commander Toad in space.* New York: Coward-McCann. (And other books in the series.)

Fourth Grade

Blume, J. (1972). *Tales of a fourth grade nothing.* New York: Dutton. (And the sequel.)

Dahl, R. (1992). *Esio trot.* New York: Viking.

Fritz, J. (1976). *What's the big idea, Ben Franklin?* New York: Coward-McCann.

Gardiner, J. R. (1980). *Stone Fox.* New York: Crowell.

Goble, P. (1988). *Her seven brothers.* New York: Bradbury. (And other books by this author.)

Haskins, J. (1989). *Count your way through Mexico.* Minneapolis: Carolrhoda.

Levine, E. (1986). *. . . If you traveled west in a covered wagon.* New York: Scholastic.

MacLachlan, P. (1985). *Sarah, plain and tall.* New York: Harper & Row.

Monjo, F. N. (1970). *The drinking gourd.* New York: Harper & Row.

Prelutsky, J. (1982). *The baby uggs are hatching.* New York: Greenwillow.

Rockwell, T. (1973). *How to eat fried worms.* New York: Franklin Watts.

Scieszka, J. (1989). *The true story of the three little pigs.* New York: Viking.

Smith, R. K. (1972). *Chocolate fever.* New York: Coward.

Spinelli, J. (1993). *Fourth grade rats.* New York Scholastic.

Thaler, M. (1985). *Cream of creature from the school cafeteria.* New York: Avon.

Van Allsburg, C. (1981). *Jumanji.* Boston: Houghton Mifflin.

Waters, K. (1991). *The story of the White House.* New York: Scholastic.

Fifth Grade

Anno, M. (1983). *Anno's USA.* New York: Philomel.

Avi. (1984). *The fighting ground.* New York: Harper & Row.

Cleary, B. (1983). *Dear Mr. Henshaw.* New York: Morrow.

Coerr, E. (197). *Sadako and the thousand paper cranes.* New York: Putnam.

Cole, J. (1989). *Anna Banana: 101 jump-rope rhymes.* New York: Morrow.

Dahl, R. (1964). *Charlie and the chocolate factory.* New York: Knopf.

Hurwitz, J. (1994). *School spirit.* New York: Morrow.

King-Smith, D. (1988). *Martin's mice.* New York: Crown.

Kline, S. (1990). *Horrible Harry in room 2B.* New York: Viking.

McAfee, A. (1987). *Kirsty knows best.* New York: Knopf.

McGovern, A. (1992). *. . . If you lived in colonial times.* New York: Scholastic.

Packard, E. (1979). *The mystery of chimney rock (Choose your own adventure).* New York: Bantam.

Pinkwater, D. M. (1977). *Fat men from space.* New York: Dell.

Schwartz, D. M. (1985). *How much is a million?* New York: Scholastic.

Taylor, M. D. (1990). *Mississippi bridge.* New York: Dial.

Van Allsburg, C. (1985). *The polar express.* Boston: Hougton Mifflin. (And other books by this author.)

Wiesner, D. (1991). *Tuesday.* New York: Clarion.

Wilder, L. I. (1953). *Little house in the big woods.* New York: Harper & Row. (And other books in the series.)

Sixth Grade

Byars, B. (1968). *The midnight fox.* New York: Viking.

Filipovic, Z. (1993). *Zlata's diary: A child's life in Sarajevo.* New York: Viking.

Figure 12–4 continued

Fleischman, S. (1990). *The midnight horse.* New York: Greenwillow.

Gilson, J. (1985). *Thirteen ways to sink a sub.* New York: Lothrop, Lee & Shepard.

Hart, G. (1990). *Ancient Egypt.* New York: Knopf.

Howe, D., & Howe, J. (1979). *Bunnicula: A rabbit-tale of mystery.* New York: Atheneum. (And other books in the series.)

Kehret, P. (1993). *Terror at the zoo.* New York: Cobble-hill.

L'Engle, M. (1962). *A wrinkle in time.* New York: Farrar, Straus & Giroux.

Lewis, C. S. (1950). *The lion, the witch and the wardrobe.* New York: Macmillan.

Lowry, L. (1989). *Number the stars.* Boston: Houghton Mifflin. (And other books by this author.)

Macaulay, D. (1975). *Pyramid.* Boston: Houghton Mifflin.

Mazer, A. (Ed.). (1993). *America street: A multicultural anthology of stories.* New York: Persea.

Naylor, P. R. (1991). *Shiloh.* New York: Atheneum.

Paterson, K. (1977). *Bridge to Terabithia.* New York: Harper & Row.

Patterson, F. (1985). *Koko's kitten.* New York: Scholastic.

Ride, S., & O'Shaughnessy, T. (1994). *The third planet: Exploring the earth from space.* New York: Crown.

Silverstein, S. (1974). *Where the sidewalk ends.* New York: Harper & Row.

Slote, A. (1991). *Finding Buck McHenry.* New York: HarperCollins.

Soto, G. (1990). *Baseball in April and other stories.* Orlando: Harcourt Brace.

Seventh Grade

Aaseng, N. (1992). *Navajo code talkers.* New York: Walker.

Avi. (1991). *Nothing but the truth.* New York: Orchard.

Caras, R. (1987). *Roger Caras' treasury of great cat stories.* New York: Dutton.

Conrad, P. (1985). *Prairie songs.* New York: Harper-Collins.

Cushman, K. (1994). *Catherine called Birdy.* New York: Dutton.

Danzinger, P. (1979). *Can you sue your parents for malpractice?* New York: Delacorte.

Fox, P. (1984). *One-eyed cat.* New York: Bradbury.

Hinton, S. E. (1967). *The outsiders.* New York: Viking.

Jukes, M. (1988). *Getting even.* New York: Knopf.

Krementz, J. (1989). *How it feels to fight for your life.* Boston: Little, Brown.

McKinley, R. (1984). *The hero and the crown.* New York: Greenwillow. (And other books by this author.)

O'Dell, S. (1960). *Island of the blue dolphins.* Boston: Houghton Mifflin.

Paulson, G. (1987). *Hatchet.* New York: Delacorte. (And other books by this author.)

Rawls, W. (1961). *Where the red fern grows.* New York: Doubleday.

Service, P. F. (1988). *Stinker from space.* New York: Fawcett.

Siebert, D. (1991). *Sierra.* New York: Harper & Row.

Wallace, B. (1992). *Buffalo gal.* New York: Holiday House.

Eighth Grade

Adams, R. (1974). *Watership down.* New York: Macmillan.

Brooks, B. (1984). *The moves make the man.* New York: HarperCollins.

Duncan, L. (1981). *Stranger with my face.* Boston: Little, Brown.

Freedman, R. (1987). *Lincoln: A photobiography.* New York: Clarion.

Gallo, D. R. (Ed.). (1993). *Join in: Multiethnic short stories.* New York: Delacorte.

George, J. C. (1989). *Shark beneath the reef.* New York: Harper & Row.

Hermes, P. (1991). *Mama, let's dance.* Boston: Little, Brown.

Janeczko, P. (Ed.). (1991). *Preposterous: Poems of youth.* New York: Orchard.

Macaulay, D. (1988). *The way things work: From levers to lasers, cars to computers—A visual guide to the world of machines.* Boston: Houghton Mifflin.

Moore, K. (1994). *. . . If you lived at the time of the Civil War.* New York: Scholastic.

Murphy, C. R. (1992). *To the summit.* New York: Lodestar.

Myers, W. D. (1990). *The mouse rap.* New York: Harper-Collins

Naylor, P. R. (1992). *All but Alice.* New York: Atheneum

Paterson, K. (1980). *Jacob have I loved.* New York: HarperCollins.

Peck, R. N. (1972). *A day no pigs would die.* New York: Knopf.

Reaver, C. (1994). *A little bit dead.* New York: Delacorte.

Sleator, W. (1986). *Interstellar pig.* New York: Dutton.

Sperry, A. (1968). *Call it courage.* New York: Collier.

Zindel, P. (1968). *The pigman.* New York: HarperCollins.

Bunnicula: A Rabbit-Tale of Mystery (Howe & Howe, 1979) are presented in Figure 12–5. These excerpts reflect the depth of students' responses to the book.

Teachers can collect students' journals periodically to monitor their responses. Wollman-Bonilla (1989) recommends writing back and forth with students, with the idea that students write more if the teacher responds. Also, teachers can model and

Figure 12–5 Excerpts from students' responses to *Bunnicula*

I think the Monroes will find out what Chester and Harold are doing.

Bunnicula must really be scared of Harold and Chester. I wouldn't trust Chester either. He's sneaky.

That was stupid! They were pounding a steak—MEAT—into the bunny's heart. That won't work!

I know how Chester and Harold feel. It's like when I got a new baby sister and everyone paid attention to her. I got ignored a lot.

I just can't stop reading. This book is so cool. And it's funny, too.

Can a bunny be a vampire? I don't think so. A bunny couldn't suck the blood out of a vegetable. They don't even have blood.

I think Chester is jealous of the baby rabbit.

Gross!!! The vegetables are all white and there are two little fang holes in each one.

I was right! I knew Harold and Chester would try to take care of Bunnicula. What I didn't know was that the Monroes would come home early.

Mrs. S., I want to write a letter to this author. I've got questions for him. Also, are there more Bunnicula books? I gotta keep reading.

I wonder why the vegetables are turning white. I know it's not Bunnicula but I don't know why.

If I were Bunnicula, I'd run away. He's just not safe in that house!

Those Monroes don't know what is happening in their own house. Are they blind?

My dog is a lot like Harold. He gets on my bed with me and he loves snacks, but you should never feed a dog chocolate.

I guess Bunnicula really is a vampire.

The Monroes got Bunnicula at a movie theater. They named him Bunnicula because they found him when a Dracula movie was on. Bunny + Dracula = Bunnicula.

This is a great book! I know stuff like this couldn't happen but it would be awesome if it could. It's just fantasy but it's like I believe it.

support students' responses in their responses. However, because responding to students' journals is very time-consuming, teachers should keep their responses brief and not respond to every entry.

Teachers and researchers have examined students' responses and noticed patterns in their responses. Hancock (1992, 1993) identified these eight categories:

1. *Monitoring understanding.* Students get to know the characters and explain how the story is making sense to them. These responses usually occur at the beginning of a book.
2. *Making inferences.* Students share their insights into the feelings and motives of a character. They often begin their comment with "I think."
3. *Making, validating, or invalidating predictions.* Students speculate about what will happen later in the story and also confirm or deny predictions they made previously.
4. *Expressing wonder or confusion.* Students reflect on the way the story is developing. They ask "I wonder why" questions and write about confusions.
5. *Character interaction.* Students show that they are personally involved with a character, sometimes writing "If I were _____, I would." They express empathy and share related experiences from their own lives. Also, they may give advice to the character.
6. *Character assessment.* Students judge a character's actions and often use evaluative terms such as "nice" or "dumb."
7. *Story involvement.* Students reveal their involvement in the story as they express satisfaction with how the story is developing. They may comment on their desire to continue reading or use terms such as "disgusting," "weird," or "awesome" to react to sensory aspects of the story.
8. *Literary criticism.* Students offer "I liked . . ./I didn't like . . ." opinions and praise or condemn an author's style. Sometimes students compare the book with others they have read or compare the author with other authors with whom they are familiar.

The first four categories are personal meaning-making options in which students make inferences about characters, offer predictions, ask questions, or discuss confusions. The next three categories focus on character and plot development. Students are more involved with the story, and they offer reactions to the characters and events of the story. The last category is literary evaluation, in which students evaluate books and reflect on their own literary tastes.

These categories can extend the possibilities of response by introducing teachers and students to a wide variety of response options. Hancock (1992, 1993) recommends that teachers begin by assessing the kinds of responses students are currently making. They can read students' journals, categorize entries, and make an assessment. Often students use only a few types of responses, not the wide range that is available. Teachers can teach minilessons and model types of responses that students aren't using, and they can ask questions in journals to prompt students to think in new ways about the story they are reading.

Some students write minimal or very limited responses in journals. It is important that students read books they find personally interesting and that they feel free to share their thoughts, feelings, and questions with a trusted audience—usually the teacher. Sometimes writing entries on a computer and using e-mail to share the entries with students in another class or with other interested readers increase students' interest in writing more elaborate responses, as the Technology Link on page 418 shows.

Technology Link   **Electronic Dialoguing About Reading, Literature, and Books**

Students can share responses about books they are reading using e-mail. Students write responses to books they are reading independently and send them to students in another classroom, older students, or preservice teachers at a university. Moore (1991) described a program set up between Eastern Michigan University and a fifth-grade class in the Ypsilanti School District in which teachers in a graduate course dialogued with students in the class. Students wrote about books they were reading, and the teachers responded. The teachers encouraged students to expand their entries, make personal connections, and reflect on their reading. One fifth grader, Chih Ping, wrote these responses about Judy Blume's *Superfudge* (1980):

11/7: I am enjoying *Superfudge*. My favorite character is Fudge. I like him because he is so funny.

11/21: I think Peter's new house is real good because in Pine Grove the apartments aren't as good. I have moved before. I just moved here and lived here like about two years. This is my second year at Chapelle. It also seemed hard for me at school. After I met Robert (one of my best friends) it became easy at school. He plays in band and I play in orchestra. I am good at playing in orchestra. I play a violin. Sometimes the teacher tells me to teach the violinist how to play a song (Violinist = people who want to play violin) while she taught other people how to play the guitar and a person how to play the viola. (p. 283)

These two entries show how this student's responses became more elaborate through dialoguing by e-mail. For more information about electronic dialoguing, see Moore (1991).

Responding in reading logs replaces doing workbook pages or worksheets. Teachers traditionally use worksheets as a management tool or because they think their use will increase students' reading levels. In *Becoming a Nation of Readers* (Anderson et al., 1985), the authors reported that children spend up to 70% of reading instructional time engaged in completing worksheets and workbook pages, even though these provide only perfunctory levels of reading practice in traditional classrooms.

During reading and responding time, there is little or no talking. Students are engrossed in reading and writing independently. Rarely do students interrupt classmates, go to the rest room, or get drinks of water, except in case of emergency. They do not use reading workshop time to do homework or other schoolwork.

www.mcps.k12.md.us

What on Earth Is Reading Workshop? See how a seventh-grade teacher uses reading workshop in his English classes.

Component 3: Sharing

For the last 15 minutes of reading workshop, the class gathers together to discuss books they have finished reading. Students talk about the book and why they liked it. Sometimes they read a brief excerpt aloud or formally pass the book to a classmate who wants to read it. Sharing is important because it helps students form a community to value and celebrate each other's accomplishments (Hansen, 1987).

Component 4: Teaching Minilessons

The teacher spends 10 to 20 minutes teaching minilessons, brief lessons on reading workshop procedures and reading strategies and skills. Topics for minilessons are usually drawn from students' observed needs, comments students make during conferences, and procedures that students need to know how to do for reading workshop. Figure 12–6 lists possible minilesson topics.

Minilessons are sometimes taught to the whole class, while at other times they are taught to small groups. At the beginning of the school year, Mrs. Donnelly teaches minilessons to the whole class on choosing books to read during reading

Figure 12–6   Minilesson topics for reading and writing workshop

Procedures	Concepts	Strategies/Skills
Reading Workshop		
Choose a book	Aesthetic reading	Identify unfamiliar words
Abandon a book	Efferent reading	Visualize
Listen to book read aloud	Comprehension	Predict and confirm
Read independently	Story genre	Engage with text
Decode unfamiliar words	Story elements	Identify with characters
Respond in reading logs	Intertextuality	Elaborate on the plot
Use double-entry journals	Sequels	Notice opposites
Give a book talk	Author information	Monitor understanding
Conference		Connect to one's own life
		Connect to previously read stories
		Value the story
		Evaluate the story
Writing Workshop		
Choose a topic	The writing process	Gather ideas
Cluster ideas	Audience	Organize ideas
Make a table of contents	Purposes for writing	Draft
Participate in writing groups	Writing forms	Revise
Proofread	Proofreaders' marks	Use metaphors and similes
Use the dictionary	Authors	Use imagery
Conference with the teacher	Illustration techniques	Sentence combining
Write an "All About the Author" page	Wordplay	Edit
Make hardcover books		Identify and correct spelling errors
Share published writing		Use capital letters correctly
Use author's chair		Use punctuation marks correctly
Use rubrics		Use dialogue
		Value the composition

Teachers teach minilessons on procedures, skills, and strategies during reading and writing workshop.

workshop; later in the year she teaches minilessons on noticing literary language and creating images in your mind as you read. She also teaches minilessons on particular authors when she introduces their stories to the whole class. In addition, she teaches minilessons on literary genres—contemporary realism, science fiction, historical fiction, folktales—when she sets out collections of books representing each genre in the classroom library. When she noticed that several students seemed unfamiliar with making predictions, she worked with that group, and when several other students questioned her about the flashback at the beginning of *The Day Jimmy's Boa Ate the Wash* (Noble, 1980), she taught a minilesson on this literary device.

Component 5: Reading Aloud to Students

Teachers often read picture books and chapter books aloud to the class as part of reading workshop. They choose high-quality literature that students might not be able to read themselves, award-winning books that they feel every student should be exposed to, or books that relate to a social studies or science theme. After reading, students participate in a grand conversation to talk about the book and share the reading experience. This activity is important because students listen to a story read aloud and respond to the story together as a community of learners, not as individuals.

WRITING WORKSHOP

Writing workshop is an excellent way to implement the writing process (Atwell, 1998; Calkins, 1994; Graves, 1994; Hornsby et al., 1992). Students write on topics that they choose themselves, and they assume ownership of their writing and learning. At the same time, the teacher's role changes from being a provider of knowledge to serving as a facilitator and guide. The classroom becomes a community of writers who write and share their writing. There is a spirit of pride and acceptance in the classroom.

In a writing workshop classroom, students have writing folders in which they keep all papers related to the writing project they are working on. They also keep writing notebooks in which they jot down images, impressions, dialogue, and experiences that they can build upon for writing projects (Calkins, 1991). Students have access to different kinds of paper, some lined and some unlined, as well as writing instruments such as pencils and red and blue pens. They also have access to the classroom library. Many times students' writing grows out of favorite books they have read. They may write a sequel to a book or retell a story from a different viewpoint. Primary-grade students often use patterns from books they have read to structure a book they are writing.

As they write, students sit at desks or tables arranged in small groups. The teacher circulates around the classroom, conferencing briefly with students, and the classroom atmosphere is free enough that students converse quietly with classmates and move around the classroom to assist classmates or share ideas. There is space for students to meet together for **writing groups,** and often a sign-up sheet for writing groups is posted in the classroom. A table is available for the teacher to meet with individual students or small groups for conferences, writing groups, proofreading, and minilessons.

Writing workshop is a 60- to 90-minute period scheduled each day. During this time students are involved in three components: writing, sharing, and minilessons. Sometimes a fourth activity, reading aloud to students, is added to writing workshop when it is not used in conjunction with reading workshop.

Component 1: Writing

Students spend 30 to 45 minutes or longer working independently on writing projects. Just as students in reading workshop choose and read books at their own pace, in writing workshop students work at their own pace on writing projects they have chosen themselves. Most students move through all five steps of the writing process—prewriting, drafting, revising, editing, and publishing—at their own pace, but young children often use an abbreviated process consisting of prewriting, drafting, and publishing. Teachers often begin writing workshop by reviewing the five steps of the writing process, setting guidelines for writing workshop, and taking students through one writing activity together. A set of guidelines for writing workshop that one seventh-grade class developed is presented in Figure 12–7.

Teachers conference with students as they write. Many teachers prefer moving around the classroom to meet with students rather than having the students come to a table to meet with the teacher. Too often a line forms as students wait to meet with the teacher, and students lose precious writing time. Some teachers move around the classroom in a regular pattern, meeting with one-fifth of the students each day. In this way they can conference with every student during the week.

Other teachers spend the first 15 to 20 minutes of writing workshop stopping briefly to check on 10 or more students each day. Many use a zigzag pattern to get to all parts of the classroom each day. These teachers often kneel down beside each student, sit on the edge of the student's seat, or carry their own stool to each student's desk. During the one- or two-minute conference, teachers ask students what they are writing, listen to students read a paragraph or two, and then ask what they plan to do

 A seventh-grade class's guidelines for writing workshop

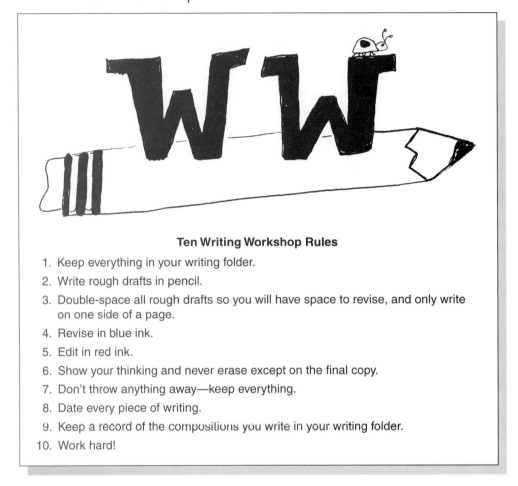

Ten Writing Workshop Rules

1. Keep everything in your writing folder.
2. Write rough drafts in pencil.
3. Double-space all rough drafts so you will have space to revise, and only write on one side of a page.
4. Revise in blue ink.
5. Edit in red ink.
6. Show your thinking and never erase except on the final copy.
7. Don't throw anything away—keep everything.
8. Date every piece of writing.
9. Keep a record of the compositions you write in your writing folder.
10. Work hard!

next. Then these teachers use the remaining time during writing workshop to more formally conference with students who are revising and editing their compositions. Students often sign up for these conferences. The teachers find strengths in students' writing, ask questions, and discover possibilities during these revising conferences. Some teachers like to read the pieces themselves, while others like to listen to students read their papers aloud. As they interact with students, teachers model the kinds of responses that students are learning to give to each other.

As students meet together to share their writing during revising and editing, they continue to develop their sense of community. They share their rough drafts with classmates in writing groups composed of four or five students. In some classrooms, teachers join the writing groups whenever they can, but students normally run the groups themselves. They take turns reading their rough drafts to each other and listen as their classmates offer compliments and suggestions for revision. In contrast, students usually work with one partner to edit their writing, and they often use red pens.

After proofreading their drafts with a classmate and then meeting with the teacher for final editing, students make the final copy of their writings. Students often want to print out their writings using the computer so that their final copies will appear professional. Many times students compile their final copies to make books during writing workshop, but sometimes they attach their writing to artwork, make posters, write letters that will be mailed, or perform scripts as skits or puppet shows. Not every piece is necessarily published, however. Sometimes students decide not to continue with a piece of writing. They file the piece in their writing folders and start something new.

Even kindergartners, first graders, and second graders can work productively during writing workshop. They often write single-draft books and use their developing knowledge of phoneme-grapheme correspondence to spell words. One page from a kindergartner's turtle book is shown in Figure 12–8. The text reads, "Turtles hide in their shells." After drawing a picture of a turtle and cutting it out for the cover of the book, William asked a parent volunteer to cut eight sheets of paper in the same shape and to help punch holes and bind the book together with yarn. William worked for several days to write and illustrate the book. He copied some of the correctly spelled words from a book on turtles that he found in the library center, and other words were spelled by a parent volunteer. Here is the complete text of the book, along with a translation:

Cover	*The Turtle Bok.*	The Turtle Book
1	*Trt hv lz*	Turtles have shells.
2	*T id in their shells.*	Turtles hide in their shells.
3	*T r gre and br*	Turtles are green and brown.
4	*Turtls etlus and fiz*	Turtles eat lettuce and flies.
5	*Tls knsm*	Turtles can swim.
6	*T lv biapd*	Turtles live by a pond.
7	*Turtles r cbd reptiles.*	Turtles are cold-blooded reptiles.
8	*I luv trlsss.*	I love turtles.

Primary-grade students make literally hundreds of little books bound with yarn and staples as they experiment with writing. Like William, many students write books about favorite animals. They also make color books, number books, pattern books, and books about their families, and they retell familiar stories such as "Little Red Riding Hood" and "The Three Billy Goats Gruff."

Parent volunteers, aides, and cross-age tutors support students as they write, encouraging them to experiment with spellings and punctuation marks. They also demonstrate how to form letters, and listen as children reread their books. Because students' spellings are not conventional, it is important that students reread their books several times to parents and tutors so that they can remember them. As students gain experience with writing, parent volunteers and cross-age tutors begin conferencing with students and guiding them into revising and editing (Baker, 1994). These volunteers help students reflect on their writing by asking pertinent questions to help them clarify or refine their thinking.

Figure 12–8   A page from a kindergartner's book about turtles

Component 2: Sharing

For the last 10 to 15 minutes of writing workshop, the class gathers together to share their new publications and make other related announcements. Younger students often sit in a circle or gather together on a rug for sharing time. If an author's chair is available, each student sits in the special chair to read his or her composition. After each reading, classmates clap and offer compliments. They may also make other comments and suggestions, but the focus is on celebrating completed writing projects, not on revising the composition to make it better. Classmates help celebrate after the child shares by clapping, and perhaps the best praise is having a classmate ask if he or she can read the newly published book.

Component 3: Teaching Minilessons

www.gallaudet.edu

🕸 *Minilessons for Writers' Workshop. Lists of minilesson topics.*

During this 10- to 20-minute period, teachers provide brief lessons on writing workshop procedures and writing strategies and skills, such as organizing ideas, proofreading, and using quotation marks in marking dialogue. In the middle and upper grades, teachers often make a transparency of an anonymous student's piece of writing (often a student in another class or from a previous year) and then display it using an overhead projector. Students read the writing, and the teacher uses it to teach the lesson, which may focus on giving suggestions for revision, combining sentences, proofreading, or writing a stronger lead sentence. Teachers also use excerpts from books stu-

Students sit in the author's chair to share their writing with classmates.

dents are reading for minilessons to show students how published authors use writing skills and strategies. Refer back to Figure 12–6 for a list of minilessons for writing workshop. These minilessons are similar to those taught in reading workshop. And for other ideas for minilessons, check *Craft Lessons: Teaching Writing K–8* (Fletcher & Portalupi, 1998), *Writing Rules! Teaching Kids to Write for Life, Grades 4–8* (Brusko, 1999), and *Reviser's Toolbox* (Lane, 1999).

Teachers also share information about authors and how they write during mini-lessons. In order for students to think of themselves as writers, they need to know what writers do. Each year there are more autobiographies written by authors. James Howe, author of *Bunnicula: A Rabbit-Tale of Mystery* (Howe & Howe, 1979), has written an autobiography, *Playing With Words* (1994), in which he reflects on his desire since childhood to make people laugh and describes his writing routine and how he makes time to read and write every day. Some of the other books in the Meet the Author series are *Firetalking,* by Patricia Polacco (1994), *Hau Kola/Hello Friend,* by Paul Goble (1994), and *Surprising Myself,* by Jean Fritz (1992).

Filmstrip and video productions about authors and illustrators are also available. For example, in American School Publishers' Meet the Newbery Author series, Arnold Lobel (1978) describes his writing process and calls his revising "unwriting." He shows how he uses a pen to cross out the unnecessary words so that his stories will fit within the 32-page picture book format. Videos are an excellent medium for authors and illustrators to demonstrate their craft. In a 27-minute video, *Eric Carle: Picture Writer* (1993), Eric Carle demonstrates how he uses paint and collage to create the illustrations for his popular picture books.

MANAGING A WORKSHOP CLASSROOM

www.jps.net

Online Writing Workshop.
A virtual middle school writing classroom with resources for every step of the writing process.

It takes time to establish a workshop approach in the classroom, especially if students are used to reading from basal readers. Students need to learn how to become responsible for their own learning. They need to develop new ways of working and learning, and they have to form a community of readers and writers in the classroom. For reading workshop, students need to know how to select books, how to read aesthetically, and other reading workshop procedures. For writing workshop, students need to know how to develop and refine a piece of writing, how to make books and booklets for their compositions, and other writing workshop procedures. Sometimes students complain that they don't know what to write about, but in time they learn how to brainstorm possible topics and to keep a list of topics in their writing workshop notebooks.

Teachers begin to establish the workshop environment in their classroom from the first day of the school year by allowing students to choose the books they read and the topics for writing. Teachers provide time for students to read and write and teach them how to respond to books and to their classmates' writing. Through their interactions with students, the respect they show to students, and the way they model reading and writing, teachers establish the classroom as a community of learners.

Teachers develop a schedule for reading and writing workshop with time allocated for each component, as was shown in Figure 12–2. In their schedules, teachers allot as much time as possible for students to read and write. After developing the schedule, teachers post it in the classroom and talk with students about the activities and discuss their expectations with students. Teachers teach the workshop procedures and continue to model the procedures as students become comfortable with the routines. As students share what they are reading and writing at the end of workshop sessions, their enthusiasm grows and the workshop approaches are successful.

Students keep two folders—one for reading workshop and one for writing workshop. In the reading workshop folder, students keep a list of books they have read, notes from minilessons, reading logs, and other materials. In the writing workshop folder, they keep all rough drafts and other compositions, a list of all compositions, topics for future pieces, and notes from minilessons.

Many teachers use a classroom chart to monitor students' work on a daily basis. At the beginning of reading workshop, students (or the teacher) record what book they are reading or if they are writing in a reading log, waiting to conference with the teacher, or browsing in the classroom library. For writing workshop, students identify the writing project they are involved in or the step of the writing process they are at. A sample writing workshop chart is shown in Figure 12–9. Teachers can also use the chart to award weekly "effort" grades, to have students indicate their need to conference with the teacher, or to have students announce that they are ready to share the book they have read or to publish their writing. Nancie Atwell (1998) calls this chart "the state of the class." Teachers can review students' progress and note which students need to meet with the teacher or receive additional attention. When students fill in the chart themselves, they develop responsibility for their actions and a stronger desire to accomplish tasks they set for themselves.

Figure 12–9 "State of the Class" chart

Names	Dates 3/18	3/19	3/20	3/21	3/22	3/25	3/26	3/27
	Writing Workshop Chart							
Antonio	4	5	5	5	5	1	1	1 2
Bella	2	2	2 3	2	2	4	5	5
Charles	3	3 1	1	2	2 3	4	5	5
Dina	4 5	5	5	1	1	1	1	2 3
Dustin	3	3	4	4	4	5	5 1	1
Eddie	2 3	2	2 4	5	5	1	1 2	2 3
Elizabeth	2	3	3	4	4	4 5	5	1 2
Elsa	1 2	3 4	4 5	5	5	1	2	2

Code:
1 = Prewriting   2 = Drafting   3 = Revising   4 = Editing   5 = Publishing

To monitor primary-grade students, teachers might use a pocket chart and have students place a card in their pocket to indicate whether they are choosing a new book, reading, or responding during reading workshop, or at which step of the writing process they are working during writing workshop.

Teachers should take time during reading and writing workshop, to observe students as they interact and work together in small groups. Researchers who have observed in reading and writing workshop classrooms report that some students, even as young as first graders, are excluded from group activities because of gender, ethnicity, and socioeconomic status (Henkin, 1995; Lensmire, 1992). The socialization patterns in elementary classrooms seem to reflect society's. Henkin recommends that teachers be alert to the possibility that boys might only share books with other boys or that some students won't find anyone willing to be their editing partner. If teachers see instances of discrimination in their classrooms, they should confront it directly and work to foster a classroom environment where students treat each other equitably.

Why Use Reading and Writing Workshop?

There are many reasons to recommend the workshop approach. In reading workshop, students select and read genuine literature that is interesting and written at their reading level. The literature has complex sentence patterns and presents challenging concepts and vocabulary. Through reading workshop, students become more fluent readers and learn to deepen their appreciation of books and reading. As students read they are developing lifelong reading habits. They are introduced to different genres and choose favorite authors. Most importantly, they come to think of themselves as readers.

In writing workshop, students create their own compositions and come to see themselves as writers. They practice writing strategies and skills and learn to choose words carefully to articulate their ideas. Perhaps most importantly, they see firsthand the power of writing to entertain, inform, and persuade.

Samway, Whang, and their students (1991) reported that the two most important benefits of reading workshop are that students become a community of learners and that they view themselves as readers. As students read and respond to books, they understand themselves and their classmates better and gain confidence in themselves as readers. In addition, their ability to choose reading materials becomes more sophisticated during the school year. Students are much more enthusiastic about reading workshop than traditional reading approaches. The authors offer advice to teachers about the necessary components of reading workshop: students want to read complete books, not excerpts; they want to choose the books they read; and they need plenty of time to read and talk about books.

Many teachers fear that their students' scores on standardized achievement tests will decline if they implement a workshop approach in their classrooms, even though many teachers have reported either an increase in test scores or no change at all (Five, 1988; Swift, 1993). Kathleen Swift (1993) reported the results of a year-long study comparing two groups of her students. One group read basal reader stories, and the other participated in reading workshop. The reading workshop group showed significantly greater improvement, and Swift also reported that students participating in reading workshop showed more positive attitudes toward reading.

Review

The workshop approach involves students in meaningful reading and writing experiences. Students read and respond to books in reading workshop, and they write and publish books in writing workshop. Effective teachers incorporate the three key characteristics of the workshop approach—time, choice, and response—in their workshops. The five components of reading workshop are reading, responding, sharing, teaching minilessons, and reading aloud to students. The components of writing workshop are similar: writing, sharing, and teaching minilessons. Sometimes teachers combine reading and writing workshop, alternate them, or use writing workshop as students complete projects related to literature focus units or content-area thematic units. A list of effective practices for the workshop approach is presented in the feature on page 429.

How Effective Teachers . . .

Conduct Reading and Writing Workshop

Effective Practices	**Ineffective Practices**
1. Teachers allow students to choose the books they want to read.	1. Teachers assign books for students to read.
2. Teachers teach students how to select books using the Goldilocks Strategy.	2. Teachers don't teach students how to select books because they assign books for students to read.
3. Teachers recognize reading workshop as an instructional approach and provide plenty of time for students to read and respond to books.	3. Teachers view reading workshop as a supplemental reading program and provide limited time for it.
4. Teachers use conferences and responses students write in reading logs to monitor their reading progress.	4. Teachers use book report forms to monitor students' progress.
5. Teachers build students' enthusiasm for reading and books through book talks and sharing.	5. Teachers deemphasize sharing.
6. Teachers teach minilessons and have students apply what they have learned through reading and writing.	6. Teachers use worksheets instead of minilessons to teach concepts and skills.
7. Teachers allow students to choose their own topics and forms for writing.	7. Teachers assign topics and forms for writing.
8. Teachers have students use the writing process to develop and refine their compositions.	8. Teachers collect single-draft compositions to edit and grade.
9. Teachers encourage students to publish their writing in books.	9. Teachers have students write compositions on sheets of paper like other school assignments.
10. Teachers have students celebrate their completed writings and share them using an author's chair.	10. Teachers don't have students share their completed compositions.

References

Anderson, R. C., Hiebert, E. H., Scott, J. A., & Wilkinson, I. A. G. (1985). *Becoming a nation of readers.* Washington, DC: National Institute of Education.

Atwell, N. (1998). *In the middle: New understandings about reading and writing with adolescents* (2nd ed.). Upper Montclair, NJ: Boynton/Cook.

Baker, E. C. (1994). Writing and reading in a first-grade writers' workshop: A parent's perspective. *The Reading Teacher, 47,* 372–377.

Barone, D. (1990). The written responses of young children: Beyond comprehension to story understanding. *The New Advocate, 3,* 49–56.

Brophy, J. E., & Good, T. L. (1986). Teacher behavior and student achievement. In M. C. Wittrock (Ed.), *Handbook of research on teaching* (3rd ed., pp. 328–375). New York: Macmillan.

Brusko, M. (1999). *Writing rules! Teaching kids to write for life, grades 4–8.* Portsmouth, NH: Heinemann.

Calkins, L. M. (1991). *Living between the lines.* Portsmouth, NH: Heinemann.

Calkins, L. M. (1994). *The art of teaching writing* (Rev. ed.). Portsmouth, NH: Heinemann.

Carle, E. (1993). *Eric Carle: Picture writer* (videotape). New York: Philomel.

Five, C. L. (1988). From workbook to workshop: Increasing children's involvement in the reading process. *The New Advocate, 1,* 103–113.

Fletcher, R., & Portalupi, J. (1998). *Craft lessons: Teaching writing K–8.* York, ME: Stenhouse.

Graves, D. H. (1994). *A fresh look at writing.* Portsmouth, NH: Heinemann.

Hancock, M. R. (1992). Literature response journals: Insights beyond the printed page. *Language Arts, 69,* 36–42.

Hancock, M. R. (1993). Exploring and extending personal response through literature journals. *The Reading Teacher, 46,* 466–474.

Hansen, J. (1987). *When writers read.* Portsmouth, NH: Heinemann.

Henkin, R. (1995). Insiders and outsiders in first-grade writing workshops: Gender and equity issues. *Language Arts, 72,* 429–434.

Hornsby, D., Parry, J., & Sukarna, D. (1992). *Teach on: Teaching strategies for reading and writing workshops.* Portsmouth, NH: Heinemann.

Hornsby, D., Sukarna, D., & Parry, J. (1986). *Read on: A conference approach to reading.* Portsmouth, NH: Heinemann.

Kelly, P. R. (1990). Guiding young students' response to literature. *The Reading Teacher, 43,* 464–470.

Lane, B. (1999). *Reviser's toolbox.* Shoreham, VT: Discover Writing Press.

Lensmire, T. (1992). *When children write.* New York: Teachers College Press.

McWhirter, A. M. (1990). Whole language in the middle school. *The Reading Teacher, 43,* 562–565.

Moore, M. A. (1991). Electronic dialoguing: An avenue to literacy. *The Reading Teacher, 45,* 280–286.

Ohlhausen, M. M., & Jepsen, M. (1992). Lessons from Goldilocks: "Somebody's been choosing my books but I can make my own choices now!" *The New Advocate, 5,* 31–46.

Prill, P. (1994–1995). Helping children use the classroom library. *The Reading Teacher, 48,* 363–364.

Samway, K. D., Whang, G., Cade, C., Gamil, M., Lubandina, M. A., & Phommachanh, K. (1991). Reading the skeleton, the heart, and the brain of a book: Students' perspectives on literature study circles. *The Reading Teacher, 45,* 196–205.

Smith, F. (1984). *Reading without nonsense.* New York: Teachers College Press.

Staton, J. (1988). ERIC/RCS report: Dialogue journals. *Language Arts, 65,* 198–201.

Swift, K. (1993). Try reading workshop in your classroom. *The Reading Teacher, 46,* 366–371.

Wollman-Bonilla, J. E. (1989). Reading to participate in literature. *The Reading Teacher, 43,* 112–120.

Children's Literature References

Blume, J. (1980). *Superfudge.* New York: Dutton.

Cleary, B. (1961). *Two dog biscuits.* New York: Morrow.

Cleary, B. (1965). *The mouse and the motorcycle.* New York: Morrow.

Cleary, B. (1977). *Ramona and her father.* New York: Morrow.

Cleary, B. (1979). *Ramona forever.* New York: Morrow.

Cleary, B. (1983). *Dear Mr. Henshaw.* New York: Morrow.

Cleary, B. (1984). *Ramona and her mother.* New York: Morrow.

Cleary, B. (1991). *Strider.* New York: Morrow.

Dahl, R. (1966). *The magic finger.* New York: Puffin.

Dalgliesh, A. (1982). *The courage of Sarah Noble.* New York: Scribner.

Fritz, J. (1958). *The cabin faced west.* New York: Coward-McCann.

Fritz, J. (1992). *Surprising myself.* Katonah, NY: Richard C. Owen.

Goble, P. (1994). *Hau kola/Hello friend.* Katonah, NY: Richard C. Owen.

Howe, D., & Howe, J. (1979). *Bunnicula: A rabbit-tale of mystery.* New York: Atheneum.

Howe, J. (1994). *Playing with words.* Katonah, NY: Richard C. Owen.

Isaacs, A. (1994). *Swamp angel.* New York: Dutton.

Kellogg, S. (1986). *Pecos Bill.* New York: Morrow.

Kellogg, S. (1988). *Paul Bunyan.* New York: Morrow.

Meet the Newbery author: Arnold Lobel. (1978). Hightstown, NJ: American School Publishers.

Noble, T. H. (1980). *The day Jimmy's boa ate the wash.* New York: Dial.

Polacco, P. (1994). *Firetalking.* Katonah, NY: Richard C. Owen.

Sachar, L. (1978). *Sideways stories from Wayside School.* New York: Avon Books.

Sachar, L. (1985). *Wayside School is falling down.* New York: Avon Books.

Basal Reading Textbooks

— Chapter Questions —

What are the advantages and disadvantages of basal reading programs?

What are the steps in a guided reading lesson?

How do teachers use literacy centers?

How do teachers determine the difficulty level of books?

Mrs. Ohashi Teaches Reading Using Basal Readers

Mrs. Ohashi's third graders are reading "The Great Kapok Tree," a selection in their *Spotlight on Literacy* basal reader program (Aoki et al., 1997). This story, which is set in the Amazon rain forest, was originally published as a trade book for children by Lynne Cherry in 1990. In the basal reader version, the text is unabridged from the original book, but because text from several pages has been printed on a single page, some illustrations from the original book version have been deleted.

The students spend one week reading "The Great Kapok Tree" and participating in a variety of related literacy activities. Mrs. Ohashi's language arts block lasts two and a half hours each morning. During the first hour she works with reading groups while other students work independently at centers. During the second hour she teaches spelling, grammar, and writing. The last half-hour is independent reading time when students read self-selected books from the classroom library or the reading center.

The skills that Mrs. Ohashi teaches each week are set by the basal reading program. She will focus on cause and effect as students read and think about the selection. The vocabulary words she will highlight in the selection are *community, depend, environment, generations, hesitated, ruins, silent,* and *squawking.* Students will learn about persuasive writing, and they will write a persuasive letter to their parents. Mrs. Ohashi will teach **minilessons** on irregular past-tense verbs, and students will study the list of spelling words provided by the basal reading program.

Mrs. Ohashi's class is divided into four reading groups, and the students in all of the groups, except one group reading at the first-grade level, can read the basal reader with her support. Her district's policy is that, in addition to reading books at their instructional level, all children should be exposed to the grade-level textbooks. Mrs. Ohashi involves all students in most instructional activities, but she reads the story to the students in the lowest group and then these students read leveled books at their level.

To choose names for the groups at the beginning of the school year, Mrs. Ohashi put crayons into a basket. A student from each group chose a crayon, and the crayon's name became the name of the group. The students who read at or almost at grade level are heterogeneously grouped into the Wild Watermelon, Electric Lime, and Blizzard Blue groups. The six remaining students form the Atomic Tangerine group.

On the first day, Mrs. Ohashi builds students' background knowledge about the rain forest by reading aloud *Nature's Green Umbrella* (Gibbons, 1994). Students talk about rain forests and together compile a list of information they have learned, including the fact that each year over 200 inches of rain fall in the rain forest. Next she introduces the selection of the week, and students "text walk" through the story, looking at the illustrations, connecting with what they already know about rain forests, and predicting events in the story. Then most students read the story with buddies, but the Atomic Tangerine group reads the selection with Mrs. Ohashi. These students join Mrs. Ohashi at the reading group table, and she reads

the story aloud while students follow along in their books. She stops periodically to explain a word, make predictions, clarify any confusions, and think aloud about the story.

After everyone finishes reading the selection, students come together to talk about the story in a **grand conversation** (see the Compendium for more information about this and all other highlighted terms in this chapter). Students respond to the story, talking about why the rain forests must be preserved. Ashley explains, "I know why the author wrote the story. On page 71 it tells about her. Her name is Lynne Cherry and it says that she wants to 'try to make the world a better place.' That's the message of this story." Then Katrina compares this story to *Miss Rumphius* (Cooney, 1982), the selection they read the previous week: "I think this story is just like the one we read before. It was about making the world more beautiful with flowers and that's almost the same."

Then Mrs. Ohashi asks what would happen if there were no more rain forests. Students mention that animals in the rain forest might become extinct because they wouldn't have homes and that there would be more air pollution because the trees wouldn't be able to clean the air. Then Mrs. Ohashi introduces a basket of foods, spices, and other products that come from the rain forest, including chocolate, coffee, tea, bananas, cashews, cinnamon, ginger, vanilla, bamboo, and rubber. Her students are amazed at the variety of things they and their parents use every day that come from the rain forest.

Next Mrs. Ohashi focuses on spelling. She explains that this week's words end with *ild* as in *mild, ind* as in *find,* and *ound* as in *found.* She administers the pretest using 15 words plus 5 challenge words provided in the basal reading program. Students take the pretest on page 83 of their Spelling Activity Book and correct their own pretests. They take these papers home and use them to practice their spelling words during the week.

Then Mrs. Ohashi introduces the grammar skill of the week: the past tense of irregular verbs. She has prepared a series of 10 sentence strips with sentences about "The Great Kapok Tree," leaving blanks for the past-tense verbs, as suggested in the teacher's guide for the basal reading program. On separate cards, she has written correct and incorrect verb forms on each side, for example: *The birds comed/came down from their trees.* She puts the sentence strips and verb cards in a pocket chart. She begins by talking about the past-tense form of regular verbs. The students understand that -*ed* marks the past tense of many verbs, as in this sentence: *The man walked into the rain forest.* Other verbs, she explains, have different forms for present and past tense. For example, *The man sleeps/slept in the rain forest.* Then students read the sentences in the pocket chart and choose the correct form of the irregular verb.

Next she explains that many irregular verbs have three forms—present tense, past tense, and past tense using *have, has,* or *had*—as in *sing–sang–sung.* She puts word cards with these 10 present-tense forms in another pocket chart: *go, give, come, begin, run, do, eat, grow, see,* and *sing.* Then she passes out additional word cards listing the two past-tense forms of each verb. As they talk about each verb, students holding word cards with the past-tense forms come and add them to the pocket chart.

During the week, students will continue to practice these irregular verbs at centers, using worksheets from the Grammar Practice Book that is part of the basal reading program, and through other minilessons.

During the last 20 minutes of the language arts block, Mrs. Ohashi introduces the 10 centers that students will work at during the week. These centers are described in Figure 13–1. The centers are arranged next to bulletin boards, at tables, or in corners of the classroom, and students follow Mrs. Ohashi as she explains each one.

During the rest of the week, Mrs. Ohashi meets with reading groups during the first hour of the language arts block while other students work independently at centers. She meets with each group two to four times during the week and uses guided reading strategies as students reread the selection and supplemental or other leveled books. She also teaches vocabulary and comprehension as directed in the teacher's guide.

Mrs. Ohashi likes to begin with the Atomic Tangerine group each morning because she feels that it gets them off to a more successful start. She uses guided reading with these students. They begin by rereading several familiar leveled books, and Mrs. Ohashi listens to the students as they read. Next, she reviews one- and two-syllable words with *ar,* and they decode these words: *car, carpet, mark, bookmark, sharp, sharpest,* and *sharks.* Mrs. Ohashi introduces their new book, *Hungry, Hungry Sharks* (Cole, 1986). Students text walk through the first eleven pages, looking at illustrations and making predictions. They put a bookmark at page 11 to remember where to stop reading. Mrs. Ohashi asks students to read to find out if sharks are dinosaurs, and they eagerly begin. Students mumble-read so that Mrs. Ohashi can hear them as they read. When students don't know a word (such as *creatures, dragons,* and *hundred*), Mrs. Ohashi helps them sound it out or, if necessary, pronounces it for them. She writes the words on word cards to review after students finish reading. As soon as they finish reading, students discuss possible answers to her question. Several believe that sharks were dinosaurs, while others disagree. So, Mrs. Ohashi rereads page 10, which says, "There are no more dinosaurs left on earth. But there are plenty of sharks." After they agree that sharks are not dinosaurs, they practice reading the word cards that Mrs. Ohashi prepared while students were reading.

Next, the students compose this sentence about sharks using interactive writing: *There are more than three hundred kinds of sharks today.* Students write on individual white boards as they take turns writing on chart paper. Then they reread the five sentences they wrote last week. During the rest of the week, students in the Atomic Tangerine group will continue reading *Hungry, Hungry Sharks* and participating in phonics, spelling, vocabulary, and writing activities with Mrs. Ohashi.

Next, Mrs. Ohashi meets with the Wild Watermelon group to reread "The Great Kapok Tree." The students read silently, but Mrs. Ohashi asks individual students to read a page aloud so that she can conduct **running records** to check their fluency. After they finish reading, Mrs. Ohashi asks the students to talk about what the man might have been thinking as he walked away from the kapok tree on the last page of the story.

Figure 13–1 The literacy centers in Mrs. Ohashi's classroom

Vocabulary Center

Students sort rain forest word cards into several categories. Also, students make word maps for three of these words from the story: *community, depend, environment, generations, hesitated, ruins, silent, squawking.* They use the glossaries in the anthologies to check the definitions.

Comprehension Center

Students examine the cause-and-effect relationships using two activities. Students match a set of pictures of the animals from the story to their reasons why the kapok tree should not be cut down. For example, the monkey's reason was that if the kapok tree is cut down, the roots will die and the soil will wash away. Mrs. Ohashi has also placed a poster in the center with the question, "What do you think would have happened if the man had chopped down the tree?" and students are encouraged to write their predictions. In addition, they complete the worksheet on page 108 in the Practice Book by answering eight comprehension questions.

Sentences Center

Students choose a favorite sentence from the story, write it on a sentence strip, and post it on the bulletin board near the center.

Reading and Rereading Center

Students read books from the text set on rain forests and supplemental books from the *Spotlight on Literacy* basal reading program. Mrs. Ohashi also has a one-minute timer at the center and students practice rereading duplicated copies of page 68 from "The Great Kapok Tree" to see how many words they can read in a minute. They read the page once for practice, then read the page and mark how many words they read in a minute. Then they read the page again and mark how many words they read this time. Students work to improve their reading speed because all third graders are expected to reach a reading speed of at least 100 words per minute.

Grammar Center

Students practice irregular past-tense verbs through several activities. Students read sentences about the story written on sentence strips and paperclip word cards with the correct form of verb to the sentence strip. Students also sort verb cards and put present, past, and past participle forms of the same verb together, such as go–went–gone. Students also complete page 71 of the Grammar Practice Book.

Listening Center

Students listen to audiotapes of "The Great Kapok Tree" or "The Mahogany Tree," and afterwards they write and/or draw a response in listening logs that are kept at the center.

Spelling Center

Students participate in a variety of activities to practice their spelling words. Lists of words are available at the center, and students build the words using linking letters. They sort spelling word cards according to spelling patterns. They complete Spelling Activity Book page 86 by identifying the correct spelling of each word. And, they write each spelling word three times in their spelling notebooks that are kept at the center.

Writing Center

Students write a rain forest book with information about plants and animals in the rain forest and the products we use that come from the rain forest.

Chart Center

Students mark the rain forest on world maps using information from pages 72–73 of their basal readers. They also add labels with names of the countries, rivers, and continents.

Computer Center

Students use a phonics program to review *r*-controlled vowels and word processing for writing activities.

Figure 13–2 A third grader's persuasive letter

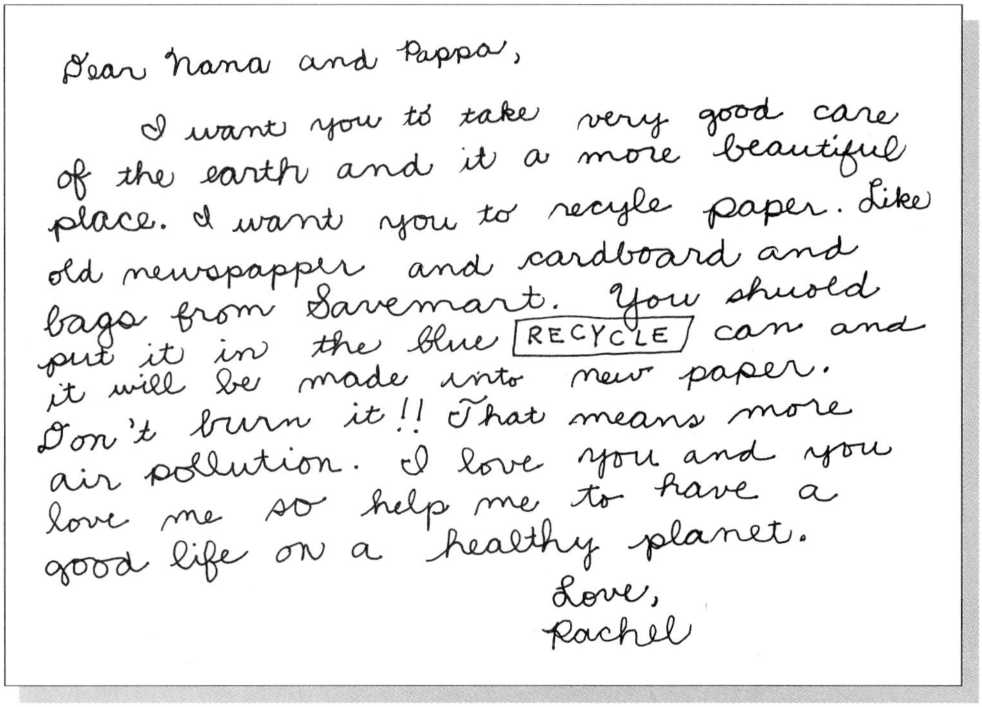

> Dear Nana and Pappa,
>
> I want you to take very good care of the earth and it a more beautiful place. I want you to recyle paper. Like old newspapper and cardboard and bags from Savemart. You shuold put it in the blue RECYCLE can and it will be made into new paper. Don't burn it!! That means more air pollution. I love you and you love me so help me to have a good life on a healthy planet.
>
> Love,
> Rachel

Next, she focuses on the cause and effect in the story. She asks the students what is causing a problem in the story, and they respond that cutting down the rain forest is the problem. When she asks what the effects of cutting down the trees might be, students mention several, including air pollution and destroying animal habitats. Then she passes out cards, each with a picture of an animal from the story, and asks students to scan the story to find the effect that that animal mentioned to the sleeping man. Students reread and then share what they found.

Then Mrs. Ohashi repeats the same activities with the other two reading groups. On the fourth and fifth days, she meets with the three reading groups that are on grade level to focus on vocabulary words from the selection.

In the second hour, Mrs. Ohashi begins a persuasive writing project. She explains that people read and write for three purposes—to entertain, to inform, and to persuade. "Which purpose," she asks, "do you think Lynne Cherry had for writing 'The Great Kapok Tree'?" The students respond that she had all three purposes, but that perhaps the most important purpose was to persuade. Then Mrs. Ohashi explains that in persuasive writing, authors use cause and effect. They explain a problem and then tell how to solve it. They also give reasons why it must be solved and tell what will happen if it isn't solved.

Figure 13–3   Mrs. Ohashi's block schedule

	MONDAY	TUESDAY	WEDNESDAY	THURSDAY	FRIDAY
8:30–9:30	Build background knowledge about the rain forest. Read aloud *Nature's Green Umbrella*. Read "The Great Kapok Tree" pp. 50–71 with buddies and Atomic Tangerines read with Mrs. O. Grand conversation	Atomic Tangerines read *Hungry, Hungry Sharks*, pp. 1–11. ML on ar- words. Interactive writing	pp. 12–23	pp. 24–35	pp. 36–47
		Wild Watermelon Electric Lime Blizzard Blue	Reread selection Take running records Focus on cause-effects using pictures of animals	Wild Watermelon Electric Lime Blizzard Blue	Review vocabulary Locate sentences Check meanings in the glossary
		Students not in reading groups work at centers			
9:30–10:30	Minilesson on irregular past-tense verbs. Pretest on spelling words. Introduce centers	Review irregular past-tense verbs. Introduce persuasive writing assignment. Brainstorm ideas. Discuss format	Spelling Practice Test. Draft and revise letters. *Remind students to get addresses	Grammar check using Grammar Practice Book p. 73. Revise and edit letters. Review friendly letter format. Begin final copies	Spelling Test. Finish letters. Address envelopes and prepare to mail
10:30–11:00	Independent Reading				Show video "The Great Kapok Tree" Read-around

The students talk about environmental problems in their community and decide to write letters to their parents and grandparents urging them to recycle and take good care of the environment. The format they will use is:

Sentence 1: Urge their parents to conserve and recycle.

Sentence 2: Tell how to conserve and recycle.

Sentence 3: Tell another way.

Sentence 4: Tell why it is important.

Sentence 5: Urge their parents to conserve and recycle.

Mrs. Ohashi and the students brainstorm many ideas and words on the chalkboard before students begin writing their rough drafts. Then on Wednesday and Thursday they revise and edit their letters, and Mrs. Ohashi meets with students to work on their letters. By Friday, most students are writing their final copies and addressing envelopes so their letters can be mailed. Before they begin recopying, Mrs. Ohashi reviews the friendly letter form so students will be sure to format the letter correctly. Rachel's letter to her grandparents is shown in Figure 13–2.

Mrs. Ohashi ends the language arts block on Friday by showing the video version of "The Great Kapok Tree," which appeared on PBS's Reading Rainbow series, and having students read their favorite sentences from the story in a **read-around.**

Figure 13–3 shows Mrs. Ohashi's block schedule for teaching "The Great Kapok Tree" using basal reading textbooks. She includes reading groups, literacy center activities, grammar and spelling minilessons, and writing activities in the schedule.

Commercial reading programs, which are commonly called basal readers, have been a staple in reading instruction for at least 50 years. In the past 20 years, however, basal readers have been criticized for their controlled vocabulary, for their emphasis on isolated skills, and for stories that lack conflict or authentic situations. In the past the stories in these textbooks have been excerpted from children's literature and rewritten, often substituting simpler or more decodable words for the author's original language (Goodman, Shannon, Freeman, & Murphy, 1988). Educators have demanded more authentic texts—selections that have not been edited or abridged— and publishers of commercial reading programs have redesigned their programs to bring them more in line with the balanced reading movement. Now many basal readers, like the series Mrs. Ohashi used in the vignette, include authentic, unabridged literature in their programs, and they are referred to as literature-based basal programs.

McCarthey and Hoffman (1995) compared newer first-grade-level literature-based basal readers with older editions and found that the newer editions were very different from the older ones. They examined five characteristics of basal readers and reported their findings:

1.   ***Word and sentence difficulty.*** The researchers reported that the total number of words was smaller in the new programs, but the newer basal readers contained more unique words. They concluded that the vocabulary was much less controlled and that there was significantly less repetition of words in the new programs.

2. *Literary characteristics.* The researchers found that the new editions included different formats. Reading materials were packaged in a variety of ways—as big books, in trade books, and in anthologies. The new editions included a wider variety of genres and had very few adaptations of children's literature.

3. *Literacy features.* The researchers also evaluated the literary quality of the selections and found that the selections in the new basals had more complex plots, more highly developed characters, and more idiomatic and metaphorical language. They concluded that the newer basals were more engaging than the older ones, but the researchers' average rating of the newer basals was only a 3 on a scale of 1 to 5.

4. *Predictability.* The researchers found that more than half of the selections in the new basal readers had predictable features, including repeated patterns, rhyme, and rhythm. In contrast, less than 20% of the stories in the older editions had predictable features.

5. *Decodability.* The researchers examined the word-level decoding demands placed on the reader and concluded that the new basal readers placed much higher decoding demands on readers than the older ones did.

McCarthey and Hoffman concluded that skills are still prevalent in newer reading textbooks, but they are slightly more integrated. They noted that assessment tools broadened from a testing-only mentality to include portfolios and other innovative assessment strategies. They also found that the tone of the teacher's manual was less prescriptive. Based on their findings, McCarthey and Hoffman recommend that teachers become decision makers and use the textbooks judiciously.

TEACHING WITH BASAL READING TEXTBOOKS

www.eduplace.com
Houghton Mifflin
www.harcourtschool.com
Harcourt Brace
www.mmhschool.com
Macmillan/McGraw-Hill
www.scottforesman.com
Scott Foresman
www.teacher.scholastic.com
Scholastic

🕸 *Check out these publishers' websites to learn about a variety of commercial reading programs.*

Publishers of basal reading textbooks tout their programs as complete literacy programs containing all the materials needed for students to become successful readers. The accessibility of reading materials is clearly one advantage of textbooks. Teachers have copies of grade-level textbooks for every student, and the newer, literature-based textbooks contain award-winning and unabridged literature.

The teacher's edition provides detailed information on how to teach the basal reading program and use the variety of supplemental materials provided with the textbook. The skills and strategies to be taught are specified in the program, and directions are provided for how to teach and assess students' learning. This information is especially useful for inexperienced and struggling teachers.

It is unrealistic, however, to assume that a commercial reading program could be a complete literacy program for all students. Teachers who have students reading below grade level need reading materials at their students' level. The same is true for teachers working with students who read above grade level. These teachers have to supplement their program with appropriate reading materials, as Mrs. Ohashi did in the vignette. In some schools, teachers share basal reading textbooks with teachers in other grades; at other schools, teachers locate sets of leveled books to use with below- and above-grade-level readers. In addition, students need many more opportunities to read and reread books than are provided in a basal reading program, so teachers stock their classroom libraries with books and provide daily time for independent reading.

Teachers appreciate the instructional and assessment tools in basal reader programs.

Materials Included in Basal Reader Programs

At the center of a basal reading program is the student textbook or anthology. In the primary grades there are two or more books at each grade level, and in fourth through sixth grade there is usually one book. Most basal reader programs end in sixth grade because seventh and eighth graders read trade books or literature textbooks. Basal readers are colorful and inviting books, often featuring pictures of children and animals on the covers of primary-level books and exciting adventures and fanciful locations on the covers of books for grades four through six. The selections in each textbook are grouped into units, and each unit includes stories, poems, and informational articles. Many multicultural selections have been added, and usually illustrations feature ethnically diverse people. Information about authors and illustrators is included for many selections. The textbooks contain a table of contents and a glossary.

Commercial reading programs provide a wide variety of materials to support student learning. Consumable workbooks are probably the best-known support material. Students write letters, words, and sentences in these books to practice phonics, comprehension, and vocabulary skills. In addition, transparencies and black-line masters of additional worksheets are available for teachers to use in teaching skills and strategies. Big books and kits with letter and word cards, wall charts, and manipulatives are available for kindergarten and first-grade programs. Black-line masters of parent letters are also available.

Some multimedia materials, including audiocassettes, CD-ROMs, and videos, are included with the programs. Teachers can use these materials at listening centers and computer centers. Collections of trade books are available for each grade level to provide supplemental reading materials. In the primary grades, many books have

www.cmsd.k12.co.us

First-Grade Classrooms. See how first-grade teachers use basal readers as part of their literacy programs.

decodable text to provide practice on phonics skills and high-frequency words; in the upper grades, the books are related to unit themes.

Basal reader programs also include a variety of assessment tools. Teachers use placement evaluations or informal reading inventories to determine students' reading levels and for placement in reading groups. They use running records to informally monitor students' reading. There are also selection and unit tests to determine students' phonics, vocabulary, and comprehension achievement. Information is also provided on how to administer the assessments and analyze the results.

A teacher's instructional guidebook is provided at each grade level. This oversize handbook provides comprehensive information about how to plan lessons, teach the selections, and assess students' progress. The selections are shown in reduced size in the guidebook, and each page includes background information about the selection, instructions for reading the selections, and coordinating skill and strategy instruction. In addition, information is presented about which supplemental books to use with each selection and how to assess students' learning.

Figure 13–4 summarizes the materials included in most basal reading programs.

Steps in a Guided Reading Lesson

www.sasked.gov.sk.ca

🕸 *Guided Reading and Thinking.*
Information about purposes, procedures, and assessment of guided reading.

Teachers use guided reading to work with small groups of students who are reading basal readers or other books at their instructional level, with approximately 90–94% accuracy (Clay, 1991). During guided reading, teachers use the reading process and support students' reading and their use of reading strategies (Depree & Iversen, 1996; Fountas & Pinnell, 1996). Students do the actual reading themselves, although the teacher may read aloud with children to get them started on the first page or two. Beginning readers often mumble the words softly as they read, and this practice helps the teacher keep track of students' reading and the strategies they are using. Older students who are more fluent readers usually read silently during guided reading. Guided reading is not round-robin reading, in which students take turns reading pages aloud to the group.

First graders build sentences using word cards during a guided reading lesson.

Figure 13–4 Materials included in basal reading programs

Textbook or Anthology	The student's book of reading selections. The selections are organized thematically and include literature from trade books. Often the textbook is available in a series of softcover books or a single hardcover book.
Big Books	Enlarged copies of books for shared reading. These books are used in kindergarten and first grade.
Supplemental Books	Collections of trade books for each grade level. Kindergarten-level books often feature familiar songs and wordless stories. First- and second-grade books often include patterned language for practicing phonics skills and high-frequency words. In grades 3 to 6, books are often related to unit themes.
Workbooks	Consumable books of phonics, comprehension, and vocabulary worksheets.
Transparencies	Color transparencies to use in teaching skills and strategies.
Blackline Masters	Worksheets that teachers duplicate and use to teach skills and provide additional practice.
Kits	Alphabet cards, letter cards, word cards, and other instructional materials. These kits are used in kindergarten through second grade.
Teacher's Guide	An oversize book that presents comprehensive information about how to teach reading using the basal reading program. The selections are shown in reduced size, and background information about the selection, instructions for teaching the selections, and instructions on coordinating skill and strategy instruction are included on each page. In addition, information is presented about which supplemental books to use with each selection and how to assess students' learning.
Parent Materials	Blackline masters that teachers can duplicate and send home to parents. Information about the reading program and lists of ways parents can work with their children at home are included. Often these materials are available in English and Spanish.
Assessment Materials	A variety of assessments, including selection assessments, running records, placement evaluations, and phonics inventories, are available along with teacher's guides.
Multimedia	Audiocassettes of some selections, CD-ROMs of some selections that include interactive components, related videos, and website connections are included.

www.connieprevatte.com

Guided Reading.
How to use guided
reading in the upper grades.

Guided reading lessons usually last 25 to 30 minutes, and over a day or two students move through all five steps of the reading process. When the students first arrive for the small-group lesson, they often reread familiar books read in previous guided reading lessons.

For the new guided reading lesson, students read books that they have not read before. Beginning readers usually read small picture books at one sitting, but older students who are reading longer chapter books take from several days to several weeks to read their books.

As for other types of reading lessons, teachers follow the five steps of the reading process for guided reading:

1. *Prereading.* Teachers introduce the new book and prepare students to read. Teachers often begin by activating or building background knowledge on a topic related to the book. Then they show the cover of the book, read the title, and talk about the book and have students make predictions. Often teachers continue with a text walk to overview the book, but they do not read the book. Then teachers introduce crucial new vocabulary. Sometimes they ask students to look through the book to locate known words and unknown words essential to the meaning of the book. One other activity that is often included in this first step is teaching or reviewing a skill or strategy that students can use as they read the book.

2. *Reading.* Teachers guide students through several readings of the book. During the first reading, students and the teacher often read the first page or two together. Then students read the book individually, reading aloud softly to themselves, or silently, depending on their reading level. Teachers prompt for strategies and word identification as needed, and then they move from student to student to listen in as the student reads. Teachers do a running record as one or two of the students read aloud. After students who are reading short picture books finish reading, they are often invited to reread the book twice, once with the teacher and once with a partner or individually.

3. *Responding.* After reading, students think about the book and make personal and literary connections. Teachers and students briefly discuss the book using grand conversation techniques. Teachers ask mainly inferential and critical-level questions to keep the discussion going, such as:

> What would happen if . . . ?
> Why did . . . ?
> If . . . , what might have happened next?
> If you were . . . , what would you . . . ?
> What did this book make you think of?
> What did you like best about this book?

After the discussion, teachers often have students create a sentence about the book and use interactive writing to write the sentence on a chart. This activity gives teachers the opportunity to review concepts about print, phonics, and spelling skills. Or, more capable writers sometimes write in **reading logs** after the guided reading lesson ends.

4. *Exploring.* Teachers teach minilessons, and students practice reading and writing words and sentences. Three types of exploring activities are:

- *Minilessons on skills.* Teachers review a skill or strategy that was evident in the text or teach a new skills lesson. Then students practice it as they reread parts of the story. Teachers also teach phonics during these minilessons.

| *Figure 13–5* | Steps in a guided reading lesson |

1. Prereading

❧ Activate or build background knowledge on a topic related to the book.
❧ Show the cover of the book and read the title.
❧ Talk about the book and have students make predictions.
❧ Do a book walk to overview the book, but do not read the book.
❧ Teach a skill or strategy that students can use as they read the book.

2. Reading

❧ Have students read the book individually, reading aloud, softly to themselves, or silently (depending on their reading level).
❧ Prompt for strategies and word identification as needed.
❧ Move from student to student to listen in as the student reads.
❧ Do a running record as one of the students reads aloud.
❧ Have students reread the book twice, once with the teacher and once with a partner or individually.

3. Responding

❧ Discuss the book with the group using a grand conversation.
❧ Ask inferential and critical-level questions, such as "What would happen if . . . ?" and "What did this book make you think of?"
❧ Use interactive writing to write a sentence about the book.
❧ Have students draw and write in reading logs.

4. Exploring

❧ Teach minilessons on skills and strategies.
❧ Practice reading and spelling high-frequency words.
❧ Use sentence strips to manipulate sentences from the book.

5. Applying

❧ Use new skills and strategies at literacy centers.
❧ Apply skills and strategies in reading and writing activities.

❧ *Word work.* Teachers review familiar high-frequency words with students and introduce a new word. Then students make the word using magnetic letters, write it on a white board, or form letters using waxy pipe cleaners to spell the word.

❧ *Sentence work.* Teachers write sentences from the book on sentence strips and cut the strips apart. Then students put the words together to re-create the sentences.

   5. *Applying.* Students practice and apply skills and strategies they are learning at literacy centers.

   The steps in a guided reading lesson are summarized in Figure 13–5.

Using Literacy Centers

Literacy centers contain meaningful, purposeful literacy activities that students can work at in small groups. Students practice phonics skills at the phonics center, sort word cards at the vocabulary center, or listen to books related to a book they are

Figure 13–6   Twenty literacy centers

Author	Information about an author that students are studying is displayed in this center. Often posters, books, and videotapes about the author are available for students to examine, and students may also write letters to the author at this center.
Class Collaborations	Students write pages to be added to a class book at this center. Each student contributes a page according to guidelines established before students visit this center. Afterwards, the teacher compiles and binds the book.
Computer	A bank of computers with word processing and drawing programs, interactive books on CD-ROM, and other computer programs are available at the center.
Data Charts	As part of social studies and science units, students compile information for data charts. Students consult informational books and reference books at the center and add information to a large class data chart or to individual data charts.
Dramatic Play	Literacy materials and environmental print are added to play centers so that primary-grade students can learn about authentic purposes for reading and writing. Food packages, for example, are placed in housekeeping centers, and street signs are added to block centers.
Library	A wide variety of books and other reading materials, organized according to topic or reading level, are available in classroom libraries. Students choose books at their reading level to read and reread.
Listening	Students use a tape player and headphones to listen to stories and other texts read aloud. Often copies of the texts are available so that students can read along as they listen.
Making Words	Letter cards, magnetic letters, and white boards that students use to spell and write words are available in this center. Students often create specific words that follow a spelling pattern or sort letters to spell a variety of two-, three-, four-, and five-letter words.
Message	Mailboxes or a bulletin board are set up in the message center so that primary-grade students can write notes and send them to classmates. Also included in the center are a list of names, stickers to use as stamps, postcards, and a variety of writing paper and envelopes.
Phonics	A variety of small objects, picture cards, magnetic letters, letter cards, and small white boards are used in this center. Students practice phonics concepts that teachers have already taught, such as matching rhyming word pictures, sorting a box of objects according to the beginning sound or vowel sound that the name of the object represents, or writing a series of words representing a word family such as *-ill.*

reading at the listening center. Figure 13–6 describes 20 literacy centers used in elementary classrooms. Centers are usually organized in special places in the classroom or at groups of tables (Fountas & Pinnell, 1996).

Literacy centers are usually associated with primary classrooms, but they can be used effectively at all grade levels, even in seventh and eighth grades. In some classrooms, all students work at centers at the same time; in other classrooms, most students work at centers while the teacher works with a small group of students.

The activities in these literacy centers relate to stories students are reading and skills and strategies recently presented in minilessons. Students often manipulate objects, sort word cards, reread books, write responses to stories, and practice skills in centers. Some literacy centers, such as reading and writing centers, are permanent,

Figure 13–6 *continued*

Pocket Charts	Teachers set out sentence strips or word cards for a familiar song or poem, and students arrange the sentence strips or words in the pocket chart so that they can read the poem or sing the song. Students often have extra sentence strips and word cards so that they create new versions and write variations.
Poetry	Charts describing various poetic forms are available in this center, and students write formula poems at this center. They often use poetic forms that teachers have already introduced to the class.
Proofreading	Students use spellcheckers, word walls of high-frequency words, and dictionaries at this center to proofread compositions they have written. Students often work with partners at this center.
Puppets	Puppets and puppet stages and small manipulative materials related to books students are reading are set out for students to use in this center. Students use the materials to retell stories and create sequels to stories.
Reading and Writing the Classroom	This center is stocked with reading wands (wooden dowel rods with eraser tips) and glasses (with the lenses removed) for students to use as they walk around the classroom and point at and read words, sentences, and books. Also included are small clipboards and pens that students use as they walk around the classroom and record familiar words and sentences posted in the classroom.
Sequencing	Students take sets of pictures about the events in a story or story boards (made by cutting apart two copies of a picture book and backing each page with poster board) and sequence them. Students can also make story boards for picture books and chapter books at this center.
Skills	Students practice skills teachers have taught in minilessons at this center. Teachers place the materials they used in the minilesson in the center for students to use. Students sort word cards, write additional examples on charts, and manipulate other materials.
Spelling	Students use white boards and magnetic letters to practice spelling words.
Word Sorts	Students sort word cards into categories according to meaning or structural forms. Sometimes students paste the sorted words on sheets of poster board, and at other times they sort the words as a practice activity and do not paste them into categories.
Writing	This center is stocked with writing materials, including pens, papers, blank books, postcards, dictionaries, and word walls, that students use for a variety of writing activities. Bookmaking supplies such as cardboard, wallpaper, cloth, paper, wide-arm staplers, yarn, brads, and marking pens are also available in this center.

but others change according to the books students are reading and the activities planned.

In some classrooms, students flow freely from center to center according to their interests; in other classrooms, students are assigned to centers or required to work at some "assigned" centers and choose among other "choice" centers. Students can sign attendance sheets when they work at each literacy center or mark off their names on a class list tacked to each center. Rarely do students move from center to center in a lockstep approach every 15 to 30 minutes; instead, they move to another center when they finish what they are doing at one center.

Figure 13–7 shows the checklist Mrs. Ohashi's students used as they worked at literacy centers. They check the box beside the name of each center when they

Figure 13–7 Mrs. Ohashi's literacy centers checklist

"The Great Kapok Tree" Centers Checklist

Name _____

❑ Vocabulary Center

❑ Comprehension Center

❑ Sentences Center

❑ Reading and Rereading Center   P

❑ Grammar Center   P

❑ Listening Center

❑ Spelling Center   P

❑ Writing Center   P

❑ Chart Center   P

❑ Computer Center

finish work at that center. Students keep their checklists in their center folders, and they add any worksheets or papers they do at a center to their folders. The P beside some centers on the center checklist in Figure 13–7 indicates that students are to complete a paper at that center and add it to their center folders. Mrs. Ohashi monitors students' progress each day, and at the end of the week she collects their folders and checks their work. Having a checklist or another approach to monitoring students' progress helps them develop responsibility for completing their assignments.

Assessing Students' Reading During Guided Reading Lessons

Teachers observe students as they read during guided reading lessons. They spend a few minutes observing each student, sitting either in front of the student or right beside the student. Teachers observe the student's behaviors for evidence of strategy use and confirm the student's attempts to identify words and solve reading problems. Some of the strategies and problem-solving behaviors that teachers look for include:

❦ self-monitoring

❦ checking predictions

Students participate in free-choice writing activities at the writing center.

❦ sounding out unfamiliar words

❦ checking to see if the word makes sense

❦ checking to see that a word is appropriate in the syntax of the sentence

❦ using all sources of information

❦ attempting to read an unfamiliar word

❦ self-correcting

❦ chunking phrases to read more fluently

Teachers take notes about their observations and use the information in deciding what minilessons to teach and what books to choose for children to read.

Teachers also take running records of one or two children during each guided reading lesson and use this information as part of their assessment. Teachers check to see that the books children are reading are at their instructional level and that they are making expected progress and continuing to progress to increasingly difficult levels of books.

DETERMINING THE DIFFICULTY LEVEL OF BOOKS

Thousands and thousands of trade books are available for elementary students, and effective teachers match students with books written at appropriate difficulty levels. Even though many books seem to be of similar difficulty because of the size of print, length of book, or number of illustrations, they are not necessarily at the same reading level. Students need books written at an appropriate level of difficulty because they are more likely to read books that are neither too hard nor too easy, and research has shown that students who do the most reading make the greatest gains in reading (Gunning, 1998).

According to the Goldilocks Strategy (Ohlhausen & Jepsen, 1992), books can be classified as too easy, too difficult, or just right for students. This classification is individualistic, so what is too difficult for one student may be too easy for another. Teachers and researchers use other terms for the three levels. "Easy" books are at the independent level, and students read these books with 95–100% accuracy in word recognition and 90–100% accuracy in comprehension. "Just right" books are books at the instructional level, where students read with 90–94% accuracy in word recognition and 75–89% accuracy in comprehension. "Too difficult" books are at the frustration level, and students read them with less than 90% accuracy in word recognition and less than 75% accuracy in comprehension.

Traditional Readability Formulas

For the past 40 years or more, teachers have used readability formulas to estimate the difficulty level of trade books and textbooks. Readability levels can serve as rough gauges of text difficulty and are reported as grade-level scores. If a book has a readability score of fifth grade, teachers can assume that many average fifth grade readers will be able to read the book. Sometimes readability scores are marked RL and a grade level, such as RL 5, on the back covers of paperback trade books.

Traditional readability scores are usually determined using vocabulary difficulty and sentence complexity, as measured by word and sentence length. The formulas don't take into account the experience and knowledge that readers bring to the reading experience. Nor do they take into account readers' cognitive and linguistic backgrounds or their motivation or purpose for reading.

www.discoveryschool.com

🕸 *Fry's Readability Graph: Directions for Use.*
More information about how to check the readability level of a text.

One fairly quick and simple readability formula is the Fry Readability Graph, developed by Edward Fry (1968). Figure 13–8 presents the Fry Readability Graph and lists the steps in using the formula to predict the grade-level score for the text, ranging from first grade through college level. Teachers should always consider using a readability formula as an aid in evaluating textbook and trade book selections for classroom use, but they cannot assume that materials rated as appropriate for a particular grade level will be appropriate for all students at that grade level. Teachers need to recognize the effectiveness of readability formulas as a tool but remember that these formulas have limitations.

Many reading selections that might seem very different actually score at the same level. For example, *Sarah, Plain and Tall* (MacLachlan, 1985), *Tales of a Fourth Grade Nothing* (Blume, 1972), *Bunnicula: A Rabbit-Tale of Mystery* (Howe & Howe, 1979), and *The Hundred Penny Box* (Mathis, 1975) all score at the third-grade level according to Fry's Readability Graph, even though some of the books are longer, have fewer illustrations, are written on very different topics, and are printed in different-sized type.

The Reading Recovery Approach to Leveling Books

Basal readers and other texts have traditionally been leveled according to grade levels, but grade-level designations, especially in first and second grade, are too broad. Reading Recovery teachers have developed a text gradient to match children to books that are neither too hard nor too easy for them (Fountas & Pinnell, 1996). Barbara Peterson (1991) examined reading materials for young children to determine the characteristics of texts that support beginning readers. She identified five criteria:

1. *Placement of text.* Books with consistent placement of text on the page are easier for children to read than books with varied placement, and books with only one line of text on a page are easier to read than books with two or more lines of text.
2. *Repetition.* Text that is highly predictable, with one or two patterns and few word changes, is easier to read than less predictable text with varied sentence patterns.

Figure 13–8 The Fry Readability Graph

Note. From "A Readibility Formula That Saves Time," by E. Fry, 1968, *Journal of Reading, 11,* p. 587.

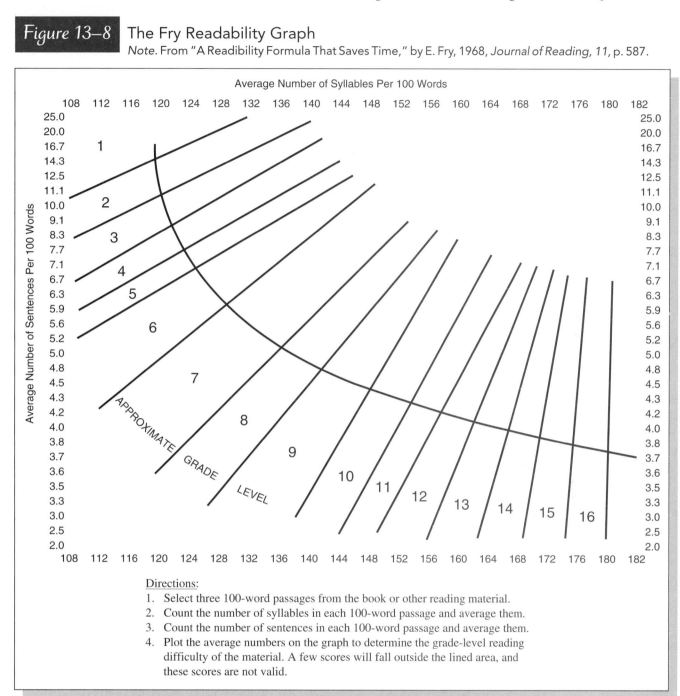

Directions:

1. Select three 100-word passages from the book or other reading material.
2. Count the number of syllables in each 100-word passage and average them.
3. Count the number of sentences in each 100-word passage and average them.
4. Plot the average numbers on the graph to determine the grade-level reading difficulty of the material. A few scores will fall outside the lined area, and these scores are not valid.

3. ***Language structures.*** Books in which the text is similar to the children's oral language patterns are easier to read than text using written language or "book" structures.
4. ***Content.*** Books about familiar objects and experiences are easier to read than books about unfamiliar topics or books using unfamiliar, specialized vocabulary.
5. ***Illustrations.*** Pictures in which the meaning of the text is visually illustrated are more supportive than illustrations that are minimally related to the text.

Figure 13–9 Trade books leveled according to Reading Recovery criteria
Fountas & Pinnell, 1999.

A   Burningham, J. (1985). *Colors.* New York: Crown.

B   Carle, E. (1987). *Have you seen my cat?* New York: Scholastic.

C   Williams, S. (1989). *I went walking.* Orlando, FL: Harcourt Brace.

D   Peek, M. (1985). *Mary wore her red dress.* New York: Clarion.

E   Hill, E. (1980). *Where's Spot?* New York: Putnam.

F   Hutchins, P. (1968). *Rosie's walk.* New York: Macmillan.

G   Shaw, N. (1986). *Sheep in a jeep.* Boston: Houghton Mifflin.

H   Kraus, R. (1970). *Whose mouse are you?* New York: Macmillan.

I   Wood, D., & Wood, A. (1984). *The napping house.* San Diego: Harcourt Brace.

J   Rylant, C. (1991). *Henry and Mudge and the bedtime thumps.* New York: Simon & Schuster.

K   Stevens, J. (1992). *The three billy goats Gruff.* New York: Holiday House.

L   Allard, H. (1985). *Miss Nelson is missing!* Boston: Houghton Mifflin.

M   Park, B. (1992). *Junie B. Jones and the stupid smelly bus.* New York: Random House.

N   Danziger, P. (1994). *Amber Brown is not a crayon.* New York: Scholastic.

O   Cleary, B. (1981). *Ramona Quimby, age 8.* New York: HarperCollins.

P   Cole, J. (1992). *The magic school bus on the ocean floor.* New York: Scholastic.

Using these criteria, Reading Recovery teachers identified 16 levels for kindergarten through third grade. A sample trade book for each level is shown in Figure 13–9, and 7,500 other leveled books are listed in *Matching Books to Readers: Using Leveled Books in Guided Reading, K–3* (Fountas & Pinnell, 1999). Primary-grade teachers are using the same criteria to level books to use in their classrooms. After they level the book, teachers code books with letters written on colored circles and place all books at the same level together in baskets or boxes.

Teachers use running records to identify each student's instructional level. Then teachers group students into homogeneous groups, but the groups remain flexible and students move from group to group according to their reading level. Teachers use leveling to organize small groups for guided reading or whenever they want to match children to books at the appropriate level of difficulty.

The Lexile Framework

The newest approach to matching books to readers is the Lexile Framework, developed by MetaMetrics and available through Scholastic, Inc. Lexile levels range from 100 to 1200, representing first through eleventh grades. Several standardized achievement tests are linked to the Lexile Framework, and students' scores are now reported in lexile levels. Or, students can determine their lexile level by completing the Scholastic Reading Inventory, a computerized reading test in which they silently read text passages and answer comprehension questions. Many trade books are also designated by lexile levels so that teachers can help students choose appropriate books according to their lexile levels.

Readers at the sixth-grade level, for example, range from 800 to 1050 lexile levels, and trade books that have been leveled in the sixth-grade range according to the Lexile Framework include *Charlie and the Chocolate Factory* (Dahl, 1964) (810), *Out of the Dust* (Hesse, 1997) (820), *Ramona Quimby, Age 8* (Cleary, 1981) (860), *Sounder* (Armstrong, 1969) (900), and *The Watsons Go to Birmingham—1963* (Curtis, 1995) (1010).

The Lexile Framework appears to be a promising program, since the wide range of possible scores allows teachers at all grade levels to more closely match students and books. As more and more books are leveled using the Lexile Framework, it seems likely that lexile levels will become increasingly important in reading instruction; however, matching students to books is often more complicated because students' background knowledge, motivation, and other individual factors influence reading success.

Review

Basal readers have been a staple of reading instruction for more than 50 years, and recently they were redesigned to include more authentic, unabridged literature and less emphasis on skills instruction. Textbook publishers tout their programs as complete reading programs, and they are especially helpful for inexperienced and struggling teachers. Students often meet in small groups to read selections in basal readers, and teachers use the guided reading procedure for the lesson. Students who are not reading often work at literacy centers and complete worksheets to practice skills they are learning. Teachers work to match students with books that they read during guided reading lessons and for other types of reading activities using traditional readability formulas, the Reading Recovery approach to leveling books, and the Lexile Framework. Guidelines for using basal reading textbooks are summarized in the feature on page 454.

How Effective Teachers . . .

Use Basal Reading Textbooks

■ **Effective Practices**	■ **Ineffective Practices**

■ Effective Practices

1. Teachers use basal reading programs together with other literacy activities.
2. Teachers match students to basal readers according to their reading levels.
3. Teachers use the variety of materials included in basal reader programs, including CD-ROMs and supplemental books.
4. Teachers use guided reading to read selections in basal readers with their students.
5. Teachers have students reread the selections or excerpts from them to practice reading.
6. Teachers teach skills as minilessons or during guided reading lessons.
7. Teachers set up centers for students to practice skills they are learning in small groups.
8. Teachers use running records to monitor students' reading and assess their use of reading strategies and skills.
9. Teachers teach students to use the Goldilocks Strategy for choosing books for independent reading.
10. Teachers use traditional readability formulas, the Reading Recovery approach to leveling books, or the Lexile Framework to determine the difficulty level of books.

■ Ineffective Practices

1. Teachers depend on basal readers as their complete reading program.
2. Teachers use the grade-level basal reader for all students in their class.
3. Teachers depend on the textbook instead of using the variety of materials included in basal reader programs.
4. Teachers assign students to read the selections independently or use round-robin reading.
5. Teachers have students read the selection only once.
6. Teachers assign worksheets instead of explicitly teaching skills.
7. Teachers don't use centers; instead, they have students complete worksheets individually, sitting at their desks.
8. Teachers use end-of-unit tests included in the basal reading textbooks to assess students' reading.
9. Teachers don't teach students how to choose appropriate books for independent reading.
10. Teachers don't know how to determine the difficulty level of trade books.

References

Aoki, E., Flood, J., Lapp, D., Martinez, M., Priestley, M., & Smith, C. B. (1997). *Spotlight on literacy (grade 3)* New York: Macmillan/McGraw-Hill.

Clay, M. M. (1991). *Becoming literate: The construction of inner control.* Portsmouth, NH: Heinemann.

Depree, H., & Iversen, S. (1996). *Early literacy in the classroom: A new standard for young readers.* Bothell, WA: Wright Group.

Fountas, I. C., & Pinnell, G. S. (1996). *Guided reading: Good first teaching for all children.* Portsmouth, NH: Heinemann.

Fountas, I. C., & Pinnell, G. S. (1999). *Matching books to readers: Using leveled books in guided reading, K–3.* Portsmouth, NH: Heinemann.

Fry, E. (1968). A readability formula that saves time. *Journal of Reading, 11,* 587.

Goodman, K. S., Shannon, P., Freeman, V. W., & Murphy, S. (1988). *Report on basal readers.* Katonah, NY: Richard C. Owen.

Gunning, T. G. (1998). *Best books for beginning readers.* Boston: Allyn & Bacon.

McCarthey, S. J., & Hoffman, J. V. (1995). The new basals: How are they different? *The Reading Teacher,* *49,* 72–75.

Ohlhausen, M. M., & Jepsen, M. (1992). Lessons from Goldilocks: "Somebody's been choosing my books but I can make my own choices now!" *The New Advocate 5,* 31–46.

Peterson, B. (1991). Selecting books for beginning readers. In D. DeFord, C. Lyons, & G. S. Pinnell (Eds.), *Bridges to literacy: Learning from Reading Recovery* (pp. 119–147). Portsmouth, NH: Heinemann.

Children's Book References

Armstrong, W. (1969). *Sounder.* New York: Harper & Row.

Blume, J. (1972). *Tales of a fourth grade nothing.* New York: Dutton.

Cherry, L. (1990). *The great kapok tree.* San Diego: Harcourt Brace.

Cleary, B. (1981). *Ramona Quimby, age 8.* New York: Morrow.

Cole, J. (1986). *Hungry, hungry sharks.* New York: Random House.

Cooney, B. (1982). *Miss Rumphius.* New York: Viking.

Curtis, C. P. (1995). *The Watsons go to Birmingham—1963,* New York: Delacorte.

Dahl, R. (1964). *Charlie and the chocolate factory.* New York: Knopf.

Gibbons, G. (1994). *Nature's green umbrella.* New York: Morrow.

Hesse, K. (1997). *Out of the dust.* New York: Scholastic.

Howe, D., & Howe, J. (1979). *Bunnicula: A rabbit-tale of mystery.* New York: Atheneum.

MacLachlan, P. (1985). *Sarah, plain and tall.* New York: Harper & Row.

Mathis, S. B. (1975). *The hundred penny box.* New York: Viking.

Chapter 14

Reading and Writing in the Content Areas

How do students use informational books, stories, and poems to learn science and social studies?

How can teachers help students read and understand content-area books?

How do students use reading and writing as tools for learning?

How do teachers develop a thematic unit?

Mrs. Roberts's Class Learns About Penguins

Mrs. Roberts's first and second graders begin their two-week unit on penguins by starting a **K-W-L chart** (Ogle, 1986) (see the Compendium for more information about this and all other highlighted terms in this chapter). Mrs. Roberts asks students what they already know about penguins and records their information in the "K: What We Know" column. Students mention that penguins live at the South Pole, that they eat fish, and that they can swim. Paula asks if penguins can fly, and Mrs. Roberts writes this question as the first entry in the "W: What We Want to Learn" column. As the discussion continues, more information and questions are added to the chart. The third column, "L: What We Learned," is still empty, but later in the unit Mrs. Roberts and her students will add entries for that column.

Students read stories and informational books about penguins during their language arts block, and they continue studying about penguins during science. During the first week of the two-week thematic unit they read *Tacky the Penguin* (Lester, 1988) and examine the beginning, middle, and end of the story. They make posters diagramming the three parts. Students also make "circles" of a **quilt** to celebrate the story. Students write their favorite quotes from the story around the outside of the circles, and in the middle of the circles they draw pictures of Tacky.

Mrs. Roberts has collected a text set of books about penguins for this thematic unit. Some are stories, and others are informational books. She also locates several poems to display on large charts. She reads some of the books aloud, such as *Little Penguin's Tale* (Wood, 1989), and students read other books during reading workshop. Still others she saves for students to read in literature circles during the second week of the unit.

Mrs. Roberts's class has reading workshop for 30 minutes each day. So that all children can read at their developmental level, Mrs. Roberts develops predictable books and other patterned books in addition to books in the text set. She created one book based on *Brown Bear, Brown Bear, What Do You See?* (Martin, 1983). The book begins this way:

Page 1: *Little penguin, little penguin, what do you see?*
Page 2: *I see a leopard seal looking at me.*
Page 3: *Leopard seal, leopard seal, what do you see?*
Page 4: *I see two gulls looking at me.*
Page 5: *Two gulls, two gulls, what do you see?*

Mrs. Roberts has also created a number book with pictures of penguins and related objects. It begins this way:

Page 1: *One fish for a hungry penguin.*
Page 2: *Two penguins standing by a nest.*
Page 3: *Three seals hunting for a penguin.*

Another book is a "T is for Tacky" book. On each page, Mrs. Roberts has drawn a picture of something beginning with *T* (e.g., a telephone, a taxi, a tiger) along with a picture of Tacky and a talking balloon. In the talking balloon is the single word for the item beginning with *T*. On the page with the telephone, the sentence at the bottom of the page says, "T is for Tacky and telephone."

Each year when Mrs. Roberts teaches this unit, she works with a small group of emergent readers in her class to create another predictable book. This year the small group decides to make a "What Can Penguins Do?" book. Students decide on these sentences:

> *Penguins can swim.*
> *Penguins can dive.*
> *Penguins can eat fish.*
> *Penguins can waddle.*
> *Penguins can sit on nests.*
> *Penguins can lay eggs.*
> *Penguins can feed babies.*
> *But, penguins cannot fly!*

Together, Mrs. Roberts and the small group of students draw and color the pictures, add the sentences, and compile the book. Then they share it with the other students in the class.

During the second week of the unit, students form literature circles. Mrs. Roberts does a **book talk** about these four informational books, and students choose one of them to read:

🎋 *It Could Still Be a Bird* (Fowler, 1990), a book that describes the characteristics of birds, using the predictable pattern "It could still be a bird."

🎋 *Penguin* (Fletcher, 1993), a book that describes the first two and a half years of a penguin's life.

🎋 *Antarctica* (Cowcher, 1990), a vividly illustrated book about penguins and other animals living in Antarctica.

🎋 *A Penguin Year* (Bonners, 1981), a book showing what penguins do during each season.

Students read the book they have chosen and talk about the book in a **grand conversation** with Mrs. Roberts or the student teacher. Later during the week, students reread the book as scientists, hunting for information about penguins to share with classmates. Students take notes on chart paper and then share what they have learned.

At the beginning of the unit, Mrs. Roberts posts a **word wall,** and she and her students add "science" words to the word wall during the unit. At the end of the unit, these words have been added:

emperor penguins	rookery	leopard seals
Adelie penguins	stand upright	birds
hatch from eggs	Antarctica	feathers
waddle	crests	flippers

swimmers	webbed feet	waterproof coat
divers	chicks	crop in throat
krill	skua gulls	nursery

Students use the words from the word wall as they write and talk about penguins, the books they are reading, and science they are learning. Students draw pictures of Antarctica and label at least eight things in their pictures using words from the word wall.

One of Mrs. Roberts's favorite vocabulary activities is "What Words Don't Belong?" (also called **exclusion brainstorming**). She makes a list of words, including some that don't relate to penguins:

penguins	polar bears	fly	swim
arctic	sing	chicks	webbed feet
krill	fur	seals	birds
wear clothes	eggs	nursery	hot
fish	ice	trees	rock nests

Students work in small groups to circle the words that don't belong, such as *polar bears, fly, hot,* and *trees.* As they share their papers with the class, students explain why the words they circled don't belong.

Mrs. Roberts uses words from the word wall as she teaches **minilessons** on phonemic awareness (segmenting and blending sounds in words), building words that rhyme with *chick* and with *coat,* and comparing *e* sounds in *egg, nests, feet,* and *seal.* She also teaches minilessons on *r*-controlled vowels, using *birds, leopard seals, nursery,* and *Antarctica* for the more advanced readers in her class.

As their project for the unit on penguins, Mrs. Roberts's students write "All About Penguins" books. They use a modified version of the writing process as they write their books. To begin, students brainstorm facts that they have learned about penguins, such as:

> *Penguins are black and white birds.*
> *Penguins are covered with feathers.*
> *Penguins are good swimmers, but they can't fly.*
> *Mother penguins lay eggs.*
> *Father penguins hold the eggs on their feet to keep them warm.*
> *Penguin chicks stay together in the rookery.*
> *Penguins look funny when they waddle on land.*
> *Penguins eat fish and krill.*
> *Leopard seals are a dangerous enemy, but people may be an even worse enemy.*

Mrs. Roberts writes these facts on sentence strips (long strips of paper that fit into pocket charts). Students read and reread these facts and think about the facts they want to include in their "All About Penguins" books.

Next, students collect five or six sheets of white paper for the inside of their books. They draw a picture and write a fact on each page. Most students invent spellings as they write, but a few locate the sentence strips and dutifully copy the fact so that their book will be written in "adult" spelling. As students write and draw, Mrs. Roberts circulates around the classroom, helping students choose facts, correcting their misconceptions about life in Antarctica, showing them how to draw penguins and other animals, and encouraging them to invent spellings. Mrs. Roberts insists that students spell *penguin* correctly, so she places word cards with the word at each table. All students are encouraged to check their spellings with words on the word wall, but Mrs. Roberts is more insistent that the more fluent writers check their spelling.

Pages from two students' penguin books are shown in Figure 14–1. The page about laying eggs was written by a second grader, and it says, "Penguins lay eggs and keep them warm with their feet and their stomachs." The page about seals eating penguins was written by a first grader who is learning English as a second language. The page says, "The seal likes to eat penguins." This first grader is experimenting with word boundaries, and he adds a dot between words. As he says the sentence, "to eat" sounds like one word to him. He also makes two word cards beside his picture.

Figure 14–1   Excerpts from two students' books about penguins

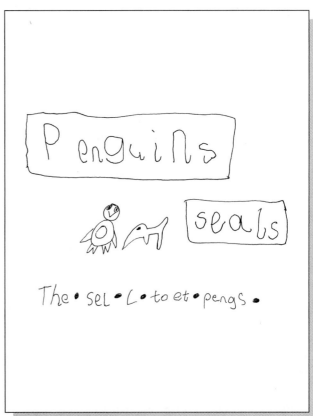

After students finish drawing and writing facts, they compile their pages and add black and orange covers—penguin colors. Before students make their covers, Mrs. Roberts teaches a brief minilesson on choosing titles and explains how to capitalize all the important words in a title. Most students title their books "The Penguin Book" or "All About Penguins," but several students experiment with other titles. One child chooses "Penguins in Antarctica," and another selects "The Adventures of Penguins." Students also add their names as the authors.

···

Students read and write all through the day as they learn science, social studies, and other content areas. Just as Mrs. Roberts's first and second graders learned about penguins by reading and writing, students at all grade levels read and write to learn about insects, World War II, rain forests, flight, and ancient civilizations.

The goal of content-area instruction is to help students construct their own understanding of big ideas. Students are naturally curious about the world, and they learn as they investigate new ideas. Students learn labels for concepts and develop new ways of expressing ideas. Reading and writing are useful learning tools, and through talking, reading, and writing, students explore concepts and make connections between what they are learning and what they already know.

Teachers organize content-area study into thematic units, and together with students, they identify big ideas to investigate. Units are time-consuming because student-constructed learning takes time. Teachers can't try to cover every topic; if they do, their students will probably learn very little. Teachers must make careful choices as they plan units, because only a relatively few topics can be presented in-depth during a school year. During thematic units, students need opportunities to question, discuss, explore, and apply what they are learning (Harvey, 1998). It takes time for students to become deeply involved in learning so that they can apply what they are learning in their own lives. The only way students acquire a depth of knowledge is by focusing on key concepts. Even the first and second graders in Mrs. Roberts's class learned key concepts about penguins. They learned (1) about the ecosystem in Antarctica, (2) how penguins have adapted to their environment, (3) about the life cycle of a penguin, and (4) that people pose a threat to the environment of Antarctica.

www.eduplace.com

Cross-Curricular Thematic Instruction. MaryEllen Vogt discusses the advantages of thematic instruction and offers suggestions for teaching and assessing units.

READING AND WRITING ARE LEARNING TOOLS

Reading and writing are tools for making sense of everyday life (Bamford & Kristo, 1998; Winograd & Higgins, 1994/1995). Many times students read entire books about content-area topics, and they may read the books aesthetically—to be carried off to Antarctica or somewhere else in the world, back in time to ancient Egypt or another period in history. Or, through a biography or autobiography, students walk in someone else's shoes and see the world from someone else's perspective—Theodore Roosevelt's or Helen Keller's, for example. At other times, students use either skimming or scanning to read rapidly through a book—especially an informational book—to get an overview or locate information.

Similarly, when students write, they brainstorm ideas, make connections among ideas, and explore their comprehension (Tompkins, 2000). Writing is more than a school activity; it becomes a tool for learning. Mrs. Roberts's students, for example, learned about penguins as they dictated facts for the K-W-L chart and wrote sentences on sentence strips, and they demonstrated their knowledge when they wrote "All About Penguins" books.

Reading Informational Books

www.carolhurst.com

Carol Hurst's Children's Literature Site.
Reviews of informational books and teaching ideas.

Children are curious, and they read informational books to find out about the world around them. Stephanie Harvey (1998, p. 70) lists these reasons why children enjoy reading informational books:

- to acquire information
- to understand the world more fully
- to understand new concepts and expand vocabulary
- to make connections to our lives and learning
- to write good nonfiction
- to have fun

They learn about whales in *Going on a Whale Watch* (McMillan, 1992), the Revolutionary War in *. . . If You Lived at the Time of the American Revolution* (Moore, 1997), bees in *The Magic School Bus Inside a Beehive* (Cole, 1996), and levers, inclined planes, and other simple machines and how they work in *Simple Machines* (Horvatic, 1989). In fact, high-quality informational books are available on almost any topic that interests children, and reading informational books is fun.

According to Horowitz and Freeman (1995), high-quality trade books play a significant role in science and other across-the-curriculum thematic units. Doiron (1994) argues that nonfiction books also have aesthetic qualities that make them very attractive and motivating for young readers.

Informational books are different from stories, and they place different demands on readers. They differ from stories in three basic ways:

1. *Organizational patterns.* Informational books are organized using expository text structures (the five basic expository patterns are explained in Chapter 9, "Becoming Familiar With the Structure of Text").
2. *Vocabulary.* Informational books include technical vocabulary related to concepts presented in the book.
2. *Special features.* Informational books include special features, including a table of contents, an index, a glossary, photo illustrations, and charts, graphs, maps, and other diagrams.

When teachers introduce informational books to students, they point out these differences and show students how they can take advantage of the special features to enhance their comprehension. Teachers also take these differences into account as they read informational books with students as part of thematic units.

Teachers help students read expository text by teaching them about expository text structures. Teachers teach students to recognize the organizational patterns and to adjust their purposes for reading to fit the structure. Students also learn about the cue words that authors use to signal structures and how to recognize them.

The four informational books about penguins that Mrs. Roberts used in the vignette at the beginning of this chapter illustrate three expository text structures. *It*

Students read biographies to learn about historical personalities such as Benjamin Franklin.

Could Still Be a Bird (Fowler, 1990) is organized using a description structure. The book points out these characteristics of birds:

1. All birds have feathers.
2. Birds have wings
3. Birds usually can fly.
4. Birds lay eggs.
5. Some birds can swim.
6. Birds can be big or little.
7. Birds can be many different colors.
8. Birds can live almost anywhere.

Both *Penguin* (Fletcher, 1993) and *A Penguin Year* (Bonners, 1981) employ a sequence structure. *Penguin* focuses on a penguin's development from hatching to age two and a half, and on the last page of the book a series of photographs reviews the sequence. *A Penguin Year* shows how penguins live from the dark winter through spring, summer, and fall. The author emphasizes that in the spring penguins return to the rookery where they were hatched in order to lay eggs, and she explains how penguin parents hatch and care for their chicks season by season.

In *Antarctica* (1990), Helen Cowcher uses a problem-solution structure to identify three of the penguins' enemies—leopard seals, skua gulls, and people—and to make a plea that people not destroy the penguins' environment. Figure 14–2 shows a chart that Mrs. Roberts's students made to emphasize the information they learned about penguins' enemies. The students shared this information with other students during a book talk.

Teachers consider the structure of text as they decide how to introduce an informational book, what type of graphic organizer or diagram to make to help emphasize the key points, and what points to emphasize in discussions. When teachers provide this type of structure, students are better able to focus on key concepts in each book rather than trying to remember a number of unrelated or unorganized facts.

Integrating Stories and Poetry

Stories bring content-area studies to life by providing a window through which students view yesterday's world and today's (Nelson, 1994; Smith & Johnson, 1994). Facts and content-area concepts are imbedded in fiction (Doiron, 1994). The settings of many stories provide historical and geographic information, and the conflict

www.booksalive.com

🕸 Books Alive Book Finder.
Use the book finder to search for nonfiction, historical fiction, and biographies related to a theme or for a grade level.

Figure 14–2 A problem-solving chart

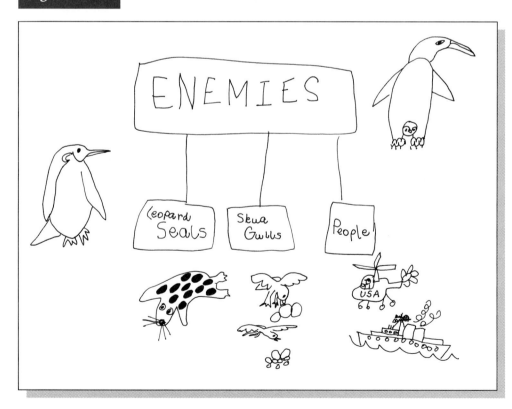

situations the characters face provide a glimpse into cultural, economic, and political issues. For example, students learn about penguins in *Tacky the Penguin* (Lester, 1988) and step into Nazi-occupied Denmark in *Number the Stars* (Lowry, 1989). They understand the discrimination that immigrants face in *Molly's Pilgrim* (Cohen, 1983), relive the dangerous days of pre–Revolutionary War Boston in *Johnny Tremain* (Forbes, 1970), and think about the consequences of pollution in *Ben's Dream* (Van Allsburg, 1990).

Whether students are reading stories as part of literature focus units, literature circles, reading workshop, or content-area units, they read aesthetically, for the lived-through literary experience. Even though students aren't reading efferently to pick out information, they are learning information and developing concepts as they read aesthetically. As they develop their understanding of a story, students often ask questions about historical settings, political situations, and unfamiliar cultural traditions during grand conversations. Stories are an important way of learning social studies and science.

Poetry is also used as part of content-area learning. Many books of poetry written for children can be used in teaching social studies and science units. Figure 14–3 presents a list of some of these poetry books. For example, *Desert Voices* (Baylor, 1981), a collection of poems written in the first person from the viewpoint of desert animals, and *Mojave* (Siebert, 1988), a book-length poem written from the viewpoint of the desert and illustrated with striking full-page illustrations, can be used in a unit on the desert.

www.acs.ucalgary.ca

The Children's Literature Web Guide. Recommended books, author biographies, links to other websites, and teaching suggestions.

Writing to Learn

Students use writing as a learning tool as they read content-area textbooks and during thematic units. They take notes, explore ideas, and organize information through writing. The focus is on using writing to help students to learn, not on spelling all the words correctly or writing neatly. Nevertheless, students should use classroom resources, such as word walls, to spell many words correctly and to write as neatly as possible so that they can reread their writing.

Learning Logs.   Students write entries in **learning logs** to record or react to what they are learning in math, science, social studies, or other content areas. Toby Fulwiler (1987) explains, "When people write about something they learn it better" (p. 9). As students write in these journals, they reflect on their learning, discover gaps in their knowledge, and explore relationships between what they are learning and their past experiences. Through these activities, students practice taking notes, writing descriptions and directions, and other writing skills. They also learn how to reflect on and evaluate their own learning (Stanford, 1988).

Science-related learning logs can take several different forms. One type of learning log is an observation log in which students make daily entries to track the growth of plants or animals. For instance, a class of second graders took a walk in the woods wearing old socks over their shoes to collect seeds, in much the same way that animals pick up seeds on their fur coats and transport them. To simulate winter, the teacher placed the students' socks in the freezer for several weeks. Then they "planted" one student's sock in the class terrarium and observed it each day as they waited for the seeds to sprout. Students kept science logs with daily entries. Two pages from a second grader's log documenting the experiment are presented in Figure 14–4. In the top entry, the student wrote "No plants so far and still dirt!" In the second entry, he wrote "I see a leaf with a point on it!"

Amon, A. (Sel.). (1981). *The earth is sore: Native Americans on nature.* New York: Atheneum. (M–U)

Asch, F. (1998). *Cactus poems.* San Diego: Gulliver. (P–M)

Baylor, B. (1981). *Desert voices.* New York: Scribner. (P–M)

Carle, E. (Sel.). (1989). *Eric Carle's animals, animals.* New York: Philomel. (P–M)

Esbensen, B. J. (1984). *Cold stars and fireflies: Poems of the four seasons.* New York: Crowell. (U)

Fisher, A. (1983). *Rabbits, rabbits.* New York: Harper & Row. (P)

Fisher, A. (1988). *The house of a mouse.* New York: Harper & Row. (Poems about mice) (P–M)

Fleischman, P. (1985). *I am phoenix: Poems for two voices.* New York: Harper & Row. (Poems about birds) (M–U)

Fleischman, P. (1988). *Joyful noise: Poems for two voices.* New York: Harper & Row. (Poems about insects) (M–U)

Goldstein, B. S. (Sel.). (1992). *What's on the menu?* New York: Viking. (Poems about food) (P–M)

Harvey, A. (Sel.). (1992). *Shades of green.* New York: Greenwillow. (Poems about ecology) (U)

Hopkins, L. B. (Sel.). (1976). *Good morning to you, valentine.* New York: Harcourt Brace Jovanovich. (See other collections of holiday poems by the same selector.) (P–M)

Hopkins, L. B. (Sel.). (1983). *A song in stone: City poems.* New York: Crowell. (M)

Hopkins, L. B. (Sel.). (1983). *The sky is full of song.* New York: Harper & Row. (Poems about the seasons) (P–M)

Hopkins, L. B. (Sel.). (1985). *Munching: Poems about eating.* Boston: Little, Brown. (M–U)

Hopkins, L. B. (Sel.). (1987). *Dinosaurs.* San Diego: Harcourt Brace Jovanovich. (M–U)

Hopkins, L. B. (Sel.). (1987). *Click, rumble, roar: Poems about machines.* New York: Crowell. (M)

Hopkins, L. B. (Sel.). (1991). *On the farm.* Boston: Little, Brown. (P–M)

Hopkins, L. B. (Sel.). (1992). *To the zoo: Animal poems.* Boston: Little, Brown. (P–M)

Hopkins, L. B. (1999). *Sports! Sports! Sports!: A poetry collection.* New York: HarperCollins. (P)

Janeczko, P. B. (Sel.). (1984). *Strings: A gathering of family poems.* New York: Bradbury Press. (U)

Larrick, N. (Sel.). (1988). *Cats are cats.* New York: Philomel. (M–U)

Larrick, N. (Sel.). (1990). *Mice are nice.* New York: Philomel. (M)

Lewis, J. P. (1998). *The little buggers: Insect and spider poems.* New York: Dial. (P–M)

Livingston, M. C. (1982). *Circle of seasons.* New York: Holiday House. (M–U)

Livingston, M. C. (1985). *Celebrations.* New York: Holiday House. (Poems about holidays) (P–M)

Livingston, M. C. (Sel.). (1986). *Earth songs.* New York: Holiday House. (M–U)

Livingston, M. C. (Sel.). (1987). *Cat poems.* New York: Holiday House. (P–M–U)

Livingston, M. C. (Sel.). (1988). *Space songs.* New York: Holiday House. (M–U)

Livingston, M. C. (Sel.). (1990). *If the owl calls again: A collection of owl poems.* New York: McElderry Books. (U)

Livingston, M. C. (Sel.). (1990). *Dog poems.* New York: Holiday House. (M–U)

Livingston, M. C. (Sel.). (1992). *If you ever meet a whale.* New York: Holiday House. (P–M)

Morrison, L. (1985). *The break dance kids: Poems of sport, motion, and locomotion.* New York: Lothrop, Lee & Shepard. (U)

Prelutsky, J. (1984). *It's snowing! It's snowing!* New York: Greenwillow. (P–M)

Prelutsky, J. (1977). *It's Halloween.* New York: Greenwillow. (See other books of holiday poems by the same author.) (P–M)

Prelutsky, J. (1983). *Zoo doings: Animal poems.* New York: Greenwillow. (P–M)

Prelutsky, J. (1988). *Tyrannosaurus was a beast: Dinosaur poems.* New York: Greenwillow. (P–M)

Provensen, A. (1990). *The buck stops here: Presidents of the United States.* New York: HarperCollins. (M–U)

Siebert, D. (1988). *Mojave.* New York: Harper & Row. (M–U)

Siebert, D. (1991). *Sierra.* New York: HarperCollins. (M–U)

Sierra, J. (1998). *Antarctic antics: A book of penguin poems.* San Diego: Gulliver. (P–M)

Sneve, V. D. H. (1989). *Dancing teepees: Poems of American Indian youth.* New York: Holiday House. (M–U)

Turner, A. (1986). *Street talk.* Boston: Houghton Mifflin. (Poems about city life) (M–U)

Yolen, J. (1990). *Bird watch: A book of poetry.* New York: Philomel. (M–U)

Yolen, J. (1990). *Dinosaur dances.* New York: Putnam. (M)

Yolen, J. (1993). *Weather report.* Honesdale, PA: Wordsong. (P–M–U)

Yolen, J. (1995). *Water music.* Honesdale, PA: Wordsong. (P–M–U)

Yolen, J. (1998). *Snow, snow! Winter poems for children.* Honesdale, PA: Wordsong. (P–M)

Figure 14—4 Two pages from a second grader's science log

Another type of learning log is one in which students make entries during a thematic unit. Students may take notes during presentations by the teacher or after reading, after viewing videos, or at the end of each class period. Sometimes students make entries in list form, sometimes in **clusters,** charts, or maps, and at other times in paragraphs.

Students often keep learning logs as part of thematic units in social studies. In their logs, students write responses to stories and informational books, note interesting words related to the theme, create timelines, and draw diagrams, charts, and maps. For example, as part of a study of the Civil War, eighth graders might include the following in their learning logs:

❦ informal **quickwrites** about the causes of the war and other topics related to the war

❦ a list of words related to the theme

❦ a chart of major battles in the war

❦ a Venn diagram comparing the viewpoints of the North and the South

❦ a timeline showing events related to the war

❦ a map of the United States at the time of the war, with battle locations marked

❦ notes after viewing several films about the Civil War era

❦ a list of favorite quotes from Lincoln's "Gettysburg Address"

❦ a response to a chapter book such as *Charley Skedaddle* (Beatty, 1987), *Brady* (Fritz, 1987), or *Across Five Aprils* (Hunt, 1987)

Through these learning log activities, students explore concepts they are learning and record information they want to remember about the Civil War.

Simulated Journals.　Students assume the role of another person and write from that person's viewpoint in simulated journals. They can assume the role of a historical figure when they read biographies or as part of social studies units. As they read stories, students can assume the role of a character in the story. In this way, students gain insight into other people's lives and into historical events. When students write from the viewpoint of a famous person, they begin by making a "lifeline," a timeline of the person's life. Then they pick key dates in the person's life and write entries about those dates. A look at a series of diary entries written by a fifth grader who has assumed the role of Benjamin Franklin shows how the student chose the important dates for each entry and wove in factual information:

December 10, 1719
Dear Diary,
My brother James is so mad at me. He just figured out that I'm the one who wrote the articles for his newspaper and signed them Mistress Silence Dogood. He says I can't do any more of them. I don't understand why. My articles are funny. Everyone reads them. I bet he won't sell as many newspapers anymore. Now I have to just do the printing.

February 15, 1735
Dear Diary,
I have printed my third "Poor Richard's Almanack." It is the most popular book in America and now I am famous. Everyone reads it. I pretend that somebody named Richard Saunders writes it, but it's really me. I also put my wise sayings in it. My favorite wise saying is "Early to bed, early to rise, makes a man healthy, wealthy, and wise."

April 19, 1752
Dear Diary,
I did a very dangerous experiment today. I wanted to learn about electricity so I flew a kite in a thunderstorm. I put a key on the string and lightning hit the kite, and there were sparks on the key. That proves lightning is electricity. But I don't want anyone else to do that experiment. It is too dangerous.

June 22, 1763
Dear Diary,
I've been an inventor for many years now. There are a lot of things I have invented like the Franklin stove (named after me) and bifocal glasses, and the lightning rod, and a long arm to get books off of the high shelves. That's how I work. I see something that we don't have and if it is needed, I figure out how to do it. I guess I just have the knack for inventing.

May 25, 1776
Dear Diary,
Tom Jefferson and I are working on the Declaration of Independence. The patriots at the Continental Congress chose us to do it but it is dangerous business. The Red Coats will call us traitors and kill us if they can. I like young Tom from Virginia. He'll make a good king of America some day.

April 10, 1785
Dear Diary,
I returned home to Philadelphia today from England. What a day it was. When my ship came to the dock, there was a crowd of people waiting to see ME. Then I heard bells ringing and cannons fired to welcome me home. I read the newspaper and it said I was a hero! What an honor.

April 16, 1790
Dear Diary,
I am dying. I only have a day or two to live. But it's OK because I am 84 years old. Not very many people live as long as I have or do so many things in a life. I was a printer by trade but I have also been a scientist, an inventor, a writer, and a statesman. I have lived to see the Philadelphia that I love so very much become part of a new country. Good-bye to my family and everyone who loves me.

Quickwriting. Quickwriting is a strategy that students use as they write in journals and for other types of impromptu writing. Students reflect on what they know about a topic, ramble on paper, generate words and ideas, and make connections among the ideas. Students write on a topic for 5 to 10 minutes and let their thoughts flow from their minds to their pens without focusing on mechanics or revisions. Younger students can do quickwrites in which they draw pictures to explore ideas.

During a thematic unit on the solar system, for example, fourth graders each chose a word from the word wall to quickwrite about. This is one student's quickwrite on Mars:

Mars is known as the red planet. Mars is Earth's neighbor. Mars is a lot like Earth. On Mars one day lasts 24 hours. It is the fourth planet in the solar system. Mars may have life forms. Two Viking ships landed on Mars. Mars has a dusty and rocky surface. The Viking ships found no life forms. Mars' surface shows signs of water long ago. Mars has no water now. Mars has no rings.

Another student wrote about the sun:

> *The sun is an important star. It gives the planets light. The sun is a hot ball of gas. Even though it appears large, it really isn't. It's pretty small. The sun's light takes time to travel to the planets so when you see light it's really from a different time. The closer the planet is to the sun the quicker the light reaches it. The sun has spots where gas has cooled. These are called sun spots. Sun spots look like black dots. The sun is the center of the universe.*

These quickwrites, which took ten minutes for students to draft, provide a good way of checking on what students are learning and an opportunity to clarify misconceptions. After students write, they usually share their quickwrites in small groups, and then one student in each group shares with the class. Sharing also takes about 10 minutes, and the entire activity can be completed in 20 minutes or less.

Clusters and Other Diagrams. Clustering is a strategy that students use as they gather and organize information they are learning in a learning log or on a chart or poster (Rico, 1983). A cluster is another name for a semantic map. Clusters are weblike diagrams with the topic or nuclear word written in a circle centered on a sheet of paper. Main ideas are written on rays drawn out from the circle, and branches with details and examples are added to complete each main idea.

Two clusters are presented in Figure 14–5. The top cluster was developed by a sixth-grade teacher during a thematic unit on birds. The purpose of the cluster was to assist students in categorizing birds such as cardinals, penguins, vultures, chickens, and ducks. As the class talked about the categories, students wrote the names of examples beside each category to complete the cluster. Later in the unit, students each chose one bird to research, and then they presented the results of their research in cluster form. The bottom cluster, on bald eagles, presents the results of one student's research. The information in the cluster is divided into four categories—life, hunters, symbol, and body—and some general information is listed at the top of the figure.

Writing to Demonstrate Learning

Students also use writing to demonstrate their learning. This type of writing is more formal, and students use the writing process to revise and edit their writing before making a final copy. Reports are the best-known type of writing to demonstrate learning. Students write many types of reports, ranging from posters, riddles, and **alphabet books** to "All About . . ." books that Mrs. Roberts's students made and other individual and collaborative reports. Too often students are not exposed to report writing until they are faced with writing a term paper in high school, and then they are overwhelmed with learning how to take notes on note cards, how to organize and write the paper, and how to compile a bibliography. There is no reason to postpone report writing until students reach high school. Early, successful experiences with informative writing teach students about content-area topics as well as how to write reports (Harvey, 1998; Krogness, 1987; Tompkins, 2000).

"All About . . ." Books. The first reports that young children write are "All About . . . " books, in which they provide information about familiar topics, such as "Signs of Fall" and "Sea Creatures" (Bonin, 1988; Sowers, 1985). Young children write an entire booklet on a single topic. Usually one piece of information and an illustration appear on each page. Mrs. Roberts's first and second graders wrote "All About Penguins" books in the vignette at the beginning of this chapter.

Figure 14–5 Two clusters on birds

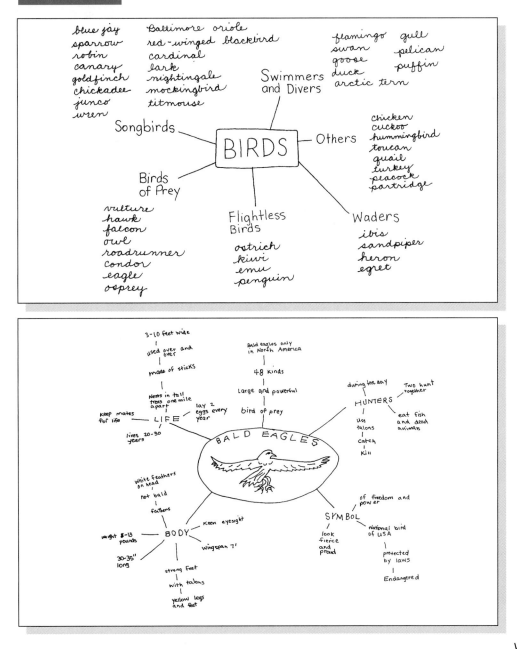

www.fredstrom.lps.org

Project Monarch Butterfly.
Fourth and fifth graders developed this website to share information on the life cycles and migration of monarch butterflies.

Collaborative Reports. Students work together to write **collaborative reports.** Sometimes students each write one page for the report, or they can work together in small groups to write chapters for the report. Alphabet books are one kind of collaborative report in which students each write a page representing one letter of the alphabet. Then the pages are compiled in alphabetical order and bound into a book. Students also create collaborative reports on almost any science or social studies topic.

Primary-grade students might make collaborative books about weather. Each student develops a page by writing one interesting fact about weather and drawing a picture illustrating the fact, and then the pages are compiled into a book. Older students might write collaborative biographies. Each student or small group writes about one event or accomplishment in the person's life, and then the pages are compiled in chronological order. Or, students work in small groups to write chapters for a collaborative report on the planets in the solar system, ancient Egypt, or the Oregon Trail.

As part of a unit on the American Revolution, a fifth-grade class developed a collaborative report. Students brainstormed a variety of topics, including the battles of Lexington and Concord, the Declaration of Independence, Betsy Ross, "No taxation without representation," and King George III. Students each chose a topic and created a page for the class book on that topic using both art and writing. Students used the writing process to revise and edit their chapters, and then they were compiled into a book. Figure 14–6 shows the page about King George III.

Figure 14–6 A page from a fifth-grade collaborative report on the American Revolution

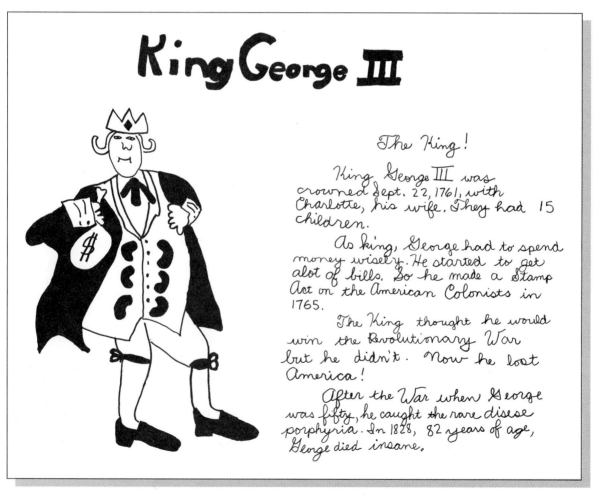

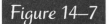 **Figure 14–7** A fifth grader's poster about bees

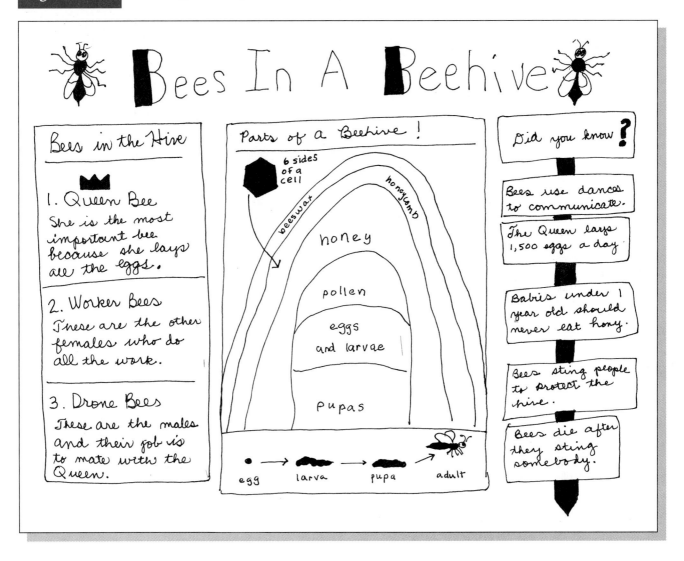

Students benefit from writing a collaborative report before writing individual reports because they learn how to write a report, with the group as a scaffold or support system, before tackling individual reports. Also, working in groups lets them share the laborious parts of the work.

Individual Reports. Students also write **individual reports** as projects during thematic units. Toby Fulwiler (1985) recommends that students do "authentic" research, in which they explore topics that interest them or hunt for answers to questions that puzzle them. When students become immersed in content-area study, questions arise that they want to explore, and increasingly students are turning to the Internet to research topics. For more information about using the Internet, check the Technology Link on pages 474–475.

Technology Link   Researching on the Internet

Students can use the vast information resources available on the World Wide Web as they prepare to write reports and present oral reports (Harvey, 1998). Displays at websites include text information, pictures, sound, video, and animated graphics, and they also provide connections to related information using hypertext links. While most websites have been developed by adults, some have been created by elementary students as part of thematic units, and students especially enjoy visiting these sites. Students can keep abreast of current news events and weather reports at some websites, investigate scientific discoveries and delve into history at other sites, or visit online museums and art galleries (Heide & Stilborne, 1999).

The World Wide Web is easy to navigate. Students locate websites with information related to their topics using search engine software. One of the best search engines for elementary students is Yahoo for Kids (www.yahooligans.com). On the search engine's homepage, students type in the topic for the search and the software program searches for websites related to the topic. A list of websites with their URL addresses and brief annotations then appears on the homepage.

Students review the list and then click on an address to connect to that website. Students overview the site, and if the site seems useful, they "bookmark" it or add it to their list of "favorites" so that they can return to it easily. Then students connect to other websites and read the information available there, take notes, and bookmark it if they want to return to it. Students can print out copies of all of the information available in the websites, but they are usually most interested in printing photographs, diagrams, maps, and other graphics to incorporate into their reports. Using the World Wide Web not only enhances students' content-area learning, it also increases their computer literacy at the same time (Leu & Leu, 1998).

Possible Pitfalls

The World Wide Web is unregulated, and some websites are not appropriate for children because of pornographic, racist, and other offensive content. All schools should

Posters.   Students also create posters during content-area units. In these posters, students combine visual and verbal elements to demonstrate learning (Moline, 1995). For example, students might:

- 🦎 draw detailed diagrams of the inner and outer planets in the solar system
- 🦎 chart the life cycle of frogs or the steps in mummification
- 🦎 identify the parts of a complex machine
- 🦎 label the clothing a Revolutionary War soldier wore and the supplies he carried
- 🦎 create timelines of a historical period
- 🦎 identify important events of a person's life on a lifeline
- 🦎 chart the explorers' voyages to America and around the world on a world map

As part of a reading and writing workshop on informational books, a fifth grader read *The Magic School Bus Inside a Beehive* (Cole, 1996) and created the poster shown in Figure 14–7.

use Internet filtering software to block children's access to inappropriate websites. While some students may be actively searching for these sites, many others stumble into them accidentally when they mistype a URL address.

There is always a possibility that information presented in websites may be inaccurate or misleading because there is no editorial review or other regulation of sites as there is in publishing books, magazines, and newspapers. Students should be alert to the possibility that some information may be incorrect, and teachers should preview websites if possible, or at least review sites whenever students raise questions.

In addition, when students freely browse the Internet, they may waste valuable instructional time as they explore websites and hypertext links. Also some students become frustrated as they end up at sites that are "under construction" or not available.

The Teacher's Role

Because of the possible problems with websites and Internet access, teachers should preview sites before students use the Internet to conduct research. Many teachers prefer to prepare a list of appropriate websites related to the topic for students rather than giving them free access to the World Wide Web. They can mark these sites with bookmarks or develop a written handout for students listing the URL addresses. Teachers can also create their own web pages that incorporate the appropriate hypertext links. Many teachers compile a list of online resources in a card file or computer database for each thematic unit to simplify their previewing.

The World Wide Web is an important complement to books, and it links students to the world of information technology. For more information, check *The Teacher's Complete and Easy Guide to the Internet* (Heide & Stilborne, 1999) and *Teaching With the Internet: Lessons From the Classroom* (Leu & Leu, 1998).

Students use a process approach to create posters such as the one shown in Figure 14–7. They plan the information they want to include in the poster and consider how to devise attention-getting displays using headings, illustrations and diagrams, captions, boxes, and rules. Students prepare a rough draft of the sections of their posters and revise and edit the sections as they do in the writing process. Then they make a final copy of each section, glue the sections onto a sheet of posterboard, and share their posters with classmates as they would share finished pieces of writing.

CONTENT-AREA TEXTBOOKS

Content-area texts are no longer viewed as the only source for learning, but they continue to be useful tools for learning across the curriculum and are available in most classrooms. Tierney and Pearson (1992) recommend that teachers shift from teaching *from* textbooks to teaching *with* textbooks and that they strive to incorporate other types of reading materials and activities into thematic units.

Content-area textbooks are often difficult for students to read—more difficult, in fact, than many informational books. One reason textbooks are difficult is that they briefly mention many topics without developing any of them in depth. A second reason is that content-area textbooks are read differently than stories. Teachers need to show students how to approach content-area textbooks by teaching students how to use specific activities to make comprehension easier. Figure 14–8 presents a list of guidelines for using content-area textbooks.

Making Content-Area Textbooks More Comprehensible

Teachers can use a variety of activities during each step of the reading process to make content-area textbooks more readable and to improve students' comprehension of what they have read.

In the prereading step, teachers activate and build students' background knowledge before reading. One activity that Mrs. Roberts used in the vignette at the beginning of the chapter is **exclusion brainstorming.** Teachers distribute a list of words, most of which are related to the main ideas presented in the reading assignment, and then ask students to mark words that they think are related to the main ideas. They read the assignment to see if they marked the right words (Johns, Van Leirsburg, & Davis, 1994). Another activity is the **prereading plan,** in which teachers introduce a key concept discussed in the chapter and students brainstorm words and ideas related to the concept (Langer, 1981).

Students view a video program to activate and build background knowledge before reading a chapter in their content-area textbooks.

Figure 14–8 Guidelines for using content-area textbooks

1. Teach Comprehension Aids

Teachers show students how to use the comprehension aids in content-area textbooks, including chapter overviews, headings that outline the chapter, helpful graphics, technical words defined in the text, and end-of-chapter summaries.

2. Create Questions Before Reading

Before reading each section of a chapter, students turn the section heading into a question and read to find the answer to the question. As they read students take notes, and then they answer the question they created after reading.

3. Identify Expository Text Structures

Teachers assist students in identifying the expository text structures used in the reading assignment, especially cause-and-effect or problem-and-solution patterns, before reading.

4. Introduce Key Terms

Teachers introduce only the key terms as part of an introductory presentation or discussion before students read the textbook assignment. After reading the teacher and students develop a word wall with the important words.

5. Focus on Big Ideas

Students focus on the big ideas instead of trying to remember all the facts or other information.

6. Include Content-Area Reading Activities

Students use activities such as exclusion brainstorming, anticipation guides, note-taking, and instructional conversations to help them comprehend textbook reading assignments.

7. Use Headings

Teachers encourage students to use headings to select and organize relevant information. The headings can be used to create a cluster, and students add details as they read.

8. Ask Self-Questions

Teachers encourage students to be active readers, to ask themselves questions as they read, and to monitor their reading.

9. Use Listen-Read-Discuss Format

Teachers use a listen-read-discuss format. To begin, the teacher presents the key concepts orally, and then students read and discuss the chapter. Or, the students read the chapter as a review activity rather than as the introductory activity.

10. Create Text Sets

Teachers supplement content-area textbook assignments with a text set of informational books, stories, poems, and other reading materials.

Teachers also guide students to set purposes for reading during this step. One of these activities is **anticipation guides.** Teachers introduce a set of statements on the topic of the chapter. Students agree or disagree with each statement and then read the assignment to see if they were right (Head & Readence, 1986).

To preview the chapter before reading, students can "text walk" through the chapter noting main headings, looking at illustrations, and reading diagrams and charts. Sometimes students turn the main headings into questions and prepare to read to find the answers to the questions. Or teachers can distribute a cluster or other graphic organizer with main ideas listed for students to complete as they read.

In the reading step, teachers help students focus on main ideas and details and organize what they are reading. Students complete graphic organizers as they read, or they can develop an outline by writing the main headings and then take notes after reading each section.

When students can't read the chapter independently, teachers have several options. They can read the chapter aloud before students read it independently. In this way, students will be familiar with the main ideas and vocabulary when they begin reading. Or, students can read with a buddy or partner, and they stop at the end of each paragraph to say something that they remember about the paragraph they just read.

During the responding step, students react to the chapter, ask questions to clarify confusions, and make connections to their own lives. Students refine their comprehension through **instructional conversations,** which are similar to grand conversations (Goldenberg, 1992/1993). In these discussions, the main ideas are discussed and students make comments, ask questions, and connect the information they are learning to background knowledge and their own lives. Teachers are the discussion leaders, and they ask questions to stimulate thinking, provide information, expand students' language using vocabulary from the chapter, and coax students to participate in the conversation.

Students also write to deepen their understanding. They reflect on their reading by writing in **learning logs** about important ideas and interesting details. Or, students can use **double-entry journals** to record quotes or important information and then write to reflect on information from the chapter.

During the exploring step, students focus on vocabulary, examine the text, and analyze the main ideas. They participate in many of the same activities used to explore stories. Students post words on word walls, make word clusters and posters to study the meaning of words, or do a **word sort** according to main ideas.

To focus on main ideas and details, students make **data charts** and list information according to main ideas. They often use this information to write reports or for other projects. Students work in small groups to make posters to highlight important information from sections of the chapter. Then each group presents the information to the class and displays the poster on the wall.

Students learn to use two special types of reading—skimming and scanning—in content-area textbook activities. In skimming, students read quickly and superficially to get the general idea; in scanning, they reread quickly to locate specific information. Students skim as they preview or to locate a word for the word wall. In contrast, students use scanning to locate details for data charts and to find specific sentences for a read-aloud.

In the applying step, students create projects to demonstrate their learning. Often students write reports or present oral reports to share what they have learned, but many other projects are possible. Students can write poems, present dramatic presentations, or create paper or cloth **quilts** with information recorded on each square.

Figure 14–9 Ways to make content-area textbooks more comprehensible

Step 1: Prereading

Teachers use these activities to activate and build students' background knowlege, set purposes for reading, and notice the structure of the text:

☞ Brainstorm words in a prereading plan.
☞ Complete an anticipation guide.
☞ Introduce a graphic organizer.
☞ Make K-W-L chart.
☞ Participate in a field trip.
☞ Participate in exclusion brainstorming.
☞ Preview the chapter.
☞ View a video.

Step 2: Reading

These activities support students so they can comprehend the main ideas more easily:

☞ Complete a graphic organizer.
☞ Listen before reading.
☞ Read with a buddy.
☞ Take notes.

Step 3: Responding

Teachers use these activities to help students clarify ideas, reflect on the main ideas presented in the chapter, and make connections with background knowledge and their own experiences:

☞ Participate in instructional conversations.
☞ Quickwrite.
☞ Write in a double-entry journal.
☞ Write in a learning log.

Step 4: Exploring

Teachers use these procedures and activities to highlight vocabulary words, examine main ideas, and connect main ideas and details:

☞ Complete a data chart.
☞ Design a main idea poster.
☞ Do a word sort.
☞ List words on word walls.
☞ Make a word cluster or poster.
☞ Participate in a read-around.
☞ Scan the text.

Step 5: Applying

Teachers provide opportunities for students to create projects and learn more about the topic of the chapter through these activities:

☞ Create an alphabet book.
☞ Design a quilt.
☞ Make a cubing.
☞ Present an oral report.
☞ Read a book from a text set.
☞ Write a poem.
☞ Write a report.
☞ Write a simulated journal.

Figure 14–9 lists these and other activities for each step of the reading process. Teachers pick from among these activities to choose the most appropriate ones for their students and for the specific chapter they are reading.

Learning How to Study

Students in the upper grades also need to learn how to use the **SQ3R study strategy,** a five-step technique in which students survey, question, read, recite, and review as they study a content-area reading assignment. The SQ3R study strategy incorporates before-, during-, and after-reading components. This study strategy was devised in the 1930s and has been researched and thoroughly documented as a very effective technique when used properly (Anderson & Armbruster, 1984; Caverly & Orlando, 1991).

Teachers introduce the SQ3R study strategy and provide opportunities for students to practice each step. At first, students can work together as a class as they use the strategy with a text the teacher is reading to students. Then students can work with partners and in small groups before using the strategy individually. Teachers need to emphasize that if students simply begin reading the first page of the assignment without doing the first two steps, they won't be able to remember as much of what they read. When students are in a hurry and skip some of the steps, the strategy will not be as successful.

Why Aren't Content-Area Textbooks Enough?

Sometimes content-area textbooks are used as the entire instructional program in social studies or science, and that's not a good idea. Textbooks typically only survey topics; other instructional materials are needed to provide the depth and understanding. Students need to read, write, and discuss topics. It is most effective to use the reading process and then extend students' learning with projects. Developing thematic units and using content-area textbooks as one resource is a much better idea than using content-area textbooks as the only reading material.

THEMATIC UNITS

www.atozteacherstuff.com
A to Z Teacher Stuff
www.proteacher.com
Proteacher
www.teachers.net
Teachers Net Lesson Bank
🕸 *Databases of lesson plans and thematic units.*

Thematic units are interdisciplinary units that integrate reading and writing with social studies, science, and other curricular areas. Students are involved in planning the thematic units and identifying some of the questions they want to explore and the activities that interest them. Students are involved in authentic and meaningful learning activities, not reading chapters in content-area textbooks in order to answer the questions at the end of the chapter. Textbooks are often used as a resource, but only as one of many available resources. Students explore topics that interest them and research answers to questions they have posed and are genuinely interested in answering. Students share their learning at the end of the unit and are assessed on what they have learned as well as the processes they used in learning and working in the classroom.

How to Develop a Thematic Unit

To begin planning a thematic unit, teachers choose the general topic and then identify three or four key concepts that they want to develop through the unit. The goal of a unit is not to teach a collection of facts but to help students grapple with several big understandings (Tunnell & Ammon, 1993). Next, teachers identify the resources

A text set is a collection of stories, informational books, and poems related to a theme.

that they have available for the unit and develop their teaching plan. Ten important considerations in developing a thematic unit are:

1. *Collect a text set of stories, informational books, and poems.* Teachers collect books, magazines, newspaper articles, and reference books for the text set related to the unit. The text set is placed in the special area for materials related to the unit in the classroom library. Teachers plan to read aloud some books to students (or tape-record them for the listening center), while some will be read independently and others will be read together by students as shared or guided reading. These materials can also be used for minilessons—to teach students, for example, about reading strategies and expository text structure. Other books can be used as models or patterns for writing projects. Teachers also write the poems on charts to share with students or arrange a bulletin board display of the poems.

2. *Set up a listening center.* Teachers select audiotapes to accompany stories or informational books, or they create their own tapes so that absent students can catch up on a book being read aloud day by day. Or, the tapes can be used to provide additional reading experiences for students who listen to a tape when they read or reread a story or informational book.

3. *Coordinate content-area textbook readings.* Teachers can teach thematic units without textbooks; however, when information is available in a content-area textbook, it should be incorporated into the unit. Teachers may decide to use the text reading to introduce the unit, or read it along with other activities, or use it to review main ideas at the end of the unit. Upper-grade students, in particular, need to learn how to read and study content-area textbooks. They learn how to use skimming and scanning, how to identify main ideas and details, and how to take notes while reading.

4. *Locate multimedia materials.* Teachers locate videos, websites, computer programs, maps, models, and other materials to be used in connection with the unit. Some materials are used to develop children's background knowledge about the unit, while others are used in teaching the key concepts. Teachers use some multimedia materials for lessons and set up other materials in centers. And, students make other materials during the unit to display in the classroom.

5. *Identify potential words for the word wall.* Teachers preview books in the text set and identify potential words for the word wall. This list is useful in planning vocabulary activities, but teachers do not simply use their word lists for the classroom word wall. Students and the teacher develop the classroom word wall as they read and discuss the key concepts and other information related to the unit.

6. *Plan how students will use learning logs.* Teachers plan for students to keep learning logs in which students can take notes, write questions, make observations, clarify their thinking, and write reactions to what they read during thematic units (Tompkins, 2000).

7. *Identify literacy skills and strategies to teach during the unit.* Teachers plan minilessons to teach literacy skills and strategies, such as using an index, scanning a text, writing an alphabet book, and conducting an interview. Students have opportunities to apply what they are learning in minilessons in reading and writing activities.

8. *Design centers to support content-area and literacy learning.* Teachers plan centers for students to work at independently or in small groups to practice strategies and skills that were first presented to the whole class and to explore topics and materials related to the unit. Possible centers include a computer center, a reading center, a listening center, a writing center, a word work center, a map- and chart-making center, a learning log center, and a project center.

9. *Brainstorm possible projects students may create to extend their learning.* Teachers think about projects students may choose to develop to extend and personalize their learning during the unit. This advance planning makes it possible for teachers to collect needed supplies and to have suggestions ready to offer to students who need assistance in choosing a project. Students work on the project independently or in small groups and then share the project with the class at the end of the theme. Projects involve reading, writing, talk, art, music, or drama. Some suggestions are:

❧ Read a biography related to the unit.

❧ Create a poster to illustrate a key concept.

❧ Make a quilt about the unit.

❧ Write and mail a letter to get information related to the unit.

❧ Write a story related to the unit.

❧ Perform a **readers theatre** production, puppet show, or other dramatization related to the unit.

❧ Write a poem, song, or rap related to the unit.

❧ Write an "All About . . ." book or report about one of the key concepts.

❧ Create a commercial or advertisement related to the unit.

❧ Create a tabletop display or diorama about the unit.

www.education-world.com

Education World. Search the database for thematic units and related sites. For the theme ancient Egypt, for instance, 592 sites were found.

www.stemnet.nf.ca

Theme-Related Resources on the World Wide Web. Links to websites related to rain forests, oceanography, machines, space, and many other themes.

www.vpds.wsu.edu

Washington Story Quilts. A primary-grade class shows how they made quilts as part of a thematic unit.

10. *Plan for the assessment of the unit.* Teachers consider how they will assess students' learning as they make plans for activities and assignments. In this way, teachers can explain to students how they will be assessed at the beginning of the unit and check to see that their assessment will emphasize students' learning of the main ideas.

Teachers consider the resources they have available, brainstorm possible activities, and then develop clusters to guide their planning. The goal in developing plans for a thematic unit is to consider a wide variety of resources that integrate listening, talking, reading, and writing with the content of the theme (Pappas, Kiefer, & Levstik, 1990).

A Primary-Grade Unit: Houses and Homes

In this three-week unit, students learn that people and animals live in different sorts of houses depending on where they live and what their needs are. They also learn about how houses are built in the United States and the types of building materials that are used. Through field trips to a site where a house is being built in town, students learn the steps in building a house. Two books are available as big books, and a variety of stories, informational books, and poems are available as small books. Students read and respond to Ann Morris's *Houses and Homes* (1992) during the first week of the unit, to *A House Is a House for Me* (Hoberman, 1978) during the second week, and to Eric Carle's *A House for Hermit Crab* (1987) during the third week. Students interview builders, carpenters, plumbers, and other people who build houses, and they manipulate some of the tools and building supplies. They learn the names for tools and building supplies as well as the names for various types of houses that people and animals live in. Students work in small groups to create projects, including making books and making a cluster of the types of houses different animals live in. A planning cluster for a unit on houses and homes is presented in Figure 14–10.

A Middle-Grade Unit: Desert Life

Students investigate the plants, animals, and people that live in the desert during this three-week unit. They learn about desert ecosystems, how deserts form, and how they change. They keep learning logs in which they take notes and write reactions to books they are reading. Students divide into book clubs during the first week to read books about the desert. During the second week of the unit, students participate in an author study of Byrd Baylor, a woman who lives in the desert and writes about desert life, and they read many of her books. During the third week, students participate in a reading workshop and read other desert books and reread favorite books. To extend their learning, students participate in projects, including writing desert riddles, making a chart of a desert ecosystem, and drawing a desert mural. Together as a class, students can write a desert alphabet book or a collaborative report about deserts. A planning cluster for a unit on desert life is presented in Figure 14–11.

An Upper-Grade Unit: Ancient Egypt

Students learn about this great ancient civilization during a month-long unit. Key concepts include the influence of the Nile River on Egyptian life, the contributions of this civilization to twentieth-century America, a comparison of ancient to modern Egypt, and the techniques Egyptologists use to locate tombs of the ancient rulers and

Figure 14–10 A planning cluster for a primary-grade unit on houses and homes

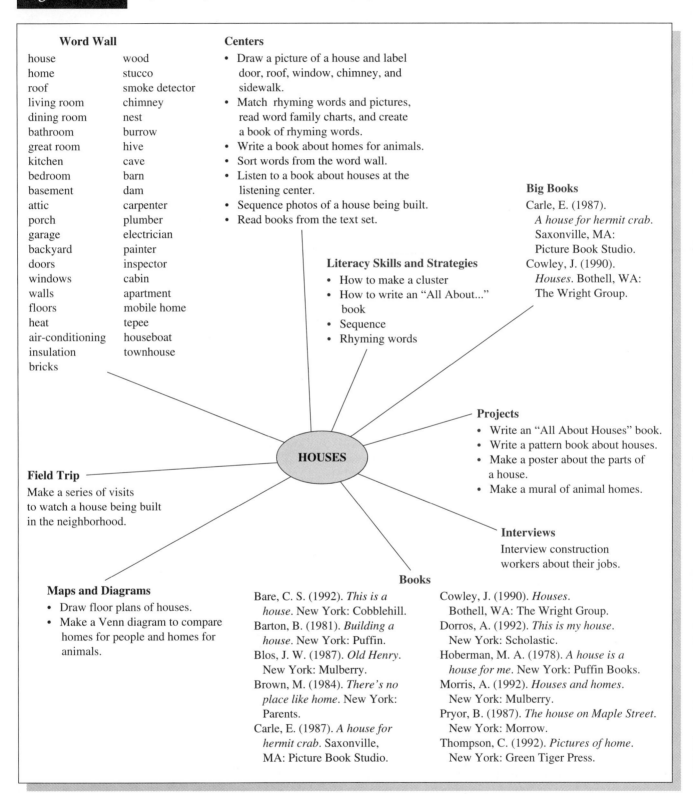

Word Wall

house	wood
home	stucco
roof	smoke detector
living room	chimney
dining room	nest
bathroom	burrow
great room	hive
kitchen	cave
bedroom	barn
basement	dam
attic	carpenter
porch	plumber
garage	electrician
backyard	painter
doors	inspector
windows	cabin
walls	apartment
floors	mobile home
heat	tepee
air-conditioning	houseboat
insulation	townhouse
bricks	

Centers

- Draw a picture of a house and label door, roof, window, chimney, and sidewalk.
- Match rhyming words and pictures, read word family charts, and create a book of rhyming words.
- Write a book about homes for animals.
- Sort words from the word wall.
- Listen to a book about houses at the listening center.
- Sequence photos of a house being built.
- Read books from the text set.

Literacy Skills and Strategies

- How to make a cluster
- How to write an "All About..." book
- Sequence
- Rhyming words

Big Books

Carle, E. (1987). *A house for hermit crab.* Saxonville, MA: Picture Book Studio.
Cowley, J. (1990). *Houses.* Bothell, WA: The Wright Group.

Projects

- Write an "All About Houses" book.
- Write a pattern book about houses.
- Make a poster about the parts of a house.
- Make a mural of animal homes.

HOUSES

Field Trip

Make a series of visits to watch a house being built in the neighborhood.

Interviews

Interview construction workers about their jobs.

Maps and Diagrams

- Draw floor plans of houses.
- Make a Venn diagram to compare homes for people and homes for animals.

Books

Bare, C. S. (1992). *This is a house.* New York: Cobblehill.
Barton, B. (1981). *Building a house.* New York: Puffin.
Blos, J. W. (1987). *Old Henry.* New York: Mulberry.
Brown, M. (1984). *There's no place like home.* New York: Parents.
Carle, E. (1987). *A house for hermit crab.* Saxonville, MA: Picture Book Studio.

Cowley, J. (1990). *Houses.* Bothell, WA: The Wright Group.
Dorros, A. (1992). *This is my house.* New York: Scholastic.
Hoberman, M. A. (1978). *A house is a house for me.* New York: Puffin Books.
Morris, A. (1992). *Houses and homes.* New York: Mulberry.
Pryor, B. (1987). *The house on Maple Street.* New York: Morrow.
Thompson, C. (1992). *Pictures of home.* New York: Green Tiger Press.

Figure 14–11 A planning cluster for a middle-grade unit on deserts

Word Wall

desert	king snake
Death Valley	jackrabbit
Sahara	Joshua trees
Mojave	spines
kangaroo rat	exoskeleton
barrel cactus	saguaro
dunes	camouflage
Gobi Desert	hawk
Bedouins	camels
oasis	tortoises
scorpion	beetles
coral snake	

Projects

- Identify deserts on world map.
- Write desert riddles.
- Draw a chart of the desert ecosystem.
- Make a tabletop desert scene.
- Write an "All About the Desert" book.
- Write an "I am" poem patterned on *Desert Voices*.
- Research a question about the desert.
- Draw a desert mural.

Literacy Skills and Strategies

- Read expository text using the efferent stance.
- Write information on a data chart.
- Use an index.
- Draw a life cycle.
- Create riddles.
- Teach problem-and-solution structure.

Maps and Diagrams

- Read landform maps.
- Draw a map of the desert.
- Draw a life cycle of a desert animal.
- Make a problem-solution chart on desert adaptations.

DESERTS

Word-Study Activities

- Make word posters and word maps.
- Do a word sort.
- Create a semantic feature analysis about desert plants and animals.

Learning Log

- Take notes.
- Write quickwrites.
- Draw diagrams.
- List vocabulary words.

K-W-L Chart

- Use to introduce the theme.
- Identify research questions.
- Use to conclude unit.

Author Study

- Share information about Byrd Baylor.
- Read her books set in the desert.
- Write letters to the author.

Centers

- Add information about desert plants and animals to a data chart.
- Listen to a book at the listening center.
- Draw a life cycle of a desert animal.
- Write a class alphabet book about deserts.
- Read Byrd Baylor's books and others from the text set.
- Write letters to author Byrd Baylor.
- Sort words from the word wall.
- Participate in making a tabletop desert diorama.

Books

Bash, B. (1989). *Desert giant.* Boston: Little, Brown.

Baylor, B. (1976). *Hawk, I'm your brother.* New York: Scribner.

Baylor, B. (1981). *Desert voices.* New York: Scribner.

Fowler, A. (1997). *It could still be a desert.* Chicago: Childrens Press.

Guiberson, B. Z. (1991). *Cactus hotel.* New York: Holt.

Hirschi, R. (1992). *Discover my world: Desert.* New York: Bantam.

Mora, P. (1994). *The desert is my mother.* Houston: Piñata Books.

Siebert, D. (1988). *Mojave.* New York: Harper & Row.

Simon, S. (1990). *Deserts.* New York: Morrow.

Taylor, B. (1992). *Desert life.* New York: Dorling Kindersley.

Word Wall

Egypt	embalming
pharoahs	Africa
Nile River	lotus
Ramses the Great	obelisk
Tutankhamun	papyrus
Nefertiti	scribes
Hatshepsut	hieroglyphs
natron	Imhotep
mummification	Champollion
canopic jars	Amun-Ra
pyramids	dynasty
Valley of the Kings	Luxor
senet	Memphis
irrigation	Rosetta stone
Old Kingdom	vizier
Middle Kingdom	Egyptologist
New Kingdom	

Cubing

Make a cube exploring the ancient Egyptian civilization.

K-W-L Chart

- Introduce K-W-L chart at the beginning of the unit.
- Identify research questions for collaborative or individual reports.
- Use to conclude the unit.

Learning Logs

Keep a learning log with quickwrites, notes, maps, charts, and diagrams.

Maps and Diagrams

- Make a timeline of ancient Egypt.
- Create a Venn diagram comparing ancient and modern Egypt.
- Read maps of ancient and modern Egypt.
- Draw maps of Egypt.

Projects

- Keep a simulated journal as an ancient Egyptian.
- Make a timeline of the ancient civilization.
- Make a poster about a god or goddess.
- Present an oral report about how to mummify someone.
- Make a salt map of Egypt and mark ancient landmarks.
- Write a collection of poems about ancient Egypt.
- Make paper.
- Present an "interview" of several ancient Egyptians.
- Write a book about the ways the Egyptian civilization has influenced ours.
- Research the Rosetta stone.
- Read two books about ancient Egypt.
- Make a chart comparing ancient and modern Egypt.

Literacy Skills and Strategies

- Use anticipation guides.
- Use the SQ3R study strategy.
- Read expository text using efferent stance.
- Make a timeline.
- Analyze root words and affixes.
- Use syllabication to identify words.

Word-Study Activities

- Make word maps.
- Do a word sort.
- Create a semantic feature analysis.
- Make a word chain.
- Write an alphabet book on Egypt.

ANCIENT EGYPT

Centers

- Draw a map of Egypt.
- Make a mummy.
- Write hieroglyphics.
- Make a god poster.
- Sort words from the word wall.
- Collect parts of speech from text set books.
- Read text set books.
- Research ancient Egypt on the Internet.

Books

Aliki. (1979). *Mummies made in Egypt*. New York: HarperCollins.

Carter, D. S. (1987). *His majesty, Queen Hatshepsut*. New York: HarperCollins.

Der Manueliàn, P. (1991). *Hieroglyphs from A to Z*. New York: Scholastic.

Giblin, J. C. (1990). *The riddle of the Rosetta stone*. New York: HarperCollins.

Gregory, K. (1999). *Cleopatra VII, daughter of the Nile*. New York: Scholastic.

Harris, G. (1992). *Gods and pharoahs from Egyptian mythology*. New York: Peter Bedrick.

Katan, N. J., & Mintz, B. (1981). *Hieroglyphs: The writing of ancient Egypt*. New York: McElderry.

Lattimore, D. N. (1992). *The winged cat: A tale of ancient Egypt*. New York: HarperCollins.

Macaulay, D. (1975). *Pyramid*. Boston: Houghton Mifflin.

McMullen, K. (1992). *Under the mummy's spell*. New York: Farrar, Straus & Giroux.

Perl, L. (1987). *Mummies, tombs, and treasure: secrets of ancient Egypt*. New York: Clarion.

Stanley, D., & Vennema, P. (1994). *Cleopatra*. New York: Morrow.

Stolz, M. (1988). *Zekmet the stone carver: A tale of ancient Egypt*. San Diego: Harcourt Brace.

Ventura, P. & Ceserani, G. P. (1985). *In search of Tutankhamun*. Morristown, NJ: Silver Burdett.

to decipher Egyptian hieroglyphics. Students will read books in literature circles and choose other books from the text set to read during reading workshop. Students and the teacher will add vocabulary to the word wall, and students will use the words in a variety of activities.

Teachers will teach minilessons on writing simulated journals, map-reading skills, Egyptian gods, mummification, and writing poems for two voices. Students will also work in writing workshop as they write reports, biographies, or collections of poetry related to the thematic unit. As a culminating activity, students will create individual projects and share them on Egypt day, when they assume the roles of ancient Egyptians, dress as ancient people did, and eat foods of the period. Figure 14–12 presents a planning cluster for an upper-grade unit on ancient Egypt.

Review

Students use reading and writing as tools for learning in the content areas. Students read informational books, stories, poems, and other materials as well as content-area textbooks. These textbooks are useful tools for thematic units, but they should never be the only reading material. Students can use a variety of activities during each step of the reading process to make textbooks more readable. They also use writing activities, such as learning logs, to explore what they are learning. Students also use writing to prepare reports to extend and document their learning. Many of the ways that effective teachers use reading and writing in thematic units are reviewed in the feature on page 488.

How Effective Teachers . . .

Use Reading and Writing in the Content Areas

■ Effective Practices

1. Teachers use informational books, stories, and poems for thematic units.
2. Teachers teach students how to read informational books, and explain the expository text structures.
3. Teachers use content-area textbooks as one resource in thematic units.
4. Teachers encourage students to use reading and writing as tools for learning.

5. Teachers teach students to use learning logs, double-entry journals, quickwrites, and clusters as learning tools.
6. Teachers have students write reports to demonstrate learning.

7. Teachers use special activities for each step of the reading process to help students comprehend content-area textbooks.
8. Teachers focus on big ideas in content-area units.
9. Teachers list important words on word walls and use a variety of activities to teach vocabulary.
10. Teachers have students create projects to extend their learning.

■ Ineffective Practices

1. Teachers teach social studies and science using content-area textbooks.
2. Teachers rarely use trade books and do not teach students about the structure of informational books.
3. Teachers use textbooks as the only resource.
4. Teachers make textbook reading assignments but do not teach students how to read the assignment effectively.
5. Teachers have students answer questions at the end of chapters and complete worksheets.
6. Teachers rarely have students use writing except to answer questions at the end of textbook chapters.
7. Teachers teach units as they are set out in content-area textbooks.
8. Teachers teach facts.
9. Teachers list vocabulary on the chalkboard and have students look up the words in dictionaries and write the words in sentences.
10. Teachers give tests.

References

Anderson, T. H., & Armbruster, B. B. (1984). Studying. In P. D. Pearson, R. Barr, M. L. Kamil, & P. Mosenthal (Eds.), *Handbook of reading research* (pp. 657–679). New York: Longman.

Bamford, R. A., & Kristo, J. V. (Eds.). (1998). *Making facts come alive: Choosing quality nonfiction literature K-8*. Norwood, MA: Christopher-Gordon.

Bonin, S. (1988). Beyond storyland: Young writers can tell it other ways. In T. Newkirk & N. Atwell (Eds.), *Understanding writing* (2nd ed., pp. 47–51). Portsmouth, NH: Heinemann.

Caverly, D. C., & Orlando, V. P. (1991). Textbook study strategies. In D. C. Caverly & V. P. Orlando (Eds.),

Teaching reading and study strategies at the college level (pp. 86–165). Newark, DE: International Reading Association.

Doiron, R. (1994). Using nonfiction in a read-aloud program: Letting the facts speak for themselves. *The Reading Teacher, 47*, 616–624.

Fulwiler, T. (1987). *The journal book*. Portsmouth, NH: Heinemann/Boynton-Cook.

Goldenberg, C. (1992/1993). Instructional conversations: Promoting comprehension through discussion. *The Reading Teacher, 46*, 316–326.

Harvey, S. (1998). *Nonfiction matters: Reading, writing, and research in grades 3–8*. York, ME: Stenhouse.

Head, M. H., & Readence, J. E. (1986). Anticipation guides: Meaning through prediction. In E. K. Dishner, T. W. Bean, J. E. Readence, & D. W. Moore (Eds.), *Reading in the content areas* (2nd ed., pp. 229–234). Dubuque, IA: Kendall/Hunt.

Heide, A., & Stilborne, L. (1999). *The teacher's complete and easy guide to the Internet.* New York: Teachers College Press.

Horowitz, R., & Freeman, S. H. (1995). Robots versus spaceships: The role of discussion in kindergartners' and second graders' preferences for science text. *The Reading Teacher, 49,* 30–40.

Johns, J. L., Van Leirsburg, P., & Davis, S. J. (1994). *Improving reading: A handbook of strategies.* Dubuque, IA: Kendall/Hunt.

Krogness, M. M. (1987). Folklore: A matter of the heart and the heart of the matter. *Language Arts, 64,* 808–818.

Langer, J. A. (1981). From theory to practice: A prereading plan. *Journal of Reading, 25,* 152–157.

Leu, D. J., & Leu, D.D. (1998). *Teaching with the Internet: Lessons from the classroom* (2nd ed.). Norwood, MA: Christopher-Gordon.

Moline, S. (1995). I see what you mean: Children at work with visual information. York, ME: Stenhouse.

Neeld, E. C. (1986). *Writing.* Glenview, IL: Scott, Foresman.

Nelson, C. S. (1994). Historical literacy: A journey of discovery. *The Reading Teacher, 47,* 552–556.

Ogle, D. M. (1986). K-W-L: A teaching model that develops active reading of expository text. *The Reading Teacher, 39,* 564–570.

Pappas, C. C., Kiefer, B. Z., & Levstik, L. S. (1990). *An integrated language perspective in the elementary school: Theory into action.* New York: Longman.

Rico, G. L. (1983). *Writing the natural way.* Los Angeles: Tarcher.

Smith, L. J., & Johnson, H. (1994). Models for implementing literature in content studies. *The Reading Teacher, 48,* 198–209.

Sowers, S. (1985). The story and the "all about" book. In J. Hansen, T. Newkirk, & D. Graves (Eds.), *Breaking ground: Teachers relate reading and writing in the elementary school* (pp. 73–82). Portsmouth, NH: Heinemann.

Stanford, B. (1988). Writing reflectively. *Language Arts, 65,* 652–658.

Tierney, R. J., & Pearson, P. D. (1992). Learning to learn from text: A framework for improving classroom practice. In E. K. Dishner, T. W. Bean, J. E. Readence, & D. W. Moore (Eds.), *Reading in the content areas: Improving classroom instruction* (pp. 85–99). Dubuque, IA: Kendall-Hunt.

Tompkins, G. E. (2000). *Teaching writing: Balancing process and product* (3rd ed.). Upper Saddle River, NJ: Merrill/Prentice Hall.

Tunnell, M. O., & Ammon, R. (Eds.). (1993). *The story of ourselves: Teaching history through children's literature.* Portsmouth, NH: Heinemann.

Winograd, K., & Higgins, K. M. (1994–1995). Writing, reading, and talking mathematics: One interdisciplinary possibility. *The Reading Teacher, 48,* 310–317.

Children's Book References

Baylor, B. (1981). *Desert voices.* New York: Scribner.

Beatty, P. (1987). *Charley Skedaddle.* New York: Morrow.

Bonners, S. (1981). *A penguin year.* New York: Delacorte.

Carle, E. (1987). *A house for hermit crab.* Saxonville, MA: Picture Book Studio.

Cohen, B. (1983). *Molly's pilgrim.* New York: Lothrop, Lee & Shepard.

Cole, J. (1996). *The magic school bus inside a beehive.* New York: Scholastic.

Cowcher, H. (1990). *Antarctica.* New York: Farrar, Straus & Giroux.

Fletcher, N. (1993). *Penguin.* London: Dorling Kindersley.

Forbes, E. (1970). *Johnny Tremain.* Boston: Houghton Mifflin.

Fowler, A. (1990). *It could still be a bird.* Chicago: Childrens Press.

Fritz, J. (1987). *Brady.* New York: Viking.

Hoberman, M. A. (1978). *A house is a house for me.* New York: Puffin Books.

Horvatic, A. (1989). *Simple machines.* New York: Dutton.

Hunt, I. (1987). *Across five Aprils.* New York: Follett.

Lester, H. (1988). *Tacky the penguin.* Boston: Houghton Mifflin.

Lowry, L. (1989). *Number the stars.* Boston: Houghton Mifflin.

Martin, B., Jr. (1983). *Brown bear, brown bear, what do you see?* New York: Holt.

McMillan, B. (1992). *Going on a whale watch.* New York: Scholastic.

Moore, K. (1997). *. . . . If you lived at the time of the American Revolution.* New York: Scholastic.

Morris, A. (1992). *Houses and homes.* New York: Mulberry Books.

Siebert, D. (1988). *Mojave.* New York: Harper & Row.

Van Allsburg, C. (1990). *Ben's dream.* Boston: Houghton Mifflin.

Wood, A. (1989). *Little penguin's tale.* San Diego: Harcourt Brace Jovanovich.

Part V

Compendium of Instructional Procedures

ALPHABET BOOKS

Students construct alphabet books much like the alphabet trade books published for children (Tompkins, 2000). These student-made books are useful reading materials for beginning readers, and students often make alphabet books as part of literature focus units and content-area units. Students can make alphabet books collaboratively as a class or in a small group. Interested students can make individual alphabet books, but with 26 pages to complete, it is an arduous task. The steps in constructing an alphabet book with a group of students are:

1. *Examine alphabet trade books.* Students examine alphabet trade books published for children to learn how the books are designed and how the authors use titles, text, and illustrations to lay out their pages. Good examples include *Eating the Alphabet: Fruits and Vegetables From A to Z* (Ehlert, 1989) and *Illuminations* (Hunt, 1989). Or, students can examine student-made alphabet books made by other classes.

2. *Make an alphabet list.* Students write the letters of the alphabet in a column on a long sheet of butcher paper for the group to use for brainstorming words for the book.

3. *Have students brainstorm words.* Students identify words related to the literature focus unit or content-area unit beginning with each letter of the alphabet, and they write these words on the sheet of butcher paper. Students often consult the **word wall** and books in the text set as they try to think of related words.

4. *Have students choose letters.* Students each choose the letter for the page they will create.

5. *Design the format of the page.* As a class or small group, students decide where the letter, the illustration, and the text will be placed.

6. *Write the pages.* Students use the writing process to draft, revise, and edit their pages. Then students make final copies of their pages, and one student makes the cover.

7. *Compile the pages.* Students and the teacher compile the pages in alphabetical order and bind the book.

Alphabet books are often used as projects at the end of a unit of study, such as the oceans, the desert, World War II, or California missions. The U page from a fourth-grade class's alphabet book on the California missions is shown in Figure 1.

ANTICIPATION GUIDES

Anticipation guides (Head & Readence, 1986) are lists of statements about a topic that students discuss before reading content-area textbooks and informational books. Teachers prepare a list of statements about the topic; some of the statements should be true and accurate, and others incorrect or based on misconceptions. Before reading, students discuss each statement and agree or disagree with it. Then they discuss the statements again after reading. The purpose of this activity is to stimulate students' interest in the topic and to activate prior knowledge. An anticipation guide about Canada might include these statements:

Canada is the second-largest country in the world.
The official language of Canada is English.
Canada is very much like the United States.

Figure 1   The "U" page from a fourth-grade class's alphabet book

Canada's economy is based on its wealth of natural resources.
Canada has always fought on the American side during wars.
Today most Canadians live within 200 miles of the American border.

The steps in developing an anticipation guide are:

1. *Identify several major concepts.* Teachers consider their students' knowledge about the topic and any misconceptions they might have as they identify concepts related to the reading assignment or unit.

2. *Develop a list of three to six statements.* Teachers write a statement about each major concept they identified. These statements should be general enough to stimulate discussion and useful for clarifying misconceptions. The list can be written on a chart, or individual copies can be duplicated for each student.

3. *Discuss the statements on the anticipation guide.* Teachers introduce the anticipation guide and have students respond to the statements. Students think about the statements and decide whether they agree or disagree with each one.

4. *Read the text.* Students read the text and compare their responses to what the reading material states.

5. *Discuss the statements again.* After reading, students reconsider their earlier responses to each statement and locate information in the text that supports or discounts the statement.

Students can also try their hand at writing anticipation guides. When students are reading informational books in literature circles, they can create an anticipation guide after reading and then share the guide with classmates when they present the book during a sharing time.

BOOK BOXES

Teachers and students collect three or more objects or pictures related to a story, informational book, or poem and put them in a box along with the book or other reading material. For example, a book box for *Sarah, Plain and Tall* (MacLachlan, 1983) might include seashells, a train ticket, a yellow bonnet, colored pencils, a map of Sarah's trip from Maine to the prairie, and letters. Or, for *Eating the Alphabet: Fruits and Vegetables From A to Z* (Ehlert, 1989), teachers can collect plastic fruits and vegetables. The steps in preparing a book box are:

1. *Read the book.* While reading the book, teachers notice important objects that are mentioned and think about how they might collect these objects or replicas of them.

2. *Choose a book box.* Teachers choose a box, basket, or plastic tub to hold the objects, and decorate the box with the name of the book, pictures, and words.

3. *Fill the book box.* Teachers place three or more objects and pictures in the box to represent the book. When students are making book boxes, they may place an inventory sheet in the box with all the items listed and an explanation of why the items were selected.

4. *Share the completed book box.* When teachers make book boxes, they use them to introduce the book and provide background information before reading. In contrast, students often make book boxes as a project during the extending step of the reading process and share them with classmates at the end of a unit.

Book boxes are especially useful for students learning English as a second language and for nonverbal students who have small vocabularies and difficulty developing sentences to express ideas.

BOOK TALKS

Book talks are brief teasers that teachers present to interest students in particular books. Teachers use book talks to introduce students to books in the classroom library, books for literature circles, or a text set of books for a unit or books written by a particular author. Students also give book talks to share books they have read during reading workshop. The steps are:

1. *Select one or more books to share.* When teachers share more than one book, the books are usually related in some way. They may be part of a text set, written by the same author, or on a related topic.

2. *Plan a brief presentation for each book.* During the one- or two-minute presentation, teachers tell the title and author of the book and give a brief summary. They also explain why they liked it and why students might be interested in it. The teacher may also read a short excerpt and show an illustration.

3. *Display the books.* Teachers show the book during the book talk and then display it on a chalk tray or shelf to encourage students' interest.

The same steps are used when students give book talks. If students have prepared a project related to the book, they also share it during the book talk.

CHORAL READING

A good way to develop students' reading fluency is through choral reading. Poems are usually the texts used for choral reading, but other texts can also be used. As students read aloud, they practice chunking words together, varying their reading speed, and reading more expressively. Students take turns reading lines or sentences of the text as they read together as a class or in small groups. Four possible arrangements for choral reading are:

❦ ***Echo reading.*** The leader reads each line, and the group repeats it.

❦ ***Leader and chorus reading.*** The leader reads the main part of the poem, and the group reads the refrain or chorus in unison.

❦ ***Small-group reading.*** The class divides into two or more groups, and each group reads one part of the poem.

❦ ***Cumulative reading.*** One student or one group reads the first line or stanza, and another student or group joins in as each line or stanza is read so that a cumulative effect is created.

The steps in choral reading are:

1. *Select a poem for choral reading.* Teachers select a poem or other text to use for choral reading and copy it onto a chart or make multiple copies for students to read.

2. *Arrange the text for choral reading.* Teachers work with students to decide how to arrange the text for reading. They add marks to the chart or have students mark individual copies so that they can follow the arrangement.

3. *Do the choral reading.* Students read the poem or other text with students several times, and teachers emphasize that students should pronounce words clearly and read with expression. Teachers may want to tape-record students' reading so that they can hear themselves.

Choral reading makes students active participants in the poetry experience, and it helps them learn to appreciate the sounds, feelings, and magic of poetry. Many poems can be used for choral reading; try, for example, Shel Silverstein's "Boa Constrictor," Karla Kuskin's "Full of the Moon," Laura E. Richards's "Eletelephony," and Eve Merriam's "Catch a Little Rhyme."

CLOZE PROCEDURE

The cloze procedure is an informal tool for assessing students' comprehension. Teachers use the cloze procedure to gather information about readers' abilities to deal with the content and structure of texts they are reading. Teachers construct a cloze passage by taking an excerpt from a book—a story, an informational book, or a content-area textbook—that students have read and deleting roughly every fifth word in the passage. The deleted words are replaced with blanks. Then students read the passage and add the missing words. Students use their knowledge of syntax (the order of words in English) and semantics (the meaning of words within sentences) to successfully predict the missing words in the text passage. Only the exact word is considered the correct answer. The following cloze activity was devised by a fourth-grade teacher to assess students' understanding during a unit on astronomy. The three paragraphs were taken from a class book, and each was written by a different student:

> *The nine planets travel around the sun. The _____ is a planet that travels around the sun once a year. The planets between the sun and the Earth are called the _____ planets and the others are the _____ planets. The planets are Mercury, _____, Earth, Mars, Jupiter, _____, Uranus, _____, and Pluto. The sun, the planets, and their _____ make up the _____ system.*
>
> *Stars are giant shining balls of hot _____. The _____ are dark, and we can only _____ them because they reflect the _____ of the sun. Planets and stars look almost the same at night, but planets do not _____. Stars stay in the same place in the _____, but planets _____ around.*
>
> *Jupiter is the _____ planet in the solar system. It is the _____ planet from the _____. Jupiter is covered with thick _____ so we can't see it from Earth. Astronomers can see a giant _____ spot on the clouds. Maybe it is sort of like a hurricane. Believe it or not, Jupiter has both _____ and _____. It is very _____ on Jupiter, but there could be life there.*

The steps in the cloze procedure are:

1. **Select a passage and retype it.** Teachers select an excerpt from a story, content-area textbook, or informational book for the cloze activity. Then they retype the text. The first sentence is typed exactly as it appears in the original text. Beginning with the second sentence, one of the first five words is deleted and replaced with a blank. Then every fifth word in the remainder of the passage is deleted and replaced with a blank. Teachers often vary the cloze procedure and delete specific content words rather than every fifth word. Character names and words related to key events in the story might be omitted. For passages from informational books, teachers often delete key terms.

2. **Complete the cloze activity.** Students read the entire text silently, and then they reread the text and predict or "guess" the word that goes in each blank. Students write the words in the blanks.

3. **Score students' work.** Teachers award one point each time the missing word is correctly identified. The percentage of correct answers is determined by dividing the number of points by the number of blanks. Compare the percentage of correct word replacements with this scale:

61% or more correct:	independent level
41–60% correct:	instructional level
less than 40% correct:	frustration level

The cloze procedure can also be used to determine whether or not an unfamiliar trade book or textbook is appropriate to use for classroom instruction. Teachers prepare a cloze passage and have all students or a random sample of students follow the procedure identified above. Then teachers score students' responses and use a one-third to one-half formula to determine the text's appropriateness for their students. If students correctly predict more than 50% of the deleted words, the passage is easy reading. If they predict less than 30% of the missing words, the passage is too difficult for classroom instruction. The instructional range is 30–50% correct predictions (Reutzel & Cooter, 1996). The percentages are different from those in the scale because students are reading an unfamiliar passage instead of a familiar one.

Clusters are weblike diagrams with the topic written in a circle centered on a sheet of paper. Main ideas are written on rays drawn out from the circle, and branches with details and examples are added to complete each main idea (Rico, 1983). Clusters are used to organize information students are learning and to organize ideas before beginning to write a composition. A third-grade class's cluster about the four layers of the rain forest is shown in Figure 2. Teachers and students can work together to make a cluster, or students can work in small groups or make clusters individually. The steps are:

CLUSTERS, MAPS, AND WEBS

Figure 2 A third-grade class's cluster about the four layers of the rain forest

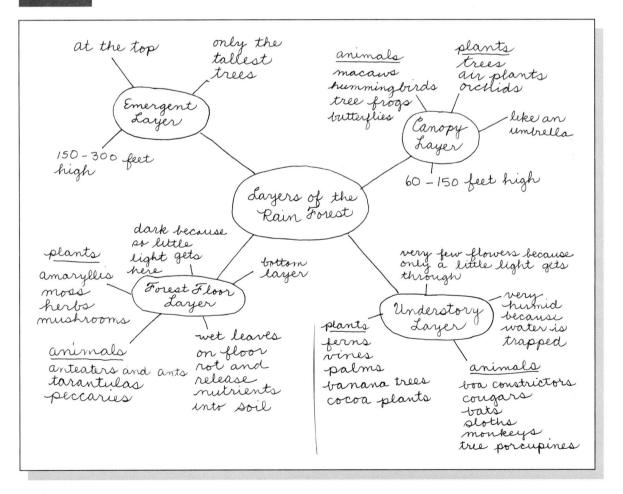

1. *Draw the center of the cluster.* Teachers or students select a topic and write the word in the center of a circle drawn on a chart or sheet of paper.

2. *Brainstorm a list of words.* Students brainstorm as many words and phrases as they can that are related to the topic, and then they organize the words into categories. The teacher may prompt students for additional words or suggest categories.

3. *Add main ideas and details.* Students determine the main ideas and details from the brainstormed list of words. The main ideas are written on rays drawn out from the circled topic, and details are written on rays drawn out from the main ideas.

Clusters are sometimes called maps and webs, and they are similar to **story maps**. In this book, the diagrams are called clusters when used for writing, and they are called maps when used for reading.

COLLABORATIVE BOOKS AND REPORTS

Students divide the work of writing an informational book or report when they work collaboratively. Students each contribute one page for a class book or work with partners or in small groups to research and write sections of the report. Then the students' work is compiled, and the book or report is complete (Tompkins, 2000). Students use a process approach as they research their topics and compose their sections of the report or book. The steps are:

1. *Choose the topic.* Students choose specific topics related to the general topic of the unit for their pages or sections. Students work in small groups, with partners, or individually to research and write their sections of the informational book or report.

2. *Plan the organization.* If students are each contributing one page for a class informational book, they might draw a picture and add a fact or other piece of information. Students working on chapters for a longer report will need to design research questions. These questions emerge as students study a topic and brainstorm a list of questions on a chart posted in the classroom. If they are planning a report on the human body, for example, the small groups that are studying each organ may decide to research the same three questions: "What does the organ look like?" "What job does the organ do?" and "Where is the organ located in the human body?"

3. *Rehearse the procedure.* Teachers and students write one section of the report or book together as a class before students begin working on their section of the report.

4. *Gather and organize ideas.* Students gather and organize information for their sections. Students writing pages for informational books often draw pictures as prewriting. Those working in small groups or with partners search for answers to the research questions. Students can use **clusters** or **data charts** to record the information they gather. The research questions are the same for each data-collection instrument. On a cluster, students add information as details to each main-idea ray; if they are working with data charts, they record information from the first source in the first row under the appropriate question, from the second source in the second row, and so on.

5. *Draft the sections of the report.* Students write rough drafts of their sections. When students are working in small groups, one student is the scribe and writes the draft while the other students dictate sentences, using information from a cluster or data chart. Next, they share their drafts with the class and make revisions on the basis of feedback they receive. Last, students proofread and correct mechanical errors.

6. *Compile the pages or sections.* Students compile their completed pages or sections, and then the entire book or report is read aloud so students can catch inconsistencies or redundant passages. Students also add front and back pages. For an informational book, students add a title page and covers. For reports, students also write a table of contents, an introduction, and a conclusion and add a bibliography at the end.

7. *Publish the informational book or report.* Students make a final copy with all the parts of the book or report in the correct sequence. For longer reports, it is much easier to print out the final copy if the sections have been drafted and revised on a computer. To make the book sturdier, teachers often laminate the covers (or all pages in the book) and bind everything together using yarn, brads, or metal rings.

8. *Make copies for students.* Teachers often make copies of the informational book or report for each student, whereas the special bound copy is often placed in the class or school library.

CUBING

Students use cubing to explore a topic from six dimensions or viewpoints (Neeld, 1986). Cubes have six sides, and there are six dimensions in this instructional procedure:

❦ ***Describe the topic.*** Students represent the topic in words, including its colors, shapes, and sizes, in order to create a mental image.

❦ ***Compare the topic to something else.*** Students consider how it is similar to or different from this other thing.

❦ ***Associate the topic with something else.*** Students explain why the topic makes them think of this other thing.

❦ ***Analyze the topic.*** Students tell how it is made or what it is composed of.

❦ ***Apply the topic.*** Students explain how it can be used or what can be done with it.

❦ ***Argue for or against the topic.*** Students take a stand and list reasons to support their argument.

Cubing involves the following steps:

1. *Construct a cube.* Students use cardboard to construct a cube and then cut six squares of paper to fit onto the sides of the cube. Or, they can use a cardboard box, such as a department store gift box that is square in shape. Later they will write and draw their responses on these square pieces of paper and attach them to the cube.

2. *Divide students into groups.* Students divide in six small groups to do the cubing. Each group examines the topic from one of the six dimensions.

3. *Examine the topic from the six dimensions.* Students in each group consider the topic from the dimension they have been assigned. They brainstorm ideas and decide on a response. Then they write and draw their response on a square sheet of paper that has been cut to fit the cube.

4. *Complete the cube.* Students attach their completed responses to each side of the cube and share their work with classmates.

Cubing is a useful procedure for helping students to think more deeply about the main ideas presented in content-area units. Middle- and upper-grade students can

Figure 3 One side of a sixth-grade class's cubing on ancient Greece

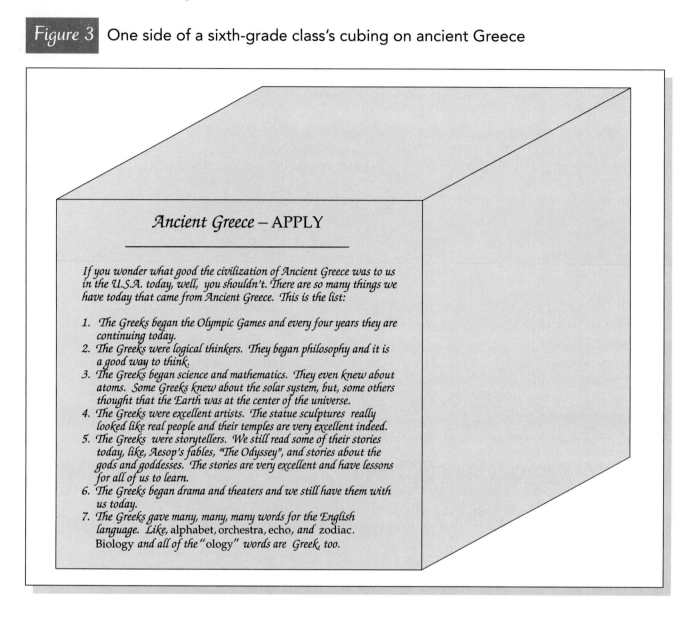

Ancient Greece – APPLY

If you wonder what good the civilization of Ancient Greece was to us in the U.S.A. today, well, you shouldn't. There are so many things we have today that came from Ancient Greece. This is the list:

1. *The Greeks began the Olympic Games and every four years they are continuing today.*
2. *The Greeks were logical thinkers. They began philosophy and it is a good way to think.*
3. *The Greeks began science and mathematics. They even knew about atoms. Some Greeks knew about the solar system, but, some others thought that the Earth was at the center of the universe.*
4. *The Greeks were excellent artists. The statue sculptures really looked like real people and their temples are very excellent indeed.*
5. *The Greeks were storytellers. We still read some of their stories today, like, Aesop's fables, "The Odyssey", and stories about the gods and goddesses. The stories are very excellent and have lessons for all of us to learn.*
6. *The Greeks began drama and theaters and we still have them with us today.*
7. *The Greeks gave many, many, many words for the English language. Like, alphabet, orchestra, echo, and zodiac. Biology and all of the "ology" words are Greek, too.*

cube topics such as Antarctica, the U.S. Constitution, endangered animals, the Underground Railroad, and ancient Greece. The "Apply" side from a sixth-grade class's cubing on ancient Greece is shown in Figure 3. Students wrote their responses on the computer and printed them out so that they would look very professional. They experimented with different fonts and varying the margin width so that their writings fit on the cube.

DATA CHARTS   Data charts are grids that students make and use as a tool for organizing information about a topic (McKenzie, 1979). In literature focus units, students use data charts to record information about versions of folktales and fairy tales, such as "Cinderella" stories, or a collection of books by an author, such as Eric Carle, Eve Bunting, or

Figure 4   A data chart for a report on the human body

Human Body Report Data Chart				
Organ _____ Researchers				
Source of information	What does it look like?	Where is it located?	What job does it do?	Other important information

Chris Van Allsburg. In content-area units, data charts are used to record information about the solar system, Native American tribes, or ancient civilizations. Students also use data charts to gather and organize information before writing reports. A data chart for a report on the human body is shown in Figure 4. The steps in making a data chart are:

1. *Design the data chart.* Teachers or students choose a topic and decide how to set up the data chart with characteristics of the topic listed across the top of the chart and examples or resources listed in the left column of the chart.

2. *Draw the chart.* Teachers or students create a skeleton chart on butcher paper for a class project or on a sheet of unlined paper for an individual project. Then they write the characteristics across the top of the chart and the examples or resources down the left column of the chart.

3. *Complete the chart.* Students complete the chart by adding words, pictures, sentences, or paragraphs in each cell.

Students use data charts in a variety of ways. They can make a chart in their **reading logs,** contribute to a class chart during a content-area unit, make a data chart with a classmate as a project after reading a book, or make a data chart as part of a writing project.

DIRECTED READING-THINKING ACTIVITY

Students are actively involved in reading stories or listening to stories read aloud in the Directed Reading-Thinking Activity (DRTA) because they make predictions and read or listen to confirm their predictions (Stauffer, 1975). DRTA is a useful approach for teaching students how to use the predicting strategy. It helps students think about the structure of stories, and it can be used with both picture book and chapter book stories. However, DRTA should not be used with informational books and content-area textbooks, because with nonfiction texts, students do not predict what the book will be about, but read to locate main ideas and details. The steps in DRTA are:

1. *Introduce the story.* Before beginning to read, teachers might discuss the topic or show objects and pictures related to the story in order to draw on prior knowledge or create new experiences. They also show students the cover of the book and ask them to make a prediction about the story using one or more of these questions:

✣ What do you think a story with a title like this might be about?

✣ What do you think might happen in this story?

✣ Does this picture give you any ideas about what might happen in this story?

If necessary, the teacher reads the first paragraph or two to provide more information for students to use in making their predictions. After a brief discussion in which all students commit themselves to one or another of the alternatives presented, the teacher asks these questions:

✣ Which of these ideas do you think would be the likely one?

✣ Why do you think that idea is a good one?

2. *Read the beginning of the story.* Teachers have students read the beginning of the story or listen to the beginning of the story read aloud. Then the teacher asks students to confirm or reject their predictions by responding to questions such as:

✣ What do you think now?

✣ What do you think will happen next?

✣ Would happen if . . . ?

✣ Why do you think that idea is a good one?

Students continue reading or the teacher continues reading aloud, stopping at several key points to repeat this step.

3. *Have students reflect on their predictions.* Students talk about the story, expressing their feelings and making connections to their own lives and experiences with literature. Then students reflect on the predictions they made as they read or listened to the story read aloud, and they provide reasons to support their predictions. Teachers ask these questions to help students think about their predictions:

✣ What predictions did you make?

✣ What in the story made you think of that prediction?

✣ What in the story supports that idea?

The Directed Reading-Thinking Activity is only useful when students are reading or listening to an unfamiliar story so that they can be actively involved in the prediction-confirmation cycle.

A special type of **reading log** is a double-entry journal (Barone, 1990; Berthoff, 1981). Students divide their journal pages into two columns. In the left column, students write quotes from the story or informational book they are reading, and in the right column they reflect on each quote. They may relate a quote to their own lives, react to it, write a question, or make some other comment. Excerpts from a fifth grader's double-entry journal about *The Lion, the Witch and the Wardrobe* (Lewis, 1950) are shown in Figure 5. The steps are:

DOUBLE-ENTRY JOURNALS

1. *Design journal pages.* Students divide the pages in their reading logs into two columns, labeling the left column "In the Text" or "Quotes" and the right column "My Responses," "Comments," or "Reflections."

Figure 5 Excerpts from a fifth grader's double-entry journal about *The Lion, the Witch and the Wardrobe*

In the Text	My Response
Chapter 1	
I tell you this is the sort of house where no one is going to mind what we do.	I remember the time that I went to Beaumont, Texas to stay with my aunt. My aunt's house was very large. She had a piano and she let us play it. She told us that we could do whatever we wanted to.
Chapter 5	
"How do you know" he asked, "that your sister's story is not true?"	It reminds me of when I was little and I had an imaginary place. I would go there in my mind. I made up all kinds of make-believe stories about myself in this imaginary place. One time I told my big brother about my imaginary place. He laughed at me and told me I was silly. But it didn't bother me because nobody can stop me from thinking what I want.
Chapter 15	
Still they could see the shape of the great lion lying dead in his bonds.	When Aslan died I thought about when my Uncle Carl died.
They're nibbling at the cords.	This reminds me of the story where the lion lets the mouse go and the mouse helps the lion.

2. *Write quotes in journals.* As students read, or immediately after reading, they copy one or more important or interesting quotes in the left column of the reading logs.

3. *Reflect on the quotes.* Students reread the quotes and make notes in the right column about their reasons for choosing the quote. Sometimes it is easier if students share the quotes with a reading buddy or in a **grand conversation** before they write comments or reflections in the right column.

Double-entry journals can be used in several other ways, too. Instead of recording quotes from the story, students can write "Reading Notes" in the left column and then add "Reactions" in the right column. In the left column students write about the events they read about in the chapter, and in the right column they make personal connections to the events. Younger students can use the double-entry format for a prediction journal (Macon, Bewell, & Vogt, 1991). They label the left column "Predictions" and the right column "What Happened." In the left column they write or draw a picture of what they predict will happen in the story or chapter before reading it. Then after reading, they draw or write what actually happened in the right column.

EXCLUSION BRAINSTORMING

Exclusion brainstorming is a preparing activity that teachers use to activate students' prior knowledge and expand their understanding about a social studies or science topic before reading (Blachowicz, 1986). Teachers present students with a list of words, and students identify words on the list that they think relate to the topic as well as those that do not belong. As they talk about the words and try to decide which ones are related to the topic, students refine their knowledge of the topic, are introduced to some key vocabulary words, and set a purpose for reading. Then after reading, students review the list of words again and decide whether or not they chose the correct words. The steps are:

1. *Choose a list of words.* Teachers choose a list of words related to a book students will read or a content-area unit that students will study and include a few words that do not fit with the topic. Then teachers write the list on chart paper and make individual copies for students.

2. *Mark the list.* Students read the list of words and work in small groups or together as a class to decide which ones are related to the topic and which are not. Then students draw circles around the words they think are not related.

3. *Learn about the topic.* Students read the book or study the unit, noticing whether the words in the exclusion brainstorming activity are mentioned.

4. *Check the list.* After reading or studying the unit, students check their exclusion brainstorming list and make corrections based on their new knowledge. They cross out unrelated words, regardless of whether or not they circled them earlier.

Exclusion brainstorming can also be used with literature when teachers want to focus on a historical setting or another social studies or science concept before reading the story. A fourth-grade teacher created the exclusion brainstorming list shown in Figure 6 before reading *The Ballad of Lucy Whipple* (Cushman, 1996), the story of a young girl who travels with her family to California during the gold rush. The teacher used this activity to introduce some of the vocabulary in the story and to help students develop an understanding of life during the California gold rush. Students

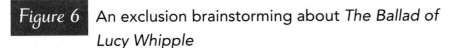

Figure 6 An exclusion brainstorming about *The Ballad of Lucy Whipple*

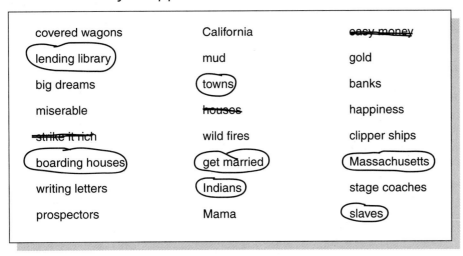

circled seven words before reading, and after reading they crossed out three words, all different from the ones they had circled earlier.

GRAND CONVERSATIONS

A grand conversation is a book discussion in which students deepen their comprehension and reflect on their feelings during the responding step of the reading process (Eeds & Wells, 1989; Peterson & Eeds, 1990). These discussions often last 10 to 30 minutes, and students sit in a circle so that they can see each other. The teacher serves as a facilitator, but the talk is primarily among the students. Traditionally, literature discussions have been "gentle inquisitions"; here the talk changes to dialoguing among students. The steps are:

1. **Read the book.** Students prepare for the grand conversation by reading the book or a part of the book, or by listening to the teacher read it aloud.

2. **Prepare for the grand conversation.** Students may respond to the book in a **quickwrite** or in a **reading log** in order to begin reflecting on the story. This step is optional.

3. **Discuss the book.** Students come together as a class or in a smaller group to discuss the book. The students take turns sharing their ideas about the events in the story, the literary language and favorite quotes, the author's craft, and the illustrations. To start the grand conversation, the teacher asks students to share their personal responses. Possible openers are "What did you think?" and "Who would like to share?" Students may read from their quickwrites or reading log entries. They all participate and may build on classmates' comments and ask for clarifications. In order that everyone gets to participate, many teachers ask students to make no more than two or three comments until everyone has spoken once. Students may refer back to the book or read a short piece to make a point, but there is no round-robin reading. Teachers can also participate in the discussion, offering comments and clarifying confusions.

4. *Ask questions.* After students have had a chance to share their reflections, teachers ask questions to focus students' attention on one or two aspects of the story that have been missed. Teachers might focus on illustrations, authors, or an element of story structure. Or, they may ask students to compare this book with a similar book, the film version of the story, or other books by the same author. Pauses may occur, and when students indicate that they have run out of things to say, the grand conversation ends. If students are reading a chapter book, teachers may ask students to make predictions before continuing to read the book.

5. *Write in reading logs.* Teachers may have students write (or write again) in a reading log. This step is optional, but students often have many ideas for reading log entries after participating in the discussion. Also, students may record their predictions before continuing to read chapter books.

Grand conversations are discussions about stories; discussions about informational books and content-area textbooks are called **instructional conversations,** and their focus is slightly different (see the section on instructional conversations on pages 507–508 to learn more).

INDIVIDUAL BOOKS AND REPORTS

Students write individual reports and informational books much like they write **collaborative books and reports.** They design research questions, gather information to answer the questions, and compile what they have learned in a report. Writing individual reports demands two significant changes: first, students narrow their topics, and second, they assume the entire responsibility for writing the report (Tompkins, 2000). The steps are:

1. *Choose and narrow topics.* Students choose topics for informational books and reports from a content area, hobbies, or other interests. After choosing a general topic, such as cats or the solar system, they need to narrow the topic so that it is manageable. The broad topic of cats might be narrowed to pet cats or tigers, and the solar system to one planet.

2. *Design research questions.* Students design research questions by brainstorming a list of questions in a **learning log.** They review the list, combine some questions, delete others, and finally arrive at four to six questions that are worthy of answering. Once they begin their research, they may add new questions and delete others if they reach a dead end.

3. *Gather and organize information.* During the prewriting step, students use **clusters** or **data charts** to gather and organize information. Data charts, with their rectangular spaces for writing information, serve as a transition for upper-grade students between clusters and note cards.

4. *Write the reports.* Students use the writing process to write their reports. They write a rough draft from the information they have gathered. Each research question can provide the basis for a paragraph, a page, or a chapter in the report. Teachers work with students to revise and edit their books or reports. Students meet in writing groups to share their rough drafts and make revisions based on the feedback they receive from their classmates. After they revise, students use an editing checklist to proofread their reports and identify and correct mechanical errors.

5. *Publish the books.* Students recopy their reports in book form and add covers, a title page, a table of contents, and bibliographic information. Research reports can also be published in several other ways; for example, as a video presentation, a series of illustrated charts or dioramas, or a dramatization.

Students often write informational books and reports as projects during literature focus units, writing workshop, and content-area units. Through these activities, students have opportunities to extend and personalize their learning and to use the writing process.

Instructional conversations are like **grand conversations** except that they are about nonfiction topics, not about literature. These conversations provide opportunities for students to talk about the main ideas they are learning in content-area units and enhance both students' conceptual learning and their linguistic abilities (Goldenberg, 1992/1993). Like grand conversations, these discussions are interesting and engaging, and students are active participants, building on classmates' ideas with their own comments. Teachers are participants in the conversation, making comments much like the students do, but they also assume the teacher role to clarify misconceptions, ask questions, and provide instruction. Goldenberg has identified these content and linguistic elements of an instructional conversation:

INSTRUCTIONAL CONVERSATIONS

1.   The conversation focuses on a content-area topic.
2.   Students activate or build knowledge about the topic during the instructional conversation.
3.   Teachers provide information and directly teach concepts when necessary.
4.   Teachers promote students' use of more complex vocabulary and language to express the ideas being discussed.
5.   Teachers encourage students to provide support for the ideas they present using information presented in content-area textbooks, text sets, and other unit-related resources in the classroom.
6.   Students and teachers ask higher-level questions, often questions with more than one answer, during the instructional conversation.
7.   Students participate actively in the instructional conversation and make comments that build upon and expand classmates' comments.
8.   The classroom is a community of learners where both students' and teachers' comments are respected and encouraged.

The steps in an instructional conversation are:

1. *Choose a focus.* Teachers choose a focus for the instructional conversation. It should be related to the goals of a content-area unit or main ideas presented in an informational book or in a content-area textbook.

2. *Prepare for the instructional conversation.* Teachers present background knowledge in preparation for the discussion, or students may read an informational book or selection from a content-area textbook to learn about the topic.

3. *Begin the conversation.* Students come together as a class or in a smaller group for the instructional conversation. Teachers begin with the focus they have identified. They make a statement or ask a question, and then students respond, sharing information they have learned, asking questions, and offering opinions. Teachers assist students as they make comments, helping them extend their ideas and use appropriate vocabulary. In addition, teachers write students' comments in a list or on a **cluster** or other graphic organizer.

    4. *Expand the conversation.* After students have discussed the teacher's focus, the conversation continues and moves in other directions. Students may share other interesting information, make personal connections to information they are learning, or ask questions. Teachers may also want to have students do a **read-around** and share important ideas from their reading.

    5. *Write in learning logs.* Students write and draw in **learning logs** and record the important ideas discussed during the instructional conversation. Students may refer to the brainstormed list or cluster that the teacher made during the first part of the discussion.

Instructional conversations are useful for helping students grapple with important ideas they are learning in social studies, science, and other content areas. When students are discussing literature, they should use grand conversations (for more information about these discussions, turn to pages 505–506).

INTERACTIVE WRITING

Students and the teacher create a message and "share the pen" as they write it on chart paper in interactive writing (Button, Johnson, & Furgerson, 1996). This instructional strategy is designed for emergent readers and writers. The message is composed by the group, and the teacher guides students as they write the message word by word on chart paper. Students take turns writing known letters and familiar words, adding punctuation marks, and marking spaces between words. All students participate in creating and writing the message—usually a sentence in length—on chart paper, and they also write the message on small white boards. Figure 7 shows a first-grade class's prediction about what will happen to Rosie written before reading *Rosie's Walk* (Hutchins, 1968). The dotted letters represent letters that the teacher wrote, and the rectangles indicate that correction tape was used to correct an error.

Figure 7 First graders' prediction about *Rosie's Walk* written interactively

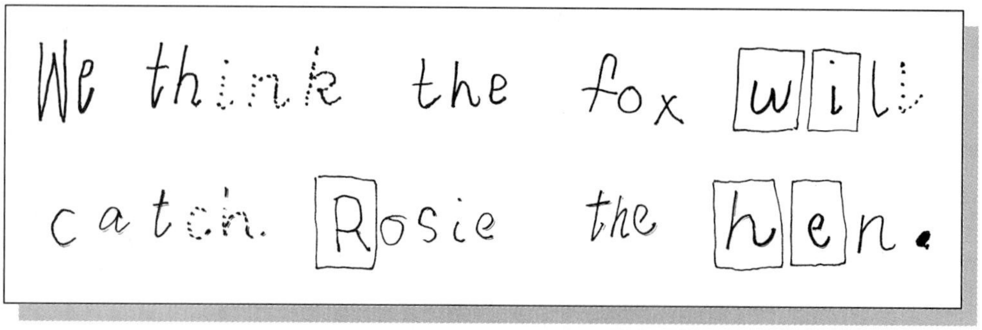

We think the fox will catch. Rosie the hen.

Interactive writing is used to show students how writing works and how to construct words using their knowledge of sound-symbol correspondences and spelling patterns (Fountas & Pinnell, 1996). The steps are:

1. ***Collect materials.*** Teachers collect chart paper, colored marking pens, white correction tape, an alphabet chart, magnetic letters, and a pointer. For individual students' writing they also collect small white boards, dry-erase pens, and erasers.

2. ***Set a purpose for the activity.*** Teachers present a stimulus activity or set a purpose for the interactive writing activity. Often they read or reread a trade book as a stimulus, but students also write daily news, compose a letter, or brainstorm information they are learning in a social studies or science unit.

3. ***Choose a sentence to write.*** Teachers negotiate the message—often a sentence or two—with students. Students repeat the sentence several times and segment the sentence into words. They also count the number of words in the sentence. The teacher also helps the students remember the message as it is written.

4. ***Pass out writing supplies.*** Teachers pass out the individual white boards, dry-erase pens, and erasers for students to use to write the text individually as it is written together on chart paper. Teachers periodically ask students to hold up their white boards so they can see what the students are writing.

5. ***Write the message.*** Students and the teacher write the first sentence word by word. Before writing the first word, the teacher and students slowly pronounce the word, "pulling" it from their mouths or "stretching" it out. Then students take turns writing the letters in the first word. The teacher chooses students to write each sound or the entire word, depending on students' knowledge of phonics and spelling. Teachers often have students use one color of pen for the letters they write, and they use another color to write the parts of words that students don't know how to spell. In that way, teachers can keep track of how much writing students are able to do. Teachers keep a poster with the upper- and lowercase letters of the alphabet to refer to when students are unsure how to form a letter, and they use white correction tape when students write a letter incorrectly or write the wrong letter. After writing each word, one student serves as the "spacer." This student uses his or her hand to mark the space between words and sentences. Teachers have students reread the sentence from the beginning each time a new word is completed. When appropriate, teachers call children's attention to capital letters, punctuation marks, and other conventions of print. This procedure is repeated to write additional sentences to complete the message. When teachers use interactive writing to write a class book, this activity can take several days or a week or longer to complete.

6. ***Display the interactive writing.*** After the writing is completed, teachers display it in the classroom and have students reread the text using shared or independent reading. Students often reread interactive charts when they "read the room." They may also add artwork to "finish" the chart.

When students begin interactive writing in kindergarten, they write letters to represent the beginning sounds in words and write familiar words such as *the, a,* and *is.* The first letters that students write are often the letters in their own names. As students learn more about sound-symbol correspondences and spelling patterns, they do more of the writing. Once students are writing words fluently, they can continue to do interactive writing as they work in small groups. Each student in the group uses a particular color pen and takes turns writing letters, letter clusters, and words. They also get used to using the white correction tape to correct poorly formed letters and misspelled words.

K-W-L CHARTS

Teachers use K-W-L charts during content-area units (Ogle, 1986, 1989). The letters *K, W,* and *L* stand for What We <u>K</u>now, What We <u>W</u>ant to Learn (What We <u>W</u>onder), and What We <u>L</u>earned. The format of a K-W-L chart is shown in Figure 8. Teachers introduce a K-W-L chart at the beginning of a content-area unit and use the chart to activate children's background knowledge and identify interesting questions. The questions often stimulate students' interest in the topic. At the end of the unit, students complete the last section of the chart, listing what they have learned. This in-

Figure 8   A K-W-L chart

K What We Know	W What We Want to Learn	L What We Learned

structional procedure helps students to combine new information with prior knowledge and develop their vocabularies. The steps are:

1. ***Post a K-W-L chart.*** Teachers post a large sheet of butcher paper on a classroom wall, dividing it into three columns and labeling the columns K (What We Know), W (What We Want to Learn or What We Wonder), and L (What We Learned).

2. ***Complete the K column.*** At the beginning of the unit, teachers ask students to brainstorm what they know about the topic. Teachers write this information in phrases or complete sentences in the K (What We Know) column. Students also suggest questions they would like to explore during the unit.

3. ***Complete the W column.*** Teachers write the questions that students suggest in the W (What We Want to Learn or What We Wonder) column. Teachers continue to add questions to the W column throughout the unit

4. ***Complete the L column.*** At the end of the unit, students brainstorm a list of information they have learned to complete the L column of the chart. It is important to note that students do not try to answer each question listed in the W column, although the questions in that column may trigger some information that they have learned. Teachers write the information that students suggest in the L column.

Older students can make K-W-L charts in small groups or create individual charts to organize and document their learning. Class charts, however, are more effective for younger children and for older students who have not made K-W-L charts before. Individual K-W-L charts may be made like flip books. Students fold long sheets of paper in half lengthwise and make two cuts to create K, W, and L flip pages, as shown in Figure 9. Students write the letters on the flip pages and lift each page to write information in each column on the chart.

Figure 9 An individual K-W-L flip book

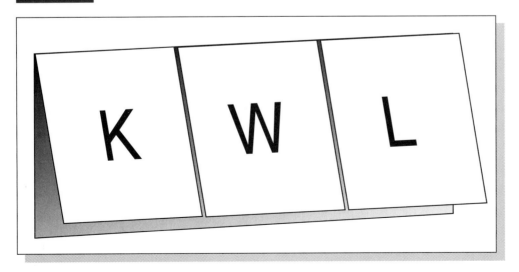

LANGUAGE EXPERIENCE APPROACH (LEA)

Children dictate words and sentences about their experiences in the language experience approach (LEA), and teachers write the dictation for the children (Ashton-Warner, 1965; Lee & Allen, 1963; Stauffer, 1970). The text they develop together becomes the reading material. Because the language comes from the children themselves and the content is based on their experiences, children are usually able to read the text easily. A kindergartner's LEA writing is shown in Figure 10. The child drew this picture of the Gingerbread Baby and dictated the sentence after listening to the teacher read Jan Brett's *Gingerbread Baby* (1999), a new version of "The Gingerbread Man" story. LEA is a type of shared writing, and reading and writing are integrated since students are actively involved in reading what they have written. The steps are:

1. *Provide an experience.* The experience serves as the stimulus for the writing. For group writing, it can be an experience shared in school, a book read aloud, a field trip, or some other experience that all children are familiar with, such as having a pet or playing in the snow. For individual writing, the stimulus can be any experience that is important for the particular child.

2. *Talk about the experience.* The teacher and children talk about the experience to generate words, and they review the experience so that the children's dictation will be more interesting and complete. Teachers often begin with an open-ended question, such as "What are you going to write about?" As children talk about their experiences, they clarify and organize ideas, use more specific vocabulary, and extend their understanding.

Figure 10   A kindergartner's LEA writing sample about *Gingerbread Baby*

The Gingerbread Baby runs and runs into the gingerbread house.

3. *Record the child's dictation.* Texts for individual children are written on sheets of writing paper or in small booklets, while group texts are written on chart paper. Teachers print neatly, spell words correctly, and preserve students' language as much as possible. It is a great temptation to change the child's language to the teacher's own, in either word choice or grammar, but editing should be kept to a minimum so that children do not get the impression that their language is inferior or inadequate. For individual texts, teachers continue to take the child's dictation and write until the child finishes or hesitates. If the child hesitates, the teacher rereads what has been written and encourages the child to continue. For group texts, children take turns dictating sentences, and the teacher rereads each sentence after writing it down.

4. *Read the text aloud, pointing to each word.* This reading reminds children of the content of the text and demonstrates how to read it aloud with appropriate intonation. Then children join in the reading. After reading group texts together, individual children can take turns rereading. Group texts can also be copied so each child has a copy to read independently.

5. *Extend the experience.* Teachers encourage children to extend the experience through one or more of these activities:

❦ Add illustrations to their writing.

❦ Read their texts to classmates from the author's chair.

❦ Take their texts home to share with family members.

❦ Add this text to a collection of their writings.

❦ Pick out words from their texts that they would like to learn to read.

The language experience approach is an effective way to help children emerge into reading. Even students who have not been successful with other types of reading activities can read what they have dictated. There is a drawback, however; teachers provide a "perfect" model when they take children's dictation—they write neatly and spell words correctly. After language experience activities, some young children are not eager to do their own writing. They prefer their teacher's "perfect" writing to their own childlike writing. To avoid this problem, young children should be doing their own writing in personal journals, at the writing center, and through other writing activities as well as participating in language experience activities. In this way they will learn that sometimes they do their own writing, while at other times the teacher takes their dictation.

LEARNING LOGS

Students write in learning logs as part of content-area units. Learning logs, like other types of journals, are booklets of paper in which students record information they are learning, write questions and reflections about their learning, and make charts, diagrams, and **clusters** (Tompkins, 2000). The steps are:

1. *Prepare learning logs.* Students make learning logs at the beginning of a unit. They typically staple together sheets of lined writing paper and plain paper for drawing diagrams and add construction paper covers.

2. *Write entries.* Students make entries in their learning logs as part of content-area unit activities. They take notes, draw diagrams, do **quickwrites,** and make clusters.

3. *Monitor students' entries.* Teachers read students' entries, and in their responses they answer students' questions and clarify confusions.

Students' writing is impromptu in learning logs, and the emphasis is on using writing as a learning tool rather than creating polished products. Even so, students should work carefully and spell words found on the **word wall** correctly.

MAKING WORDS

Making words is an activity in which students arrange letter cards to spell words. As they make words using letter cards, they review and practice phonics and spelling concepts (Cunningham & Cunningham, 1992; Gunning, 1995). Teachers choose key words that exemplify particular phonics or spelling patterns for students to practice from books students are reading or from a content-area unit. Then they prepare a set of letter cards that small groups of students or individual students can use to spell words. The teacher leads students as they create many, progressively longer words using the letters. A making words activity that a sixth-grade class completed while studying ancient Egypt is shown in Figure 11. The steps in making words are:

1. *Make letter cards.* Teachers make a set of small letter cards (one- to two-inch-square cards) for students to use in word-making activities. For high-frequency letters (vowels, *s, t,* and *r*) make three or four times as many letter cards as there are students in the class. For less frequently used letters, make one or two times as many letter cards as there are students in the class. Print the lowercase letter form on one side of the letter cards and the uppercase form on the other side. Package cards with each letter separately in small boxes, plastic trays, or plastic bags. Teachers may also want to make a set of large letter cards (three- to six-inch-square cards) to display in a pocket chart or on the chalkboard during the activity.

2. *Choose a word for the activity.* Teachers choose a word to use in the word-making activity, but they do not tell students what the word is. The word is often taken from a **word wall** in the classroom and relates to a book students are reading or to a content-area unit. The word should be long enough and have enough vowels that students can easily make at least ten words using the letters.

3. *Distribute letter cards.* A student distributes the needed letter cards to individual students or to small groups of students, and students arrange the letter cards on one side of their desks. It is crucial that students have letter cards to manipulate; it is not sufficient to write the letters on the chalkboard, since students can spell more words using the cards and some students need the tactile activity to be able to spell the words.

4. *Make words using the cards.* Students manipulate the letter cards to spell two-letter words. As students spell words, teachers make a chart and record the words that students spell correctly using the letter cards on the chart. Teachers can also use the large letter cards to spell words along with the students or to help students correctly spell a tricky word. After spelling all possible two-letter words, students spell three-letter words, four-letter words, and so forth, until they use all of the letter cards and figure out the chosen word.

5. *Repeat the activity at a center.* After completing the word-making activity, teachers put the chart the class created and several sets of letter cards in a literacy center so that students can repeat the word-making activity. As students make words, they write them on a chart. First they list two-letter words, then three-letter words, and so forth. Students can refer to the chart, if needed.

Figure 11   A sixth-grade making words activity using the word *hieroglyphics*

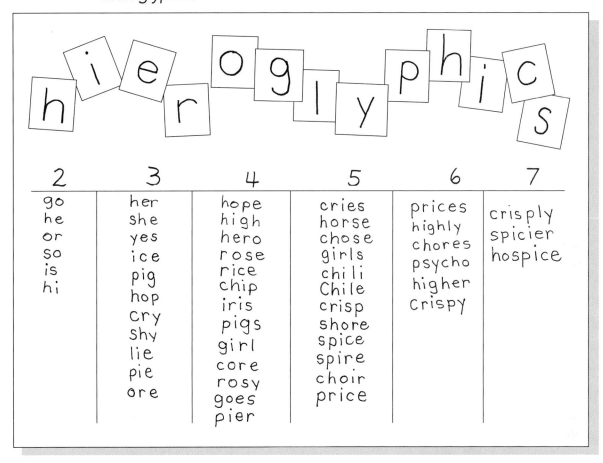

Students can also use letter cards to practice spelling rimes. For example, to practice the *-ake* rime, students use the *b, c, f, h, l, m, r, s, t,* and *w* letter cards and the *-ake* rime card. Using the cards, students make these words: *bake, shake, cake, make, flake, rake, lake, take,* and *wake.* Teachers often add several other letter cards, such as *d, p,* and *v,* to make the activity more challenging.

Teachers teach minilessons on literacy procedures, concepts, strategies, and skills (Atwell, 1987). These lessons are brief, often lasting only 15 to 30 minutes. Minilessons are usually taught as part of the reading process during the exploring step, or as part of the writing process during the editing step. The steps in conducting a minilesson are:

MINILESSONS

1. ***Introduce the topic.*** Teachers begin the minilesson by introducing the procedure, concept, strategy, or skill. They name the topic and provide essential information about it.

2. *Share examples of the topic.* Teachers share examples taken from books students are reading or students' own writing projects.

3. *Provide information about the topic.* Teachers provide additional information about the procedure, concept, strategy, or skill and make connections to students' reading or writing.

4. *Provide opportunities for guided practice.* Teachers involve students in guided practice activities so that students can bring together the information and the examples introduced earlier.

5. *Create a poster.* Students create a poster about the procedure, concept, strategy, or skill to review the information they have learned. The poster is displayed in the classroom so that students can refer to it when necessary.

6. *Provide authentic practice opportunities.* Teachers provide additional opportunities for students to use the procedures, concepts, strategies, or skills they are learning in meaningful ways.

Teachers present minilessons to the whole class or to small groups to introduce or review a topic. The best time to teach a minilesson is when students will have immediate opportunities to apply what they are learning.

OPEN-MIND PORTRAITS

To help students think more deeply about a character and reflect on story events from the character's viewpoint, students draw an open-mind portrait of the character. These portraits have two parts: the face of the character is on one page, and the mind of the character is on the second page. A fourth grader's open-mind portrait of Sarah, the mail-order bride in *Sarah, Plain and Tall* (MacLachlan, 1983), is shown in Figure 12. The steps are:

1. *Make a portrait of a character.* Students draw and color a large portrait of the head and neck of a character in a book they are reading.

2. *Cut out the portrait and open-mind pages.* Students cut out the character's portrait and trace around the character's head on one or more sheets of paper. Students may make open-mind portraits with one "mind" page or with several pages in order to show what the character is thinking at important points in the story or in each chapter of a chapter book. Then they cut out the mind pages and attach the portrait and mind pages with a brad or staple to a heavy sheet of construction paper or cardboard. The portrait goes on top. It is important that students place the brad or staple at the top of the portrait so that there will be space to write and draw on the mind pages.

3. *Design the mind pages.* Have students lift the portrait and draw and write about the character, from the character's viewpoint, on the mind pages. Students focus on what the character is thinking and doing at various points in the story.

4. *Share completed open-mind portraits.* Have students share their portraits with classmates and talk about the words and pictures they chose to include in the mind of the character.

PREREADING PLAN

The prereading plan is a diagnostic and instructional procedure used when students are reading informational books and content-area textbooks (Tierney, Readence, & Dishner, 1995). Teachers use this strategy to diagnose students' prior knowledge and

Figure 12   An open-mind portrait of Sarah of *Sarah, Plain and Tall*

provide necessary background knowledge so that students will be prepared to understand what they will be reading. The steps are:

1. *Discuss a key concept.* Teachers introduce a key concept to students using a word, phrase, or picture to initiate a discussion. Then students brainstorm words about the topic and record their ideas on a chart. Teachers help students make connections among the brainstormed ideas. Teachers present additional vocabulary and clarify any misconceptions, if necessary.

2. *Quickwrite about the topic.* Students write a **quickwrite** or draw pictures about the topic using words from the brainstormed list.

3. *Share the quickwrites.* Students share their quickwrites with classmates, and teachers ask questions to help students clarify and elaborate their quickwrites.

This activity is especially important when students have little technical vocabulary or background knowledge about a topic, and for students who are learning English as a second language.

QUICKWRITES

Students use quickwriting as they write in response to literature and for other types of impromptu writing. Quickwriting, originally called "freewriting" and popularized by Peter Elbow (1973), is a way to help students focus on content rather than mechanics. Students reflect on what they know about a topic, ramble on paper, generate words and ideas, and make connections among the ideas. Young children often do quickwrites in which they draw pictures and add labels. Some students do a mixture of writing and drawing. Figure 13 presents a first grader's quickwrite made after reading *Sam, Bangs, and Moonshine* (Ness, 1966). In this Caldecott Medal story, a girl named Sam tells "moonshine" about a make-believe baby kangaroo to her friend Thomas. The results are almost disastrous. In the quickwrite, the child writes, "If you lie, you will get in big trouble and you will hurt your friends." The steps are:

1. ***Choose a topic.*** Students identify a topic for their quickwrite and write it at the top of the paper.

2. ***Write or draw about the topic.*** Students write sentences or paragraphs and/or draw a picture related to the topic. Students should focus on interesting

Figure 13 A first grader's quickwrite after reading *Sam, Bangs, and Moonshine*

ideas, make connections between the topic and their own lives, and reflect on their reading or learning.

   3. *Share quickwrites.* After students write, they usually share their quickwrites in small groups or during grand conversations, and then one student in each group shares with the class.

   Students do quickwrites for a variety of purposes in several of the steps of the reading process, including:

❦   to activate background knowledge before reading

❦   as an entry for **reading logs**

❦   to define or explain a word on the **word wall**

❦   about the theme of a story

❦   about a favorite character

❦   to compare book and film versions of a story

❦   about a favorite book during an author study

❦   about the project the student is creating

Students also do similar quickwrites during content-area units.

Students make squares out of construction paper and arrange them to make a quilt to respond to a book they have read or to present information they have learned in a content-area unit. Quilts about stories are designed to highlight the theme, reinforce symbolism, and recall favorite sentences in a book students have read. A square from a quilt about *Fly Away Home* (Bunting, 1991), a story about a homeless boy and his dad who live at an airport, is shown in Figure 14. The third graders created a modified "wedding ring" quilt pattern for their quilt. The steps in making a quilt are:

QUILTS

   1. *Design the quilt square.* Teachers and students choose a design for the quilt square that is appropriate for the story—its theme, characters, or setting—or reflects the topic of the content-area unit. Students can choose a quilt design or create their own design that captures an important dimension of the story or unit. They also choose colors for each shape in the quilt square.

   2. *Make the squares.* Students each make a square and add an important piece of information from the unit or a favorite sentence from the story around the outside of the quilt square or in a designated section of the square.

   3. *Compile the quilt.* Teachers tape the squares together and back the quilt with butcher paper, or staple the squares side by side on a large bulletin board.

   Quilts can be made of cloth, too. As an end-of-the-year project or to celebrate Book Week, teachers cut out squares of light-colored cloth and have students use fabric markers to draw pictures of their favorite stories and add the titles and authors. Then teachers or other adults sew the squares together, add a border, and complete the quilt.

A quilt square from a quilt about *Fly Away Home*

READ-AROUNDS

Read-arounds are celebrations of stories and other books, usually performed at the end of literature focus units or literature circles. Students choose favorite passages from a book to read aloud. Read-arounds are sometimes called "Quaker readings" because of their "unprogrammed" format. The steps are:

1. ***Choose a favorite passage.*** Students skim a book they have already read to locate one or more favorite passages (a sentence or paragraph) and mark the passages with bookmarks.

2. ***Practice reading the passage.*** Students rehearse reading the passages so that they can read them fluently.

3. ***Read the passages.*** Teachers begin the read-around by asking a student to read a favorite passage aloud to the class. Then there is a pause and another student begins to read. Teachers don't call on students; any student may begin reading when no one else is reading. The passages can be read in any order, and more than one student can read the same passage. Teachers, too, read their favorite passages. The read-around continues until everyone who wants to has read.

Students like participating in read-arounds because the featured book is like a good friend. They enjoy listening to classmates read favorite passages and noticing literary language. They seem to move back and forth through the story, remembering events and reliving the story.

Students keep reading logs to write their reactions and opinions about books they are reading or listening to the teacher read aloud. Students also add lists of words from the **word wall,** diagrams about story elements, and information about authors and genres (Tompkins, 2000). For a chapter book, students write after reading every chapter or two. The steps are:

1. *Prepare the reading logs.* Students make reading logs by stapling paper into booklets. They write the title of the book on the cover and add an appropriate illustration.

2. *Write entries.* Students write their reactions and reflections about the book or chapter they have read or listened to the teacher read aloud. Instead of summarizing the book, students relate the book to their own lives or to other literature they have read. Students may also list interesting or unfamiliar words, jot down quotable quotes, and take notes about characters, plot, or other story elements. The primary purpose of reading logs, though, is for students to think about the book, connect literature to their lives, and deepen their understanding of the book.

3. *Read and respond to the entries.* Teachers read students' entries and write comments back to students about their interpretations and reflections. Some teachers read and respond to all entries, and other teachers, because of time limitations, read and respond selectively. Because students' writing in reading logs is informal, teachers do not expect them to spell every word correctly, but it is not unreasonable to expect students to spell characters' names and other words on the word wall correctly.

Readers theatre is a dramatic production of a script by a group of readers (Martinez, Rose, & Strecker, 1998/1999). Each student assumes a role and reads the character's lines in the script. Readers interpret a story without using much action. They may stand or sit, but they must carry the whole communication of the plot, characterization, mood, and theme by using their voices, gestures, and facial expressions. Readers theatre avoids many of the restrictions inherent in theatrical productions: students do not memorize their parts; elaborate props, costumes, and backdrops are not needed; and long, tedious hours are not spent rehearsing. For readers theatre presentations, students can read scripts in trade books and textbooks, or they can create their own scripts. The steps are:

1. *Select a script.* Students and the teacher select a script and then read and discuss it as they would any story.

2. *Choose parts.* Students volunteer to read each part and mark their lines on the script. They also decide how to use their voice, gestures, and facial expressions to interpret the character they are reading.

3. *Rehearse the production.* They read the script several times, striving for accurate pronunciation, voice projection, and appropriate inflections. Less rehearsal is needed for an informal, in-class presentation than for a more formal production; nevertheless, interpretations should always be developed as fully as possible.

4. *Stage the production.* Readers theatre can be presented on a stage or in a corner of the classroom. Students stand or sit in a row and read their lines in the script. They stay in position through the production or enter and leave according to

the characters' appearances "onstage." If readers are sitting, they may stand to read their lines; if they are standing, they may step forward to read. The emphasis is not on production quality; rather, it is on the interpretive quality of the readers' voices and expressions. Costumes and props are unnecessary; however, adding a few small props enhances interest and enjoyment as long as they do not interfere with the interpretive quality of the reading.

REPEATED READINGS

Teachers often encourage students to reread the featured book several times during literature focus units and to reread favorite books during reading workshop. Students become more fluent readers when they reread books, and each time they reread a book their comprehension deepens. Jay Samuels (1979) has developed an instructional procedure to help students increase their reading fluency and accuracy through rereading. The steps in the individualized procedure are:

1. *Conduct a pretest.* The student chooses a textbook or trade book and reads a passage from the book aloud while the teacher records the reading time and any miscues.

2. *Practice rereading the passage.* The student practices rereading the passage orally or silently several times.

3. *Conduct a post-test.* The student rereads the passage while the teacher again records the reading time and notes any miscues.

4. *Compare pre- and post-test results.* The student compares his or her reading time and accuracy between the first and last readings. Then the student prepares a graph to document his or her growth between the first and last readings.

This procedure is useful for students who are slow and inaccurate readers. When teachers monitor students' readings on a regular basis, students will become more careful readers. Making a graph to document growth is an important component of the procedure, since the graph provides concrete evidence of the student's growth.

RUNNING RECORDS

Teachers observe individual students as they read aloud and take running records of students' reading to assess their reading fluency (Clay, 1985). Through a running record, teachers calculate the percentage of words the student reads correctly and then analyze the miscues or errors. Running records are easy to take, although teachers need some practice before they are comfortable with the procedure. Teachers make a check mark on a sheet of paper as the child reads each word correctly. Teachers use other marks to indicate words that the student doesn't know or pronounces incorrectly. The steps in conducting a reading record are:

1. *Choose a book.* Teachers have the student choose an excerpt 100 to 200 words in length from a book he or she is reading. For beginning readers, the text may be shorter.

2. *Take the running record.* As the student reads the excerpt aloud, the teacher makes a record of the words read correctly as well as those read incorrectly.

The teacher makes check marks on a sheet of blank paper for each word read correctly. Errors are marked this way:

❧ If the student read a word incorrectly, the teacher writes the incorrect word and the correct word under it:

<u>gentle</u>
generally

❧ If the student self-corrects an error, the teacher writes *SC* (for self-correction) following the incorrect word:

<u>bath SC</u>
bathe

❧ If the student attempts to pronounce a word, the teacher records each attempt and adds the correct text underneath:

<u>com- com- company</u>
companion

❧ If the student skips a word, the teacher marks the error with a dash:

<u>—</u>
own

❧ If the student adds words that are not in the text, the teacher writes an insertion symbol (caret) and records the inserted words:

<u>where he</u>
∧

❧ If the student can't identify a word and the teacher pronounces the word for the student, the teacher writes *T*:

<u>T</u>
routine

❧ If the student repeats a word or phrase, the repetition is not scored as an error, but the teacher notes the repetition by drawing a line under the word or phrase (marked in the running record with check marks) that was repeated:

<u>✓✓✓</u>

A sample running record was shown in Figure 3–5.

3. *Calculate the percentage of miscues.* Teachers calculate the percentage of miscues or oral reading errors. When the student makes 5% or fewer errors, the book is considered to be at the independent level for that child. When there are 6–10% errors, the book is at the instructional level, and when there are more than 10% errors, the book is too difficult—the frustration level.

4. *Analyze the miscues.* Teachers looks for patterns in the miscues in order to determine how the student is growing as a reader and to determine what skills and strategies the student should be taught. A miscue analysis of a running record was shown in Figure 3–6.

Many teachers conduct running records with all students in their classrooms at the beginning of the school year and at the end of grading periods. In addition, teachers do running records more often during guided reading groups and with students who are not making expected progress in reading in order to track their growth as readers and make instructional decisions.

SAY SOMETHING

When students are reading with a buddy, they can use the say something strategy to stop and talk about their reading. By sharing their responses, they will improve their comprehension (Harste, Woodward, & Burke, 1984). Children of all ages enjoy reading with a buddy and using the say something strategy to clarify misconceptions, make predictions, and share reactions. The steps are:

1. ***Divide students into pairs for reading.*** Teachers divide students into pairs for buddy reading. Students can read stories, informational books, basal reader selections, or content-area textbooks.

2. ***Read one page.*** Students read a page of text before stopping to talk. They can read silently or mumble-read, or one student can read to the other. The type of reading depends on the level of the book and the students participating in the activity.

3. ***Briefly talk about the page.*** After they finish reading the page, students stop to talk. They each make a comment or ask a question before continuing to read. Sometimes the discussion continues longer because of a special interest or a question, but after a brief discussion, students read the next page and then stop to talk again. For content-area textbooks, students often stop after reading a single paragraph to talk about their reading because the text is often densely written and clarification is needed.

Teachers often use a book they are reading aloud to the class to model the procedure. After they read a page, they make a comment to the class and one student is chosen to make a response. With this practice, students are better able to use the say something strategy independently.

SQ3R STUDY STRATEGY

In the SQ3R study strategy (Anderson & Armbruster, 1984), students use five steps—survey, question, read, recite, and review—to read and remember information in content-area reading assignments. This strategy is very effective when students know how to apply it correctly. The five steps are:

1. ***Survey.*** Students preview the reading assignment, noting headings and skimming (rapidly reading) the introduction and summary. They note the main ideas that are presented. This step helps students activate prior knowledge and organize what they will read.

2. ***Question.*** Students turn each heading into a question before reading the section. Reading to find the answer to the question gives students a purpose for reading.

3. ***Read.*** Students read the section to find the answer to the question they have formulated. They read each section separately.

4. ***Recite.*** Immediately after reading each section, students recite from memory the answer to the question they formulated and other important information they have read. Students can answer the questions orally or in writing.

5. *Review.* After finishing the entire reading assignment, students take a few minutes to review what they have read. They ask themselves the questions they developed from each heading and try to recall the answers they learned by reading. If students took notes or wrote answers to the questions in the fourth step, they should try to review without referring to the written notes.

Story boards are cards to which the illustrations and text (or only the illustrations) from a picture book have been attached. Teachers make story boards by cutting apart two copies of a picture book. Students use story boards to sequence the events of a story, to examine a picture book's illustrations, and for other exploring activities. The steps in making story boards are:

1. *Collect two copies of a book.* It is preferable to use paperback copies of the books because they are less expensive to purchase. In a few picture books, all the illustrations are on either the right-hand or left-hand page, and only one copy of these books is needed for illustration-only story boards. In Chris Van Allsburg's *The Mysteries of Harris Burdick* (1984), for example, all illustrations are on the right-hand pages.

2. *Cut the books apart.* Teachers remove the covers and separate the pages. Next, they trim the edges of the cut-apart sides.

3. *Attach the pages to pieces of cardboard.* Teachers glue each page or double-page spread to a piece of cardboard, making sure that each page in the story will be included.

4. *Laminate the cards.* Teachers laminate the cards so that they can withstand use by students.

5. *Use the cards in sequencing activities.* Teachers pass out the cards in random order to students. Students read their pages, think about the sequence of events in the story, and arrange themselves in a line around the classroom to sequence the story events.

Story boards can also be used when there are only a few copies of a picture book so that students can identify words for the **word wall,** notice literary language, and examine the illustrations.

For chapter books, students can create their own story boards, one for each chapter. Students can divide into small groups, and each group works on a different chapter. Students make a poster with a picture illustrating the chapter and a paragraph-length summary of the chapter. A group of eighth graders created the story board presented in Figure 15. It summarizes Chapter 2 of *Dragonwings* (Yep, 1975), the story of Moon Shadow, a young boy who comes from China to San Francisco in 1903 to join the father he has never met.

Teachers and students make a variety of diagrams and charts to examine the structure of stories they are reading (Bromley, 1991; Claggett, 1992; Macon et al., 1991). Six types of story maps are:

❦ Beginning-middle-end diagrams to examine the plot of a story

❦ Character clusters to examine the traits of a main character (Macon et al., 1991)

Figure 15 An eighth-grade story board from *Dragonwings*

Chapter 2
"The Company"

Moon Shadow meets his Uncle Bright Star. He had worked in the California Gold Rush and building the railroad. Then Windrider, Moon Shadow's dad, shows Moon Shadow around, to make him feel safe at home. They go past the Barbary Coast where the white demons live to his new home in Chinatown, the town of the Tang People. It looks like his old home in China. Moon Shadow's dad gave him a kite to fly. It was like a blue and green butterfly. Moon Shadow loved his new kite. Moon Shadow hasn't flown his kite yet, but I bet that he can't wait! They all go into a big house called the Company of the Peach Order Vow and then Uncle Bright Star's son named Black Dog comes. He is in a gang and he takes drugs. He tells everyone that the demons hate them and want to kill them. Then they heard the sound of a window shattering. So they went downstairs and they saw that a window was broken and the white demons were yelling and shouting at them. Moon Shadow is scared but Windrider protects him.

🌿 Venn diagrams to compare book and film versions of a story or for other comparisons

🌿 Plot profiles to chart the tension in each chapter of a chapter book (Johnson & Louis, 1987)

🌿 Sociograms to explore the relationships among characters (Johnson & Louis, 1987)

🌿 **Clusters** to probe the theme, setting, genre, author's style, or other dimensions of the story

"Skeleton" diagrams for these six types of story maps are presented in Figure 16. Students use information from the story they are reading and add words, sentences, and illustrations to complete the story maps.

Figure 16   Six types of story maps

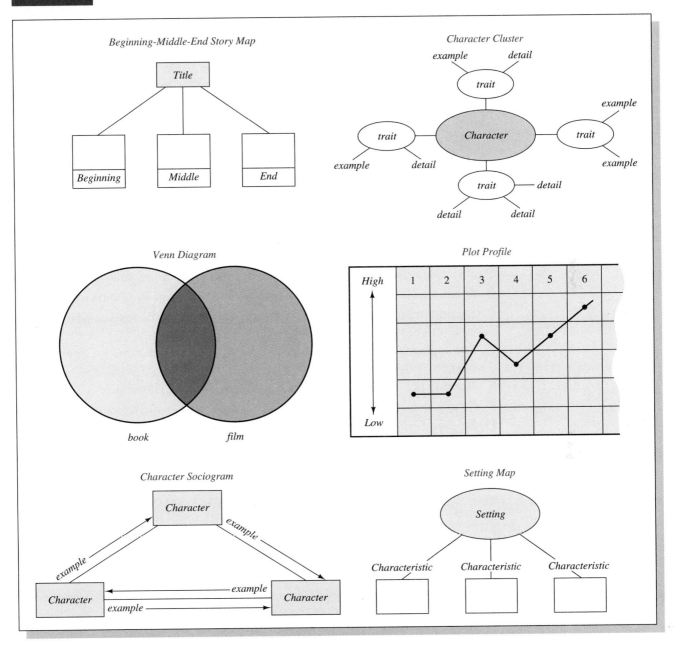

The steps in using story maps are:

1. *Choose a story map.* Teachers choose the type of story map that is appropriate for the story and the purpose of the lesson.

2. *Draw the diagram.* Teachers make a "skeleton" diagram on the chalkboard or on a chart.

3. Complete the diagram. Teachers work with students to complete the diagram. Students usually work together as a class the first time they do a story map. The next few times they do the story map, they work in small groups. After this experience, students make maps individually. For most story maps, students use a combination of words and pictures.

Students often make story maps as an exploring activity, but they can also choose to make a story map as a project. There are many other types of story maps students can make, and teachers can invent their own maps to help students visualize other structures and relationships in stories.

WORD SORTS

Students examine words and their meanings, sound-symbol correspondences, or spelling patterns using word sorts (Morris, 1982; Schlagal & Schlagal, 1992). Students sort a group of words (or objects or pictures) according to one of these characteristics:

🦋 Conceptual relationships, such as words related to one of several characters in a story or words related to the inner or outer planets in the solar system

🦋 Rhyming words, such as words that rhyme with *ball, hit,* or *flake*

🦋 Consonant sounds, such as pictures and objects of words beginning with *r* or *l*

🦋 Sound-symbol relationships, such as words in which the final *y* sounds like long *i* (*cry*) and words in which the final *y* sounds like long *e* (*baby*)

🦋 Spelling patterns and rules, such as long-*e* words with various spelling patterns (*sea, greet, be, Pete*)

🦋 Number of syllables, such as *pig, happy, afternoon,* and *television*

🦋 Syllable division rules, using words such as *mag-net, can-dle, ti-ger, stor-y,* and *po-et*

🦋 English, Latin, and Greek etymologies of words, using words such as *teeth* (English), *nation* (Latin), and *thermometer* (Greek)

Sometimes teachers determine the categories for the sort and at other times students choose the categories. When teachers determine the categories, it is a closed word sort, and when students choose the categories, it is an open word sort (Bear, Invernizzi, Templeton, & Johnston, 2000). The steps in this instructional strategy are:

1. Compile a list of words. Teachers compile a list of 10 to 20 words that exemplify a particular pattern and write the words on small cards. With younger children, small objects or picture cards can be used.

2. Determine the categories for the sort. Teachers determine the categories for the sort and tell students, or students read the words and determine the categories themselves. They may work individually or together in small groups or as a class.

3. Sort the cards. Students sort the words into two or more categories and write the sorted words on a chart or glue the sorted word cards onto a piece of chart paper.

4. Share the completed sorts. Students share their word sort with classmates, emphasizing the categories they used for their sort.

Many of the words chosen for word sorts should come from high-frequency **word walls,** books students are reading, or content-area units. Figure 17 shows a

Figure 17 A first-grade word sort using words from Nancy Shaw's "Sheep" books

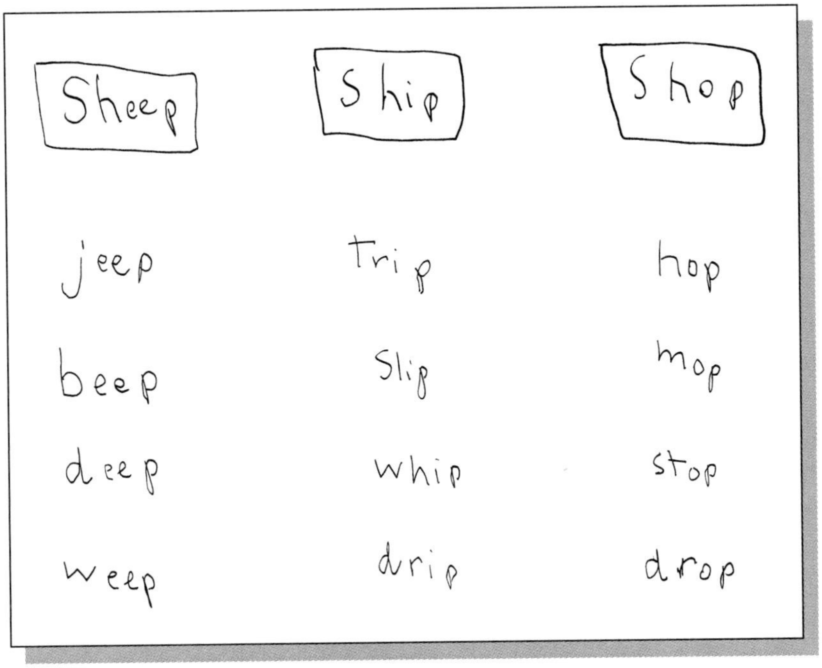

Sheep	Ship	Shop
jeep	trip	hop
beep	slip	mop
deep	whip	stop
weep	drip	drop

first-grade word sort using words from Nancy Shaw's *Sheep in a Jeep* (1986), *Sheep on a Ship* (1989), and *Sheep in a Shop* (1991) books. Students sorted the words according to three rimes—*eep, ip,* and *op.*

WORD WALLS

Word walls are alphabetized collections of words posted in the classroom that students can refer to when they are reading and writing and for word-study activities. Words for the word wall can be written on large sheets of butcher paper or on cards displayed in pocket charts, and they are often written in alphabetical order so that students can locate the words more easily.

There are three types of word walls. One type is a high-frequency word wall, and primary teachers post the 100 highest-frequency words on this word wall (Cunningham, 2000). A second type of word wall is a content-area word wall, and teachers and students write important words related to the unit on the word wall. A third type of word wall is a literature word wall, and teachers and students write interesting, confusing, and important words from the story they are reading. A literature word wall for *Sarah, Plain and Tall* (MacLachlan, 1983) is shown in Figure 18. The three types of word walls should be posted separately in the classroom because if the words are mixed, students will have difficulty categorizing the words.

The steps in using a literature word wall are:

1. *Prepare the word wall.* Teachers hang a long sheet of butcher paper on a blank wall in the classroom and divide it into alphabetical categories. Or, teachers can display a large pocket chart on a classroom wall and prepare a stack of cards on which

Figure 18 A literature word wall for *Sarah, Plain and Tall*

AB	C	D	E
Anna	Caleb	dough	eagerly
biscuits	coarse	dunes	energetic
bonnet	carpenter		
ayuh	cruel		
	chores		
	collapsed		
FG	**H**	**IJ**	**KL**
gophers	hearthstones	Indian paintbrush	longing
feisty	homely		
fogbound	hollow		
	harshly		
	housekeeper		
M	**NO**	**P**	**QR**
mild mannered	nip	Papa	rascal
Maine	oyster	prairie	roamer
	offshore	paddock	
		pesky	
		preacher	
		pitchfork	
S	**T**	**UVW**	**XYZ**
sing	troublesome	widened	
Sarah	tumbleweed	woodchuck	
shovel	treaded (water)	wooly ragwort	
slippery		wild-eyed	
squall		windbreak	
suspenders		wretched	
shuffling			

to write the words. Then they add the title of the book students are reading at the top of the word wall.

    2. *Introduce the word wall.* Teachers introduce the word wall and add character names and other several key words during preparing activities before reading.

    3. *Add words to the word wall.* After reading a picture book or after reading each chapter of a chapter book, students suggest additional "important" words for the word wall. Students and the teacher write the words in alphabetical categories on the butcher paper or on word cards, making sure to write large enough so that most students can see the words. Or, if a pocket chart is being used, students arrange the word cards in alphabetical order.

4. *Use the word wall for exploring activities.* Students use the word wall words for a variety of vocabulary activities, such as **word sorts** and **story maps.** Students also refer to the word wall when they are writing in **reading logs** or working on projects.

For other types of word walls, teachers follow a similar approach to post words on the word walls and highlight the words through various activities.

During the revising step of the writing process, students meet in writing groups to share their rough drafts and get feedback on how well they are communicating (Tompkins, 2000). Revising is probably the most difficult part of the writing process because it is difficult for students to stand back and evaluate their writing objectively. Students need to learn how to work together in writing groups and provide useful feedback to classmates. The steps are:

WRITING GROUPS

1. *Read drafts aloud.* Students take turns reading their rough drafts aloud to the group. Everyone listens politely, thinking about compliments and suggestions they will make after the writer finishes reading. Only the writer looks at the composition, because when classmates and teacher look at it they quickly notice and comment on mechanical errors, even though the emphasis during revising is on content. Listening as the writing is read aloud keeps the focus on content.

2. *Offer compliments.* After listening to the rough draft read aloud, classmates in the writing group offer compliments, telling the writer what they liked about the composition. These positive comments should be specific, focusing on strengths, rather than the often-heard "I liked it" or "It was good." Even though these are positive comments, they do not provide effective feedback. When teachers introduce revision, they should model appropriate responses because students may not know how to offer specific and meaningful comments. Teachers and students can brainstorm a list of appropriate comments and post it in the classroom for students to refer to. Comments may focus on organization, introductions, word choice, voice, sequence, dialogue, theme, and so on. Possible comments are:

I like the part where . . .
I'd like to know more about . . .
I like the way you described . . .
Your writing made me feel . . .
I like the order you used in your writing because . . .

3. *Ask clarifying questions.* After a round of positive comments, writers ask for assistance with trouble spots they identified earlier when rereading their writing, or they may ask questions that reflect more general concerns about how well they are communicating. Admitting the need for help from one's classmates is a major step in learning to revise. Possible questions to ask classmates are:

What do you want to know more about?
Is there a part I should throw away?
What details can I add?
What do you think the best part of my writing is?
Are there some words I need to change?

4. *Offer other revision suggestions.* Members of the writing group ask questions about things that were unclear to them and make suggestions about how to revise the composition. Almost any writer resists constructive criticism, and it is especially difficult for elementary students to appreciate suggestions. It is important to teach students what kinds of comments and suggestions are acceptable so that they will word what they say in helpful rather than hurtful ways. Possible comments and suggestions that students can offer are:

> I got confused in the part about . . .
> Do you need a closing?
> Could you add more about . . . ?
> I wonder if your paragraphs are in the right order because . . .
> Could you combine some sentences?

5. *Repeat the process.* The writing group members repeat the process so that all students have an opportunity to share their rough drafts. The first four steps are repeated for each student's composition. This is the appropriate time for teachers to provide input as well.

6. *Make plans for revision.* At the end of the writing group session, each student makes a commitment to revise his or her writing based on the comments and suggestions of the group members. The final decision on what to revise always rests with the writers themselves, but with the understanding that their rough drafts are not perfect comes the realization that some revision will be necessary. When students verbalize their planned revisions, they are more likely to complete the revision step. Some students also make notes for themselves about their revision plans. After the group disbands, students make the revisions.

References

Anderson, T. H., & Armbruster, B. B. (1984). Studying. In P. D. Pearson, R. Barr, M. L. Kamil, & P. Mosenthal (Eds.), *Handbook of reading research* (pp. 657–679). New York: Longman.

Ashton-Warner, S. (1965). *Teacher.* New York: Simon & Schuster.

Atwell, N. (1987). *In the middle: Writing, reading, and learning with adolescents.* Portsmouth, NH: Heinemann.

Barone, D. (1990). The written responses of young children: Beyond comprehension to story understanding. *The New Advocate, 3,* 49–56.

Bear, D. R., Invernizzi, M., Templeton, S., & Johnston, F. (2000). *Words their way: Word study for phonics, vocabulary, and spelling instruction.* Upper Saddle River, NJ: Merrill/Prentice Hall.

Berthoff, A. E. (1981). *The making of meaning.* Montclair, NJ: Boynton/Cook.

Blachowicz, C. L. Z. (1986). Making connections: Alternatives to the vocabulary notebook. *Journal of Reading, 29,* 643–649.

Bromley, K. D. (1991). *Webbing with literature: Creating story maps with children's books.* Boston: Allyn & Bacon.

Button, K., Johnson, M. J., & Furgerson, P. (1996). Interactive writing in a primary classroom. *The Reading Teacher, 49,* 446–454.

Claggett, F. (1992). *Drawing your own conclusions: Graphic strategies for reading, writing, and thinking.* Portsmouth, NH: Heinemann.

Clay, M. M. (1985). *The early detection of reading difficulties* (3rd ed.). Portsmouth, NH: Heinemann.

Cunningham, P. M. (2000). *Phonics they use: Words for reading and writing* (3rd ed.). New York: Harper-Collins.

Cunningham, P. M., & Cunningham, J. W. (1992). Making words: Enhancing the invented spelling-decoding connection. *The Reading Teacher, 46,* 106–115.

Eeds, M., & Wells, D. (1989). Grand conversations: An exploration of meaning construction in literature study groups. *Research in the Teaching of English, 23,* 4–29.

Elbow, P. (1973). *Writing without teachers.* London: Oxford University Press.

Fountas, I. C., & Pinnell, G. S. (1996). *Guided reading: Good first teaching for all children.* Portsmouth, NH: Heinemann.

Goldenberg, C. (1992/1993). Instructional conversations: Promoting comprehension through discussion. *The Reading Teacher, 46,* 316–326.

Gunning, T. G. (1995). Word building: A strategic approach to the teaching of phonics. *The Reading Teacher, 48,* 484–488.

Harste, J. C., Woodward, V. A., & Burke, C. L. (1984). *Language stories and literacy lessons.* Portsmouth, NH: Heinemann.

Head, M. H., & Readence, J. E. (1986). Anticipation guides: Meaning through prediction. In E. K. Dishner, T. W. Bean, J. E. Readence, & D. W. Moore (Eds.), *Reading in the content areas* (2nd ed.) (pp. 229–234). Dubuque, IA: Kendall/Hunt.

Johnson, T. D., & Louis, D. R. (1987). *Literacy through literature.* Portsmouth, NH: Heinemann.

Lee, D. M., & Allen, R. V. (1963). *Learning to read through experience* (2nd ed.). New York: Meredith.

Macon, J. M., Bewell, D., & Vogt, M. E. (1991). *Responses to literature, grades K–8.* Newark, DE: International Reading Association.

Martinez, M., Roser, N. L., & Strecker, S. (1998/1999). "I never thought I could be a star": A readers theatre ticket to fluency. *The Reading Teacher, 52,* 326–334.

McKenzie, G. R. (1979). Data charts: A crutch for helping pupils organize reports. *Language Arts, 56,* 784–788.

Morris, D. (1982). "Word sort": A categorization strategy for improving word recognition. *Reading Psychology, 3,* 247–259.

Neeld, E. C. (1986). *Writing* (2nd ed.). Glenview, IL: Scott Foresman.

Ogle, D. M. (1986). K-W-L: A teaching model that develops active reading of expository text. *The Reading Teacher, 39,* 564–570.

Ogle, D. M. (1989). The know, want to know, learn strategy. In K. D. Muth (Ed.), *Children's comprehension of text: Research into practice* (pp. 205–223). Newark, DE: International Reading Association.

Peterson, R., & Eeds, M. (1990). *Grand conversations: Literature groups in action.* New York: Scholastic.

Reutzel, D. R., & Cooter, R. B., Jr. (1996). *Teaching children to read: From basals to books* (2nd ed.). Englewood Cliffs, NJ: Merrill/Prentice Hall.

Rico, G. L. (1983). *Writing the natural way.* Los Angeles: Tarcher.

Samuels, S. J. (1979). The method of repeated readings. *The Reading Teacher, 32,* 403–408.

Schlagal, R. C., & Schlagal, J. H. (1992). The integral character of spelling: Teaching strategies for multiple purposes. *Language Arts, 69,* 418–424.

Stauffer, R. G. (1970). *The language experience approach to the teaching of reading.* New York: Harper & Row.

Stauffer, R. G. (1975). *Directing the reading-thinking process.* New York: Harper & Row.

Tierney, R. J., Readence, J. E., & Dishner, E. K. (1995). *Reading strategies and practices: A compendium* (4th ed.). Boston: Allyn & Bacon.

Tompkins, G. E. (2000). *Teaching writing: Balancing process and product* (3rd ed.). Upper Saddle River, NJ: Merrill/Prentice Hall.

Children's Book References

Brett, J. (1999). *Gingerbread Baby.* New York: Putnam.

Bunting, E. (1991). *Fly away home.* New York: Clarion.

Cushman, K. (1996). *The ballad of Lucy Whipple.* New York: Clarion.

Ehlert, L. (1989). *Eating the alphabet: Fruits and vegetables from A to Z.* Orlando, FL: Harcourt Brace Jovanovich.

Hunt, J. (1989). *Illuminations.* New York: Bradbury Press.

Hutchins, P. (1968). *Rosie's walk.* New York: Macmillan.

Lewis, C. S. (1950). *The lion, the witch and the wardrobe.* New York: Macmillan.

MacLachlan, P. (1983). *Sarah, plain and tall.* New York: Harper & Row.

Ness, E. (1966). *Sam, Bangs, and moonshine.* New York: Holt, Rinehart & Winston.

Shaw, N. (1986). *Sheep in a jeep.* Boston: Houghton Mifflin.

Shaw, N. (1989). *Sheep in a ship.* Boston: Houghton Mifflin.

Shaw, N. (1991). *Sheep in a shop.* Boston: Houghton Mifflin.

Van Allsburg, C. (1984). *The mysteries of Harris Burdick.* Boston: Houghton Mifflin.

Yep, L. (1975). *Dragonwings.* New York: HarperCollins.

Award-Winning Books for Children

Caldecott Medal Books

The Caldecott Medal is named in honor of Randolph Caldecott (1846–86), a British illustrator of children's books. The award is presented by the American Library Association each year to "the artist of the most distinguished American picture book for children" published during the preceding year. The award was first given in 1938 and is awarded annually. The winning book receives the Caldecott Medal, and one or more runners-up are also recognized as "Honor" books.

2000 *Joseph had a little overcoat,* Simms Taback (Viking). **Honor books:** *Sector 7,* David Wiesner (Clarion); *The ugly duckling,* Jerry Pinkney (Morrow); *When Sophie gets angry—really, really angry,* Molly Bang (Scholastic); *A child's calendar,* John Updike, illustrated by Trina Schart Hyman (Holiday House).

1999 *Snowflake Bentley,* Jacqueline Briggs Martin (Houghton Mifflin). **Honor books:** *Duke Ellington: The piano prince and his orchestra,* Andrea Davis Pinkney, illustrated by Brian Pinkney (Hyperion); *No David!,* David Shannon (Scholastic); *Snow,* Uri Shulevitz (Farrar Straus Giroux); *Tibet through the red box,* Peter Sis (Farrar Straus Giroux).

1998 *Rapunzel,* Paul O. Zelinsky (Dutton). **Honor books:** *The gardener,* Sarah Stewart, illustrated by David Small (Farrar Straus Giroux); *Harlem,* Walter Dean Myers, illustrated by Christopher Myers (Scholastic); *There was an old lady who swallowed a fly,* Simms Taback (Viking).

1997 *Golem,* David Wisniewski (Clarion). **Honor books:** *Hush! A Thai lullaby,* Minfong Ho, illustrated by Holly Meade (Orchard); *The graphic alphabet,* David Pelletier (Orchard); *The paperboy,* Dav Pilkey (Orchard); *Starry messenger,* Peter Sis (Farrar Straus Giroux).

1996 *Officer Buckle and Gloria,* Peggy Rathmann (Putnam). **Honor books:** *Alphabet city,* Stephen T. Johnson (Viking); *Zin! Zin! Zin! A violin,* Lloyd Moss, illustrated by Marjorie Priceman (Simon & Schuster); *The faithful friend,* Robert D. San Souci, illustrated by Brian Pinkney (Simon & Schuster); *Tops and bottoms,* Janet Stevens (Harcourt Brace).

1995 *Smoky night,* Eve Bunting, illustrated by David Diaz (Harcourt Brace). **Honor books:** *Swamp angel,* Anne Isaacs, illustrated by Paul O. Zelinsky (Dutton); *John Henry,* Julius Lester (Dial); *Time flies,* Eric Rohmann (Crown).

1994 *Grandfather's journey,* Allen Say (Houghton Mifflin). **Honor books:** *Peppe the lamplighter,* Elisa Bartone (Lothrop); *In the small, small pond,* Denis Fleming (Holt); *Owen,* Kevin Henkes (Greenwillow); *Raven: A trickster tale from the Pacific northwest,* Gerald McDermott (Harcourt Brace Jovanovich); *Yo! Yes?* Chris Raschak (Orchard).

1993 *Mirette on the high wire,* Emily McCully (Putnam). **Honor books:** *Seven blind mice,* Ed Young (Philomel); *The stinky cheese man and other fairly stupid tales,* Jon Scieszka, illustrated by Lane Smith (Viking); *Working cotton,* Sherley Anne Williams, illustrated by Carole Byard (Harcourt Brace Jovanovich).

1992 *Tuesday,* David Wiesner (Clarion). **Honor book:** *Tar beach,* Faith Ringgold (Crown).

1991 *Black and white,* David Macaulay (Houghton Mifflin). **Honor books:** *Puss in boots,* Charles Perrault, illustrated by Fred Marcellino (Farrar Straus Giroux); *"More, more, more" said the baby,* Vera B. Williams (Morrow).

1990 *Lon Po Po, A Red Riding Hood story from China,* Ed Young (Philomel). **Honor books:** *Bill Peet: An autobiography,* William Peet (Houghton Mifflin); *Color zoo,* Lois Ehlert (Lippincott); *Herschel and the Hanukkah goblins,* Eric A. Kimmel, illustrated by Trina Schart Hyman (Holiday House); *The talking eggs,* Robert D. San Souci, illustrated by Jerry Pinkney (Dial).

1989 *Song and dance man,* Jane Ackerman, illustrated by Stephen Gammel (Knopf). **Honor books:** *Goldilocks,* James Marshall (Dial); *The boy of the three-year nap,* Diane Snyder, illustrated by Allen Say (Houghton Mifflin); *Mirandy and Brother Wind,* Patricia McKissack, illustrated by Jerry Pinkney (Knopf); *Free fall,* David Wiesner (Lothrop).

1988 *Owl moon,* Jane Yolen, illustrated by John Schoenherr (Philomel). **Honor book:** *Mufaro's beautiful daughters: An African tale,* John Steptoe (Morrow).

1987 *Hey, Al,* Arthur Yorinks, illustrated by Richard Egielski (Farrar Straus Giroux). **Honor books:** *Alphabatics,* Suse MacDonald (Bradbury); *Rumplestiltskin,* Paul O. Zelinsky (Dutton); *The village of round and square houses,* Ann Grifalconi (Little, Brown).

1986 *The polar express,* Chris Van Allsburg (Houghton Mifflin). **Honor books:** *King Bidgood's in the bathtub,* Audrey Wood (Harcourt Brace Jovanovich); *The relatives came,* Cynthia Rylant (Bradbury).

1985 *Saint George and the dragon,* Margaret Hodges, illustrated by Trina Schart Hyman (Little, Brown). **Honor books:** *Hansel and Gretel,* Rika Lesser, illustrated by Paul O. Zelinsky (Dodd, Mead); *Have you seen my duckling?* Nancy Tafuri (Greenwillow); *The story of jumping mouse,* John Steptoe (Lothrop, Lee & Shepard).

1984 *The glorious flight: Across the channel with Louis Bleriot,* Alice and Martin Provensen (Viking). **Honor books:** *Little red riding hood,* Trina Schart Hyman (Holiday); *Ten, nine, eight,* Molly Bang (Greenwillow).

1983 *Shadow,* Blaise Cendrars, translated and illustrated by Marcia Brown (Scribner). **Honor books:** *A chair for my mother,* Vera B. Williams (Greenwillow); *When I was young in the mountains,* Cynthia Rylant, illustrated by Diane Goode (Dutton).

1982 *Jumanji,* Chris Van Allsburg (Houghton Mifflin). **Honor books:** *On Market Street,* Arnold Lobel, illustrated by Anita Lobel (Greenwillow); *Outside over there,* Maurice Sendak (Harper & Row); *A visit to William Blake's inn: Poems for innocent and experienced travelers,* Nancy Willard, illustrated by Alice and Martin Provensen (Harcourt Brace Jovanovich); *Where the buffaloes begin,* Olaf Baker, illustrated by Stephen Gammell (Warne).

1981 *Fables,* Arnold Lobel (Harper & Row). **Honor books:** *The Bremen-Town musicians,* Ilse Plume (Doubleday); *The gray lady and the strawberry snatcher,* Molly Bang (Four Winds); *Mice twice,* Joseph Low (Atheneum); *Truck,* Donald Crews (Greenwillow).

1980 *Ox-cart man,* Donald Hall, illustrated by Barbara Cooney (Viking); **Honor books:** *Ben's trumpet,* Rachel Isadora (Greenwillow); *The garden of Abdul Gasazi,* Chris Van Allsburg (Houghton Mifflin); *The treasure,* Uri Shulevitz (Farrar Straus Giroux).

1979 *The girl who loved wild horses,* Paul Goble (Bradbury). **Honor books:** *Freight train,* Donald Crews (Greenwillow); *The way to start a day,* Byrd Baylor, illustrated by Peter Parnall (Scribner).

1978 *Noah's ark: The story of the flood,* Peter Spier (Doubleday), **Honor books:** *Castle,* David Macaulay (Houghton Mifflin); *It could always be worse,* Margot Zemach (Farrar Straus Giroux).

1977 *Ashanti to Zulu,* Margaret Musgrove, illustrated by Leo and Diane Dillon (Dial). **Honor books:** *The amazing bone,* William Steig (Farrar Straus Giroux); *The contest,* Nonny Hogrogian (Greenwillow); *Fish for supper,* M. B. Goffstein (Dial); *The Golem: A Jewish legend,* Beverly Brodsky McDermott (Lippincott); *Hawk, I'm your brother,* Byrd Baylor, illustrated by Peter Parnall (Scribner).

1976 *Why mosquitoes buzz in people's ears,* Verna Aardema, illustrated by Leo and Diane Dillon (Dial). **Honor books:** *The desert is theirs,* Byrd Baylor, illustrated by Peter Parnall (Scribner); *Strega Nona,* Tomie de Paola (Prentice-Hall).

1975 *Arrow to the sun,* Gerald McDermott (Viking). **Honor book:** *Jambo means hello: A Swahili alphabet book,* Muriel Feelings, illustrated by Tom Feelings (Dial).

1974 *Duffy and the devil,* Harve and Margo Zemach (Farrar Straus Giroux). **Honor books:** *Cathedral: The story of its construction,* David Macaulay (Houghton Mifflin); *The three jovial huntsmen,* Susan Jeffers (Bradbury).

1973 *The funny little woman,* Arlen Mosel, illustrated by Blair Lent (Dutton). **Honor books:** *Hosie's alphabet,* Hosea, Tobias, and Lisa Baskin, illustrated by Leonard Baskin (Viking); *Snow-White and the seven dwarfs,* translated by Randall Jarrell from the Brothers Grimm, illustrated by Nancy Ekholm Burkert (Farrar Straus Giroux); *When clay sings,* Byrd Baylor, illustrated by Tom Bahti (Scribner).

1972 *One fine day,* Nonny A. Hogrogian (Macmillan). **Honor books:** *Hildilid's night,* Cheli Duran Ryan, illustrated by Arnold Lobel (Macmillan); *If all the seas were one sea,* Janina Domanska (Macmillan); *Moja means one: Swahili counting book,* Muriel Feelings, illustrated by Tom Feelings (Dial).

1971 *A story, a story.* Gail E. Haley (Atheneum). **Honor books:** *The angry moon,* William Sleator, illustrated by Blair Lent (Atlantic-Little); *Frog and Toad are friends,* Arnold Lobel (Harper & Row); *In the night kitchen,* Maurice Sendak (Harper & Row).

1970 *Sylvester and the magic pebble,* William Steig (Simon & Schuster). **Honor books:** *Alexander and the wind-up mouse,* Leo Lionni (Pantheon); *Goggles!* Ezra Jack Keats (Macmillan); *The judge: An untrue tale,* Harve Zemach, illustrated by Margot Zemach (Farrar Straus Giroux); *Pop Corn and Ma Goodness,* Edna Mitchell Preston, illustrated by Robert Andrew Parker (Viking); *Thy friend, Obadiah,* Brinton Turkle (Viking).

1969 *The fool of the world and the flying ship,* Arthur Ransome, illustrated by Uri Shulevitz (Farrar Straus Giroux). **Honor book:** *Why the sun and the moon live in the sky: An African folktale,* Elphinstone Dayrell, illustrated by Blair Lent (Houghton Mifflin).

1968 *Drummer Hoff,* Barbara Emberley, illustrated by Ed Emberley (Prentice-Hall). **Honor books:** *Frederick,* Leo Lionni (Pantheon); *Seashore story,* Taro Yashima (Viking); *The emperor and the kite,* Jane Yolen, illustrated by Ed Young (Harcourt Brace Jovanovich).

1967 *Sam, Bangs & Moonshine,* Evaline Ness (Holt, Rinehart & Winston). **Honor book:** *One wide river to cross,* Barbara Emberley, illustrated by Ed Emberley (Prentice-Hall).

1966 *Always room for one more,* Sorche Nic Leodhas, illustrated by Nonny Hogrogian (Holt). **Honor books:** *Hide and seek fog,* Alvin Tresselt, illustrated by Roger Duvoisin (Lothrop); *Just me,* Marie Hall Ets (Viking); *Tom tit tot,* Evaline Ness (Scribner).

1965 *May I bring a friend?* Beatrice Schenk de Regniers, illustrated by Beni Montresor (Atheneum). **Honor books:** *Rain makes applesauce,* Julian Scheer, illustrated by Marvin Bileck (Holiday House); *The wave,* Margaret Hodges, illustrated by Blair Lent (Houghton Mifflin); *A pocketful of cricket,* Rebecca Caudill, illustrated by Evaline Ness (Holt).

1964 *Where the wild things are,* Maurice Sendak (Harper & Row). **Honor books:** *Swimmy,* Leo Lionni (Pantheon); *All in the morning early,* Sorche Nic Leodhas, illustrated by Evaline Ness (Holt); *Mother Goose and nursery rhymes,* illustrated by Philip Reed (Atheneum).

1963 *The snow day,* Ezra Jack Keats (Viking). **Honor books:** *The sun is a golden earring,* Natalia M. Belting, illustrated by Bernarda Bryson (Holt); *Mr. Rabbit and the lovely present,* Charlotte Zolotow, illustrated by Maurice Sendak (Harper & Row).

1962 *Once a mouse . . . ,* Marcia Brown (Scribner). **Honor books:** *The fox went out on a chilly night: An old song,* Peter Spier (Doubleday); *Little bear's visit,* Else Holmelund Minarik, illustrated by Maurice Sendak (Harper & Row); *The day we saw the sun come up,* Alice E. Goudey, illustrated by Adrienne Adams (Scribner).

1961 *Baboushka and the three kings,* Ruth Robbins, illustrated by Nicolas Sidjakov (Parnassus). **Honor book:** *Inch by inch,* Leo Lionni (Obolensky).

1960 *Nine days to Christmas,* Marie Hall Ets & Aurora Labastida, illustrated by Marie Hall Ets (Viking). **Honor books:** *Houses from the sea,* Alice E. Goudey, illustrated by Adrienne Adams (Scribner); *The moon jumpers,* Janice May Udry, illustrated by Maurice Sendak (Harper & Row).

Newbery Medal Books

The Newbery Medal is named in honor of John Newbery (1713–67), a British publisher and bookseller in the 1700s. Newbery is known as the "father of children's literature" because he was the first to propose publishing books specifically for children. The award is presented each year by the American Library Association to "the author of the most distinguished contribution to American literature for children" published during the preceding year. The award

was first given in 1922 and is awarded annually. The winning book receives the Newbery Medal, and one or more runners-up are also recognized as "Honor" books.

2000 *Bud, not Buddy,* Christopher Paul Curtis (Delacorte). **Honor books:** *Getting near to baby,* Audrey Coulombis (Putnam); *26 Fairmont Avenue,* Tomie de Paola (Putnam); *Our only May Amelia,* Jennifer L. Holm (HarperCollins).

1999 *Holes,* Louis Sachar (Farrar Straus Giroux). **Honor book:** A long way from Chicago, Richard Peck (Dial).

1998 *Out of the dust,* Karren Hesse (Scholastic). **Honor books:** *Ella enchanted,* Gail Carson Levine (HarperCollins); *Lily's crossing,* Patricia Reilly Giff (Delacorte); *Wringer,* Jerry Spinelli (HarperCollins).

1997 *The view from Saturday,* E. L. Konigsburg (Atheneum). **Honor books:** *A girl named Disaster,* Nancy Farmer (Orchard); *The moorchild,* Eloise Jarvis McGraw (McElderry); *The thief,* Megan Whalen Turner (Greenwillow); *Belle Prater's boy,* Ruth White (Farrar Straus Giroux).

1996 *The midwife's apprentice,* Karen Cushman (Clarion). **Honor books:** *What Jamie saw,* Carolyn Coman (Front Street); *The Watsons go to Birmingham—1963,* Christopher Paul Curtis (Delacorte); *Yolanda's genius,* Carol Fenner (McElderry); *The great fire,* Jim Murphy (Scholastic).

1995 *Walk two moons,* Sharon Creech (HarperCollins). **Honor books:** *Catherine called Birdy,* Karen Cushman (Clarion); *The ear, the eye and the arm,* Nancy Farmer (Orchard).

1994 *The giver,* Lois Lowry (Houghton Mifflin). **Honor books:** *Crazy Lady!,* Jane Leslie Conly (HarperCollins); *Dragon's gate,* Laurence Yep (HarperCollins); *Eleanor Roosevelt: A life of discovery,* Russell Freedman (Clarion).

1993 *Missing May,* Cynthia Rylant (Orchard). **Honor books:** *The dark-thirty: Southern tales of the supernatural,* Patricia McKissack (Knopf); *Somewhere in the darkness,* Walter Dean Myers (Scholastic); *What hearts,* Bruce Books (HarperCollins).

1992 *Shiloh,* Phyllis Reynolds Naylor (Atheneum). **Honor books:** *Nothing but the truth,* Avi (Orchard); *The Wright brothers: How they invented the airplane,* Russell Freedman (Holiday House).

1991 *Maniac Magee,* Jerry Spinelli (Little, Brown). **Honor book:** *The true confessions of Charlotte Doyle,* Avi (Orchard).

1990 *Number the stars,* Lois Lowry (Houghton Mifflin). **Honor books:** *Afternoon of the elves,* Janet Taylor Lisel (Orchard); *Shabanu, daughter of the wind,* Susan Fisher Staples (Knopf); *The winter room,* Gary Paulsen (Orchard).

1989 *Joyful noise: Poems for two voices*, Paul Fleishman (Harper & Row). **Honor books:** *In the beginning*, Virginia Hamilton (Harcourt Brace Jovanovich); *Scorpions*, Walter Dean Myers (Harper & Row).

1988 *Lincoln: A photobiography*, Russell Freedman (Clarion). **Honor books:** *After the rain*, Norma Fox Mazer (Morrow); *Hatchet*, Gary Paulsen (Bradbury).

1987 *The whipping boy*, Sid Fleischman (Greenwillow). **Honor books:** *A fine white dust*, Cynthia Rylant (Bradbury); *On my honor*, Marion Dane Bauer (Clarion); *Volcano: The eruption and healing of Mount St. Helen's*, Patricia Lauber (Bradbury).

1986 *Sarah, plain and tall*, Patricia MacLachlan (Harper & Row). **Honor books:** *Commodore Perry in the land of the Shogun*, Rhoda Blumberg (Lothrop, Lee & Shepard); *Dog song*, Gary Paulsen (Bradbury).

1985 *The hero and the crown*, Robin McKinley (Greenwillow). **Honor books:** *Like Jake and me*, Mavis Jukes (Knopf); *The moves make the man*, Bruce Brooks (Harper & Row); *One-eyed cat*, Paula Fox (Bradbury).

1984 *Dear Mr. Henshaw*, Beverly Clearly (Morrow). **Honor books:** *The sign of the beaver*, Elizabeth George Speare (Houghton Mifflin); *A solitary blue*, Cynthia Voigt (Atheneum); *Sugaring time*, Kathryn Lasky (Macmillan); *The wish giver*, Bill Brittain (Harper & Row).

1983 *Dicey's song*, Cynthia Voigt (Atheneum). **Honor books:** *The blue sword*, Robin McKinley (Greenwillow); *Doctor DeSoto*, William Steig (Farrar Straus Giroux); *Graven images*, Paul Fleischman (Harper & Row); *Homesick: My own story*, Jean Fritz (Putnam); *Sweet Whispers, Brother Rush*, Virginia Hamilton (Philomel).

1982 *A visit to William Blake's inn: Poems for innocent and experienced travelers*, Nancy Willard (Harcourt Brace Jovanovich). **Honor books:** *Ramona Quimby, age 8*, Beverly Clearly (Morrow); *Upon the head of the goat: A childhood in Hungary, 1939–1944*, Aranka Siegal (Farrar Straus Giroux).

1981 *Jacob have I loved*, Katherine Paterson (Crowell). **Honor books:** *The fledgling*, Jane Langton (Harper & Row); *A ring of endless light*, Madeleine L'Engle (Farrar Straus Giroux).

1980 *A gathering of days: A New England girl's journal, 1830–1832*, Joan W. Blos (Scribner). **Honor book:** *The road from home: The story of an Armenian girl*, David Kerdian (Greenwillow).

1979 *The westing game*, Ellen Raskin (Dutton). **Honor book:** *The great Gilly Hopkins*, Katherine Paterson (Crowell).

1978 *Bridge to Terabithia*, Katherine Paterson (Crowell). **Honor books:** *Anpao: An American Indian odyssey*, Jamake Highwater (Lippincott); *Ramona and her father*, Beverly Clearly (Morrow).

1977 *Roll of thunder, hear my cry*, Mildred Taylor (Dial). **Honor books:** *Abel's Island*, William Steig (Farrar Straus Giroux); *A string in the harp*, Nancy Bond (Atheneum).

1976 *The grey king*, Susan Cooper (Atheneum). **Honor books:** *Dragonwings*, Laurence Yep (Harper & Row); *The hundred penny box*, Sharon Bell Mathis (Viking).

1975 *M. C. Higgins, the great*, Virginia Hamilton (Macmillan). **Honor books:** *Figgs and phantoms*, Ellen Raskin (Dutton); *My brother Sam is dead*, James Lincoln Collier and Christopher Collier (Four Winds); *The perilous guard*, Elizabeth Marie Pope (Houghton Mifflin); *Philip Hall likes me, I reckon maybe*, Bette Green (Dial).

1974 *The slave dancer*, Paula Fox (Bradbury). **Honor book:** *The dark is rising*, Susan Cooper (Atheneum).

1973 *Julie of the wolves*, Jean C. George (Harper & Row). **Honor books:** *Frog and Toad together*, Arnold Lobel (Harper & Row); *The upstairs room*, Johanna Reiss (Crowell); *The witches of worm*, Zilpha Keatley Snyder (Atheneum).

1972 *Mrs. Frisby and the rats of NIMH*, Robert C. O'Brien (Atheneum). **Honor books:** *Annie and the old one*, Miska Miles (Atlantic-Little); *The headless cupid*, Zilpha Keatley Snyder (Atheneum); *Incident at Hawk's Hill*, Allan W. Eckert (Little, Brown); *The planet of Junior Brown*, Virginia Hamilton (Macmillan); *The tombs of Atuan*, Ursula K. LeGuin (Atheneum).

1971 *The summer of the swans*, Betsy Byars (Viking). **Honor books:** *Enchantress from the stars*, Sylvia Louise Engdahl (Atheneum); *Kneeknock rise*, Natalie Babbitt (Farrar Straus Giroux); *Sing down the moon*, Scott O'Dell (Houghton Mifflin).

1970 *Sounder*, William Armstrong (Harper & Row). **Honor books:** *Journey outside*, Mary Q. Steele (Viking); *Our Eddie*, Sulamith Ish-Kishor (Pantheon); *The many ways of seeing, An introduction to the pleasures of art*, Janet Gaylord Moore (Harcourt Brace Jovanovich).

1969 *The high king*, Lloyd Alexander (Holt, Rinehart & Winston). **Honor books:** *To be a slave*, Julius Lester (Dial); *When Shlemiel went to Warsaw and other stories*, Isaac Bashevis Singer (Farrar Straus Giroux).

1968 *From the mixed-up files of Mrs. Basil E. Frankweiler*, E. L. Konigsburg (Atheneum). **Honor books:** *The black pearl*, Scott O'Dell (Houghton Mifflin); *The Egypt game*, Zilpha Keatley Snyder (Atheneum); *The fearsome inn*, Isaac Bashevis Singer (Scribner); *Jennifer, Hecate, Macbeth, William McKinley, and me, Elizabeth*, E. L. Konigsburg (Atheneum).

1967 *Up a road slowly,* Irene Hunt (Follett). **Honor books:** *The jazz man,* Mary Hays Weik (Atheneum); *The King's Fifth,* Scott O'Dell (Houghton Mifflin); *Zlateh the goat and other stories,* Isaac Bashevis Singer (Harper & Row).

1966 *I, Juan de Pareja,* Elizabeth Borton de Trevino (Farrar Straus Giroux). **Honor books:** *The animal family,* Randall Jarrell (Pantheon); *The black cauldron,* Lloyd Alexander (Holt, Rinehart & Winston); *The noonday friends,* Mary Stolz (Harper & Row).

1965 *Shadow of a bull,* Maia Wojciechowska (Atheneum). **Honor book:** *Across five Aprils,* Irene Hunt (Follett).

1964 *It's like this, cat,* Emily Neville (Harper & Row). **Honor books:** *The loner,* Ester Wier (McKay); *Rascal,* Sterling North (Dutton).

1963 *A wrinkle in time,* Madeleine L'Engle (Farrar Straus Giroux). **Honor books:** *Thistle and thyme: Tales and Legends from Scotland,* Sorche Nic Leodhas (Holt); *Men of Athens,* Olivia Coolidge (Houghton Mifflin).

1962 *The bronze bow,* Elizabeth George Speare (Houghton Mifflin). **Honor books:** *Frontier living,* Edwin Tunis (World); *The golden goblet,* Eloise McCraw (Coward); *Belling the tiger,* Mary Stolz (Harper & Row).

1961 *Island of the blue dolphins,* Scott O'Dell (Houghton Mifflin). **Honor books:** *America moves forward,* Gerald W. Johnson (Morrow); *Old Ramon,* Jack Schaefer (Houghton Mifflin); *The cricket in Times Square,* George Selden (Farrar Straus Giroux).

1960 *Onion John,* Joseph Krumgold (Crowell). **Honor books:** *My side of the mountain,* Jean Craighead George (Dutton); *America is born,* Gerald W. Johnson (Morrow); *The gammage cup,* Carol Kendall (Harcourt Brace Jovanovich).

Index of

Authors and Titles

Subject Index